658.014 ROB

D1338753

IMI
Information Centre & Library

Organisation Theory

CONCEPTS AND CASES

PEARSON
Education
Australia

STEPHEN P. ROBBINS AND NEIL BARNWELL

5th
EDITION

Organisation Theory

CONCEPTS AND CASES

Copyright © Pearson Education Australia (a division of Pearson Australia Group Pty Ltd) 2006

Pearson Education Australia
Unit 4, Level 3
14 Aquatic Drive
Frenchs Forest NSW 2086

www.pearsoned.com.au

The *Copyright Act 1968* of Australia allows a maximum of one chapter or 10% of this book, whichever is the greater, to be copied by any educational institution for its educational purposes provided that that educational institution (or the body that administers it) has given a remuneration notice to Copyright Agency Limited (CAL) under the Act. For details of the CAL licence for educational institutions contact:
Copyright Agency Limited, telephone: (02) 9394 7600, email: info@copyright.com.au

All rights reserved. Except under the conditions described in the Copyright Act 1968 of Australia and subsequent amendments, no part of this publication may be reproduced, stored in a retrieval system or transmitted in any form or by any means, electronic, mechanical, photocopying, recording or otherwise, without the prior permission of the copyright owner.

Acquisitions Editor: Frances Eden
Project Editor: Sandra Goodall
Editorial Coordinator: Roisin Fitzgerald
Copy Editor: Kathryn Lamberton
Proofreader: Ron Buck
Cover design by Nada Backovic Designs
Internal design by Nada Backovic Designs and Dizign Pty Ltd
Typeset by Midland Typesetters, Australia

Printed in China(EPC)

2 3 4 5 10 09 08 07

National Library of Australia
Cataloguing-in-Publication Data

Robbins, Stephen P., 1943– .
Organisation theory : concepts and cases.

5th ed.
Includes index.
For tertiary students
ISBN 978 0 73397 471 7.

ISBN 0 7339 7471 6.

1. Organizational behavior. 2. Organizational change – Australia. I. Barnwell, Neil. II. Title.

658.00994

Every effort has been made to trace and acknowledge copyright. However, should any infringement have occurred, the publishers tender their apologies and invite copyright owners to contact them.

PEARSON
Prentice Hall

An imprint of Pearson Education Australia
(a division of Pearson Australia Group Pty Ltd)

Contents

Detailed Contents

Preface

We are pleased to present the fifth edition of *Organisation Theory: Concepts and Cases* to our readers. This edition follows a similar approach to that used in previous editions. It is intended primarily for business students and the material has been selected and presented in a way that will assist them in understanding organisations and their management. It is expected that it will be of most use to undergraduate students and postgraduate students in the early stages of their courses.

The theme continues that of previous editions in that it concentrates on material that will be of practical value to those faced with the task of managing or working in an organisation. In the case of organisational theory, this is not as easy as it may appear. Organisation theory is a multidisciplinary study that includes elements of sociology, anthropology and corporate strategy. It is also influenced by philosophy, in the sense that people have different orientations about organisations and their management. This contributes to these areas being contested terrain, where various approaches vie to attract attention and dominate discourse. Inevitably, in drawing upon this material, judgements must be made as to what is important and of value to students. In this task we have been guided by the material's practical value.

This does not mean that the text does not have a firm academic base. The material is drawn from studies published in respected academic journals and, in some cases, business publications. Each chapter is extensively referenced and contains a guide to further reading for those interested in broadening their study of the topic.

Although most of those using the text will be undertaking business degrees, the basic principles and theories discussed apply to all organisations. The book is therefore also of use to those charged with managing government departments, charities and various non-government organisations.

As with previous editions, we open each chapter with an illustrative case study and we conclude with a closing case study which is intended to be discussed in class. Each chapter also contains review questions which test students' knowledge of the material. Many illustrative boxes are dispersed throughout the text showing how the material may be applied to current business situations. The book also contains a useful glossary and concluding case studies.

A new chapter has been added for this edition. It covers organisational knowledge and learning, areas of increasing importance to contemporary organisations. All the other chapters have been thoroughly revised and brought up to date.

We hope that students and instructors will find this book both useful and easy to read. And as a final authorship task, we extend our thanks to those too many to mention who have provided support and encouragement throughout its writing and production.

Stephen P Robbins
Neil Barnwell (neil.barnwell@uts.edu.au)

PART 1

Introduction to Organisation Theory

part 1

CHAPTER 1

An overview

After reading this chapter you should be able to:

- understand what the discipline of organisation theory covers
- compare organisation theory and organisational behaviour
- explain the benefits of studying organisation theory
- describe the systems perspective
- describe the life-cycle perspective
- discuss how systems and life cycles are part of the biological metaphor
- introduce the concepts of critical theory and postmodernism as they apply to organisation theory
- discuss how the book is organised and what will be covered in subsequent chapters.

Introduction

Virgin Blue takes to the skies

One of the most prominent businessmen of the past 20 years is Sir Richard Branson, the originator of the widely known Virgin brand. Virgin brand goods and services range from a cola drink to banking and mobile phones.[1] Branson's business approach is to take on dominant players in established industries and carve out a niche for himself, promoting his product by flamboyant marketing techniques. In some cases the name is used as a marketing tool, with services and expertise provided by specialists. But in other cases entirely new organisations are created.

One of Branson's early ventures was into the airline industry, through the establishment of Virgin Atlantic. This pitted him in head-to-head competition against British Airways, a competitive stoush which he immensely enjoyed. He also operates a European airline, Virgin Express, which he uses when travelling around the region. As owner of the airline he often sits and chats with the pilots during the flight. On one such flight in the late 1990s one of the pilots, an Australian, was complaining about the fact that there were only two airlines in Australia and that as a result air travel was expensive. There seemed to be room for at least one more airline offering a lower cost product. Branson's entrepreneurial spirit was aroused, and he determined on the spur of the moment to start a new airline to service the Australian market.

Air transportation is not an industry for the faint-hearted. It is legendary for the enormous amount of capital it consumes, often with little return. It is also difficult to be a small player. Economies favour established airlines with large fleets, extensive networks and frequency of service. Owing to the distance of Australia from the rest of his airline operations, Branson's new airline could not be an extension of one he already owned; he had to start a new organisation from scratch.

His first move was to appoint a chief executive. He chose Brett Godfrey, a 37-year-old finance manager with Virgin Express. Godfrey's task was formidable. He needed to identify essential tasks and refine these into areas of responsibility. Managers were then appointed to be responsible for those areas. They in turn had to build their departments by hiring the appropriate staff, allocating tasks and recommending investment decisions. A decision had to be made on the location of the head office and appropriate accommodation found. Suitable aircraft had to be leased and maintenance facilities established. One of the greatest hurdles for the new company was negotiating with the various government bodies that control aviation. Procedure manuals had to be written and presented to the Civil Aviation and Safety Authority for approval. Test flights were needed to prove the capacity of the airline to perform and to handle emergencies appropriately before an air operator's certificate could be issued. Landing slots had to be negotiated with the various airport authorities, a particular problem in Sydney with its capacity constraints. Suitable terminal access had to be arranged—no easy task, given that most airports catered only for the then two dominant carriers, Ansett and Qantas. In addition, IT systems had to be developed and hardware and software purchased and installed. Booking and information systems were put on line. A call centre had to be established, maintenance and supply contracts negotiated and Human Resource Management policies written.

The airline even needed a new name. Singapore Airlines owned a 49% share of Virgin Atlantic and the right to the Virgin brand name as it applied to airlines. The Virgin airline in Australia would be totally financed by Sir Richard Branson himself, with no direct relationship to his other aviation investments. Thus the name Virgin Blue was born.

If Virgin Blue was to be successful, it had to seek points of difference between itself and the other airlines. One of these points was obvious: it was to pitch its price lower than Ansett and Qantas. The other was the feel of the airline: being a new start-up, Virgin Blue could hire those who reflected the image it wanted to create. This was particularly relevant to those who worked at the customer interface. Not surprisingly, Virgin Blue wanted to create a youthful persona, full of smiles and freshness and not too bureaucratic. It was also important that staff possess a can-do approach and a positive attitude, and that they be flexible in their work, if the start-up airline were to be successful. The feeling that they were part of a historic shift in the airline industry was a major motivator. It called this persona the 'Virgin flair'.

Virgin Blue also used its choice of head office location to advantage. Drawn to Brisbane by concessions and grants from the Queensland government, it identified considerable advantages in weaving itself into the fabric of Queensland society. All of its initial routes originated from Brisbane, and it promoted itself heavily in that state as a local airline for local people. The atmosphere of the 'Sunshine State' started to permeate its culture.

The unexpected collapse of Ansett created new opportunities and challenges for Virgin Blue. Suddenly Qantas was the only competitor and Branson and Godfrey sensed that they would have little difficulty in competing with a bureaucratic, inefficient and slow-moving rival. Ambitious goals were developed based upon reaching at least 50% of the domestic market. This involved major purchases of new aircraft and a significant expansion of the organisation. There was also a change in the ownership of the airline with Chris Corrigan's Patrick Corporation purchasing a large shareholding. In 2004 there were further ownership changes as Virgin Blue raised capital from the public and listed on the Australian Stock Exchange. But Virgin Blue experienced the inevitable growing pains in part, self-inflicted through overconfidence. Qantas proved itself a formidable competitor, particularly with the introduction of Jet Star. Virgin Blue overcommitted itself to expansion and found it had too many aircraft for the passengers on offer, depressing profit margins. There were also rumours of staff discontent and high turnover rates. Faced with increased competition and pressure on margins, the strategic direction of the airline was not clear and in 2005 Patrick Corporation moved to increase its stake in the airline to over 50% which gave it management control. The excitement of starting a new airline had evolved into the more mundane task of managing a mature organisation in a highly competitive environment.

Brett Godfrey created an organisation. Within 18 months of the idea being formed, the red aircraft of Virgin Blue became a familiar sight. The task was beyond the capacity of any one person. We can see in Virgin Blue's formation all the features of an organisation that we will discuss in this book. Goals had to be set and key areas of responsibility, necessary to achieve the goals, identified. Departments were formed and coordination mechanisms established. Pressures from the environment had to be identified and responded to. As well, the culture of the organisation, including the standards of behaviour and attitudes towards work, needed to reflect the values and attitudes necessary for the organisation's survival. Finally, over just a few years the organisation moved from being a new start-up company to one grappling with the problems of maturity and hostile competition, leading to subsequent changes in the organisation's goals. Although there were many factors responsible for Virgin Blue's successful establishment, the correct organisational structure and design played a prominent part. And although many other factors will determine whether Virgin Blue thrives, the discipline of organisation theory, which is the subject of this book, will have a major part to play.

Some basic definitions

The Virgin Blue story illustrates the creation and growth of an organisation. But what precisely do we mean by the term *organisation*? Perhaps not so obviously, Virgin Blue's senior management was also involved with *organisation structure, organisation design, organisation theory* and *organisational behaviour*. As all four terms are important and are often confused, let's clarify them.

What is an organisation?

organisation
a consciously coordinated social entity, with a relatively identifiable boundary, which functions on a relatively continuous basis to achieve a common goal or set of goals

An **organisation** is a consciously managed and coordinated social entity, with an identifiable boundary, which functions on a relatively continuous basis to achieve a common goal or set of goals. That's a mouthful of words, so let us break it down into its more relevant parts.

The words, *consciously managed and coordinated*, imply that there is a management hierarchy involved in decision making in the organisation. *Social entity* means that the unit is composed of people or groups of people who interact with each other. The interaction patterns that people follow in an organisation do not just emerge—rather, they are deliberately channelled in directions which promote the organisation's interests. It follows that the interaction patterns of the organisation's members must be balanced and harmonised to minimise duplication yet ensure that critical tasks are completed. The result is that our definition assumes explicitly the need for coordinating the interaction patterns of people and monitoring the results of that interaction.

An organisation has an *identifiable boundary*. This boundary can change over time and may not always be perfectly clear, but a definable boundary must exist in order to distinguish members from non-members. Such a boundary tends to be created through explicit or implicit contracts between members and their organisation, for example, through an employment relationship. In social or voluntary organisations, members contribute in return for prestige, social interaction or the satisfaction of helping others. But every organisation has a boundary that differentiates who is and who is not part of that organisation.

People in an organisation have some *continuing bond*. This bond, of course, does not mean lifelong membership. On the contrary, organisations face constant change in their memberships, although while they are members the people in an organisation participate with some degree of regularity. For a clerk in the National Australia Bank, that may require being at work eight hours a day, five days a week. Alternatively, someone functioning on a relatively continuous basis as a member of the Country Women's Association may attend only a few meetings a year or merely pay the annual dues. At the other extreme, military and religious orders often demand total commitment from members.

Finally, organisations exist to achieve something. What they set out to achieve is reflected in the organisation's *goals*, and they are usually unattainable by individuals working alone or, if attainable individually, are achieved more efficiently through group effort. While it is not necessary for all members to actively endorse the organisation's goals, or even fully understand what they are, our definition implies that disagreement with or objection to the goals of the organisation would lead to a person terminating their membership.

Notice how all the parts of our definition align with our description of the development of Virgin Blue. The goals of Virgin Blue are to provide cost-effective air travel to the people of Australia, achieve an adequate market share and make an acceptable return on funds employed. Staff were hired and inducted into the Virgin Blue vision and values. In undertaking their tasks they developed a formal set of relationships which were the patterns of interaction of the organisation. These patterns included people undertaking specialised tasks and a hierarchy of workers and managers.

Members of Virgin Blue are identified as employees, owners or board members. In return for their work effort or other contribution they receive pay and other forms of compensation. Finally, the organisation's life exists beyond that of any of its members. Employees may leave, but they can be replaced so that the activities they perform can continue without any change in the nature of the organisation. Even the ownership of Virgin Blue has changed, with little effect on its day-to-day operations.

What is organisation structure?

Our definition of *organisation* recognises the need for formally coordinating the interaction patterns of organisation members and managing their activities. **Organisation structure** defines how tasks are to be allocated, areas of responsibility and authority, reporting relationships, and the formal coordinating mechanisms and interaction patterns that will be followed. We define an organisation's structure as having three components: complexity, formalisation, and centralisation. (We review each of these in detail in Chapter 4.)

organisation structure the degree of complexity, formalisation, and centralisation in an organisation

Complexity considers the extent of differentiation within the organisation. This includes the degree of specialisation or division of labour; in other words how many different occupations and tasks exist in the organisation, the number of levels in the organisation's management hierarchy and the extent to which the organisation's units are dispersed geographically. As tasks at Virgin Blue became increasingly specialised and more levels were added to the hierarchy, the organisation became increasingly complex. Complexity, of course, is a relative term. A small business, for instance, has a long way to go to approach the complexity of BHP Billiton or the ANZ Bank, where there are hundreds of occupational specialties, many management levels between production workers and the chief executive officer, and organisational units dispersed in countries throughout the world.

The degree to which an organisation relies on rules and procedures to direct the behaviour of employees is known as *formalisation*. Some organisations operate with a minimum of such standardised guidelines; others, even those quite small in size, have all kinds of regulations instructing employees as to what they can and cannot do. But not all formalisation exists as written rules and regulations. Much formalisation is internalised through the socialisation process which establishes what behaviours are acceptable.

Centralisation considers where the responsibility for decision-making authority lies. In some organisations, decision making is highly centralised. Problems flow upwards and just a few senior executives, or even one person, make the relevant decisions. In other cases, decision making is decentralised. Authority is dispersed downwards in the hierarchy and a greater number of people are involved in decision making. It is important to recognise that, as with complexity and formalisation, an organisation is not *either* centralised or decentralised. Centralisation and decentralisation represent two extremes on a continuum. Organisations *tend* to be centralised or *tend* to be decentralised. The placement of the organisation on these continuums, however, is one of the major factors in determining what type of structure exists.

What is organisation design?

organisation design the construction and change of an organisation's structure

Our third term, organisation design, emphasises the management side of organisation theory. **Organisation design** is concerned with constructing and changing an organisation's structure to achieve the organisation's goals. Constructing or changing an organisation is not unlike building or remodelling a house: both begin with a goal which includes a vision of what is to be achieved; the designer then creates a plan to achieve the goal, including the means of how to get there. In house construction, plans exist as drawings, or lines on a computer screen; in organisation design, the corresponding document is an organisation chart.

As you proceed through this text, you will see a consistent concern with offering prescriptions for how organisations can be *designed* to facilitate the attainment of their goals. The concern should not be surprising, as this book is intended for business students, and managers who have responsibility for designing organisations. A further reason is that organisation design options are fairly easy to describe and comprehend and hence, in many ways, manage. So there is a natural tendency to orient our thoughts to those things that can be more readily understood and as a result provide useful tools for management to apply.

What is organisation theory?

organisation theory the discipline that studies the structure and design of organisations

From our previous definitions, it is not too difficult to identify that **organisation theory** includes the study of the structure and design of organisations. But organisations have a life which is far more complex than that laid down in formal organisational design. Organisations develop personalities, which we call culture. Whether or not the culture assists an organisation in attaining its goals is important to managers. And as environments and technologies are never fixed, so organisations must adapt to the changes that affect them. These include changes in societal attitudes and expectations which require an organisational response. Hence areas such as sustainability and gender, which were previously not of any great importance, are attracting greater research interest. There is also a political element in organisational theory. Organisations play a significant part in the society we live in and undertake fundamental roles in governance, wealth creation and distribution. So organisations become both a focal point for activists and a means by which activists themselves leverage their influence. As organisations are not homogeneous, they may also be analysed in terms of who gets to be members, who exercises power and how that power is exercised. So, in addition to structure and design, organisational theory includes the study of these less clearly defined areas and makes suggestions as to how they can contribute to organisational effectiveness.

At the end of this chapter, we introduce a model that identifies explicitly the major subparts that make up this discipline we call organisation theory. Chapter 2 presents a brief overview of the evolution of organisation theory over time.

Contrasting organisation theory and organisational behaviour

As we are clarifying terminology, it might be helpful in this section to differentiate between the subject matter of organisation theory and that of organisational behaviour. Many students of management and organisations will take courses in both areas, and a brief comparison of the two should assist you in understanding their different emphases as well as their areas of overlap.

Organisational behaviour is the study of the way in which individuals and teams behave in the workplace. It focuses on behaviour in organisations and on a narrow set of employee performance and attitude variables—employee productivity, absenteeism, turnover and job satisfaction are those most often looked at. Topics relating to the individual typically studied in organisational behaviour include perception, values, learning, motivation and the personality–task interface. Group topics include roles, status, leadership, power, communication and conflict.

organisational behaviour a field of study that investigates the impact of individuals and small-group factors on employee performance and attitudes

In contrast, organisation theory takes a macro-perspective. Its unit of analysis is the organisation itself or its primary subunits, such as departments or divisions. Organisation theory focuses on the behaviour of organisations and uses a broader definition of organisational effectiveness. It is concerned not only with employee performance and attitudes but also with the overall organisation's ability to achieve its goals and adapt to its environment.

This micro–macro distinction creates some overlap; for instance, the way an organisation is structured has an impact on employee behaviour. Students of organisational behaviour should therefore consider the structure–behaviour relationship. Similarly, some micro-topics are relevant to the study of organisation theory. However, where micro- and macro-issues overlap, their emphasis is often different: for instance, the topic of culture in organisational behaviour tends to focus on the way that culture influences interpersonal relationships within groups; when studied by organisational theorists, on the other hand, the emphasis is on how culture contributes to the organisation's goals and the extent to which it is manageable. While the student of organisational behaviour is likely to see culture as arising from the actions of individuals and being a people issue, the student of organisation theory tends to see the same culture as arising from the way that tasks and departments are structured, the way that the organisation allocates rewards and sanctions, and the patterns of communication and reporting relationships. The issue of course is not that one is right and the other wrong. Rather, organisational behaviour and theory emphasise different levels of organisational analysis.

The biological metaphor

Organisations are intangible: that is, they do not exist as a physical presence but as a set of relationships among people. Given this intangibility, a **metaphor** is a popular device for making comparisons. The use of metaphors can be extremely helpful in explaining or providing insight into the workings of two phenomena, by drawing upon one which you already understand fairly well and applying it to one which you are

metaphor a figure of speech in which a descriptive term is used to refer to another object to which it seems to bear no relationship

trying to understand. In this section we will look at organisations (a phenomenon we will assume you are technically unfamiliar with) as if they were living organisms, like plants, animals or human beings (phenomena we will assume you *are* reasonably familiar with). We call this comparison the biological metaphor. This comparison is not a random one. As organisations are composed of individuals, it may not be surprising that they reflect the way of life of individuals and their life cycle.

The use of the biological metaphor has drawn criticism. Some scholars have questioned whether the biological metaphor is appropriate for application to organisations.[2] For example, while few would dispute that organisations are born, grow and require continual nourishment for survival, organisations are not predestined to die, as all living organisms are. Death may be a part of biological life, but it is not inevitable for organisations. Churches and government departments, for instance, seem to have an almost indefinite life, and constant mergers and acquisitions in business make defining organisational death problematic. Further, many business organisations are established with the intention of being sold when an appropriate opportunity emerges. So while the biological metaphor is not perfect, it has benefits as a conceptual framework for understanding organisations and simplifying complex phenomena.

OT CLOSEUP

Ten different ways of looking at organisations, or what you see is what you get!

Organisations have been conceptualised in numerous ways.[3] The following represent some of the more OFTEN used descriptions:

Rational entities in pursuit of goals. Organisations exist to achieve goals, and the behaviour of organisational members can be explained as the rational pursuit of those goals.

Coalitions of powerful constituencies. Organisations are made up of groups, each of which seeks to satisfy its own self-interest. These groups use their power to influence the distribution of resources within the organisation.

Open systems. Organisations are input–output transformation systems that depend on their environment for survival.

Meaning-producing systems. Organisations are artificially created entities. Their goals and purposes are symbolically created and maintained by management.

Loosely coupled systems. Organisations are made up of relatively independent units that can pursue dissimilar or even conflicting goals.

Political systems. Organisations are composed of internal constituencies that seek control over the decision process in order to enhance their position.

Instruments of domination. Organisations place members in job 'boxes' that constrain what they can do and with whom they can interact. Additionally, they are given a boss who has authority over them.

Information-processing units. Organisations interpret their environment, coordinate activities and facilitate decision making by processing information horizontally and vertically through a structural hierarchy.

Psychic prisons. Organisations constrain members by constructing job descriptions, departments, divisions, and standards of acceptable and unacceptable behaviours. When accepted by members, they become artificial barriers that limit choices.

Social contracts. Organisations are composed of sets of unwritten agreements whereby members perform certain behaviours in return for compensation.

The first metaphor used is that of the *systems perspective*, which views the organisation as a system which interacts with its environment in a repetitive cycle of events. The second is the *life-cycle perspective*, which views the organisation as a living organism which grows, passes through predictable stages of development, undergoes a series of predictable transitions and deteriorates if the energy used in daily activities is not replaced by new inputs. Describing organisations as systems and as proceeding through a life cycle provides new insight into their make-up.

The systems perspective

There is wide agreement among organisational theorists that a systems perspective offers important insight into the workings of an organisation.[4] The following pages introduce the idea of systems, contrast *open* and *closed* systems, and demonstrate how an open-systems approach can assist you in better understanding what organisations do.

Definition of a system

A **system** is a set of interrelated and interdependent parts which interact to produce a unified output. Organisations are systems, and so too are cars, plants and human bodies. Inputs go through a transformation process to emerge as outputs, which are different in form to the inputs.

system a set of interrelated and interdependent parts arranged in a manner that produces a unified whole

The unique characteristic of the systems viewpoint is the interrelationship of parts within the system. Every system is characterised by two diverse forces: differentiation and integration. A system is differentiated into specialised functions. In the human body, for instance, the lungs, heart and liver are all distinct functions. Similarly, organisations have divisions and departments with each performing specialised activities. At the same time, in order to maintain unity and purpose among the differentiated parts, every system has a process of integration. In organisations, this integration is typically achieved through coordinating devices such as actions of management, rules, procedures and policies, and the monitoring of performance. Every system, therefore, requires differentiation in order to identify its subparts and integration to ensure that the system does not break down into separate elements which act randomly.

The subsystems of an organisation may in turn be broken down into further subsystems. The Commonwealth Bank, for instance, may be viewed as a system; funds management as a subsystem; and parts of funds management, such as marketing, as yet a further subsystem. This highlights a dilemma for both managers and researchers: what is to be our level of analysis? By examining the complete system we may be taking too broad a view for effective analysis. But if we concentrate on minor subsystems, we may miss important features of the whole system that impinge on subsystem effectiveness.

Types of systems

Systems are classified typically as either closed or open. Closed-system thinking views the system as self-contained. Its dominant characteristic is that it essentially ignores the effect of the environment on the system. A **closed system** would be one that received no energy from an outside source and from which no energy was released into its surroundings. This implies there is no environmental interaction. The closed-system perspective is more of a conceptualisation rather than something that actually exists and has little applicability to the study of organisations.

closed system a self-contained system that has no interaction with its environment

open system a dynamic system that interacts with and responds to its environment

In contrast, an **open system** recognises the interaction of a system with its environment and its dependence upon it. A simplified graphic representation of the open system appears in Figure 1.1.

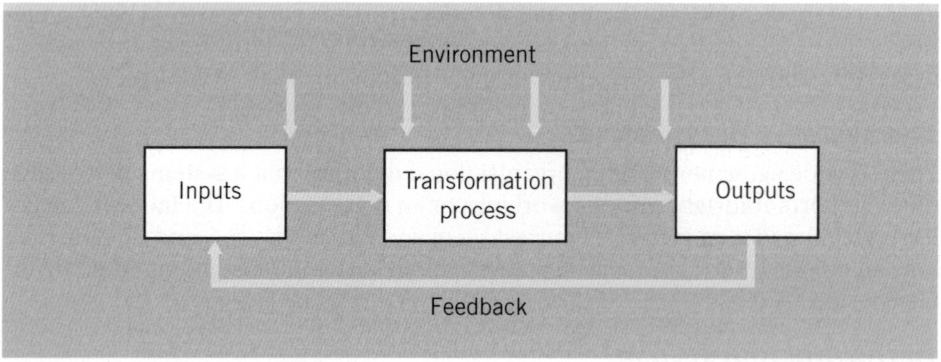
Environment
Inputs
Transformation process
Outputs
Feedback

FIGURE 1.1 Basic open system

No one who studies organisations could build much of a defence for viewing them as closed systems. Utopian communities, hunter–gatherers or self-contained religious organisations may qualify as a closed system, at least for a period of time. But the concept has little applicability in our society. Business organisations obtain their raw materials and human resources from the environment. They depend on clients and customers in the environment to absorb their output. And all the while, the environment creates new pressures ranging from the actions of competitors to changes in technology and legislative requirements. For instance, banks take in deposits, convert them into loans and other investments, and use the surpluses arising from lending to cover their costs, to fund growth, and pay dividends and taxes. The banking system, for example, interacts actively with its environment, which is made up of people with savings to invest, those in need of loans, potential employees, those willing to provide equity capital to the bank, regulatory authorities, and increasingly public attitudes.

An organisation's environment is far more complex than obtaining raw materials and inputs into the production process and distributing outputs. Major environmental changes that have occurred in recent years includes deregulation, privatisation of government enterprises and the growth in globalisation. These have generally combined to greatly increase the levels of competition and environmental demands. Community expectations are also a significant environmental influence on organisations, with those that can exploit emerging attitudes and values, such as The Body Shop, generally performing extremely well.

Figure 1.2 provides a more complex picture of an open system as it would apply to an industrial organisation. We see inputs of materials, labour and capital. We see a technological process created for transforming raw materials into finished product. The finished product, in turn, is sold to customers. Financial institutions, the labour force, suppliers and customers are all part of the environment, as is government.

As we have seen, it is difficult to conceive of any system as being fully closed. All systems must have some interaction with their environments if they are to survive. Probably the most relevant way in which to look at the closed–open dichotomy is to consider it as a range rather than as two clearly separate classifications. In this way,

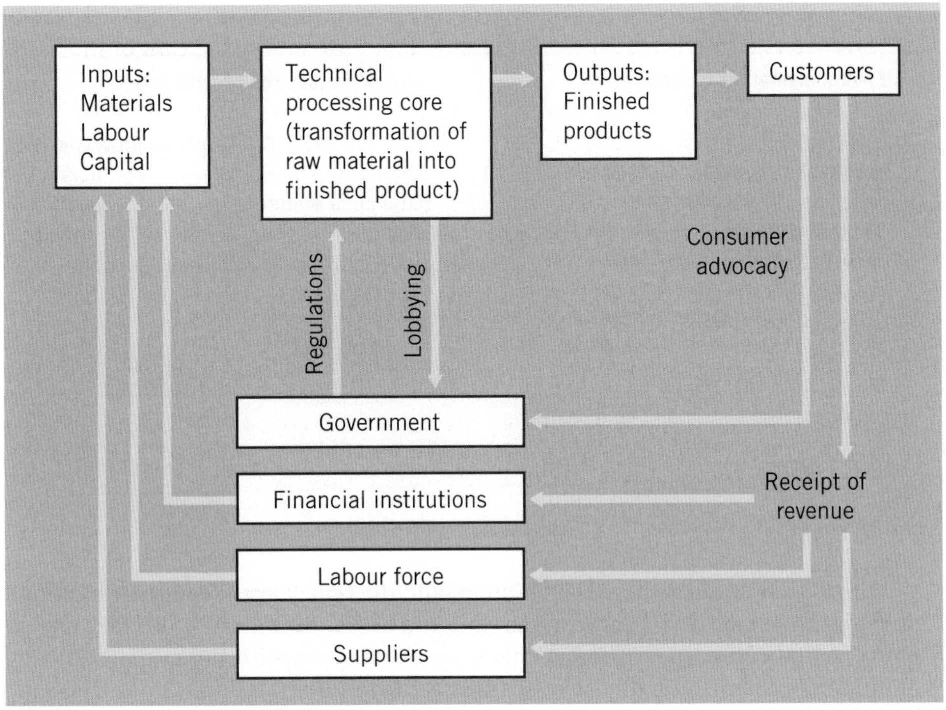
Inputs:
Materials
Labour
Capital
Technical processing core (transformation of raw material into finished product)
Outputs: Finished products
Customers
Consumer advocacy
Regulations
Lobbying
Government
Financial institutions
Receipt of revenue
Labour force
Suppliers

FIGURE 1.2 An industrial organisation as an open system

we can explain that the degree to which a system is open or closed varies between systems. An example of a system which is more closed than open would be the prison system, which has limited environmental interaction. Organisations such as media and fashion companies, which rely upon catering to fickle changes in tastes and attitudes, are more open to the environment. An open system, for instance, may become more closed if contact with the environment is reduced over time. The reverse would also be true. The experience of many government instrumentalities, such as electricity-generating authorities and Telstra, illustrate how systems may move to become more open.

Characteristics of an open system

All systems have inputs, transformation processes and outputs. They take such things as raw materials, energy, information and human resources and convert them into goods and services, waste materials and the like. Open systems, however, have some additional characteristics of relevance to those of us studying organisations. These are summarised in Table 1.1.[5]

- **Environment awareness.** One of the most obvious characteristics of an open system is its recognition of the interdependence between the system and its environment. Changes in the environment affect one or more of the systems or subsystems. Because of the interrelationships of subsystems, a change in one subsystem affects others which form the system. Conversely, changes in the system affect its environment. Some companies make major technological innovations, for instance, which affect the environment of other organisations.

environment awareness the organisation consistently interacts with its environment

TABLE 1.1 Characteristics of an open system

Environmental awareness: the organisation consistently interacts with its environment	**Movement towards growth and expansion:** the more sophisticated the system, the more it is likely to grow and expand
Feedback: the system adjusts to information from its environment	**Balance of maintenance and adaptive activities:** to be effective the system must ensure that its subparts are in balance and that it maintains its ability to adapt to the environment
Cyclical character: the system consists of cycles of events	**Equifinality:** there are a number of ways to achieve the same objective
Tendency towards growth: without active intervention, the system runs down or disintegrates	
Steady state: there is an input or energy to counteract the winding-down properties	

Source: Adapted from Daniel Katz & Robert L. Khan, *The Social Psychology of Organizations*, 2nd edn, New York: John Wiley, 1978.

Without a boundary there is no system, and the boundary or boundaries determine where systems and subsystems start and finish. Boundaries may take a legal form, in that companies are legal entities entitled to employ staff and own assets. Boundaries can also be physical, such as the international boundaries that may form an impediment to trade. They can also be maintained psychologically through symbols, such as titles, uniforms and indoctrination rituals. They may even take the form of a shared belief system, which is characteristic of religious organisations. At this point, it is sufficient to acknowledge that the concept of boundaries is required for an understanding of systems. Somehow we must make a judgement as to what is part of the system and what is not.

feedback receipt of information pertaining to individual or system effectiveness

- **Feedback**. Open systems continually receive information from their environment. This helps the system to understand and adjust to environmental changes by taking corrective action to rectify deviations from its planned course. We call this receipt of environmental information feedback—that is, a process that allows a portion of the output to be returned to the system as input (e.g. information or money) so as to modify succeeding outputs from the system.

cyclical character the system consists of repetitive cycles of events

- **Cyclical character**. Open systems consist of cycles of events. The system's outputs furnish the means for new inputs that permit the repetition of the cycle. This is demonstrated in Figure 1.2; the revenue received from the customers of an industrial firm must be sufficient to pay creditors and the wages of employees and to repay loans if the cycle is to be perpetuated and the organisation to survive.

tendency towards growth without active intervention, the system runs down or disintegrates

- **Tendency towards growth**. A closed system, because it does not import energy or new inputs from its environment, will run down over time as equipment wears out, workforces age and products become dated. In contrast, an open system is able to import energy from its environment. As a consequence it can repair itself, maintain its structure, avoid death and even grow, because it has the ability to import more energy than it puts out. In technical terms, this tendency towards growth is called negative entropy. In a business, examples of imported energy are capital and loans, employees with new skills, or updated plant or equipment.

steady state the result of an input of energy to counteract winding-down properties

- **Steady state**. There is generally a balance between inputs from the environment and those expended to counteract the winding down of the system. This results in a relatively steady state with the character of the system remaining almost unchanged over long periods of time. Most motor vehicle and oil companies, although involved in major interactions with their environment, maintain their character over many years. Many organisations draw resources from their environment, not with the intention of undergoing radical change but to expand existing operations. Such expansion rarely results in changes to the system.

- **Movement towards growth and expansion**. To ensure survival, large and complex systems operate in such a way as to acquire some margin of safety beyond the immediate level of existence. The many subsystems within the system—to avoid winding down—tend to import more energy from the environment than is required for the system's output. The result is that the steady state is applicable to simple systems but, at more complex levels, becomes one of preserving the character of the system through growth and expansion. We see this in large corporations and government bureaucracies which, not satisfied with the status quo, attempt to increase their chances of survival by actively seeking opportunities to grow and expand.

  A final point on this characteristic needs to be made: the basic system does not change directly as a result of expansion. The most common growth pattern is one in which there is merely a multiplication of the same type of cycles or subsystems. The quantity of the system changes while the quality remains the same. Most colleges and universities, for instance, expand by doing more of the same thing rather than by pursuing new or innovative activities.

movement towards growth and expansion the more sophisticated the system, the more it is likely to grow and expand

- **Balance of maintenance and adaptive activities**. Open systems seek to reconcile two, often conflicting, sets of activities. **Maintenance activities** ensure that the various subsystems are in balance and that the total system conforms to its environment. This, in effect, prevents rapid changes that may unbalance the system. In contrast, **adaptive activities** are necessary so that the system can adjust over time to variations in internal and external demands. Maintenance activities seek stability and preservation of the status quo through the purchase, maintenance and overhaul of machinery, the recruitment and training of employees, and mechanisms such as the introduction and enforcement of rules and procedures. Adaptive activities focus on change through planning, market research, recruitment and training, new product development and the like.

  Both maintenance and adaptive activities are required if a system is to survive. Stable and well-maintained organisations that do not adapt as conditions change will not be long-lasting. Similarly, the adaptive but poorly maintained organisation will be inefficient and unlikely to survive for long.

balance of maintenance and adaptive activities to be effective the system must ensure that its subparts are in balance and that it maintains its ability to adapt to the environment

maintenance activities activities that provide stability to a system and preserve the status quo

adaptive activities change activities that allow the system to adapt over time

- **Equifinality**. The concept of equifinality argues that a system can reach the same final state from differing initial conditions and by a variety of paths. This means that an organisational system can accomplish its objectives with varied inputs and transformation processes. Thus different car companies can use different design and production methods and be organised in different ways but still produce a mass market car. As we discuss the managerial implications of organisation theory, it will be valuable for you to keep the idea of equifinality in mind. It will encourage you to consider a variety of solutions to a given problem rather than to seek a single optimal solution.

equifinality a system can reach the same final state from differing initial conditions and by a variety of paths

Importance of the systems perspective

The systems point of view is a useful framework for students of management trying to conceptualise organisations. For managers and future managers, the systems perspective makes it possible to see the organisation as interdependent subsystems which need to be integrated to form a complete and effective system. It prevents, or at least deters, lower level managers from viewing their jobs as managing static, isolated elements of the organisation. It encourages all managers to identify and understand the changing nature of the environment in which their system operates, and the way the environment nurtures, and threatens, the organisation. It helps them to see the organisation as stable patterns and actions within boundaries and to gain insight into why organisations may be resistant to change. Finally, it directs their attention to alternative inputs and processes for reaching their goals.

However, the systems perspective is not the only way in which we can view organisations. One of its greatest limitations is that it is an abstract concept. When viewing an organisation using a systems perspective, an observer sees a complex interaction of systems, subsystems and environments. The tendency is to consider that everything depends on everything else. This makes it difficult to isolate specific problems and to offer to management suggestions as to what precisely will change and to what degree, if a certain action is taken.

A further problem arises in that it has poor explanatory power as to how and why organisations change over time. What brings them into existence and why do they fail? What are the stages they pass through in their passage from being a small organisation to a large one or from a mature organisation to one that finally fails? Our next perspective, the life cycle, provides valuable insight into these problems.

The life-cycle perspective

We have seen that organisations are brought into existence, grow and eventually die (though it may take 100 years or more). New organisations are formed daily. At the same time, hundreds of organisations cease to exist each day. We see this birth and death phenomenon especially among small businesses. But the formation and turnover rate of business organisations in market-based economies is high and is facilitated by a legal system which makes buying and selling of businesses easy. But no organisation is immune. Charities which were formed to cater to the specialist needs of particular groups, such as polio victims or war veterans, eventually find that as the need for their services declines so their existence is threatened.

In this section, we will draw upon the biological metaphor which suggests that organisations proceed through predictable life-cycle stages. Like living organisms, it argues, all organisations are conceived, live and die. Like any living organisms, some develop faster than others and some do a far better job of ageing than others. Also, as with biological growth and ageing, there are also predictable phases that organisations pass through. As a result, the metaphor of the life cycle remains a useful way to conceptualise the life of an organisation.

Definition of a life cycle

organisational life cycle the pattern of predictable change through which the organisation moves from start-up to dissolution

The **organisational life cycle** refers to the pattern of predictable change through which the organisation moves from start-up to dissolution. We suggest that organisations evolve through a standardised sequence of transitions as they develop over time. By applying the life-cycle metaphor to organisations, we are saying that there are distinct stages through which organisations proceed, that the stages follow a consistent pattern, and that the transition from one stage to another is a predictable rather than a random occurrence.

Life-cycle stages

The life-cycle concept has received a great deal of attention in the strategy and marketing literature. Marketers identify that products move through four stages: birth or formation, growth, maturity, and decline. The implication is that products must be continually refreshed, and new ones introduced, in order for sales to be maintained. We could use these life-cycle stages in describing organisations, but organisations are not products, and they have some unique characteristics which require some modifications in our description. Research into the organisation life cycle leads us to a five-stage model:[6]

1 *Entrepreneurial stage.* This stage is synonymous with the formation stage in the product life cycle. The organisation is in its infancy. Goals tend to be fluid or ambiguous. Creativity and managerial input is high. Progression to the next stage demands acquiring and maintaining a steady supply of resources such as capital and labour.
2 *Collectivity stage.* This stage continues the innovation of the earlier stage, but now the organisation's mission is clarified and its chances of survival have increased. Communication and structure within the organisation remain essentially informal. Members put in long hours and demonstrate high commitment to the organisation. The organisation is generally quite small, with intensive, hands-on management.
3 *Formalisation-and-control stage.* In the third stage, as the organisation grows and its production of goods and services becomes more established, the operation of the organisation stabilises. Predictability increases, permitting formal rules and procedures to be imposed. Innovation is de-emphasised, while efficiency and stability take on greater importance. Established management positions emerge as decision making within the organisation is clarified. Decision making takes on a more conservative orientation as it seeks to protect existing investments and market position. It also concentrates more upon day-to-day problems and issues. At this stage, the organisation exists beyond the presence of any one individual. Roles have been clarified and defined so that changes in organisational membership cause no severe threat to the organisation.
4 *Elaboration-of-structure stage.* In this stage the organisation has reached a large size with the characteristics of a bureaucracy. Management searches for new products and growth opportunities to maintain the momentum of expansion. The organisation structure becomes more complex and elaborated. Decision making is decentralised.
5 *Decline stage.* As a result of competition, poor management, fashion changes, technological obsolescence or similar forces, the organisation in the decline stage finds the demand for its products or services shrinking. Management searches for ways to hold markets and looks for new opportunities. Employee turnover, especially among those with the most saleable skills, escalates. Conflicts prompted by shortage of resources and disagreements over strategy increase within the organisation. New people assume leadership in an attempt to arrest the decline. Decision making becomes more centralised in this stage. Eventually the organisation ceases to exist.

Do all organisations proceed through the five stages? Not necessarily! If possible, management would like to avoid having the organisation reach stage 5. However, excluding this stage from our model assumes that organisations follow an unending growth curve or at least remain stable. This obviously is an optimistic assumption. No organisation, or society for that matter, can endure for eternity. But some can last for a very long time and outlive any of their members. Westpac Bank (formerly the Bank of New South Wales) dates back to the early 1800s. The Universities of Sydney and Melbourne are over 150 years old, quite young compared with their European counterparts, such as Oxford and the Sorbonne. The Roman Catholic Church has an existence which goes back almost 2000 years. Whether these organisations are now in the decline stage is questionable, even though they are still doing basically the same thing as they did when they started in business. What is apparent is that if basic technologies or competitive conditions change, organisations can face rapid decline and death. Steam locomotive manufacturers entered the 1950s as major industrial enterprises. By the beginning of the 1960s, most had passed from the scene. Within the space of 20 years, companies in the United Kingdom moved from dominating world ship-building to almost ceasing to exist. When the transistor was introduced to commercial production in the late 1950s, it foreshadowed the end of many manufacturers of technologically out-of-date thermionic valves. And during the tech boom of the late 1990s, organisations were established, grew and became extinct within the space of a couple of years.

Do the life-cycle stages correlate with the number of years an organisation has been established? Not at all! Observation confirms that some organisations have reached stages 3 and 4 less than five years after being formed, while others are 40 years old and still in their collectivity stage. In fact, some successful organisations seek to stay in the early stages. For example, Country Road, the successful designer, manufacturer and retailer of fashion clothing products, realises that it must retain many of the attributes of a stage 2 company to remain competitive. In considering this issue, it is sometimes not easy to determine the stage a company is at. Is Microsoft still at the growth stage or at the maturity or even decline stage? BP, an oil company with an almost 100-year history, is positioning itself to be a major player in sustainable energy to take it beyond the oil age. Where does this place the company in relation to our model? On the other hand, some organisations never die. Police services, for instance, are often subject to various inquiries into corruption, misuse of power, neglect of duty and selective enforcement of justice. Regardless of the criticisms sustained by police forces and their quality of management, the need for their services guarantees their existence.

Is it possible to reconcile our five-stage organisation life-cycle model with the more traditional four-stage model of formation, growth, maturity, and decline? The answer is yes. As shown in Figure 1.3, formation and the entrepreneurial stage are closely related. Collectivity is essentially comparable with growth. Stages 3 and 4 in our model—formalisation and elaboration—appear to align reasonably well with maturity. Finally, of course, decline, and death, is consistent in both models.

Importance of the life-cycle perspective

One of the benefits of viewing organisations from a life-cycle perspective is that it encourages us to view them as dynamic entities. Organisations cannot isolate themselves from the forces acting upon them. The life-cycle perspective suggests that a number of these forces present themselves in a predictable sequence. As a result, organisations evolve and change in an expected pattern over time.

Additionally, the life-cycle metaphor is valuable when we consider what management can do to make an organisation more effective. The actions that are

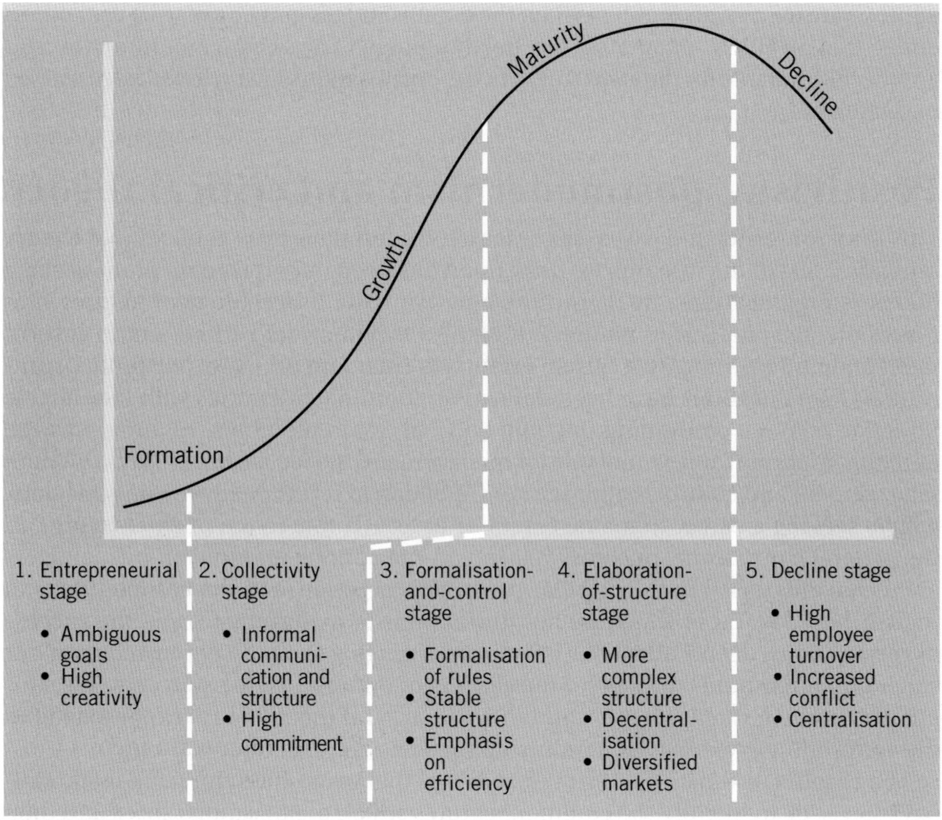
Maturity
Decline
Growth
Formation
1. Entrepreneurial stage
• Ambiguous goals
• High creativity
2. Collectivity stage
• Informal communication and structure
• High commitment
3. Formalisation-and-control stage
• Formalisation of rules
• Stable structure
• Emphasis on efficiency
4. Elaboration-of-structure stage
• More complex structure
• Decentralisation
• Diversified markets
5. Decline stage
• High employee turnover
• Increased conflict
• Centralisation

FIGURE 1.3 Organisational life cycle

OT CLOSEUP

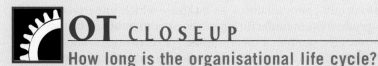

How long is the organisational life cycle?

The concept of the organisational life cycle has considerable empirical support, particularly for business organisations. But it does beg the question, 'How long is the life cycle?' In many cases it is tied to the basic technology of the company's products. Banking has been a long-established industry and will continue to be so. As a result, it is common to see long-established banks which are nowhere near the end of their life cycle. Westpac was established in 1817 and shows no sign of decline—although it has had a few brushes with insolvency in its history.

On the other hand, disruptive technologies can send organisations with old technology into decline in the space of a few years, no matter how effective their management systems. Polaroid's bankruptcy in the face of digital imaging is a good case in point. Others enter a premature mature or decline phase and struggle for legitimacy and new markets. Examples are travel agents faced with competition from the Internet and newspapers faced with electronic forms of disseminating information.

One company which appears to have gone through all of the stages of the life cycle in little more than 30 years is Microsoft. Its growth rapidly paralleled that of the personal computer, but as the personal computer matured, so did Microsoft. As the technology stabilised, competitors started to erode Microsoft's market. Free systems such as Linux posed a threat, and a bureaucratic Microsoft found it was slow to respond to the challenge of search engines such as Google. There is no shortage of advice being proffered to Microsoft as to how to respond to the competitive environment, but the fact that there is no obvious way to maintain the growth of the past points to what may be a long, slow decline.

appropriate for a given problem when the organisation is growing may be very different if that problem occurs in the decline stage. The management styles and approaches suitable for different stages in the organisation's life cycle will be discussed in Chapter 14.

Positivism, postmodernism and critical theory

This book presents and discusses research undertaken by organisational theory scholars. Most of the research we draw upon has been undertaken on profit-seeking business organisations. By definition, and using the terminology of politics, this makes them capitalistic in nature. But we also include work carried out on government undertakings and, to a certain extent, charities and other not-for-profit organisations. Organisations have been defined as coordinated entities with identifiable boundaries and a continuing ongoing bond between members. In doing this, we imply an important and central role for management. Indeed, an organisation without management and control is almost a contradiction in terms. Many reading this book will be seeking a career in management or at least a role in the business world. In the general community, business issues and the actions undertaken by managers are widely discussed in the popular press. This is because in the competitive and market-based world in which we live, the actions of management, and the success of corporations, deeply affect our lives in ways ranging from the performance of our superannuation funds through to the success of our careers. Many accept this situation as normal; it reflects the world they see around them and is acknowledged as the conventional way in which industrial societies are structured.

The empirical studies that form the basis of this book share the same methodology: they seek to identify the common features which organisations share and then determine what may give rise to these common features. These techniques are called observational, in that the researcher observes various organisational practices. As a result of this form of inquiry we find that organisations in turbulent and changing environments share certain commonalities, as do those which undertake routine tasks such as mass-production manufacturing or the operation of rail systems. The subject of research may be a sample of organisations, parts of organisations or one organisation studied intensively. In many cases, we develop a series of propositions, or hypotheses, which are logical statements of association often derived from previous research and which are then tested for their validity. In either case, data are gathered and often statistical analysis is conducted with conclusions drawn from the data.

Such studies are undertaken in order to expand our understanding of what influences organisational structure and practices. In doing this we can expand knowledge and contribute to the more effective management of organisations. An additional reason for undertaking research of this nature is that it satisfies our curiosity about the world around us.

This approach has certain shortcomings. In many instances, correlations and other statistical tests identify only weak associations between variables. This does not provide us with confidence that an unambiguous cause-and-effect relationship exists. It also often occurs that a hypothesis that is strongly supported by theory receives little support when subjected to experimental investigation. Methodological difficulties also create problems. We often have to contend with problems such as how to measure intangibles, such as the relationships between people and the structures of organisations. Nevertheless, a number of landmark theories which have wide applicability have emerged from past research efforts and these will be discussed in subsequent chapters.

This process is called **positivism** and can be described as an assumption that the world may be known and improved by extending knowledge through research. Positivism leads to the development of normative theories. These words require explanation. Positivism implies that we are attempting to do things which lead to some improvement. In this case we are trying to improve organisational effectiveness. **Normative** means that we are trying to develop theories which may be applied across a wide range of situations.

positivism an assumption that the world may be known and improved by extending knowledge through research

normative theories that apply across a wide range of situations

But there are many organisational theorists who are not comfortable with our approach. A brief glance through academic journals dealing with matters relating to organisational theory will show that only some studies, in some journals only, actually follow the methodology we have described. A number of researchers have no doubt been discouraged by the lack of strong associations, and have diverted their attention to other research approaches. Some have moved from analysing populations of organisations to methodologies concentrating on smaller groups or even individuals. And other researchers now promote the position that the future of organisation theory lies not with positivism but with postmodernism and critical theory. These later approaches to organisational theory stand as a counterpoint to that taken by this book. It is therefore worthwhile identifying what these approaches are.

Post means after, so postmodernism is the period after modernism. This leads to the question: what is modernism? The modern world started to emerge in the 18th century, when ideas of individual responsibility and the rights of 'man' (as they were referred to then) were widely debated. The Industrial Revolution was gathering pace at that time and modern capitalism began to emerge. Over the next 200 years or so, significant scientific discoveries were made, and their commercialisation saw the growth of the business corporation with which we are familiar. Accompanying the Industrial Revolution was a great expansion of world trade as companies sought materials and markets for finished products. Modernism is the period associated with this economic expansion. The institutions and organisations that grew to dominance during this period are also called modern. These organisations generally are profit seeking, have private ownership, are actively managed and respond to market forces. Although most people work in small organisations, it is the large organisations that dominate the business landscape and capture most researchers' attention.

You would probably agree that we live in a world dominated by modernist thought and institutions. But the expansion of capitalism has not been without its critics. These critics—among the more widely known being Marx and Engels—viewed capitalism as a passing phase of economic organisation. They proposed that increasingly workers were becoming marginalised and exploited in the interests of capital. The workers, who they called the proletariat, would eventually rise up and overthrow the existing order. Thus capitalism was just one stage in an evolution. Both postmodernism and critical theory, in their own way, draw on the idea of the evolution of capitalism to another state. Postmodernism promotes a world after modern institutions have been overtaken by events. No doubt you are confused with what this has to do with organisational theory and this book. Our discussion will start with critical theory, as it is perhaps easiest to place within this evolution.

Critical theory

It is obvious from its name that **critical theory** sets out to criticise.[7] So what is it criticising? In some circles, particularly in some parts of universities, there is wide

critical theory an approach to studying organisations which concentrates on their perceived shortcomings and deficiencies discussion about the benefits and disadvantages of capitalism and the modern and increasingly multinational orientation of business enterprise. It is not the intention of this book to engage in this particular debate. However, critical theory attempts to highlight one particular aspect of capitalism, which is the experience of lower level workers within organisations.

So here is one of the counterpoints to this book. Assess the material contained in it for a moment from the viewpoint of a worker. To locate this worker's experience, let's say this person is a call centre operator. The worker may be low paid, subject to constant surveillance and control, and located in an area—as many call centres are—with few other employment opportunities. If we give this person (let's call him Peter) *voice*, that is the opportunity to be heard rather than remain *marginalised*, he may view the material in this book as irrelevant. He may consider that it acts against his interests by promoting a system that keeps him in tedious work, lacking challenge and choice. Peter may prefer an approach to teaching that promotes greater awareness of organisational control and surveillance and is more sensitive to the social problems arising from low wages and lack of choice. Further, Peter may look around at his fellow workers and find that many are from disadvantaged groups with little career choice and almost no chance of promotion. As competition increases in the industry he works in, there is greater pressure upon him and his workers to work even harder to keep their jobs. Critical theorists would take the point of view of the worker; what they are criticising is the capitalist system, and the organisations which it spawns, exploiting and marginalising (i.e. pushed to the edge of discussion so their opinions are not heard) those hired to work in the lower levels of organisations.

Critical theorists, along with postmodernists, would attack positivist methodologies as laying false scientific claims to world knowledge. The idea that we can quantify, categorise and analyse organisations or social systems to any degree of accuracy is considered by them to be misleading. Much exists within organisations that defies easy explanation. Further, much of the research on organisations serves the narrow interests of managers and the owners of capital, rather than the wider interests of the worker.

Critical theory therefore has a heavy social activist overlay. It considers that work in a capitalist system is inherently dehumanising, oppressing and exploitative, particularly of minorities. It also tends to view managers not as an essential part of the organisation but as an exploitative group allied with the forces of capital and management as the agent of capital against the worker, a position obviously inspired by Marxist thought. But most critical theorists do not seek to overthrow the social system. They seek to create conditions, and organisational structures and practices, which promote the emancipation of people. This is promoted by theorising, research and awareness building.

Postmodernism

postmodernism an approach to studying organisations, which emerged from European philosophical origins and rejects traditional approaches to studying organisations

We often speak of critical theory and **postmodernism** in the same breath, but they have different origins.[8] A group of philosophers, later known as postmodernists, emerged in Europe after World War II ended in 1945. The most widely known and quoted are Wittgenstein, Lyotard, Foucault and Derrida. They came to maturity at a tumultuous time, with wars in Europe having devastated populations and created human suffering on a scale impossible to imagine. The end of the second world war brought further tensions as Europe became one of the main arenas of conflict between communism and capitalism. The age in which they lived was characterised by abuse of power, so it is not surprising that power became a central focus in their writings.

Their philosophies envisaged a social system which was shorn of much of the prejudice and power relations of the past. We have used the term philosophy deliberately in the sense that this group were philosophers in the traditional sense of the word, not management researchers seeking better ways to manage. Consequently, postmodernism should be seen as part of a school of philosophical thought with its own language, jargon and terminology. The use of postmodernist language enables easy identification of papers written from this perspective.

In reviewing postmodernism, it is helpful to remember that organisational theory is not just a subset of management inquiry. It is a cross-disciplinary study, drawing on sociology, anthropology, social psychology and even philosophy. Each of these disciplines contributes in its own way to knowledge in the area and each, in turn, influences the way that knowledge evolves. As the functioning of organisations is of great importance to management researchers, they in turn have influenced the way that organisational theory has been constructed, researched and interpreted. In some ways it is helpful to view postmodernist approaches as emerging from the non-management disciplines.

Postmodernism is not an easy approach to describe. There are different schools of thought in organisation theory, each with its own interpretation. Some approaches are driven by fashions and fads in thinking, others by favoured academic elites who influence knowledge through control of important journals. We will concentrate on describing the four areas of postmodernism relevant to this book. These are how knowledge is generated and defined, the power/knowledge connection, the role of language in researching organisations, and postmodernism's political agenda.

The generation of knowledge

Earlier we described the way that most of the knowledge in this text has been generated. Postmodernists would consider that this approach has major flaws. Postmodernists challenge the claim that science is objective and impartial. They claim it falsely promotes the concept that the world is capable of being known and controlled through reason. They propose that positivist approaches structure knowledge in ways that do not represent what is occurring in organisations. This is called *reification*—that is, giving physical attributes to something that does not exist in a tangible form. Through the process of reification we have shaped knowledge into certain forms that suit the researcher's purpose. This has become the way we have learnt to know the world and the way in which reality is represented. This leads to one of the central points of difference between postmodernism and scientific methodology: that is, that postmodernists consider knowledge to be socially constructed and interpreted. Drawing upon the concept of the social construction of knowledge, postmodernists would take a view of organisations which reflects the interests of management and perpetuates the position of those who traditionally exercise power in organisations. This group is generally termed the *elite*.

Postmodernists consider that this process of inquiry has devalued *the other*—those silent voices which have not participated in our research. Postmodernists would consider that we have created a situation where managerial elites exert *hegemony* and *domination* over marginalised groups and, as a result, have ignored the issues of class, gender and ethnicity.

OT CLOSEUP
A postmodernist glossary

Postmodernists have developed their own vocabulary, which is commonly drawn upon in their publications. Some of the more commonly used and easy to describe terms are listed below. A number of these terms are not exclusive to postmodernism and have quite wide application, but an understanding of them is necessary to appreciate the meanings behind postmodernist writing. Many postmodernist articles are difficult to interpret, not because the ideas behind them are hard to grasp but because meanings are hidden behind arcane terminology. Interpretation also depends upon understanding the philosophy underpinning the writing.

Deconstruction. Pulling apart in order to understand. Anything may be deconstructed, including society, but postmodernists generally apply the word to the use of language.

Discourse. Communication through words. The wider meaning is associated with not just sentences but streams of thought.

Domination. One group attempting to rule or govern another.

Elite. Those holding power and influence.

Hegemony. Dominance over a group of people.

Marginalisation. Ignoring the attitudes and experiences of groups or the individual.

Metanarratives. A group of narratives or stories which inform the dominant discourse or communication.

Other. Those excluded by the dominant group.

Postcolonial analysis. Attitudes and values attributed to the Third (postcolonial) World. Most research is oriented to First World experience.

Privileged position. Those whose opinions, or voice, are heard. Often refers to those whose opinions dominate research.

Reflexivity. Derives from the word 'reflect' and refers to the need for researchers constantly to consider the implications and effectiveness of their research.

Reification. Converting something intangible into concrete form.

Signification. The meaning behind something.

Voice. An opinion or point of view. When a group or person does not have voice, it implies that their opinions or attitudes are not being heard.

The power/knowledge connection

Power is at the heart of postmodernist concerns. Power is generally seen in a negative light, as a vehicle for exploitation, rather than as a means of achieving goals. Power becomes the way in which domination is exercised in organisations. Postmodernists also consider that there is a power/knowledge nexus. Power emerges from knowledge and knowledge is kept within the empowered group by the control and exercise of language.

The role of language

In undertaking empirical research, we use language as *representation*; it represents certain things we wish to research. Postmodernists, in contrast, claim that language shapes our concept of reality, and that reality is a social construction based on language. Control of language in turn influences the way in which events are interpreted and acted upon. By such use of language we have generated an image of organisations that serves the interests of the elite.

Postmodernists regard language not as a passive describer of objects and events but as a changing, living representation of relationships within organisations. Consequently, we should concentrate on language as action. It is primarily through language that knowledge and power is exercised and through minutely analysing and pulling apart language that true knowledge of organisational practices will be revealed. This process is called *deconstruction*.

The political agenda

We noted earlier that the study of organisations is cross-disciplinary. Many scholars in these disciplines generally do not view business activities in a sympathetic light. Drawing upon socialist and collectivist ideas, they consider business organisations as inherently discriminatory and managers as an exploitative elite seeking to reproduce their own privileges. Given this, it is not surprising that postmodernism has a political edge and has developed as a form of opposition to capitalistic business enterprises. Postmodernists are particularly concerned with the modern organisation as being a form of social control. The strongest evidence in this may be found in the language used by postmodernists. Such terms as elites, marginalisation, power, domination and hegemony reveal a preoccupation with stratified social processes rather than goals, means and ends. Most postmodernists accept that their approach involves the active promotion of a political agenda.

One school of postmodernist thought makes its political agenda explicit: this is critical postmodernism. It combines the political activism of critical theory with postmodernist thought to form a critique of modern business. It actively seeks to promote research and theorising aimed at demonstrating the inherent inequality of business organisations. The aim is not to develop ways of making large organisations less oppressive but to engineer their replacement with smaller, more inclusive units.

Overall, the view of human nature taken by postmodernists is not particularly complimentary. They view the world as being divided between the oppressed and the oppressor, the elite and the marginalised, the powered and the disempowered. The only purposeful activity that is acknowledged by them is the exercise and reinforcement of power by elites for reasons which are never articulated but which may be assumed to be for the purposes of exploitation. The marginalised, downtrodden and victims of the exercise of power are assumed not to have the motivation, power or ability to change their situation. As a result, power and control are viewed in a negative light.

Postmodernist research

Postmodernism has found its expression more in theorising than in research output. There are a number of studies, however, which illustrate a postmodernist approach. One study identified that 'just-in-time' inventory management and 'total quality control' are associated with an increase in management control and reduced worker autonomy.[9] But there is very little research that can specifically be identified as postmodern.

Postmodernists reject the positivist approach to research and advocate that researchers concentrate their efforts on micro-texts, that is, language deconstruction, and individual encounters, rather than on researching total organisations. As a result, postmodernist researchers concentrate on analysis of text and vocabulary in order to peel away layers of meanings. One of the reasons for the low volume of postmodernist research may be that many organisational researchers lack skills in language interpretation and text analysis. Another is that the focus of postmodernist inquiry leads to research difficulties. It is tricky, for instance, to measure such phenomena as power, influence and exploitation. Not only are these subjective, but they are constantly

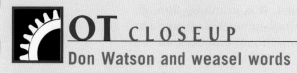

OT CLOSEUP
Don Watson and weasel words

Language is never static and the way that it changes often leads to controversy. One of the leading critics of some of the changes to language usage is Don Watson, the speechwriter to former prime minister Paul Keating. Watson has two main complaints about the use of language: that business is developing its own vocabulary and jargon, which is increasingly obscure and turgid, and that management's approach to language is infiltrating the general discourse of the community. Not only do these words confuse rather than clarify issues, but they are often misleading. In particular, Watson points to the constant use of the words, 'enhanced', 'inputs' and 'implement', as obscuring matters. Librarians have now become 'information needs identifiers'. Everyone becomes a 'customer' and 'going forward' means some time in the future.

War also provides examples of obscure vocabulary. 'Collateral damage' describes civilian casualties and destruction of items not meant to be destroyed, a 'target rich' environment means that there is a lot to shoot at, 'servicing the target' means 'firing at it' and 'self harm incidents' refer to attempted suicides.

Source: Drawn from Don Watson, *Death Sentence: The Decay of Public Language*, Random House, Sydney, 2003.

shifting within organisations. And what one person considers exploitation may be welcome employment for another. Making hamburgers in fast food establishments is a case in point. As a result of these factors it is not surprising that postmodernist research has little application to solving business problems.

Yet another postmodernism

Some researchers apply a different interpretation to the term postmodernism.[10] They regard modernism as the period dominated by large bureaucratic organisations. They see such organisations as being outdated, inefficient and unable to respond to change. They are characterised by high levels of control and provide low levels of autonomy to workers. The current age, which is that after modernism, is characterised by fast-changing technologies and environments and higher levels of competition and globalisation. Large, inward looking, modernist, bureaucratic organisations are seen to be ill suited to this environment. This has led to the emergence of postmodernist organisations. These are small and nimble with low levels of hierarchy and control, increased worker autonomy, and fewer rules and regulations.

It can be seen that this interpretation of postmodernism is different from that previously discussed. It approaches business organisations in a conventional manner and proposes that a new organisational form is emerging in response to environmental changes. We will expand on the new organisational forms in later chapters.

Critical theory and this book

Researchers and theorists study organisations for many different reasons. As forming organisations is a fundamental human activity, it is not surprising that so many different disciplines have an interest in the area. It is also understandable that the study of organisations has been influenced by political considerations.

This book draws on one subset of organisational inquiry. It uses as its subject organisations which operate within a business environment. These are primarily business organisations but may include not-for-profit organisations such as hospitals, educational institutions and government departments. The structure and management of these organisations reflect certain patterns and these patterns are capable of rational inquiry and interpretation. The results of research to determine these patterns form a coherent discipline, which we explore in later chapters. Hence we are relying on scientific methodology.

We approach the study of organisations from the point of view of their management. In this we take a sympathetic view of the manager's task, not in the sense that managers deserve sympathy but in the sense that managers in the current environment face a difficult task. Our aim is to assist managers and those likely to be managers later in their career, in unravelling some of the difficulties associated with the organisational part of their job. Where postmodernist interpretation assists this, and it does in areas such as culture, we include it in the text. However, remember that this book is about the total organisation and its structure. Much postmodernist theorising has greater relevance to the individual–organisational interface. This area is more the concern of organisational behaviour.

A further reason for adopting our approach is that, along with an introductory organisational behaviour unit, this is probably the first subject you have taken in organisational studies. As such, it needs to be fairly easily understood and to concentrate on those aspects of organisations which can be described and discussed with reasonable clarity. It is possible to do this when discussing reporting relationships but difficulties arise when elusive phenomena such as power are discussed. Power is fluid in nature and difficult to measure. Its study requires probably more subtlety and ability to be comfortable with intangibles than those undertaking early courses, and lacking work experience, may possess.

There is much that is not understood about organisations. They are, after all, an abstract construct, a human invention that exists within our imagination; it is this abstract nature that leads to the manipulative and political behaviour characteristic of organisational life. But they do exist to achieve goals. They use technologies that are measurable and observable and have structures that may be traced through areas of responsibilities and reporting relationships. They exist within environments that may be classified and apply strategies that may be identified and categorised. It is at this level of application that this book is aimed.

A managerial approach does push to the periphery other ways in which organisations are experienced by their members. To use the terminology of many organisational theorists, the voice of the marginalised is excluded and their experiences of organisations ignored. But the aim of this book is to create more effective organisations. If organisations are achieving their goals, and are well managed and competitive in their chosen markets, then job satisfaction and quality of work life for all organisation members should be improved. Organisations are not static entities; they are actively managed and managers have choices. This book hopes to guide managers towards appropriate choices which will benefit all in the organisation.

Coming attractions: the plan of this book

This book is concerned with applying organisation theory to answering the following five questions:

1 How do we know whether an organisation is successful?
2 How may we classify and describe the components of an organisation?

3 What influences the structure an organisation adopts?
4 What options do managers have for designing their organisation, and in what circumstance should each be applied?
5 How may knowledge of organisation theory be applied to help managers to solve current organisational problems?

The issue of an organisation's success is subsumed under the topic of *organisational effectiveness*. This is *the* dependent variable; it is the primary object of our attention. However, what constitutes organisational effectiveness is itself not easy to determine. In Chapter 3, four approaches to defining and measuring organisational effectiveness are presented. We consider what it is that organisations are trying to do and how various constituencies may define and appraise the same organisation's effectiveness differently. We also provide guidelines to help you evaluate an organisation's effectiveness.

Organisation structure has a definite but complicated meaning. As noted previously, the three primary components or *dimensions of an organisation* are complexity, formalisation, and centralisation. They represent the variables that, when combined, create different organisational designs. Chapter 4 takes an in-depth look at each of these dimensions of organisation structure. We also describe the five basic structural forms that organisations adopt.

An ongoing debate in organisational theory surrounds the question of what determines structure. Attention has focused on five determinants: the organisation's overall *strategy*; *size*, or the number of people employed by the organisation; the degree of routineness in the *technology* used by the organisation to transform its inputs into finished products or services; the degree of uncertainty in the organisation's *environment*; and the self-serving preferences of those individuals or groups who hold *power and control* in the organisation. The first four of these determinants have been labelled 'contingency variables' because their supporters argue that structure will change to reflect changes in them.[11] So, for example, if structure is contingent on size, a change in size will result in a change in the organisation's structure. The power–control perspective, however, is non-contingent. Its supporters propose that, in all instances, an organisation's structure is determined by the interests of those in power and that these individuals will always prefer the structural design that maximises their control. In Chapters 5 to 9, we review the five determinants and assess under what conditions each can become the major cause of an organisation's structure. Chapter 10 integrates the previous chapters by discussing how environmental and technological changes have led to new, emergent forms of organisations.

Certain issues are currently receiving the bulk of attention by organisational theorists as they attempt to offer solutions to organisational problems presently challenging managers. These include *managing the environment, organisational change, organisational culture, evolution, organisational knowledge* and *gender in organisations*. Chapters 11 to 16 look at each of these issues and demonstrate how organisational theory concepts can assist in their management. Following Chapter 16 you'll find a set of cases. These provide additional opportunities to apply the concepts introduced in the book to the solution of management problems.

Figure 1.4 summarises the plan of this book and how it has been translated into topics and chapters. Our primary concern is with the impact of various structures on effectiveness. Therefore, we begin with a discussion of organisational effectiveness. Then we define structural components and the determinants of structure. This is followed by a section on the various design options that can be constructed out of

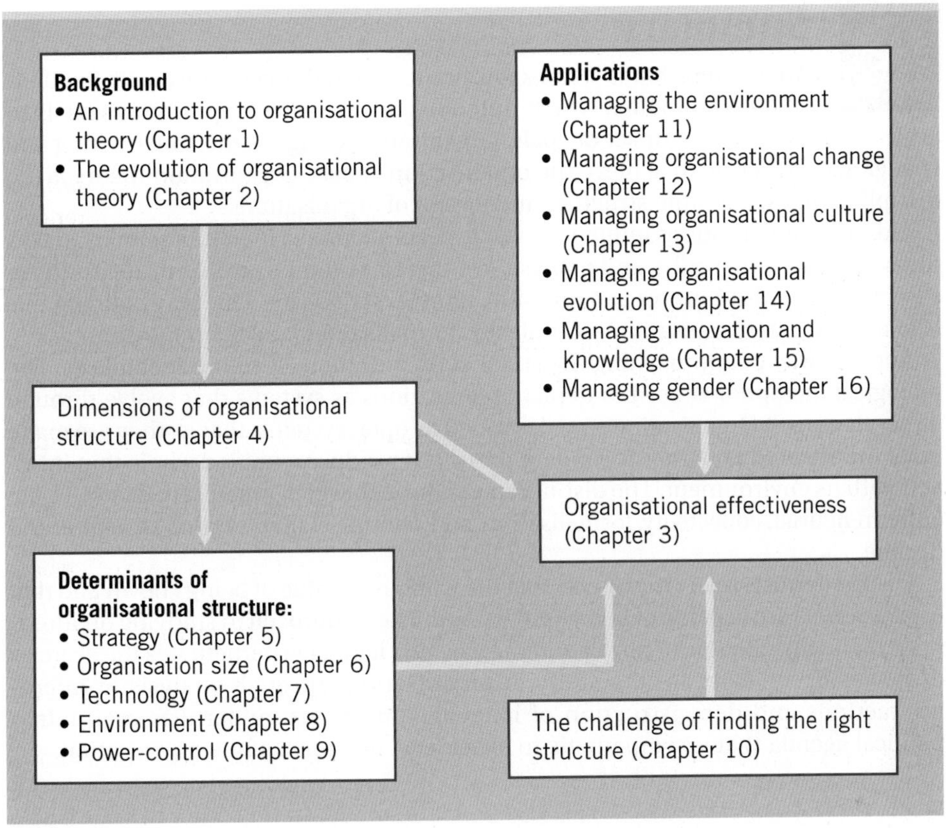
Background
• An introduction to organisational theory (Chapter 1)
• The evolution of organisational theory (Chapter 2)
Applications
• Managing the environment (Chapter 11)
• Managing organisational change (Chapter 12)
• Managing organisational culture (Chapter 13)
• Managing organisational evolution (Chapter 14)
• Managing innovation and knowledge (Chapter 15)
• Managing gender (Chapter 16)
Dimensions of organisational structure (Chapter 4)
Organisational effectiveness (Chapter 3)
Determinants of organisational structure:
• Strategy (Chapter 5)
• Organisation size (Chapter 6)
• Technology (Chapter 7)
• Environment (Chapter 8)
• Power-control (Chapter 9)
The challenge of finding the right structure (Chapter 10)

FIGURE 1.4 Framework for analysing organisation theory

the structural components. Attention is continually focused on linking structural designs with effectiveness. After reviewing the various structural options, you should be able to ascertain under what conditions each is preferable. The section on applications demonstrates how organisation theory concepts relate to six current managerial issues.

A final point needs to be made here: organisational theory concepts apply to subunits of an organisation as well as to the overall organisation. Although we will focus in this book on the structure and design of entire organisations, this is not the only level of analysis to which this book is applicable. The concepts to which you will be introduced in the following chapters are relevant to analysing divisions, departments and similar subunits within organisations as well as to organisations in their entirety. In fact, most large organisations are too diverse and internally heterogeneous to be treated as a single structural entity. Consequently, when we say that an organisation is structured in a certain singular way, in many cases this is a generalisation. A closer look typically reveals several different structural forms within most organisations, especially those that are large and complex.

Summary

An organisation is a consciously coordinated social entity, with an identifiable boundary, which functions on a relatively continuous basis to achieve a common goal or set of goals. Organisation design is the constructing and changing of structure to achieve the organisation's goals. Organisation theory is the discipline that studies the structure and design of organisations.

Although organisations influence most aspects of our life, their intangibility makes them difficult to describe and analyse. We therefore tend to concentrate on those aspects of organisations we can measure, or at least describe. One way of doing this is to measure an organisation's complexity, formalisation, and centralisation.

Another way of approaching the study of organisations is to use metaphors. The biological metaphor is used to depict organisations as systems that evolve through life-cycle stages. Organisations are described as open systems, that is, they are made up of interrelated and interdependent parts that produce a unified whole that interacts with its environment. The distinct stages through which organisations evolve are entrepreneurial, collectivity, formalisation-and-control, elaboration-of-structure, and decline.

Postmodernists reject the notion that the world is capable of being known and that organisations are capable of being understood. Their approach to studying organisations highlights the role of power and the way that language perpetuates the exercise of power. They advocate the study of organisations through analysis of micro-interactions and deconstruction of language. Most postmodernists maintain a political agenda that is sympathetic to lower level members of the organisation.

For review and discussion

1. Are all groups organisations? Discuss.
2. Can organisation theory be applied to a small business with only two or three employees? Discuss.
3. What research methodologies are generally used to study organisation theory?
4. How can the systems perspective help you better understand organisations?
5. Compare *open* and *closed* systems.
6. What are the characteristics of an open system?
7. Why do organisations tend towards growth?
8. Give an example of how the environment affects an organisation you are familiar with.
9. At what stage of their life cycle are the following organisations:
   - Virgin Blue
   - The educational institution you are studying at
   - Shell
   - Department of Foreign Affairs and Trade
   - ABC?
10. Is organisational decline inevitable? Defend your position.
11. Contrast organisation structure and organisation design.
12. Contrast organisational behaviour and organisation theory.

13 Describe the approach of critical theory. Does it complement organisation theory or does it replace it?

14 Identify the way that postmodernists approach organisation theory. In what way may postmodernist theories be of use to managers?

15 Being as specific as possible, identify the inputs, transformation processes, utputs, relevant subsystems and environment of each of the following organisations:
- Red Cross Blood Bank
- Greek Orthodox Church
- Carlton Football Club
- Royal Australian Navy
- St Vincent's Hospital
- Westfield shopping centre.

CASE FOR CLASS DISCUSSION

Who would want to manage CityRail?

Most cities have their mass transit systems, particularly rail systems, which are relied upon to move people into CBDs and other areas of high population density. One of their main tasks is to reduce congestion on the roads. But they have other responsibilities as well: the less well-off section of the population, who generally don't have cars, are heavily reliant upon public transport, and school children often depend upon trains. Because of this, substantial discounts on fares are offered to pensioners, the retired and others on reduced incomes. So the mass transit systems are not just a way of moving workers to their place of employment; they are also essential components of the social welfare system.

Because very few commuter rail systems make a profit, most are owned and operated by governments. Sydney's commuter rail system, CityRail, provides a good example of the problems facing mass transit rail networks. The background to the main problems is that rail systems are very expensive to build and they never cover the cost of financing; they are generally fortunate if they cover their running costs. Money must be provided by government, which has to make difficult decisions as to how to allocate scarce funds. Will they spend the money on railways, hospitals, schools, other welfare expenditure or something else? Generally transit systems are towards the end of the list of priorities. Consequently investment in rail systems always lags technical advances and rarely matches the depreciation of existing equipment. The end result is breakdowns and late running of trains. Commuters also now expect air-conditioning and other comfort standards which also require heavy capital expenditure on carriages.

The basic rail system of Sydney has been established for over a century. It has grown piecemeal by adding lines when money has become available. However, rather than consisting of a number of separate lines, Sydney's system is highly integrated, with delays on one line quickly leading to delays on others. As a result, CityRail has developed a well-deserved reputation for late running trains. Thus senior management found itself in a difficult position.

An ideal CityRail management from the government's point of view was one that managed to do more with less and kept the trains from the front page of the newspapers. However, this was not always possible as many of the tasks placed upon management such as improving on-time running and keeping capital expenditure low were incompatible. As a consequence, morale was low and there was constant turnover in management ranks.

The staffing of CityRail also presented problems. The system had remained largely static over decades and there was little labour turnover in key skill areas, such as train drivers. Many drivers were recruited from the baby boomer generation when they were young and they had spent their whole working life with the one employer. This was good for CityRail as it kept recruitment and training budgets lower than they otherwise would have been. But the result was an ageing workforce, the consequences of which were highlighted when a train crash, which cost a number of lives, was attributed to a driver with a poor health record collapsing at the controls of the train. A health check of the remaining drivers resulted in over one hundred having to be stood down because they did not pass their medical test. This led CityRail to cancel many trains and played havoc with schedules. There was no easy answer to this shortage as it took up to two years to train a driver.

The problem for the state government was that, as it owned and operated CityRail, these issues were having a direct influence upon its credibility. If something was not done quickly then seats could easily be lost at the next election. But the billions of dollars needed to untangle the system and improve on-time running, let alone build new lines to areas in need of them, had to be justified against other competing claims for government funds. Attempting to reconcile all of the challenges faced by CityRail was not proving to be an inexpensive or easy task.

QUESTIONS

1 Use CityRail to illustrate the open-system perspective of organisations.
2 Discuss whether the life-cycle perspective can be usefully applied to the CityRail case.
3 Discuss how organisation theory may assist CityRail in improving its effectiveness. Are postmodernist and critical approaches to organisational theory relevant to CityRail? Why or why not?

FURTHER READING

William Berquist, *The Postmodern Organization: Mastering the Art of Irreversible Change*, San Francisco: Jossey-Bass, 1993.

Robert Chia, 'From Modern to Post Modern Organizational Analysis', *Organization Studies*, 16(4), 1995, pp. 580–604.

Robert Gephart, 'Critical Management Studies', *Academy of Management Review*, 18(4), 1993, pp. 798–803.

Kenneth J. Gergen & Tojo Joseph Thatchenkery, 'Organization Science as Social Construction: Postmodern Potentials', *Journal of Applied Behavioral Science*, 40(2), 2004, pp. 228–50.

Daniel Katz & R.L. Khan, *The Social Psychology of Organizations*, 2nd edn, New York: Wiley, 1978.

John Kimberley & R.H. Miles, eds, *The Organizational Life Cycle*, San Francisco: Jossey-Bass, 1980.

Gareth Morgan, *Images of Organization*, 2nd edn, Thousand Oaks, CA: Sage, 1997.

NOTES

1 The material for this case study has been drawn from Ben Sandilands, 'Virgin Fills Airline Brand Vacuum', *The Australian Financial Review*, 13 September 2000; Sharon McDonald-Leigh, 'My Job', *The Sydney Morning Herald*, 23 September 2000; Lachlan Colquhoun, 'Newcomers Score in Dogfights: Early Rounds', *Business Review Weekly*, 13 October 2000.

2 John R. Kimberly, 'The Life Cycle Analogy and the Study of Organizations: Introduction', in J.R. Kimberly & R.H. Miles, eds, *The Organizational Life Cycle*, San Francisco: Jossey-Bass, 1980, pp. 6–9.

3 See, for example, Gareth Morgan, *Images of Organizations*, 2nd edn, Thousand Oaks, CA: Sage, 1997.

4 See Donde P. Ashmos & George P. Huber, 'The Systems Paradigm in Organization Theory: Correcting the Record and Suggesting the Future', *Academy of Management Review*, October 1987, pp. 607–21.

5 This section is adapted from Daniel Katz & Robert L. Kahn, *The Social Psychology of Organizations*, 2nd edn, New York: Wiley, 1978, pp. 22–30.

6 Adapted from Kim S. Cameron & David A. Whetten, 'Models of the Organization Life Cycle: Applications to Higher Education', *Research in Higher Education*, June 1983, pp. 211–24.

7 Robert Gephart, 'Critical Management Studies', *Academy of Management Review*, 18(4), 1993, pp. 798–803.

8 The following are a selection of articles relevant to the postmodernist approach to organisation theory: John Hassard, 'Post Modern Organizational Analysis: Towards a Conceptual Framework', *Journal of Management Studies*, 31(3), 1994, pp. 303–24; Robert Chia, 'From Modern to Postmodern Organizational Analysis', *Organization Studies*, 16(4), 1995, pp. 580–604; Howard Schwartz, 'The Postmodern Organization: Mastering the Art of Irreversible Change; Managing in the Postmodern World: America's Revolution Against Exploitation', *Academy of Management Review*, 20(1), 1995, pp. 215–21; Kenneth Gergen & Tojo Thatchenkery, 'Organization Science as Social Construction: Postmodern Potentials', *Journal of Applied Behavioral Science*, 40(2), 2004, pp. 228–50; Marta Calas & Linda Smircich, 'Past Postmodernism? Reflections and Tentative Directions', *Academy of Management Review*, 24(4), 1999, pp. 649–71; Mats Alvesson & Stanley Deetz, 'Critical Theory and Postmodernism: Approaches to Organizational Studies', in Stewart Clegg, Cynthia Hardy & Walter Nord, eds, *Handbook of Organizational Studies*, London: Sage, 1996; and Steven Feldman, 'The Levelling of Organization Culture: Egalitarianism in Critical Postmodern Organization Theory', *Journal of Applied Behavioral Science*, 35(2), 1999, pp. 228–44.

9 Thomas Lawrence & Nelson Phillips, 'Commentary: Separating Play and Critique: Postmodern and Critical Perspectives on TQM/BPR', *Journal of Management Inquiry*, 7(2), 1998, pp. 154–60.

10 Richard Daft & Arie Lewin, 'Where are the Theories for the "New" Organizational Forms: An Editorial Essay', *Organizational Science*, 4(4), 1993, i–iv.

11 See, for instance, George Schreyogg, 'Contingency and Choice in Organization Theory', *Organization Studies*, 3, 1980, pp. 305–26; and Henry L. Tosi, Jr & John W. Slocum, Jr, 'Contingency Theory: Some Suggested Directions', *Journal of Management*, Spring 1984, pp. 9–26.

CHAPTER 2

The evolution of organisation theory

After reading this chapter you should be able to:

- describe the evolution of the different approaches to organisation theory
- identify the early management theories
- explain the influence of the behavioural school
- discuss the role of sociotechnical systems
- discuss the complexity of decision making in organisations
- describe the various parts of contingency theory
- explain the contribution of critical theory and postmodernism
- describe the emergence of paradigm proliferation
- explain the meaning of paradigm proliferation
- contrast the rational and political perspectives of organisations
- examine some contemporary organisational approaches.

Introduction

The Toyota way

Toyota holds a central place in the mythology of business and management. Rising from the ashes of a defeated Japan, it is now one of the world's most studied business organisations. From making cheap and cheerful cars in the 1950s, it now produces one in every ten cars made. Its reputation for quality and price is unrivalled. In its second half century, it is showing few signs of the slowdown which often afflicts companies as they mature. There appears little bureaucratic inertia and innovation is proceeding apace.

Much of the work which is carried out in Toyota plants would be familiar to most observers. There is the well-known production line which is closely associated with motor vehicle assembly, workers undertaking specialised tasks and the subdued buzz of constant activity. Neither equipment, nor workers or material are idle. If you had the money and the interest you could travel to every Toyota plant around the globe, of which there are many, and would find every one to be a clone of the other. And interestingly, Toyota would not stop you studying their company; they are remarkably open about their production system. One reason is that they know how difficult it would be for another manufacturer to replicate.

The reputation of the Toyota management system was built upon the application of a few principles. First, the customer must be satisfied. Cars must be competitively priced, reliable and meet customer needs; there is no point in doing anything unless it leads to customer satisfaction. Second are the operations management techniques such as Kanban, just in time and material requirements planning, all aimed at eliminating wasted time and resources. But there are subtle management techniques which are more difficult to observe. Workers are responsible for quality and are their own quality inspectors. The company also works intensively with subcontractors to improve their performance and keep costs down.

However, there is one aspect of the Toyota system which is difficult to copy and that is that everyone is a problem solver. One of the rules-in-use at Toyota is that everyone in the organisation designs the solution to a problem which they face, applies the solution, tests it for conformance and then tries to improve upon the results. The combination of specialisation and everyone being a problem solver can lead to fragmentation, but Toyota has developed extensive integrating devices to manage the complexity of the system and prevent communication bottlenecks.

Needless to say, this system takes time to implement and is difficult for any other organisation, particularly a large one, to copy. Toyota places great stress on hiring the right people for entry level positions and then training them extensively. It rarely hires managers from outside; it promotes from within its workforce. It also operates the equivalent of a university, The Toyota Institute, which is attended by most of its senior managers. The programs it operates are oriented towards promoting the Toyota Way.

Toyota subsumes within its system many of the different approaches to organisational thought which have emerged over the last 100 years. One of these is the application of job specialisation and division of labour. Another is the concern with people and the realisation that people lie at the heart of productivity. Yet another is the development of a management system to reduce complexity and facilitate decision making. More recently is harnessing the energy and knowledge of everyone in the organisation to solve problems and contribute ideas. As we shall see in this chapter, the Toyota Way has emerged from many different branches of management thought and development.

The study of organisational theory has undergone an evolutionary process. The current state of inquiry is the result of different perspectives that have emerged in response to technological, environmental and social changes. The attention given to analysing organisations by both academics and practitioners has gathered pace over the past century. Not surprisingly, as those who comment and theorise on organisations come from a wide variety of disciplinary backgrounds, there are often divergent views as to how best to study organisations and for whose purpose they should be analysed.

The purpose of this chapter is to provide a brief overview of the main contributions and demonstrate how we got to where we are today. In doing this we will show how technological and environmental changes and paradigm shifts have influenced the study of organisations. One of the themes of this chapter will be that current organisation theories reflect a cycle of evolutionary development. Theories have been introduced, evaluated and refined over time, with new insights reflecting and supplementing areas that earlier theory overlooked. New theories and approaches sometimes emerge as a result of problems that managers face, such as those currently challenging multinational corporations and government departments. Others emerge from theorising and research on the part of academics.

Although organisational theory is subject to fashions and trends in thinking and research, few approaches are entirely discredited; generally the more useful parts of each theory find a continuing place in management thought. So if you want to understand what is happening today in organisation theory, you need to look back along the path from which it has come.

Developing a framework

Most systematic study of organisation theory has taken place since about 1900. This is not surprising, as by this time the industrialised world had started to take the form with which we are familiar. Most inventions that were to shape the 20th century had been devised and it was left to subsequent efforts to commercialise them. The growth in industrial organisations was paralleled by the growth of educational institutions to study them and management consultancies to advise them. There were a few major pre-20th-century milestones, and we will discuss them in the next section. However, for us the real problem lies in developing a framework that can adequately demonstrate the evolutionary nature of contemporary organisation theory. That is, how do you *organise* organisation theory?

It has been suggested that there are two underlying dimensions in the evolution of organisation theory and that each dimension, in turn, has opposing perspectives.[1] The first dimension reflects the fact that organisations are *systems*. The concept of the organisation being viewed as a system was introduced and described in Chapter 1. We saw that organisations can be viewed as open systems, which interact with their environment. Or they may be viewed as closed systems, which are almost self-sufficient entities. Before about 1960, organisation theory tended to be dominated by a closed-system perspective. Organisations were seen as essentially autonomous and sealed off from their environment, or at least that was what management attempted to achieve. During the 1960s, however, organisation theory began to take on a distinctly open-system perspective. Analyses that had previously placed the primary focus on the internal characteristics of an organisation gave way to approaches that emphasised the importance for the organisation of events and processes external to it.

The second dimension deals with the *ends* of organisation structure. Here again are two opposing positions. The rational or strategic perspective argues that the structure of an organisation is conceived as a vehicle for effectively achieving specified objectives and that this perspective is the main influence on organisational design. In contrast, the social perspective emphasises that structure is primarily the result of conflicting forces of the organisation's constituents, who seek power and control.

In addition to viewing the evolution of organisation theory along these two dimensions, we shall identify the main environmental, technological and political forces that have influenced ways of thinking in relation to organisations. By doing this we are developing tools of analysis that enable us to understand the current state of research and practice.

A further important reason for developing our framework is to enable students to identify the background and approaches taken by the authors of journal articles and books which they may be reading. Few publications in the organisational theory area explicitly identify the author's approach to the topic; it is left to the reader to place what they are reading into context. This chapter hopes to provide that context to those undertaking further reading in this discipline.

Early contributions

The concept of a person whose main task is to 'manage' is of quite recent origin. It evolved with the growth of the modern industrial undertaking, whose complex operations required large numbers of administrators. Prior to this, managerial tasks were undertaken as a by-product of the position a person held. Civil engineers, for instance, oversaw the work of those constructing their projects. Naval architects superintended the construction of ships. Management was something that went with their job!

There is no shortage of examples of organisational structures in classical times. Both the words 'administrator' and 'superintendent' have Latin origins. The structure of organisations was even referred to in the Bible, where Moses' father-in-law refers to leaders of tens, fifties, hundreds and thousands. The Roman army had a similar structure, with the centurion being the leader of the 'hundreds'. Until the growth of the modern corporation, the largest organisations were associated with the church and the army (and sometimes navy). The structures and practices of these organisations provided the template for most organisations that followed. They inducted members and socialised them into their ways. Membership implied disciplined conformance. There was a ranking of administrators and managers according to levels of responsibility, with each level of management having its badges of rank and symbols of office. This led to pyramid-shaped organisations. Loyalty and predictable performance were outcomes of the culture of the organisation, enabling operations to take place over a wide geographic spread. Armies also developed the concept of line and staff, with the 'line' being those engaged in actual warfare and 'staff' describing those who provided the services supporting them, such as planning, victualling and transport. Napoleon further introduced the concept of the 'division' in his armies, being a self-contained part of a larger organisation.

The experience of preindustrial organisations foreshadowed many of the problems faced by modern managers.[2] The English East India Company, for instance, incorporated in the 1600s, was faced with the problem of profitably exploiting trade with the Far East, a region stretching from India to China. Its greatest problems were those of maintaining discipline among its workforce, determining where it was making and losing money, and managing significant cultural diversity. It never surmounted the first problem: distances were too great, and a sense of entrepreneurialism and adventure led to most employees looking after their own interests rather than the company's. The second problem, that of knowing where it was making and losing money, was similarly never solved: management accounting was in its infancy, and accounts for some voyages were years late. Some commentators claim that lack of up-to-date financial data was the main reason for the company's demise. The issue of managing cultural diversity was partly solved by setting up a company college in London where local history, culture and languages were taught to those heading for the Far East, an early and comprehensive form of 'pre-departure training'.

The 18th century provides us with the first systematic analyses of the basis of modern organisational life, that of **division of labour**. The division of labour is the breaking down of tasks into simple components which can be undertaken on a repetitive basis by job specialists. Since antiquity, there had always been an element of division of labour. There were those who specialised in warfare, engineering, tax gathering and the like. But most were born into a station in life, such as peasant or labourer, and most grew their own food and led a life of self-sufficiency. Son followed father and daughter followed mother in occupation and activity.

division of labour functional specialisation; job broken down into simple and repetitive tasks

Not surprisingly, productivity was low. Adam Smith, observing what was happening around him in an industrialising Britain, wrote in 1776 about the economic advantages of the division of labour in the pin-manufacturing industry.[3] Smith noted that 10 individuals, each doing a specialised task, could produce about 48 000 pins a day among them. He proposed, however, that if each were working separately and independently, the 10 workers would be lucky to make 200 or even 10 pins between them in one day. Smith concluded then what most practising managers now accept as common sense: namely, that division of labour can bring about significant efficiencies.

The concept of the division of labour had widespread implications for organisations and their management. No longer was one person producing all his/her own needs according to his/her own wants. The division of labour implied that someone had to decide what to produce, how to produce it, provide the capital equipment and then staff what was, in effect, a small production line. These are all, of course, functions of management. The other implication was that a far more sophisticated system of exchange was required to trade the outputs of the division of labour. Adam Smith identified that market forces played this role, and he was the first to describe the role of markets and the price system as mediators in economic exchange.

The 19th century saw the development of two other industrial innovations with far-ranging implications for organisation theory. These were the emergence of mass production and the introduction of the railways.[4] These days we hardly give these two major innovations a second thought. But the organisational structures needed to make them work were the forerunners of the modern industrial undertaking.

First, mass production! Folklore has it that Henry Ford's model-T production line was the first example of mass production, but this is not the case. Ford was greatly influenced by previous attempts at mass production, including the Chicago abattoirs with their moving production line. The first modern use of mass production emerged in the United States around the 1840s. A large array of industrial and consumer goods, ranging from harvesters and sewing machines through to locks and armaments, was built on production lines using specially constructed capital equipment. The many components were accurately built to very fine tolerances, which enabled the interchanging of parts. This was in contrast to the craft method of production, where a craftsman built a complete item such as a lock using just sheet metal and basic tools as inputs. Needless to say, using this system, no two locks were the same, and no part was interchangeable with a lock made by another craftsman.

Using modern terminology, mass production 'dumbed down' labour in that craftsmen disappeared and were replaced by low-skilled assembly-line workers. The system was, however, knowledge-intensive. The extent of engineering input, including product design and knowledge of metals, alloys and machining, as well as tooling and capital equipment manufacturing, led to the production line as the 'high-tech' phenomenon of its day. One of the greatest achievements of mass production was at the Springfield armaments factory in the 1860s. So well known were the mass production techniques at this plant that the system used on the Ford production line was initially known as the Springfield system.

Out of the mass production system emerged the modern industrial structure, with workers, foremen, superintendents, works managers and general managers. We also see a type of line and staff arrangement, with the designers and administrators comprising the staff and the assembly-line workers forming the line. Departments such as accounting, finance and planning emerged to improve flows of information and assist management control, whilst research and development and engineering departments promoted innovation and the introduction of new techniques and products. Socially, we see the widespread introduction of working for wages. Prior to the modern factory, most workers were self-employed either as farmers or contractors. The emergence of the wage earner as the urban proletariat had significant implications for political activity and the structure of society.

The second major 19th-century innovation was the railway. Although still a transport backbone in most countries, the railways' neglect in some parts of the world gives them an air of run-down obsolescence. From today's perspective it is difficult to appreciate how innovative railways were, or to comprehend the many management challenges their administration posed. At the height of railway construction in the 1850s and 60s, railway companies were being floated at a rate hardly matched until the dot-com boom of the late 1990s. Railways were very knowledge-intensive. They posed significant engineering challenges, in both the construction of the railway and its equipment, such as engines and rolling stock. And matters were no easier when it came to their organisation. They had to be run profitably in order to pay dividends to those who subscribed capital to build them. Large numbers of people had to be employed with many different job specialisations. Extensive training in new skills was required. The railways were a 24-hour per day operation, and long distances and often different time zones had to be accommodated. Safety and profitability required the development of timetables and schedules. A workforce culture had to be developed to reinforce strict timekeeping.

It is not surprising that the army provided a basis for the management systems that were adopted. The railways were structured along departmental lines, with each department specialising in a particular task. Planning staff undertook the task of scheduling and timetabling. Uniforms with badges of rank reinforced strict hierarchical control and concepts of the 'general manager' emerged. In Prussia station staff even stood to attention as a train passed.

The structure that evolved promoted effective work effort and minimised complexity. Clear lines of authority were introduced and areas of responsibility spelt out. High levels of coordination were achieved through planning and scheduling and the division of labour was promoted through hiring and training. All of these will be familiar to most readers, even though the technologies we now use are radically different.

Turning to contributions made during the 20th century, we will begin with the organisational forms that emerged to exploit the new technological discoveries of the late 19th and early 20th centuries.

From 1900 to the 1930s—early management theories

The main aim of theorists during the **1900–1930s** was to identify universal principles and management techniques that could be applied to management. The challenges of management seemed to be much the same everywhere, no matter what the industry or occupations involved. Given this perception it is natural that a simple set of solutions was sought for problems. As this period saw the emergence of the first systematised approach to organisation theory, we call the output of the various theorists the classical school. In a sense it is misleading to call those whose work is described below 'theorists'. They were in fact practical people, generally successful managers, who drew on their experiences to inform their publication and lecturing.

1900–1930s Need to reduce production costs leading to improving efficiency. Achievement of rational goals with closed system perspective. Focus of analysis was work practices

Managers during this period were responding to the challenge of how to manage the large-sized civilian organisations that were emerging at the end of the 19th century. This was the beginning of the age of mass production, when the products of technological innovation had an extensive market if they could be produced in quantity at a low price. As a result, organisations that produced them had to be of a large size.

However, additional social factors emerged which complicated the management of organisations. It was a period of great industrial unrest, with bitter strikes in large companies and continuous agitation by many workers in support of major political and social change. Both complicating and contributing to this were the tensions caused by wars and depressions. Additionally, most governments were attempting to isolate their economies through high tariff barriers and other restrictions on trade. Given the environmental uncertainties, most managers took a similar attitude and attempted to isolate their organisations from outside influence.

The classical theorists had in common the view that organisations were established, and managed, to achieve rational goals such as profit or return on assets. As we have seen, there was a very strong desire to reduce the costs of production in order to expand the market for products so one of the main aims of the classical theorists was to improve the productive efficiency of the organisations. They viewed the ideal organisation as a closed system created to achieve goals efficiently. As a result they viewed the organisation as being rational, and once efficient processes had been established, predictable outcomes could be expected. This is often called the classical view of organisations. Let's now examine the contributions of the main contributors to this approach.

Frederick Taylor and scientific management

The publication in 1911 of Frederick Winslow Taylor's *Principles of Scientific Management* marked the beginning of serious theory building in the field of management and organisations.[5] Taylor was a mechanical engineer by training, employed by the Midvale and Bethlehem steel companies in Pennsylvania. He strongly believed, on

scientific management a movement initiated by Frederick Taylor to achieve production efficiencies by systematising and standardising jobs to achieve the 'one best way' they should be done

the basis of his observation of work methods at the time, that worker output was only about one-third of what was possible. He set out to correct the situation by applying the scientific method to jobs on the shop floor. His desire to find the 'one best way' in which each job should be done would be part of what today we would call work design.

After years of conducting experiments with workers, he proposed four principles of **scientific management**, which, he argued, would result in significant increases in productivity: (a) the replacement of inexact methods for determining each element of a worker's job with scientific determination; (b) the scientific selection and training of workers; (c) the cooperation of management and labour to accomplish work objectives, in accordance with the scientific method; and (d) a more equal division of responsibility between managers and workers, with the former doing the planning and supervising and the latter doing the execution.

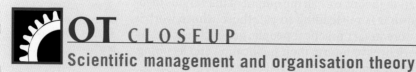

OT CLOSEUP

Scientific management and organisation theory

Most writings on scientific management concentrate on organising work on the factory floor. But Taylor and his colleagues made a major contribution to the management of the modern corporation. Large organisations are certainly not new: most civilisations have had to grapple with the problems of government and the need to organise armies and navies. Churches and other religious bodies are also large organisations that have had to develop the means of coping with large size and geographic spread. The growth of the large corporation, however, raised its own problems. From the beginning of the 20th century it became clear that the large corporation would become the pre-eminent organisation form, which would define industrialised life. Corporations did not become big because it was easy to manage large numbers of people; in fact, the opposite applied. Corporations became large because of the need for large-scale capital investment, the complexity of the product, such as with motor cars, or the economies arising from mass production. Large workforces had to be managed as a result of these other imperatives. The need to monitor costs and provide many of the clerical services necessary to run a complex business contributed to the growth of the workforce.

Taylor's organisational innovation was the functional foreman, who acted as a link between management and shop floor worker. But Russell Robb, of the then newly formed Harvard Business School, attempted a compromise between the old military style and the new conditions of industry. He claimed that all organisations differ, depending on their methods and what they are trying to achieve. Robb noted that the modern corporation had much to learn from the military, particularly the military's stress on fixing responsibility and authority, clearly defining duties and channels of communication, and providing order and discipline.

However, in the military, order and discipline were stressed far more than was needed in the modern corporation. The industrial corporation was built on extensive division of labour and needed greater coordination of effort than did the military. Success in industry was not based on obedience but on economy of effort, and as a result the industrial corporation had to be different. Also, civilian workforces could not be disciplined in the same way as military forces. There should be more stress placed on worker and management selection and training, processes had to be arranged to keep costs low, and the manager needed to be aware of the organisation as a system.

These problems rose in prominence as the corporation moved from the entrepreneurial stage, which was managed by its founder and owner, into the stage where ownership and management were distinctly separate.

Source: Adapted from Daniel A. Wren, *The Evolution of Management Thought*, 4th edn, New York: John Wiley, 1994.

The early theorists such as Taylor and Fayol were primarily practical people, who were closely associated with the operation of the companies they worked for or advised. In contrast, the background of many theorists who emerged in the 1930s was in the behavioural sciences. The 20th century saw the emergence of disciplines such as psychology and anthropology and their application to the workplace. It became clear to this group, which we will call the human relations school, that one of the major impacts on organisational effectiveness was the motivations and actions of the workforce. One of the characteristics of this period was the recognition of the social nature of organisations. These theorists, who are often referred to as forming the human relations school, viewed organisations as made up of both tasks and people. Below we discuss the contribution of a number of influential thinkers from this period.

Elton Mayo and the Hawthorne studies

Elton Mayo probably does not deserve his prominent place in the pantheon of management history. He was an academic researcher called in to explain some unusual findings which emerged from some simple experiments being undertaken between 1924 and 1927 at an electrical manufacturing plant in the United States. His research became known as the **Hawthorne studies**. These studies, which would eventually be widely expanded and would carry on through the early 1930s, emerged from work being undertaken by Western Electric industrial engineers at the Hawthorne plant to examine the effect of various lighting levels on worker productivity. Control and experimental groups were established. Lighting for the experimental group was raised and lowered in intensity, while the control group worked under unchanging illumination levels. The engineers had expected individual output to be directly related to the intensity of light. However, there were contradictions in their findings. As the light intensity was raised in the experimental unit, output rose for both the experimental and control group. To the surprise of the engineers, as the light level was lowered in the experimental group, productivity continued to rise in both groups. In fact, a productivity decrease was observed in the experimental group only when the light intensity had been reduced to that of moonlight. The engineers concluded that illumination intensity clearly was not directly related to group productivity, but they could not explain the behaviour they had witnessed.

Hawthorne studies a series of studies which identified the behavioural basis of organisational outcomes

The Western Electric engineers asked the Harvard psychologist, Elton Mayo, and his associates to join the study as consultants. This began a relationship that would last until the end of 1932 and encompass numerous experiments covering the redesign of jobs, changes in the length of the work day and work week, introduction of rest periods, and individual versus group wage plans.[9] For example, in one experiment the researchers sought to evaluate the effect of a piecework incentive pay system on group productivity. The results indicated that the wage-incentive plan was less of a determining factor for a worker's output than were group pressure and acceptance and the feeling of security. Social norms of the group, therefore, were concluded to be the key determinants of individual work behaviour.

It is generally agreed by management scholars that the Hawthorne studies had a dramatic impact on the direction of management and organisation theory. It ushered in an era of organisational humanism. Managers would no longer consider the issue of organisation design without including the effects on work groups, employee attitudes and manager–employee relationships.

Chester Barnard and cooperative systems

Merging the ideas of Taylor, Fayol and Weber with the results from the Hawthorne studies led to the conclusion that organisations were cooperative systems. They are composed of tasks and people that have to be maintained at an equilibrium state. Attention only to technical jobs or to the needs of people who do the jobs sub-optimises the system. Therefore, managers need to organise around the requirements of the tasks to be performed and the needs of the people who will perform them.

The notion that an organisation is a cooperative system is generally credited to Chester Barnard. He presented his ideas in *The Functions of the Executive*, in which he drew on his years of experience with American Telephone and Telegraph, including in senior management positions.[10]

In addition to being one of the first to treat organisations as systems, Barnard offered other important insights. He challenged the classical view that authority flowed from the top down by arguing that authority should be defined in terms of the response of the subordinate; he introduced to organisation theory the role of the informal organisation; and he proposed that the manager's major roles were to facilitate communication and to stimulate subordinates to high levels of effort. Chester Barnard's work predated those of later chief executives, such as Jack Welch of General Electric, whose widely read memoirs helped propagate ideas as to how organisations should be managed.

Douglas McGregor: Theory X and Theory Y

One of the most often mentioned contributions to the behavioural school is Douglas McGregor's thesis that there are two distinct views of human beings: one basically negative—Theory X—and the other basically positive—Theory Y.[11] After reviewing the way managers dealt with employees, McGregor concluded that a manager's view of the nature of human beings is based on a certain grouping of assumptions and on the fact that he or she tends to mould his or her behaviour towards subordinates according to those assumptions.

Under Theory X, the four assumptions held by managers are:

1. Employees inherently dislike work and, whenever possible, will attempt to avoid it.
2. As employees dislike work, they must be coerced, controlled or threatened with punishment to achieve desired goals.
3. Employees will shirk responsibilities and seek formal direction whenever possible.
4. Most workers place security above all other factors associated with work and will display little ambition.

In contrast to these negative views of human beings, McGregor listed four other assumptions that he called Theory Y:

1. Employees can view work as being as natural as rest or play.
2. Human beings will exercise self-direction and self-control if they are committed to the objectives.
3. The average person can learn to accept, even seek, responsibility.
4. Creativity—that is, the ability to make good decisions—is widely dispersed throughout the population and is not necessarily the sole province of those in managerial functions.

What are the implications of McGregor's Theory X and Theory Y for organisation theory? McGregor argued that Theory Y assumptions were preferable and that they should guide managers in the way they designed their organisations and motivated their employees. Much of the enthusiasm, beginning in the 1960s, for participative decision making, the creation of responsible and challenging jobs for employees and developing good group relations can be traced to McGregor's advocacy that managers follow Theory Y assumptions.

Warren Bennis and the death of bureaucracy

The strong humanistic theme of this period culminated with a eulogy on the passing of bureaucracy.[12] Warren Bennis, for example, claimed that bureaucracy's centralised decision making, impersonal submission to authority and narrow division of labour were being replaced by decentralised and democratic structures organised around flexible groups. Influence based on authority was giving way to influence derived from expertise. Whilst Weber argued that bureaucracy was the ideal organisation, Warren Bennis argued the other extreme: conditions now pointed to flexible adhocracies as the ideal organisational form.

The Tavistock Institute and sociotechnical systems

Two of the characteristics of the post-World War II period were chronic industrial disputation, which mainly took the form of strikes by workers, and socialist ideologies, which emphasised worker autonomy. For most of the 20th century, much of the work undertaken in organisations was extremely tedious and lacked challenge or opportunity for advancement. The factory production line was typical of much of the work at that time. **Sociotechnical systems** was an approach to organising which attempted to make work more interesting and challenging and involve workers more in decision making with the intention of reducing industrial conflict by improving the quality of working life.[13] The Tavistock Institute in London was an early advocate of this approach. It was also a prominent movement in Scandinavia where government legislation mandated workers' rights to decision making. Sociotechnical systems did not advocate one best way to manage, but promoted certain principles by which jobs should be designed. These included an end to repetitive, short-cycle work, eliminating repressive management, dignity for workers and worker involvement in the way that work was organised and structured. The sociotechnical systems approach was multidisciplinary in that it drew on many of the behavioural sciences to better understand the behaviour of workers. One of the most widely discussed outcomes of this approach is that of autonomous work groups, which were common in the Scandinavian motor industry in the 1970s.

sociotechnical systems an attempt to make work more interesting and challenging by improving the quality of working life

Sociotechnical systems was an attempt by the behavioural sciences to contribute to a reduction in social tensions and to improve quality of working life. In many ways the circumstances which prompted it was overtaken by time; automation eventually eliminated much of the drudgery at work, and globalisation saw many routine jobs exported. There are still unfulfilling jobs around but many of these are undertaken on a short-term basis, such as those in McDonald's, or are widely dispersed, such as domestic workers, making organising workers difficult.

Contribution of the human relations school

In 50 years we had essentially moved from one extreme position to another. The human relations school still regarded organisations as closed systems, but they stressed the social aspects of the system rather than the nuts and bolts of production. By the 1960s, most managers were aware of the influence that human behaviour had on organisational outcomes. One of the problems facing them was how to classify this behaviour and to incorporate the more humanistic attitude in organisational structures and practices. This had to be achieved in such a way that did not compromise efficiency. Both Barnard and McGregor proposed classifications that advanced the understanding of workplace behaviour and permitted managers to incorporate these understandings into organisational practices. This process did not end with the 1960s. Although the period under review was a productive time in theory development and practical understanding, the task of balancing organisational and human needs is ongoing. The approach of this group laid the groundwork for later organisation researchers and theorists who stressed that organisations were far from being rational and predictable and that the point of inquiry should move from a management perspective to a lower level employee perspective. Given that the pressures of globalisation on organisations appear to be leading to longer work hours and less job security, we may in the future see a re-emergence of the human relations school.

1950s–1970
A period concerned with improving the manageability and decision-making processes of organisations

From 1950 to 1970—the unmanageable organisation and decision making

By the 1950s very large and complex organisations had emerged. Although they were subject to environmental pressures, making them open systems, they acted as if they were closed systems with the result that their focus was often to look inward to processes rather than outward to customers or the environment. These organisations often had hundreds of thousands of employees, and controlling them appeared to present insuperable problems. In fact, management control was often tenuous with workforces frequently on strike or on go-slows. Administration took the form of more and more complex bureaucracies in which it was difficult to make decisions and in which no one seemed to have responsibility. Lifetime employment was the norm, and the basis for promotion was often seniority rather than merit.

A number of theorists highlighted the difficulties inherent in managing organisations of this nature, particularly in relation to decision making, and suggested that they almost had an existence beyond rational intervention. This theme was taken up by a number of popular satirists whose work was widely read, particularly by office workers and managers to whom it was directed.

This section is also instructive in that it highlights the difference between populist and academic approaches to studying organisations, a trend which started to emerge during this period. Populist approaches tend to use humour and satire to draw the attention of readers to phenomena they may not have been aware of, or may have experienced but not been able to articulate or express. Academic researchers, in contrast, seek deeper underlying themes and explanations which generally lack popular appeal and which often require specialist knowledge to interpret. Their writings tend to be arcane and are aimed at other academics, although of course there are exceptions, such as Chester Barnard in the previous section. Our explanation will start with the populists and then move on to academic writers.

The Peter Principle

The Peter Principle was proposed by Laurence Peter and Raymond Hull.[14] They suggested that in large, stable, hierarchical bureaucracies which offered lifetime employment, managers would be promoted until they reached a level at which they were incompetent. They had, in effect, reached their 'level of incompetence' and, at that level, promotion ceased. However, this meant that in the absence of redundancies and downsizing, many managers were essentially incompetent, limiting the amount of effective work being accomplished in the organisation. Peter and Hull suggested that in a process called 'lateral arabesque' incompetent managers were moved laterally at their same level in the organisation and were often given longer job titles in the process.

Parkinson's laws

C. Northcote Parkinson proposed a number of laws relating to organisations.[15] The best known of these is that work expands to fill the time available for its completion. He also noted the expansion of the number of administrators compared with those actually doing the work. For instance, he observed that staff numbers in the British Colonial Office were greater after Britain had divested itself of colonies than when it still administered them. Another of Parkinson's laws noted that in meetings the time spent on any item on an agenda is in inverse proportion to its importance. Many of Parkinson's observations are exaggerated for effect but his book found ready readers amongst those frustrated by the organisations they worked in.

Herbert Simon and satisficing

On a more serious note, the academic Herbert Simon and his collaborators studied the process of decision making in complex organisations.[16] They proposed that the

OT CLOSEUP

The organisation man

The growth of the large corporation, particularly in the United States, led to a large section of the workforce being known as 'organisation men', a concept popularised in the 1950s. These were seen as faceless individuals foregoing all their individuality to the numbing conformity of the organisation. This conformity extended beyond the workplace: organisation men shared similar values, family life and ways of living. Indeed, the suburbs they lived in and the cars they drove all suffered from the same uniformity. This raised particular concern in the USA, where the mythology of the rugged individual was seen to be giving way to a collectivism that subjugated the individual to the group.

The writings on the organisation men were sociological in origin. The 'men' part obviously excluded women who were generally invisible in the organisation, at least as far as promotion and careers were concerned. The writings also had a white-collar orientation, omitting reference to those who might be termed working class from the shop floor. And with the notable exception of Frederick Taylor, few of the other theorists we discuss have much to say about work on the factory floor.

Although the era of the organisation man may have passed, along with the social contract that underpinned the role, the impact of the organisation on its workers is as current as it was in the 1950s. Rather than worrying about numbing uniformity, we are now concerned about overwork, lack of security, and the impact of travel and work demands on family life. To many of those caught between career and family demands, the role of the 1950s' organisation man must seem extremely comfortable.

Source: Adapted from Anthony Sampson, *The Company Man: The Rise and Fall of Corporate Life*, (Copyright © Estate of Anthony Sampson 1995) by permission of PFD <www.pfd.co.uk> on behalf of the Estate of Anthony Sampson.

assumption of rationality in decision making, as typified by 'economic man' is misplaced. Rather, they invented the term 'administrative man' to describe decision-making behaviour. Whilst rational decision makers sought to optimise the outcomes of decision making, 'administrative man' was content to satisfice, that is, to adopt a course of action that was satisfactory or 'good enough'. This occurred because it was not possible to fully process all the information which was available in organisations. As a result, optimal decisions were unattainable. Simon and his colleagues proposed that decision making could be placed upon a continuum with programmed and non-programmed decision making at either end. With great foresight he suggested that advances in information technology would lead to a move towards more programmed decision making and, hence, greater rationality in decision making.

The complexity of decision making

In considering how decisions were made in organisations, James March and his colleagues noted that a business firm is constrained by the problems of coordinating the flow of information, constantly changing and difficult to understand external environments, and limitations in the capacity to process, store and utilise information. Under these circumstances, it is unlikely that decisions would conform to the concept of being rational. March and a number of other colleagues went on to propose that organisations faced a 'garbage can of choices' in which the decision-making process was not closely linked to the decisions being made.[17] In a similar manner, Charles Lindblom proposed that decision making in organisations was too complex and too much influenced by political considerations for rationality to prevail.[18] He suggested that the result of the decision-making process could be summarised as the science of 'muddling through', which was the practical alternative to rational decision making.

In highlighting the irrational nature of much decision making in organisations, the writers described in this section led the way in identifying the role that power and politics play in organisations.

1960–1980
Determining the most appropriate structural form. Achieving rational goals with an open systems perspective. Focus of analysis was the total organisation and its structural form

From 1960 to 1980—the study of contingency

There was a gap in the various approaches so far considered. What was missing was consideration of organisation structure. Was there a structure that was right for all occasions? Or did different circumstances give rise to the need for different structures? The contingency approach views the structure of organisations as contingent—that is, dependent on pressures that can be identified and analysed. It was noted that organisations do not have an infinite number of forms. Their structures are predictable depending on the contingency factors. Researchers at this time used the methodology of sampling large numbers of organisations and then looking for cause-and-effect relationships between structures and environmental relationships. They therefore viewed the organisation as an open system. Their research had the purpose of improving organisational effectiveness by providing managers with guidance as to the most appropriate structure, given the contingency factors. This has sometimes been described as developing a general theory of management.

This period was very productive for organisational research. Many of the theories and studies described in subsequent chapters derive from this time. The contingency approach was facilitated by the more stable social and political conditions of the period. Technological change was slow and there were high levels of government ownership of business and regulation of industry. Globalisation had yet to make its presence felt. The most influential researchers of this period are described below.

Herbert Simon and the principles backlash

We have already highlighted the work of Herbert Simon in the previous section. He was an observer and a prolific theorist of organisations over a long period of time, and contributed to new ways of looking at them. He foreshadowed the rise of the contingency movement as early as the 1940s, and subsequently developed the intellectual template for others to follow. Simon noted that most classical principles were nothing more than proverbs, and many contradicted each other. He argued that organisation theory needed to go beyond superficial and oversimplified principles to a study of the conditions under which competing principles were applicable.[19] Nevertheless, the 1950s and 60s tended to be dominated by simplistic principles—of both the mechanistic and the humanistic variety. It took approximately 20 years for organisation theorists to respond effectively to Simon's challenge.

Katz and Kahn's environmental perspective

Daniel Katz and Robert Kahn's *The Social Psychology of Organizations* was a major impetus towards promoting the open-systems perspective on organisation theory.[20] Their book provided a convincing description of the advantages of an open-systems perspective for examining the important relations of an organisation with its environment and the need for organisations to adapt to a changing environment if they were to survive.

Since Katz and Kahn's work, numerous theorists have investigated the environment–structure relationship. Various types of environments have been identified, and much research has been conducted to evaluate which structures conform best with these different types of environments. The classic studies of Burns and Stalker and Lawrence and Lorsch, described in later chapters, stand out as leaders in the field. No current discussion of organisation theory would be complete without a thorough assessment of environment as a major contingency factor influencing the preferred form of structure.

The case for technology

Research in the 1960s by Joan Woodward and Charles Perrow, as well as the conceptual framework offered by James Thompson, have made an impressive case for the importance of **technology** in determining the appropriate structure for an organisation.[21] As with environment, no contemporary discussion of organisation theory would be complete without consideration of technology and the need for managers to match structure with technology. This period largely predated the expanding influence of information technology and the rise of the service industries. Research on these influences necessarily belongs to a later period but is influenced by the work of researchers such as Perrow and Thompson.

technology the information, equipment, techniques and processes required to transform inputs to outputs

The Aston Group and organisation size

In addition to advocates of environment and technology, theorists from this period include those who identified **organisation size** as an important factor influencing structure. This position has been most zealously argued by researchers associated with the University of Aston in England.[22] Large organisations have been shown to have many common structural components. So, too, have small organisations. Most

organisation size the total number of employees in the organisation

important perhaps, the evidence suggests that certain of these components follow an established pattern as organisations expand in size. Such evidence has proven valuable to managers in helping them make organisation-design decisions as their organisations have grown.

Miles and Snow and the strategic imperative

The study of corporate strategy gathered pace in the 1970s, and in 1978 an influential book written by Raymond Miles and Charles Snow was published categorising strategy.[23] They then proposed that successful implementation of the chosen strategy required an appropriate structure to be adopted. They were arguing in support of the strategic imperative: that is, that one of the determinants of structure is the strategy which an organisation adopts. The study of strategy has expanded over the past 20 years, with the research of Michael Porter being widely disseminated and influencing how the organisation can profitably exist within its environment.[24]

Paradigm proliferation—from 1980 to the present

It is in the nature of academic research to be continually exploring new areas of interest.[25] And as with any behavioural science, areas of inquiry emerge which dominate thinking for a period before other areas attract the interest of researchers. This process does not invalidate previous areas of interest; research continues to refine and complement established concepts. Sometimes old ideas emerge in new guises, a contemporary interpretation attracting new interest. For instance, Taylorism is far from dead; we hear echoes of it every time we discuss job specialisation. And the idea of organisational culture experienced a resurgence in the 1980s.

A paradigm is a model used as a framework of ideas. The paradigm which informed Taylorism sought to raise the productive efficiency of organisations. Since then other paradigms have emerged, such as contingencies, which inform an organisation's structure and the role that power and politics plays in organisations. **Paradigm proliferation** refers to the emergence of a number of new frameworks with which to view organisations. These have emerged because the study of organisations is multidisciplinary and also because researchers approach their task from varying perspectives. And of course there has been a great increase in the number of researchers who have contributed in different ways to knowledge in the area.

paradigm proliferation the emergence of a number of new frameworks with which to view organisations

The different disciplines which contribute to organisational theory include sociology, anthropology and social psychology, as well as management. Some, like management, concentrate on applied research aimed at improving organisational effectiveness. Applied research is practical research which aims to identify cause and effect relationships such as linking environmental changes with organisational responses. It seeks to be of use to practitioners and to inform teaching in the management disciplines. Other disciplines seek to reveal previously unexplored phenomena and often view organisations holistically rather than as an agglomeration of subsystems or something to be managed. Often their subjects of research differ from those of interest to managers. Anthropologists, for example, study societies rather than organisations, whilst social psychologists bring knowledge of behaviour and human processes to organisations, something that most managers could not hope to duplicate. Yet a further audience for academic research is other academics. Many academics do not research or publish for a wide audience; they intend it to be primarily read, and cited, by other academics. This inevitably influences the nature of what they research and how they present their findings.

Also during this period, aspects of organisation theory intersected with elements of philosophy to create a more theoretical approach to the subject area. Many theories and interpretations which were incapable of empirical testing were proposed. Increasingly, much organisational theory writing is not intended to inform practice, but is aimed at informing a specialised academic audience.

An unspoken but ever present influence on organisation studies is the political orientation of the researcher. An old observation is that researchers normally find what they set out to find. So if you are researching discrimination in organisations, chances are you will find it. For experienced researchers and those familiar with interpreting research findings, the orientation of the researcher is fairly apparent from their writings. Different orientations include those of Marxists, feminists, labour process interpretations, postmodernists and critical theorists. We referred to a number of these approaches in the previous chapter. Many of these differing interpretations have emerged from those trained in non-business disciplines and who have subsequently moved into business schools. Many in fact are anti-business and anti-management in orientation, and make little effort to improve the way that business is organised. One of the consequences of these different approaches is the paradigm proliferation referred to in the heading of this section.

To be fair, much of this paradigm proliferation emerged from the limitations thrown up by the search for a general theory of management. Empirical findings often identified only weak relationships, and generalisations were difficult to make. It was from these limitations that contingency theory emerged. But organisation theorists found themselves operating in a difficult area in which theories were too general to have a specific application or alternatively too specific to be of general use. The postmodernists went so far as to suggest that there were no generalised explanations.

One theme running through organisation theory over the past 20 years is that of the political nature of organisations. In part this emerged from the limitations of the contingency theory approach and the search for a general theory of management. While having its merits, and providing significant insight into organisations, the search for a general theory of management proved elusive. The contingency factors could explain part of what was happening in organisations, but there were significant variations in structures that seemed to defy easy explanation. From the 1980s, the influence of power and politics was promoted as being able to account for many of the unexplained areas. It further became apparent that, with the growth of large organisations, there were limitations on the ability of managers to cognitively, that is mentally, process all that was going on about them. This prompted various researchers to develop theories as to how managers coped with the limitations on their ability to process information and how they lived with uncertainty. An early formulation of this position was made by James March and Herbert Simon, but it has been extensively refined by Jeffrey Pfeffer.

In many ways it is surprising that organisation researchers took so long to incorporate the realities of power in their theories. In one way it is understandable: power is difficult to understand, elusive and almost impossible to measure. But its influence on all human interactions, including formal organisations, has been well documented for as long as humans have been recording their history. Classical organisational theorists ignored power issues by concentrating on the scientific structuring of jobs and organisational structures but they had an implicit assumption that all power should reside with the management of the organisation. The behavioural theorists thought that power issues could be bypassed by creating more people-friendly organisations and by devolving power to work groups and other structures lower in the organisation. The contingency theorists did not take power into account in their research. By the 1980s, it was clear that issues relating to power could not be ignored and that any study of organisations should include consideration of power.

March and Simon's cognitive limits to rationality

In the previous section it was noted that a number of writers challenged the idea of rational decision making in organisations. As a result of their observations that organisations tended to make decisions which were 'good enough', March and Simon argued for a revised model of organisation theory—one very different from the rational cooperative systems view.[26] This revised model would recognise the limits of a decision maker's rationality and acknowledge the presence of conflicting goals. It also provided the theoretical foundation for power and politics to play a part in the way in which organisations are structured and managed.

Pfeffer's organisations as political arenas

Jeffrey Pfeffer has built on March and Simon's work to create a model of organisation theory that encompasses power coalitions, inherent conflict over goals, and organisational design decisions that favour the self-interest of those in power.[27] Pfeffer proposed that control in organisations becomes an end rather than a means of achieving goals. Organisations are coalitions composed of varying groups and individuals with different demands. An organisation's design represents the result of the power struggles by these diverse coalitions. Pfeffer argues that if we want to understand how and why organisations are designed the way they are, we need to assess the preferences and interests of those in the organisation who have influence over the design decisions.

Critical theory and postmodernism

Critical theory and postmodernism were discussed in Chapter 1. They are included here because chronologically this is where they fit. Also they are often concerned with issues of power, although not perhaps in the sense considered by most organisational writers. Critical theory and postmodernism are often considered together as they share the basic feature of acting as a counterpoint to the business and organisational structures with which we are familiar. Critical theory seeks to describe organisations not as mechanisms of production and exchange, or collaborative effort, but as arenas of exploitation and marginalisation. This exploitation may be of lower level workers in the organisation or of minorities. The perception that business organisations destroy Third World cultures and values through their global operations, and the undesirability of this, form part of critical theory. So do many of the gender studies we will discuss in Chapter 16.

Postmodernism is a more difficult construct. Not surprisingly, postmodernism reflects a world which is held to exist after modernism. Modernism grew out of the enlightenment in Europe, in which science and reason replaced superstition and intuition as the way towards progress. Our society and the organisations in it are based on modernistic ideas. Postmodernism would consider that these are now in decay, and that a new concept of progress will result. This new way to progress largely rests on redefining equality, reordering power relationships and a reduced role for science in relation to symbolism and meaning.[28]

Both critical theory and postmodernism consider that what industrialised societies define as progress is in reality a means of exploitation and marginalisation. To build a new and better world, the existing order needs to be deconstructed—that is, pulled apart—before a new and more equitable order can be built. However, apart from generalised statements regarding the rights of the individual and the promotion of equality, no concrete proposals have been made representing a new order that can be debated.

In researching organisations from a critical or postmodern perspective, stress is placed on power systems; the use of language or dialectics, which define knowledge and relationships; and the multiple roles and loss of meanings associated with organisational life. The approach tends to stress the experiences of lower level members of the organisation.

OT CLOSEUP

Is there an Australian organisational form?

There is probably little that is unique in Australia's business structures. We have been heavily influenced by the writings of management theorists in the United Kingdom and the United States, and their ideas on management reach Australian shores very quickly after they are released overseas. Moreover, Australian organisations that are subsidiaries of companies based in those countries tend to take on a structure dictated from the head office. The management of Australian multinationals is influenced in turn by the practices they see in overseas countries. And there is no reason to believe that a steel mill in Australia would have a structure that was radically different from a steel mill in most parts of the world: the skills and knowledge to run it are much the same as steel mills everywhere. This is the concept of *mimetic isomorphism*—that is, organisations faced with similar environments and using similar technologies could be expected to develop similar structures.

The effects of the country's size and geographic location have influenced the type of structure favoured by Australian multinationals. Given the small population base and isolation from the large population centres—in contrast to Japan, Germany and the US—few Australian companies would be able to micromanage extensive overseas operations. Micromanage means having extensive day-to-day input into decision making. Examples of the types of companies which need to micromanage are those producing complex products with extended supply chains such as motor vehicle manufacturers and electronics companies. A further group of activities which small countries cannot undertake are those requiring extensive finance, such as aircraft manufacture, which necessitates greater capital bases than small countries have. Capital goods manufacture often requires a dense network of suppliers of specialist products, which is difficult to build in small economies.

What structural form tends to emerge from these influences? Most Australian firms adopt a *multidomestic structure*, that is, one which is largely self-managed in the country in which it is based. The business often is not part of a global brand, but carries branding and symbols relevant to the country in which it is domiciled. NAB's British banking, Boral's brick operations in the US and Brambles' Chep business in Europe are examples. The large mining companies also conform to a multidomestic strategy with each mine largely operating on a stand-alone basis.

But as the economy grows, globalisation expands and areas of specialisation emerge there will always be exceptions. Fonterra, the New Zealand dairy company, has transmogrified over the past few years from being an exporter to becoming more deeply involved in the markets in which it operates. Some companies are so successful overseas that they move their top management closer to overseas markets to be near where they make most of their money. James Hardie and CSL provide good examples.

You may wonder why organisations figure so prominently in the writings of the critical and postmodern school. The reason is that organisations are inherently more powerful than individuals, and by their nature have hierarchies in which not all are, or can be, of equal status. Similarly, organisations consume resources from their environment, as well as producing products and services for consumption by those in the environment. They therefore have a major influence in shaping the societies of which they are a part.

Postmodernism is more a philosophy than a disciplinary approach; it rejects the modern world and bases its rejection upon a selective assessment of what it considers to be disadvantageous. It has not yet progressed to formulating what it considers to be a superior system of organising. As it rejects empiricism (that is testing hypotheses through research) it can hardly use research to support its contentions. At the same time, theories which cannot be tested must always have limited applicability. The relevance of postmodernism largely depends upon what type of knowledge a researcher or practitioner wants and to what purpose it is to be put.

Symbolic-interpretive perspectives—from the 1980s

symbolic-interpretive perspective views the organisation as a social construct

Nominating the 1980s as the beginning of the **symbolic-interpretive perspective** is to a certain extent misleading. Anthropologists and sociologists have long realised that organisations provide a sense of meaning and belonging to their members. The role of symbols as a means of identifying organisations and their members predates the Roman Empire. The cross of the Christian Church is probably the pre-eminent example of an organisational symbol. Myths, legends and stories have also been extensively studied as a way of interpreting a culture and for their role in transmitting a culture from one generation of members to another.

The symbolic-interpretive approach concerns itself more with behavioural than with structural issues but it has relevance for a number of chapters in this book, primarily those on culture and gender. The approach concentrates on how organisational participants interpret language and symbols in organisations and attribute meanings to relationships between people. It then examines how these interpretations and meanings influence the interactions between organisational participants. One of the difficulties of this approach is that of achieving impartiality in interpreting the symbols and evaluating the interactions. Many researchers using the symbolic-interpretive framework have acknowledged points of view which precondition them to interpret their observations in certain ways. As critiques of scientific methodology and impartiality are currently fashionable, many researchers do not see this as a significant issue. An associated problem is that many studies, such as those relating to gender, only concentrate on one side of an interaction. In this way a holistic view of complex social phenomena is not achieved.

A further problem in using this perspective is that it requires knowledge of specialist types of research, which is not common amongst those who study business. Further, knowledge of psychology, anthropology and other behavioural disciplines aids in interpreting data. Many business researchers are lacking in such knowledge.

Anthropological and psychological techniques are still used to study organisations and provide valuable insight into their operation. But the movement of the symbolic-interpretive perspective to a central focus in organisation theory developed as a result of three emerging observations. The first was by Karl Weick, who claimed that an organisation is a social construct—that is, it is enacted by its members. The second was the publication of *In Search of Excellence* in 1980, which popularised the idea that organisations had an identifiable culture and that the appropriateness of this culture was a major contributor to organisational effectiveness. The third emerged from studying the role of gender in organisations. It was felt by many researchers that research techniques common in the business disciplines failed to reveal the subtleties necessary to adequately describe the experience of women in organisations. Since these observations, the symbolic-interpretive approaches have taken a central place within organisational theory.

Karl Weick and enactment theory

Karl Weick's *The Social Psychology of Organizing* was influential in directing researchers' attention to the intangible nature of organisations.[29] Prior to Weick's work, organisations had tended to be viewed as something tangible and solid, and hence capable of easy interpretation and study. Weick claimed that this reification of organisations—that is, attributing real properties to an intangible body—was a process where the phenomenon was created by the observer. He called this **enactment**; we can make a culture, an environment or an organisation appear, but it is then difficult to identify the difference between that creation and reality. In particular, Weick was interested in the way that intangible factors had an impact upon non-programmed decision making in organisations.

enactment a process where structures and process take form through the actions of individuals

Berger and Luckman's social construction of reality

Two German sociologists, Peter Berger and Thomas Luckman, in their book *The Social Construction of Reality*, proposed that human relationships were built up through a process of negotiations between people and a common interpretation of shared history and experience.[30] What sustains social order is at least a minimum agreement as to how events are to be perceived and the meanings that are attached to them. These interpretations take on a life beyond that of abstract occurrences, but nevertheless remain socially constructed. Although aimed at societies, Berger and Luckman's insights also apply to the way business organisations create and interpret their reality.

Peters and Waterman's *In Search of Excellence*

Writing for a business audience, Peters and Waterman popularised the idea that organisational culture had a significant impact on effectiveness.[31] Although only one of a number of factors identified as characteristic of excellent companies, their observations popularised the notion of the culture of business organisations and redirected the research attention of management and business researchers. Also popularising the importance of culture was the extensive literature relating to the culture of Japanese companies. Such books as *The Art of Japanese Management* by Pascale and Athos dwelt heavily on the way in which national and corporate culture was the key to the strength of Japanese companies.[32]

Recently developed perspectives

A number of other approaches to organisation theory have been developed and refined over the past 20 years and have emerged in mainstream thinking. These approaches have little in common and this has contributed to the idea of paradigm proliferation in the field. Future researchers may find common threads between the different approaches. We will describe each of them briefly in turn.

Organisational economics

The link between organisations and economics was first proposed by the economist, Ronald Coase, in1937.[33] In addressing the basic problem of why organisations exist, he proposed that organisations could sometimes mediate exchanges between members more easily and cheaply than markets can. If the price system was used to determine what each worker was to do, it would involve a complex round of negotiations in relation to discovering what comparable prices were elsewhere, negotiating and renegotiating contracts, monitoring performance and settling disputes. These costs are called transaction costs and they are incurred in determining the scale, scope and price of a task. In contrast, an employee, within reason, can be told by management what task to carry out, thus minimising transaction costs.

Williamson has developed organisational economics further by taking Coase's analysis and building it into an exploration of the relationships between hierarchies and markets.[34] Hierarchies are well known to most of us as the chain of command in organisations that instructs lower level employees what to do. Markets in turn are a social construct, with ongoing participants who contract with each other to provide goods and services. The form that dominates will reflect what is cheapest to run in any given situation. This will be a reflection of the costs of each transaction between individuals and groups. Also, markets compared with hierarchies are often poor at handling uncertainty and risk. Consequently, in many cases, the cost of running hierarchical organisations is lower than that for organising performance through markets.

Another application of economics to organisation theory is that of agency theory.[35] A manager in an organisation has a number of subordinates, who are considered to be the manager's agents. The manager has the natural motivation to obtain as much benefit from his or her agents as possible, and the agents in turn have the incentive to shirk or otherwise cheat on the contract. The resulting behaviour is an outcome of the bargaining process. Another common application of agency theory is where the managers of a company are the agents of the shareholders. Agency theory examines these relationships, particularly where there is asymmetrical knowledge—that is, where more is known about the transaction by one party than the other.

The picture painted of managers by those who study organisational economics, particularly agency theory, is not particularly flattering. The assumptions made are that it is human nature for managers and workers to act in selfish and opportunistic ways. It has little explanatory power when considering issues such as voluntary effort or acts of cooperation or collaboration which don't involve some form of extrinsic reward. For this reason, organisational economics has been called an anti-management theory.[36] However, the increasing use of market controls in organisations, as evidenced by the popularity of divisionalisation of large companies and the extensive use of outsourcing and subcontracting, suggests that organisational economics makes a major contribution in explaining why certain structures are adopted.

Institutional theory

Institutional theory claims that organisational responses are often repetitive and products of past actions and practices. That is, over time, responses become institutionalised. These institutionalised practices are often the result of social pressures to conform to convention. As a result, we find that many organisational actions and management decisions are imitations of past practices. And as institutional theory tends to look at groups of organisations, many management decisions are seen to be cloning the practices of other successful organisations.[37]

Managing the multinational corporation

Managing multinational corporations, such as Toyota, General Electric, Sony, BP and Nestlé, presents the greatest organisational challenge of our time. Other challenges, such as managing small- and medium-sized enterprises, may be more common, but the large multinational places significantly greater demands upon organisational design and management ability. The sun literally never sets upon their activities, with operations which span the globe and operate 24 hours per day, 7 days per week. Such organisations are only made possible by an acute understanding of management challenges. These range from accommodating local cultures to maintaining quality. Much has been written on their management and they remain the focus of research effort.[38] Although the multinational corporation is often the subject of anti-globalisation protesters, most researchers interested in them focus on issues related to improving their effectiveness.

Gender in organisations

Until 30 years ago, few questioned the gender segregation obvious in most organisations. Men and women had their respective jobs, and men were dominant in management. However, women increasingly objected to their exclusion from key parts of the organisation and, even when the obvious barriers were removed, women were still underrepresented in many areas. This started a field of research that has as its foundation the role of gender in organisations. This has developed into feminist approaches to organisational structuring and research.

There are many subgroups of feminist thought.[39] Most will be familiar with the women in management literature, which seeks to research and promote the interests of women within existing organisational structures. But many may not be so well known, including the socialist, psychoanalytic and Third World/postcolonial viewpoints.

One strand of feminist literature takes the view that organisations are run as patriarchies that marginalise women's participation. This strand may extend to challenging our businesses and organisations as constructs of exploitation. Another strand of literature proposes that the way males exercise power and influence is detrimental to sound management and the feminisation of management would lead to more productive and collaborative organisations. Feminist research methods have extended beyond normal survey and statistical processing into the analysis of language, called dialectics, non-verbal communication patterns, and the use of empathic case studies where the researcher adopts a partial and sympathetic approach to the subject. The result of such research is mixed and, not surprisingly, outcomes reflect the positions of those undertaking the research. In complex organisations and social systems it is difficult to identify the mechanisms through which social forces and processes operate. As with power, these mechanisms are largely invisible.

The research into gender in organisations is part of the wider analysis of the role that gender plays in the functioning of society. (We discuss gender in organisations in Chapter 16.)

Popular management writers

Management thinkers writing for a mass market adopt a different approach to academic researchers. Book sales are important to them so they must grab the attention of potential readers. These writers rarely emerge from the intellectual background of universities; they have largely drawn upon industry experience, particularly in management consulting or as chief executive officers (CEOs).

Many management thinkers and writers have an extensive following. Most use the written word as well as seminars and even television to communicate their message. In contrast to the postmodernists, they seek to make organisations more productive by helping them use their resources, including human ones, more innovatively and effectively. We will discuss the ideas of a few of the better known management writers.

Tom Peters

Tom Peters came to prominence through his co-authorship with Bob Waterman of the modern management book, *In Search of Excellence*. In this they describe the characteristics of America's most successful large corporations. Since that time, Tom Peters has continued to develop the theme of the most appropriate organisational form for modern organisations.[40] He claims that the environment in which business operates is becoming more unpredictable and competitive. In response, organisations need to improve communications, become more innovative and nimble, and respond to environmental changes in shorter time frames that in the past.

Peters sees organisational structure as having an important role in business becoming more responsive. He claims that 'crazy times call for crazy organisations'. He advocates the reduction of management layers and the widening of the span of control, even to the extent of each supervisor having up to 70 subordinates. Middle managers should become boundary spanners and facilitators rather than experts and guardians of functional units. Lower level employees should form self-managing teams, unhindered by restrictive bureaucracy. The result of these moves would be a far more decentralised and responsive organisation.

Charles Handy

Charles Handy is a British management theorist who also stresses the need for innovation and flexibility in organisations.[41] But he advocates a far softer role for organisations and management through stressing the human side of the organisation. Whereas Peters was seeking to create organisations with a harsh edge which could be fiercely competitive, Handy promotes the idea of organisations as places where people would like to work as well as being competitive entities.

Handy's main contribution was to identify, in terms understandable to most, what he called the tribes and gods who make up the corporate world. Tribes reflect the corporate culture, and gods, the attributes of individuals within the culture. No one tribe or god is more important than the other, but both within and between organisations the various tribes and gods interact to produce productive and innovative companies. He also claims that employees should identify what type of person they are and seek organisations that complement their talents. Handy seeks to improve the way organisations are managed by advocating a greater understanding of organisational behaviour. In this he is an educator rather than an innovative management thinker.

Ricardo Semler

Ricardo Semler is a Brazilian industrialist who inherited a metals manufacturing company from his parents.[42] Becoming disillusioned with traditional management practices, which emphasised command and control, he turned much of the management of the company over to his employees. They determined the rates of pay for each worker, working hours, how the work was to be organised, who was responsible for what task, what to produce and who to hire and fire. In order to facilitate this, most of the workforce operated as teams of no more than 10 people.

Semler's contribution was to devolve decision-making power to his employees, eliminating most of the input from the management hierarchy. He also set up many employees as subcontractors, who supplied goods to his main plants. It is still too early to determine the extent of the success of Semler's work, as long-term decisions such as financing and adapting to technological change still have to be faced. But it does indicate that many tasks relevant to organising work in the factory or office may be undertaken by lower level workers.

Michael Hammer and re-engineering

Although there are a number of theorists who have promoted re-engineering, Hammer is the person commonly associated with it.[43] The proponents of re-engineering observed that traditional organisational structures are hierarchies that are constructed around role specialisations. Re-engineering seeks to build the structure of the organisation around multidisciplinary processes, which can then be grouped together to create the totality of the organisation's effort. The structure of the organisation therefore represents a series of largely self-contained tasks, rather than a hierarchy built around occupational specialists.

Jack Welch and the General Electric experience

A significant publishing industry has emerged over the past 20 years based upon the reminiscences of retired chief executives. Typically, these are from managers who have had a significant impact upon their companies and whose names are well known within the business world and even the wider community. One of the best known and widely read of the former managers is Jack Welch, the former CEO of General Electric.[44] His ideas as to the way large companies should be structured and managed have been widely discussed and adopted and a number have become common practice. One of his ideas was to reduce bureaucratic inertia and increase productivity by reducing the number of layers of management and downsizing the number of employees. Another was to decentralise decision making in order to put the customer uppermost in decision makers' minds and promote faster decision making. He also stressed that the quality of management was a company's most important asset.

Summary

Modern organisation theory began with the scientific management approach, which emerged at the beginning of the 20th century. This approach relied heavily on simplistic and universal principles, developing models of organisation that stressed rationality and the mechanistic nature of organisations. Subsequent approaches in the 1930s, to a large degree represented a counterpoint to the rational-mechanistic view. The focus moved away from the division of labour and centralised authority towards democratic organisations. The human factor, which tended to be treated as a predictable 'given' by the scientific management approach, moved to dominate new thinking in organisation theory in the years between 1930 and 1960.

The two early approaches have been supplemented by new ways of thinking and the current state of organisation theory more fully reflects subsequent schools of thought. Contingency advocates have taken the insights provided by the earlier theorists and reframed them to reflect the pressures emerging in a given situation. The contingency view, in addition to recognising that there is not 'one best way', has made significant strides in identifying those contingency variables that are most important for determining the right structure. The political perspective, which emerged in the 1970s, builds on our knowledge of behavioural decision making and political science, and has significantly improved our ability to explain organisational phenomena that the contingency advocates' rational assumptions overlooked.

Contemporary approaches to organisational theory may be divided into two groups. The first comes from an intellectual analysis of features of organisational operations. These investigations include organisational economics, institutional theory and gender in organisations. Critical theory and postmodernism create a new paradigm, or basic set of assumptions, in the way that organisations are viewed. Researchers who approach their tasks from these perspectives would emphasise the inequalities of organisations, in both the sense of power and rewards. They would also stress the coercive nature of organisations.

The second contemporary approach to organisations is to make them more efficient and to improve their use of resources, particularly people. Ever since organisations started to grow large, managers and theorists have been grappling with the need to balance control with decentralising decision making. They are also constantly challenged by the problems of organisational change. Much of the modern thinking regarding organisations approaches these old problems in ways applicable to today's workforces and levels of technology.

Table 2.1 summarises the various approaches to the study of organisations and the period in which they emerged.

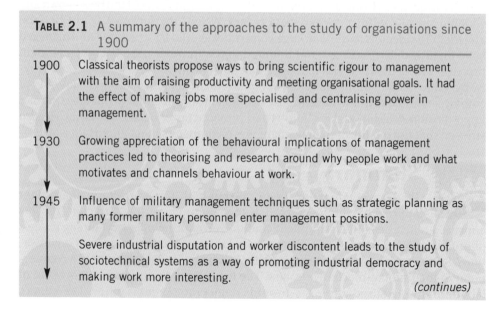

TABLE 2.1 A summary of the approaches to the study of organisations since 1900

1900	Classical theorists propose ways to bring scientific rigour to management with the aim of raising productivity and meeting organisational goals. It had the effect of making jobs more specialised and centralising power in management.
1930	Growing appreciation of the behavioural implications of management practices led to theorising and research around why people work and what motivates and channels behaviour at work.
1945	Influence of military management techniques such as strategic planning as many former military personnel enter management positions.
	Severe industrial disputation and worker discontent leads to the study of sociotechnical systems as a way of promoting industrial democracy and making work more interesting.

(continues)

1950 Researchers and theorists grapple with the difficulties of information processing and decision making in large, impersonal and bureaucratic organisations. The increasing complexity of business and the information it generates anticipates the role of information processing and the computer.

A number of satirists parody management and organisational shortcomings to popular acclaim.

1960 The idea of the organisation as a system with extensive environmental interactions starts to emerge.

Researchers seek to identify universal management principles which will form a general theory of management. The search fails but ushers in an appreciation of how contingencies such as environment, technology and strategy influence an organisation's structure.

Population ecology seeks to link environmental capacity with organisational survival.

1980 Researchers begin to appreciate that successful companies are more than just a collection of assets, they are also social movements. This promotes the symbolic-interpretive perspective which influences research through the study of culture and organisational meaning.

Researchers determine that organisational size and structure may be explained by organisational economics.

Globalisation, deregulation and privatisation significantly increase the competitive environment. The study of the structure of multinationals and organisational networks expands.

Downsizing reverses the trend towards continuous organisational growth.

1990 The study of gender in organisations seeks to explain the low numbers of women in management positions.

Postmodernism and critical theory attempts to link European philosophical traditions and insights to organisation research and theory.

The diversity in approach and research practice since 1980 has been termed paradigm proliferation.

For review and discussion

1. What was the nature of the problems which classical management theory set out to solve?
2. Explain how the behaviourist and power approaches to organisations share a social perspective.
3. How relevant are scientific management principles today?

4 Evaluate whether there is a relationship between theory and practice in organisation theory.
5 Discuss how military organisations have affected approaches to structuring organisations.
6 Contrast Taylor's and Fayol's levels of organisational analysis.
7 How relevant are Fayol's principles today?
8 'As most large organisations today are bureaucracies, Weber's views could be considered highly influential.' Do you agree or disagree? Discuss.
9 What are the implications of the Hawthorne studies for contemporary organisation theory?
10 Do you think most managers have Theory X or Theory Y views of people? How might this view affect their organisation design decisions?
11 What are the key contingency variables that researchers identified in the 1960s and 70s?
12 Why has power emerged as an important area of study for organisational theorists?
13 Why is it difficult to classify modern approaches to organisational theory as one coherent type?
14 Why have a number of modern theories regarding organisations been called anti-management?
15 How applicable is critical theory and postmodernism to managers of organisations?
16 Contrast the approach to organisations of postmodernists with that of the popular management writers.
17 Of the recently developed perspectives, including the modern management writers, which do you think will have the greatest long-term impact? Why?

CASE FOR CLASS DISCUSSION

The Japanese transplant car factory

The opening case in this chapter introduced Toyota as one of the most admired of modern companies. Much of this admiration is built upon Toyota's reputation for building quality cars.[45] Although not to everyone's taste (even the managing director of Toyota Australia has been known to refer to his products as refrigerators on wheels), Toyotas are rarely rivalled in the fields of build quality and durability. Once only built in Japan, from the 1980s the Japanese manufacturers started to establish transplant factories around the world. This presented them with a major management problem. The capital equipment of the factory was easy to establish in foreign fields; the unique Japanese production system, which in part reflected Japanese cultural characteristics, proved much more difficult. To maintain quality, and keep production costs low, the Japanese relied on teamwork and quality circles. Their management system, at least on the factory floor, was very flat, with little in the way of hierarchy. The problem was how to instil this way of working in a foreign workforce.

The setting up of a greenfields factory in the United States (i.e. one completely new and built on a 'green field') provides a good example of how Toyota has tackled the problem. Toyota selected staff who had never worked in a factory before. It had no shortage of applicants: 58 000 applied for 1200 jobs. To select those it wanted, Toyota put all applicants through an extensive series of tests. These included measurements of reading and maths skills, group exercises, and an extensive interview aimed at identifying certain personality and attitudinal traits and communication skills. This process took 20–25 hours.

From this process, team leaders were selected. (Teams form the basis of Toyota's production system, and so the role of the team leader is critical.) The team leaders were sent to Japan for up to four weeks for training. They spent nine hours a day on the shop floor, learning the processes they would be using back home. They also spent their leisure time together, thus developing a camaraderie they would be expected to take back to their own factory. Team leaders have managerial responsibilities for immediate production activities. They play a crucial role in the organisation, design and allocation of work on a daily basis.

The training of 'new hires' is extensive. The first week is given over to training activities both in the classroom and on the production line. This process is called assimilation. It includes extensive safety and quality training. There are just a few job classifications, and everyone in the team is capable of undertaking all tasks allocated to the team. Jobs are rotated in order to avoid repetitive strain injuries. The team members themselves largely determine how tasks will be undertaken and who will undertake them. As the vehicle moves down the assembly line, each team is encouraged to regard the next team as its customers. There are meetings at the start of each work day to review the previous day's work and plan for the current one. At this time the team also discusses any problems that may have arisen.

Suggestions aimed at improving quality and reducing costs are encouraged and expected. In many cases they are rewarded with monetary payments. This is part of the management philosophy of delegating managerial authority and responsibility to shop floor workers.

The attempts at building a common bond between workers and encouraging community of spirit are further enhanced by the dining arrangements. All personnel, from management to cleaners, eat in the same cafeteria. Dress standards encourage uniformity of outlook. Similarly, managers do not have walled-in offices but sit at desks in large, open areas adjacent to the production facility.

Source: Adapted from Greg Gardner, 'Tracking Toyota's Tundra' *Ward's Auto World*, 34(10), 1998, pp. 42–4.

QUESTIONS

1 Identify and describe the similarities and differences between scientific management and the Toyota manufacturing system.

2 Does the evidence of the use of power in the above case make Pfeffer's ideas relevant only to Western cultures? Discuss.

3 What evidence is provided in the case of the other approaches to organisation theory discussed in this chapter?

FURTHER READING

Thomas Clarke & Stewart Clegg, *Changing Paradigms: The Transformation of Management Knowledge in the 21st Century*, London: HarperCollins, 1998.

Lex Donaldson, *American Anti-Management Theories of Organization: a Critique of Paradigm Proliferation*, Cambridge: Cambridge University Press, 1995.

Charles Handy, *Inside Organisations: 21 Ideas for Managers*, London: BBC Books, 1990.

Daniel Katz & Robert Khan, *The Social Psychology of Organizations*, New York: John Wiley, 1966.

Tom Peters, *Thriving on Chaos*, New York: Knopf, 1988.

Anthony Sampson, *Company Man: The Rise and Fall of Company Life*, London: HarperCollins, 1995.

W. Richard Scott, 'Theoretical Perspectives', in Marshall W. Meyer, ed., *Environments and Organizations*, San Francisco: Jossey-Bass, 1978.

Ricardo Semler, *Maverick: The Success Story behind the World's Most Unusual Workplace*, New York: Warner, 1993.

Jack Welch, *Jack: What I've Learned from Leading a Great Company and Great People*, London: Headline, 2001.

Oliver Williamson, *Markets and Hierarchies, Analysis and Antitrust Implications*, New York: Free Press, 1975.

Daniel Wren, *The Evolution of Management Thought*, 4th edn, New York: John Wiley, 1994.

NOTES

1 This selection is based on W. Richard Scott, 'Theoretical Perspectives', in Marshall W. Meyer, ed., *Environments and Organizations*, San Francisco: Jossey-Bass, 1978, pp. 21–8.

2 John Keay, *The Honourable Company: A History of the English East India Company*, London: HarperCollins, 1993.

3 Adam Smith, *An Inquiry into the Nature and Causes of the Wealth of Nations*, New York: Modern Library, 1937. Originally published in 1776.

4 Daniel Wren, *The Evolution of Management Thought*, 4th edn, New York: John Wiley, 1994.

5 Frederick W. Taylor, *The Principles of Scientific Management*, New York: Harper & Row, 1911.

6 Henri Fayol, *Administration lndustrielle et Générale*, Paris: Dunod, 1916.

7 Max Weber, *The Theory of Social and Economic Organizations*, ed. Talcott Parsons, trans. A.M. Henderson & Talcott Parsons, New York: Free Press, 1947.

8 See, for example, Ralph C. Davis, *The Principles of Factory Organization and Management*, New York: Harper & Row, 1928; and *The Fundamentals of Top Management*, New York: Harper & Row, 1951.

9 Elton Mayo, *The Human Problems of Industrial Civilization*, New York: Macmillan, 1933; and Fritz J. Roethlisberger & William J. Dickson, *Management and the Worker*, Cambridge: Harvard University Press, 1939.

10 Chester I. Barnard, *The Functions of the Executive*, Cambridge: Harvard University Press, 1938.

11 Douglas McGregor, *The Human Side of Enterprise*, New York: McGraw-Hill, 1960.

12 Warren G. Bennis, 'The Coming Death of Bureaucracy', *Think*, November–December 1966, pp. 30–5.

13 For a contemporary description of sociotechnical systems, see Enid Mumford, *Redesigning Human Systems*, London: Information Science Publishing, 2003.

14 Dr Laurence J. Peter & Raymond Hull, *The Peter Principle*, London: Pan Books, 1970.

15 C. Northcote Parkinson, *Parkinson's Law, or The Pursuit of Progress*, London: John Murray, 1958.

16 Herbert A. Simon, *Administrative Behavior: A Study of Decision-Making Processes in Administrative Organizations*, New York: Macmillan, 1947.

17 Michael D. Cohen, James G. March & Johan P. Olsen, 'A Garbage Can Model of Organizational Choice', *Administrative Science Quarterly*, 17, 1972, pp. 1–25.

18 Charles E. Lindblom, 'The Science of Muddling Through', *Public Administration Review*, 19, 1959, pp. 79–88.

19 Herbert A. Simon, *Administrative Behavior: A Study of Decision-Making Processes in Administrative Organizations*, New York: Macmillan, 1947.

20 Daniel Katz & Robert L. Kahn, *The Social Psychology of Organizations*, New York: John Wiley, 1966.

21 Joan Woodward, *Industrial Organization: Theory and Practice*, London: Oxford University Press, 1965; Charles Perrow, 'A Framework for the Comparative Analysis of Organizations', *American Sociological Review*, April 1967, pp. 194–208; and James D. Thompson, *Organizations in Action*, New York: McGraw-Hill, 1967.

22 See, for example, Derek S. Pugh, David J. Hickson, C.R. Hinings & C. Turner, 'The Context of Organization Structures', *Administrative Science Quarterly*, March 1969, pp. 91–114.

23 Raymond Miles & Charles Snow, *Organizational Strategy, Structure and Process*, New York: McGraw Hill, 1978.
24 Michael Porter, *Competitive Strategy*, New York: The Free Press, 1980.
25 For a discussion on paradigm proliferation, see Karl Weick, 'Theory Construction as Disciplined Reflexivity: Tradeoffs in the 90s', *Academy of Management Journal*, 24(4), October 1999, pp. 797–807.
26 James G. March & Herbert Simon, *Organizations*, New York: John Wiley, 1958.
27 Jeffrey Pfeffer, *Organizational Design*, Arlington Heights, IL: AHM Publishing, 1978; and *Power in Organizations*, Marshfield, MA: Pitman Publishing, 1981.
28 See S. Clegg, C. Hardy & W. Nord, *Handbook of Organisation Studies*, London: Sage, 1996. See also M. Foucault, *Power/Knowledge*, New York: Pantheon, 1980; and R. Cooper, 'Modernism, Postmodernism and Organization Analysis: The Contribution of Jaques Derrida', *Organization Studies*, 10(4), 1989, pp. 479–602.
29 Karl Weick, *The Social Psychology of Organizing*, Reading MA: Addison Wesley, 1969.
30 Peter Berger & Thomas Luckman, *The Social Construction of Reality: A Treatise in the Sociology of Knowledge*, Garden City, NY: Doubleday, 1966.
31 Thomas Peters & Robert Waterman, *In Search of Excellence: Lessons from America's Best-Run Companies*, New York: Harper & Row, 1982.
32 Richard Pascale & Anthony Athos, *The Art of Japanese Management*, New York: Simon & Schuster, 1981.
33 Robert Coase, 'The Nature of the Firm', *Economics*, 4, 1937, pp. 386–405.
34 Oliver Williamson, *Markets and Hierarchies, Analysis and Antitrust Implications*, New York: Free Press, 1975.
35 Agency theory literature derives from that concerning property rights. See, for instance, A.A. Alchian & H. Demsetz, 'Production, Information Costs and Economic Organization', *American Economic Review*, 62, 1972, pp. 777–95.
36 Lex Donaldson, *American Anti-Management Theories of Organization: a Critique of Paradigm Proliferation*, Cambridge: Cambridge University Press, 1995.
37 See Walter W. Powell & Paul DiMaggio, eds, *The New Institutionalism in Organizational Analysis*, Chicago: Chicago University Press, 1991; and Lynne G. Zuker, *Institutional Patterns and Organisations: Culture and Environments*, Cambridge: Balinger, 1988.
38 See, for instance, Christopher Bartlett & Sumantra Ghoshal, *Managing Across Borders*, Boston, MA: Harvard Business School Press, 1991.
39 Clegg, Hardy & Nord, op cit.
40 Tom Peters, *Thriving on Chaos*, New York: Knopf, 1988.
41 Charles Handy, *Inside Organisations: 21 Ideas for Managers*, London: BBC Books, 1990.
42 Ricardo Semler, *Maverick: The Success Story Behind the World's Most Unusual Workplace*, New York: Warner, 1993.
43 Michael Hammer, *Re-engineering the Corporation: A Manifesto for Business Revolution*, London: Nicholas Brealey, 1993.
44 Jack Welch, *Jack: What I've Learned from Leading a Great Company and Great People*, London: Headline, 2001.
45 This section is drawn from Martin Kennly & Richard Florida 'The Transfer of Japanese Management Styles in Two US Transplant Industries: Autos and Electronics', *Journal of Management Studies*, 32(6), 1995, pp. 789–802; Greg Gardner, 'Tracking Toyota's Tundra', *Ward's Auto World*, 34(10), 1998, pp. 42–4; and Terry Besser, 'Rewards and Organizational Goal Achievement: A Case Study of Toyota Motor Manufacturing in Kentucky', *Journal of Management Studies*, 32(3), 1995, pp. 383–99.

CHAPTER 3

Organisational effectiveness

After reading this chapter you should be able to:

- explain four approaches to organisational effectiveness
- list the assumptions of each of the organisational effectiveness approaches
- describe how managers can operationalise each approach
- identify key problems with each approach
- explain the value of each approach to practising managers
- compare the conditions under which each is useful for managers.

Introduction

Are you sure you know what effectiveness is?

Take any group of people and ask them to name an organisation they 'like'. Many may associate their choice with pleasant things, organisations which take you on holidays perhaps, their local hospital for giving them a sense of security, maybe a favourite restaurant or recreation club. Now ask them to suggest an organisation they think does its job well. A different set of answers is likely to emerge. Maybe the supermarket they patronise, a favourite clothing boutique, perhaps a charity such as the Salvation Army or an environmental group such as Greenpeace.

What about those organisations which they really don't like? The taxation department would hardly rank highly on most people's list of great organisations; nor would most government departments. Some may not like McDonald's because of health concerns; others love it because it gives great children's parties. Anti-globalisers probably don't like Nike and greenies don't like oil companies.

If we asked for a list of organisations that are well managed we may get blank looks, but those familiar with business may come up with Toyota, General Electric or perhaps a food company such as Nestlé. If we asked if BHP Billiton's profit meant that it was efficient, well managed or exploitative we would find that we would be offered a variety of conflicting answers.

This imaginary discussion highlights the difficulties faced in suggesting ways to improve organisations. We may make them efficient, but they still may not do their job well, or they may be doing things which are not socially acceptable to many people. On the other hand, organisations which do things that really no one can criticise because they contribute to the greater good—charities spring to mind—may in actual fact not be efficient and in some cases may make no impression on situations they are trying to improve.

Addressing this problem lies at the heart of this book. Using terminology relevant to organisational theory we are trying to create effective organisations. But what is an effective organisation? We will attempt to answer this question as the chapter progresses.

Organisations exist! People have formed formal organisations for as long as they have led settled lives. The earliest formal organisations were armies and the bureaucracies of kings and monarchs, closely followed by religious organisations. We could immediately identify many of the features of the organisations of antiquity: a hierarchy of management, symbols of rank and position, functional areas charged with undertaking specialised tasks and, on the behavioural side, often the development of a common culture associated with the sharing of values and goals. No civilisation ever became great without being organised: the Roman Empire and China provide good examples. As industrialisation advanced in the 19th and 20th centuries we became a far more organised society. Instead of production taking place in owner operated workshops or peasant farmed land, production increasingly moved to factories. Many of these factories grew in size to become the large industrial firms and multinationals which we are so familiar with today. But organisations exist for doing far more than producing goods and services for the marketplaces of the world. Government departments, charities, lobby groups, educational institutions, sporting clubs and multilateral bodies such as the United Nations are all organisations. Further, we generally accept that organisations in our society take a legal form, that is, they are incorporated under law and may take different forms of ownership. A business organisation, for example, has a different form of ownership and control to a religious body. The law also facilitates the extinguishment of organisations, particularly business organisations which are legally structured as shareholder owned companies. Every year thousands of organisations cease to exist as they merge with other organisations or fail, with their assets being liquidated.

This discussion leads us to the dilemma of how to identify a 'successful' organisation. Given the wide range of organisations we are likely to have to evaluate, this is no easy task; and the broader the areas that organisations exist in, the more difficult it becomes. For organisational theorists, issues such as these are considered under the general heading of *organisational effectiveness*. As you will see, researchers have had considerable difficulty in trying to agree on what this term means and how to apply it across a wide range of organisations. Yet almost all these same researchers are quick to acknowledge that this term is the central theme in organisational theory: what we are trying to do is expand our knowledge of organisations in order to generate more effective ones. In fact, it is difficult to conceive of a theory of organisations that does not include the concept of effectiveness.[1]

Importance of organisational effectiveness

Every discipline in the administrative sciences contributes in some way to helping managers make organisations more effective. Marketing, for instance, guides managers in identifying market needs and promoting and selling products. Financial concepts assist managers in making the optimum use of funds invested in the organisation. Production and operations management concepts offer guidance in designing efficient production processes and controlling supply chains. Accounting principles assist managers by providing information that can enhance the quality of the decisions they make.

Organisation theory presents another answer to the question of what makes an organisation effective. That answer is: an appropriate organisation structure! This book will demonstrate that the way we put people and jobs together and define their roles and relationships is an important determinant in whether an organisation is successful. As we will demonstrate in later chapters, some structures work better under certain conditions than do others. Importantly, those managers who understand their structural options and the conditions under which each is preferred will have a definite advantage over their less informed counterparts. Organisation theory, as a discipline, clarifies which organisation structure will lead to, or improve, organisational effectiveness.

In addition to studying the structure of an organisation, organisation theory also studies issues that arise when we view the organisation as a collective of people. Organisation behaviour examines the actions of individuals through such fields of study as leadership, motivation and teamwork. In contrast, organisation theory is concerned with such organisation-wide features as culture and organisational change.

We also consider the interaction of the organisation with its environment, and how organisations transform themselves over time in response to environmental and technological change and the process of growth and decline.

Ideas as to effectiveness have changed over time in response to changes in investor preferences, government policy, community expectations and management paradigms. Funds managers looking to invest large amounts of savings are seeking sound investments with good growth prospects. Those companies that can provide this need never be short of capital. However, the opposite is also true. Many organisations have found that their lack of access to funds has crimped growth prospects and in some cases forced them into liquidation. Major shifts in government policy over the past 20 years, including deregulation and privatisation, have led to new demands being placed on organisations to respond to emerging environmental pressures. Improving quality has led to a reappraisal of many established practices and technological innovation has been rapid, altering the way organisations relate to their environment. As well, globalisation has greatly increased the level of competition under which companies operate. Finally, all organisations, from churches and the taxation department through to consumer products firms, are under close scrutiny from a community concerned about breaches of trust and ethical standards.

All this has meant that issues relating to organisational effectiveness are very much of concern to the community. But what is effectiveness, and how do we go about assessing it?

In search of a definition

If you had been a student of organisational theory in the 1950s you would have had a deceptively simple way of assessing organisational effectiveness. At that time effectiveness was considered to be related to whether an organisation achieved its goals or not.[2] Although simple in concept and straightforward to understand, when it came to putting the *goal attainment approach* into practice, many difficulties emerged that limited research into the topic, as well as its application by managers. For example: Whose goals? Short-term goals or long-term goals? The organisation's stated goals or the goals which inform the actions of managers?

Another simple approach to measuring effectiveness is to consider *survival* a necessary precondition for success.[3] If there is anything an organisation seeks to do, it is to survive. But the use of survival as a criterion presumes the ability to identify when an organisation ceases to exist. Unfortunately, the death of an organisation is nowhere as clear as a biological death. Some organisations clearly do die. They become insolvent; assets, if any, are sold; and employees are paid off. But, in fact, most organisations don't die—they're remade. They merge, reorganise, sell off major parts or move into totally new areas of endeavour. The business pages of newspapers carry daily reports of mergers, acquisitions and takeovers, which often occur in the name of organisational effectiveness. Although it is less common, even churches merge. Charities evolve from catering to one sector of the community to another as needs change. For example Legacy, which was set up to cater for the needs of the children and widows of deceased servicemen who had served overseas, now sees itself as promoting the interests of youth generally. The RSL has moved from an almost exclusive emphasis on ex-servicemen and women to include a community service obligation. Other organisations can survive long periods of time while not being considered effective. For some organisations—and common targets for most people include government departments and large corporations—death practically never

Assumptions

The assumptions underlying a systems approach to organisational effectiveness are much the same as those discussed in Chapter 1. A systems approach to effectiveness implies that organisations are made up of interrelated subparts. If any one of these subparts performs poorly, it will negatively affect the performance of the whole system. Effectiveness also requires awareness of, and successful interaction with, important environmental constituencies. It highlights that management should maintain good relations with customers, suppliers, government agencies, shareholders, the community and other constituencies that have the power to disrupt the stable operation of the organisation.

Survival requires a steady replenishment of resources consumed in production. Raw materials and other inputs must be secured, vacancies created by employee resignations and retirements must be filled, depreciated plant and outdated technology requires replacement, declining product lines must be revamped, changes in the economy and the tastes of customers or clients need to be anticipated and reacted to, and so on. The resources of the system are not just productive machinery and physical assets. They include such intangibles as ideas, inventions and patents, brand names, customer goodwill and the skills of the management team. Failure to replenish these as they decay, either because of management neglect or lack of resources in the environment, will result in the organisation's decline and, possibly, death.

Making systems operative

Let us turn now to the issue of how the systems approach to effectiveness may be applied. First, we look at a sampling of criteria that systems advocates consider relevant; then we consider the various ways in which managers measure these criteria.

The systems view looks at factors such as the ability to ensure continued receipt of inputs into the system and the distribution of outputs, flexibility of response to environmental changes, the efficiency with which the organisation transforms inputs to outputs, the clarity of internal communications, the level of conflict among groups and rates of innovation. These measures may be benchmarked against other organisations doing similar things. In contrast to the goal-attainment approach, the systems approach focuses on the means necessary to ensure the organisation's continued survival. And it should be noted that systems advocates do not neglect the importance of specific end goals as a determinant of organisational effectiveness. Rather, they question the validity of the goals selected and the measures used for assessing the progress towards these goals.

In operationalising the systems approach, it has been suggested that important systems interrelationships can be converted into organisational effectiveness variables or ratios.[13] These could include output/input, transformations/input, transformations/output, changes in input/input, and so on. Table 3.2 gives some examples of measurement criteria that could be used, together with these variables in a business firm, a hospital and a university.

Operations managers and management accountants use many of these measures when they assess the effectiveness of the transformation process. In keeping with the systems idea of environmental interaction, many organisations, including charities and government departments, benchmark many of their measures, often called critical ratios, against their competitors and industry standards.

Yet another systems application of organisational effectiveness is the concept of added value, popularised by a professor at the London Business School, John Kay.[14]

TABLE 3.2 Examples of effectiveness measures of systems for different types of organisations

System variables	Business firm	Hospital	University
Output/input	Return on investment	Average length of patient stay	Number of publications per staff member
Transformations/input	Inventory turnover	Staff per patient	Staff/student ratio
Transformations/output	Sales volume	Total number of patients treated	Number of students graduated
Changes input/input	Change in working capital	Change in number of patients treated	Change in student enrolment

Source: Adapted from William M. Evan, 'Organization Theory and Organizational Effectiveness: An Exploratory Analysis', in S. Lee Spray, ed., *Organizational Effectiveness: Theory, Research, Utilization*, Kent, OH: Kent State University Press, 1976, pp. 22–3. Reproduced with permission.

The cycle of absorbing inputs from the environment, turning them into usable products and services and then marketing these should leave a surplus of cash over and above that needed to maintain the system in its repetitive cycle. This surplus is called the value added, and Kay suggests that the larger it is the more successful the company. Kay considers that a commercial organisation that does not add value (i.e. one that contributes no more than the value of its inputs) cannot justify its existence in the long run.

The determination of added value starts with money received from sales to customers. From this are deducted salaries and wages, capital costs and payments to suppliers. These groups are called stakeholders, and payment to them ensures their future cooperation. What is left is the added value. This is less than the operating profit of the firm, because return to shareholders is included in the capital costs. But it represents the effectiveness with which resources are used in the organisation, including shareholders' funds. This approach has a finance orientation and concentrates on profit-making organisations, so it has little applicability to government or charitable organisations.

Problems

The two most telling shortcomings of the systems approach relate to measurement and the issue of whether means really matter.

While some process variables may be specific and easy to measure, such as hours to build a motor vehicle, or expense to income ratios, other critical ratios are not so easy to quantify. Rates of innovation, quality of the management team and community goodwill, all necessary for organisational strength, defy easy measurement. Environments may also change very quickly, rendering one set of measures superfluous and raising the importance of what previously was not considered significant. The entry of low-cost airlines into Australia, for instance, very quickly changed the environmental landscape for the established airlines, leading Qantas to establish its own low-cost subsidiary.

OT CLOSEUP
How effective is the United Nations?

Researchers and theorists have expended large amounts of time attempting to develop ways of assessing organisational effectiveness. The main thrust of their efforts has been directed towards profit-seeking organisations, making the task of measuring effectiveness a little easier as profitability is often included as an assessment criterion. But some organisations seem to defy any means of assessing their effectiveness. A prime example of such an organisation is the United Nations. Now over 50 years old, it reflects the power balances existing at the conclusion of the Second World War. Its shortcomings, from failing to stop genocide to the corruption associated with the oil for food program in Iraq, are widely publicised. The squabbles of its members are such that there is little agreement on reform.

The main powerbrokers in the Security Council regard the UN as politically useful at times but capable of being ignored at others. Some members use the body only for political grandstanding. It is famous for passing resolutions which are ignored and never enforced. Areas of concern to the modern world, such as terrorism and rebuilding countries after civil war, are not covered by its charter and therefore no efforts are made to address these issues. It would be easy to say that the UN is a fairly ineffective organisation. Certainly if it was a business it would have ceased to exist years ago.

But many of its constituent bodies, such as the World Health Organization, do considerable good and economic institutions like the IMF help to maintain economic stability. Also, who could imagine the world without the UN? It therefore may be possible to say that the UN is fairly effective because, even though it has such significant problems, nations—its most important strategic constituency—still want it to exist.

would argue that effective organisations align their goals with important areas of the environment. When management give profits highest priority, for instance, they make the interests of owners paramount. Similarly, adaptability to the environment, customer satisfaction and a supportive work climate favour the interests of society, clients and employees, respectively.

Making strategic constituencies operative

The management of most organisations would intuitively know what groups are important to the organisation in the environment, and what is needed to satisfy these groups. However, these groups, as in all things political, are constantly changing. Intuitive managers read their environment well and respond accordingly. However, very large organisations with multiple environments may need to conduct a more formal review of the importance of each strategic group. Management wishing to apply this perspective might begin by asking key members of the management team to identify the constituencies they consider to be critical to the organisation's survival. This input can be combined and synthesised to arrive at a list of strategic constituencies.

As an example, Caltex, which refines and markets petroleum products, may have as its strategic constituencies the suppliers of crude oil, state and local governments concerned with pollution and safety issues, and unions representing workers at the plant. It would also include shareholders, who provide capital, and banks through which the company might have short-term loans. Finally, wholesalers and retailers who distribute the product would be critical to the company's success.

The above list could then be evaluated to determine the relative power of each constituency. Basically, this means looking at each one in terms of how dependent on it the organisation is. Does it have considerable power over the organisation? Are there alternatives to what this constituency provides? How do these constituencies compare in the impact they have on the organisation's operations?

The third step requires identifying the expectations that these constituencies hold for the organisation. What do they want of it? Given that each constituency has its own set of special interests, what goals does each seek to impose on the organisation? Shareholders' goals may be in terms of profit or appreciation in share prices, and the union's may be in terms of acquiring job security and high wages for its members, whereas the Environmental Protection Authority will want the firm's manufacturing plants to meet all minimum air-, water- and noise-pollution requirements. Table 3.3 contains a list of strategic constituencies which a business firm might confront and the typical organisational-effectiveness criteria each is likely to use.

The strategic-constituencies approach would conclude by comparing the various expectations, determining common expectations and those that are incompatible, assigning relative weights to the various constituencies and formulating a preference ordering of these various goals for the organisation as a whole. This preference order, in effect, represents the relative power of the various strategic constituencies. The organisation's effectiveness would then be assessed in terms of its ability to satisfy these goals.

The stakeholder approach to effectiveness

As we have seen, the strategic-constituencies approach is an overtly political way of assessing effectiveness. The stakeholder approach recognises not only the importance of strategic constituencies but also those who may not have the political power to influence the existence of the organisation or even its direction. To the list in Table 3.3 we could add such groups as families of workers, environmentalists, residents near the plant and those generally concerned to see that ethical decision making is maintained. All of these groups, even though they may not be formally organised as a pressure group, are considered to be affected by the organisation and should therefore be considered when important decisions are made. Sometimes the aims of these

TABLE 3.3 Typical organisational effectiveness criteria of selected strategic constituencies

Constituency	**Typical OE criteria**
Owners	Return on investment; growth in earnings
Employees	Pay; benefits; satisfaction with working conditions and career prospects
Customers	Satisfaction with price; quality; service
Suppliers	Satisfaction with payments; future sales potential
Creditors	Ability to pay debts
Unions	Competitive wages and benefits; satisfactory working conditions; willingness to bargain fairly
Local community officials	Involvement of organisation's members in local affairs; lack of damage to the community's environment; provision of employment
Government agencies	Compliance with laws; avoidance of penalties and reprimands

groups are not all that obvious and the pressures they can bring are difficult to predict; McDonald's responding to health activists is a case in point.

The stakeholder approach has been developed by theorists such as Archie Carroll[17] as a counterpoint to the view that business organisations exist only to maximise profits for their shareholders. Carroll considers that this not only leads to a narrow focus in decision making but also neglects the community of which the organisation is a part. The stakeholder approach considers that an organisation is effective only if it takes into account the wider community that has an interest in the decisions of the organisation, even if this is at the cost of profits.

The advocates of the stakeholder approach see its advantage as taking the harsh edge from organisational decision making and civilising what may seem to be a system purely focused on profit. However, most organisations are aware of at least some of their wider responsibilities. And the interests of shareholders and other stakeholders may coincide when profits are increased because customers are satisfied, or when superior employment conditions attract the best staff.

Problems

As with the previous approaches, strategic constituencies is not without problems. The task of separating the strategic constituencies from the larger environment is easy to talk about but difficult to do. Because the environment changes rapidly, what was critical to the organisation yesterday may not be so today and may be entirely different tomorrow. For example, the privatisation of government enterprises introduced a whole new set of constituencies for organisations. An example of an even quicker change in strategic constituencies is provided by banks, which exist on the goodwill and confidence of their depositors. If word is spread that a bank is insolvent, the resulting run on the bank by depositors can put it out of business in an afternoon. This highlights that strategic constituencies are not static but are constantly shifting as circumstances change.

Even if the constituencies in the environment can be identified and are assumed to be relatively stable, what separates the strategic constituencies from the 'almost' strategic constituencies? Where do you draw the line? And won't the interests of each member of the management team strongly affect what he or she perceives as strategic? An executive in finance is unlikely to see the world—or the organisation's strategic constituencies—in the same way as an executive in the supply chain management function. Finally, identifying the expectations that the strategic constituencies hold for the organisation presents a problem. How do you tap that information accurately?

The strategic-constituencies approach also assumes that an organisation's basic goal is survival. This may not be the case in many instances. Organisations are often established with the idea of selling them to someone else once they reach a certain size. Any company listed on the stock exchange has effectively put itself up for sale. Many businesses realise that they must merge with another in order to achieve some form of economies of scale, and management then negotiates the best deal that it can. Even charities and not-for-profit organisations such as hospitals or recreation clubs realise that independence may not be the best policy for their strategic constituents. Amalgamations and mergers then follow.

Value to managers

If survival is important for an organisation, it is incumbent on managers to understand just who it is (in terms of constituencies) that survival depends upon. By

OT CLOSEUP

Halliburton—a company activists love to hate

Business critics may hold a dislike for most businesses, but they can't criticise all of them all of the time; they normally concentrate on one or two high-profile cases. In the United States a company which raised the ire of activists for some time was Nike. Critics lambasted it for child labour abuses, unhealthy working conditions and miserly pay for workers. Over the past few years, Nike and similar companies have gone to great lengths to address the accusations and, as a result, much of the sting has been removed from criticism levelled at them.

Many activists in the US have moved on to another company called Halliburton. Halliburton conducts a range of businesses, including maintenance of oil rigs and oil fields, construction activities and provision of catering for the US army in Iraq. It has been embroiled in bribery scandals and it has been accused of being granted high-value contracts without tendering. Critics argue that these have been acquired because of the company's close links with the White House. The Vice-President of the United States, Dick Cheney, once headed the company.

Halliburton is the biggest US contractor in Iraq, having won work worth over US$15 billion. It also stands to benefit from the reconstruction work associated with Hurricane Katrina which devastated New Orleans. Halliburton's critics are extremely well organised and their website <www.halliburtonwatch.org> shows correlations between Halliburton's share price and the number of soldiers killed in Iraq. It was also noted that the share price rose as Hurricane Katrina struck in anticipation of lucrative rebuilding contracts.

Perhaps Halliburton's high profile amongst activists is less of a problem than that which was presented to Nike. Nike sold consumer goods and the reputation of its brand was important to it. Halliburton's customers are mainly government departments and other large companies and, provided that it maintains key contacts, it can afford to ignore most of the criticism aimed at it. It can be confident that there are not too many companies with the skills and financial resources to undertake major contracts, particularly in areas such as Iraq where the risk profile can be extremely high. So even politicians who may be wary of dealing with Halliburton because of all the bad publicity would probably have to turn to it for assistance. As long as Halliburton keeps the critical constituency of government onside, then it can ignore most of the criticism. But activists have keen political antennas; that is why most of their activism is aimed at severing the Halliburton–government relationship.

operationalising the strategic-constituencies approach, managers decrease the chance that they might ignore or severely upset a group whose power could significantly hinder the organisation's operations. If management knows whose support it needs if the organisation is to maintain its health, it can modify its preferred ordering of goals as necessary to reflect the changing power relationships with its strategic constituencies.

The balanced scorecard approach

Organisations can be very confusing and difficult to comprehend. Notwithstanding advances in management techniques and the ability to process information, the complexity associated with the activities and interactions of large numbers of people working in multiple subsystems defies easy analysis and understanding. The technologies of even a medium-sized organisation are beyond the grasp of one person and areas of waste and inefficiency are often difficult to identify. Environments are constantly changing, and the demands on the organisation for performance, and indeed to justify its existence, never seem to diminish. Whether an organisation is performing well or poorly may not even be obvious to senior management, at least in the short term. Given this complexity, it is easy for those managing and working in an organisation to concentrate their energies on a few, easy-to-grasp measures that are easy to arrive at.

So far in this chapter we have identified the importance of ends, means and processes in measuring organisational effectiveness. We have also identified that responding innovatively to environmental pressures contributes to the effectiveness of an organisation. The **balanced scorecard** attempts to integrate all of these approaches.[18]

balanced scorecard the balanced scorecard seeks to balance the various demands on the organisation with its capabilities

In generating the various measures used in the balanced scorecard, one seeks to balance (hence the name) the various demands on the organisation with its capabilities. As a result, developing the measures becomes a diagnostic tool—a management technique to align the organisation with its environment and a measurement system to identify whether goals are being met. It is also seen as a means of developing and implementing strategy.

The balanced scorecard, developed by Kaplan and Norton, is an attempt to provide an integrated measure of organisational effectiveness. As with the approaches previously discussed, it proposes that there is no one measure that can assess an organisation's performance or that can focus attention on critical areas of the business. Financial measures are historical rather than future oriented and are limited as to what can be measured in monetary terms. Operational measures, such as process times and defect rates, often lack the ability to differentiate between items of greater and lesser importance. The balanced scorecard attempts to view performance in several areas simultaneously and identify not just results but how the results were achieved.

Making the balanced scorecard operative

The various components of the balanced scorecard are illustrated in Figures 3.1a–b. The various performance measures are linked, highlighting that they are interrelated. The components attempt to identify four basic questions facing any organisation. These are:

- How do important financial providers perceive us? (*Financial Perspective*) All organisations must have access to finance and hence they have financial demands and constraints. Financial measures enable an organisation to determine how profitable it is and its rate of return on assets. It can also be used by charities to identify how successful they are at raising funds or government departments in accessing budget increases. In short, the financial measures indicate whether an organisation's strategy and its execution are contributing to profitability, or covering costs.
- How do customers see us? (*Customer Perspective*) Goals and measures under this heading typically include assessment of time to delivery, product utility, and performance and service which, when combined, show how the product or service contributes to creating value for customers. Market share is also a good measure of customer satisfaction.
- What must we excel at? (*Internal Perspective*) These measures concentrate on what the company must do internally to meet the customers' expectations. This is a process-driven measure, examples of which may include on-time running, quality

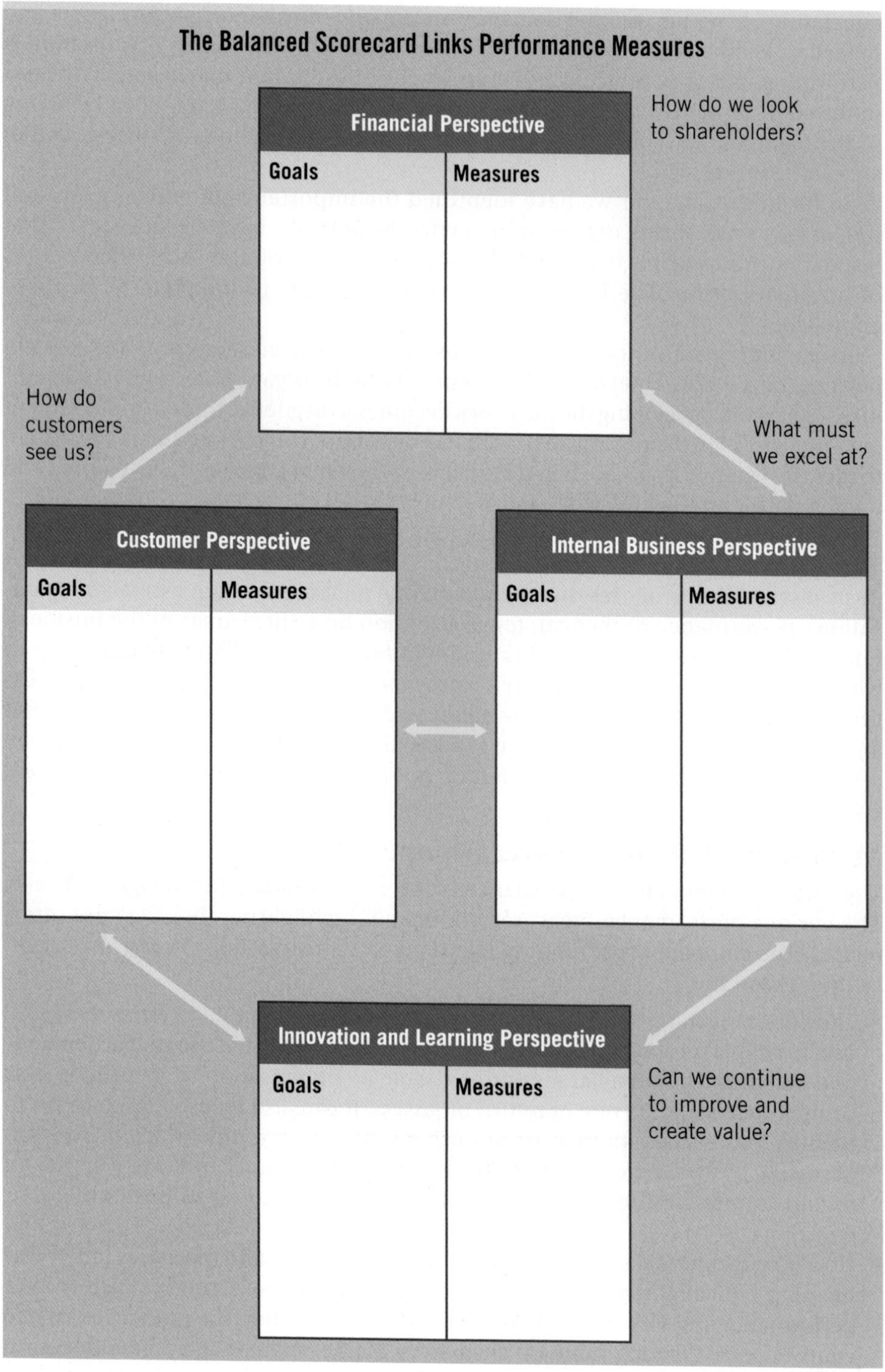
The Balanced Scorecard Links Performance Measures
Financial Perspective
Goals
Measures
How do we look to shareholders?
How do customers see us?
What must we excel at?
Customer Perspective
Goals
Measures
Internal Business Perspective
Goals
Measures
Innovation and Learning Perspective
Goals
Measures
Can we continue to improve and create value?

FIGURE 3.1A Representation of the balanced scorecard

Source: Robert Kaplan & David Norton, 'The Balanced Scorecard—Measures that Drive Performance', *Harvard Business Review*, Jan/Feb 1992, pp. 71–79.

Railco's Balanced Business Scorecard

Financial Perspective	
Goals	**Measures**
Reduce reliance on government subsidy	Increase % of revenue from fares
Accelerate system upgrade	Increase number of joint venture undertakings

Customer Perspective	
Goals	**Measures**
Be a preferred means of transportation	Increase % of travellers choosing rail transport
Increase comfort levels	Complete air-conditioning of fleet Clean carriages at terminus stops

Internal Business Perspective	
Goals	**Measures**
Improve on time running	Undertake signals upgrade Introduce planned maintenance
Reduce staffing costs	Benchmark staffing levels against worlds best practice

Innovation and Learning Perspective	
Goals	**Measures**
Reduce environmental impact	Instal environmentally friendly air-conditioning
Reduce energy usage	Develop new generation of rolling stock
Improve response times to unexpected events	Computerise timetabling and station information boards

FIGURE 3.1B Application of the balanced scorecard to a city rail system

attainment, availability of equipment, cycle times for introduction of new product, after-sales service and costs of production.
- Can we continue to improve and create value? (*Innovation and Learning Perspective*) This goal is associated with the ability to develop and introduce new products of value to customers or clients. It also includes measures of continuous improvement and production efficiencies.

Kaplan and Norton stress that it is possible to have too many measures of organisational performance. Management should identify just a few goals for each of the four perspectives. The measures developed for each goal should be easy to understand and contribute to deciding whether the goal has been achieved or not. The goals and measures will of course vary between organisations. In one way, the balanced scorecard is similar to the goal-attainment approach. Where it differs is that it formalises the way in which goals are determined. It also proposes that there are multiple goals, which exist within a network of interrelationships. Choosing what to measure is very important, as measurements guide actions, but it is difficult to avoid subjectivity. An example of goals and measures for a city-based rail system is shown in Figure 3.1b.

The first benefit attributed by Kaplan and Norton to the balanced scorecard is that it brings together in a single report many areas of importance to an organisation's competitiveness. These include both short-term efficiency issues and those relating to the long-term adaptability of the organisation. Second, the scorecard acts to guard against suboptimisation. By forcing senior managers to consider all important operational issues together, they are compelled to evaluate whether improvement in one area may have been achieved at the expense of creating problems in another. For instance, there is always the temptation within organisations to achieve superior short-term performance at the expense of long-term viability. A good example is that equipment maintenance can be curtailed, improving short-term cash flows but leading to unreliable plant and higher costs in the future. The balanced scorecard should be able to identify where unwise compromises have been made.

The balanced scorecard also puts into perspective the use of financial measures as a means of information to managers. Financial measures tend to be backward-looking, as they provide information only on what has occurred in the past. They fail to reflect contemporary value-creating actions, such as innovation and new product development. Money also is a symbolic measure which lacks the diagnostic ability of those which, for example, use time, defects or consumption rates as their unit of measure. Financial measures are important, but must be considered in combination with other sources of information in order to allow a comprehensive picture of the organisation to emerge.

Although it may appear that the balanced scorecard is applicable only to business organisations, it is of use to organisations in the non-profit sector as well. No organisation can ignore resource constraints; organisations must derive their funds from somewhere. Likewise, all organisations have some form of consumer group that must be satisfied. And in the not-for-profit sector, these groups can be difficult to define. Should charities, for instance, regard donors as customers? However they are regarded, they must be satisfied that their donations are being put to good use, or they will take their donations elsewhere. The balanced scorecard allows all of these competing interests to be assessed and incorporated in decision making.

Finally, the underlying theme of the balanced scorecard is organisational survival. It aligns important environmental constituencies with measures aimed at satisfying

the failure to adequately provide these services led to GSL receiving a fine of over $500 000 for breach of contract. GSL was found to have mistreated detainees by refusing them access to toilet facilities during transit, and detainees were also denied adequate food, water and medical treatment. Further problems arose for GSL in providing psychological and psychiatric treatment to detainees, many of whom were deeply disturbed. This was held to be inadequate and a number of high-profile cases of detainees attempting suicide or sewing their lips together reached the mass media. All of this was made public by a small group of activists who monitor the condition of detainees in detention centres and regularly keep touch via the Internet. The press also takes a keen interest in events taking place in detention centres.

GSL responded to the fine by dismissing a number of officers and improving training. It also undertook to work with the Department of Immigration to improve services to detainees. The Department of Immigration itself undertook to reduce the level of coercion when it detained non-citizens. It has removed all children from detention and reduced the levels of surveillance and the prison-like atmosphere of many of the detention centres. It has moved most female detainees and low-risk males to motel-style accommodation.

But GSL has been tarnished through association with the old system. It would argue that it was caught up in having to implement an excessively harsh detention policy with a level of coercion that was not necessary. As a result, psychological problems multiplied. This led to frustration on the part of its employees, compounded by the desperation of many of those detained. In the end it was a contract which involved far more than providing food and doing the cleaning.

QUESTIONS

1. What is the best method of assessing the effectiveness of GSL? Using this method how would you rate its effectiveness?
2. What are GSL's critical constituencies? Is it possible to satisfy them all? If not, which is the most important?
3. How closely is the effectiveness of GSL linked to Department of Immigration policies? What is the best way for GSL to manage this relationship?
4. In answering the above questions, to what extent were you influenced by a) your attitude towards the detention of asylum seekers, and b) your attitude towards the government contracting out work of this nature.

FURTHER READING

Kim Cameron, 'Effectiveness as Paradox: Consensus and Conflict in Conceptions of Organizational Effectiveness', *Management Science*, 32(5), 1986, pp. 539–53.

Kim Cameron & Dave Whetton, eds, *Organizational Effectiveness: A Comparison of Multiple Models*, New York: Academic Press, 1983.

Michael Hitt, 'The Measuring of Organizational Effectiveness: Multiple Domains and Constituencies Management', *International Review*, 28(2), 1988, pp. 28–40.

Robert Kaplan & David Norton, 'The Balanced Scorecard—Measures that Drive Performance', *Harvard Business Review*, Jan/Feb 1992, pp. 71–9.

Robert Kaplan & David Norton, *The Balanced Scorecard: Translating Strategy into Action*, New York: McGraw Hill, 1996.

Arie Lewin & John Minton, 'Determining Organizational Effectiveness: Another Look and an Agenda for Research', *Management Science*, 32(5), 1986, p. 538.

Jeffrey Pfeffer & Gerald Salancik, *The External Control of Organizations*, New York: Harper & Row, 1978.

NOTES

1 Paul S. Goodman & Johannes M. Pennings, 'Perspectives and Issues: An Introduction', in P.S. Goodman, J.M. Pennings & Associates, eds, *New Perspectives on Organizational Effectiveness*, San Francisco: Jossey-Bass, 1977, p. 2.

2 Amitai Etzioni, *Modern Organizations*, Englewood Cliffs, NJ: Prentice Hall, 1964, p. 8.

3 John R. Kimberly, 'Issues in the Creation of Organizations: Initiation, Innovation, and Institutionalization', *Academy of Management Journal*, September 1979, p. 438.

4 Jeffrey Pfeffer, 'Usefulness of the Concept', in Goodman et al., *New Perspectives on Organizational Effectiveness*, p. 139; and H. Kaufman, *Are Government Organizations Immortal?*, Washington, DC: Brookings Institution, 1976.

5 John P. Campbell, 'On the Nature of Organizational Effectiveness', in Goodman et al., *New Perspectives on Organizational Effectiveness*, p. 15.

6 Kim S. Cameron, 'A Study of Organizational Effectiveness and its Predictors', *Management Science*, January 1986, p. 88.

7 Kim S. Cameron, 'Effectiveness as Paradox: Consensus and Conflict in Conceptions of Organizational Effectiveness', *Management Science*, 32(5), 1986, pp. 539–53.

8 Charles Perrow, 'The Analysis of Goals in Complex Organizations', *American Sociological Review*, December 1961, pp. 854–66.

9 Charles K. Warriner, 'The Problem of Organizational Purpose', *Sociological Quarterly*, Spring 1965, pp. 139–46.

10 Karl Weick, *The Social Psychology of Organizing*, Reading, MA: Addison-Wesley, 1969, p. 8 (author's emphasis).

11 Warriner, 'The Problem of Organizational Purpose', p. 140.

12 Ephraim Yuchtman & Stanley E. Seashore, 'A Systems Resource Approach to Organizational Effectiveness', *American Sociological Review*, December 1967, pp. 891–903.

13 William M. Evan, 'Organization Theory and Organizational Effectiveness: An Exploratory Analysis', in S. Lee Spray, ed., *Organizational Effectiveness: Theory, Research, Utilization*, Kent, OH: Kent State University Press, 1976, pp. 21–4.

14 John Kay, *Foundation of Corporate Success: How Business Strategies Add Value*, Oxford: Oxford University Press, 1993.

15 Jeffrey Pfeffer & Gerald Salancik, *The External Control of Organizations*, New York: Harper & Row, 1978.

16 Robert H. Miles, *Coffin Nails and Corporate Strategies*, Englewood Cliffs, NJ: Prentice Hall, 1982.

17 Archie Carroll, *Business and Society: Ethics and Stakeholder Management*, 3rd edn, Cincinnati, OH: South Western College Publishing, 1996; and Ian March, *Stakeholder Capitalism and Australian Business, Politics and Public Policy*, Sydney: AGSM, 1996.

18 Drawn from Robert Kaplan & David Norton, 'The Balanced Scorecard—Measures that Drive Performance', *Harvard Business Review*, Jan/Feb 1992, pp. 71–9; and Robert Kaplan & David Norton, *The Balanced Scorecard: Translating Strategy into Action*, New York: McGraw Hill, 1996.

PART 2

Comparing Organisations

part 2

CHAPTER 4

Dimensions of organisation structure

After reading this chapter you should be able to:

- explain the key terms commonly used to compare organisations
- describe the three components comprising complexity
- identify the benefits that accrue from formalisation
- list the common formalisation techniques
- discuss why the centralisation debate is important
- identify the importance of coordination
- describe the five basic structural configurations
- explain the benefit of metaphors to describe organisations.

Introduction

Australia is restructuring

In order to meet the challenge of a highly competitive and aggressive Woolworths, Coles Myer launched 'Operation Right Now'. It was a major restructuring of the business, aimed at cutting costs and responding to the changes in consumer demand.[1] But Coles Myer isn't alone. In the past couple of years, as competition has increased and globalisation and technological innovation have thrown up new challenges and opportunities, almost all firms have had to restructure. Not only business firms but charities such as Red Cross and the Smith Family, the University of Newcastle and the Department of Foreign Affairs and Trade have all undergone major restructures in recent years. In fact, it is difficult to find a well-managed organisation now that has not recently restructured to cut costs, become more responsive to customers or competitors, or to achieve some similar aim. But what is it that these organisations are restructuring? And when we compare these organisations what measures and terms are available to us to use? This chapter will address these questions.

We often read references, particularly in publications aimed at a management and business readership, to the structure of an organisation. And, of course, when changes are made to an organisation's structure we call it restructuring. The structure of an organisation refers to its overall dimensions, characteristics and areas of responsibility. We need terms to describe these as we often need to compare organisations and describe them to others. As organisations are often changing, it is helpful to have the language and vocabulary to describe the changes which are taking place. There is also a link between an organisation's structure and its effectiveness so understanding what structure is emerges as being of great importance. But as organisations are intangible—that is, as they lack physical properties—use of conventional measures is not possible. For instance, we can describe the dimensions of a room by its length, breadth and height. We cannot 'measure' an organisation in a similar manner. And measures such as number of employees or financial indicators provide us with little guidance as to the nature of the organisation or how it is managed. So what measures are available to us? We are largely reduced to identifying characteristics and then describing where organisations 'fit' in relation to the measures chosen. This chapter introduces and describes what those measures are. We will draw on the dimensions described in later chapters as we further our understanding of organisations.

Needless to say, not everyone would agree with the dimensions we have chosen; some may feel that they reflect a dated way of looking at organisations.[2] They may also feel that the measures reflect a tangibility which it is not possible to achieve when researching organisations. Further, many organisational researchers would take the view that in nominating the dimensions we have, we have chosen to 'know' organisations in this way, and this would not be their preferred way of interpreting organisational phenomena. However, discussion of the nominated dimensions provides us with the basic vocabulary that managers and consultants commonly use. We will start by looking at the various components of complexity.

Complexity

What do we mean by the term *complexity*, what makes an organisation complex and why is complexity important? The purpose of this section is to answer these three questions.

Definition

Complexity refers to the degree of differentiation that exists within an organisation.[3] *Horizontal differentiation* considers the number of different occupational, task and administrative groupings within the organisation. *Vertical differentiation* refers to the number of layers of management in the organisation. *Spatial dispersion* describes the extent to which the organisation's facilities and personnel are spread over a wide geographical area. An increase in any one of these three factors will increase an organisation's complexity.

complexity the degree of horizontal, vertical and spatial differentiation in an organisation

Horizontal differentiation

Horizontal differentiation refers to the degree to which an organisation is separated into different units on the basis of the tasks performed by organisational members, their education and training, and their administrative groupings. The larger the number of different occupations within an organisation that require specialised knowledge and skills, the more complex the organisation. This is because diverse skills and orientations make it more difficult for organisational members to communicate and more difficult for management to coordinate their activities. For instance, when managers create specialised groups or departments, they differentiate each one from the other, making interactions between them more complex. This is often termed 'creating organisational silos'. If the organisation is staffed by people who have similar backgrounds, skills and training, they are likely to see the world in similar terms. Conversely, diversity increases the likelihood that they will have different goal emphases, time orientations and even a different work vocabulary. *Job specialisation*, sometimes called the division of labour, reinforces differences: the chemical engineer's job is clearly different from that of a recruitment specialist. Their training and skills are different. They have different ways of viewing the organisation's environment. The vocabulary that they use on their respective jobs is different, and they are typically assigned to different departments which are based in different locations.

horizontal differentiation the degree of differentiation among units based on the orientation of members, the nature of the tasks they perform, and their education and training

Almost all organisations, whether they are profit-, government- or community-based, rely on job specialisation. So it is worthwhile briefly identifying why this is so common in organisations. First, in highly sophisticated and complex operations, physical limitations mean that no one person can perform all required tasks. If one person had to build a complete motor car alone, even possessing the hundreds of skills necessary, it would take months of full-time effort. Second, limitations of knowledge act as a constraint. Some tasks require highly developed skills; others can be performed by the untrained. The greater the skill levels required, the more likely jobs will be highly specialised, making it impossible for employees to undertake a range of tasks. Additionally, to have highly trained workers undertaking tasks requiring lower level skills is a waste to the organisation. In addition to skill levels, special knowledge may be required in order to respond to local conditions or the needs of particular groups of customers.

Another element in favour of division of labour is efficiency. Skills and knowledge of a task increase through repetition and concentration on a particular specialised area. Moreover, training is simplified. It is easier and less costly to train workers to undertake a specific and repetitive task than to train them for difficult and complex activities. In addition, all workers have unique talents and abilities. It makes sense for workers to concentrate on what they are good at rather than to undertake a whole range of tasks, many of which they may have little talent for.

Division of labour creates groups of specialists which are normally organised into departments. Departments can be created on the basis of simple numbers, task or function, product or service, client, geography or process. Most large corporations will use all six. On the other hand, in a very small organisation simple numbers represent an informal and highly effective method by which people can be grouped.

Job specialisation leads to the organisation defining areas of responsibility. This is often spelt out in a job description. Most job descriptions are in writing and agreed to by each party, but in some cases may contain general statements or are verbal agreements. In the case of lower level workers, they may be part of an industrial enterprise agreement. Through defining the areas of responsibility, management attempts to ensure that all important areas and tasks have someone responsible for them and that coordination and cooperation is promoted.

OT CLOSEUP

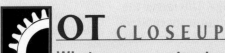

What are we restructuring and what are we aiming to achieve?

To put restructuring into perspective, the following examples of restructuring by prominent Australian institutions provide us with a glimpse of what senior managers are attempting to achieve.

Commonwealth Bank. Introduced a new structure aimed at aligning the bank's products with delivery to customer segments. This involved the creation of four new business divisions: Retail Banking, Premium Services, Investment and Insurance Services, and Institutional and Business Services. It aimed to improve clarity, speed of decision making and responsibility by making the various customer groups the main focus of the structure. Branches were refurbished and ATMs replaced.[4]

Coles Myer. 'Operation Right Now', referred to in the introduction, brought together general merchandising and apparel under one management. This was in order to create clear differentiation between the various businesses to minimise cannibalising of each other's sales. Merchandising (selecting and buying what is to be sold in stores) was to be centralised for some items such as shoes and manchester. One thousand head office positions were abolished to reduce costs and increase flexibility. Clear roles and accountabilities were defined to enable staff to concentrate on improving performance.[5] The process to sell the Myer stores was started in 2005.

ANZ Bank. The branch network was restructured in order to raise its strategic effectiveness. This involved closing poorly located branches and opening others in high traffic areas. Others were merged. The aim was to make more intensive use of the branch network.[6]

Newcastle University. Eleven faculties were reduced to five and administration departments were combined. The aim was to produce a one-stop approach for students and staff.[7]

Pacific Dunlop's South Pacific Tyre Division. Rationalisation of three Victorian manufacturing plants is reducing both costs and the range of tyres produced.[8]

PMP. PMP is a magazine publisher, which was faced with falling demand. Magazine sorting and delivery to retailers was subcontracted to freight forwarders. Warehouses in Adelaide, Brisbane and Perth were closed. About 440 staff were laid off. The aim was to reduce the cost base.[9]

The areas of responsibility reflect the complexity of the organisation. A small manufacturing organisation may make a verbal agreement with the production manager in relation to his or her tasks. On the other hand, a large multinational organisation may define in close detail the responsibility and authority of the holder of a particular position. The greater the complexity of the organisation, the more likely it is that the areas of responsibility of a particular position will be more highly defined. Top management does not escape these restrictions. Often included along with their responsibilities are targets and goals for the organisation to achieve, as well as limitations on their authority.

As specialisation increases, so does complexity. This is because an increase in specialisation requires more sophisticated and expensive methods of coordination and control. Later in this chapter we will analyse the techniques available to organisations to coordinate their specialists.

Vertical differentiation

Vertical differentiation refers to the depth of the structure of an organisation, and is often referred to as the number of *layers of management* from the lowest level workers to the chief executive officer. The greater the number of layers of management, the more complex an organisation becomes. The more levels that exist between top management and lower level workers, the greater the potential for communication breakdown, the more difficult it is to coordinate the decisions of managerial personnel, and the more likely it is that political and power plays will slow decision making and create administrative bottlenecks.

vertical differentiation the number of hierarchical levels between top management and operatives; sometimes referred to as layers of management

Organisations with the same number of employees need not have the same degree of vertical differentiation. Organisations can be tall, with many layers of hierarchy, or flat, with few levels. The determining factor is the span of control.

Span of control defines the number of subordinates that a manager can supervise effectively. If this span is wide, managers will have a large number of subordinates reporting to them. If it is narrow, managers will have few subordinates. All things being equal, the narrower the span of control, the taller the organisation (that is, the more layers of management it will have). Simple arithmetic will show that the difference between an average management span of, say, four, and one of eight in a company of 4000 non-managerial employees can make a difference of two entire levels of management and of nearly 800 managers.

span of control the number of subordinates that a manager can supervise effectively

This statement is illustrated in Figure 4.1. You will note that each of the operative (lowest) levels contains 4096 employees. All the other levels represent management positions: 1365 managers (levels 1–6) with a span of 4, and 585 managers (levels 1–4) with a span of 8. The narrower span of 4 creates high vertical differentiation and a tall organisation. The wider span creates a flatter organisation.

The various layers of management may broadly be classified into three main areas. The first is top management, whose main responsibility is setting the strategic direction of the organisation. This normally comprises the top layer or two of management. The next group down is middle management. A strict definition of middle management is that they implement the plans of senior managers. But in addition they supervise lower level managers and provide input into the decisions made by top management. In many ways middle managers are an information conduit for information flowing up and down the organisation. Lower level management is primarily concerned with the day-to-day tasks of supervising the production of goods and services.

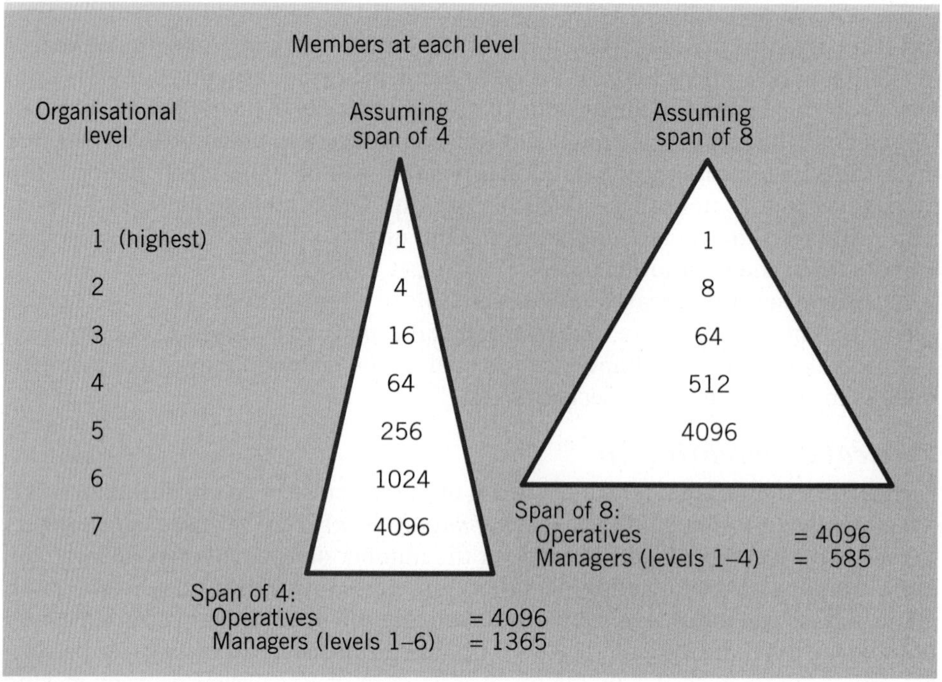
Members at each level
Organisational level
Assuming span of 4
Assuming span of 8
1 (highest)
2
3
4
5
6
7
1
4
16
64
256
1024
4096
1
8
64
512
4096
Span of 8:
Operatives = 4096
Managers (levels 1–4) = 585
Span of 4:
Operatives = 4096
Managers (levels 1–6) = 1365

FIGURE 4.1 Contrasting spans of control

Information technology has had an impact on both the span of control and the extent of vertical differentiation in organisations.[10] The use of computers and computer-based communication technologies, such as email, has facilitated the flow of communication across and up and down the organisation. This has removed the need for large numbers of managers who previously acted as communication channels. It has also made it easier for managers to gather and process information.

There has also been a shift in management attitudes over the past 15 years towards giving greater responsibility to lower level employees. Computers have again helped by allowing employees as diverse as production workers and accounts clerks to access a far greater range of information than had previous generations of workers. Combined with higher levels of education in the workforce and better selection of employees, this has allowed many tasks previously undertaken by management to be undertaken by the workers themselves.

Spatial dispersion

spatial dispersion the degree to which the location of an organisation's facilities and personnel is dispersed geographically

The third element in complexity is spatial dispersion. **Spatial dispersion** refers to the degree to which the location of an organisation's offices, plant and personnel is dispersed.

Spatial dispersion is high when the operations of an organisation are geographically widely spread. This would apply to large multinational organisations whose operations span the globe. Alternatively, it is low when operations take place in a very small geographic area: spatial dispersion would be low if one building held all organisational members. The HSBC Banking Corporation, with its worldwide operations, has a high level of spatial dispersion. On the other hand, The Adelaide Bank, which

OT CLOSEUP

Are organisations becoming flatter?

Although there is not a great deal of evidence to support the fact that flatter organisations are either cheaper or more effective to run, most organisation restructuring in recent years has involved the flattening of the organisation. For instance Boral, which has operations in Australia, Europe and the USA, has only 5 layers of management from the shop floor to the managing director. Many large organisations and government departments had a legendary number of management layers. Sydney Water and its predecessor reduced its management structure from 14 to 7 layers. Indeed, for most organisations the majority of consultants will recommend that the number of layers of management be reduced. If the numbers at the bottom of the organisation remain unchanged, this in effect means that the span of control should be increased.

Tom Peters, one of the authors of *In Search of Excellence*, claims that there is great scope in Western organisations to increase spans of control.[11] He notes that in Japan spans of control are often 100 and, in some cases, 200. In Western organisations, spans of control are often only 10, although it should be noted that different methods of counting are often used.[12] Comparisons of this nature are also often complicated by cultural factors. Peters claims that no organisation needs any more than 5 layers as a maximum. In fact, many large companies have reduced their layers of management to five and sometimes less.

Peters proposes that all organisations should aim for 3 layers of management, with a span of control at the supervisory level of 25–75. He admits that his solution is a radical response to making organisations more flexible and responsive, but it is a point of view that all companies should consider. Certainly, when restructuring, unless some limits are placed on the number of layers of management, or goals set and progress towards them monitored, then layers of management can continue to grow without check.

is focused on the South Australian market, has a low level of geographic dispersion. In the finance industry, a small company-based credit union with operations in one location would present an even lower level of geographic dispersion.

A lower level of spatial dispersion generally presents fewer problems for management. The geographic distance between staff is small and therefore fewer communication problems should arise; most staff should know each other, making problem solving easier; and as all staff members are drawn from the same geographic area and work within the same environment, behaviour patterns, attitudes and values should be similar. A high level of spatial dispersion leads to greater amounts of time and effort, hence cost, in managing these issues. Managing across different time zones also can present management with difficult control problems, particularly if day-to-day micro-management is involved.

The rise in the number of organisations with overseas operations has increased the level of complexity. This also applies to charities and not-for-profit organisations, which now often have a worldwide constituency. If senior executives reside in one city, middle managers in half a dozen other cities and lower level managers in a hundred different offices around the world, complexity is increased. This increases the amount of information the organisation must process.

In summary, spatial dispersion is the third element in defining complexity. It tells us that even if horizontal and vertical differentiation were to remain the same across spatially separated units, the physical separation of parts of the organisation would increase complexity.

Why is complexity important?

Why is the issue of complexity important for managers? The various specialised subsystems of organisations require communication, coordination and control if they are to be effective. The more complex an organisation, the greater the need for effective communication, coordination and control devices. In other words, as complexity increases, so do the demands on management to ensure that differentiated and dispersed activities are working smoothly and together towards achieving the organisation's goals. The need for coordination devices such as committees, computerised information systems and formal policy manuals is reduced for organisations that are low in complexity. So one way of answering the 'What does complexity mean to managers?' question is to say that it creates different management tasks and influences the way in which managers use their time. The higher the complexity, the greater the amount of attention management must give to dealing with problems of communication, coordination and control, and the maintenance of the organisation itself. Increased complexity also contributes to greater difficulties in managing organisational change.

This has been described as a paradox in the analysis of organisations.[13] Management's decision to increase differentiation is made typically in the interests of economy and efficiency or in order to accommodate company expansion. But these decisions create pressure to add managerial personnel to facilitate control, coordination and management of conflict. Thus the economies that increased size generates must be set against the increased burden and cost of managing a more complex organisation. Rarely are large organisations effective or efficient simply because they are large. The benefits of large size emerge from efficiencies in other areas, such as production or financial economies. Managers must balance economies from these areas with the diseconomies of having to manage large, complex organisations.

Formalisation

The second component of organisation structure is formalisation. In this section we define formalisation, explain its importance, explain the more popular formalisation techniques and show how formalisation contributes to complexity.

Definition

formalisation the degree to which jobs and procedures within the organisation are standardised

Formalisation refers to the degree to which jobs and procedures within the organisation are standardised.[14] If a job is highly formalised, those doing the job have a minimum amount of discretion over what is to be done, when it is to be done, and how it should be done. Employees are expected to undertake tasks in exactly the same way; this results in a consistent and uniform output. Where formalisation is high, there are clear job descriptions, many organisational rules to follow and clearly defined procedures covering work processes in the organisation. Where formalisation is low, employees' behaviour is relatively non-programmed. Such jobs would offer employees a great deal of discretion in undertaking their work. Thus one way of viewing formalisation is as a measure of standardisation of work.

Formalisation may also take the less tangible form of predictable thought patterns and approaches to problem solving within the organisation. In addition, organisational effectiveness requires the voluntary cooperation of members and actions that promote a positive environment within the organisation. Where this is achieved, high formalisation may also be seen to be present as it is possible to predict the behaviour of organisation members in non-routine situations. While the existence of extensive policy manuals and highly defined job descriptions may be evidence of written formalisation, similarity in the ways of thinking of organisational members is also evidence of behavioural formalisation.

Range of formalisation

It's important to recognise that the degree of formalisation can vary widely between and within organisations. Counter sales staff at McDonald's have little discretion in how they go about their work. There are fixed procedures to follow and their work is closely supervised. Additionally, their hours of work are closely monitored and any deviation from predetermined schedules is immediately identified and corrected. On the other hand, head office staff has far more freedom in how they do their job, including their hours of work. It is generally true that the narrowest of unskilled jobs—those that are simplest and most repetitive—are most amenable to high degrees of formalisation. The greater the professionalisation of a job, the less likely it is to be highly formalised. Yet there are obvious exceptions. Public accountants and consultants, for instance, are required to keep detailed records of their minute-by-minute activities so that their companies can bill clients appropriately for their services, and lawyers need to follow strict procedures in dealing with legal matters. In general, however, the relationship holds. The jobs of lawyers, engineers, social workers, librarians and professionals tend to rate low on formalisation.

For any given organisation, formalisation also differs with the level of the employee or manager and the work of their department. Employees higher in the organisation are increasingly involved in activities that are less repetitive and more conceptual in nature. The discretion that managers have increases as they move up the hierarchy. So formalisation tends to be inversely related to level in the organisation. Moreover, the kind of work in which people are engaged influences the degree of formalisation. Jobs in production are typically more formalised than are those in sales or research. That is because production tends to be concerned with stable and repetitive activities. Such jobs lend themselves to standardisation. In contrast, the sales department must be flexible in order to respond to the changing needs of customers, while research must be flexible if it is to be innovative.[15]

Why is formalisation important?

Organisations use formalisation because of the benefits that accrue from regulating employees' behaviour. Standardising behaviour reduces variability. Retailers such as David Jones and Woolworths ensure that their store presentation and standards of service are the same regardless of where they are located. Formalisation permits cars to flow smoothly down the assembly line, as each worker on the line performs highly standardised and coordinated activities. Formalisation also permits all members of the organisation to anticipate how others will act in certain situations and lays down guidelines to follow. For instance, it prevents members of a paramedic unit or fire-fighting team from standing around at the scene of an accident and arguing about who is to do what.

There are also economic benefits from formalisation. The greater the formalisation, such as procedures to be followed at a supermarket checkout, the less discretion is required from a job incumbent. As a result, their pay is low. However, jobs that are low on formalisation demand greater judgement and organisations must pay for the skill and knowledge to exercise that judgement. Typically, hiring employees with a professional background is far more expensive than hiring those with little formal training.

Formalisation may also be used to manage risks. Airline pilots follow strictly defined procedures. Most managers have limitations placed on them in relation to expenditure of money and other major decisions. Foreign exchange dealers are limited in the trades they can make and banks have strict policies for lending money. The aim of these restrictions is to reduce the amount of risk arising from the actions of any one person.

Formalisation techniques

Managers have at their disposal a number of techniques which promote the standardisation of employee behaviour. However, not all formalisation techniques are internal to the organisation. When professional employees are hired, they come with extensive formalisation acquired through years of study in their chosen profession. Membership of a professional body commits a member to certain values and standards of behaviour. In hiring such employees, the organisation can be reasonably confident that these standards will become part of formalised behaviour patterns of employees. We call this external formalisation, as it has been acquired external to the organisation.

The formalisation of most members occurs, however, as a result of direct action on the part of management and others in the organisation. In this section, we review the most common formalisation techniques used by organisations.

Selection

Organisations do not choose employees at random. Even though there is a comprehensive body of laws to eliminate discrimination against target groups in hiring, this still leaves companies a fair amount of discretion as to who to hire. And even though the ability to do the job is the main criterion for selection, there are still generally a number of employees from whom to select. As a consequence, interviewers will always be looking at the ability of a person to fit into the organisation and reflect its values as one of the prime requirements for selection.[16]

Role requirements

Individuals in organisations fulfil roles. Every job carries with it task requirements and expectations about how the incumbent is supposed to behave. Role requirements may be explicit and defined in great detail; in such cases, the degree of formalisation is high. Other roles allow employees freedom to react to situations in unique ways and minimum constraints are placed on the person doing the job. In this case, formalisation is lower, at least in relation to the tasks a person does.

rules explicit statements that tell an employee what he or she ought or ought not to do

procedures specific standardised sequences of steps that result in a uniform output

Rules, procedures and policies

Rules are explicit statements that tell an employee what he or she ought or ought not to do. Examples of rules are limits on credit card sales approvals, specified hours of work, limitations on managers approving expenditure, and forms for annual and sick leave approval. Rules generally leave no room for employee judgement or discretion. They state a particular and specific required behaviour pattern.

Procedures are a series of interrelated sequential steps that employees follow in the accomplishment of their tasks. These are established to ensure standardisation of work processes. The same input is processed in the same way, and the output is the same each day. Procedures are aimed at establishing a specific standardised sequence that results in a uniform output.

policies statements that guide employees, providing discretion within limited boundaries

Policies are guidelines that set constraints on decisions that employees make. They are largely developed to guide and regulate behaviour in situations where it is difficult or impossible to define the problem to be faced. Policies leave greater discretion for decision makers than do rules. Rather than specifying an exact set of procedures to follow, policies provide the parameters which guide decision making. The discretion is created by including judgemental terms (e.g. 'best', 'satisfied', 'competitive'), which the employee is left to interpret. Policies need not be written to control discretion. Employees may absorb an organisation's implied policies merely by observing the actions of members around them. This is part of the process of socialisation, and the behavioural constraints and motivations reflected in the implied policies become part of the organisation's culture.

Socialisation

socialisation an adaptation process by which individuals learn the values, norms and expected behaviour patterns for the job and the organisation of which they will be a part

Socialisation refers to an adaptation process by which individuals absorb the values, norms and expected behaviour patterns for the job and the organisation of which they will be a part. This may be likened to learning the organisation's culture. Most socialisation occurs on the job, through a process of observation, behaviour modification and interaction with existing organisational members. But for professionals, socialisation into the standards of their profession mostly occurs before they join the organisation.

OT CLOSEUP

Extremes of formalisation

In organisations where the members are fully included, there is little distinction between the organisation members and the organisation itself. Some religious orders provide examples of this. The Roman Catholic order of the Jesuits was renowned for the rigour of its training and the length of time it took to become a full member of the order. Novitiates were secluded in seminaries for years where they absorbed the standards and practices of the order and the behaviours which were expected of its priests. Up to 14 years could pass before final vows were taken and, in that time, seminarians had to demonstrate full commitment to the organisation, its standards, culture and way of thought. At the end of the process, there was virtually no distinction between the organisation and the individual. The individual could always be counted on to act in the organisation's best interest and, in turn, what they did determined the organisation's standards. At its extreme there was no need for management because the individual's and the organisation's goals were one and the same.

The same process can be seen in military systems, which take in a wide variety of recruits from diverse backgrounds. All armies have a process of recruit training where newly recruited soldiers are withdrawn from the world for up to 12 weeks and are intensively inculcated with standards, practices, technology and expectations of the army. Their former personas are stripped from them and a new person emerges, highly formalised in the ways of the army.

Such full inclusion is in contrast to the much more common partial inclusion where membership of the organisation is only part of a person's time commitment.

Training

Many organisations provide training for employees. This includes the on-the-job variety, where development programs and apprenticeship methods are used to teach employees preferred job skills, knowledge and attitudes. It also includes off-the-job training, such as classroom lectures, films, demonstrations, simulation exercises and programmed instruction. Again, the intention is to instil in employees preferred work behaviour and attitudes.

New employees are often required to undergo a brief orientation program in which they are familiarised with the organisation's objectives, history, philosophy and rules, as well as with relevant personnel policies such as hours of work, pay, procedures, overtime requirements and benefit programs. In many cases, this is followed by specific job training. The aim of such training is to reduce variability in the behaviour of organisational members.

Rituals

rituals processes by which members prove their trustworthiness and loyalty to the organisation by participating in various behaviours in which predetermined responses are expected

We are all familiar with **rituals** in organisations. Churches and the armed forces are the best known examples of organisations that regularly require members to show their loyalty by taking part in ceremonies in which all members participate. Business organisations also have their rituals, which all those who aspire to higher management positions must attend. Even lower level employees and those who do not want promotion are often obliged to take part.

In business organisations rituals are essentially communal activities which bring people and groups together. Typical examples are attending Christmas parties, sales or other departmental conferences, informal lunches and after-dinner drinks and

OT CLOSEUP

Do sophisticated information systems change the basic organisation dimensions?

In this chapter so far we have described two ways in which we compare organisations. Although we have referred to the impact of information technology in different parts of the chapter, we are left with the question as to whether information technology will render the measures we have discussed obsolete.

There is no doubt that information technology will alter the way in which organisations are structured and managed. But we can say that the basic organisational dimensions described in this chapter will still be those which are used for organisational comparison. Why? Because no matter what their technology, organisations will still conform to the basic definition given in Chapter 1, namely that each will be a consciously coordinated social entity, with an identifiable boundary, which aims to meet certain goals. Part of the need for an identifiable boundary arises from the legal requirement to incorporate an organisation, and the need to hire employees and to have managers responsible for the operation of the company. Furthermore, most organisations produce complex products, which is one of the reasons that organisations, as opposed to single traders, exist. This implies a division of labour, the need for supervision and coordination, and the need for managers to determine the strategic direction of the company. All of these mean that it is necessary to determine where decisions are made and how formalised and complex the organisation will be.

Even though each of these dimensions of organisation structure may be affected by changes in the way an organisation gathers and processes information, we will still have to use the measures of organisational structure discussed in this chapter.

taking part in outdoor and other training exercises. Some companies even have company songs and chants in which groups of employees participate. Rituals can also extend to the style of clothes that are the accepted form of dress and which indicate membership of a particular group and hence adherence to its values. Merchant bankers with their power dressing are clad differently from workers in the Toyota factory, with their monogrammed work shirts and zip-up jackets. But each group is uniformly clad, thus showing a common bond between them and the organisation. Taking part in rituals is a way for a manager, and those aspiring to management, to show loyalty to the organisation and adherence to established practices and attitudes. They thereby show that they can be trusted to reflect the organisation's norms and values.[17]

Centralisation

Where are decisions made in the organisation: at the top by senior management, or down low where the decision makers are closest to the action? Are they made by one person, or are many individuals and groups involved? These questions introduce the last of the components making up organisation structure. The subject of this section is centralisation and its counterpart, decentralisation.

Definition

centralisation the degree to which decision making is concentrated in a single point in the organisation, usually top management

Centralisation is the most difficult to define of the three components. Most organisational theorists agree that the term refers to the degree to which decision making is concentrated at a single point in the organisation. When applied in common usage, the 'single point' in the organisation is normally the top few managers. On the other hand, where decision making is widely dispersed within the organisation, the term *decentralisation* is normally used. Centralisation, therefore, is the degree to which the formal authority to make discretionary choices is concentrated in an individual, a unit or a level (usually high in the organisation), thus permitting employees (usually low in the organisation) minimum input into their work.

This elaborate definition highlights the following points in relation to centralisation:

1 Centralisation is concerned only with the formal structure, not the informal organisation. It applies only to formal authority.
2 Centralisation looks at decision discretion. Where decisions are delegated downwards but extensive policies exist to constrain the discretion of lower level members, there is increased centralisation. Policies can therefore act to override decentralisation.
3 Concentration at a single point can refer to an individual, a unit or a level, but the single point *implies* concentration at a high level.
4 Information processing can extend top management control, but the decision choice may still lie with the low-level member. Thus, an information-processing system may closely monitor decentralised decisions.
5 The transference of all information requires interpretation. The filtering that occurs as information passes up and down through layers of management is a fact of life. Control of information input is a form of de-facto decentralisation and is a highly political activity. Management decisions are centralised if concentrated at the top, but the more the information input to those decisions is filtered through others, the less concentrated, controlled and well informed are the decisions.

OT CLOSEUP
The centralisation dilemma

Decision making always presents a problem for large organisations, particularly if it has strategic implications. Decision making centralised on one person or group may be fast and responsive but it has its disadvantages. In large organisations, full information may not be accessed or processed or different opinions sought or evaluated. And there are always the shortcomings associated with human decision making: information overload, the influence of emotion and the personal desires of the decision maker, and the tendency to manipulate information to conform to desired outcomes.

BHP provides a good example of how centralised decision making can lead to poor decisions being made. In the 1990s, BHP comprised three divisions: Minerals, Oil and Steel. Over time its head office had devolved much of its strategic oversight and decision making to the divisions. This made the divisional heads very powerful and in due course they became used to operating at arm's length from the head office.

Each division had plans for growth and BHP Minerals based its strategy on growing its copper assets and becoming a global copper player. The price of copper at that time had been rising and continuing demand was expected to push the price up even further. The CEO of BHP Minerals at the time, Jerry Ellis, had already made overtures to take over the American company, Magma Copper, but had been rebuffed. However, in 1995, with the copper price at an all-time high, Ellis was contacted by the head of Magma Copper, J. Burgess Winter, and advised that Magma was ready to do a deal if BHP made an offer higher than the market price of Magma shares. Ellis jumped at the opportunity and without doing due diligence (a process where a company's business, financial and material assets are subject to close scrutiny and examination) quickly sealed the deal with the ready acquiescence of the BHP board.

The deal was a disaster. The price of copper was being artificially inflated by speculative deals by a rogue trader employed by Sumitomo. When the deals were exposed the price of copper crashed by 35%, leaving the economics of the purchase in disarray. But further trouble loomed! As BHP took control it found that Magma's assets were not what they had seemed. The mines were high cost and lacked reserves and the copper smelters had significant environmental problems. In short, Ellis had overpaid for inferior assets.

BHP eventually wrote off the $3.2 billion it paid for Magma, all the more damaging for having been raised through debt rather than equity. But the Magma purchase could easily have been avoided. Inputs from finance, engineering, mining and other experts should have been sought and incorporated into collective decision making. The head office, and the board, should have insisted upon due diligence being carried out and the personal relationship between Ellis and Winter should not have influenced the decision. Centralisation of decision making was the main cause of BHP's problems.

Source: Robert Gottliebsen, *The ten best and ten worst decisions of Australian CEOs*, Penguin, Melbourne, 2003.

Why is centralisation important?

The heading of this section may mislead you, because it implies that centralisation, in contrast to decentralisation, is important. The term *centralisation* in this context is meant to be viewed in the same way as complexity and formalisation should be viewed in this chapter. It represents a range—from high to low. It may be clearer, therefore, if we ask: why is the centralisation–decentralisation issue important?

In addition to being collections of people, organisations are decision-making and information-processing systems. They facilitate the achievement of goals through

When should you use it?

The machine bureaucracy is most efficient when matched with large size, a stable environment and a technology that permits standardised, routine work. You see its effectiveness when you go into the main post office in any major city, visit a motor vehicle production line or book an airline ticket. The machine bureaucracy is appropriate only as long as its environment remains stable and its technology routine. But this design configuration is not conducive to making changes either rapidly or efficiently. This can be seen in the efforts of large organisations to introduce programs of change. Such processes may take decades and, in many cases, fail to meet the expectations held of them.

Given these strengths and weaknesses, where are you likely to find machine bureaucracies? In mass-production firms, such as those in the car and steel industries; service organisations with simple, repetitive activities, such as banks, insurance and telephone companies; government agencies with routine work, such as post offices and the taxation department; and organisations that have special safety needs, such as airlines and railways. All these organisations have routine and highly standardised activities. Most of their activities have occurred many times before and are therefore predictable and amenable to formalised procedures. Such formalised procedures are also critical for safety and maintenance of quality.

The weakness in the machine bureaucracy does not arise because it becomes too big, although some machine bureaucracies are extremely large with hundreds of thousands of employees. It arises because it tries to do too much. It may be producing too diverse a product range or operating over too wide a geographic area. In this case the inefficiencies arising from attempting to manage the resulting complexity lead to the machine bureaucracy becoming inappropriate. The answer is to divide the machine bureaucracy into a number of self-contained divisions. The divisional structure is our third configuration.

The divisional structure

The **divisional structure** is a set of autonomous self-contained units, each typically configured as a machine bureaucracy. CSR, ANZ Bank, Boral, Wesfarmers and Rio Tinto are examples of organisations that use the divisional structure. As Figure 4.7 illustrates, the dominant part of the divisional structure lies with middle

divisional structure a structure characterised by a set of self-contained, autonomous units coordinated by a central headquarters

FIGURE 4.7 The divisional structure

Source: Henry Mintzberg, *Structure in Fives: Designing Effective Organizations*, © 1983. Reprinted by permission of Pearson Education, Upper Saddle River, NJ.

management. They report to, and are overseen, by a head office which is often located close to a central business district. As the divisions are autonomous, this allows middle management—the divisional managers—a great deal of control over their individual businesses.[23]

The use of the term middle managers needs some clarification in this context. Chief executives of large businesses (i.e. the divisions) are not normally described as middle managers. But in the context of divisionalisation they are middle managers. They are answerable to the senior managers in the head office and they supervise lower level managers. Thus they meet the role requirements normally associated with middle managers.

Figure 4.8 shows how the divisional form is utilised at Wesfarmers. Each of its major areas of responsibility—groups headed by a senior executive—represents a separate division. As with most divisional structures, each division is generally autonomous, with the divisional managers responsible for its performance. The divisional general managers generally hold major strategic and operating decision-making authority in relation to their businesses. This form also has a central head office that provides support services to the divisions. This typically includes financial, legal and tax services. Additionally, of course, the headquarters acts as an external overseer, evaluating the performance of each division and deciding which receives capital for investment. This task is facilitated by the divisions being run as profit centres. That means each division is run as a separate business, showing a profit or loss. Divisions, therefore, are autonomous within the parameters laid down by the head office.

Rather than have one large organisation undertaking many different and unrelated tasks, what divisionalisation does is not to make the total organisation smaller, but to break it up, or divide it, into a smaller number of manageable parts, all of which report to a head office. The organisation may be divided on a number of bases. First, it may be by product. This may be seen in the Wesfarmers' structure. A second basis for divisionalisation is by geographic area. This is particularly relevant to service industries. The third method is by customer. For example, large manufacturers often have a defence division, which is solely aimed at serving defence customers. Similar divisions may exist for railways, aerospace and so forth. The divisions may extend

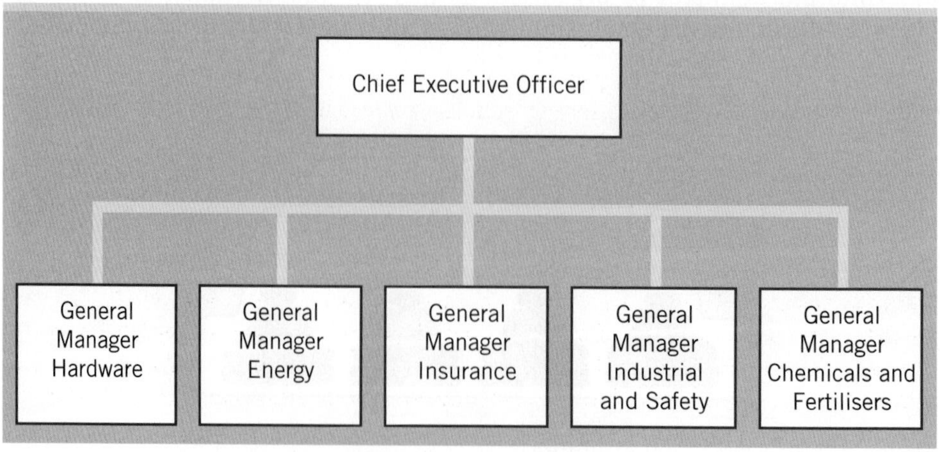
Chief Executive Officer
General Manager Hardware
General Manager Energy
General Manager Insurance
General Manager Industrial and Safety
General Manager Chemicals and Fertilisers

FIGURE 4.8 Modified organisational chart of Wesfarmers Limited

Source: www.wesfarmers.com, 2006.

quite deep into the organisation's structure. For instance, Blue Scope Steel may have divisions extending two or three layers deep into the structure even to the level of each plant.

The divisional form is probably the most common form of large business structure. Given its dominance, it is surprising that the divisional structure is relatively new. It was introduced by Alfred Sloan in the early part of the last century when he put together General Motors from a group of previously independent car manufacturers.

Strengths and weaknesses

One of the strengths of the divisional structure is that it provides clear accountability and responsibility for the performance of each division. The divisional manager is more focused on outcomes—that is, the profit or loss of his/her division—than on internal processes.

Another strength of the divisional structure is that it frees head office staff from involvement with day-to-day operating details so that they can pay attention to the long term. Big-picture, strategic decision making is done at headquarters. At Wesfarmers, for instance, senior executives can wrestle with the strategic problems of the total organisation, while the division managers can concentrate on producing fertilisers and distributing building material products as effectively as possible.

The autonomy and business focus of the divisional form make it an excellent vehicle for training and developing general managers. For instance, a large corporation with 15 divisions has 15 division managers, who are developing the kind of generalist perspective that is needed in the organisation's top spot.

Another strength of the divisional form is that, as each division is autonomous, it can be sold or disposed of with minimal effect on the entire organisation. And it follows that businesses may be added with little disruption to existing businesses. Also, ineffective performance in one division has little effect on the other divisions. Consequently, the divisional structure spreads risk by reducing the chance that a poorly performing part of the organisation will take down other parts of the organisation with it.

It is evident that the real strengths of the divisional form come from the creation of self-contained businesses 'within a business'. The divisions are responsive to their own environment, are accountable, derive the benefits of specialisation, and are able to process information as if they were organisations unto themselves.

In the divisional form, the head office is generally responsible for the allocation of capital and making major investment decisions. Returning to our example of Wesfarmers, the board of Wesfarmers itself will decide whether to invest in expanding the hardware chain or the fertiliser business. Wesfarmers can also use its strong credit rating to obtain finance at a cheaper rate than if the hardware group acted as a separate corporation independent of Wesfarmers.

Let us turn now to the weaknesses of the divisional structure. First is the duplication of activities and resources. Each division, for instance, will have its own accounts department. In the absence of autonomous divisions, an organisation's accounting tasks might be centralised and carried out for a fraction of the cost that divisionalisation requires. The divisional form's duplication of functions raises the organisation's costs and reduces efficiency. This is overcome to a certain extent by the creation of shared resource units. These typically provide services such as logistics, warehousing and transport, financial services, purchasing, and buying of advertising space for each division.

Another disadvantage is the propensity of the divisional form to make cooperation between divisions difficult. There is little incentive with this structural design to encourage cooperation among divisions. Conflict is generated as divisions and head office argue about where to locate support services. The more the divisions succeed in having these services decentralised to their level, the less dependent they are on headquarters and, hence, the less power headquarters personnel can wield over them.

The autonomy of the divisions, to the degree that it is more theory than practice, can breed resentment in the division managers. While the structure gives autonomy to the divisions, this autonomy is exercised within constraints. The division manager is held fully accountable for results in the unit, but because the manager must operate within the uniform policies imposed from head office there is likely to be resentment and for his/her authority to be less than his/her responsibility.

Finally, the divisional form creates coordination problems. Personnel are often unable to transfer between divisions, especially when the divisions operate in highly diverse product or service markets. Personnel in Wesfarmers' Bunnings hardware stores would find it difficult to transfer to the fertiliser division. This reduces the flexibility of head office executives to allocate and coordinate personnel. Additionally, the divisional form may make coordination of customer relations and product development a problem. If the divisions are in competing or closely adjoining markets, they may compete with each other for the same sale. To many prospective shoppers, Kmart and Target are different chains, selling similar merchandise to discount shoppers. However, as both are owned by Coles Myer, they both compete for the same dollar as if they were owned by separate companies.

Similarly, the competition between divisions over product development can be dysfunctional. The classic illustration is the NDH (not developed here) syndrome. An innovation developed by one division and then authorised by head office to be instituted in all divisions often fails because it was NDH. This rivalry and territorial protectionism by the individual divisions can make coordination by headquarters extremely difficult.

When should you use it?

The primary reason for using the divisional structure is product or market diversity. When an organisation chooses a diversification strategy—to become a multiproduct or multimarket organisation—the divisional form becomes preferable to a machine bureaucracy. When an organisation diversifies, complexity leads to management becoming too complex and a change in structural design becomes necessary.

Other contingency factors include size, technology and environment. As size increases, it becomes more difficult to coordinate functional units and to keep members' attention focused on the organisation's goals. Organisational size and goal displacement appear to be highly correlated. With growing size, communication channels become strained and unable to handle the greater complexity. Growth in size encourages movement to the divisional structure.

Not all technologies are compatible with the division form. To be applicable, the organisation's technology must be divisible: 'Divisionalization is possible only when the organization's technical system can be efficiently separated into segments, one for each division'.[24] It is difficult, for instance, for IAG Insurance to divisionalise because economies of scale and the commitment of hundreds of millions of dollars to very high fixed-cost technical systems basically preclude divisibility. Finally, the environment affects preference for the divisional form. The divisional structure works best where the environment is neither very complex nor very dynamic. This is because highly complex and dynamic environments are associated with non-standardised processes and outputs, yet the divisional form is a lot like the machine bureaucracy in its emphasis on standardisation. The divisional form, therefore, tends to have an environment that is more simple than complex and more stable than dynamic.

The professional bureaucracy

The past quarter of a century has seen the emergence of a new structural configuration called the professional bureaucracy. The **professional bureaucracy** is a decentralised configuration in which highly trained specialists form the operating core but where the benefits of standardisation and decentralisation are still achieved.

professional bureaucracy a structural form that has highly skilled professionals, high complexity, decentralisation and the use of internalised professional standards in place of external formalisation

The jobs that people do today increasingly require a high level of specialised expertise. Hospitals, schools, universities, museums, libraries, engineering design firms, management consultancies, social service agencies, and public accounting and legal firms are just some of the types of organisations where the majority of key staff have professional expertise. The employment of professionals has created the need for an organisational design that permits high levels of expertise to be applied to unique problems.

Figure 4.9 illustrates the configuration for professional bureaucracies. The power in this design rests with the operating core because they have the critical skills that the organisation needs and they have the autonomy—provided through decentralisation—to apply their expertise. The only other part of the professional bureaucracy that has a large complement of employees is the support staff, but their activities are focused on serving the operating core.[25]

You can see what a professional bureaucracy looks like in Figure 4.10. The Legal Aid Commission of New South Wales relies on the skills of lawyers in various specialties as well as other professionals in such areas as social work and child support. These professionals acquired their skills through years of study, leading to their admission to professional bodies. They perform their activities relatively autonomously, but the structure is high in complexity and there are many rules and regulations; however, the formalisation is internalised rather than imposed by the organisation itself. The Legal Aid example also illustrates a fact about most professional bureaucracies, which is that they also typically include machine bureaucracies within them. In Legal Aid, for example, the support staff that assist the professionals—secretaries, clerks, computer services, library, human resources and so on—will not have decentralised

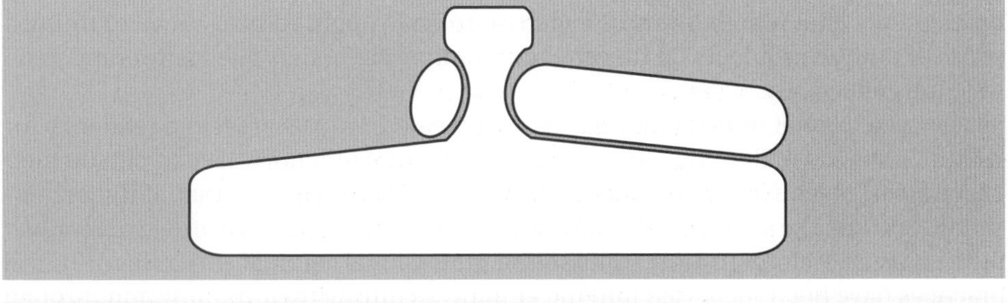

FIGURE 4.9 The professional bureaucracy

Source: Henry Mintzberg, *Structure in Fives: Designing Effective Organizations*, © 1983, p. 159. Reprinted by permission of Pearson Education, Upper Saddle River, NJ.

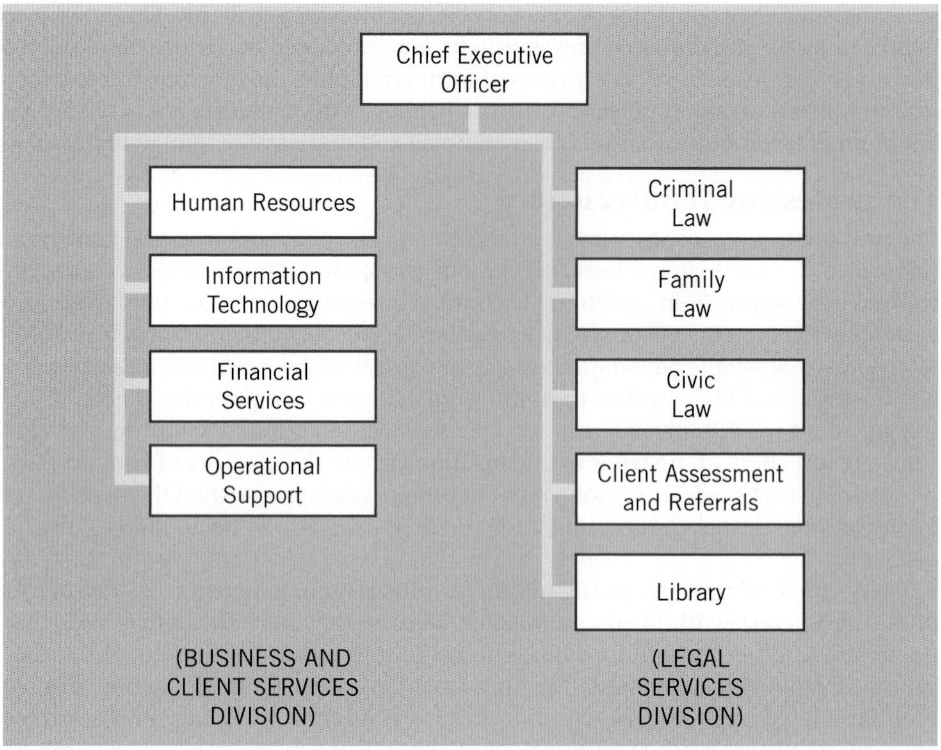
Chief Executive Officer
Human Resources
Information Technology
Financial Services
Operational Support
Criminal Law
Family Law
Civic Law
Client Assessment and Referrals
Library
(BUSINESS AND CLIENT SERVICES DIVISION)
(LEGAL SERVICES DIVISION)

FIGURE 4.10 Abbreviated organisational chart of the Legal Aid Commission of New South Wales

Source: Annual Report 2004/5.

authority, and their formalisation will be externally imposed by the rules and regulations surrounding their work.

Strengths and weaknesses

The strength of the professional bureaucracy is that it can perform specialised tasks—those that require the skills of highly trained professionals—with the same relative efficiency as the machine bureaucracy. One of the characteristics of tasks undertaken by professionals is that few of the problems faced are the same. The professional bureaucracy allows high levels of expertise to be brought to bear on a continuous series of unique problems. In this environment, professionals need autonomy to do their jobs effectively.

The professional bureaucracy has its weaknesses. First, there is the tendency for subunit conflicts to develop. The various professional functions seek to pursue their own narrow objectives, often placing their own self-interest over that of the organisation. Second, the specialists in the professional bureaucracy are often constrained by the rules of their profession: standards of professional conduct and codes of ethical practices have been socialised into the employees during their training and through membership of professional bodies. This means that they cannot be managed in the same way as employees in other structural configurations. This leads to difficulties when organisations need to adapt to changing circumstances.

A further management problem is the difficulty in coordinating the work of the various professionals. In the professional bureaucracy, work is compartmentalised and allocated to the person with the necessary skills and training to carry it out. Rarely do professionals coordinate with each other, leading to limitations on the complexity of work that can be carried out. Another weakness is that in the professional bureaucracy it is difficult to set strategic priorities. This is because it has no clear strategic apex. Many professional bureaucracies exist as partnerships, where all partners are equal. This contrasts with a conventional business which has a board of directors and clear areas of responsibility for strategic matters. No one therefore has the clear-cut authority typically associated with the strategic apex. Many professional bureaucracies have introduced the position of managing partner in order to provide overall direction to the organisation and have therefore minimised this problem.

When should you use it?

The professional bureaucracy is at its best when matched with a complex and stable environment. The organisation's operating core will be dominated by skilled professionals who have internalised difficult-to-learn but nevertheless well-defined procedures. The complex and stable environment means that the organisation requires the use of difficult skills that can be learned only in formal education and training programs, and there is enough stability for these skills, but not the problems faced, to be well defined and standardised.

The growth of professional services has made the professional bureaucracy a commonly applied form. As organisations have hired more and more technical specialists, they have been forced to come up with an alternative to the machine bureaucracy. The professional bureaucracy provides such an alternative by decentralising decision making, while maintaining many of the other advantages of the machine form.

The adhocracy

When Peter Weir or George Lucas makes a film, they bring together a diverse group of professionals. This team—composed of producers, scriptwriters, film editors, set designers and hundreds of other specialists—exists for the one purpose of making a single film. They may be called back by Weir or Lucas when either of these directors begins another film, but that is irrelevant when the current project begins. These professionals often find themselves with overlapping activities because no formal rules or regulations have been provided to guide members of the team. While there is a production schedule, it must often be modified to take into consideration unforeseen contingencies. The film's production team may be together for a few months or, in some unusual cases, for several years, but the organisation is temporary. In contrast to bureaucracies or divisional structures, these film-making organisations have no entrenched hierarchy, no permanent departments, no formalised rules, and no standardised procedures for dealing with routine problems. This leads to our last design configuration.

adhocracy an organisational form characterised by high horizontal differentiation, low vertical differentiation, low formalisation, intensive coordination, and great flexibility and responsiveness

The **adhocracy** is a decentralised form which is characterised by high horizontal differentiation, low vertical differentiation, low formalisation, intensive coordination, and great flexibility and responsiveness.

Horizontal differentiation is significant because adhocracies are staffed predominantly by professionals with a high level of expertise. Vertical differentiation is low because the many levels of administration would restrict the organisation's ability to adapt. Also, the need for supervision is reduced because professionals have internalised the behaviours that management wants. However, coordination is quite extensive as it is important for tasks to be carried out in the correct sequence.

We have already found professionalisation and formalisation to be inversely related. The adhocracy is no exception. There are few rules and regulations. Those that exist tend to be loose and unwritten. Again, the objective of flexibility demands an absence of formalisation. Rules and regulations are effective only where standardisation of behaviour is sought. However, the adhocracy is far more intensively coordinated than the professional bureaucracy, often having specific individuals whose only role is to coordinate the activities of others.

Decision making in adhocracies is decentralised. This is necessary for speed and flexibility and because senior management cannot be expected to possess the expertise needed to make all decisions. So the adhocracy depends on decentralised teams of professionals and highly skilled employees for decision making.

The adhocracy is a very different design from those we encountered earlier. This can be seen in Figure 4.11. Because the adhocracy has little standardisation or formalisation, the technostructure is almost non-existent. Because middle managers, the support staff and operatives are typically all professionals in orientation, the traditional distinctions between supervisor and employee and line and staff become blurred. The result is a central pool of expert talent that can be drawn upon to innovate, solve unique problems and perform flexible activities. Power flows to anyone in the adhocracy with expertise, regardless of his or her position.[26]

Adhocracies are best conceptualised as groups of teams. Specialists are grouped together into flexible teams that have few rules, regulations or standardised routines. Coordination between team members is through mutual adjustment, but often a team member's main role is to coordinate the efforts of others. As conditions change, so do the activities of the members. However, adhocracies do not have to be devoid of horizontally differentiated departments. Departments may be used for clarity and then department members deployed into small teams—which cut across functional units—to perform their tasks.

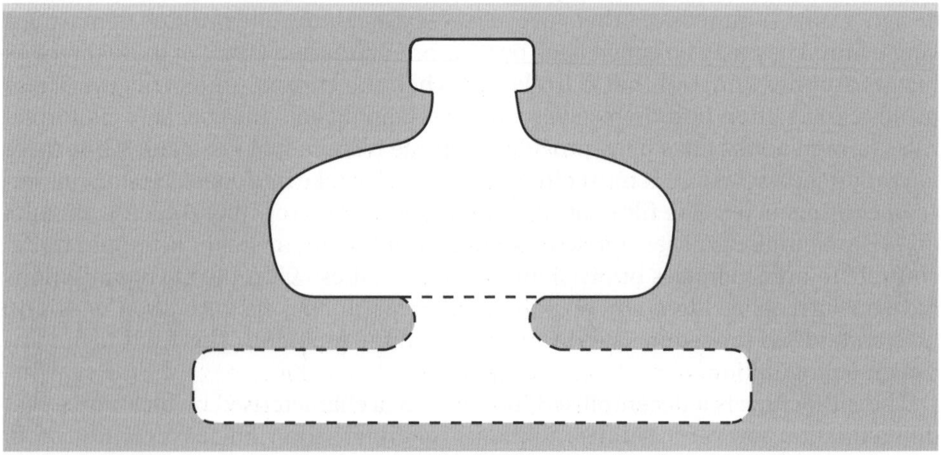

FIGURE 4.11 The adhocracy

Source: Henry Mintzberg, *Structure in Fives: Designing Effective Organizations*, © 1983, p. 262. Reprinted by permission of Pearson Education, Upper Saddle River, NJ.

OT CLOSEUP

The network structure and the Jabiru

Unless you are a light aircraft aficionado, it is unlikely that you have heard of the Jabiru. It is a small training and sports utility aircraft built in Bundaberg, Queensland. It is the brainchild of Phil Ainsworth and Rod Stiff, two sugar cane harvester manufacturers who thought of the idea of producing a light aircraft in 1987. Their ideas proved so successful that up to 500 have been delivered and over 100 are on order. Most of the aircraft are sold in kit form: that is, the various parts are put into a shipping container with the customer being responsible for final assembly. Some, however, are fabricated in Bundaberg and flown to final customers.

The aircraft has been so successful that Ainsworth and Stiff soon realised that they did not have the space to manufacture the numbers being ordered. As most of the parts were not large (the Jabiru is no jumbo jet), they made their employees an offer to set up their own businesses fabricating the parts of the aircraft that they were already trained for. This mainly involved fibreglassing and light metal work. Local families have found new skills, with some parts being made by 'Gran and Grandad' in the shed, while the more sophisticated parts are made by teams of five or six workers who lease a hangar at the airport. The engine is made in Bundaberg by another subcontractor, CAMit. The parts are machined from solid blocks of metal. This allows design changes to be easily incorporated through a simple change to the computer program controlling the machine. Over 35 engines are produced per month.

Ainsworth and Stiff derive considerable advantage from using their network of suppliers. They don't have to worry about day-to-day management of a workforce. They can concentrate their efforts on design and marketing. They have no layers of middle management. The system has the flexibility of being able to expand and contract the production schedule with minimum disruption to the company; most of Ainsworth's and Stiff's costs are variable and dependent on the number of aircraft ordered. The subcontractors themselves are free to seek other work commensurate with their skills and interests. CAMit, for example, supplies engines for many different types of small aircraft.

The network structure used to manufacture the Jabiru offers considerable advantages in flexibility and workforce management. It comes as no surprise that networks are becoming more common in industry.

Source: Adapted from Tony Arbon, 'Australia's Jabiru Flies High', *Australian Aviation*, September 2001, pp. 34–6.

The Sydney Theatre Company is a typical example of an adhocracy (see Figure 4.12). Developed around the concept of mounting a continuously changing range of productions, it relies heavily on the flexibility inherent in the adhocratic form. Most of its employees and contract staff work in teams built around productions. Each team is composed of experts who are under the coordination of the director for each production. The distinction between managers and workers is minimised, as the organisation is essentially staffed by professionals. All employees enjoy a great deal of autonomy, within the limits of having to coordinate with other employees. The Sydney Theatre Company's structure is based on the constant need to change and update its repertoire, rather than on narrow functional specialties. Instead of being permanently part of a team, employees have tenure on a specific team, depending on how long it takes for that team to accomplish its task.

Strengths and weaknesses

The history of adhocracy can be traced to the development of taskforces during World War II, when the military created ad-hoc teams that were disbanded after completion

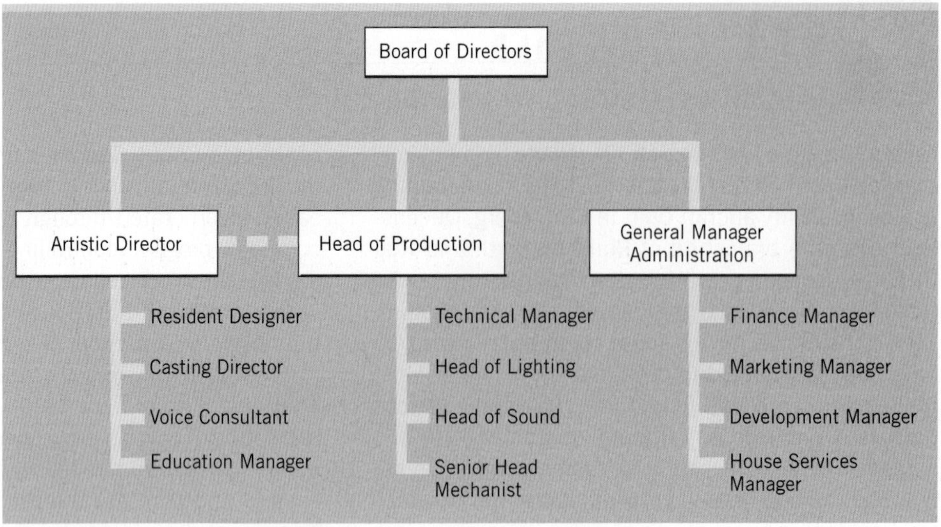
Board of Directors
Artistic Director
Head of Production
General Manager Administration
Resident Designer
Casting Director
Voice Consultant
Education Manager
Technical Manager
Head of Lighting
Head of Sound
Senior Head Mechanist
Finance Manager
Marketing Manager
Development Manager
House Services Manager

FIGURE 4.12 Modified organisational chart of the Sydney Theatre Company, 2005

Source: www.sydneytheatre.com.au

of their missions. There was no rigid time span for their existence: teams could last a day, a month or a year. Roles performed in the teams were interchangeable and, depending on the nature and complexity of the mission, the group could be divided into subunits, each responsible for different facets of the job to be done. The advantages of these ad-hoc teams included their ability to respond rapidly to change and innovation and to facilitate the coordination of diverse specialists. Over 50 years have passed since the end of World War II, but the advantage of ad-hoc teams, or what we call adhocracy, continues today. When it is important that the organisation be adaptable and creative, when individual specialists from diverse disciplines are required to collaborate to achieve a common goal and when tasks are technical, non-programmed and too complex for any one person to handle, the adhocracy represents a viable alternative.

On the negative side, conflict is a natural part of adhocracy. There are no clear boss–subordinate relationships. Ambiguities exist over authority and responsibilities. Activities cannot be compartmentalised. In short, adhocracy lacks the advantages of standardised work.

Adhocracy can create social stress and psychological tensions for members. It is not easy to set up and quickly dismantle work relationships on a perpetual basis. Some employees find it difficult to cope with rapid change, living in temporary work systems and having to share responsibilities with other team members.

In contrast to bureaucracy, adhocracy is clearly an inefficient configuration. It is also a vulnerable design. As one author noted, 'Many of them either die early or else shift to bureaucratic configurations to escape the uncertainty'.[27] So why, you might ask, would it ever be used? Because its inefficiencies, in certain circumstances, are more than offset by the need for flexibility and innovation.

There are other, informal ways in which organisations may be described. One of these is the use of metaphors, as when we use something familiar to us to describe an organisation. While metaphors may provide a powerful and rich description of an organisation, they lack the precision to permit organisational comparison.

For review and discussion

1 Identify and briefly describe the measures of complexity. Are the three measures related to each other? Discuss.
2 Identify and briefly describe the common formalisation techniques.
3 What are the benefits and disadvantages of formalisation to an organisation?
4 Compare the formalisation of unskilled workers with that of professionals.
5 Why is the issue of centralisation important to an organisation?
6 In what ways would working in a centralised organisation be different from working in a decentralised one?
7 Discuss how job satisfaction could be maintained in a highly formalised and centralised organisation.
8 Identify and describe the different types of coordination used in organisations.
9 Identify and briefly describe an organisation you are familiar with which is likely to have (a) high formalisation and centralisation, (b) low formalisation and centralisation, (c) high formalisation and decentralisation.
10 What is authority? How is it related to centralisation?
11 How may metaphors be used to better understand people's perceptions of organisations?
12 Identify and describe the five component parts of most organisations.
13 Identify and describe the five basic structural configurations.
14 Discuss how it is possible for a large organisation to possess the characteristics of a number of the basic structural configurations.
15 Which of the structural configurations would be most attractive to a potential graduate? Why?

CASE FOR CLASS DISCUSSION

Flight Centre's families, villages and tribes

Flight Centre travel agencies with their red and white signs are a familiar sight in most shopping centres in Australia and increasingly overseas. Established in the late 1970s and headquartered in Brisbane, Flight Centre now has over 1000 shops in 6 countries (Australia, New Zealand, South Africa, Canada, Britain and the USA). Having grown at over 20% compound per year up to 2000, it was one of Australia's fastest growing companies, and its fourth largest retailer, with a share price to match. At first glance, you might consider that Flight Centre would be managed in much the same way as any other large organisation. But a quick look at the spread of the shops indicates that this may not be the case. They are all small, with only a few staff in each, and there are often two or three outlets in the one city shopping block. No economies of scale or centralised bureaucratic control here. But that is not the only thing that makes Flight Centre different.

The structure of Flight Centre emanates from the beliefs of the founder, Graham Turner. He claims that after 200 years of industrialisation, people are still hard-wired to work in small groups within larger groups. Flight Centre's basic structure is built on the 'family' of three to seven people who form a retail shop. A family can also be an administrative or head office team, providing services such as HR, IT or marketing. Next comes the 'village' of seven to ten families. This is roughly a department or an area. Further on is 'tribal' country, which is roughly equivalent to a regional office of three or four villages from the same tribe. 'Tribes' are also the different brands within the company, such as Corporate Traveller, Flight Centre and Student Flights. The company also has extensive interests in corporate travel.

The 'country' is the business unit that buys the services, such as training, recruitment, holiday packages and marketing for the families and villages. When 'countries' become too big, they are split into smaller countries. 'Countries' don't have to buy the service from another Flight Centre business unit. Travel consultants can buy products from any wholesaler, and are free to negotiate with whomever they want if they can get a better deal. Flight Centre wholesale products are run as profit centres. Innovation and new business development is handled through national and global SWOT teams (strengths, weaknesses, opportunities and threats), which try out new ideas.

This results in a flat structure with no more than three levels from the bottom to the top of the company. It also allows for expansion to be accommodated within the structure without too much of a problem. The company has rapidly expanded overseas over the last seven years.

The company discovered one of its basic management ideas early in its existence, when a shop in Melbourne made $200 000 in its first year with 6 staff, the same profit the next year with 14 staff and $120 000 in the third year with 18 staff. That's when the benefits of keeping the shops small became apparent. With 6 staff the manager knew everyone and had regular contact with the staff. With 18 staff this was not possible; administration work piled up, morale and motivation slumped, and staff turnover rose. Graham Turner realised that, to be successful, units needed to be small and dynamic.

The managers of Flight Centre shops take 10% of the shop's profit as an incentive and may own up to 20% of their shop. Travel consultants, those staff dealing with the customers, are paid a guaranteed base salary plus a share of the shop's profit. Team managers normally stay at their job for 10 years and then move on, often to other tasks within the company. Women make up 60%–65% of staff, and most staff are aged between 25 and 35. Entry age is normally about 25 years. The company goes to great lengths to foster communication between staff and develop a community of feeling. 'Buzz nights' are held once a month, and there are other less formal get-togethers. Turner feels that 100 people are about the maximum that staff can know and interact with.

Apart from activities such as negotiating bulk deals with service providers such as airlines, the structure seemed fairly simple to manage and infinitely expandable, as could be seen by the integration of the overseas takeovers. In 2002, Graham Turner decided to wind down his involvement with the company and decentralise decision making by appointing a joint managing director responsible for overseas operations. But just as this occurred, the Internet started to impact heavily upon Flight Centre's business. No longer was the competition similar chains of agencies, which could be out-competed with better organisational structure and staff incentives, now it was online booking agencies and the Web pages of the airlines, particularly discount airlines. Potential travellers could 'surf the Web' looking for the best deal, and they did so in increasing numbers. Airlines also reduced the commission paid to travel agencies to almost zero.

Flight Centre's profit was hit and the answer, however imperfect it might be, had to be found in offering a competitive website which did the surfing for the customer. To combat this threat to the company's profitability, Graham Turner centralised decision making and became the sole managing director. But the full impact of the Web still has to work its way through the company and it has the potential to destabilise what was considered to be a great structural innovation.

Source: Adapted from Elizabeth Johnson, 'Fly Boys', *The Australian Financial Review*, Boss Magazine, 8 June 2001, p. 26; Darryl Blake, *Skroo the Rules*, Brisbane: Information

Australia, 2001; and Mandy Johnston, *Family, Village and Tribe*, Sydney: Random House, 2005.

QUESTIONS

1 Relate the organisational structure at Flight Centre to as many relevant aspects as you can identify in this chapter.

2 Using Mintzberg's classification scheme, how would you classify Flight Centre's structure? Nominate points of similarity with and difference from the classification you have identified.

3 From the case, provide evidence of the roles of functional and social specialisation. Show how both are necessary for Flight Centre to function effectively.

4 With what advantages does the use of metaphors provide the managers and workers at Flight Centre?

5. How might the greater use of the Internet lead to a change in the way that Flight Centre does business? How might it affect the structure?

FURTHER READING

Jay Galbraith, *Designing Organizations: An Executive Briefing on Strategy, Structure and Process*, San Francisco: Jossey-Bass, 1995.

Richard H. Hall, *Organizations: Structure and Process*, 3rd edn, Upper Saddle River, NJ: Prentice-Hall, 1982, p. 84.

Henry Mintzberg, *The Structuring of Organizations*, Upper Saddle River, NJ: Pearson Education, 1979, pp. 91–2.

Charles Perrow, *Complex Organizations: A Critical Essay*, 3rd edn, New York: Random House, 1986.

D.S. Pugh, D.J. Hickson, C.R. Hinings & C. Turner, 'Dimensions of Organization Structure', *Administrative Science Quarterly*, June 1968, p. 75.

NOTES

1 Coles Myer Ltd press release, 25 September 2001.

2 For a critique of the methodology by which complexity, formalisation and centralisation have come to dominate the definitions of major structural dimensions, and for presentation of an alternative approach, see Richard Blackburn & Larry L. Cummings, 'Cognitions of Work Unit Structure', *Academy of Management Journal*, December 1982, pp. 836–54.

3 See, for example, James L. Price & Charles W. Mueller, *Handbook of Organizational Measurement*, Marshfield, MA: Pitman Publishing, 1986, pp. 100–5.

4 Commonwealth Bank Media Release, 20 December 2001.

5 Coles Myer, op. cit.

6 Anthony Hughes, 'ANZ Bank to Restructure Branch Network', *Sydney Morning Herald*, 25 August 2001, p. 47.

7 Anonymous, 'Uni Plans to Restructure No Answer', *Newcastle Herald*, 8 May 2001, p. 12.

8 Ian Porter, 'SPT Factory Revamps to Boost PacDun Shares', *The Age*, 28 September 2001, p. 1.

9 Annie Lawson, 'PMP to Trim 120 Jobs to Cut Gordon and Gotch Losses', *The Age*, 7 September 2001.

10 H. Gleckman et al., 'The Technology Payoff', *Business Week*, 14 June 1993, p. 57–68; M. Liu, H. Denis, H. Kolodny & B. Stymne, 'Organization and Design for Technological Change', *Human Relations*, 43, January 1990, pp. 7–22; George, Huber, 'A Theory of the Effects of Advanced Information Technologies on Organizational Design, Intelligence and Decision Making', *Academy of Management Review*, 14, 1990, p. 47–71.

11 Tom Peters, *Thriving on Chaos*, New York: Knopf, 1988, pp. 354–65.

12 ibid.

13 Richard H. Hall, *Organizations: Structure and Process*, 3rd ed., Englewood Cliffs, N.J.: Prentice-Hall, 1982, p. 84.
14 D.S. Pugh, D.J. Hickson, C.R. Hinings & C. Turner, 'Dimensions of Organization Structure', *Administrative Science Quarterly*, June 1968, p. 75.
15 Henry Mintzberg, *The Structuring of Organizations*, Upper Saddle River, N.J.: Pearson Education, 1979, pp. 91–2.
16 Benjamin Schneider, 'The People Make the Place', *Personnel Psychology*, Autumn 1987, pp. 437–52.
17 Charles Perrow, *Complex Organizations: A Critical Essay*, Glenview, Ill.: Scott, Foresman, 1972, p. 100.
18 Herbert A. Simon, *Administrative Behavior*, 3rd edn, New York: Free Press, 1976, p. 294.
19 James Stoner, Roger Collins & Philip Yetton, *Management in Australia*, Sydney: Prentice-Hall, 1985.
20 See, e.g., Henry Mintzberg, *Structure in Fives: Designing Effective Organizations*, Upper Saddle River, NJ: Pearson Education, 1983.
21 All the information in relation to the five basic structural configurations is drawn from Henry Mintzberg, *Structuring in Fives: Designing Effective Organizations*, Upper Saddle River, NJ: Pearson Education, 1983.
22 Mintzberg, *Structure in Fives: Designing Effective Organizations*, p. 217.
23 Mintzberg, *The Structuring of Organizations*, pp. 397–8.
24 Mintzberg, *Structure in Fives: Designing Effective Organizations*, p. 194.
25 ibid, p. 261.
26 Henry Mintzberg, *Structure in Fives: Designing Effective Organizations*, p. 261.
27 Danny Miller & Peter H. Friesen, *Organizations: A Quantum View*, Upper Saddle River, N.J.: Pearson Education, 1984, p. 85.
28 Henry Mintzberg, 'Structuring in 5s: A Synthesis of the Research on Organization Design', *Management Science*, March 1980, pp. 336–8.
29 Mintzberg, *The Structuring of Organizations*, p. 449.
30 See, for instance, Ian Palmer & Richard Dunford. 'Conceptualising Metaphors: Reconceptualising Their Use in the Field of Organizational Change', *Academy of Management Review*, 21(3), 1996, pp. 691–717.
31 Simon, *Administrative Behavior*.

PART 3

Contingencies

part 3

CHAPTER 5

Strategy

After reading this chapter you should be able to:

- define organisation strategy
- compare business-level with corporate-level strategy
- describe Chandler's 'structure-follows-strategy' thesis
- list and define Miles and Snow's four strategic types
- explain the structural implications of Porter's competitive strategies
- describe how globalisation strategies lead to different structures
- explain the industry–structure relationship
- explain the strategy of networks.

Introduction

Cochlear—hear now, and always

The ability of implants, the 'bionic ear', to assist the deaf in hearing has been one of the great advances in modern medicine.[1] Not perhaps as spectacular as life-saving innovations, it has nonetheless made a major contribution to the quality of life of over 60 000 recipients across the globe. The world's leader in ear implants is an Australian company, Cochlear.

The initial idea for implants to assist the deaf emerged from research conducted by Professor Graham Clark of the University of Melbourne. Motivated by the experiences of his deaf father, he combined his extensive knowledge of the anatomy of the ear with emerging technologies based upon miniaturisation of electronic circuits. His major innovation was to place electrodes in the cochlea in the inner ear and directly stimulate them externally. Later implants were combined with portable speech processors. A company called Cochlear was established to commercialise the invention.

Progress initially tended to be slow as new systems underwent development, but the first implant, an unsophisticated product by modern standards, was carried out in 1978. The results were encouraging, but capital was required to further develop the product and the company received a grant from the Australian government and management assistance from Nucleus, a heart pacemaker company. Commercial implants soon followed and, in 1981, Cochlear established its global headquarters in Sydney.

Apart from the inevitable setbacks inherent with medical products, the company has continuously expanded and now is the largest such company in the world. Many of its 850 employees are scientists engaged in developing increasingly sophisticated implants. It has also grown by acquisition, using its cash flow to buy out struggling competitors who may have complimentary products but lack the capital and economies of scale to compete successfully against Cochlear.

If we think in terms of strategy, to be successful Cochlear combines two main goals: it must focus on a specific market niche, in this case ear implants, and it must be global in orientation in order to achieve economies of scale. A brief examination of Cochlear would reveal that both of these goals are reflected in its structure: large laboratories to undertake research and development, offices and staff located around the world, and mechanisms in place to promote knowledge sharing throughout the company. We could therefore conclude that strategy has a significant influence upon Cochlear's structure.

imperative a variable that dictates structure

Over the next five chapters we will be examining in some detail what influences an organisation's structure. In this chapter we look at the way that strategy can *cause* an organisation's structure to take a certain form. We consider strategy as being an **imperative** (an imperative *dictates* something; in our usage, strategy is dictating is structure). Of the imperatives we consider, strategy has probably the longest history. The study of strategy goes back to the early days of modern organisations, and an awareness of how strategy influences structure gradually developed over subsequent years. Up to 40 years ago, strategy was considered to be the only influence upon organisational structure. Since then the influence of other imperatives has become clearer. But strategy remains one of the fundamental influences on the way organisations are managed. This is possibly because decisions on strategy are closely linked to the fundamental purpose of the organisation, and what it sets out to achieve.

The early study of organisations did not differentiate clearly between goals and strategy. Organisations were considered to be machine-like in nature. Clear and identifiable goals were determined, and the organisation's structure subsequently evolved to attain the goals. This process reflected the assumptions inherent in rational choice theory. These assumptions included the following:[2]

- The organisation has a goal or goals towards which it strives.
- It moves towards its goals in a 'rational' manner.
- The organisation exists to transform economic inputs to outputs.
- The environment within which the organisation operates is stable and rarely changes.

There were times when such assumptions were valid. For much of the 20th century economies were isolated from each other, and firms attempted to control their environments in such a way that they almost existed as a closed system. The growth of globalisation and the promotion of competition by governments, as well as rapid technological innovation, have altered the environments in which organisations operate. Research has also thrown more light on how goals and strategies are determined. As discussed in Chapter 3, they are no longer considered as the rational outcome of a purposeful, deliberative process. Regardless of these limitations, we can still identify how strategy influences structure.

A word of warning regarding the limitations inherent in this chapter is in order here! Most of the research and theory building informing this chapter has been carried out on profit-seeking organisations operating in a market economy and has excluded many large organisations such as government departments, educational establishments, military systems, and not-for-profit organisations and charities. This does not mean that these organisations do not have strategies; often their strategies are more explicit than those in the profit-seeking sector. But theory building and research in this area have not yet progressed sufficiently to identify trends and categories appropriate for linking strategy to structural characteristics.

For the profit-seeking sector, however, we are fortunate that strategy lends itself to easy classification. As a result, a number of useful models have been developed that may be applied to any organisation which has choices. Basically this refers to those organisations operating in a market economy. However, first we need to identify what strategy is.

What is strategy?

Whenever management is discussed, *strategy* and *strategic* suffer from being the two most overused and clichéd words in the management vocabulary. As a result, they have lost much of their specific meaning and relevance. But for our purposes, we can revert to the origins of business strategy and define it in a way which gives it an exact meaning. It is necessary to do this in order to undertake a systematic study of its impact on organisation structures.

strategy the adoption of courses of action and the allocation of resources necessary to achieve the organisation's goals

According to Chandler, **strategy** may be defined as the determination of the basic long-term goals and objectives of an enterprise, and the adoption of courses of action and the allocation of resources necessary for carrying out these goals.[3] Decisions to merge with another company, expand into overseas markets, diversify into a new line of business or increase the product range involve the defining and setting of new goals. In order to implement decisions, plans must be drawn up, areas of responsibility defined and tasks allocated. In other words, goals must be accompanied by a plan of implementation if they are to be of any use.

There is a distinction between *strategy* and *tactics*. Strategic decisions establish the general purpose and direction of the enterprise and the methods by which they will be achieved. The day-to-day decisions associated with implementing plans and operating the enterprise may be described as tactical decisions, although common usage of the term 'strategy' has seen it being used for almost any decision which is made.

It can also be seen from the above definition and discussion, that *goals* and *strategy* are not the same thing. Goals refer to ends: what we wish to achieve by a certain point in time. Strategy refers to both means and ends, that is, where we wish to be at some point in the future and how we intend to get there. Of course, not all goals have strategic implications. Many relate to performance improvements, financial objectives, sales targets or other measures, and as a result are not relevant when the structural implications of strategy are considered.

Our definition does not tell us how an organisation determines its strategy. With anything as important and complex as strategy it is not surprising that there are different approaches as to how it will be determined. Two approaches emerge: the first views strategy as the outcome of a rational deliberation process; the other sees strategy as emerging from a string of minor incremental decisions.[4]

planning mode strategy as an explicit and systematic set of guidelines developed in advance

The first view can be called a **planning mode**. Planning mode views strategy as a plan or explicit set of guidelines developed in advance. Managers identify where they want to go; then they develop a systematic and structured plan to get there. This approach may be viewed as almost scientific in its practice. It reduces the determination of strategy to a well-thought-out process where rationality plays a significant role. Proponents would regard the planning mode as the ideal form of strategy determination, and until recently this viewpoint dominated the organisation theory literature.

The planning mode is widely practised. Virtually all large firms have a strategic plan that sets out what the organisation is attempting to achieve and how it intends to get there. This applies particularly to those firms listed on the stock exchange, where external analysts are continually assessing performance and prospects of firms with a view to making investment decisions. But environments are never stable, competitors rarely predictable, and strategy can change with the fortunes of the various factions constantly jostling for influence within the organisation. Further, what managers say they are trying to achieve and what plans they have in their head, or their top drawer, may be two different things. So supplementing the formal strategy process there emerges a stream of significant decisions based upon unanticipated opportunities and threats. A sudden change in economic conditions, a lucky oil strike, a technological breakthrough by a competitor or even changes in the political balance within companies can all lead to sudden and unanticipated changes in strategy.

evolutionary mode a strategy that evolves over time as a pattern in a stream of significant decisions

A perspective that acknowledges the unpredictable processes involved in strategy formation, and stands in contrast to the planning mode, is called the **evolutionary mode**. The evolutionary mode does not necessarily view strategy as a well-thought-out and systematic plan. Rather, it views strategy as a stream of significant decisions evolving over time. The strategies of many organisations follow the evolutionary mode to take into account such occurrences as an unexpected opportunity, the changing perceptions of the board of directors and senior management, the unanticipated actions of competitors, or the realisation that changes in technologies and tastes have led to products becoming mature and not providing the growth companies aspire to. Technological and environmental change can create opportunities in one area while closing them in another. Organisations have no alternative but to evolve with these changes or cease to exist. But their response to them is often halting and does not follow an even pace of change. Any firm that has been in existence for more than a few years has faced situations in which its original strategy has been overtaken by events. For those established over 100 years, changes in strategy often have led to companies changing their entire line of business. CSR, for instance, started out as a sugar refiner but now is basically a building material manufacturer. BHP Billiton has long since ceased to have any association with Broken Hill or with steel making. In many cases, both the buying and the selling of assets were made opportunistically rather than as a result of long-range planning. Figure 5.1 illustrates the difference between the planning and the evolutionary mode.

Organisational behaviour provides further insight into how strategy may evolve in ways other than as a well-thought-out process. The actions of people in organisations even call into question whether some decisions in the strategy area may be called rational at all. Simon introduced the concept of 'bounded rationality' to describe the situation where the human mind has difficulty in grasping a situation because of its complexity.[5] In other words, the decision maker does not have perfect knowledge of all variables. Decisions are therefore made under a number of psychological and external constraints that lead to a decision maker 'satisficing'; that is, they will stop searching for an alternative as soon as the minimum requirements for a decision have been met. We can see that these limitations may lead to a strategy formulation that simply evolves from one state to another. Lindblom has called this 'the science of muddling through', which highlights the fact that planning and decision execution are seldom orderly and sequential but emerge from situations of

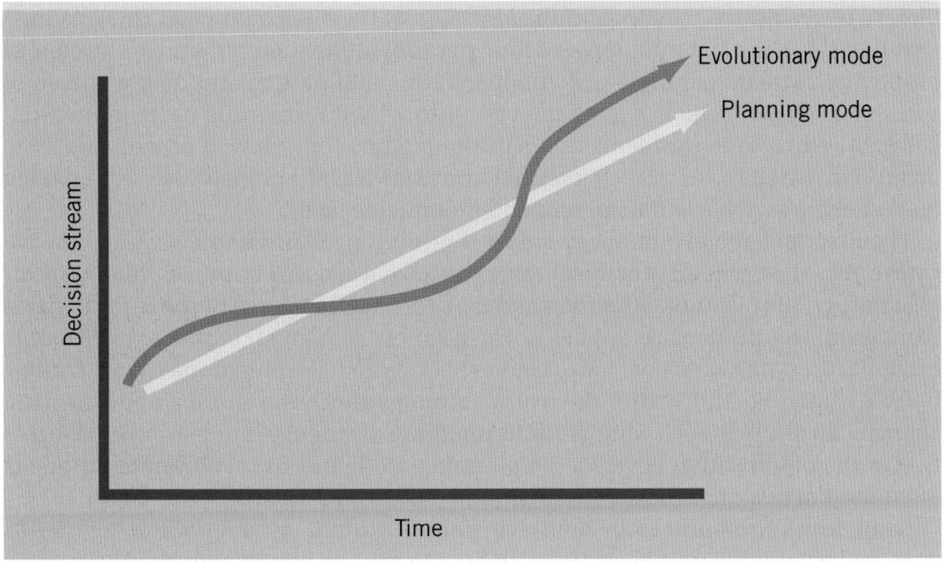
Evolutionary mode
Planning mode
Decision stream
Time

FIGURE 5.1 Comparison of planning and evolutionary mode of decision making

OT CLOSEUP

Strategy and not-for-profit organisations

The strategy–structure relationship is not just for profit-seeking organisations. Charities and not-for-profit organisations also face demanding environments in which important strategic directions must be determined and then structures put in place to implement the strategies. The case of the main associations serving the blind and vision-impaired in eastern Australia provides a good example. New South Wales and Victoria have been served over the last hundred years by well-known local organisations, the Royal Blind Society and the Royal Victorian Institute for the Blind. More lately Vision Australia has offered complementary services. As the competition for charitable donations is intense, in 2002 the three organisations decided to amalgamate their operations to form one organisation. They felt that this would enable them to build a stronger organisation which would have a greater presence when seeking donations and underwriting fund-raising activities. Having 'one voice' would also mean a stronger voice. But they also identified that other economies could be achieved from a merger. They would have a stronger base from which to expand into other parts of Australia, greater economies in purchasing and administration could be achieved, and service delivery would be enhanced. There would also be greater opportunities for other partnerships and alliances. The new organisation became known as Vision Australia.

The structure chosen was a federation, which loosely conforms to the private-sector divisionalised structure. Whilst the organisation was given a new name, each state has a strong local presence and close linkages with their communities. A head office was established to present a common front to interested parties in the environment, to seek economies and provide common services, such as financial and HR services to the state operations. The structure can be clearly seen to reflect the goals and aspirations of the organisation.

chance and the internal workings of the firm.[6] Further insight into decision making was made by Cohen, March and Olsen who challenged the pre-existence of goals to direct organisational choices and the logicality of the choice process. They claimed that decisions are the outcomes of four partially dependent streams: a stream of problems, a stream of potential solutions, a stream of participants, and a stream of solutions. These formed a 'garbage can' into which numerous participants had contributed various problems and solutions. Thus they viewed organisations as organised anarchies, very much removed from the ideal of a rational, decision-making body seeking to achieve transparent and identifiable goals.[7]

The planning and evolutionary modes, however, need not be viewed as exclusive categories. All successful organisations must take a rational approach to determining strategy; they cannot leave themselves entirely at the mercy of short-term incrementalism. This particularly applies to organisations that must commit large amounts to capital spending which has a 10-year payback period. But environments are continuously changing, and within the overall strategy there is room for opportunistic changes. So one way of viewing the determination of strategy is that the overall direction of the organisation is set by the planning mode but the evolutionary mode is often used in response to short-term opportunities and threats.

Some firms confound us by not having an identifiable strategy when logic leads us to believe they should have one. Needless to say, we do not consider these firms to be leaders in their field, or hold them up as examples for others to follow. Such

OT CLOSEUP
BHP Billiton and Chandler's thesis

BHP Billiton, one of Australia's largest private-sector companies, can be seen as fitting Chandler's thesis—at least in its early stages. Incorporated in 1885 to exploit the rich silver, lead and zinc lode at Broken Hill in New South Wales, the company built its smelters at Port Pirie in South Australia to convert the ore to purified metal. In the smelting process iron-stone was used as a flux, and this was obtained from the nearby Iron Monarch deposit.

Iron Monarch and its nearby neighbour, Iron Knob, were rich deposits, and a trial smelting in 1905 convinced the company that it could profitably make iron from the deposit. In 1915 the company set up its first iron-making facility at Newcastle, carrying the ironstone around the Australian coast by ship. Further expansion occurred in the steel industry when it bought the Port Kembla-based Australian Iron and Steel in 1935. Using its basic steel-making capacity, BHP, as it then was, expanded into downstream activities such as wire drawing, sheet steel rolling, and tube and pipe making. The company also became involved in coal mining, initially to service the steel industry. In 1936 it joined a number of other companies in establishing the Commonwealth Aircraft Corporation and in 1941 began to build ships at Whyalla, in South Australia. During World War II it was involved in the manufacture of various types of munitions and in the substitution of local material for imports unavailable because of the war. In addition to opening new iron ore mines in Western Australia, BHP opened a manganese mine at Groote Eylandt in 1966.

In 1967 BHP, in partnership with Esso, discovered commercial quantities of oil in Bass Strait. This led to a major expansion of interest in an area with little connection to its steel-making activities. Later, in 1976, BHP joined Shell in proving the enormous North West Shelf natural gas deposits.

During the 1970s, BHP continued its expansion in the mineral area with the opening of coal and iron mines, aimed at the export market, and with the OK Tedi project in New Guinea. In 1983, BHP bought Utah International, the mining subsidiary of General Electric. Utah has mining interests in the United States, Canada, Brazil, Chile and other countries, as well as in Australia. BHP also bought a number of oil exploration companies, the main one being the US-based Energy Resources Group.

Up to this point we can draw clear parallels between Chandler's thesis and the growth of BHP. As its product range expanded, BHP introduced a divisionalised structure based upon its main product groups. Divisions reached deep into the heart of the structure, with each mine and steel plant being a profit centre. But BHP also illustrates the flaws in Chandler's analysis. During the 1990s BHP fell on hard times, with a string of poor decisions that weakened the company. New management was appointed to set the company back on a growth path. But the world situation had changed. At that time, mineral prices were low and mining companies realised that they must consolidate in order to have some influence over price, and so a merger with Billiton, the former Shell mining interest, was executed. Subsequently, BHP Billiton exited the steel industry in order to focus on mining activities. Along with many other companies of its size, it attempted to simplify its structure, not make it more complicated by adding new businesses.

All of the companies studied by Chandler have had chequered histories as they have struggled to adapt to technological change, inbred management and innovative actions of competitors. Perhaps new historical analysis will provide more light on the strategy–structure nexus.

and the multidivisional form.[12] One researcher essentially supported Chandler's findings, although he used a different classification scheme for defining strategy.[13] Organisational strategies were labelled as single business (no diversification), dominant business (70–95% of sales coming from one business or a vertically integrated chain), related business (diversified in related areas, with no one business accounting for more than 70% of sales) and unrelated business (diversified in unrelated areas, with no one business accounting for more than 70% of sales). The researcher found that the related and unrelated business strategies were linked to machine bureaucracies or functional structures. No single structure was found consistently in the dominant-business category.

Summarising Chandler's contribution

Chandler's claim that strategy influences structure seems well supported, but this support must be qualified by the difficulty involved in generalising his conclusions to a wider population of companies. He looked only at large, profit-making organisations. He focused on growth as a measure of effectiveness rather than profitability. Moreover, his definition of strategy, based on product differentiation, is far from all-inclusive. Strategy can, for instance, include concern with market segmentation, financial strengths and leverage opportunities, actions of competitors, assessment of the organisation's comparative advantage vis-à-vis its competition, and the like. There is also the problem of generalisation inherent in all historical analysis: Chandler's analysis refers only to one phase of industrial expansion, and its applicability to current industrial experience and technologies may be limited. In particular, companies at the current time are more likely to be narrowing their product range rather than broadening it. Nevertheless, 'there appears to be little doubt that strategy influences structure at the organisation wide level, as opposed to the department or work group level. The evidence on this point is overwhelming'.[14]

Contemporary strategy–structure theories

As we noted previously, strategy is a broad concept and can be described along a number of dimensions. Since Chandler's work in the early 1960s, one of the classic works on the strategy–structure relationship has been undertaken by Miles and Snow. In addition, the landmark work of Michael Porter on competitive strategies has direct relevance to the strategy–structure relationship, while Bartlett and Ghoshal's study includes the applicability of the strategy–structure relationship as it applies to multinational corporations. Below we review each of those three contributions.

Miles and Snow's four strategic types

Raymond Miles and Charles Snow classify organisations into one of four strategic types based on the rate at which they change their products or markets. They call these types defenders, prospectors, analysers, and reactors.[15] While the four categories are distinct types, it is not implied that firms necessarily fit them perfectly. For instance, the divisions of multidivisional firms may belong to different strategic types. However, the categories are sufficiently broad, but yet specific enough, for us to identify which organisations are likely to fit into them.

defenders organisations whose strategy is to produce a limited set of products directed at a narrow segment of the total potential market

Defenders seek stability by producing only a limited set of products directed at a narrow segment of the total potential market. Within this limited niche, or domain, defenders strive aggressively to prevent competitors from taking market share or customers from them. Organisations do this through standard competitive actions, such as aggressive pricing or production of high-quality products. But defenders tend to ignore developments and trends outside their current areas of interest, choosing instead to grow through market penetration and perhaps some limited product development. There is little or no scanning of the environment to find new areas of opportunity, but there is intensive planning oriented towards cost and other efficiency issues. The result is a structure made up of high horizontal differentiation with highly specialised tasks, centralised control and decision making, and an elaborate formal hierarchy for communications and coordination. Over time, true defenders are able to carve out and maintain small niches within their industries that are difficult for competitors to penetrate.

An example of a defender strategy is the grocery chain, Woolworths. Although it is not exclusively a grocery retailer (it owns Big W and the Dick Smith and Tandy electronic chains), the company maintains its focus on grocery retailing. It is aggressive in protecting its market share and loses little opportunity to expand within its narrow sector of food retailing. It maintains its competitiveness through constant pressure on suppliers' prices and economies of scale in areas such as warehousing and purchasing. Any firm seeking to challenge the dominance of Woolworths would face a formidable task.

There are more defenders around than initially meet the eye. Many of the more complex manufactured goods whose brand names are well known have as components the output of many smaller, specialised firms. These firms, which are unknown outside a small industry circle, specialise in areas as diverse as motor vehicle brake shoes, small electric motors for such things as mirrors and electric windows, railway signalling equipment, air compressor valves and fast ferry construction. They dominate one small, clearly defined area through being at the leading edge of both knowledge and manufacturing techniques, making it difficult for others to displace them. They have adopted a classic defender strategy.

prospectors
organisations whose strategy is to find and exploit new product and market opportunities

Prospectors are almost the opposite of defenders. The prospector's strength lies in finding and exploiting new product and market opportunities. Innovation may be more important than high profitability. When thinking of prospectors, Internet and biotechnology companies immediately spring to mind. But they also include firms in lower technology areas, such as magazine publishers that introduce new magazine titles almost monthly in an attempt to identify new market segments. Fashion companies, such as Mambo and Billabong, grew to prominence on their reputation as innovators. Advertising agencies also rise or fall on their ability to innovate and there are big rewards for property developers who can create desirable and fashionable developments.

The prospector's success depends on developing and maintaining the capacity to survey a wide range of environmental conditions, trends and events and then introduce new products based on that research. Therefore, prospectors invest heavily in personnel who seek potential opportunities. As flexibility is critical to prospectors, the structure will also be flexible. It will rely on multiple technologies that have a low degree of routinisation and standardisation. There will be numerous decentralised units. The structure will be low in formalisation and have decentralised control, with lateral as well as vertical communications: 'In short, the prospector is effective—it can respond to the demands of tomorrow's world. To the extent that the world of tomorrow is similar to that of today, the prospector cannot maximise profitability because of its inherent inefficiency.'[16]

analysers
organisations whose strategy is to move into new products or markets only after their viability has been proven

Analysers attempt to minimise risk by adopting innovations after they have been proven by others. They try to capitalise on the best of both of the preceding types. They seek to minimise risk and maximise opportunity for profit. Their strategy is to move into new products or new markets only after viability has been proven by prospectors. Analysers live by imitation. They take the successful ideas of prospectors and copy them or, as happens in some cases, take them over and greatly expand their production. Manufacturers of mass-marketed fashion goods that are copies of designer styles follow the analyser strategy. This label also probably characterises such well-known firms as Unilever, Pacific Brands and Nestlé. Retailers can also be prospectors, as illustrated by Coles Myer establishing Officeworks and Harvey Norman moving into retailing computers. They essentially follow their smaller and more innovative competitors with imitation products, but only after their competitors have demonstrated that the market is there.

Analysers must have the ability to respond to the lead of key prospectors, yet at the same time maintain operating efficiency in their stable product and market areas. They tend to have smaller profit margins in the products and services that they sell than do prospectors, but they are more efficient as they are generally better financed and can achieve economies of scale. Prospectors have to have high margins to justify the risks that they take and to cover their productive inefficiencies.

Analysers seek both flexibility and stability. They respond to these supposedly contradictory goals by developing a structure made up of dual components. Parts of these organisations, such as manufacturing and distribution, have high levels of standardisation, routinisation and automation to attain efficiencies. But they are sufficiently flexible to introduce new product lines. However, once introduced, they are mass produced. Other parts, such as marketing and product development, are adaptive in order to enhance flexibility. In this way, they seek structures that can accommodate both stable and dynamic areas of operation. But in this compromise there can be costs. If situations change rapidly, demanding that organisations move fully in either direction, their ability to take such action is severely limited.

reactors a residual strategy that describes organisations that follow inconsistent and unstable patterns

Reactors represent a residual strategy. The label is meant to describe the inconsistent and unstable patterns that arise when one of the other three strategies is pursued improperly. In general, reactors respond inappropriately, perform poorly and, as a result, are reluctant to commit themselves aggressively to a specific strategy for the future. What can cause this? Top management may have failed to make the organisation's strategy clear. Management may not have fully shaped the organisation's structure to fit the chosen strategy. Management may have maintained its current strategy–structure relationship despite overwhelming changes in environmental conditions or despite the fact that its products or services may be obsolete. Whatever the reason, however, the outcome is the same. The organisation lacks a set of response mechanisms with which to face a challenging environment. Decline and extinction are often the outcomes of this strategy.

Table 5.1 summarises Miles and Snow's strategic typologies. It shows the goal(s) of each, the type of environment that each faces, and the structural mechanisms that management would choose to achieve the goal(s). The reactor strategy is omitted for the obvious reason that it results in ineffective performance.

The key element in Miles and Snow's strategy–structure theory is management's assessment of environmental uncertainty. If management selects a defender strategy, for instance, this suggests that it perceives the environment as stable. Of course, perceptions of environmental uncertainty vary from manager to manager. Managers in two organisations can face exactly the same environment and perceive it very differently.

The dropping of tariffs in the clothing industry has revealed that there are significant differences in opinion about what this will mean for the industry. On the one

nationalisation puts many strains on established practices and management systems. New organisational control mechanisms take time to develop and implement and are subject to considerable political lobbying. This is particularly so for the behavioural aspects of control, such as organisational culture. Perhaps this is one of the reasons that so few truly global companies have emerged over the past 30 years.

The strategic types of Barlett and Ghoshal, and those of Miles and Snow and Porter, bear little relationship to each other. They are not, however, mutually exclusive. Miles and Snow and Porter concentrate on a strategy aimed at a single market. Barlett and Ghoshal develop strategies appropriate to internationalising firms. The theories do have in common the proposition that once a strategy is determined it will be ineffective without an appropriate organisational structure. In other words, strategy causes structure.

OT CLOSEUP

The worldwide matrix

Miles and Snow's and Porter's theories are based upon the existence of fairly simple environments. But the environments of most multinationals are complex and each element of the complexity requires that it be responded to. The matrix is a structure which aims at responding to two different environmental segments at the same time. It is normally considered to be a subset of adhocracy, discussed in Chapter 4, and became very fashionable in the 1970s. One version of it exists within the highest levels of management of multinational corporations. Multinationals face two seemingly irreconcilable pressures: deriving the benefits of global integration, and being sensitive to the needs of local markets. If global integration takes precedence, then organisations are structured along global product lines; in such cases, the heads of the major product divisions, such as exploration, oil, and chemicals, report to the CEO. If local sensitivities are important, then an area-based structure would be preferred. In such a structure the head of the major regions, for instance, Europe, North America and Asia, would answer directly to the CEO.

But what if the pressures for global integration and local responsiveness exist in equal measure? A number of large multinationals have attempted to address this problem by adopting a structural solution known as the global matrix. In this structure a manager is responsible for product, and another is responsible for geographic area. Senior managers within a region answer to both managers. While at first glance this appears to be an ideal solution to the problem of responsiveness, it is not without its difficulties and, in some cases, companies have abandoned the structure and returned to one based on either product or area.

So what are some of the problems with the global matrix? It can become easily unbalanced: through the interactions of personalities and other pressures, either the business unit or area manager may end up making most of the important decisions. Managers often have conflicting priorities, which can lead to decisions either being made slowly or not made at all as proponents of product and area fight turf wars and engage in power plays. Also, no one is clearly accountable for poor performance; the other party to the matrix may easily be blamed for any problems that arise. These problems may be exacerbated by the fact that top managers don't see each other very often as they are commonly located in different parts of the world. So the day-to-day interaction and communication, which may contribute to negotiated trade-offs, doesn't occur.

As a result of these factors, multinationals are abandoning global matrices and reverting to simpler structures. In place of dual reporting relationships, they are putting more emphasis on hiring and training and using improved communication techniques, both face to face and through technologies such as email, to make managers more aware and responsive to the trade-offs required.

Limitations to the strategy imperative

We have presented the positive case for strategy determining structure. We argue that once an organisation establishes its strategy it must adopt a structure which leads to the successful implementation of the strategy. The structures adopted are not random; they fall within predictable categories. But, not surprisingly, as with many issues in organisation theory, there is another side to the debate.

Few argue that strategy *cannot* determine structure. The questioning of the strategy imperative emerges from doubts about the amount of discretion that managers actually have in determining strategy. Once established, basic strategies change very rarely because any changes lead to major organisational upheavals. Following from this, it seems logical that the influence of strategy upon structure would be greater in the early development period of an organisation when it is just being established. It is at this time that organisations have the greatest choice of strategy. Once personnel have been hired, capital equipment has been purchased, and procedures and policies have been established, they are much more difficult to change. When the organisation is in its infancy, vested interests and political considerations have yet to emerge to influence decision making. But once a firm becomes established, managers may be severely restricted in their discretion. Organisations cannot easily change their basic technologies. Similarly, it is logical that the capital-to-labour ratio in an organisation will affect the impact of strategy on structure. If the ratio is low—that is, it is labour-intensive—managers have much more flexibility, and hence discretion, to effect change and influence structure. Clothing manufacturers, for instance, can easily change the cut, style and colour of clothing. In contrast, cement manufacturers have little alternative but to make cement.

Another challenge to the strategy imperative relates to the lag factor. When management implements a new strategy, there is often no immediate change in structure. Does this suggest that structure does not follow strategy? Advocates of a strong strategy–structure relationship say no. They point out that there is often a time lag between a change in strategy and the emergence of a new structure. At the extreme, this lag argument can almost be considered an excuse for advocating the strategy–structure relationship.[20] If researchers fail to find a strategy–structure relationship in the study of an organisation, they can always claim that there is a lag and that structure just hasn't caught up yet. More realistically, however, we find that this lag is not a purely random phenomenon. Some organisations are slower to adapt their structures to changes in strategy than are others. The major factor affecting response is the degree of competitive pressure. The less competition an organisation faces, the less rapid its structural response.[21] Without competition, the pressure for efficiency is reduced. So we could conclude that where an organisation faces minimal competition, there is likely to be a significant lag between changes in strategy and modifications in structure.

A further factor to consider is that although we talk about strategy as a stand-alone topic it does not exist independently of other influences on organisational structure such as technology and environment. Motor vehicle manufacturers, for instance, are in the business of mass production regardless of the preferences of senior management. This implies that their strategic options are limited; the technology of mass production limits the extent to which cars can be customised. Those firms producing commodities similarly face restrictions on their strategic choice. Producers of minerals, electricity, cement, basic building materials and agricultural products find it difficult to differentiate their product. The only strategy open to them is one based on cost containment and price leadership.

Applicability of the strategy imperative

The research and theories which inform the strategy–structure imperative confine their examination of the relationship to the organisation-wide level. This is not surprising as the study of strategy is normally concerned with the organisation as a whole or the major business units or divisions. This leads to the observation that the strategy–structure relationship may only be valid for the top layers of structure. The daily work of the organisation for lower level managers and workers continues in much the same way regardless of the strategy adopted. There are exceptions, of course. Those in companies that conform to the prospector strategy would find that their working lives would be spent differently from those in an organisation conforming to the defender strategy. However, particularly for large organisations, we would expect that the strategy–structure relationship would be strongest at the top of the organisation. Imperatives such as technology, environment and size, discussed in later chapters, are likely to have a greater influence at the work group and unit level.

Could strategy follow structure?

Is it possible that strategy and structure are positively related but that the causal arrow is the opposite from what we've assumed? Perhaps structure determines strategy! One author acknowledges at least the logical possibility, 'as when a multidivisional structure is installed because everyone else is doing it and then an acquisitions strategy is developed to make the structure viable'.[22] Structure may limit strategic choices and channel strategy in certain directions. This position is informed by the continuous streams of fads and fashions which emerge in the management literature.

A little thought would certainly suggest that structure could influence strategy. Structure can motivate or impede strategic activity as well as simply constrain strategic choices. For instance, strategic decisions made in a centralised structure are typically going to have less diversity of ideas and are more likely to be consistent over time than in a decentralised organisation where input is likely to be diverse and the people providing that input will change.

The influence of power and politics, to be discussed in Chapter 9, also informs this point of view. Power holders are always reluctant to reduce their power, and one of the best ways to preserve it is to resist any change to an organisation's structure. As a consequence, although strategies may change to adapt to emerging circumstances, structure will lag because of political considerations.

A further pointer to structure influencing strategy is the existence of what are called legacy systems (see Figure 5.7). Any company of long standing has legacy systems; these are the established ways of doing things, often reflected in rules and regulations and standard operating procedures. These take time to establish and once in place channel thinking into predetermined patterns. Problems are defined and interpreted in ways that make sense to the organisation. Solutions are based on what the organisation can put in place through its standard practices. As a result, strategy becomes a projection of past actions based on what the organisation can structurally achieve. Of course, organisations can change their structure, but this is not undertaken without difficulty, as we will see in later chapters.

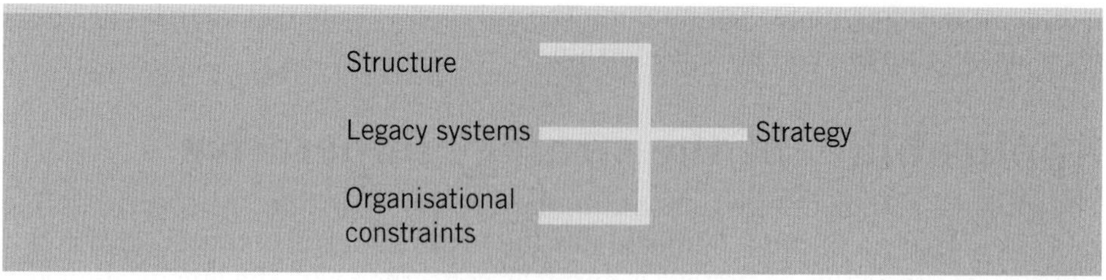
Structure
Legacy systems
Organisational constraints
Strategy

FIGURE 5.7 Structure–strategy relationship

OT CLOSEUP

Cemex's structure leads its strategy

When thinking of multinational companies, Mexico and cement don't immediately spring to mind. But one of the most successful cement manufacturers in the world is Cemex, a Mexican cement manufacturer. It is managed by Lorenzo Zambrano, the grandson of the founder, who happens to be a great believer in the benefits of using information technology to better manage his business. Cement is basically a commodity, so the greatest returns go to the cheapest producer. Zambrano has used information technology to relentlessly reduce costs in his Mexican plants. On taking up the CEO's position in 1985, he chafed at the lack of ready data to identify how well his plants were performing. He set up an IT department to devise programs to provide him with automated plant reports. Over time, a system was set up to transmit performance data from satellite plants to the head office in Monterey in northern Mexico. Automation has not only reduced staffing—it has permitted ongoing functions such as quality control, kiln temperatures and even sales to be constantly monitored from a central location. Cemex was an early user of email, constantly keeping touch with managers in the plants and asking them to explain any deviation from optimal operations or sales targets.

Once the cement is mixed and loaded onto one of the ready-mixed concrete trucks it must be poured within 90 minutes. Cemex has developed a program to improve the logistics of its delivery system to meet the tight time frames. By putting a computer and global positioner in each truck, Cemex has been able to introduce a system that not only calculates which truck should go where but enables dispatchers to redirect trucks as the need arises.

These innovations give Cemex an edge in a fragmented industry and have made it a leading industry consolidator. Potential acquisitions go through a thorough process of strict financial evaluation before a takeover occurs. Although big in the US, Cemex likes to operate in regions where the market is growing and where its technologies and management skills can make a difference. This often means developing countries where there is expanding demand for cement for infrastructure and building. Once a firm is acquired, Cemex applies its management systems and style through integration teams, a well-practised function which has been used on many occasions. These teams are both multidisciplinary and multicultural and help integrate the acquisition into the Cemex business. Cemex is quite comfortable operating in political environments that the more cautious may avoid.

Through applying its own management systems it can readily spread innovation in research and development and new product applications throughout the group. What Cemex successfully avoids is each plant becoming isolated from the rest of the group, thus losing the benefits of technology transfer.

Cemex's strategy, which includes both goals and the means to get there, predetermines what Cemex does. In a sense it is a strategy which relies upon growth, and would atrophy if Cemex settled into a steady state. So we can claim that in Cemex's case, structure leads its strategy.

What is the research indicating that structure determines strategy? A study of 110 large manufacturing firms found that strategy followed structure.[23] Another study of 54 large firms found that structure influences and constrains strategy, rather than the other way round.[24] If further research were to support these conclusions, we could state that as a structural determinant, strategy is of limited importance.

The industry–structure relationship

Closely related to the issue of strategy's impact on structure is the role of industry as a determinant of structure. There are distinguishing characteristics of industries that affect the strategies they will choose.[25] As a result, strategy may be merely an intermediate step between the unique characteristics of the industry in which the organisation operates and the structure it implements to achieve alignment. This relationship is shown in Figure 5.8.

Industries differ in terms of growth possibilities, regulatory constraints, barriers to entry, capital requirements and numerous other factors: 'Simply knowing the industry in which an organization operates allows one to know something about product life cycles, required capital investments, long-term prospects, types of production technologies, regulatory requirements, and so forth'.[26] Public utilities such as water supply companies, for example, face little competition, normally produce a single product such as water or electricity, and so can have more tightly controlled structures. Similarly, if a firm is in the motor vehicle industry and seeks to competitively produce cars to sell in the $18 000–$25 000 range, it will need to be extremely large in size and use standardised operations—in other words, a global firm. In some industries, strategic options are relatively few. The home computer industry, as a case in point, is rapidly becoming the exclusive province of companies that compete on a high-volume, low-cost basis. The alcoholic beverage industry supports a much broader range of strategic options—competing on manufacturing, marketing or product-innovation bases.

In order to illustrate how an industry can affect an organisation's structure, let us take two variables that tend to differ by industry category—capital requirements for entry, and product-innovation rates. Figure 5.9 shows four industry categories with examples for each. Type A industries rate high on both variables, while type C industries are high on capital requirements and low on product innovation. The high capital requirements tend to result in large organisations and a limited number of competitors. Access to capital becomes a key success factor. Firms in type A and C industries will have high complexity and standardised procedures, with the type As being more decentralised to facilitate rapid response to innovations introduced by competitors. Type B and D industries, because of low capital requirements, tend to be made up of a large number of small firms. Type D, however, is likely to have more task specialisation and greater formalisation than type B, because low product innovation allows greater standardisation. In the same way as capital requirements influence organisational size and number of competitors, we should expect high product-innovation rates to result in less formalisation and more decentralisation of decision making.

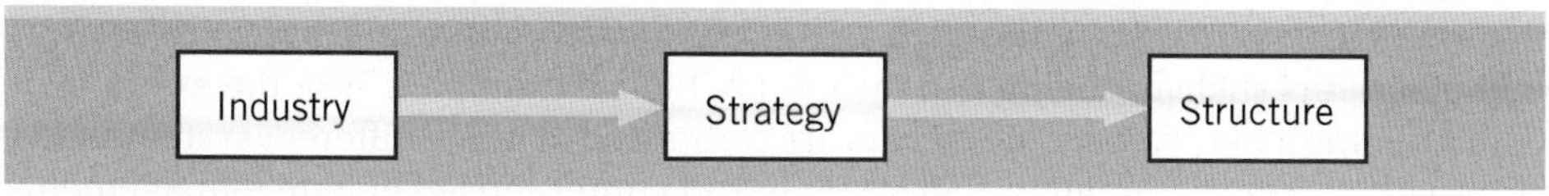
Industry
Strategy
Structure

FIGURE 5.8 Industry–structure relationship

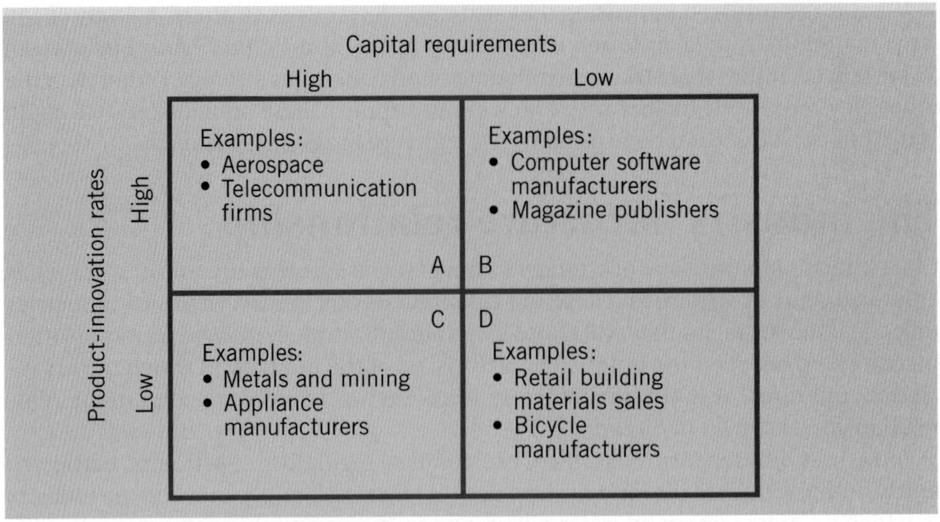
Capital requirements
High
Low
Product-innovation rates
High
Low
Examples:
• Aerospace
• Telecommunication firms
A
Examples:
• Computer software manufacturers
• Magazine publishers
B
C
Examples:
• Metals and mining
• Appliance manufacturers
D
Examples:
• Retail building materials sales
• Bicycle manufacturers

Figure 5.9 Two variable analyses of industries

The preceding analysis argues that industry categories *do* influence structure. While there are certainly intra-industry differences—Colgate-Palmolive and Avon are both in personal-care products but use very different marketing channels—there is a high degree of similarity within industry categories. These similarities lead to strategies that tend to have largely common elements and, in turn, these result in structural characteristics that are very similar.

The power of combinations—the strategy of industrial networks

This chapter has concentrated on the strategies, and the corresponding structures, of individual companies. It draws upon our definition of organisations which views them as having identifiable boundaries and a large measure of autonomy in determining how they are structured and managed. However, recent years have seen the emergence of combinations of firms which are so closely connected and mutually dependent that the boundaries between them are difficult to identify, not so much in the legal sense, but in the operational sense.[27] This suggests that in many cases **networks** of companies, as well as individual companies, implement strategies. It also suggests that the strategies of individual companies are both shaped and constrained by other companies with which they have close and ongoing mutual dependencies, such as with a strategic alliance.

networks groups of companies that pool their resources in various ways

We can identify a number of different forms of networks and strategic alliances. The first is where there is a dominant company which clearly leads a group of subcontractors.[28] Motor car companies such as Ford, General Motors and Toyota, and aircraft manufacturers such as Boeing and Airbus, are typical examples. Take the example of Ford building a new Falcon. Motor cars are composed of many different systems such as brakes, gearboxes, engines, fuel systems and computerised engine management. Ford, as project manager, defines broadly what it wants from, say, the brake manufacturer and then lets the brake manufacturer design and manufacture the brake system. As a result, a Falcon is composed of the cooperative efforts of the brake manufacturer and a large number of different specialist suppliers, all working together as a *network*. The aircraft manufacturers such as Boeing take the sharing of research and development and manufacturing a step further. Hawker De Haviland in Australia may undertake to design part of the wing for the Boeing 777. But it does this for a share in the 777 project. If the aircraft is successful, Hawker shares the profits with Boeing: if it fails, Hawker may be lucky to make money from the venture. The attraction for Boeing is that the risks associated with introducing a new aircraft, which are always high, are shared among many different designers and manufacturers. Should the aircraft not prove to be commercially successful, Boeing's survival is not threatened. An example of an industrial network is given in Figure 5.10.

Another type of network arises when there is not a leading company or project manager to offer direction or control.[29] The personal computer industry provides us with a good example. The personal computer is made up of many different parts, such as the monitor, hard disc, power supply, microprocessors and motherboard. Designing and putting into production each of these requires extensive research and development and investment in manufacturing capacity. It is an industry that is very dispersed and decentralised, and no one company leads the industry. The industry comprises mutually dependent companies but evolves in accordance with technological developments and customer demand. So each company concentrates on what it is good at, selling its components to computer assemblers, who are generally close to the customer. There is even a futures market for the output of the specialist manufacturers.

Networks of these types are often called *clusters* and are generally coordinated by market forces.[30] Networks in the computer industry have developed in places such as Silicon Valley in California and the southern China–Hong Kong–Taiwan axis. Similar networks have developed in other industries. The entertainment industry has a cluster around Los Angeles. New York and London form a cluster in banking and financial services. In Australia there are clusters of tourism and financial services around

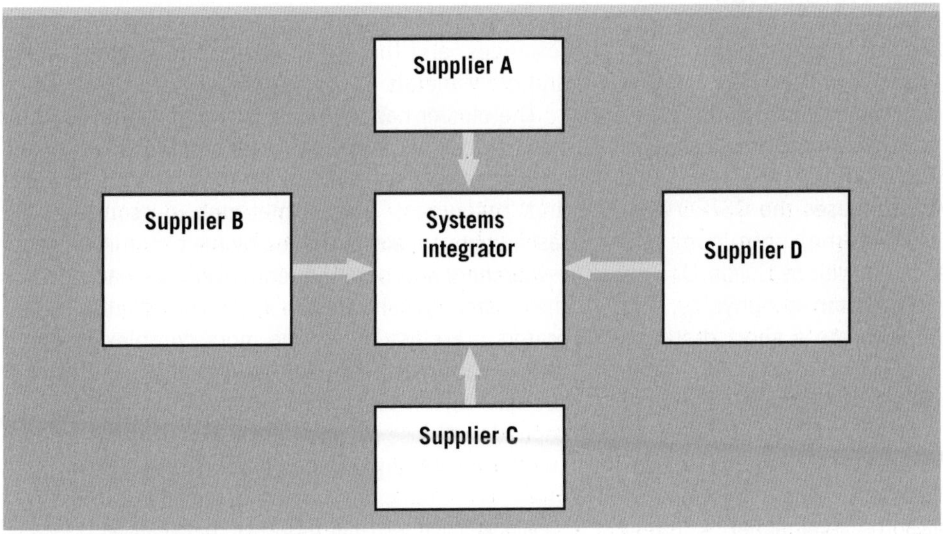
Supplier A
Supplier B
Systems integrator
Supplier D
Supplier C

FIGURE 5.10 Example of an industrial network

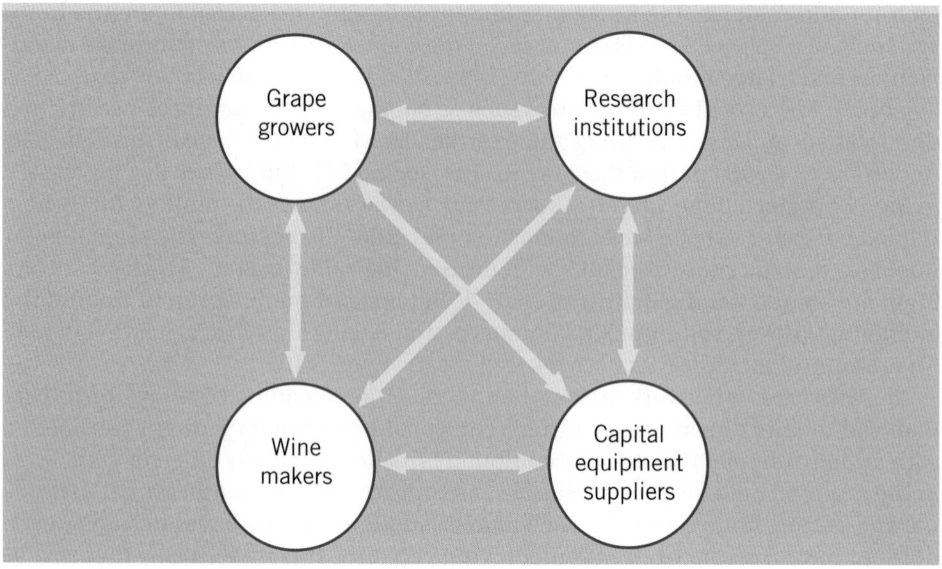
Grape growers
Research institutions
Wine makers
Capital equipment suppliers

FIGURE 5.11 Example of an industrial cluster

Sydney, a wine cluster in South Australia, and the motor vehicle industry is clustered around the Melbourne-based car manufacturers (see Figure 5.11). There is also a cluster of fast-ferry manufacturers around Kwinana in Western Australia.

A third type of relationship is the *strategic alliance*. The strategic alliance is a management term for two or more companies which cooperate in a venture by each

OT CLOSEUP

Underground visionaries

It is becoming increasingly common for technologically leading-edge industries to exist as clusters. One of these clusters, based on mineral exploration technology, has developed in Perth around the Australian Resources Research Centre (ARRC). The ARRC is a purpose-built centre which houses the CSIRO divisions of exploration and mining, petroleum and mineral products research, as well as Curtin University's department of exploration geophysics. Rio Tinto's research laboratories are a short distance away.

Scattered around Perth are many independent, and sometimes informal, research efforts funded by mining companies and specialty research teams. These are undertaking research into mining industry-related fields such as airborne aeromagnetics, three-dimensional computer modelling of underground resources, and the use of bacteria to liberate nickel and other metals from low-grade ore.

The cluster has no formal membership or association; it does not exist as a legal entity. But each part supports the other with information, sharing of ideas and resources, and sometimes personnel. Top researchers are also attracted by the proximity of other researchers and potential employers. As each part of the cluster concentrates on a specialised area, collaborators are close by for the more complex research tasks. And, of course, the educational institutions, such as Curtin, benefit from drawing on the research capabilities close by, and the cluster benefits from the supply of skilled graduates produced by Curtin.

Source: Adapted from Tim Treadgold, 'Underground Visionaries', *Business Review Weekly*, 20 April 2001, p. 76.

some relationships were statistically significant, enough deviant cases existed to question seriously the assumption that large organisations were necessarily more complex than small ones. Hall sided with Aldrich's structure-causes-size thesis when he concluded, 'If a decision is made to enlarge the number of functions or activities carried out in an organization, it then becomes necessary to add more members to staff the new functional areas'.[22] However, in terms of objectivity, it must be noted that the evidence was more inconsistent than rejecting the link between size and the other variables. Hall and associates, therefore, may question the size–structure relationship, but their research has certainly not demonstrated that the two are unrelated.

A final consideration relates to the status of the management in an organisation. A study of 142 small- and medium-sized businesses found that changes in size were related to changes in structure among those firms that were run by professional managers but that no such relationship appeared among the businesses that were controlled by owner-managers.[23] Specifically, it was found that increases in size were associated with more horizontal differentiation, more formalisation and more delegation of decision making only in firms controlled by professional managers. While it is dangerous to generalise from a single study, this research may help to explain some of the diverse findings in previous studies where there have been a large number of business firms in the sample but no control for the type of ownership. If, for example, owner-managers are unwilling to dilute their personal power over their organisations by decentralising decision making—even though this unwillingness reduces their organisation's effectiveness—we should expect the relationship between a business organisation's size and its structure to be moderated by the kind of management the firm has.

Is it possible to isolate size as a contingency?

The above discussion highlights the difficulties involved in isolating size as a contingency. The motor vehicle industry provides a good example of this problem. Let's look at a large manufacturer, say Ford. By any measure, Ford is a large organisation with all the complexity that one would expect of its size. But it also manufactures a complex product, requiring extensive design, planning and production capability. As a manufacturer catering to most sections of the market, it must keep its costs low. This leads to mass production. It also means spreading its fixed costs over a large number of units, leading to worldwide operations. Its suppliers are similarly dispersed. In summary, Ford does not have the luxury of being a small organisation. What is driving its size is its strategy of being a mass-market manufacturer. This leads to the technologies appropriate to mass production. Such strategy and production techniques are predicated on a stable environment: designs of cars changing slowly and demand is fairly constant. Therefore, if we study the forces leading to Ford's organisational structure, how do we isolate the influence of size from other variables such as strategy and technology?

Researchers have attempted to overcome this problem by undertaking longitudinal studies. These allow us to look at the same sample of organisations over a given period of time, typically during their growth phase. We have quoted a number of these in the previous section. But as we are looking at the effects of size, we do not need to be too exact as to what caused it: size itself is capable of being isolated. But it does mean that we must exercise caution in drawing conclusions as to cause and effect.

Ford's case raises a further issue with size; that is, that parts of organisations may develop different structures as they grow in response to different work demands. As

Ford grew, different parts of the company developed their own approach to work, not all of the ways of working reflecting the large size of the organisation. We would expect to see the classic symptoms of large size in such areas as manufacturing, motor vehicle assembly and routine office functions. But in areas such as design and engineering, many of the structural features of large size may not be present. Design studios are often located far away from assembly plants and their structure is reflected in the organic form. Much the same applies to engineering. So the differentiation implied by large size may not always be associated with the high level of formalisation associated with bureaucracy.

A further reason for considering size as a contingency is that most observers, including employees and people in the community generally, realise that large organisations are 'different' from small ones. They also require different skills to manage. Most observers may not be able to articulate what these differences are, but their intuition is probably not misplaced. It is the role of scholarship to identify and quantify these differences. As with all organisational research, researchers are limited by their methodology and measuring instruments. Organisations defy easy measurement and analysis, and it is possible that the differences we intuitively expect to find between large and small organisations are difficult to determine using traditional research techniques. There is a bias throughout this book to rely on quantifiable measures, and it is recognised that these do not capture the subtleties of organisational life. However, the subtleties in turn defy easy measurement, and in some cases may be difficult for organisational members themselves to articulate and describe.

Conclusions on the size–structure relationship

In overview terms, the relationship between size and structure is not clear.[24] Although some have found a strong relationship and argue for its causal nature, others have challenged these findings on methodological grounds or have argued that size is a consequence, rather than a cause of structure. But when we look at the research in more specific terms, a clearer pattern seems to evolve. We will demonstrate that size certainly does not dictate all of an organisation's structure but that it is important in predicting some dimensions of structure which have widespread applicability.

Size and complexity

Blau found that the impact of size on complexity was at a decreasing rate. As noted by Argyris, this conclusion may apply only to government-type agencies with the unique characteristics of the unemployment offices studied. Meyer's findings, however, certainly cannot be ignored. Although they were also restricted to government offices, he demonstrated strong evidence in favour of the size imperative. We might conclude tentatively that size affects complexity, but at a decreasing rate, in government organisations. Whether this holds for business firms is questionable. It may well be that in business organisations, where managers have greater discretion, structure causes size. Consistent with the strategy imperative, if managers have discretion they may choose to make their structure more complex (consistent with management theory) as more activities and personnel are added. Neither can it be ruled out that the size–structure relationship is circular. There is evidence indicating that size generates differentiation and that increasing differentiation also generates increasing size.[25] This shows itself in the proportionately greater number of administrative positions in large organisations.

The strongest case can be made for the effect of size on vertical differentiation, that is, the number of layers of management.[26] In fact, one study found that size alone was the dominant predictor of vertical differentiation, explaining between 50% and 59% of the variance.[27] A less strong but certainly solid case can be made for the relationship between size and horizontal differentiation. That is, the larger the organisation, the more pronounced (at declining rates) the division of labour within it, the same being true of the functional differentiation of the organisation into divisions.[28]

The relationship between size and spatial differentiation is problematic. Blau's high correlations are almost certainly attributable to the kind of organisations he studied. Other efforts to assess this relationship have failed to generate Blau's strong positive relationship; yet other investigations support Blau.[29] Further research covering diverse types of organisations is needed before conclusions of any substance can be drawn.

What about the criticism of the Aston Group's work and Hall's research? Our position is that they have not demonstrated the importance of size. More longitudinal studies are needed to clarify the size–structure causation. But in the interim, we propose that the critics have pointed out methodological problems with several of the important studies confirming the impact of size on complexity and have suggested potential alternative hypotheses, although they certainly have not demonstrated size to be irrelevant. Even Hall noted that 6 of his 11 measures of complexity were significantly related to size.[30] These observations highlight the difficulty in separating size, as an independent variable, from other organisational dimensions. It is part of many interrelationships which are discussed in this book.

Size and formalisation

The Aston findings supported the view that size affects formalisation. Hall's conclusion was that formalisation could not be implied from knowledge of organisation size, but he acknowledged that it could not be ignored either. A recent comprehensive review of 27 studies covering more than 1000 organisations concluded that the relationship between size and formalisation was high, positive and statistically significant.[31]

There would appear to be a logical connection between an increase in size and increased formalisation. Management seeks to control the behaviour of employees. Two popular methods are surveillance by the management hierarchy and the use of high formalisation. While not perfect substitutes for each other, as one increases the need for the other should decrease. Because surveillance costs should increase rapidly as organisations expand in size, it seems reasonable to propose that there would be economies if management substituted formalisation for direct surveillance as size increased. The evidence supports this contention.[32] Rules and surveillance are both aspects of control. The former are impersonal; the latter requires such activities as supervising work closely and inspecting the quantity and quality of work. In small organisations, control through surveillance may be achieved relatively easily through informal face-to-face relationships. But as the organisation grows there are more subordinates to supervise, so that it becomes increasingly efficient to rely more on rules and regulations for exerting control. Rules and regulations also provide for uniformity of control across a wide range of employees. We can expect, therefore, to find an increase in formal rules and regulations within an organisation as that organisation increases in size.

After reviewing the size–formalisation literature, one author proposed that 'the larger the organization, the more formalized its behavior'.[33] His explanation, however, emphasised that larger organisations formalise those activities that tend to recur often. The larger the organisation, the more behaviours repeat themselves, and hence management is motivated to handle them more efficiently through standardisation. With increased size comes greater internal confusion. Given management's general desire to minimise this confusion, they seek means to make behaviour at lower levels in the hierarchy more predictable. Management turns to rules, procedures, job descriptions and other formalisation techniques to bring about this predictability.

A final point about the size–formalisation relationship should be noted: we cannot ignore whether the organisation is independent or is a subsidiary of a larger organisation.[34] Parent firms often impose rules and regulations to maintain financial and reporting consistencies that would be unnecessary if the small firm were independent. So a moderating factor in size's effect on formalisation would be whether the organisation was a subsidiary of a larger firm. If so, expect the former to have higher formalisation than its size alone would dictate.

Size and centralisation

'It is only common sense that it is impossible to control large organizations from the top: because much more is happening than an individual or set of individuals can comprehend, there is inevitable delegation.'[35] But what is the evidence in support of this statement? As we concluded, formalisation increases with size. These rules and regulations *allow* top management to delegate decision making while at the same time ensuring that the decisions are made in accordance with the desires of top management. But the research is mixed in demonstrating that size leads to decentralisation.[36] In fact, one comprehensive review concluded that the correlation between size and centralisation is not significantly different from zero.[37] Precisely why this occurs is not clear. One possibility is that as an organisation increases in size some activities remain centralised and move further up the growing hierarchy while others are decentralised leaving no change in centralisation. The influence of the ownership of the organisation may also play a part. Yet further problems may arise from difficulties in being able to measure centralisation with any degree of accuracy.

When does an organisation become large?

Throughout this chapter we have tried to assess what effect, if any, changes in an organisation's size have on its structure. One interesting finding has been that size's influence seems to diminish as the number of employees expands. Once an organisation becomes large in size, it tends to be high in complexity, high in formalisation and decentralised, and that further increases in the number of employees have no noticeable further influence on structure. This conclusion, then, begs the question: how big is big? Put another way: at what point do additional employees become irrelevant in determining an organisation's structure?

Our answer can only be an approximation. However, most estimates tend to fall in the range of 1500–2000 employees.[38] Organisations with fewer than 1500 employees tend to be labelled as 'small'. Chances are that in an organisation up to this size, most people will have met, or at least know of, everyone else in the organisation. Employees may have greater understanding of the business as they are in contact with a greater number of activities that are undertaken. There may still be a fair amount of informal coordination, and the full range of formalisation techniques is probably

OT CLOSEUP

Rethinking organisational size

The relative benefits of being small and big continue to challenge managers of all types of organisations. One author has attempted to identify the benefits and disadvantages of being large. He identifies the benefits as follows:

Size provides the leverage for capturing significant market share. This leads to increased profitability, and is of considerable benefit in such consumer products as motor vehicles, pharmaceuticals and information technology. The increased profitability derives from economies of scale, better access to shelf space in shops, acquisition of cheaper inputs, price setting and establishing orderly markets.

Size improves access to low-cost capital. Many investors identify size with financial stability. The bigger the company, the more likely it is to be included in major investment indices and be covered by financial analysts. It is also likely to have a superior credit rating. Access to lower cost capital reduces the cost of acquisitions and investment in new plant and equipment.

Size brings improved brand recognition and advertising benefits. A recognisable brand has its benefits. Firms like Nike, Sony and IBM can introduce new products without the perceived risks of an unknown brand.

Size permits greater investment in research and development. The advantages of investment in R&D, particularly in areas such as biotechnology and information technology, are obvious. New products are often developed by those who can afford to spend on R&D.

Size permits global reach. Accessing new markets is often risky and requires large amounts of capital—particularly in emerging markets such as China. Larger companies are more able to bear the high costs involved in establishing a market position.

Size facilitates expertise and systems development. Compared to their smaller counterparts, large firms can hire specialists in areas such as finance and human resources. They can also invest in corporate infrastructure such as information systems and financial control systems, investments that would often be prohibitively expensive for smaller companies.

But size does bring its disadvantages. These include:

Size leads to lower employee satisfaction. Larger organisations suffer from increased employee turnover, lowered job satisfaction, higher absenteeism. The link in the employees' mind between their actions and the company's success becomes blurred, leading to lower motivation and potentially weaker company performance.

Size leads to resistance to innovation. Large firms harbour individuals with a strong vested interest in the status quo and who actively resist change. As a result, innovation is lower and new products and services are not developed well or rapidly.

Size leads to coordination problems. Large firms need expensive and extensive infrastructure to coordinate actions. They develop layers of management and elaborate staff groups which can easily become insulated from the market. These developments result in a system biased towards measuring internal performance rather than external value to customers.

Size leads to high formalisation. High formalisation need not be a problem, but when associated with bureaucracy it can lead to poor customer service and uninspired products. Further, managers in such bureaucracies rarely see the need for change, and often block the initiatives of those who are more in touch with the market.

Large organisations are often highly scrutinised. Such organisations are particular targets for attention from governments and activist organisations such as Greenpeace. They are also more likely to be sued.

Source: Adapted from Edward Lawler III, 'Rethinking Organizational Size', *Organizational Dynamics*, 26(2), 1997, pp. 24–35.

not present. On the other hand, when an organisation or any of its subunits starts to exceed 2000 employees, it becomes increasingly difficult to coordinate without introducing new subunits, creating formalised rules and regulations, or delegating decision making downwards. So we'll define a large organisation as one having approximately 2000 or more employees.

The preceding definition now allows us to make two important statements. First, adding employees to an organisation once it has approximately 2000 members should have a minimal impact on its structure. Second, a change in size will have its greatest impact on structure when the organisation is small. The big organisation, with 5000–10 000 employees, can double its size and you're not likely to see any significant changes in its structure. But if an organisation with 500 employees doubles its size, you should expect this to be followed by significant structural changes. Going from 100 to 200 employees would have an even greater impact on structure.

Special issues relating to organisation size

In this section we address three issues related to size. First, how can organisation theory assist managers of large organisations? Second, is organisation theory applicable to small organisations? Lastly, we will consider the issue of downsizing.

The problems of large size

In this chapter we have seen that the structure of an organisation has reached its full development when the number of employees reaches about 2000. However, within the world of business and government there are organisations of enormous size. For instance, IBM has 240 000 employees and Royal Dutch Shell 106 000. Coles Myer is Australia's largest employer with just over 152 000 employees, many of them part-time. But these all pale into insignificance with the armies of the United States, Russia and China, which each have well over one million members.

OT CLOSE

OT CLOSEUP
The big and the small in the mining industry

Those who are given to worry about the world being dominated by large companies may have little to be concerned about; there is plenty of room for small ones as well. The mining industry provides a good example. The world of mining seems to be dominated by a few very large corporations: BHP Billiton, Rio Tinto, AngloAmerican and Xtrata are always in the press. But these companies are only interested in very large, long-life deposits of minerals. They have access to the large amounts of capital needed to develop new mines, they can bring considerable knowledge to bear on potential problems and they have well-connected marketing departments dealing in a range of commodities. Small mines are of little interest to them.

Small mines can be managed far more successfully by organisations which are smaller in size. Such organisations have lower overheads, shorter communication channels and a senior management team that is far closer to operations and better informed as to any problems and issues which may arise. For Rio Tinto, managing a small mine would be a nuisance, as it would attempt to apply large company control techniques to a small organisation. This would result in such large overheads in areas like supervision, controls and generating management reports that it would be hardly worthwhile operating the mine.

Needless to say, large size presents management with problems that are either not present in a smaller organisation or may be more difficult to manage. In this section we consider what additional problems arise in managing large organisations, and how managers can use the structure of the organisation to assist them in alleviating the problems of size.

Given that managing large organisations consumes a significant amount of time and effort, it is worth considering why large organisations exist. The reason is that there are other significant economies in their operations that outweigh the diseconomies of employing and managing large numbers of people. The large costs involved in designing a car and equipping a factory to manufacture it means that small car companies are not an option. The risks and capital involved in discovering, refining and distributing oil products indicate why there are few small, integrated oil companies. And in government services, such as social security and foreign affairs, the need to apply uniform standards and deliver services over a large area dictates the size of the organisation.

We can identify a number of problems that are common to most large organisations. These are listed below, and they are summarised in Table 6.1:

1 *The growth of bureaucracy.* The high formalisation of bureaucracy, such as rules and regulations, tends to increase as managers try to maintain control over an increasingly unwieldy organisation. However, the extent of bureaucracy means that most large organisations have a tendency towards inertia. Top managers are often remote from workers and customers and incentives largely favour predictability. But the environment often changes faster than the rules and regulations, leading to a misfit between what the organisation is actually doing and what the environment is demanding.[39]

2 *The need to gather and process information and turn it into knowledge.*[40] There are significant amounts of data and information in large organisations. But data in themselves are of little use: the organisation must find a way to process data into a useful format that the organisation can act on.

3 *The need to adapt to changing technologies and product life cycles.*[41] Most organisations grow large because they have exploited a given technology. Toyota and cars, Microsoft and personal computer software, Kodak and photographic film are examples. However, all of these technologies can be overtaken by new innovations. The challenge for companies is to adapt to new technologies as they develop.

TABLE 6.1 Summary of large size problems and structural solutions

Problems associated with large size organisations	Structural contributions to solutions
Growth of bureaucracy	Divisionalisation
Turning information to knowledge	Outsourcing
Adapting to changing technologies	Decentralisation
Long time frames for action	Structuring to facilitate change
Need for accurate costing information	Allocating responsibilities
Managing over a wide geographic spread	
Bounded rationality	

4 *Extended time frames for action.*[42] In large organisations it can take a long time before realising that change is required. Stagnation may have set in for some time before management realises that action is necessary. During this time an organisation can 'live off its fat'—that is, run down its assets while maintaining its activities. Further, once remedial action has been taken, it can take a number of years to determine whether it is working or not.
5 *Knowing where profits are being made and costs incurred.*[43] In large organisations it is often difficult to allocate costs and revenues to individual products. For instance, how does Sony allocate overheads across its wide product range? How can the costs of information technology be allocated to each part of the organisation? And how does a large bank determine the costs and benefits of each customer or product? These issues are important for effective management.
6 *Difficulty in managing over a wide geographic area.*[44] By their nature, most large organisations operate in different markets and regions. Indeed, the multinational corporation is the dominant form of business in our time. But managing such firms leads to problems of employing people from different cultures, adapting products and services to suit local conditions, and maintaining control over operations that are located far away from the head office.
7 *Bounded rationality.*[45] The scale and scope of operations of large organisations means that it is impossible for one person, or even a group of people, to fully understand all that is going on. Procedures must therefore be introduced to reduce this complexity into bits of information that are capable of being grasped by the senior managers of the company.

Given these difficulties, how can structure contribute to the efficient management of large organisations? Remember that structure is the way we allocate responsibilities, the extent of formalisation and the location of decision making. The following structural solutions can be applied to problems we have identified above:

1 *Dividing the organisation into manageable parts.*[46] This is called divisionalisation. Each division operates largely as a separate business, with its own identifiable goals, management, staff and facilities. It enables a clearer identification of costs and revenues and places decision making close to where business is transacted. It also reduces the amount of communication needed for day-to-day operations.
2 *Outsourcing.*[47] Organisations can reduce many problems arising from size by not doing everything themselves. Airlines often outsource maintenance and baggage handling. Computer services are often bought in, and other companies have specialist firms undertake their cleaning, distribution, logistics or warehousing. Each of these actions removes the need for managing large staff numbers.
3 *Finding a balance between what decisions to centralise and decentralise.* Managers often tend to centralise decision making in order to maintain control. However, decision making should be made as close as possible to where the problem lies while controlling factors such as risk and access to information. Successful large companies have managed to find a balance between centralisation and decentralisation.
4 *Structuring to facilitate change.*[48] There is no easy way to combat the bureaucratic tendency. However, part of the response involves adopting an appropriate organisational structure. In seeking to reduce the tendency towards bureaucracy, managers should aim to reduce power distances, develop means of facilitating communication, and support new ways of recognising and solving problems.

Further, they should seek to reward actions that promote flexibility rather than adherence to fixed ways of responding to problems. The structure should also reflect the current and future needs of the organisation, rather than past practices. In addition, many of the elements of formalisation, those that are not intended to minimise risk for instance, should be taken as guides to action, rather than absolute rules to be followed on penalty of discipline.

5 *Ensuring that important tasks have someone responsible for them.* If important tasks have noone responsible for them, chances are they will be neglected or overlooked. Managers must also be aware of how environmental changes create the need for new responsibilities. For instance, mining companies are finding that they now need environmental and local community liaison managers. Quality-control managers in manufacturing and the growth in the number of human resource managers are all examples of responsibilities that have been generated to address important functions. Over the past twenty years we have seen the emergence of new positions such as chief information officer and chief financial officer in response to the need to clarify responsibilities in these areas.

6 *Physically separate those areas of the organisation which undertake different types of work.* Large organisations normally undertake a wide variety of different tasks. A motor vehicle manufacturer has different parts of the organisation specialising in body design, engineering, assembly, research into fuel cells, supply chain management, customer finance, accounting tasks and so forth. Many of these are undertaken where it makes most sense. Body design is often in 'hip' cities such as London or Los Angeles, assembly is drifting towards lower wage countries or those where inducements are given to invest, research is located close to the source of talented scientists and so on. Often call centres are located in regional areas where wages are lower and labour turnover less. Developments in communication and information technology have permitted the wider geographic spread of operations. The advantage this offers firms is that they may apply management styles appropriate to the task at each location. Designers, for instance, work in a different way to assemblers, and clerks in turn work differently from research scientists. By physically separating the workplaces, optimum work and management conditions may be applied.

In summary, we see that organisation theory makes a contribution to the management of large organisations. Although the set of structural options open to large organisations may be extensive, the consequences of choosing the wrong one can lead to significant problems. We have argued that successful large organisations manage best by actually becoming small—that is, by dividing themselves into units of such a size as to enable managers to understand the operations of their area and to respond accordingly. Formal mechanisms to promote adaptation to change are also necessary for large organisations.

Organisation theory and small businesses

We live in a society dominated by large organisations. Although 97% of all enterprises may be classified as small—that is, as having fewer than 10 employees—over 50% of the workforce can be found in the remaining 3% of organisations.[49] While there may be a great number of small organisations, large organisations have the greatest impact on our society and attract most press attention and commentary.

But before we progress too far on this section, our definition of what is a 'small' and 'large' organisation needs clarification. Earlier in the chapter we referred to an

OT CLOSEUP

Obtaining the benefits of being small while being big

The benefits of a small organisation are fairly well known: there are fewer impediments to communication, creativity is heightened, innovations can be introduced far more quickly and, as workers and management are closer to the customer, they are more responsive to customers' needs. These are the very attributes that large businesses often lack, and one of the great management challenges of the present day is to try to derive many of the benefits of being small while being a big business.

For most of the 20th century, large organisations advertised their power by the architecture of their head office. It was generally located in a fashionable area of the city and was large and imposing, with grand entrances and state-of-the-art materials. Inside, there were thousands of head office employees maintaining close oversight of the far-flung divisions. The large head office turned out to be an impediment to change, and one of the features of the past 20 years has been the downsizing of the head office, with most staff either being made redundant or moving to the divisions.

Adopting divisionalised structures has also assisted the management of large organisations. Divisions are essentially profit centres and they can penetrate deep into an organisation's structure. What in effect they do is substitute market controls for supervision by a management hierarchy. If management wishes to know what the profitability of a division is, it only needs to look at the profit and loss statement. Of course, management is more complex than this; subjective judgements as to performance still need to be made, but the existence of profit centres simplifies management's task. Divisionalisation also permits divisions to adopt a structure which is appropriate to the work being undertaken. But problems of coordination between divisions can pose communication issues and extensive divisionalisation is often inappropriate when high levels of coordination and cooperation are required.

Nevertheless, the idea of small operating units which are profit centres that agglomerate into a larger organisation is a popular way to capture the benefits of being small.

Another method used to improve creativity in large organisations is introducing a 'skunk-works'. This is a group of people isolated from the main, highly formalised processes of the organisation, charged with the task of creating innovative products. Motor vehicle manufacturers often use skunk-works to generate concept cars or new means of motive power. A skunk-works of young people may be created, for instance, to generate ideas for a car aimed at the youth market. Many innovations in aerospace are undertaken in skunk-works. The layout of the skunk-works is extremely informal, with few offices and physical barriers in the workplace. Timekeeping is informal and there is little in the way of hierarchy. There is generally intensive use of IT for design and communication purposes. The skunk-works highlights the long-standing practice of firms locating their operations where most benefit is to be derived. Research and development laboratories are located at some distance from production facilities, and mining companies locate their main administrative offices in a financial centre, their operations where the mines are and their marketing staff where the customers are.

Corporate culture, or what may be termed 'social software', also contributes to managing large size. The structure of an organisation often only makes a small contribution to managerial effectiveness. In particular, it frequently creates conditions where hundreds of managers can say 'no' but few can say 'yes'. The past 20 years has seen the symbiotic evolution of communication technology and an appreciation of corporate culture as a control and motivating device. Managers of large organisations realise that self control is far better than externally imposed control and, as a consequence, go to great lengths and expense to build a common culture amongst staff.

Communication barriers can be tackled by using inexpensive air travel to promote face-to-face meetings, whilst emails and intranets facilitate day-to-day contact amongst dispersed workers. Greater understanding of these management techniques has emboldened managers to embark on mergers and create large companies which they otherwise may have been reluctant to do.

organisation with under 1500 people as being 'small'. Most people would clearly not regard an organisation of this size as being small. The problem of definition has arisen largely because researchers study different aspects of the influence of size and consequently apply different measures of it. For instance, in the study which considered an organisation of under 1500 people as being small, elements of complexity were being researched. However, in the previous paragraph, the commonwealth statistician required a measure which identified the many family owned businesses in existence.

The problems of terminology generate difficulties when seeking to compare studies. Researchers tend to define small, medium and large organisations by the number of employees. This is understandable as it is one of the easiest parts of an organisation to measure. But there is also a behavioural aspect to size, such as the extent of formalisation or the way management is practised, which is more difficult to measure. So as you read through this section, bear in mind the purpose for which the research or study was carried out as this informs the concept of organisational size.

These considerations have not been lost on those who study organisation theory. Studies are almost exclusively of medium-sized and large organisations, those with hundreds of employees or more. Even textbook authors fall prey to this bias: you'll find references in this book to large statutory authorities and government departments, or firms the size of BHP Billiton, Woolworths and National Australia Bank, but rarely a mention of small business, particularly the owner-managed firm. It may therefore be appropriate to ask whether the organisation theory being described in this book has any application to those who manage or expect to manage a small business, such as one owned by one person or a family?

The answer is definitely yes! The right structural design is critical if a small business is to succeed. An important point, however, is that small businesses do not face the same problems as large organisations; therefore, we should expect a different priority to be assigned to organisation theory issues by the small-business manager.

The influence of the owner

Although many definitions of small business are based on number of employees (this varies, and definitions up to 500 employees in manufacturing have been used), a small business could more accurately be described as one where one person, generally the owner, makes all the major decisions. These would include where to locate, what to produce, the target market, the source of inputs, and who to hire and fire. This should give us the clue that a small business is often a reflection of the owner's personality and management style. So not all small businesses will be structured the same. Some may have decentralised decision making for operational decisions, while in other small businesses of a similar type nothing goes on without the owner's knowledge and permission. Other businesses may have created positions for relatives or friends, even though there may not be much work for them to do. And many small start-up high-technology companies reflect the owner's passion for innovation and unstructured work hours.[50]

The world view of owner-managers—that is, their personality, attitudes and beliefs—influences the way that small businesses are structured and managed.[51] On the whole they tend to prefer a relatively unstructured workplace, where roles and responsibilities are not clearly defined. But decision making, including even day-to-day decisions, is highly centralised. Organisational structure tends to follow the decisions that have been made, rather than anticipating them. And when staff is recruited, they are chosen because of situational factors rather than a rational assessment of requirements.[52]

This does not mean that in a small business anything passes as a satisfactory design. There is the same need for the structure to suit the environment, the technology and the strategy in a small organisation as in a big one. But following the principle of equifinality, discussed in Chapter 1, there is likely to be a large number of variations between the structures of organisations doing much the same thing. This does not prevent us from making generalisations about what structure small businesses are likely to adopt.

The foregoing discussion highlights the close relationship between management and ownership in a small business. In a large organisation, management acts as agents for the owners. This has the implication that they may act only within the parameters given to them by the owners. But in the small business there is no agency relationship; management and ownership are essentially one and the same. As a consequence, there are fewer constraints on the owner-manager to act.

Issues of reduced importance

All the structural variables are less important to the small-business manager, because the range of variation in small businesses is typically limited. Small businesses tend to have a minimal degree of horizontal, vertical and spatial differentiation, and most are characterised by low formalisation, at least of the written kind, and high centralisation. There is also a fewer range of jobs within the organisation. For instance, instead of having full-time accountants and lawyers on staff, their services can be bought as needed. The reduced horizontal differentiation means that in occupations such as accounting, the accountant may do all the accounting work rather than specialise in one particular part of it. Vertical differentiation in small businesses is usually low for the obvious reason that these structures tend to be flat. Similarly, spatial differentiation is usually low because small businesses don't spread their

OT CLOSEUP

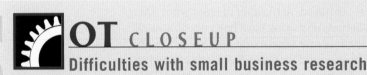

Difficulties with small business research

One of the problems with small-business research is reaching agreement on what constitutes a small organisation.[53] Researchers have, in the past, used number of employees, but this measure is simply an administrative convenience. Some researchers claim that perceptions of size by those in the sample should be taken into account when determining whether a business is small or large. They claim that the parties involved will show general agreement as to what is small and large in their sector, and that this should guide research. So key participants' perceptions and beliefs take precedence over a numerical measure.

Data on many small businesses remain hard to come by, which may account for the lack of organisational research. Generally, gathering data means speaking to the owner or manager or seeking his or her permission to interview or submit a questionnaire to employees. But owners are often busy people with little time, or sympathy, for research. They are generally practical people, with a strong distrust of abstract and theoretical constructs. Data gathering is also time-consuming, with each entry to a workplace having to be negotiated separately but yet, because of the size of the business, yielding relatively few data. It is hardly surprising that medium- and large-sized businesses are the main subject of research.

5 *Greater entrepreneurship.* Downsizing should lead to greater decentralisation of functions, which should lead to more innovative behaviour on the part of management.
6 *Increased productivity.* Downsizing rarely leads to less work being undertaken. Those who are left are expected to do much the same amount of work with fewer people.

A favourite target of downsizing has been the large head offices organisations built up over many years. In some companies, managers in the field had control over only 30% of their costs, so they had little incentive to search for economies or instigate change. By reducing the number of head office staff and making the business managers responsible for a greater proportion of their costs, managers were more likely to be more careful in spending money. As well, the impact of information technology allowed many of the functions of head office to be undertaken at a decentralised location.

The effects of downsizing

Downsizing rarely achieves all of the benefits attributed to it. A number of studies have shown that the benefits of downsizing have fallen short of the set objectives. In a survey in the USA of 1005 firms, only 46% felt that they had reduced costs in accordance with expectations; fewer than one in three felt that profits grew as much as expected, and only 20% reported satisfactory improvement in shareholders' return on investment.[56]

Not only are the financial returns of downsizing often not as great as anticipated, but companies frequently handle poorly the problem of how to make the best use of those who remain. Studies consistently show that after a downsizing has occurred, the surviving employees become narrow-minded, self-absorbed and risk-averse. There is a lowering of commitment and morale, more job insecurity, productivity often drops and, needless to say, management fails to maintain the trust of other employees.[57] These symptoms are so common that they are called survivor's syndrome.

Most companies start downsizing programs with few policies or programs in place to minimise the negative effect of cutting back. Senior managers easily forget that organisations rely on a complex web of communication channels and interrelationships to get things done. Once these relationships are severed, new ones must be established, and this can take time. In many cases this problem is exacerbated by major decisions regarding cuts being made by consultants who lack a firm understanding of how the organisation operates. The remaining managers and lower level employees can feel misused and alienated, and rather than productivity increasing it can actually drop. The reserve of trust that organisations need to operate effectively takes a long time to be re-established.

Further problems with downsizing can arise because the skills of those remaining in the organisation are not able to replace those who have been dispensed with. Part of the collective memory of the organisation walks out the door with the employees who leave the firm. Because of this, many companies that have downsized have found that they have had to re-employ managers and lower level workers either as consultants or other part-time help at a higher cost than having them on the payroll. This has contributed to the cost savings of downsizing being lower than most companies anticipated.[58]

The way that downsizing is implemented can also have an influence on its success. Downsizing is often attempted in a random manner, with the intention of reducing headcounts rather than considering the ongoing needs of the organisation. Table 6.3 lists a number of ineffective downsizing practices. Poorly thought out downsizing

TABLE 6.3 Ineffective downsizing practices

The use of voluntary early retirement practices
Making across-the-board layoffs
Eliminating training and development programs
Cutting too deeply into the numbers of personnel
Placing remaining employees into jobs for which they have insufficient skills
Emphasising employee accountability over employee involvement
Expecting survivors to 'row harder'
Implementing layoffs slowly in phases over time
Promising high monetary rewards rather than careers

Source: Adapted from M.A. Hitt, B.W. Keats, H.F. Harback and R.D. Nixon 'Rightsizing: Building and Maintaining Strategic Leadership and Long-Term Competitiveness', *Organizational Dynamics*, Autumn 1994, p. 25.

practices can see those with considerable experience leaving the organisation, without anyone to take their place. This is a typical effect of the voluntary redundancy and early retirement schemes open to all employees. Another counterproductive way of implementing downsizing is to phase it in over time: productivity and morale plummets as everyone wonders who will be next to go.

One of the problems of downsizing is that managers are often neither well informed nor experienced in implementing it. Unfortunately, managers do not enjoy perfect knowledge of how the organisation works or the detailed roles of those in the organisation. The larger the organisation, the more remote senior management will be from the day-to-day running of it. Under these conditions, their judgements in relation to downsizing are often only best guesses. And those who are expert in downsizing often cannot perform in any other role. The American manager, Al Dunlap, has earned the nickname 'Chainsaw' for his attack on corporate staffing and overheads. But his tenure is typically only 18 months in a company before he moves on. He was employed by the late Kerry Packer in the early 1990s to reduce the costs and staffing levels of Consolidated Press.[59]

In the 1980s downsizing came as a shock to most employees, including managers. Although they were familiar with layoffs during economic downturns, the laying off of large numbers of employees during otherwise prosperous times by healthy companies challenged the implicit idea of the social contract between employer and employee. Since that time, downsizing has become part of normal management practice and one which no longer comes as a shock to employees. In many cases companies are hiring whilst they are downsizing; in effect, they are changing their workforce composition. Most disputes these days are not about the practice but about the amount of compensation to be paid when downsizing occurs.

The need to maintain investment in the future

It may be difficult for managers to be downsizing on the one hand and managing for the future on the other. But one factor that is easy to forget during the downsizing phase is that the future of the organisation should be as high in management's mind as the present. New products need to be brought to market, distribution channels and product image maintained, management development undertaken, and the general entropy associated with organisations as open systems constantly resisted. This

OT CLOSEUP

Downsizing in Australia

Australian industry has experienced its fair share of downsizings. Public corporations, such as water supply and electricity authorities, and the finance industry, especially banking, have shed large numbers of employees over the past 10 years. One of the reasons that downsizing has attracted so much media publicity is that, while reducing workforces because of economic downturn has been common in the past, current downsizing owes little to economic decline. It has created enormous social stress as families have lost income and workers career prospects. It has also led to many workers taking retirement earlier than they would have wanted owing to their inability to find other employment. Identifying the reasons for downsizing is difficult, but technological change, heightened levels of competition and a desire to increase productivity have played their part.

Two Australian researchers, Peter Dawkins and Craig Littler, have undertaken a major study into the effects of downsizing. They studied data from over 4000 large Australian firms over the period 1990 to 1998. Over 80% of the firms they studied downsized during that time, and downsizing appears to have permeated Australian business organisations.

Their study revealed that downsizing almost always led to a loss of skills and knowledge within the organisation. Laying people off to reduce numbers is a random exercise which often leads to what has been termed 'cesspool syndrome' where less qualified employees rise to the top.

Downsizing firms are far more likely than their non-downsizing peers to substitute temporary or part-time staff. In some cases, employees who have been made redundant through downsizing return soon afterwards as contractors. The use of temporary staff, however, does not stem the loss of skills from the organisation.

In relation to individual exposure to downsizing, Dawkins and Littler found that:

- men were more likely than women to experience downsizing
- older workers were significantly more exposed to downsizing than younger workers
- education and skill levels provided no protection against downsizing
- primary industry workers and those in regional areas were less likely to experience downsizing than were urban dwellers.

Older workers are more likely than younger workers to be affected by downsizing. They are more likely to be employed by downsizing firms and, when laid off, their chances of finding comparable employment opportunities are slim. Most downsized workers experience a loss of job satisfaction in their new jobs.

Downsizing appears to have little effect on rates of unemployment generally. An expanding economy generates as many jobs as have been lost. But downsizing firms don't appear to increase their profitability as a result of laying off staff. Indeed, most report that the aims of downsizing are rarely met.

Source: Drawn from Peter Dawkins & Craig Littler, eds, *Downsizing: Is it Working for Australia?*, Melbourne: Institute of Applied Economic and Social Research, University of Melbourne, 2001.

cannot be achieved if an organisation is staffed and structured to produce only for the present range of tasks, with no resources allocated to preparing for the future. Cuts in staff, systems and equipment that are too hard and too deep are generally counterproductive. In times of declining profit, research staff may seem to be a luxury, maintenance engineers easy to cut, investment in new processes and skills unnecessary, and market development a waste. However, it is from these areas that future profitability springs. And even though there may be a short-term gain, the long-term future of the company will be put at risk if areas such as these are neglected for too long.

Summary

Organisational size is defined as the total number of employees. Strong arguments have been proposed indicating that size is the major determinant of structure, but there has been no shortage of critics of this position.

A review of the evidence indicates that size has a significant influence on vertical differentiation. The effect of size on spatial differentiation is unclear. Increases in formalisation appear to be related closely to increases in organisational size. Finally, although common sense suggests that size and centralisation would be inversely related, research reveals mixed findings.

Large organisations present managers with a range of significant problems to solve. These include the tendency towards bureaucracy, the need to adapt to changing technologies and product cycles, identifying the sources of revenues and costs, and the difficulty of managing over a wide geographic area. Structure was found to contribute to the successful management of large organisations by reducing complexity to manageable parts, locating decisions at the right place in the organisation and ensuring that important tasks have someone responsible for them.

We noted that organisation theory is based on studies almost exclusively of medium- and large-sized organisations. Small businesses face different problems and have different priorities in terms of important organisation theory concepts. In addition to the fact that small businesses have a different organisation theory agenda, their managers have a more limited set of structural options.

Finally, we looked at the issue of downsizing. Almost all large organisations have downsized at some time during the past few years. However, few have achieved the goals they set themselves. We examined the aims of downsizing and found that there were many reasons for it apart from reducing costs. Other reasons included attempting to make a more nimble and responsive organisation. All downsizing had a negative impact on those left in the organisation, but the effects could be far worse than they need be if it was implemented inappropriately.

For review and discussion

1 Which of the following indicators of size has the greatest impact upon structure? Why?
   - turnover
   - market capitalisation
   - geographic spread
   - number of employees
   - complexity of product
   - number of different divisions and departments

2 'One of the strongest cases for the size imperative has been made by Meyer.' What is the support for this statement?

3 'Size is the major determinant of structure.' Construct an argument to support this statement. Then construct one to refute it.

4 Discuss the difficulties of separating the effects of size from that of technology and other organisational variables.

5 What is the relationship between size and complexity?

6 What is the relationship between size and formalisation?

Does it influence the whole organisation or only parts of it? Does it have a greater impact on some areas than on others? Do some technologies have a more significant impact than others? As with so many concepts in organisational theory, the way in which it is defined and measured influences subsequent research and comparison of findings. There is probably no construct in organisational theory where diversity of measurement has produced more multiple findings and confusion than research into technology. Both Pacific Brands and John Cutler convert inputs into outputs. The way they do this has some bearing on structure.

Defining technology

Although intuitively we accept that technology must have an influence on the way organisations are structured (that is, the relationship has face validity), it is extremely difficult to develop a definition of technology that is capable of guiding research. As long as we adopt a generalised approach which is applicable to all organisations and their productive processes, there is general agreement among organisational theory researchers that **technology** refers to the information, equipment, techniques and processes required to transform inputs into outputs in an organisation. This definition permits us to include within the technology construct not just physical processes but also mental concepts which are part of the information required to complete a task. That is, technology looks at *how* the inputs are converted to outputs. There is also agreement that the concept of technology, despite its IT or manufacturing connotation, is applicable to all types and kinds of organisations. As discussed in Chapter 1, all organisations turn inputs into outputs. Regardless of whether the organisation is a manufacturing firm, a bank, a hospital, a social service agency, a research laboratory, a newspaper or a military unit, or an environmental lobby group, it will use a technology of some sort to produce its product.

technology the information, equipment, techniques and processes required to transform inputs into outputs

The problems begin when we move from the concept to its application. At issue is basically the question: given the wide diversity of organisations and what they do, how is it possible to measure technology? Researchers have used a number of technology classifications. A partial list would include operations techniques used in work-flow activities; characteristics of the materials used in the work flow; varying complexities in the knowledge system used in the work flow; the degree of continuous, fixed-sequence operations; the extent of automation; and the degree of interdependence between work systems. Each of these measures of technology is slightly different, and you would expect different results even if they were applied to the same organisation.

But this introduces several additional problems—that is, accommodating varying types and sizes of organisations and different levels of analysis. Some studies have been limited to manufacturing firms. Some have included only very large organisations, while others have concentrated upon the work group and even individuals. Still others have been directed to the total organisation, yet the researchers attempt to compare their findings with studies directed at the work unit or job level. Not surprisingly, the breadth of these efforts, and the attempt to generalise to all organisations from samples that differ greatly, might be expected to end up producing inconsistent results. And that is exactly what has happened.

In summary, we lack the precision to create a universal and generalised measure of technology. So how can we then progress our understanding of the relationship? There have been a number of landmark contributions linking technology to various aspects of organisational structure. We let these studies put forward their own arguments, and we will then evaluate them to see whether we can identify any linkages between them. To minimise confusion, we will restrict our discussion to the landmark contributions to the technology–structure debate. The four studies we describe take very different perspectives on technology, but they will give you the basics for understanding what we know about how technology affects structure. After reviewing these four positions, we tie them together, ascertain where we stand today on the technological imperative, and determine what specific statements we can accurately make about the impact of technology on structure. Later in the chapter we will examine various specific aspects of technology, particularly the impact of information technology upon organisations.

The initial thrust: Woodward's research

The initial interest in technology as a determinant of structure can be traced to the mid-1960s and the work of Joan Woodward.[1] Her research, which focused on production technology, was the first major attempt to view organisation structure from a technological perspective. Woodward's study does not pretend to be applicable to all organisations: it applies only to manufacturing industries. Woodward was searching for a link between technology and the most appropriate structure, which if it could be identified, might then be incorporated into management practice and teaching. The research methodology she used is also relevant to us and raises questions as to its general applicability. Subsequent studies have used the same methodology, although in recent times not on such a broad scale. As we can see from Chapter 1, those influenced by postmodernist thinking would reject the survey-type methodology used by Woodward.

Background

Woodward chose approximately 100 manufacturing firms in the south of England. These ranged in size from fewer than 250 employees to over 1000. The data she gathered were quite extensive, but our discussion will concentrate on the structural variables. The data allowed her to compute various measures of structure: the number of hierarchical levels, the span of control, the administrative component, the extent of formalisation and the like. She also gathered financial data on each firm (e.g. profitability, sales, market share), which allowed her to classify the companies as above-average or below-average in terms of success or organisational effectiveness. Her objective was straightforward: is there a correlation between structural form and effectiveness? Her proposition, derived from the classical prescriptions of management theorists, was that there is one optimum form of organisational structure that contributes to organisational effectiveness.

Her efforts to link common structures to effectiveness were unsuccessful. The structural diversity among the firms in each of her effectiveness categories was so great that it was impossible to establish any relationship or draw any valid conclusions between what was regarded as sound organisational structure and effectiveness. It was only after Woodward had grouped the firms according to their typical mode of production technology that relationships between structure and effectiveness became apparent.

Woodward categorised the firms into one of three types of technologies: **unit, mass** or **process production**. She treated these categories as a scale with increasing degrees

unit production technology where units are custom-made and work is non-routine

mass production large-batch or mass-produced technology

process production highly controlled, standardised and continuous processing technology

of technological complexity, unit being the least complex and process the most complex. Unit producers would manufacture custom-made products such as locomotives, turbines for hydroelectric installations or special-purpose vehicles. Mass producers would make large-batch or mass-produced products such as refrigerators or motor cars. The third category, process production, included heavily automated continuous-process producers such as oil and chemical refiners.

Woodward's findings

Woodward found that there were distinct relationships between these technology classifications and the subsequent structure of the firms, and that the effectiveness of the organisations was related to the 'fit' between technology and structure.

For example, the degree of vertical differentiation increased with technical complexity. The median number of management levels for firms in the unit, mass and process categories were three, four and six respectively. More important, from an effectiveness standpoint, the above-average firms in each category tended to cluster around the median for their production group.

Woodward also found that the administrative component varied directly with the type of technology: that is, as technological complexity increased, so did the proportion of administrative and support staff personnel as distinct from those actually involved in the production process. However, not all the relationships were linear. For instance, the mass-production firms had the smallest proportion of skilled workers and scored high in terms of overall complexity and formalisation, whereas the unit and process firms tended to rate low on these structural dimensions.

A careful analysis of her findings led Woodward to conclude that for each category on the technology scale (unit, mass, process) and for each structural component, there was an optimal range around the median point that encompassed the positions of the more effective firms. That is, within each technological category, the firms that conformed most nearly to the median figures for each structural component were the most effective (see Table 7.1). The mass-production technology firms were highly differentiated, relied on extensive formalisation, and did relatively little to delegate authority. Both the unit and process technologies, in contrast, were structured more loosely. Flexibility was achieved through less vertical differentiation, less division of labour and more group activities, more widely defined role responsibilities and decen-

TABLE 7.1 Summary of Woodward's findings on the relationship between technological complexity and structure

	Low	Technology	High
Structural characteristic	**Unit production**	**Mass production**	**Process production**
Number of vertical levels	3	4	6
Supervisor's span of control	24	48	14
Manager/total employee ratio	1:23	1:16	1:8
Proportion of skilled workers	High	Low	High
Overall complexity	Low	High	Low
Formalisation	Low	High	Low
Centralisation	Low	High	Low

tralised decision making. High formalisation and centralised control apparently were not feasible with unit production's custom-made, non-routine technology and not necessary in the heavily automated, inherently tightly controlled continuous-process technology.

Woodward's investigation demonstrated a link between technology, structure and effectiveness. Firms that most nearly approximated the typical structure for their technology were the most effective. Firms that deviated in either direction from their ideal structure were less successful. Therefore, Woodward argued that effectiveness was a function of an appropriate technology–structure fit. Organisations that developed structures that conformed to their technologies were more successful than those that did not.

Woodward was also able to explain the disparity between her findings and the classical prescriptions of management theorists: these prescriptions must have been based on the theorists' experiences with organisations that used mass-production technologies. The mass-production firms had clear lines of authority, high formalisation, a low proportion of skilled workers achieved through a high division of labour, wide spans of control at the supervisory level and centralised decision making. But as not all organisations use mass-production technology, these prescriptions lacked generalisability. Thus Woodward's research spelt the beginning of the end for the view that there were universal principles of management and organisation applicable to all organisations. Her work was to represent the initial transition by organisation theory scholars from a universal principles perspective to a contingency theory of organisations.

Evaluation

Several follow-up studies have supported Woodward's findings, but she has also had her share of criticism. Let us review what others have had to say about Woodward's research. Edward Harvey was an early advocate of Woodward.[2] He believed that the underlying foundation of Woodward's scale was technical specificity. That is, he assumed that more specific technologies present fewer problems requiring new or innovative solutions than do more diffuse or complex technologies. So he took 43 different industrial organisations and rated them as technically diffuse (which closely paralleled Woodward's unit production), technically intermediate (similar to mass production) and technically specific (similar to Woodward's process production). These categories were based on the number of major product changes that the sample firms had experienced in the 10 years before the study. Harvey found a relationship between technical specificity and structure which was consistent with Woodward's technological imperative. Basically, organisations with specific technologies had more specialised subunits, more authority levels and higher ratios of managers to total personnel than did those with diffuse technologies.

Woodward's findings were also supported in another study of manufacturing firms.[3] The researcher, like Woodward, found no evidence of such a thing as a universally optimum structural form. His data constituted strong evidence to confirm Woodward's claim that unit, mass and process production result in different structural forms and that proper fit within categories increases the likelihood that the organisation will be successful.

Woodward's research and analysis by no means developed a watertight case for the technological imperative. Criticisms have been made at a number of levels.[4] Her measure of technology has been criticised as unreliable. Her methodology, as it relied primarily on subjective observations and interviews, may lead to differing conclusions being drawn. Woodward implies causation, yet her methodology can allow her to claim only association. This is a problem common to all statistical analysis. Her measures of organisational success may be criticised as lacking rigour. Finally, as her firms were all British companies engaged almost exclusively in manufacturing, any generalisations to all organisations, or even to manufacturing firms outside Great Britain, must be guarded. And, of course, the advance of new technologies, such as information technology, has the capacity to render Woodward's findings meaningless to present-day organisations.

Another criticism derives from her research objectives. More recent organisational scholars would reject the survey approach used by Woodward as being of limited use in understanding organisations. They would concentrate more on the experiences of individuals and the greater subtleties revealed by in-depth case studies. Additionally, many organisational scholars are not from a management or business disciplinary background, or do not view organisations the way that managers might view them. So an approach, such as Woodward's, would not appeal to them.

Notwithstanding these criticisms, Woodward's work remains a significant contribution to the area. Her methodology may not be widely replicable or the findings resonate with contemporary organisations, but whenever technology and organisations are mentioned, her work justly stands as a landmark contribution.

Knowledge-based technology: Perrow's contribution

One of the major limitations of Woodward's perspective on technology was its manufacturing base. As manufacturing firms represent less than a third of all organisations, technology needs to be operationalised in a more general way if the concept is to have meaning across all organisations. Charles Perrow proposed such an alternative.[5]

Background

Perrow concentrated upon knowledge technology rather than production technology. He defined technology as 'the action that an individual performs upon an object, with or without the aid of tools or mechanical devices, in order to make some change in that object'.[6] He then proceeded to identify what he believed to be the two underlying dimensions of knowledge technology.

task variability the number of exceptions encountered in performing a task

problem analysability the type of search procedures followed to find successful methods for adequately responding to task exceptions, from well-defined and analysable to ill-defined and unanalysable

The first dimension, labelled **task variability**, considers the number of exceptions encountered in one's work. These exceptions will be few in number if the job is high in predictability. Jobs that normally have few exceptions in their day-to-day practice include those on a motor vehicle assembly line or a cook at McDonald's. At the other end of the spectrum, if a job has a great deal of variety a large number of exceptions can be expected. Typically, this characterises top management positions, consulting jobs or the work of professionals. So task variability appraises work by evaluating it along a variety–predictability continuum.

The second dimension, called **problem analysability**, assesses the type of search procedures followed to find successful methods for responding adequately to task exceptions. The search may, at one extreme, be described as well defined. If your car does not start, the mechanic works through a series of well-defined procedures to identify the cause—is the battery flat, is there petrol in the tank, is there a fuel blockage and so on? Using this kind of logic, where various alternatives are eliminated, it is possible to find the source of the problem and rectify it.

The other extreme is ill-defined problems. If you are an architect with a brief to design a building which 'reflects its environment but whose style will be noteworthy' then you will hardly follow a formulae to reach an optimum solution. You will not use a formal search technique. You will have to rely on your prior experience, judgement and intuition to find a solution. Through walking around the site, looking at the environment, sketching ideas and applying trial and error you might arrive at an acceptable choice. This dimension ranged from well defined to ill defined.

These two dimensions—task variability and problem analysability—can be used to construct a two-by-two matrix. This is shown in Figure 7.1. The four cells in this matrix represent four types of technology: routine, engineering, craft, and non-routine:

routine technology containing few exceptions and easy-to-analyse problems

engineering technology containing a large number of exceptions, but can be handled in a rational and systematic manner

craft technology containing relatively difficult problems but with a limited set of exceptions

non-routine technology containing many exceptions and difficult-to-analyse problems

- **Routine technologies** (cell 1) have few exceptions and easy-to-analyse problems. The mass-production processes used to make steel or motor cars or fast food belong in this category. A bank teller's job is also an example of activities subsumed under routine technology.
- **Engineering technologies** (cell 2) have a large number of exceptions, but they can be handled in a rational and systematic manner. The construction of office buildings would fall into this cell, as would the activities performed by accountants.
- **Craft technologies** (cell 3) deal with relatively difficult problems but with a limited set of exceptions. This would include custom tailoring, furniture restoring or the work of performing artists.
- **Non-routine technologies** (cell 4) are characterised by many exceptions and difficult-to-analyse problems. Examples of non-routine technologies would be strategic planning and basic research activities.

In summary, Perrow argued that if problems can be studied systematically, using logical and rational analysis, cells 1 or 2 will be appropriate. Problems that can be handled only by intuition, insight or experience require the technology of cells 3 or 4.

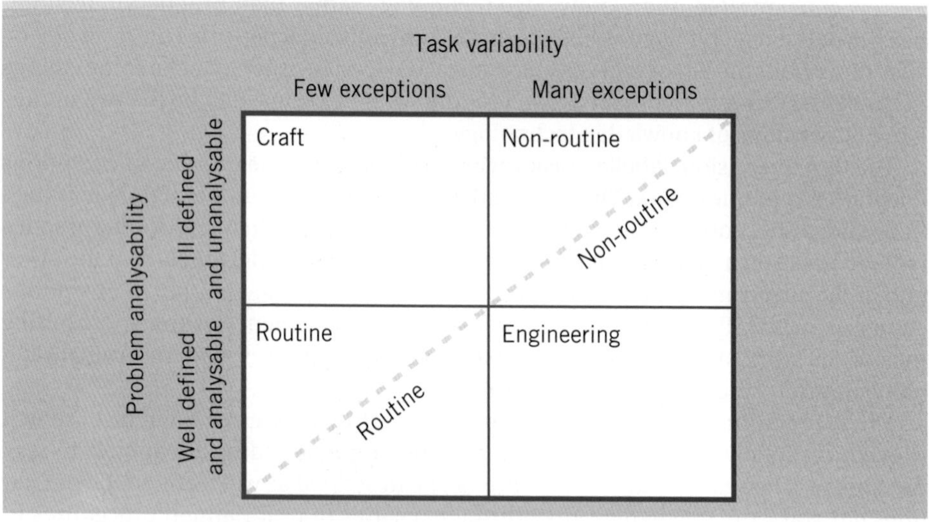
Task variability
Few exceptions
Many exceptions
Problem analysability
Ill defined and unanalysable
Well defined and analysable
Craft
Non-routine
Routine
Engineering
Non-routine
Routine

Figure 7.1 Perrow's technology classification

Similarly, if new, unusual or unfamiliar problems appear regularly, they will be in either cells 2 or 4. If problems are familiar, then cells 1 or 3 are appropriate.

Perrow also proposed that task variability and problem analysability were positively correlated. By that he meant that it would be unusual to find instances where tasks had very few exceptions and search was clearly unanalysable or where tasks had a great many exceptions and search was well defined and easily analysable. Thus the four technologies can be combined into a single routine–non-routine dimension. This is shown in Figure 7.1 as a diagonal line.

Perrow argued that control and coordination methods should vary with technology type. The more routine the technology, the more highly structured the organisation should be. Conversely, non-routine technologies require greater structural flexibility. Perrow then identified the key aspects of structure that could be modified to the technology:

- the amount of *discretion* that can be exercised for completing tasks
- the *power* of groups to control the unit's goals and basic strategies
- the extent of *interdependence* between these groups
- the extent to which these groups engage in *coordination* of their work, using either feedback or the planning of others.

How are these aspects of structure linked to the categories of technology? Most routine technology (cell 1) can be accomplished best through standardised coordination and control. These technologies should be aligned with structures that are high in both formalisation and centralisation. This is because the production process is repetitive and easily understood and the exceptions may be anticipated and planned for. At the other extreme, non-routine technologies (cell 4) demand flexibility. Basically, they would be decentralised, have high interaction among all members and be characterised as having a minimum degree of formalisation. The low formalisation derives from an inability to write rules about a constantly changing set of problems. In between, craft technology (cell 3) requires that problem solving be done by those with the greatest knowledge and experience. That means decentralisation. Engineering technology (cell 2), because it has many exceptions but analysable search processes, should have decisions centralised but should maintain flexibility through low formalisation. Table 7.2 summarises Perrow's predictions.

TABLE 7.2 Perrow's technology–structure predictions

		Structural characteristic			
Cell technology		**Formalisation**	**Centralisation**	**Span of control**	**Coordination and control**
1	Routine	High	High	Wide	Planning and rigid rules
2	Engineering	Low	High	Moderate	Reports and meetings
3	Craft	Moderate	Low	Moderate—wide	Training and meetings
4	Non-routine	Low	Low	Moderate—narrow	Group norms and group meetings

Evaluation

The two-by-two matrix of technologies and the predictions of what structural dimensions are most compatible with these technologies were not examined empirically by Perrow. But others have tested the theory.

One study, of 14 medium-sized manufacturing firms that looked only at the two extreme cells—routine and non-routine technologies—found support for Perrow's predictions.[7] Another, covering 16 health and welfare agencies, confirmed that organisations do have diverse technologies and that the more routine the work, the more likely it is that decision making will be centralised.[8]

State employment-service agencies were the set of organisations analysed in yet another test of Perrow's theory.[9] In this study, technology was operationalised at the unit rather than the organisational level, in the belief that if routineness of technology actually affects structure this effect should be greatest at the unit level. Again, the results proved consistent with Perrow's predictions: work that was high in routineness was associated with high formalisation.

Unlike Woodward, Perrow did not intend that his typology should be applied to the whole organisation, particularly if it was a large one. He viewed technology as being best measured at the work-group or individual level. Hence Perrow's model is applicable to all types of work in all nature of industries—provided we use the appropriate unit of analysis. This is because he viewed technology as a mental process, rather than a physical activity. So no matter whether a person is a clerk in the public service, a motor mechanic or the managing director of a large public corporation, the technology we use may be classified according to Perrow's typology.

In summary, there appears to be considerable support for Perrow's conclusions. Organisations and organisational subunits with routine technologies tend to have greater formalisation and centralisation than do their counterparts with non-routine technologies.

One note of caution before we move on! Perrow's original theory went somewhat beyond what we have presented here. He predicted, for instance, relationships between the type of technology and structural aspects such as hierarchical discretion levels and types of coordination. These other relationships have found limited support by way of empirical studies.[10] In part this arises because the more specific and detailed any theory becomes, the less it is able to be generalised to all situations. We point this out to acknowledge that Perrow has his critics and that there is a basis for attacking his theory. But at the general level—and by that we mean the issues of whether technologies can be differentiated on the basis of routineness and whether more routine technologies are associated with higher degrees of formalisation and centralisation—the evidence is largely supportive.

Technological uncertainty: Thompson's contribution

The third major contribution to the technology–structure literature has been made by James Thompson.[11] In contrast to Woodward and Perrow, Thompson is not a member of the technological-imperative school. Rather, as will be shown, Thompson's contribution lies in demonstrating that technology determines the selection of a strategy for reducing uncertainty and that specific structural arrangements can facilitate uncertainty reduction. It may be considered that his theory is more an environmental theory than one associated with technology, but it is normally considered under the general rubric of technology and we will continue the convention.

Background

Thompson sought to create a classification scheme that was sufficiently general to deal with the range of technologies found in complex organisations. He proposed three types that are differentiated by the tasks an organisational unit performs.

Long-linked technology

Long-linked technology was associated with tasks or operations which were sequentially interdependent. This technology is characterised by a fixed sequence of connected steps, as shown in Figure 7.2A. That is, activity A must be performed before activity B, activity B before activity C and so forth. Examples of **long-linked technology** include mass-production assembly lines and taking an aeroplane journey.

long-linked technology a fixed sequence of connected steps: sequentially interdependent tasks

Arising from sequential interdependence, efficiency requires a high level of coordination between activities. This leads to the major uncertainties facing management being on the input and output sides of the organisation. Acquiring raw materials, for instance, and disposing of finished goods become major areas of concern. As a result, management tends to respond to this uncertainty by controlling inputs and outputs.

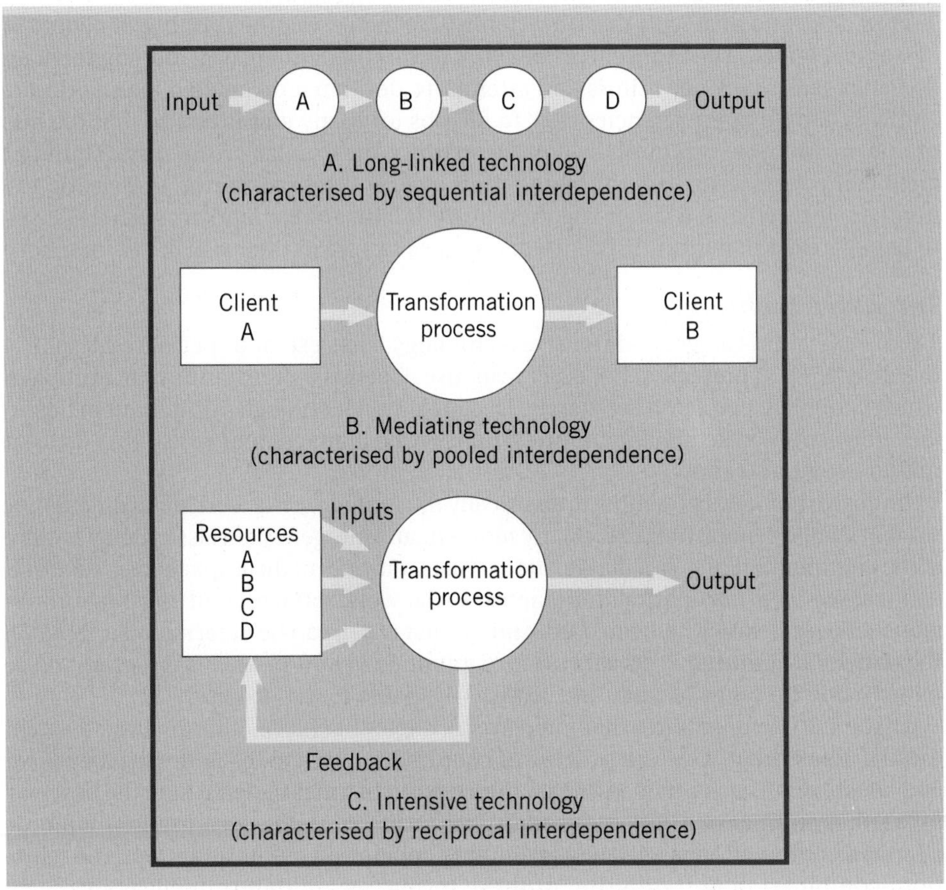
Input
A
B
C
D
Output
A. Long-linked technology
(characterised by sequential interdependence)
Client
A
Transformation
process
Client
B
B. Mediating technology
(characterised by pooled interdependence)
Resources
A
B
C
D
Inputs
Transformation
process
Output
Feedback
C. Intensive technology
(characterised by reciprocal interdependence)

FIGURE 7.2 Thompson's technology classification

One of the best means of achieving this is to integrate vertically—forwards, backwards, or both. This allows the organisation to encompass important sources of uncertainty within its boundaries. Comalco, for example, has large plants for manufacturing aluminium foil. It integrates backwards by controlling its inputs, operating aluminium smelters and refineries that provide the raw materials to the foil plants. It integrates forwards by controlling its output, marketing much of its foil through supermarkets under its own name.

Mediating technology

mediating technology the process of linking together different clients in need of each other's services: pooled interdependence

Thompson identified **mediating technology** as one that links clients on both the input and output side of the organisation. Banks, telephone companies, retail stores, insurance companies, employment and welfare agencies, and post offices are examples. As shown in Figure 7.2B mediators perform an interchange function, linking units that are otherwise independent. The linking unit responds by standardising the organisation's transactions and reducing variability in client expectations and behaviour. Banks, for instance, bring together those who want to save (depositors) with those who want to borrow. Neither of the groups knows each other, but the bank's success depends on attracting both. As a result, the managers of mediating technologies face uncertainty arising from the organisation's potential dependence on a small number of clients and the risks inherent in client transactions.

How does one deal with this uncertainty? By increasing the number of clients or customers served. The more clients one has, the less dependence on any single client. So banks seek many depositors and attempt to develop a diversified loan portfolio. Similarly, employment agencies seek to fill jobs for many employers so that the loss of one or two major accounts will not jeopardise the organisation's survival. Insurance companies also seek to reduce their overall levels of risk by increasing the numbers insured and diversifying their portfolio. Insurance markets such as Lloyds of London exist to permit insurance companies to spread their risk in this manner.

Intensive technology

intensive technology the utilisation of a wide range of customised responses, depending on the nature and variety of the problems: reciprocal interdependence

Thompson's third category—**intensive technology**—represents a specialised response to a diverse set of problems. The exact response depends on the nature of the problem which cannot be predicted accurately. This includes technologies dominant in hospitals, universities, research laboratories, full-service management consulting firms or military combat teams.

Intensive technology is most dramatically illustrated by the work of an emergency ward of a large general hospital. At any moment an emergency admission may require some combination of X-ray, diagnostic services, various medical specialties, pharmaceutical services, occupational therapies, social work services, and spiritual or religious services. Those which are used, and in what order, can be determined only when the patient is admitted.[12] What is pre-programmed is not the treatment given to the patient, but the range of skills and services available to the hospital.

Figure 7.2C demonstrates that intensive technology achieves coordination through mutual adjustment. This is a process of coordination where those involved observe and consult with each other and share information in order to determine the best way forward. A number of different resources are available to the organisation, but only a limited combination is used at a given time depending on the situation. The selection, combination and ordering of these resources are determined by feedback relating to the task being undertaken. Because of this need for flexibility of response, the major uncertainty that managers confront is the problem itself. They respond by ensuring the availability of a variety of resources to prepare for any contingency. As in our hospital example, the organisation has a wealth of specialised services and skills available with which it can respond to a variety of situations.

Structural implications

The structural implications from Thompson's framework are less straightforward than those derived from the work of Woodward or Perrow. Basically, each technology creates a type of interdependence. Long-linked technology is accompanied by *sequential interdependence*—the procedures are highly standardised and must be performed in a specified serial order. Mediating technology has *pooled interdependence*—two or more units each contribute separately to a larger unit. Intensive technology creates *reciprocal interdependence*—the outputs of units influence each other in a reciprocal fashion. Each of these interdependencies, in turn, demands a certain type of coordination that will facilitate organisational effectiveness yet minimise costs.

In general terms, we can translate Thompson's insights into structural terminology. He argued that the demands placed on decision making and communication as a result of technology increased from mediating (low) to long-linked (medium) to intensive (high). Mediating technology is coordinated most effectively through rules and procedures. It can do this because both sets of customers are grouped into predetermined categories and rules and regulations are set up for each category. Any customer who can't be categorised is rejected. This process also reduces organisational complexity by reducing the need for coordination and management of exceptions. Long-linked technology should be accompanied by extensive planning and scheduling. This process increases organisational complexity because of the need to accommodate changes to plan. This leads to a moderate level of formalisation: tasks can be standardised but there needs to be flexibility to respond to change. Intensive technology requires mutual adjustment. This implies high complexity arising from the needs of non-standardised problems. And because of this, formalisation must be low as there is little of a routine nature to standardise tasks and procedures around. These conclusions may be summarised as follows:

- mediating technology = low complexity and high formalisation
- long-linked technology = moderate complexity and formalisation
- intensive technology = high complexity and low formalisation.

Evaluation

There is, unfortunately, a shortage of data against which Thompson's predictions can be judged. The only study of consequence using Thompson's dimensions measured not structure but the relationship between technology and organisational effectiveness.[13] Analysing 297 subunits from 17 business and industrial firms, investigators were able to support part of Thompson's model. Long-linked and mediating technologies were associated closely with the use of standardisation, rules and advanced planning, whereas intensive technologies were characterised by mutual adjustments to other units. The investigators concluded that the criterion of effectiveness varies with the type of technology used by the organisational unit.

The lack of data makes it impossible to conclude whether Thompson's framework is empirically supported, but it does have face validity: that is, it appears to be a comprehensive model that explains the behaviour of organisations. It certainly permits a wide range of varying organisations to be compared. Its value, however, may lie far more in offering a rich and descriptive technology classification than in providing insight into the relationship between technology and structure.

Task uncertainty: Galbraith's contribution

We have seen that organisational technology involves transforming inputs into outputs. This process of transformation has different levels of uncertainty.[14] Jay Galbraith defined uncertainty as '. . . the difference between the amount of information required to perform a task and the amount of information already possessed by the organization'.[15] An example of a certain task with a high level of existing knowledge would be that undertaken by a checkout operator at a supermarket. An example of an uncertain task with smaller levels of existing knowledge would be designing a new type of jet aircraft, such as the 'stealth' bomber.

Background

The extent of uncertainty of the task itself was not of primary importance to Galbraith. Rather, he considered that as task uncertainty increased, so did the amount of information that had to be processed among decision makers in order to achieve the desired level of organisational performance. The amount of information, and how this information was processed, became the major determinant of the structure of the organisation.

Figure 7.3 shows how Galbraith has identified different organisation design strategies to accommodate different levels of uncertainty and information processing. In a straightforward routine task, such as the checkout operator mentioned above, rules and programs that reflect the existing knowledge of the organisation may be used. Any exception encountered is referred to a manager further up the hierarchy. Another method used to deal with uncertainty is the use of goals or targets. A complex task such as reconditioning a locomotive is guided by the fact that the task must be completed by a certain date. Those undertaking the reconditioning of the various subsystems, such as the electrics and the brakes, will be guided by the completion date. Once the goal is known, tasks can progress independently of each other.

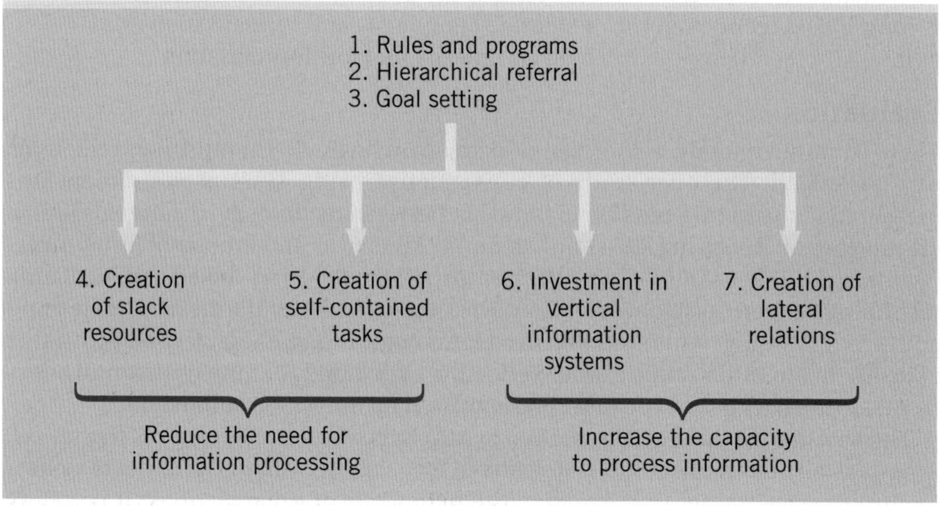
1. Rules and programs
2. Hierarchical referral
3. Goal setting
4. Creation of slack resources
5. Creation of self-contained tasks
6. Investment in vertical information systems
7. Creation of lateral relations
Reduce the need for information processing
Increase the capacity to process information

FIGURE 7.3 Galbraith's organisation design strategies

many parts, then shouldn't these parts, or subunits, exhibit variations in the technologies they use?

This differentiation has led to almost all large organisations and many of moderate size having multiple technologies. Averaging these subunits to arrive at a composite measure, or simply identifying one technology from among several and calling it the dominant technology, leads to diluting the effects of technology. We should expect studies assessing the technology–structure relationship at the organisational level of analysis, where there is a great deal of variation in technology between subunits, to result in aggregate measures that are likely to be meaningless. As we will see, this is precisely what happens.

Technology research has been undertaken at the organisational and work-unit levels. Both view technology as the means by which tasks are accomplished, but one considers the organisation as the unit of analysis and the other considers the work unit as the primary unit. Organisational-level analysis starts with the major product or service offered, which leads it to focus on the dominant conversion technology. Work-unit-level analysis starts with the tasks performed by the individual employees or the work unit, which in turn becomes the unit of study.

When these two types of studies are combined, it is difficult—if not impossible—to draw useful conclusions. However, when they are separated, a clear pattern emerges. The organisational-level studies are still mixed, with few consistent relationships appearing between technology and structure. But the work-unit-level studies have produced more consistent results. In an evaluation of the relationship between technology and a set of structural variables in eight work-unit-level studies, one study found that at least half the correlations were significant and all were in the same direction.[20]

Why do work-unit-level studies support the technological imperative, whereas those at the organisational level do not? Several explanations have been offered.[21] First, work-unit-level studies have far fewer conceptual and methodological problems. They have a simpler concept of technology, and similarity of work patterns amongst subjects is greater. The other reason for the high correlation between technology and structure at the work-unit level is undoubtedly related to size. Work-unit-level studies are researching technology at the operating core. If there is a technological imperative, this is where it should be most evident because technology's impact should be greatest closest to the core. Organisational-level studies have difficulties in defining and measuring technology in a manner appropriate for this level of analysis. This is particularly so in large organisations. The resultant inconsistent findings suggest that the technological imperative may have its greatest impact on small organisations or mid-sized organisations which are dominated by one technological type.

Special issues in organisational technology

There are a number of special issues in organisational technology, all of which will be discussed in some detail below.

Manufacturing and service technologies

Most studies investigating the impact of technology on organisation structure have been carried out on manufacturing organisations. However, an increasing number of the workforce is involved in providing services. There is also a third group, which can be called combined product and service firms. Figure 7.5 shows how service and manufacturing firms form the ends of a continuum and the typical industries in each category.

Most are familiar with the typical manufacturing firm, but what are the features of the service industries that make them different?[22] First, there is simultaneous production and consumption. Examples are a hairdresser cutting hair, the journey to work on the train, and services provided by a doctor. This also means that the customer is part of the production process and that the output is customised to the consumer's needs. Even mass-transit journeys are customised, to the extent that passengers are getting on the train or bus all the time at places to suit their requirements.

Another major difference is that the output of the service industries is often intangible: that is, it cannot be inventoried, stored or even seen. Watching a movie, undertaking a journey and attending a concert are all activities that cannot be inventoried to be drawn on in the future. Lastly, many services are labour-intensive. Hairdressing, medical services and personal fitness training all involve a labour intensity that is difficult to automate.

Do the characteristics of the service industries have an impact on their structure? Research shows that they do. One of the features of the service industries is that those providing the service come into direct contact with the customers of the organisation.[23] We continuously interact with transport, banking and retail employees, but rarely with those that make our cars or televisions. This means that service providers must stress interpersonal skills, which in turn indicates higher levels of training in the service industries, at least in communication and customer interface skills. It would

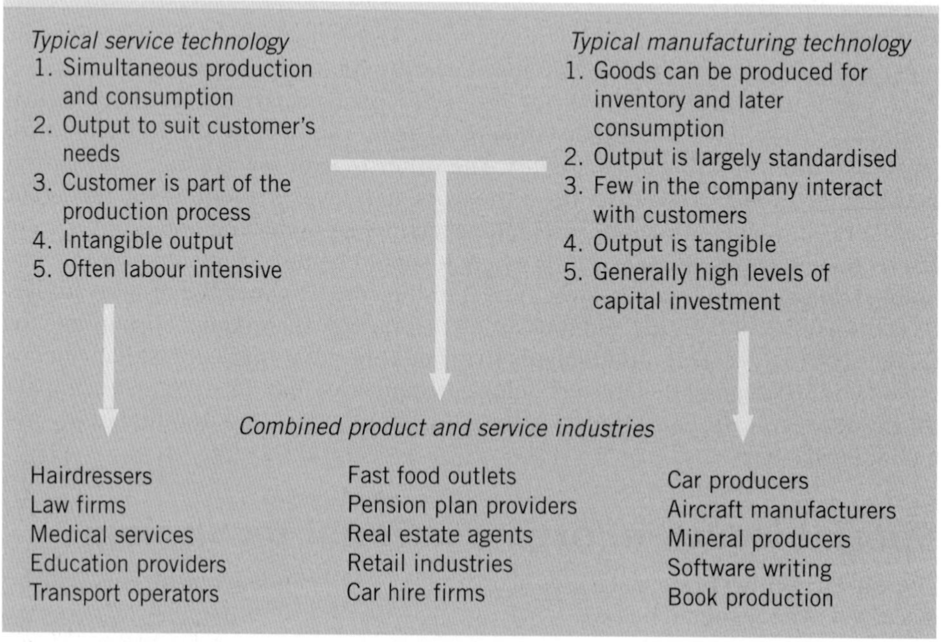
Typical service technology
1. Simultaneous production and consumption
2. Output to suit customer's needs
3. Customer is part of the production process
4. Intangible output
5. Often labour intensive
Typical manufacturing technology
1. Goods can be produced for inventory and later consumption
2. Output is largely standardised
3. Few in the company interact with customers
4. Output is tangible
5. Generally high levels of capital investment
Combined product and service industries
Hairdressers
Law firms
Medical services
Education providers
Transport operators
Fast food outlets
Pension plan providers
Real estate agents
Retail industries
Car hire firms
Car producers
Aircraft manufacturers
Mineral producers
Software writing
Book production

FIGURE 7.5 Examples of service and manufacturing technologies

Source: Adapted from David E. Bowen, Caren Siehl & Benjamin Schneider, 'A Framework for Analyzing Customer Service Orientations in Manufacturing', *Academy of Management Review*, 14, 1989, pp. 75–95.

make little difference to us if our car was assembled by grumpy workers, but irritable flight attendants can put an airline out of business.

Because of the need for customer interaction in service industries, decision making in relation to how the task is carried out tends to be more decentralised than in manufacturing. This applies not only in the professions, such as law and medicine: it extends to those in lesser skilled occupations such as hairdressers and taxi drivers, who must customise their output.

OT CLOSEUP
Customer contact requirements in the service industries

We noted that in the service industries those working in the operating core of the organisation came into regular contact with customers and, as a consequence, are part of the image which the company was trying to project. Alternatively, manufacturing employees were buffered from the environment and rarely or never came into customer contact. It is possible to identify the consequences of this by looking at the employee requirements in the two different types of industries.

Virgin Blue, for instance, is keen to project an image of fun, enthusiasm, innovation and freshness. Its cabin staff must meet the minimum requirements of drive for achievement, guest service orientation, teamwork and a desire to create a memorable and positive experience for all. Applicants must be punctual and reliable and enthusiastic and happy, and have a high standard of grooming.

The requirements for those working in the motor trades, however, are far more mundane. The minimum requirements of one car company is that applicants enjoy manual and practical work, have good hand–eye coordination, an eye for detail and a technical aptitude, and be interested in design and fabrication using metal and other products. Whilst having a pleasing personality and being well groomed would no doubt be an advantage, it is not a requirement for the job.

Another feature of service industries that influences their structure is that many tend to be both smaller and more geographically dispersed than manufacturing companies. In many service operations, such as hairdressers and restaurants, it is difficult to achieve economies of scale. And most services must be taken to where the customers are. This means that most service organisations are segregated into smaller operating units which may be managed on a decentralised basis.

How do manufacturing industries interact with their customers? They have what are termed 'boundary spanners', whose main task it is to interact with customers.[24] The boundary spanners have the effect of protecting the operating core from intrusions by customers, thus allowing work to proceed without interruptions. If we buy a new car and want to make an inquiry about the car's performance, we do not speak to a production-line worker who built the car, or to one of the engineers who designed it. Rather, we speak to a boundary spanner, such as a salesperson or distributor, who can generally handle our inquiry. We will address the issue of boundary spanners again in Chapter 8 when the impact of environment is discussed.

Technology and information processing

One of the greatest technological innovations of the past 40 years has been the application of computers to various organisational tasks. Often called the 'computer revolution', 'information technology' or 'high-tech', the new technologies originally applied computers to traditional tasks such as scheduling, coordination, storage of data and routine information manipulation and processing. In recent years, computers have been applied more intensively to communications and intercompany linkages, facilitating the emergence of modified organisational forms. Our interest in this technology concentrates upon the influence which it has upon organisational structure. To identify this influence, it is necessary to examine the forms that the new technologies have taken.

Before we do this, a word of warning! Research in this area has been greatly hampered by the difficulty in generating an appropriate definition of information technology suitable for research purposes.[25] As well, while the impact of computerisation may be found in just about every business activity, devising a unit of measurement for it is extremely difficult; there is no equivalent of the 'standard metre' in information technology research. Likewise, separating computerisation from other variables that can influence structure is a complex task with so many variables complementing each other. For instance, emails do not displace face-to-face or voice communication but rather change the nature of both. The influence of new technology is subtle and, in many cases, unpredictable as people and units learn to incorporate it into their working practices. Notwithstanding these difficulties, researchers have identified certain influences, which form the basis for our discussion.

information technology (IT) a generic term covering the application of computerised information-processing techniques to organisational operations

The technologies we consider may be grouped together under the heading of **information technologies (IT)**. IT is a general term covering a number of different categories of information processing.[26] The first is the one most usually associated with computers, that of undertaking tasks associated with the *day-to-day operations* of the organisation. Examples are routine accounting tasks, inventory control, information storage, and payroll calculations. The effect of this application is to improve efficiency, particularly in resource usage. The second grouping comprises *technologies that improve communication.* Examples include email, the Internet, intranets, file sharing and teleconferencing. These technologies help bring people together by creating a shared workspace, thus reducing the restraints imposed by geography and time and enabling them to do things they may not otherwise have been able to do. It also promotes coordination between individuals and subunits and, through the creation of central data banks, permits the wide dispersion of information throughout the organisation. Such linkages facilitate innovation and are particularly important for organisations which have a wide geographic spread and a complex range of tasks to undertake. The third grouping comprises *control systems.* These monitor and evaluate the performance of the organisation. They undertake much of the routine work associated with control. Such tasks as stock management, monitoring bank balances, maintaining budgets and keeping track of the costs of a vehicle fleet are typical control functions. They were often designed to conform to the existing control mechanisms of the organisation, but with the emergence of proprietary programs such as SAP, organisations are finding that in many cases they must restructure to fit the dictates of the program. The fourth application of IT is that of acting as a *decision support system.* In this role it supports the intellectual process of planning and decision making but cannot replace the intuitive insight of the decision maker. Functions such as calculating potential rates of return, generating spreadsheets, analysis of various financial projections, scenario planning and the use of computers to undertake quality-control evaluation are examples of this function. The fifth function of IT is *codifying the knowledge base.* Humans may be creative but their capacity to remember is limited and is subject to decay. This is particularly so when knowledge of a complete process is shared between individuals or units. Advances in IT have permitted the codification of knowledge and its dissemination throughout the organisation. This facilitates the ability to apply past and current knowledge to organisational problems. The fifth application of IT is to *promote innovation.* No longer do those involved in such areas as research, design, strategy and other innovative activities need to be located close to each other. They may now be dispersed, often across continents, and may communicate with each other using new technologies. Even those located close to each other benefit from access to databases and other information which may be shared more readily between team members. The last grouping is that which supports *interorganisational systems.* This facilitates the movement of information from the boundary of one organisation to another. IT therefore may be seen as providing a boundary-spanning role. The external environment may also be scanned faster using IT. We have previously mentioned email and the Internet, but many organisational networks have a need for their computer-based systems to communicate with one another. These may be based on business-to-business Internet linkages but may also include electronic data interchange. The links between airlines and travel agencies and between retailers and wholesalers, interbank transfers, and graphical and data interchanges between organisations producing different parts of a product are examples of interorganisational systems.

OT CLOSEUP

The death of distance

One of the great innovations of our time has been the development of technology to transmit information over vast distances at relatively little cost. How is this likely to affect the organisations we work for and manage? Frances Cairncross proposes that organisations will be affected in a number of ways. She identifies the following as being likely outcomes of the so-called information revolution.

The death of distance. Distance will no longer determine the cost of communicating electronically. Some types of work, such as share and futures trading, financial services and call centres, will work three shifts a day across the world's three main time zones.

Location will become unimportant. Companies will locate any screen-based activity wherever the best combination of skills and cost can be found.

Size will become irrelevant. Small companies will be able to offer services that previously could be offered only by large companies. Individuals anywhere with great ideas will attract global capital.

More customised content. Improved networks will allow individuals to order customised products.

A deluge of information. As information becomes plentiful and cheap, there will be a significant role for those who can filter, sift, process and edit it.

The loose-knit corporation. Many companies will become networks of independent specialists, leading to more employees working in smaller units or alone.

More minnows, more giants. On the one hand, the costs of starting a new business will decline and some barriers to entry will fall. Companies are also more likely to outsource to smaller companies. On the other, communication will amplify the strengths of brands and the power of networks.

Increased power of the brand. Anything fashionable—be it music, a clothing label or a travel destination—will receive wide exposure, increasing profitability.

Source: Adapted from Frances Cairncross, *The Death of Distance*, London: Orion Publishing, 1997.

These influences may be summarised as providing *information efficiencies* and *information synergies*.[27] Information efficiencies are the cost and time savings that result when IT permits individual employees to become more productive. This may be by facilitating simple tasks such as filing, maintaining records and paper processing. But it may also emerge from improving such functions as decision making, employee communication and the ability to access and analyse data, and by permitting employees to perform more complex tasks. Information synergies, on the other hand, emerge when two or more individuals or subunits use IT to collaborate across organisational boundaries. The subsequent benefits contribute to the innovativeness of the organisation and to organisational learning.

The influence of IT on structure

Isolating the influence of IT upon organisational structure, as distinct from contingency factors such as strategy, size and environment, is one which is fraught with methodological difficulties. But research indicates that relationships do exist. IT is an *enabling technology*, that is, it enables organisations to do things which they would not have otherwise been able to do. As a result, it differs from the other contingencies we have discussed in that its impact often generates opposite outcomes. For instance, IT may promote centralisation as well as decentralisation or large size as well as small size. Another way of putting this is that IT moderates the effect of other variables. The findings of the impact of IT on the main structural variables are discussed below and are summarised in Table 7.4.

TABLE 7.4 Summary of the influence of information technology usage on organisational structure

- **Extent of IT usage.** Most organisations use some form of IT. But those with dynamic and less routine work tend to use IT more intensively.
- **IT and formalisation.** IT facilitates formalisation of processes and systems but also reduces the need for routine tasks.
- **Impact on communication and coordination.** IT's ability to facilitate communication and coordination has permitted more complex work to be undertaken.
- **Impact on middle managers.** IT usage has led to a reduction in the number of middle managers in centralised organisations. In decentralised organisations, middle managers have tended to increase.
- **Impact on decision making.** IT tends to support lower-level, routine decision making rather than higher-level, conceptual decision making.
- **Impact of communication technologies.** IT has facilitated the dispersion of organisational activities and the formation of networks and clusters. It has reduced the cost of coordination and integration.
- **IT and size.** IT has facilitated the emergence of extremely large and complex organisations, but also smaller organisations which work together as networks.
- **Structure of IT departments.** These tend to reflect the structure of the organisation. If the organisation is centralised, so too will the IT department be centralised. The opposite also holds.

Source: Drawn from a discussion paper presented by Henry Ergas at the Reserve Bank of Australia Conference on Productivity and Growth, 1995, <www.rba.gov.au/PublicationsandResearch/Conferences/1995/>.

QUESTIONS

1 The case study highlights a number of changes that have occurred at NAB since the introduction of information technology. Link the changes to the type of technology introduced.

2 Use the information in the case to either support or reject the observation that technology has its greatest impact lower in the organisation and at the level of the individual or work group.

3 In this chapter the differences between service and manufacturing industries were discussed. Drawing upon the case, evaluate whether, for the average NAB employee, there is little difference in being in either a service or a manufacturing industry.

4 The case study portrays jobs which have become narrow in scope and closely monitored as a result of information technology. However, within a bank environment, many jobs have changed for the better as a result of IT. Where are these jobs likely to be located and how would IT impact upon them?

FURTHER READING

Louis W. Fry, 'Technology–Structure Research: Three Critical Issues', *Academy of Management Journal*, September 1982, pp. 532–52.

Jay Galbraith, *Designing Effective Organizations*, Reading, MA: Addison Wesley, 1973.

Michael Hammer and James Champy, *Reengineering the Corporation*, London: Nicholas Brealey, 2001.

Charles Perrow, 'A Framework for the Comparative Analysis of Organizations', *American Sociological Review*, April 1967, pp. 194–208.

Alain Pinsonneault & Kenneth L. Kraemer, 'The Impact of Information Technology on Middle Managers', *MIS Quarterly*, 17(3), 1993, pp. 271–92.

James D. Thompson, *Organizations in Action*, New York: McGraw-Hill, 1967.

Bob Travica, 'Information Aspects of New Organizational Designs: Exploring the Non-Traditional Organization', *Journal of the American Society for Information Sciences*, 49(13), 1998, pp. 1224–44.

Joan Woodward, *Industrial Organization: Theory and Practice*, London: Oxford University Press, 1965.

NOTES

1 Joan Woodward, *Industrial Organization: Theory and Practice*, London: Oxford University Press, 1965.

2 Edward Harvey, 'Technology and the Structure of Organizations', *American Sociological Review*, April 1968, pp. 247–59.

3 William L. Zwerman, *New Perspectives on Organization Theory*, Westport, CN: Greenwood Publishing, 1970.

4 See, for example, Lex Donaldson, 'Woodward Technology, Organizational Structure, and Performance—A Critique of the Universal Generalization', *Journal of Management Studies*, October 1976, pp. 255–73.

5 Charles Perrow, 'A Framework for the Comparative Analysis of Organizations', *American Sociological Review*, April 1967, pp. 194–208.

6 ibid.

7 Karl Magnusen, 'Technology and Organizational Differentiation: A Field Study of Manufacturing Corporations', Doctoral dissertation, University of Wisconsin, Madison, 1970.

8 Jerald Hage & Michael Aiken, 'Routine Technology, Social Structure, and Organizational Goals', *Administrative Science Quarterly*, September 1969, pp. 366–77.
9 Andrew H. Van de Ven & André L. Delbecq, 'A Task Contingent Model of Work-Unit Structure', *Administrative Science Quarterly*, June 1974, pp. 183–97.
10 See, for example, Lawrence Mohr, 'Operations Technology and Organizational Structure', *Administrative Science Quarterly*, December 1971, pp. 444–59.
11 James D. Thompson, *Organizations in Action*, New York: McGraw-Hill, 1967.
12 ibid, p. 17.
13 Thomas A. Mahoney & Peter J. Frost, 'The Role of Technology in Models of Organizational Effectiveness', *Organizational Behavior and Human Performance*, February 1974, pp. 122–38.
14 Jay Galbraith, *Designing Effective Organizations*, Reading, MA: Addison Wesley, 1973.
15 ibid, p. 5.
16 It is interesting that a careful review of a recent study that proposes to give renewed support to the technological imperative (see Robert M. Marsh & Hiroshi Mannari, 'Technology and Size as Determinants of the Organizational Structure of Japanese Factories', *Administrative Science Quarterly*, March 1981, pp. 33–57) finds that complexity and formalisation are a function of size and that centralisation varies randomly in relation to both technology and size.
17 See, for example, David J. Hickson, D.S. Pugh & Diana C. Pheysey, 'Operations Technology and Organization Structure: An Empirical Reappraisal', *Administrative Science Quarterly*, September 1979, pp. 378–97; and D.S. Pugh, D.J. Hickson, C.R. Hinings & C. Turner, 'The Context of Organization Structures', *Administrative Science Quarterly*, March 1969, pp. 91–114.
18 Hickson et al., 'Operations Technology and Organization Structure: An Empirical Reappraisal'.
19 Donald Gerwin, 'Relationships between Structure and Technology at the Organizational and Job Levels', *Journal of Management Studies*, February 1979, p. 71; and James L. Price & Charles W. Mueller, *Handbook of Organizational Measurement*, Marshfield, MA: Pitman, 1986, pp. 209–14.
20 Donald Gerwin, 'Relationships between Structure and Technology at the Organizational and Job Levels'.
21 ibid; and Louis W. Fry, 'Technology–Structure Research: Three Critical Issues', *Academy of Management Journal*, September 1982, pp. 532–52.
22 David E. Bowen, Caren Siehl & Benjamin Schneider, 'A Framework for Analyzing Customer Service Orientations in Manufacturing', *Academy of Management Review*, 14, 1989, pp. 79–95; Peter K. Mills & Newton Margulies, 'Towards a Core Typology of Service Organisations', *Academy of Management Review*, 5, 1980, pp. 225–65; and Peter K. Mills & Dennis J. Moberg, 'Perspectives on the Technology of Service Operations', *Academy of Management Review*, 7, 1982, pp. 467–78.
23 Richard B. Chase & David A. Tansik, 'The Customer Contact Model for Organization Design', *Management Science*, 29, 1983, pp. 1037–50.
24 ibid.
25 Karlene H. Roberts & Martha Grabowski, 'Organizations, Technology and Structuring', in Stewart Clegg, Cynthia Hardy & Walter Nord, eds, *Handbook of Organization Studies*, London: Sage, 1996.
26 This classification is derived from Daniel Robey, *Designing Organizations*, 2nd edn, Homewood, Ill: Irwin, 1986; and Todd Dewett & Gareth Jones, 'The Role of Information Technology in the Organization: A Review, Model and Assessment', *Journal of Management*, 27(3), 2001, p. 313.
27 Dewett & Jones, ibid. Much of the discussion in this section is drawn from this article.
28 Lorin Hitt & Erik Brynjolfsson, 'Information Technology and Internal Firm Organization: An Exploratory Analysis', *Journal of Management Information Systems*, 14(2), 1997, pp. 81–101.

29 Bob Travica, 'Information Aspects of New Organizational Designs: Exploring the Non-Traditional Organization', *Journal of the American Society for Information Sciences*, 49(13), 1998, pp. 1224–44.
30 Nicholas Argyris, 'The Impact of Information Technology on Coordination: Evidence from the B2 "Stealth" Bomber', *Organization Science*, 10(2), 1999, pp. 162–80.
31 Erik Brynjolfsson, 'Information Assets, Technology and Organization', *Management Science*, 40(12), 1994, pp. 1645–62.
32 Dewett & Jones op. cit.
33 Alain Pinsonneault & Kenneth L. Kraemer, 'The Impact of Information Technology on Middle Managers', *MIS Quarterly*, 17(3), 1993, pp. 271–92; Daniel Robey, 'Computers and Management Structure: Some Empirical Findings Re-examined', *Human Relations*, 30, 1977, pp. 963–76; and Teresa Heintze and Stuart Bretschneider, 'Information Technology and Restructuring in Public Organizations: Does Adoption of Information Technology Affect Organizational Structures, Communications and Decision Making' *Journal of Public Administration Research and Theory*, Oct 2000, pp. 801–30.
34 C. Ferioli & P. Migliarese 'Supporting Organizational Relations through Information Technology in Innovative Organizational Forms', *European Journal of Information Systems*, 5(3), 1996, pp. 196–207.
35 Dewett & Jones, 'The Role of Information Technology in the Organization: A Review, Model and Assessment'.
36 Andrew Stein, 'Re-engineering the Executive: The 4th Generation of EIS', *Information Management*, 29(1), 1995, pp. 55–62.
37 H. Simon, 'Applying Information Technology to Organization Design', *Public Administration Review*, 1973, pp. 268–78.
38 Roberts & Grabowski, 'Organizations, Technology and Structuring'.
39 Pinsonneault & Kraemer, 'The Impact of Information Technology on Middle Managers'.
40 Roberts & Grabowski, 'Organizations, Technology and Structuring'.
41 See, for instance, David Pearce Snyder, 'Extra-preneurship: Reinventing Enterprise for the Information Age', *The Futurist*, July–August 2005, pp. 47–53.
42 Dewett & Jones, 'The Role of Information Technology in the Organization: A Review, Model and Assessment'.
43 Huber G.P. 'A Theory of the Effects of Advanced Information Technologies on Organizational Design, Intelligence, and Decision Making', *Academy of Management Review*, 15(1), 1990, pp. 47–71.
44 Dewett & Jones, 'The Role of Information Technology in the Organization: A Review, Model and Assessment'.
45 Michael J. Mandel, 'The New Business Cycle', *Business Week*, 31 March 1997, pp. 48–54.
46 Kirk Fiedler, Varun Grover & James T.C. Teng, 'An Empirically Derived Taxonomy of Information Technology Structure and its Relationship to Organization Structure', *Journal of Management Information Systems*, 13(1), Summer 1996, pp. 9–34.
47 ibid; and William King & Vikram Sethi, 'An Empirical Assessment of the Organization of Transnational Information Systems', *Journal of Management Information Systems*, 15(4), 1999, pp. 7–28.
48 Joan Graef, 'Getting the Most from R and D Information Services', *Research-Technology Management*, 41(4), 1998, pp. 44–7.
49 See, for instance, Majed Al-Mashari & Abdullah Al-Mudimigh, 'ERP Implementaion; Lessons from a Case Study', *Information, Technology and People*, 16(1), 2003, pp. 21–34; and Fawzy Soliman & Mohamed A. Yousef, 'The Role of SAP Software in Business Process Reengineering', *International Journal of Productions and Operations Management*,18(9/10), 1998, p. 886.
50 For an Australian example, see Ian Martin & Yen Cheung, 'SAP and Business Process Reengineering', *Business Process Management Journal*, 6(2), 2000, p. 113.
51 Wanda J. Orlikowski, 'Using Technology and Constituting Structures: A Practice Lens for Studying Technology in Organizations', *Organization Science*, July/August, 2000, pp. 404–30.

52 Ibid.

53 Patricia L. Nemetz & Louis W. Fry, 'Flexible Manufacturing Organizations: Implications for Strategy Formulation and Organization Design', *Academy of Management Review*, October 1988; and Wayne F. Cascio & Raymond F. Zammuto, 'Societal Trends and Staffing Policies', in Wayne F. Cascio, ed., *Human Resource Planning, Employment and Placement*, Washington, DC: BNA/ASPA, 1989.

54 See, for example, Stanley H. Udy, Jr, *Organization of Work*, New Haven, CN: HRAF Press, 1959; Hickson et al., op. cit.; and Raymond G. Hunt, 'Technology and Organization', *Academy of Management Journal*, September 1970, pp. 235–52.

55 Gerwin, 'Relationships between Structure and Technology at the Organizational and Job Levels'.

56 Hage & Aiken, 'Routine Technology, Social Structure, and Organizational Goals'.

57 Andrew Van de Ven, André Delbecq & Richard Koenig, Jr, 'Determinants of Coordination Modes within Organizations', *American Sociological Review*, April 1976, pp. 322–38.

58 Jerald Hage & Michael Aiken, 'Relationship of Centralization to Other Structural Properties', *Administrative Science Quarterly*, June 1967, pp. 72–92.

CHAPTER 8

Environment

After reading this chapter you should be able to:

- define environment from an organisational theory perspective
- differentiate between the specific and the general environment
- explain the key dimensions of environmental uncertainty
- describe the contributions of Burns and Stalker, Lawrence and Lorsch, and Duncan
- review the contributions of population ecology, institutional theory and resource dependence
- describe the effect of environmental uncertainty on complexity, formalisation and centralisation.

Introduction

James Hardie—from fibro in suburbia to mesothelioma and the US siding market

Any organisation which has been established for over a century has had to adapt to considerable environmental change over time. Most face significant technological, legal, economic and social change, and James Hardie has had to adapt to all four. Established in the late 19th century by two Scotsmen, James Hardie and Andrew Reid, James Hardie grew to prominence manufacturing the humble sheet of fibro, a building material commonly used to clad the outside of low-cost housing. Fibro is short for fibrous plaster, and its main components were asbestos and cement, mixed together and then dried to form a sheet. It is now widely known that when breathed in asbestos causes extensive disabilities and can even lead to deadly lung diseases such as mesothelioma.

Fibro was used extensively up to the 1980s, but was not the only form of asbestos used. Asbestos was applied extensively in industry, particularly as a form of insulation, much of it supplied by companies other than James Hardie. Up to the late 1970s, sales of fibro were buoyant and James Hardie was one of the more successful companies in Australia, with profitability increasing year by year. But first slowly, then in an increasing rush, the health impact of using asbestos became more widely known. Knowledge linking asbestos to health issues had been around for some time and James Hardie, and other companies in Australia and overseas, found themselves facing significant legal liability to their workers and to the users of asbestos. In the US, many companies with asbestos liabilities filed for bankruptcy and claims against insurance companies brought many almost to their knees, including many syndicates of Lloyds of London.

Faced with the almost complete elimination of its core product, James Hardie attempted to diversify into entirely different industries ranging from telecommunications to healthcare. But it was research into a new form of fibre sheeting, this time using cellulose from trees in place of asbestos, which was to play the largest part in James Hardie's resurgence. Finding a ready market for the product, particularly as external walling, or siding, for houses in the US, the company decided to sell all its unrelated businesses and become a pure fibre cement manufacturer.

But James Hardie had to deal with the legacy of liabilities arising from its days as an asbestos manufacturer. As most of its operations were now overseas, and because of a more favourable tax regime, in 2001 James Hardie moved its legal registration as a company to the Netherlands but kept its ASX listing. In order to cover claims against it, it set up a trust fund with $293 million, to compensate victims of asbestos.

By 2005, it became apparent that the trust fund was at least $1.5 billion underfunded and accusations circulated that James Hardie had left Australia to avoid its legal liabilities and, in the process, had avoided adequately compensating victims of asbestosis. Unions, governments and the media all entered into the debate and claims of unethical conduct against James Hardie became a common theme. Subsequent moves by James Hardie to top up the fund did little to quell community concern and threats of boycotts against James Hardie products were made. During the controversy the managing director was forced to resign. James Hardie found itself facing multiple, conflicting environments. On the one hand, it was operating a successful business with expanding US sales and promising markets elsewhere, but at the same time it was fending off claims of unethical conduct involving avoiding its legal liabilities.

Intuitively we accept that there is a close interaction between an organisation and its environment. Similarly, most of us have witnessed the establishment and demise of many organisations. One framework which is widely accepted as explaining the dependency of the organisation upon its environment is that of the open-systems framework, discussed in Chapter 1. Using that framework, we identified that the key to understanding organisations as open systems was the recognition that organisations exist within an environment which they must respond to. But since that introduction we have said little about the environment and its interaction with the organisation. In this chapter, that omission will be rectified.

A common theme in organisation theory is that organisations must adapt to their environments if they are to maintain or increase their effectiveness. In open-system terms, we can think of organisations as developing mechanisms to monitor their environment, adapting their behaviour to suit the environmental changes they identify and feeding the subsequent changes back into the environment. At James Hardie, management first found that the environment was supportive of its activities and the high demand for its products led to company-wide expansion. However, its environment slowly changed. Its products were found to be injurious to health and it reacted with confusion as to what to do about it. Though a new path for expansion was eventually found, old liabilities refused to go away and continued to plague the company. Again the company misjudged the environmental pressures upon it. The company found that it was running a successful business, but an unsuccessful public relations exercise, and the two were beginning to merge and threaten the whole business.

In this chapter we clarify what we mean by the term environment and assess the relationship between environment and structure. This relationship forms a central part of organisational theory because of the many and varied complex linkages between an organisation and its environment. Arising from the centrality of this relationship, there is no shortage of theorising and empirical work associated with it. We will be introducing much of this work as the chapter unfolds. An important theme running through the early part of the chapter is that different organisations face varying degrees of environmental uncertainty. As managers do not like uncertainty, they try to minimise its impact on their organisation. We demonstrate that structural design is a major tool that managers may draw upon for controlling and living with environmental uncertainty. In the latter part of the chapter, we will discuss a number of theories which take a more macro view of how the organisation draws upon, and influences, its environment.

Defining environment

There is no shortage of definitions of environment. Their common thread is that it consists of factors outside the organisation itself. For instance, the most popular definition identifies the environment as everything outside an organisation's boundaries. Another author has proposed that ascertaining an organisation's environment appears simple enough: 'Just take the universe, subtract from it the subset that represents the organisation, and the remainder is environment'.[1] We agree with this writer when he adds that, unfortunately, it isn't that simple. First, let us differentiate between an organisation's general environment and its specific environment.

General versus specific environment

An organisation's environment and general environment are essentially the same. The latter includes everything, such as economic factors, political conditions, the social

general environment conditions that potentially have an impact on the organisation

milieu, the legal structure, the ecological situation and cultural conditions. The **general environment** encompasses conditions that *may* have an impact on the organisation, but their relevance is not particularly clear. Consider the price and availability of petrol in the general environment of cinema chains such as Greater Union. At first glance it may appear that Greater Union has little to worry about in relation to petrol supply, as it is not a major input into its business. But should there be a significant increase in the price of petrol, or a shortage either through strikes or some other interruption, then Greater Union is likely to be hard hit. This is because many cinema patrons travel by car, and if petrol is either unavailable or expensive, they are likely to be more careful as to what trips they make. However, for most of the time, the price and availability of petrol is a distant concern for Greater Union: most of its attention is paid to the specific environment.

specific environment the part of the environment that is directly relevant to the organisation in achieving its goals

The **specific environment** is that part of the environment that is directly relevant to the organisation in achieving its goals. At any given moment, it is that part of the environment with which management will be concerned, because it is made up of the critical constituencies that can positively or negatively influence the organisation's effectiveness. It is unique to each organisation and it changes with conditions. Typically, it will include clients or customers, suppliers of inputs, competitors, governments, unions, trade associations and public pressure groups. The operator of Sydney airport is in the specific environment of Air New Zealand but in the general environment of Woolworths. On the other hand, the bakers of Tip Top bread are in the specific environment of Woolworths but in the general environment of Air New Zealand. Figure 8.1 shows the general and specific environments of a refrigerator manufacturer.

domain an organisation's niche that it has staked out for itself with respect to products or services offered and markets served

An organisation's specific environment will vary depending on the domain it has chosen. **Domain** refers to the claim that the organisation stakes out for itself with respect to the range of products or services offered and markets served. It identifies the organisation's niche. Volkswagen and Mercedes-Benz are both German firms that manufacture motor vehicles, but they operate in distinctly different domains. Similarly, Toowoomba TAFE and James Cook University are both higher education institutions in Queensland, but they do substantially different things and appeal to different segments of the higher education market. These two institutions have identified different domains.

Why is the concept of domain important? It is because the domain of an organisation determines the points at which it is dependent on its specific environment.[2] Change the domain and you will change the specific environment. And it is from the specific environment that most of the pressure on organisations is initially felt.

Actual versus perceived environment

Any attempt to define environment requires making a distinction between the objective or actual environment and the one that managers perceive. Evidence indicates that measures of the actual characteristics of the environment and measures of characteristics perceived by management are not highly correlated.[3] Furthermore, it is perceptions—not reality—that lead to the decisions that managers make regarding organisation design. In other words, managers enact, that is act upon, the environment they perceive.

Unfortunately, we lack the ready means of assessing and measuring how fast an environment is changing or how stable it might be. We must rely upon comparing environments and making informed judgements as to the differences between them. There may be general agreement that new technologies in the telecommu-

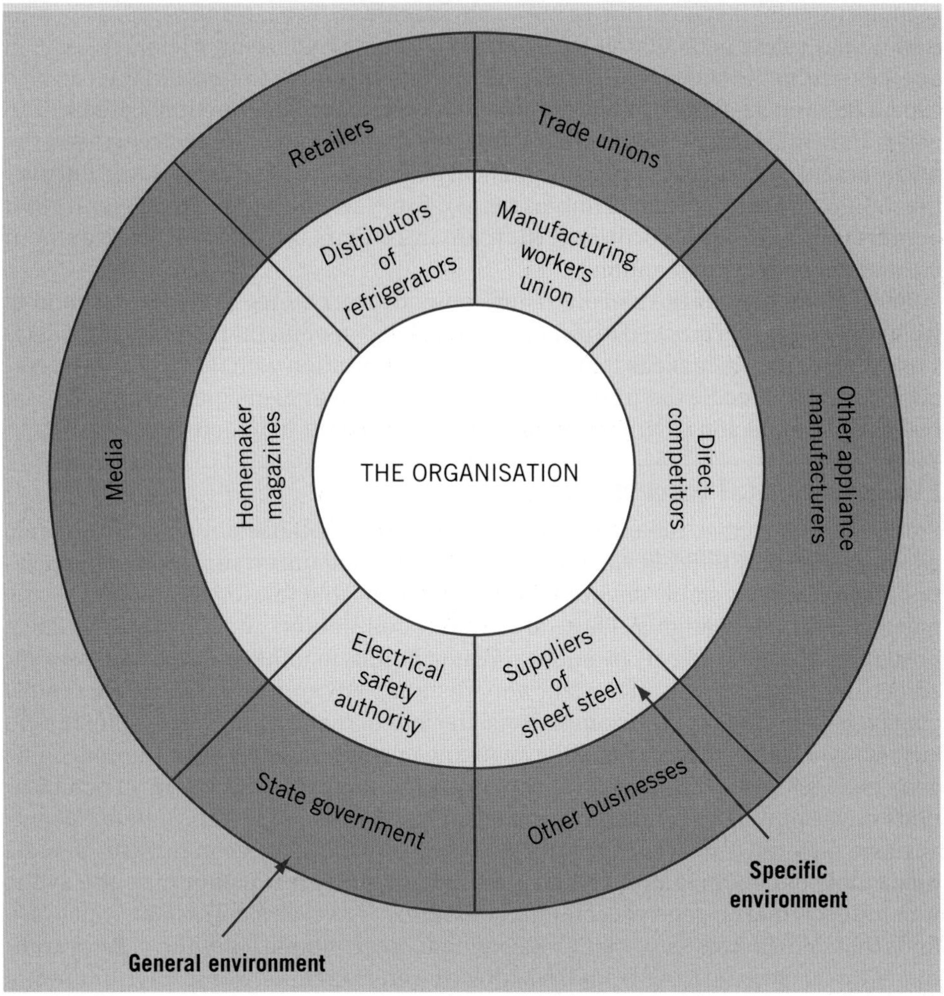
Retailers
Trade unions
Distributors of refrigerators
Manufacturing workers union
Media
Homemaker magazines
THE ORGANISATION
Direct competitors
Other appliance manufacturers
Electrical safety authority
Suppliers of sheet steel
State government
Other businesses
Specific environment
General environment

FIGURE 8.1 The general and specific environment of a refrigerator manufacturer

nications industry are leading to rapid environmental change for those in the industry, and that manufacturers of basic foods, such as noodles and breakfast cereals, face a stable environment. But the same environment that one organisation perceives as unpredictable and complex may be seen as static and easily understood by another organisation.[4] The bakers of Tip Top bread may feel that their environment is unstable, with variations in the price of inputs and demanding distributors to contend with. But compared to a fire-fighting organisation, Tip Top enjoys the most stable of environments.

Classifying environments which are partly stable and partly changing raises further issues. For instance, part of an airline's environment, for example, ticketing, is very stable, predictable and repetitive, but actions of competitors and of the weather can very quickly create instability in the environment. A further problem arises with determining what is specific. There are obvious things in the environment which are important to an organisation, the price of jet fuel to an airline and iron ore to a steel manufacturer for instance. But, in not so obvious areas, those in one part of an organisation may select parts of that environment as being important, whereas people in another part of the same organisation see something else as important. You can also expect differences based on background, education and the functional area within which individuals work. Even senior managers in the same firm are likely to see the environment dissimilarly and many political power games have been played out over the right to determine what is important in a firm's environment. This suggests that organisations construct or invent their environments and that the environment created depends on perception.

Remember that it is the perceived environment that counts. Managers respond to what they see. As we proceed in our discussion, keep in mind that the structural decisions that managers make to better align their organisation with the degree of uncertainty in their specific environment depend on the managers' perception of what makes up the specific environment and their assessment of uncertainty.

Environmental uncertainty

From our perspective, the environment is important because not all environments are the same. They differ in what we call environmental uncertainty. Some organisations face relatively stable environments; this means that few forces in their specific environment are changing. There are no new competitors, no new technological breakthroughs, little activity by public pressure groups to influence the organisations, and so on. Other organisations face very dynamic environments: there are rapidly changing technologies, new competitors, the loss of major customers, difficulties in acquiring raw materials, continually changing customer preferences, unpredictable price changes and so on. The number of uncertainties that may exist in an organisation's environment also influences management action. For instance, hotels generally face only one major uncertainty, and that is the level of demand. This may be predictable depending upon known seasonal and other factors but may also swing widely depending on general economic conditions. However, a rail system, which also finds that demand for its services is dependent on economic conditions, faces additional uncertainty arising from breakdowns and accidents. Some environmental uncertainties are easier to predict, and therefore manage, than others. Mining companies know that their main uncertainty is the price of the commodity they produce; they can manage this uncertainty by hedging, being prudent with borrowings and constantly monitoring costs. Retail stores know that the level of economic growth affects their sales; low growth leads to low sales. As they have been through this cycle many times before, they have a set of responses they have learned from experience to handle the situation (e.g. sales, discounting and various forms of promotion). But most importantly they know that there is little alternative but to wait until growth rates improve. Alternatively, some environmental change is difficult to understand. This particularly applies to technological change. The introduction of the Internet and e-commerce saw many managers facing difficult decisions. Managers felt that unless they embraced the new technologies their companies would be disadvantaged. Their confusion was compounded by the considerable overselling of many of the benefits of e-commerce by early-adopting proponents. But its impact was poorly understood, difficult to predict, and at least in the short term not as great as expected. As most managers had no experience of a similar technology to fall back on, and were afraid of being 'left behind', their perceived environmental uncertainty was high.

Stable environments and those that are easier to predict create significantly less uncertainty for managers than do dynamic ones, and as uncertainty is a threat to an organisation's effectiveness management will try to minimise it.[5] Later in this chapter we show that managements' concern is with reducing the impact of environmental uncertainty upon the organisation, and that this can be accomplished through the adoption of an appropriate organisation structure.

OT CLOSEUP

How easy is it to read the environment?

Reading this chapter may give the impression that understanding the environment and responding to it is a fairly easy task. Certainly, in some ways it is. A transport company, for instance, knows the relationship between how much fuel it uses, its price and the profitability of the company. But major technological innovations are more difficult to identify and respond to. Most major technological innovations have taken time to disseminate throughout the business world, and managers have had to ride the experience curve to determine how innovations can best be used. The steamship, the telephone, aircraft, motor transport and computerisation are just a few innovations that have had a slow introduction but which, when the technology was fully developed, pushed aside all competing technologies.

So how do you know when one of these major innovations has been made and, more importantly, how do you know how to respond? Andy Grove provides some useful insight. Andy Grove is a co-founder of Intel, one of the icons of the microprocessor age. His observations derive from the impact of computerisation on organisations. He sees the Internet as having a similar, if not greater, long-term impact than any of the other major innovations to date, even though many of the benefits were overhyped by e-commerce proponents in the late 1990s. (Remember that the Internet was no overnight introduction: its use dates back to the 1970s.)

Grove calls major technological innovations strategic inflection points. So how do you know you are at a strategic inflection point? Most of the time, recognition takes place in stages. First is the subtle uneasiness that something is different. Customers' attitudes change and new competitors emerge from out of nowhere armed with the new technology. Second, there is a dissonance between what your company thinks it is doing and what is actually happening within the organisation. This type of chaos always exists, but at strategic inflection points it is quantitatively different. Eventually a new set of actions emerges, which is more like a rebirth than the normal adaptation process. Often this occurs under a new management with a fundamentally different understanding of how the new technology affects the business.

So when is the right moment to take appropriate action? Unfortunately, you don't know, but you cannot afford to be late. The company must change while it is still healthy and generating cash, and that implies acting when not everything is known. This places a premium on judgement, intuition and instinct; nothing else will get you through. Grove is ever-hopeful. He claims that it is possible to pick the strategic inflection points by looking at them using a different frame, or mindset, from the one we have been used to. The signals are out there and capable of being read by those with the appropriate perception.

Of course, the strategic inflection points may put you out of business if you are right where they are operating. Intuition and judgement did not save sailing ship owners or horse-drawn carriage manufacturers.

Source: Adapted from Andy Grove, *Only the Paranoid Survive: How to Exploit the Crisis Points which Challenge Every Company and Career*, New York: HarperBusiness, 1996.

The enacted environment

The process through which the actual and perceived environments interact in relation to environmental uncertainty has been explained in an interpretation called the enacted environment.[6] Proponents of the enacted environment claim that uncertainty and the environment exist simultaneously within the decision maker's head. There then commences a cycle of searching for information in order to reduce uncertainty, leading to a perception of more uncertainty because of the information gathered. This feeds into a need to gather more information, and so environmental uncertainty becomes enacted within the decision maker's mind. Uncertainty is not reduced by more information, but rather the amount of information increases uncertainty. Because this approach highlights how environments are enacted in the decision maker's mind, it is sometimes called the social constructionist view of environments and may be seen to be related to the postmodern concept of the social constructionist view of reality.

Environmental enactment explains how the introduction of computers may have increased uncertainty. Take the example of a breakfast cereal manufacturer. Whereas 30 years ago the manufacturer may have simply produced the cereal, put it on the supermarket shelves and received quarterly sales reports, the same manufacturer is now able to process information as to who is buying the product and why, how competing products are selling, and how sales vary between different demographics and geographic regions. Pressure to improve performance can therefore be exerted on poorly performing brands. With all this considered, it would not be surprising if the cereal manufacturer considered that the environment had become far more uncertain and exerted a greater impact upon the organisation than it did 30 years ago.

As much as enactment theory helps explain how environments are perceived, for most of this chapter we will take what may be called a normative view of environments. That is, it is possible, at least for our purposes, to consider environments along certain dimensions, such as uncertainty, and that managers perceive environments in fairly predictable ways. Further, the response to these perceptions, particularly the structural responses, conforms to patterns which may be categorised. The next section introduces landmark studies which inform the environmental imperative.

Landmark contributions

There is no shortage of research on the influence of environments on organisations. But much of the research may be summarised in the work of just a few researchers who have made landmark contributions. Here we have summarised the work of Burns and Stalker, Lawrence and Lorsch, and Duncan.

Burns and Stalker

Tom Burns and G.M. Stalker studied 20 English and Scottish industrial firms to determine how their organisational structure and managerial practice might differ depending on different environmental conditions.[7] Using interviews with managers and their own observations, they evaluated the firms' environmental conditions in terms of the rate of change in their scientific technology and their relevant product markets. What they found was that the type of structure that existed in rapidly changing and dynamic environments was significantly different from that in organisations with stable environments. Burns and Stalker labelled the two structures organic and mechanistic, respectively.

Mechanistic structures are characterised by high complexity, formalisation and centralisation. Job specialisation is high, with each worker only making a small contribution to the final output. Efforts are concentrated on improving technical processes rather than the final product. Power and knowledge reside in the management hierarchy, which decides how work will be accomplished. They also decide on the rights and responsibilities of workers. Most flow of information and communication is vertical, that is, up and down the hierarchy. Emphasis is placed upon knowledge of internal processes rather than general knowledge of the environment.

mechanistic structure a structure characterised by high complexity, formalisation and centralisation

Organic structures are relatively flexible and adaptive, with an emphasis on knowledge. There is an emphasis on lateral communication, that is, between individuals wherever they are located, rather than communication up and down a hierarchy. As a result of this network of communication, tasks are continuously redefined through interaction with others. Commitment to the firm is valued more highly than obedience and adherence to established procedures. Power and influence derives from knowledge and expertise, rather than position in the hierarchy, and top managers are not considered to be the repository of all knowledge. Problems are not passed up the hierarchy or passed onto others, but are addressed by the person experiencing the problem. The content of communication consists mainly of information and advice rather than instructions and decisions. The characteristics of these structures are summarised in Table 8.1.

organic structure flexible and adaptive structures, with emphasis on lateral communication, non-authority-based influence and loosely defined responsibilities

Burns and Stalker believed that the most effective structure is one that adjusts to the requirements of the environment, which means using a mechanistic design in a stable, certain environment and an organic form in a turbulent environment. However, they recognised that the mechanistic and organic forms were types which formed two ends of a continuum; they did not present themselves as polar opposites from which one must be selected. No organisation is purely mechanistic or purely organic but rather tends towards one or the other. Moreover, Burns and Stalker emphasised that one was not preferred over the other. The nature of the organisation's environment determined which structure was superior. Large firms may even have some parts which are organic and others which are mechanistic. For instance, motor vehicle manufacturers may apply largely mechanistic practices in their assembly plants, but the design studios, which develop the body shape and look of the car, may be organic and located far away from the assembly plant.

Efforts to test Burns and Stalker's conclusions have met with general support.[8] For instance, engineering consultants must deal with an endless series of unpredictable problems.[9] They require a structure that can allow the organisation to respond and adapt to continual change. It should not be surprising, therefore, to find that their structure closely follows the characteristics of an organic form.

TABLE 8.1 Comparing mechanistic and organic structures

Characteristic	Mechanistic	Organic
Task definition	Rigid	Flexible
Communication	Vertical	Lateral
Formalisation	High	Low
Influence	Authority	Expertise
Control	Centralised	Diverse

Lawrence and Lorsch

Paul Lawrence and Jay Lorsch, both of the Harvard Business School, have complemented the work of Burns and Stalker in exploring the relationship between environmental differences and effective organisation structures.[10] They chose 10 firms in 3 industries—plastics, food, and containers—in which to carry out their research.

Lawrence and Lorsch deliberately chose these three industries because they appeared to be the most diverse (in terms of environmental uncertainty) they could find. Bear in mind that they undertook their research in the 1960s. The plastics industry was highly competitive: the life cycle of any product was historically short, and firms were characterised by considerable new-product and process development. The container industry, on the other hand, was quite different. There had been no significant new products in two decades and sales growth had only kept pace with population growth. Lawrence and Lorsch described the container firms as operating in a relatively certain environment, with no real threats to consider. The food industry was midway between the two. There had been substantial innovation, but new-product generation and sales growth had been lower than in the plastics industry and higher than in the container industry.

Lawrence and Lorsch sought to align the internal environments of these firms with their respective external environments. They hypothesised that the more successful firms within each industry would have better alignments than the less successful firms. Their measure of the *external* environment sought to tap the degree of uncertainty. This measurement included the rate of change in product innovation over time, the clarity of information that management had about the environment, and the length of time it took for management to get feedback from the environment on actions taken by the organisation. But what constituted an organisation's *internal* environment? Lawrence and Lorsch looked at two separate dimensions: *differentiation* and *integration.*

differentiation task segmentation and attitudinal differences held by individuals in various departments

The term **differentiation**, as used by Lawrence and Lorsch, closely parallels our definition of horizontal differentiation. However, Lawrence and Lorsch argued that, in addition to job specialisation, managers in various departments can be expected to have different attitudes and behave differently in terms of their goal perspective, time frame and interpersonal orientation. Different interests and differing points of view mean that members of each department often find it difficult to see things the same way or to agree on integrated plans of action. Each is also responsible for only a small part of the work of the organisation. Therefore, the degree of differentiation becomes a measure of complexity and indicates more complications and a need to process information. The other dimension that interested Lawrence and Lorsch was **integration**, the quality of collaboration that exists among interdependent units or departments that are required to achieve unity of effort. Integration devices that organisations typically use include rules and procedures, formal plans, the authority hierarchy and decision-making committees.

integration the quality of collaboration that exists among interdependent units

The unique, and probably the most important, part of Lawrence and Lorsch's study was that they did not assume the organisation or the environment to be uniform and composed of a single element. In contrast to previous researchers, they perceived both the organisation and the environment as having subsets: that is, that *parts* of the organisation deal with *parts* of the environment. They were proposing that an organisation's internal structure could be expected to differ from department to department, reflecting the characteristics of the subenvironment with which it interacts. They postulated that a basic reason for differentiating into departments or subsystems was to deal more effectively with subenvironments. For example, in each of the 10 organisations that Lawrence and Lorsch studied, they were able to identify market, technical–economic and scientific subenvironments. These three subenvironments corresponded to the sales, production, and research and development functions within the organisations.

Lawrence and Lorsch proposed that the more turbulent, complex and diverse the external environment facing an organisation, the greater the degree of differentiation among its subparts. If the external environment was very diverse and the internal environment was highly differentiated, they further reasoned, there would be a need for an elaborate internal integration mechanism to avoid having units going in different directions. The need for increased integration to accommodate increases in differentiation related to the different goals of departmental managers. In all three industries, the researchers found manufacturing people to be most concerned with cost-efficiency and production matters. Research and engineering people emphasised scientific matters. Marketing staff's orientation was towards the marketplace.

In reference to their three industries, Lawrence and Lorsch hypothesised that the plastics firms would be the most differentiated, followed by food firms and container firms, in that order. And this is precisely what they found. When they divided the firms within each industry into high, moderate and low performers, they found that the high-performing firms had a structure that best fitted their environmental demands. In diverse environments, there were more differentiated subunits than in homogeneous environments. In the turbulent plastics industry this meant high differentiation. The production units had relatively routine activities, in contrast to sales, research and engineering. Where the greatest standardisation existed, in the container industry, there was the least differentiation. Departments within the container firms generally had similar structures. The food firms, as postulated, were in the middle ground. Furthermore, the most successful firms in all three industries had a higher degree of integration than their low-performing counterparts.

What does all this mean? First, the environments are composed of a number of subenvironments, each with different degrees of uncertainty. Second, successful organisations' subunits meet the demands of their subenvironments. As differentiation and integration represent opposing forces, the key is to match the two appropriately, creating differentiation between departments to deal with specific problems and tasks facing the organisation and getting people to integrate and work as a cohesive team towards the organisation's goals. Successful organisations have more nearly solved the dilemma of providing both differentiation and integration by matching their internal subunits to the demands of the subenvironment. Finally, Lawrence and Lorsch present evidence to confirm that the environment in which an organisation functions—specifically in terms of the level of uncertainty present—is of foremost importance in selecting the structure appropriate for achieving organisational effectiveness.

Before we leave Lawrence and Lorsch, it should be mentioned that they have been sharply criticised for their use of perceptual measures of environmental uncertainty.[11] As noted earlier, actual and perceived degrees of uncertainty are likely to differ. Attempts to replicate Lawrence and Lorsch's work using objective measures of uncertainty have often failed, which suggests that their results may be a function of their measure.[12] From a research standpoint, this criticism is valid. However, from the practising manager's perspective, it is his or her perception that counts. So while we should recognise that Lawrence and Lorsch have used perceptual measures and that defining the environment in terms of certainty/uncertainty criteria is by no means simple, we should also recognise that the findings of Lawrence and Lorsch represent an important contribution to our understanding of the impact of the environment on organisational structure.

OT CLOSEUP

How do firms differentiate and integrate?

Lawrence and Lorsch found that firms facing high levels of environmental uncertainty differentiated to meet each environmental segment, and then integrated the various differentiated parts in order to provide a coordinated organisation-wide response to the uncertainty. In practical terms, what forms do differentiation and integration take? No two organisations would emerge with identical practices, but the following are the most common mechanisms used.

Differentiation is mainly achieved through the creation of departments, or parts of departments. This is a structural initiative. For instance, the uncertainties in an oil company may surround procurement of crude oil, shipping, and refining. There may also be uncertainties with currency exchange rates, insurance, and environmental risk. The uncertainty surrounding all of these would take a different form and we would expect to find a department, or part of a department, dealing with each segment. These would be staffed by experts who would constantly monitor their area of responsibility. Each would take steps to reduce uncertainty, perhaps by the use of hedging or futures markets or long-term contracts or, in the case of shipping, by owning the ships. In the oil company, the size of the departments would suggest that the main reason for differentiation of the firm would be to meet the requirements of different environmental segments. Refining and accounting departments, which both experience low uncertainty, are likely to be extremely large. Alternatively, crude oil supply and insurance are likely to be very small and answer to high in the organisation's structure.

Integration may take many forms, including integrating structural positions. These may be departments, such as planning and scheduling, which are of critical importance to transport companies. Or there may be positions in the structure which are solely aimed at integrating the work of others. Typical titles are project manager, program manager, and various types of coordinators. The more differentiated the organisation, the more integrators we are likely to find.

Integration may also take the form of formalised programs and schedules. Motor vehicle companies, for instance, make a sales forecast up to six months ahead and this becomes the master scheduling plan, governing what is to be produced in the assembly plants and the myriad of suppliers' factories. This would also be the case with an oil company. Once a decision is made as to what the likely demand during the next year will be, then the supply department will know how much oil will need to be purchased, shipping will know how many ships to charter and so on. But, of course, all predictions are uncertain. In the case of the prediction being optimistic, excess crude oil could be sold on futures markets and shipping could be released from its charter arrangements.

Duncan's complexity and change framework

Robert Duncan classified environments along two dimensions.[13] The first is the *rate of change* of environments. Some environments change only slowly; for example, the environments of brewers, cement manufacturers and banks change only gradually over time. On the other hand, the fashion and telecommunications industries are characterised by rapid change. The second dimension identified by Duncan is that of *environmental complexity.* The greater the number of elements there are in an environment, the more complex the environment. Airlines face a complex environment because of the large number of environmental elements they face, while companies growing timber and baking bread face a small number of environmental elements. The interaction of environmental complexity and stability forms a two by two matrix, where different levels of uncertainty may be identified. Each of these levels of uncertainty leads to the adoption of different structural responses. Although Duncan did not expand on these, it is not difficult to identify what they are likely to be (see Figure 8.2).

The combination of a stable environment and low complexity leads to *low uncertainty* for organisations. Breweries, bakeries and soft-drink manufacturers all face this type of environment. The nature of the environment they face permits them to centralise their operations, as there is a low level of need to gather and process infor-

	Complex	Simple
Dynamic	**High uncertainty** Large number of unpredictable external elements *Examples:* Telecommunication companies Aerospace firms Biotechnology companies *Structural elements:* • Decentralised, organic structure • Many different departments, extensive use of boundary spanners • Extensive integration mechanisms and use of coordination and liaison roles • Extensive planning and forecasting	**Moderate to high uncertainty** Few environmental elements but each element changes often and unpredictably *Examples:* Fashion clothing Music industry Computer games Television programming *Structural elements:* • Decentralised with an emphasis on teamwork • Constant environmental monitoring by boundary spanners • High levels of coordination in order to promote imitation and innovation • Production facilities often mechanistic
Static	**Low to moderate uncertainty** Large number of dissimilar external elements which change only slowly *Examples:* Motor vehicle manufacturers Banks Oil companies Retail chains *Structural elements:* • Centralised, formalised and mechanistic structure • Differentiated into many departments to meet environmental elements • Large numbers of boundary spanners • Programmed coordination and use of planning for integration	**Low uncertainty** Small number of easily understood environmental elements which change slowly *Examples:* Cement manufacturers Soft-drink bottlers Breweries Bakeries *Structural elements:* • Centralised with high formalisation, mechanistic • Few departments • Coordination by programs and planning

FIGURE 8.2 Duncan's environmental framework

Source: Adapted from Robert Duncan, 'Characteristics of Organizational Environments and Perceived Environmental Uncertainty', *Administrative Science Quarterly*, 17, 1972, pp. 313–27.

mation. There are also relatively few decisions to make. The small amount of change in their productive activities permits high levels of formalisation. There are few departments, as there is not a large number of environmental elements to respond to. Because there is little change in the way goods or services are produced, production processes are highly formalised. Coordination is by program and planning, with few roles for coordinators. In summary, the structure is mechanistic in operation.

A stable environment combined with a high level of complexity leads to *low to moderate uncertainty*. In this environment, there are many different elements, but each changes only slowly, if at all. This describes the environment of educational institutions, motor vehicle manufacturers, banks and large retail chains. The stability of the environment leads to centralisation and high formalisation. Operations are mechanistic in nature. But the organisation differentiates itself into many different departments to meet the environmental elements. Because of the complexity of the environment, there are a large number of boundary spanners, both individuals and departments, whose role is to monitor the environment. But as there is little change in day-to-day operations, programmed coordination dominates.

An unstable environment combined with low levels of complexity leads to *moderate to high uncertainty*. In this environment, there are only a few elements, but each element changes in an unpredictable manner. Examples include fashion clothing, the music industry, computer games and television broadcasters. As there is a heightened need to process information and respond to it, management is decentralised. Teamwork is emphasised in order to facilitate communication. There is extensive use of boundary spanners and intensive coordination devices to enable the organisation to respond to environmental pressures. However, production processes are more stable and tend towards being mechanistic.

When organisations are both complex and unstable, *high uncertainty* ensues. This is the most demanding environment for management, and it places great demands on the organisation's structure. Industries in which we are likely to find high uncertainty are in telecommunications, biotechnology and aerospace. In highly uncertain environments, firms are decentralised as it is not possible for one person to grasp the full nature of the challenges facing the company. Structures consist of many different departments and are organic in nature. Extensive and expensive coordination and integration devices are used, including project managers, coordinators and liaison staff. There is also extensive use of scenario planning and forecasting.

Duncan's framework did not emerge from an empirical study, but it does encapsulate most of the variables that have been identified as defining organisational environments. It draws on Lawrence and Lorsch's findings that environments are not single elements but are composed of a number of elements; the greater the number of elements, the greater the complexity. The rate of change of these elements determines the stability of the environment. Stability enables decision making to be centralised and permits high levels of formalisation; it is not possible to formalise something that is constantly changing. But complexity comes with the need to gather, process and respond to numerous environmental elements, each with their own demands. This leads to decentralisation and a greater need for coordination.

As with other environmental classifications, Duncan's framework may be criticised because of its inability to actually measure stability and complexity: perceptual differences will lead to differing interpretations.[14] But notwithstanding this, it stands as a powerful reminder of the influence of environment on structure.

The role of the boundary spanner

In the previous chapter, we introduced the role of the boundary spanner. As the name implies, the role is relevant to the area where the organisation interacts with its environment, that is, at the boundary of the organisation. Boundary spanners may refer to individuals or departments. They may be seen as liaising between the organisation and its environment. Staff who undertake this role are called by a multitude of titles, many being organisationally specific and almost uninterpretable to outsiders.

Why do organisations have boundary spanners? Organisations have a core which concentrates upon the basic production of goods and services. It is best if this core proceeds with its work with the minimum of distraction. If there is to be any interruption to the flow of work it should proceed through an established channel, which can filter the information from the environment into a form that is useful to the core. Similarly, if the core wishes to communicate with the environment, it often does so through one of the boundary spanners.

So the boundary spanner may be seen to be making a number of contributions to managing environmental uncertainty. First, they have expertise in understanding and interpreting the environmental segment which they are concerned with. Second, they filter and process environmental information into a form which is useful to the organisation and then transmit this information through established channels. Third, they protect the core from undue disruption by removing the need for it to interact directly with the environment. And finally, they represent the organisation to the environment.

Let's consider the role of boundary spanners at a motor vehicle manufacturer. The main boundary spanner is actually an institution—the car dealer. When you buy a car, you almost exclusively interact with the dealer, not the manufacturer. If you find that the windscreen wipers don't work, you don't telephone the manufacturer and ask to speak to the assembler of the windscreen wipers; you contact the dealer—but not just anyone at the dealer. Their service centre has staff whose specific role is to interact with customers. You rarely get to speak with a mechanic as the service centre is set up to separate you from the workshop. Neither are many customers able to speak to the manufacturer directly, and if they do attempt to do so it will be with a specific person whose role is to liaise with customers.

The role of the boundary spanner is consistent with the findings of Lawrence and Lorsch. Although they did not specifically mention the boundary spanner role, the task of interaction with specific environmental segments was central to Lawrence and Lorsch's theory. But the role does suggest that some parts of the organisation have little direct interaction with the environment, implying that many parts of the organisation may be operating largely insulated from the environment.

The use of information technology in complex environments

We have noted that complex and dynamic environments require extensive environmental scanning and flexible organisational responses. Specific structural units and positions are often created to undertake this function. But regardless of the structural response, such environments place a heavy burden upon communication processes. It is not surprising that, as a result, research indicates that organisations facing such environments are intense users of information technology.[15] Organic structures, for instance, place a heavy emphasis upon lateral communication, something that information technology handles extremely well. In addition, the integrative functions identified by Lawrence and Lorsch may be facilitated by the intensive use of information technology. There are a number of outcomes of the application of communication technology in such situations. First, existing organisations may increase their effectiveness in handling difficult-to-predict environments, as managers and other staff will be better informed and response times will be faster. Second, environments which were considered to be unpredictable and difficult to operate in will become more manageable as information becomes more readily and widely available. Environments may then be perceived as being more stable. Third, other organisations may consider that they now have the capacity to operate in more unstable environ-

OT CLOSEUP

How Macquarie Bank manages risk

All banks do not do the same thing. Banking can roughly be divided into two main areas of activity: the traditional role of taking deposits and making loans, and investment banking. All banking has risks but the traditional banks, such as the NAB and the Commonwealth, minimise theirs by only making loans on the security of assets. A house mortgage is a typical example. Investment banks, however, undertake a far greater range of financing activities, often making investments on their own behalf and 'putting their balance sheet' behind a project (that is, risking their own capital). Macquarie Bank, for instance, typically finances infrastructure projects, such as airports and tollways, puts them into a publicly listed trust, then collects a management fee for ongoing administration. Macquarie also buys companies for on-sale in more favourable markets. It is also involved in funds management and stockbroking, property development and treasury activities, such as currency and commodity trading. It is far more innovative than traditional banks, constantly on the lookout for new profit opportunities—the more innovative, the better. Its staff are bright, restive and competitive, and are rewarded generously through bonuses, which they must earn by high levels of performance. Put these characteristics together and they add up to staff who are anxious to take on high levels of risk. One difficulty for Macquarie is that as it is a global company operating on a geographic basis it is possible for the different divisions to unknowingly take on the same risk, for example, in exposure to a certain currency. This would multiply the bank's risk beyond a level with which it would be comfortable.

Macquarie realises that control of risk is basically a structural issue. Systems and structures must be put in place to manage it. This starts with a board level committee, which establishes the parameters of what level of risk is appropriate to the bank and a framework in which risk may be assessed against the bank's risk-management policies. Day-to-day risk-management assessment is undertaken by the Risk Management Division, which reports to the managing director. It is independent of all other operating divisions of the bank and is charged with the responsibility of assessing risk from a global perspective and maintaining prudential limits, that is, adequate reserves to meet any anticipated eventuality. All new proposals must pass through the Risk Management Division, and if new proposals are approved, a constant monitoring brief is maintained in the light of changing circumstances. As a simple illustration, the Risk Management Division constantly monitors the amount that is lent to individuals to buy shares, known as margin loans, and makes continuous adjustment in the light of the state of the market, interest rates, economic outlook, the extent of underlying security and the other risks the bank has taken on. No investment, capital expenditure or commitments in areas such as futures and currency trades may be undertaken without approval of the Risk Management Division.

Source: Drawn from Macquarie Bank Annual Report 2005.

ments and, as a result, may be tempted to move from the predictability of stable environments.

This discussion highlights the interrelationships of the contingencies. For instance, technology and environment combine to facilitate certain structural outcomes, which in turn are favoured by those in power in the organisation. As you progress through the chapters you will uncover other interrelationships, many of which we will discuss.

A synthesis: the organisation and environmental uncertainty

In this section, we look for common threads among studies on the environment. As our goal is integration and clarity rather than merely the presentation of many diverse research findings, it is important to seek some common ground in the environmental literature. Recent research suggests that there are three key dimensions to any organisation's environment—capacity, volatility, and complexity.[16] These three dimensions synthesise much of the literature previously discussed.

The **capacity** of an environment refers to the degree to which it can support growth. This refers, for instance, to the availability of finance, customers, resource inputs and even managerial skill. Rich and bountiful environments are characterised by plentiful resources. These may be drawn upon by organisations to facilitate growth and expansion. They also protect the organisation against shortages in times of scarcity. The resources provide the sustenance for organisations to grow. Scarce environments, in contrast, provide few inputs for organisations and they struggle to survive. In the late 1990s, for instance, dot.com companies experienced an abundant supply of finance, leading to the formation of many new companies with few questions asked about their viability. Companies in the petroleum-refining industry, on the other hand, faced relative scarcity of capital as financiers questioned the profitability of the industry, resulting in the companies struggling to raise finance for modernisation.

capacity the degree to which an environment can support growth

The degree of instability in an environment is captured in the **stability** dimension. Where there is a high degree of unpredictable change, the environment is *dynamic*. At the other extreme is a *stable* environment. Financial markets are often dynamic, with change occurring unpredictably, whilst a cement manufacturer exists in a stable environment. In the latter case the only real uncertainty is the level of demand for the final product.

stability the extent to which there is little change in the environment

Finally, the environment needs to be assessed in terms of **environmental complexity**—that is, the degree to which the environment is concentrated on just a few elements. *Simple environments* have a few concentrated elements. This might describe a small mining company, which might have only a few inputs and only one output. It is easy in such an organisation for only one person to monitor the environment. In contrast, *complex environments* have many different elements in them which may not be related to one another and which may vary at different rates. A shipping company faces a complex environment. It must deal with various port authorities, freight forwarders, shipbuilders, suppliers and so on.

environmental complexity the degree to which the environment is concentrated on just a few elements

Figure 8.3 summarises our definition of the environment along its three dimensions. The arrow in this figure points towards higher uncertainty. Thus organisations that operate in environments characterised as scarce, dynamic and complex face the greatest degree of uncertainty. This is because they have a diverse set of elements in the environment to constantly monitor, many of which are unpredictable. Should

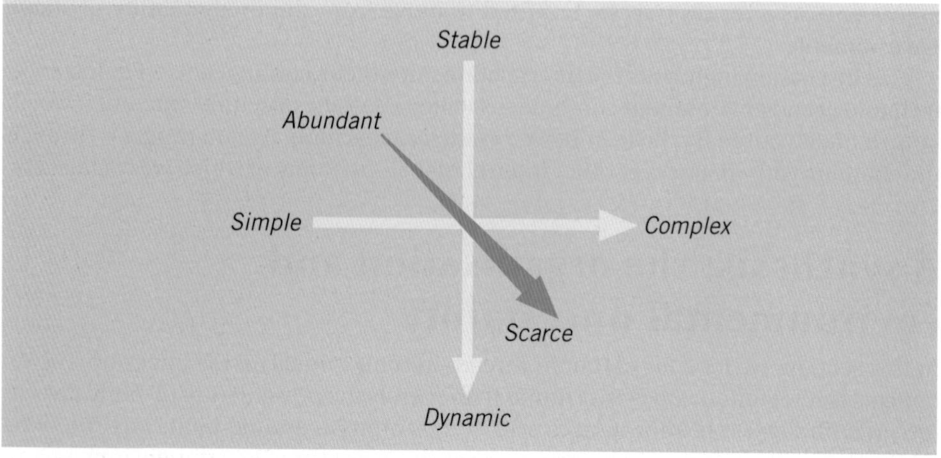
Stable
Abundant
Simple
Complex
Scarce
Dynamic

FIGURE 8.3 Three-dimensional model of the environment

they read their environment incorrectly, there are few resources in the environment to draw upon to compensate for the resulting problems.

Given this three-dimensional definition of environment, we can offer some general conclusions. There is evidence that relates the degree of environmental uncertainty to different structural arrangements. Specifically, the more scarce, dynamic and complex the environment, the more preferable will be the organic structure. The more abundant, stable and simple the environment, the more appropriate will be the mechanistic structure. Note how the preceding conclusions align with the discussion of technology and structure in the previous chapter. Routine technologies operate in relative certainty, whereas non-routine technologies imply relative uncertainty. High environmental uncertainty and technology of a non-routine nature both require organic-type structures. Similarly, low environmental uncertainty and routine technology can be managed more effectively in mechanistic structures.

The environmental imperative

As a result of our previous analysis, you should now have a reasonable understanding of what environment is and what some scholars have found in their efforts to better understand the environment–structure relationship. You now have the background to interpret more fully the cases for and against the environmental imperative.

The case for

The case for the argument that environment determines structure has been made by Burns and Stalker, Lawrence and Lorsch, and Duncan. Basically, they consider that environmental pressures create conditions which must be met by firms adopting appropriate structures. Further, these structures may be categorised according to the nature of the environment faced.

The open-systems perspective provides further support for the environmental perspective. But a word of warning is in order. The research we discussed earlier in the chapter is very specific. It links certain environmental conditions with specific structural responses. The open-systems perspective is nowhere near as specific as this and makes no suggestions as to how firms should respond to their environments. It identifies that organisations are dependent on acquiring inputs and disposing of outputs if they are to continue to survive. These inputs and outputs flow from and to the environment. Because of this dependency, organisations cannot ignore their environments.

It is true that some organisations need to be more environmentally aware than others and that in large organisations different subunits must monitor their subenvironments more closely than other subunits, but no organisation is so autonomous that it can insulate itself completely from its environment.

Further, not all of these environments behave in the same way. Some cannot be predicted with any degree of confidence. Some behave in random ways, while others vary along predictable dimensions. Also, new elements in the environment are constantly emerging while other unpredictable elements progressively come under greater control, such as through the development of futures markets. Past problem areas often become more predictable over time or greater knowledge of them reduces the uncertainty surrounding them. All told, environmental dependence creates uncertainty for managers. Environments are not amenable to easy control. The less management can control its environment, the greater the uncertainty for managers. Managers do not like making decisions under conditions of high uncertainty. We will discuss in Chapter 11 the ways in which managers seek to control their environment. But they cannot eliminate uncertainty, so they look to options within their control that can reduce it. One of those options is designing the organisation so as to be able to respond best to uncertainty. If uncertainty is high, therefore, the organisation will be designed along flexible lines to adapt to rapid changes. Managers are also more likely to use boundary spanners to interact with the environment. If uncertainty is low, management will opt for a structure that is most efficient and offers the highest degree of managerial control, which is the mechanistic form.

Current trends in organisational strategy have the effect of reducing uncertainty for the firm. Organisations have increasingly moved towards focusing on core competencies. In simple terms, this means concentrating on those areas in which the firm has a comparative advantage. This often means divesting itself of non-core businesses, but it also includes outsourcing of such tasks as logistics, information technology, catering and maintenance. One of the main effects of doing this is to reduce uncertainty by operating in a market segment which is sufficiently narrow to understand and to respond to in an informed way. For instance, if a company ran its own delivery operation, it would have to deal with the complexities and uncertainties associated with fuel and capital equipment supplies, labour unions, insurance and reliability of delivery. Through outsourcing this function, it transfers much of this responsibility to another company, hence reducing its uncertainty.

Information technology also assists in reducing uncertainty. Greater amounts of information about the environment can be processed, which leads to better knowledge, more informed decisions, and faster and speedier organisational response. It also enables greater differentiation by promoting the means of integration. Integration may be facilitated by information and communication technologies, providing management with both the structural means, and the confidence, to differentiate the organisation to meet environmental challenges. Lastly, information and communication technologies appear to facilitate the emergence of specialised firms operating in an environmental niche which they understand well. Linked through complex supply chains and networks, these individual organisations contribute to the emergence of the virtual corporation. One of the characteristics of this form of industry structure is that each organisation faces a relatively stable, simple environment, but the virtual organisation may face more complex and dynamic conditions. So the resilience and adaptability of the virtual corporation to environmental shocks and uncertainties would appear to be more than that of its individual parts.

OT CLOSEUP

The innovator's dilemma

A feature of innovation that has always puzzled observers is that often new technologies that create new markets and displace old technologies rarely emerge from companies which are well established in the old technologies. An extreme example is that of digital photography, which was developed by companies in the electronic industries rather than by the established photographic companies such as Kodak or Polaroid. Another is the MP3-based iPod which was developed by Apple, rather than Sony, which could have been expected to be the natural innovator in the area.

A book by Clayton Christensen called *The Innovator's Dilemma* explores why this might be so. His proposals, which blend considerations of strategy and environment, fit neatly with issues relating to managers' selective perception of the environment and how they enact that environment in their decision making.

Christensen proposed that technologies could be divided into two types: sustaining and disruptive. Sustaining technologies enhance current trends in an industry, whilst disruptive technologies are innovations which herald the wave of the future. Disruptive technologies often start on a small scale and are only of relevance to a specialised market segment. It is only over time that they grow to displace the sustaining technologies. However, they have the capacity to completely obliterate sustaining technology companies, as can be seen from the demise of Polaroid.

So why do those companies which are dominant in the sustaining technologies find it difficult to introduce disruptive technologies? Christensen proposed that there were five reasons for this. First, successful companies find it difficult to allocate resources to areas which are not aligned to the demands and wishes of their major customers and investors. Second, the initial markets for disruptive technologies are only small and don't seem worthwhile to allocate time and effort to. Third, because it appears that the markets are only small, they don't present as having the potential to satisfy the growth needs of large companies. Fourth, as a market for disruptive technologies does not appear to exist, it cannot be analysed and companies are reluctant to engage in guesswork. They stress the importance of satisfying existing large customers who in turn cannot articulate the need for technologies which don't exist. Lastly, an organisation's capabilities also define its disabilities. An organisation's capabilities are to be found in its processes and values. But these processes and values are aimed at supporting and promoting the sustaining technologies. These limit the support for new ideas and new products and make the organisation captive of its sustaining technologies.

The Innovator's Dilemma highlights that managers view the environment through the lens of the capabilities of their own companies. Their orientation is to satisfy customers' needs and they view this as largely doing what they are doing a little better and a little cheaper. They are reluctant to give credibility to new technologies, the introduction of which may lead to major changes in the organisation, often at the expense of their political power base. They are in effect enacting what they see as important in the environment, but what they see as important may not be important in the future; they may quite well have overlooked an important disruptive technology, which will have a significant impact upon their organisation in the future.

Source: Drawn from Clayton Christensen, *The Innovator's Dilemma*, Cambridge, Mass: Harvard Business School Press, 1997.

The case against

If the environment does have an impact upon structure, it may be limited to those subunits or departments that interact directly with the environment. As we have seen, these departments are often termed boundary spanners. For instance, the structure of the purchasing and marketing functions may be a direct response to their dependence on, and interaction with, the environment. Yet it may have little or no impact on production, research and development, accounting and similarly activities which have no environmental interaction. It may also be that, as environments are perceived and enacted from within the organisation, what is perceived is reflected in the structure of the organisation.[17] If environments are creations, it is possible that structures differentiated into many different parts will perceive a heterogeneous environment or that decentralised structures will perceive more environmental uncertainty because of their structural arrangement. This reflects the social constructionist view of environments and may, in fact, explain Lawrence and Lorsch's findings.

A major argument of the environmental imperative supporters is that organisations structure themselves to minimise the impact of uncertainty—that is, environmental changes that organisations cannot forecast. As noted earlier in our discussion of the specific environment, not all uncertainty in the environment may have consequences for the organisation. Uncertainty, therefore, is relevant only when it occurs along with the organisation being dependent upon that part of the environment.[18] Moreover, uncertainty is *unplanned* variation. For a retailer a drop in demand because of seasonal variations would not constitute uncertainty; it has been experienced before and it will be experienced again. Further, if there is constant rate of change, such as consistent and incremental improvements in motor vehicles over time, there is no guarantee that the situation is uncertain. Indeed, it is possible to argue that as constant technological innovation has characterised the past 150 years, such change represents stability rather than unpredictability.

Finally, it has been said that the environmental imperative is just not in agreement with observed reality.[19] Not only do organisations that operate in seemingly similar environments have different structures, they often show no significant difference in effectiveness. Furthermore, many organisations have similar structures and very diverse environments. This latter point is consistent with our observation that there is no shortage of organisations with the mechanistic form. Businesses of all kinds, government departments and even charities possess many of the structural elements of the mechanistic form. This suggests that the environmental imperative may have been overstated or perhaps there are very few turbulent environments. Yet another reason may be that the organisations in turbulent environments have a limited life span and so rarely exist long enough to be studied.

Are environmental changes leading to new organisational forms?

Since the early 1990s, organisational researchers have suggested that environmental and technological changes have created the conditions for the emergence of new organisational forms which differ considerably from traditional organisational structures.[20] They suggest that environmental change is speeding up, necessitating a fresh approach to organisational structuring. Structures and management practices now need to respond to faster search procedures, greater demands for coordination and information processing, and a multidisciplinary approach to decision making. It has even been suggested that, in periods of rapid change, by the time information has been received it is often obsolete, inaccurate or of little use.[21] In this case, only partial processing of information takes place and organisational learning is incomplete.

Researchers and theorists have suggested that given these conditions new organisational forms are emerging, variously called the virtual organisation, the network or the spaghetti organisation. They also see two main trends in organisational response. The first is for organisations to become more focused in their strategy, that is, to rely more upon core competencies. This means that they operate in a smaller environmental segment, which is more readily understood and which places less demand upon information processing. The trend to concentrate often, but not always, leads to smaller organisations, each contributing to part of the supply chain. Each individual organisation then has to process a smaller and more manageable amount of information. Hence networks of interrelated firms emerge creating a virtual organisation.

When the structure of the organisation is considered, the proponents of the new organisational design suggest that hierarchies and command and control mechanisms will be replaced by lateral communication facilitated by information technologies. Organisational charts will become obsolete. Information technology will also facilitate the integration of many minor decisions needing to be made in response to environmental turbulence. Traditional management will be replaced by leaders who are most suited to the task at hand.

Whilst the emergence of the new organisational form has intuitive appeal, there are few organisations which conform to it. In this it echoes the early days of the matrix structure, which was more spoken of than applied. Further, many of the structural responses were identified and described by earlier researchers such as Burns and Stalker and Lawrence and Lorsch. So whilst proponents of emerging organisational forms may put forward strong theoretical arguments, there is little evidence of such forms becoming common.

Further issues relating to organisational environments

So far in this chapter we have considered the ways in which an organisation may be structured in order to respond to its environment. We have mainly discussed the structural responses that managers may adopt in order to reduce uncertainty. However, scholars have developed other perspectives on the environment–organisation relationship. These help explain how organisations come into being, factors which affect their survival and, in some cases, the structures they adopt. We will consider the three most important of these perspectives: population ecology, institutional theory, and resource-dependence theory.

population-ecology view the environment selects certain types of organisations to survive and others to perish based on the fit between their structural characteristics and the characteristics of their environment

The population-ecology approach to organisational selection

The past 20 years have seen the growth and development of what stands as an extreme environmental-imperative position. This position, which has been labelled the natural selection or **population-ecology** view,[22] argues that the environment selects certain types of organisations to survive and others to perish on the basis of the fit between their structural characteristics and the characteristics of their environment. Population ecologists argue that organisational forms must either fit their environmental niches or fail.

Population ecology relies heavily on biology's survival-of-the-best-adapted doctrine. This doctrine argues that there is a natural selection process that allows the strongest and most adaptable species to survive over time. Population ecology applies the same kind of thinking to organisations. The environment 'naturally' selects 'in' some organisations and selects 'out' others. Those selected 'in' are the survivors, while those selected 'out' perish. More specifically, population ecologists would argue that organisations that survive have resources, management advantages and structural dimensions that the casualties didn't have.

In any given population of organisations there are variations in such characteristics as structure, management skills, knowledge and attitudes, and access to resources. Population ecologists argue that certain organisations survive based on the fit between the organisation and its environment. Those that are selected to survive are those that are best adapted to their environment. Another way of looking at this process is that the environment selects certain organisations to survive based on their environmental fit. But population ecology has no predictive power: it cannot provide managers in advance with suggestions as to steps that should be taken in order to improve the chances of an organisation's survival.

The population-ecology view is somewhat like the biological metaphor discussed in Chapter 1, but it looks at whole populations rather than an individual organisation. In this, it may be viewed as applying the concept of natural selection to a population of organisations. It seeks to explain what happened, and what is happening, rather than to make predictions as to which particular organisation is likely to survive. Those organisations that survive would, according to population ecologists, be the best adapted to their environments.

Some clarification of what survival is would be useful. As population ecology concentrates on populations of organisations, there needs to be a number of organisations doing similar things within a given environment for the theory to apply. This infers typical private-sector industries such as retailers, banks and manufacturers. Any company within these industries may merge with another or become insolvent and their assets be disposed of; generally only those which have adapted to their environment survive. So survival, according to population ecology, is maintenance of an independent existence.

Organisations such as key government departments are virtually guaranteed existence. Departments of taxation, defence and foreign affairs, for instance, are set up by acts of parliament as monopolies. As a result, a population of such organisations does not exist and hence the ideas of population ecology have limited application in their case.

Assumptions of population ecology

In order to understand population ecology better, we should be familiar with the assumptions underlying its approach. First, the population-ecology perspective operates at a different level of analysis from many of the studies in this book. It focuses on groups or populations of organisations, not on individual organisations. You would use a population-ecology approach to explain why, from hundreds of producers of motor cars in 1920, only a handful now remain, and why just a few companies dominate domestic appliance manufacturing. It also provides a sound framework on which to base analysis of industries with high failure rates such as hospitality and retail. Second, population ecology defines organisational effectiveness as simply survival. At any time, the organisations that operate in any industry are defined as effective because they are among the survivors. Third, population ecologists assume that the environment is totally determining. In direct contrast to the theme in Chapter 5, where strategy is described as determining structure, the population-ecology view assumes that management—at least in the short or intermediate term—has little impact on an organisation's survival. Managers are not seen as proactively managing or influencing the organisation's interactions with its environment. Success, therefore, is a result of events beyond management's control.

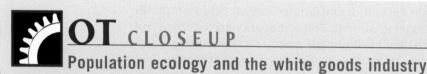

OT CLOSEUP

Population ecology and the white goods industry

White goods are household appliances that are generally white, such as refrigerators, washing machines, cooking appliances and dishwashers. Although taken for granted now, they were once every householder's dream and possession of them marked entrée to the modern world. Their manufacture was also at the cutting edge of production technology, and appliance manufacturing was an attractive and high-profile investment.

Australia now does not have any locally owned appliance manufacturers. The last one was Email, which was bought by Swedish manufacturer Electrolux in 2000. The only other local manufacturer is Fisher and Paykel, a New Zealand company. But there was a time when there was no shortage of white goods manufacturers in Australia: there were more than 30 independent manufacturers in the 1950s, supplying what was then an ever-expanding market. Local manufacture was protected by high tariffs, and agreements among manufacturers set prices and territories for each manufacturer to sell into.

By the 1980s the environment had begun to change. Trade practices legislation outlawed agreements among manufacturers and promoted competition. High tariffs were progressively falling, with a resulting increase in price competition. Markets had also matured, with customers buying products only when old ones wore out or when a new household was established.

So what happened to the 30 manufacturers of white goods? One by one they merged, or went out of business, as their management realised that they could not all survive. Many could not achieve the economies of scale necessary to keep costs down. Some plants were too small and could not be refinanced; for others the designs were found wanting and the money or the will were not available to update them. The ongoing consolidation of retailing into a fewer number of chains had the effect of reducing the number of outlets for the many manufacturers. Those manufacturers with less market strength or weak brand names found it increasingly difficult to get their product onto the showroom floor. The weakest went first. Brands such as Malleys, Pope, Hallstrom, Silent Knight and Electrice disappeared. By the 1990s only a few manufacturers were left. Eventually Email emerged as the only Australian-owned manufacturer, it having become clear that the local market could support only one manufacturer. Its stable of brands, ranging from Simpson, Kelvinator, Westinghouse and Hoover through to Dishlex and Vulcan, revealed the path of its mergers.

But the scale of the Australian market was against even Email. Its manufacturing facilities were up-to-date and low-cost, but it needed better access to overseas markets than it alone could forge. It also needed engineering and design input from better financed design labs. In the event, Email did not so much fail as suffer from lack of shareholder belief that adequate returns could be made from domestic appliances. In order to diversify, Email had acquired a profitable metals-distribution business. This was of great interest to other metals businesses and they acquired Email and put the appliance part of the business back on the market. The only company that could extract sufficient economies from Email was Electrolux, which duly acquired full control. There were few other interested parties.

A fourth assumption of population ecology is that the carrying capacity of the environment is limited. There are only so many hospitals, for instance, that a given community's size can absorb. This sets up a competitive arena, where some organisations will succeed and others will fail. Finally, population ecology assumes the existence of a three-stage process that explains how organisations operating in similar environmental niches often have common structural dimensions. The process proposes that forces of change are generated in the environment rather than from managerial action. This three-stage process is described in the next section.

The organisational change process

How do organisations change to better fit with the environment they face? The answer can be found in a three-stage process of change that recognises *variations* within and between organisations, the *selection* of those variations that are best suited to their environments, and a *retention* mechanism that sustains and reproduces those variations that are positively selected (see Figure 8.4).

Within any population of organisations (e.g. fast-food restaurants, chemical firms, hospitals and private schools) there will be variations in organisational forms. These can be planned or random variations, but the key point is that there will be diversity. Some of these variations, however, are better suited to their environments than others. Those that are better suited survive, while the others fall out of the set and perish. Organisations that have a form that fits their environment are positively selected and survive, while others either fail or change to match their environmental requirements. This finally leads to the retention of those variations that are positively selected. Over time, selected organisational forms tend to emerge in populations that share common needs for economies of scale, technologies and control systems.

As a result of the above process, we should expect to find similar organisational practices and structural characteristics within the same population. The reason is that those organisations that were different were less able to compete. There are not enough resources in any environment to support an unlimited number of organisations, so there is a natural selection process that reproduces organisational structures that best fit with their environment. Over the very long run, of course, even the positively selected variations are likely to be selected 'out' because environments change and, in so doing, favour a different set of variations.

Every industry is made up of sets of organisations that can be divided into populations with common resources and technologies. But there is only so much money and so many customers, market segments and other resources available in the environment. Organisations can select a niche for themselves—emphasising low cost, quality, convenience of location, hours of service or the like—but there is still competition. The survivors will be those that have best adjusted their internal resources to their environment.

We can see support for the population-ecology viewpoint in the actions of venture capitalists in places such as Silicon Valley.[23] Venture capitalists specialise in funding start-ups whose only asset is a good idea. All venture capitalists are hoping to back

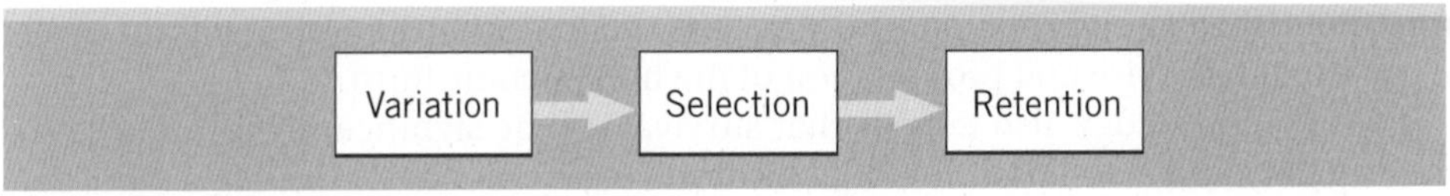
Variation
Selection
Retention

FIGURE 8.4 Population-ecology view of the change process

the next Microsoft, but as there is no security for the loans that they give, these loans are inherently risky. In addition, it is virtually impossible to pick in advance which investments will pay off handsomely and which will lose money. Venture capitalists, therefore, spread their investments over a wide range of promising options, knowing that only one or two will be outstanding successes and just a few more will pay their way. They are reduced to allowing the environment do the selection.

Limitations to the population-ecology view

Population ecology is not a general theory to explain why and how organisations survive. As its critics have shown, it has clear limitations.[24]

The theory ignores managerial motives and abilities. But management can often influence their environment to their advantage. Corporate influence may not be all-powerful, as it is often depicted in management textbooks or imagined by businesses critics; however, neither is it irrelevant. Management can choose the domains or niches it wants to compete in and, especially in the long term, change or influence its domain. Similarly, organisations can reinvent themselves by changing to suit a new set of environmental circumstances. The more resources they have or can acquire, the greater their chance of successful transformation. Further, few managers undertake major change programs without drawing upon the experience and example of other organisations facing similar circumstances. So there is much that organisations may do through their own efforts to adapt to their environment.

Population ecology appears to have reduced application to large and powerful organisations. The reason is that these organisations can often insulate themselves against failure. They have strong constituencies in government that will protect them. Moreover, as we show in Chapter 11, large organisations can control their environments because many elements in their environments—suppliers, customers, unions and the like—are dependent on them and accede to their demands. This reveals much to us about the nature of organisational environments themselves. In many cases they are not taken as given, but made up of constituencies which may be influenced by lobbying and other similar activities.

A further limitation of population ecology is that in public-sector organisations efficiency and adaptation are not effectiveness criteria—we simply do not let police forces, treasuries and law courts go out of business.[25] So population ecology may best be described as a special theory, applicable to small and powerless organisations. Reality tells us that most large organisations, as well as almost all those organisations in the public sector such as the police force, tend to be relatively immune to threats to their existence from the environment and as a consequence are rarely selected 'out'.

Implications

Population ecology provides an explanation of why organisations in common populations tend to have common structural characteristics and why certain types of organisations survive while others die. It can explain why small organisations so often fail, why the divisional structure became popular in the 1960s and why organic structures flourished as environments became less stable. Perhaps most important of all, it can explain the rise and proliferation of the bureaucratic form.[26]

Population ecology also tells us that survival will be significantly influenced by the capacity and stability of the organisation's environment. Is the capacity of the environment rich or lean? The richer the environment, the more organisations that will survive. Over the past 10 years we have seen the consolidation of the motor vehicle industry into just a few groups which can achieve the necessary economies of scale to survive. Few financiers would fund the establishment of a new motor vehicle manufacturer. Alternatively, the significant growth of superannuation has seen the number of investment managers expand in order to handle the large volume of funds to be invested; new funds managers are constantly emerging as others go out of business. Furthermore, the more stable the environment, the harder it is for new organisations to enter and compete. This is because stable, certain environments tend to retain large organisations that have achieved significant economies with high market shares. These tend to react aggressively to fend off any challenge to their dominance.

Population ecologists challenge the research methodologies often used in organisation theory. Organisation theory researchers have traditionally looked at different structural relationships and sought to relate them to varying degrees of organisational effectiveness. Population ecologists have correctly noted that such research is biased: it doesn't survey *all* organisations, merely the survivors. The truly 'ineffective' organisations are not studied because they died too soon. Thus the value of organisational research is likely to improve if researchers look at organisations that have failed as well as those that have survived.

Acceptance of population ecology as a mainstream theory, at least among students of management and business, is not likely to occur, because it runs counter to the doctrine of rational attribution. This doctrine holds that organisations may be actively managed in order to increase their effectiveness. Outcomes which cannot be predicted—those which may be attributed to luck, chance or random selection—cannot, by definition, be managed. A view that organisational success is pure chance is not likely to be widely accepted in schools of business and management, whose survival is based on a proactive view of managers and their ability to influence an organisation's survival and growth.

Institutional theory

Institutional theory is difficult to pin down because of the large number of meanings we can attribute to the word institution. Another name for an organisation is an institution; and many organisations have 'Institute' as part of their name. But the word can also be used to describe a situation where outside pressures induce repetitive behaviours in organisations. These repetitive behaviours then become accepted practice. When this occurs we call it institutionalising behaviour, and it is from this use of the word that institutional theory derives. But there is yet another meaning. Pressures upon organisations can be random or they may emerge from a formalised pressure group or from groups acting in combination. Where pressures emerge as a result of combined action by groups or through legal bodies such as government, we call them institutional pressures. Generally, institutional pressures are more powerful than the pressures exerted by individuals. Where these external pressures have a significant impact on an organisation we call it an institutionalised environment. Provided that the institutional pressures in an environment are similar for most organisations, it is not surprising that we would expect most organisations to look somewhat alike, with similar structures and practices.[27]

Institutional theory proposes that organisations are influenced not only by their internal processes but also by the need to adapt to the institutional pressures in the external environment. This need for adaptation then leads to behaviours being repeated and becoming 'institutionalised'. This process lies behind the emergence of similar types

institutional theory an approach which integrates an organisation's past actions and the social and environmental pressures on it to explain organisational practices

of organisations and is called isomorphism. We can divide institutional demands into two broad types. The first is economic and technical demands, which may be seen most clearly in the expectation that profit-seeking organisations show a profit, innovate and respond to change. Management must develop organisational structures to meet these demands. Institutionalised demands may also emerge from government regulations and laws. For instance, equal opportunity laws require organisations of a certain size to have an equal opportunity officer, and this person must report to a senior person in the organisation. Hence, it is not surprising that all large companies have such a position. Also, defence departments often require certain organisational structures and quality assurance procedures be adopted by their contractors.

The second is social demands, which reward organisations for conforming to societal values, norms and expectations. These are basically cultural expectations. Organisations tend to reflect the cultural values of the society in which they exist. Additional social demands arise from the pressure to conform to the practices of other organisations—that is, to mimic them. Managers are consistently studying other organisations and copying innovations they feel may be of use to them. This sometimes leads to organisations following the ideas of the latest fashion or trend in management thinking, often with inadequate consideration as to whether it would be of benefit to them. MBA programs have often been criticised for creating institutionalised management, with critics arguing that MBA programs teach managers to manage in the same way. Certainly the fact that managers move seamlessly between organisations suggests that organisations are managed in a similar fashion.

Although all organisations must respond to both economic and social demands, for many one group clearly dominates. Firms in the profit-making sector may place commercial and technical demands uppermost in their consideration. Alternatively, Amnesty International and Greenpeace, among similar organisations, rely heavily for their existence on the values, norms and beliefs of important groups of supporters, regardless of how inefficiently they may be using resources.

Evaluation of institutional theory

One of the more useful contributions of institutional theory is the explanation of the way in which social, economic and legal pressures influence organisational structures and practices. An organisation's ability to adapt to these plays a part in favouring organisational survival. Greenpeace and Amnesty International, for instance, have been greatly favoured by the appeal they have for many sections of the population. Alternatively, many large and supposedly powerful corporations have been humbled by the social pressures exerted by critics or other constituencies. The oil company, Shell, was greatly embarrassed by public reaction to its operations in Nigeria, even though a strong case could be made that Shell had little influence on the course of events. Yet the management and accountability of Greenpeace and Amnesty International are far more opaque than that of many multinationals.

We can see cultural and social pressures operating at another level. Most multinational companies are clearly far from being stateless. It does not take long to identify the practices of the home country in their operations. Toyota is clearly Japanese, Siemens is clearly German, and McDonald's is considered to be the ultimate embodiment of American culture. While the influences of the home country may be identified, most of the overseas operations of the companies mentioned have been significantly modified by the local culture. Indeed, their overseas success depends on adapting to local conditions and expectations.

Overall, the claim that organisations must conform to the institutionalised environment is not very different from our observations in Chapter 3 regarding strategic constituencies. We noted in that discussion that certain groups in the organisation's environment had to be satisfied in order for the organisation to survive. What institutional theorists have done is provide a useful elaboration and understanding of how this occurs.

Resource-dependence theory

In Chapter 1 we introduced the concept of the open system. This concept highlights the interaction of the organisation and its environment. Resource-dependence theory draws on the concept of the open system to promote the ways in which the organisation depends on the environment for its resources—hence the name resource-dependence theory.[28] However, resource dependence brings with it the capacity of suppliers to exert power on organisations, and as a result makes them vulnerable to the exercise of this power. The dependent organisation will in turn take various actions to minimise the impact of its resource dependence. The action that the organisation takes depends on the criticality of the resource. Typical resource dependencies are the dependence of steel mills on the supply of raw materials, bakeries on flour supplies, start-up businesses on capital, universities on government funding and oil refineries on supplies of crude oil. High-profile management consultancies are also dependent on hiring from the limited pool of talented and well-informed consultants.

One of the ways of looking at resource-dependence theory is that dependence on resources increases uncertainty for the organisation. As we have seen, managers do not like uncertainty and will act to reduce it. Lawrence and Lorsch's theory indicates that organisations are likely to differentiate themselves to meet each environmental threat. But this does not reduce the threat so much as make it easier to focus management's attention on the problem. Most active responses must be external to the organisation. These include taking an equity stake in a supplier or distributor, long-term contracts, buffering (i.e. building up emergency supplies), diversifying suppliers, lobbying and building personal relationships. We discuss these more fully in Chapter 11, where we consider the ways in which an organisation manages its environment.

Resource-dependence theory is a useful way for us to analyse threats to the organisation. Dependency creates uncertainty, but while the direction of the uncertainty is generally predicable, its magnitude is not. For instance, an outbreak of war in the Middle East would be likely to interrupt crude oil supplies. Airlines can easily predict that this will affect both the supply and price of jet fuel. The uncertainty arises from not knowing how much the supply and the price will change. As airlines are heavily dependent on fuel as a resource, we would expect to find that their organisational structure has been differentiated to meet this dependency. We would also expect airlines to take action external to the organisation, to minimise interruptions to supply.

The environment–structure relationship

It is time to attempt some specific formulations on the environment–structure relationship. As in the previous chapters, we look at the effect on complexity, formalisation and centralisation. However, before we make these formulations, several general predictions about the environment–structure relationship are offered.

Every organisation depends on its environment to some degree, but we cannot ignore the fact that some organisations are much more dependent on the environment and certain subenvironments than are others. This dependency creates vulnerabilities for the organisation, which managers attempt to minimise.[29]

The evidence demonstrates that a dynamic environment has more influence on structure than a static environment does.[30] A dynamic environment will push an organisation towards an organic form, even if large size or routine technology suggests a mechanistic structure. But not all parts of the environment change at the same rate. When operating in a dynamic environment, firms differentiate themselves into various parts based on the needs of each environmental segment. Arising from this, we would expect more intensive coordination in a dynamic environment. We would also expect organisations actively to devise ways to reduce their dependency when facing dynamic environments.

The computer manufacturer, Dell, illustrates this point. Personal computer manufacturing is essentially a routine operation; the basic design of computers has not changed for over 20 years. As a result, it is a highly competitive industry. Manufacturers such as Dell are essentially assemblers of component manufacturers' products. But there has been a consistent drop in the price of components ever since computers have been manufactured. So those firms that are dependent upon the supply of components are vulnerable to their falling price level. Assemblers and marketers who can take advantage of the latest prices, which are generally lower, have a price advantage over other assemblers who work from an inventory of components. Dell manages this vulnerability by not keeping inventories and only buying components as it needs them. Hence it has lower costs than its competitors and has established itself as a leader in the industry.

Environment and complexity

Environmental uncertainty and complexity are directly related. That is, high environmental uncertainty tends to lead to greater complexity. In order to respond to a dynamic and more complex environment, organisations differentiate themselves into multiple environments and subunits. An organisation faced with a volatile environment will need to monitor that environment more closely than one that is stable. This is typically accomplished by creating specialist units facing each environmental segment. Similarly, a complex environment requires the organisation to buffer itself with a greater number of departments and specialists.

Environment and formalisation

We predict that stable environments should lead to high formalisation because stable environments create a minimal need for rapid response, and economies exist for organisations that standardise their activities. But we caution against assuming that a dynamic environment must lead to low formalisation throughout the organisation. Management's preference will undoubtedly be for insulating operating activities from uncertainty. If successful, a dynamic environment is likely to lead to low formalisation of boundary activities while maintaining relatively high formalisation within other functions.

Environment and centralisation

The more complex the environment, the more decentralised the structure.[31] Regardless of the static–dynamic dimension, if a large number of dissimilar factors and components exist in the environment, the organisation can best meet the uncertainties that this causes through decentralisation. It is difficult for management to understand a highly complex *environment* (note that this is different from a complex *structure*). Management information-processing capacity becomes overloaded, so decisions are divided into subsets and are delegated to others.

Disparities in the environment are responded to through decentralisation.[32] When different responses are needed to different subenvironments, the organisation creates decentralised subunits to deal with them, so we can expect organisations to decentralise selectively. This can explain why, even in organisations that are generally highly centralised, marketing activities are typically decentralised. This is a response to a disparity in the environment: that is, even though the environment is generally static, the market subenvironment tends to be dynamic.

Finally, the evidence confirms that extreme hostility in the environment drives organisations, at least temporarily, to centralise their structures.[33] A wildcat strike by the union, an interruption of supplies or the sudden loss of a major customer all represent severe threats to the organisation, and top management responds by centralising control. When survival is in question, top management wants to oversee decision making directly. Of course, you may note that this appears to contradict an earlier prediction. You would expect this dynamic environment to meet with decentralisation. What appears to happen is that two opposing forces are at work, with centralisation the winner. The need for innovation and responsiveness (via decentralisation) is overpowered by top management's desire for coherent and consistent responses.

Summary

The theme of this chapter has been that different organisations face different degrees of environmental uncertainty and that structural design is a major tool that managers can use to eliminate or minimise the impact of environmental uncertainty.

The environment was defined as everything outside an organisation's boundaries. Our concern, however, is with the specific environment—that part most relevant to the organisation. Management desires to reduce uncertainty created by this specific environment.

Three landmark contributions were cited. Burns and Stalker argued that an organisation's structure should be mechanistic in a stable, certain environment and organic when the environment is turbulent. Lawrence and Lorsch's major contributions included the recognition that there are multiple specific environments with different degrees of uncertainty, that successful organisations' subunits meet the demands of their subenvironments and that the degree of environmental uncertainty is of the utmost importance in the selection of the right structure. Duncan identified four different structural types drawn from the interaction of environmental complexity and environmental change. We synthesised the studies into three dimensions: capacity (abundant–scarce), volatility (stable–dynamic), and complexity (simple–complex).

The environment–structure relationship is complicated, but we concluded that:

1 The environment's effect on an organisation is a function of dependence.
2 A dynamic environment has more influence on structure than does a stable one.
3 Complexity and environmental uncertainty are inversely related.

4 Formalisation and environmental uncertainty are inversely related.
5 The more complex the environment, the greater the decentralisation.
6 Extreme hostility in the environment leads to temporary centralisation.

The summary so far approaches the influence of the environment from the perspective of managerial action. But there are a number of other approaches, which study environmental influence from a different perspective. Population ecologists view the environment as having limited carrying capacity. Environments select those organisations to survive that are best adapted to their environment. Population ecologists therefore seek to identify the processes through which the environment selects organisations to succeed or fail. Institutional theory helps explain how forces in the environment, including formal and informal ones, help influence organisational structure and practices. And resource-dependence theory helps explain how dependence on scarce resources influences organisational actions to increase the chance of organisational survival.

For review and discussion

1 What is the difference between an organisation's general environment and its specific environment?

2 What does the 'enacted environment' mean? Provide an example from your experience.

3 Why do managers dislike environmental uncertainty? What are some of the ways they can reduce it?

4 Describe the technology and environment that fit best with (a) mechanistic and (b) organic structures.

5 Why would an organic structure be inefficient in a stable environment?

6 Discuss whether Duncan's typology oversimplifies the impact of the environment upon an organisation.

7 What was Lawrence and Lorsch's main contribution to organisational theory?

8 Are differentiation and integration opposing or complementary forces? Support your answer.

9 Define each of the following environmental dimensions:
(a) capacity (b) volatility (c) complexity.

10 Under what conditions is environment likely to be a major determinant of structure?

11 According to the population-ecology view, how do organisations change?

12 Why is a limited carrying capacity within the environment critical to the population-ecology view? Provide support for your answer by referring to the OT Closeup on the Australian white goods industry.

13 If the population ecologists are right, what can management do to make their organisations more effective?

14 Describe how institutional theory helps explain the structure and practices of an organisation you are familiar with.

15 Select an organisation with which you are familiar and identify its key resource dependencies. How does it seek to reduce uncertainty arising from the resource dependencies?

CASE FOR CLASS DISCUSSION

Qantas faces its environment

There is only one word to describe the airline industry and that is brutal. Capital costs are high, with one jumbo jet costing over $250 million. Add to that the cost of terminals, maintenance facilities and a significant investment in IT and a billion dollars hardly gets you started. But finding finance is only the first of your problems. One of the greatest difficulties is the cyclical nature of the industry. An outbreak of SARS or bird flu, a terrorist attack or an economic downturn and the profitability of an airline disappears overnight. This is because air travel for most is a discretionary purchase; it is not a 'must have' in order to stay alive. Holidays requiring air travel can be postponed indefinitely. Even business can get by with greatly reduced levels of travel if need be. All of this adds up to an industry with high costs but wildly fluctuating demand. It is not surprising that downturns take a toll on the financially weakest as can be seen in the aftermath of the terrorist attacks in 2001.

But there are ways in which uncertainty can be managed, and Qantas provides a good example. In 1992 Qantas, which flew only to overseas destinations, merged with Australian Airlines, a purely domestic carrier. Both were owned by the federal government and the merger formed what was the 12th largest airline in the world in terms of passenger-kilometres flown. The merger between the two airlines was in preparation for the federal government privatising the airline in 1995. In an industry where profitability is hard to come by it has had an enviable record of being profitable ever since.

Although air transport is high in glamour, Qantas' operations can basically be classified as mechanistic. Its activities are undertaken in a repetitive cycle, which dominate the working life of most employees. Its operations conform to a timetable that it updates approximately every six months, and aircraft maintenance is performed in accordance with fixed schedules. Planning to reduce uncertainty is a major function at Qantas, ensuring that for the time horizon being considered all major eventualities are covered. A constant brief must be kept on political factors affecting the airline and its competitors, and a politically savvy chief executive is almost a must. International air routes are governed by agreements between countries as to landing rights. Although this form of international cartel is coming under pressure, governments still intervene far more often in this than in most other industries. Factors affecting political instability in the countries in which the airline operates must be constantly monitored.

All industries have critical functions that can affect profitability. One of the keys to success in transport is to keep capital equipment earning revenue all the time. To do this, Qantas has developed advanced management information systems which allow it instant updates on the level of booking for each flight in any part of the world. It has a function that airlines call yield management, which could loosely be called pricing. This function is to fill an aircraft with passengers paying the maximum fare that can be extracted from them. Yield management plays demand off against availability, using the price of a ticket as the variable in keeping the planes full. Hence, there are such variables as seasonal fares, discounts for times of day, holiday excursions and so on. The business person who must travel at short notice, however, pays the full fare. Out of the 400 people in a jumbo jet, few will be paying the standard fare for their travel. They range from first-class full-fare passengers to tourists on super-apex excursions and staff going on holidays at greatly discounted rates.

There are numerous departments interfacing with the environment at Qantas. From fuel supply futures to juggling currency in hedging operations, every contingency that can be thought of is covered. These departments form larger groupings for management purposes. For instance, all specialist maintenance functions, such as engines and avionics, combine to form a larger department. Some departments exist to form an interface with outside suppliers of services, such as airport authorities, advertising agencies and regulatory agencies. Shareholders form one of Qantas' critical constituencies; keeping shareholders informed of the financial position of the company is an important function. It also concentrates management's minds upon the need to improve profit performance.

The large number of departments and the continuous nature of operations place a heavy burden upon communication and coordination within the organisation. Computerised information systems are supplemented by a wide range of coordinators and project managers. IT systems also store information on such things as bookings of passengers and cargo, performance of aircraft, availability of spares and crew schedules.

There is constant downward pressure on prices in the airline industry. Basically, air travel is a commodity, with all airlines offering the same services. Most of the travelling public are price-sensitive, and seek the cheapest deals commensurate with their needs. Qantas has one of the higher cost structures in the industry, particularly when ranked against its Asian competitors, and it is faced with the need to trim staff and lower operating costs. The introduction of Australian Airlines, and more lately Jetstar as stand-alone operations with their own management has allowed Qantas to operate as both a low-cost and a full-service operator, something which few airlines around the world have managed to do.

One of the problems facing Qantas is that many of its strongest competitors are either government owned or government supported and are not allowed to fail. This is particularly so of many Asian and Middle Eastern airlines. It means that the normal shake-out which occurs in most industries to clean out the poorly managed and undercapitalised participants does not occur in the airline industry; bankruptcy is avoided by governments providing various forms of handouts.

Strategic and technological opportunities and threats also contribute to an uncertain environment. Provided costs can be kept under control, size is a good protection against unexpected downturns. Economies in purchasing and overheads can be achieved, thus pushing costs lower, and the more extensive the network serviced, the more passengers are likely to be drawn to the airline. So Qantas is always evaluating its strategic options in relation to mergers and acquisitions. Technological changes are promising a new approach to network development. Ultra-long-range aircraft being delivered or under development are bringing more ports into non-stop flying distance from Australia. This, combined with their smaller size, will open new opportunities for Qantas to serve ports it has withdrawn from and bypass hubs such as Singapore.

QUESTIONS

1 How closely does Qantas' structure conform to the theories of Lawrence and Lorsch? Support your position showing areas of similarity and difference.

2 Identify how changes in Qantas' environment have affected important tasks in the organisation. How have these affected Qantas' strategy?

3 To what extent does the nature of the task that Qantas is engaged in determine its structure? Given your answer to question 1, what do you consider has a greater impact, technology or environment?

4 How could you apply the population-ecology view to the airline industry? In the Qantas case, what indicates a practical limitation to the population-ecology viewpoint?

5 How does Qantas seek to control uncertainty? How has it incorporated this into its structure?

FURTHER READING

Howard Aldrich, *Organizations and Environments*, Englewood Cliffs, NJ: Prentice Hall, 1970.

Tom Burns & G.M. Stalker, *The Management of Innovation*, London: Tavistock, 1961.

Robert Duncan, 'Characteristics of Organizational Environments and Perceived Environmental Uncertainty', *Administrative Science Quarterly*, 17, 1972, pp. 313–17.

Paul Lawrence & Jay W. Lorsch, *Organization and Environment: Managing Differentiation and Integration*, Boston: Division of Research, Harvard Business School, 1967.

Walter Powell & Paul DiMaggio, eds, *The New Institutionalism in Organizational Analysis*, Chicago, IL: University of Chicago Press, 1991.

NOTES

1 Robert H. Miles, *Macro Organizational Behavior,* Santa Monica, CA: Goodyear Publishing, 1980, p. 195.

2 James D. Thompson, *Organizations in Action,* New York: McGraw-Hill, 1967, p. 27.

3 H. Kirk Downey, Don Hellriegel & John W. Slocum, Jr, 'Environmental Uncertainty: The Construct and Its Application', *Administrative Science Quarterly,* December 1975, pp. 613–29.

4 William H. Starbuck, 'Organizations and Their Environments', in Marvin D. Dunette, ed., *Handbook of Industrial and Organizational Psychology,* Chicago: Rand McNally, 1976, p. 1080.

5 William R. Dill, 'Environment as an Influence on Managerial Autonomy', *Administrative Science Quarterly,* March 1958, pp. 409–43.

6 Karl Weick, *The Social Psychology of Organizing,* Reading, MA: Addison Wesley, 1969; and Robert Duncan, 'Characteristics of Organizational Environments and Perceived Environmental Uncertainty', *Administrative Science Quarterly,* 17, 1972, pp. 313–27.

7 Tom Burns & G.M. Stalker, *The Management of Innovation,* London: Tavistock, 1961.

8 See Henry Mintzberg, *The Structuring of Organizations,* Englewood Cliffs, NJ: Prentice Hall, 1979, pp. 270–2.

9 Margaret K. Chandler & Leonard R. Sayles, *Managing Large Systems,* New York: Harper & Row, 1971, p. 180.

10 Paul Lawrence & Jay W. Lorsch, *Organization and Environment: Managing Differentiation and Integration,* Boston: Division of Research, Harvard Business School, 1967.

11 See, for example, Henry L. Tosi, Ramon J. Aldag & Ronald G. Storey, 'On the Measurement of the Environment: An Assessment of the Lawrence and Lorsch Environmental Subscale', *Administrative Science Quarterly,* March 1973, pp. 27–36; and H. Kirk Downey & John W. Slocum, Jr, 'Uncertainty: Measures, Research, and Sources of Variation', *Academy of Management Journal,* September 1975, pp. 562–78.

12 Ramon J. Aldag & Ronald G. Storey, 'Environmental Uncertainty: Comments on Objective and Perceptual Indices', in Arthur G. Bedeian, A.A. Armenakis, W.H. Holley, Jr & H.S. Field, Jr, eds, *Proceedings of the Annual Meeting of the Academy of Management,* Auburn, AL: Academy of Management, 1975, pp. 203–5.

13 Robert Duncan, 'Characteristics of Perceived Environments and Perceived Environmental Uncertainty', *Administrative Science Quarterly,* 17, 1972, pp. 313–27.

14 Weick, *The Social Psychology of Organizing.*

15 Aimin Yan & Meryl Rice Louis, 'The Migration of Organizational Functions to the Work Unit Level: Buffering, Spanning and Bringing up Boundaries', *Human Relations,* 52(1), 1999, pp. 25–48; Roger Sor, 'Information Technology and Organisational Structure: Vindicating Theories from the Past', *Management Decision,* 42(1/2), 2004, pp. 316–25; and Choong C. Lee & Varun Grover, 'Exploring Mediation between Environmental and Structural Attributes: The Penetration of Communication Technologies in Manufacturing Organizations', *Journal of Management Information Systems,* 16(3), 1999/2000, pp. 187–218.

16 Gregory G. Dess & Donald W. Beard, 'Dimensions of Organisational Task Environments', *Administrative Science Quarterly,* March 1984, pp. 52–73.

17 Weick, *The Social Psychology of Organizing.*

18 Jeffrey Pfeffer, *Organizational Design,* Arlington Heights, IL: AHM Publishing, 1978, p. 133.

19 John Child, 'Organizational Structure, Environment, and Performance: The Role of Strategic Choice', *Sociology,* January 1972, pp. 1–22.

20 This section is drawn from Nicolaj Siggelkow & Jan W. Rivkin, 'Speed and Search: Designing Organizations for Turbulence and Complexity', *Organization Science,* April 2005, pp. 102–22.

21 Kathleen Eisenhardt & L. J. Bourgeois III, 'The Politics of Strategic Decision Making in High Velocity Environments', *Academy of Management Journal,* December 1998, pp. 737–71.

22 Michael T. Hannan & John H. Freeman, 'The Population Ecology of Organizations', *American Journal of Sociology*, March 1977, pp. 929–64; Howard E. Aldrich, *Organizations and Environments*, Englewood Cliffs, NJ: Prentice Hall, 1970; Douglas R. Wholey & Jack W. Brittain, 'Organizational Ecology: Findings and Implications', *Academy of Management Review*, July 1986, pp. 513–33; Dave Ulrich, 'The Population Perspective: Review, Critique and Relevance', *Human Relations*, March 1987, pp. 137–52; John Betton & Gregory Dess, 'The Application of Population Ecology Models to the Study of Organizations', *Academy of Management Review*, 10(4), 1985, pp. 750–7; and Alessandro Lomi, 'The Population Ecology of Organizational Founding: Location Dependence and Unobserved Heterogeneity', *Administrative Science Quarterly*, 40(1), 1995, pp. 111–14.
23 See, for instance, J. Alay, 'The Heart of Silicon Valley', *Fortune*, 136(1), 1997, p. 66; and L.H. Dobkins, 'Regional Advantage, Culture and Competition in Silicon Valley and Route 128', *Journal of Economic Behavior and Organization*, 32(1), 1997, pp. 161–3.
24 Charles Perrow, *Complex Organizations: A Critical Essay*, 3rd edn, Glenview, IL: Scott, Foresman, 1986, pp. 211–16; Andrew H. Van de Ven, 'Review of Organizations and Environments by H.E. Aldrich', *Administrative Science Quarterly*, June 1979, pp. 320–6; Wai Fong Foo, John C. Oliga & Anthony G. Puxty, 'The Population Ecology Model and Management Action', *Journal of Enterprise Management*, June 1981, pp. 317–25; and Amos H. Hawley, 'Human Ecology: Persistence and Change', *American Behavioral Scientist*, January/February 1981, pp. 423–44.
25 ibid.
26 John Langston, 'The Ecological Theory of Bureaucracy: The Case of Josiah Wedgwood and the British Pottery Industry', *Administrative Science Quarterly*, September 1984, pp. 330–54.
27 Paul DiMaggio & Walter Powell, 'The Iron Cage Revisited: Institutional Isomorphism and Collective Rationality in Organizational Fields', *American Sociological Review*, 48, 1983, pp. 147–60; Walter Powell & Paul DiMaggio, eds, *The New Institutionalism in Organizational Analysis*, Chicago, IL: University of Chicago Press, 1991; Richard Scott, 'The Adolescence of Institutional Theory', *Administrative Science Quarterly*, 32, 1987, pp. 493–511; Lynn Zucker, ed., *Institutional Patterns and Organizations: Culture and Environment*, Cambridge, MA: Ballinger, 1988, W. Richard Scott & Soren Christensen, eds, *The Institutional Construction of Organizations*, Thousand Oaks, Ca.: Sage, 1995.
28 This section is mainly drawn from Jeffrey Pfeffer & Gerald Salancik, 'The External Control of Organizations: A Resource Dependence Perspective', New York: Harper & Row, 1978.
29 David Jacobs, 'Dependency and Vulnerability: An Exchange Approach to the Control of Organizations', *Administrative Science Quarterly*, March 1974, pp. 45–59.
30 Mintzberg, *The Structuring of Organizations*, p. 272.
31 ibid., pp. 273–6.
32 ibid., pp. 282–5; and Edward F. McDonough III & Richard Leifer, 'Using Simultaneous Structures to Cope with Uncertainty', *Academy of Management Journal*, December 1983, pp. 727–35.
33 Mintzberg, *The Structuring of Organizations*, pp. 281–2.

CHAPTER 9

Power-control

After reading this chapter you should be able to:

- discuss the arguments in support of strategic choice for managers
- distinguish between power and authority
- describe how an individual or group gains power
- define politics
- explain the power-control model of how structures emerge
- describe the power-control interpretation of technology and environment's role in structure
- explain the power-control view of structural change
- examine how power and politics interact within organisations
- discuss at what levels in the organisation the five contingencies are likely to have their strongest influence.

Introduction

The 'car guys' take charge at General Motors

General Motors in the USA has a reputation for producing stodgy cars.[1] It was traditionally an engineering-dominated company with an emphasis on producing at reasonable cost. But starting in the 1980s, it watched as its market share slowly but continuously eroded, first to the Japanese and then to a host of other imports and smarter local producers. The only cars it made money on were SUVs, pick-up trucks, favoured by Americans, and a few four-wheel-drives and luxury vehicles. The main reason the GM cars were not selling was that they were just plain boring and indistinguishable from one another.

This reflected the combination of an emphasis on brand management and cost cutting. The marketers, who had gained the upper hand at GM, promised that by astute marketing and brand management they could arrest the decline in sales. They pushed consistent brand imagery and strong marketing, rather than innovative styling, to sell cars. Many rigid design rules were in place that resulted in boring cars. Stylists had to consult lengthy design manuals for each division, including up to 40 pages describing the crest for each brand. Adding to these problems were the powerful engineers, who were more interested in cost cutting than producing attractive cars.

To try to overcome these problems, GM appointed Robert Lutz as vice-chairman for product development. He is a classic 'car guy' with a passion for product and a flair for design. He is obsessed with producing cars not to a formula or a price but to a design that will grab customers and become a must-have product. His is a powerful position. He reigns supreme over every aspect of vehicle operations, from the design studio to the factory floor. He is trying to convince executives that unless the design is right, no marketing in the world will sell the product. He has thrown away the instruction book and told designers to be innovative. He approves all designs and has rejected some out of hand as being too stodgy.

Lutz has help. He has found allies in the organisation and has key positions reporting to him. The resistance of the engineers and manufacturers has crumbled; the past history of poor market performance has left them without a power base to challenge Lutz's authority.

The 'car guys' story introduces another perspective on how organisation structures evolve. Organisation members, looking to satisfy their self-interest or point of view, seek to gain power and then use it to create structures that work to their benefit.

In the previous four chapters we have looked at strategy, size, technology and environment as independent determinants of structure. We found that while each of these contingency variables could explain some of the variations to be found in organisational structures, none could explain all of the variations identified. Each contributed by explaining a part, but only a part. Is it possible that the variables interrelate? That is, by combining them, could we get a whole greater than the sum of the parts? For instance, do large size, routine technology, stable environment and analyser strategy go together? Efforts in this direction suggest that there is an interaction among the

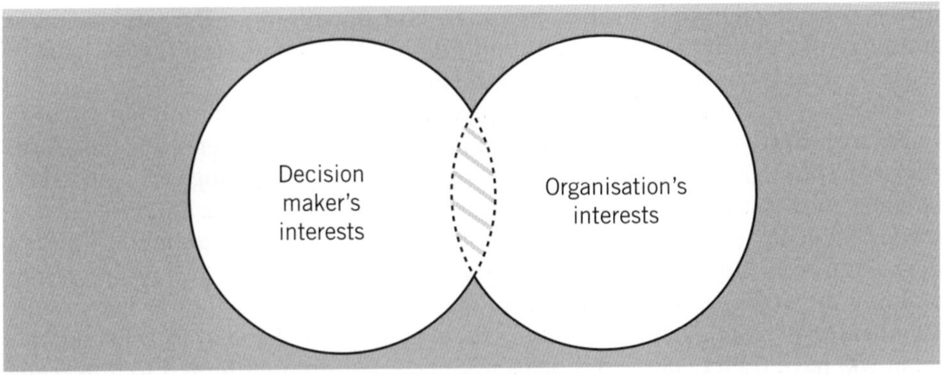
Decision
maker's
interests
Organisation's
interests

FIGURE 9.1 Interplay of the decision maker's and the organisation's interests

Although it would be highly desirable, in terms of organisational effectiveness, for the two circles (representing the individual's interests and the organisation's interests) to align perfectly, that is far more likely to be the exception than the rule. Given that the two circles do not align, what can we predict, and what does it mean to decision making?

It is unreasonable for us to expect that decision makers will neglect their self-interest. As a result, their decision choices will reflect the criteria and preferences compatible with the shaded area. That is, for much of the time, the decision maker is likely to let his or her own interests, both personal and strategic, influence decision making. Moreover, if confronted with a set of choices, all of which meet the 'good enough' criterion, the decision maker would obviously choose the one most beneficial either personally or to their point of view, or both. In Figure 9.1, the overlapping area of the circles represents the region in which the decision maker's interests and those which promote organisational effectiveness coincide. In this area, for instance, we can expect managers to be concerned with economic efficiencies and to prefer an organisation structure that would facilitate them. This area also represents the discretionary range in which—given the constraints of size, technology and environment—managers still have room for making choices that are also self-serving, that is in the decision maker's interests.

Modern management techniques aim to merge the interests of the decision maker and those of the organisation, thus reducing the influence of the manager's self-interest. This has the effect of increasing the area of overlap shown in Figure 9.1. This may be achieved in a number of ways. Reward systems are often aimed at inducing decisions which benefit the organisation. The most obvious are rewarding sales staff for what they sell and top management for achieving profit goals. Managers are also rewarded for achieving targets such as profitability. But socialisation also plays a part, by reinforcing preferred behaviour standards. And on an organisation-wide basis, a strong culture can serve to keep the interests of the organisation uppermost in managers' minds.

Dominant coalitions

The individuals who make up the organisation coalesce into groups with similar interests or values. These are called coalitions and they flourish largely because of the differences of opinion surrounding goals, strategy, organisational effectiveness and what is considered to be in the best interests of the organisation. The action of these groups reinforces the political nature of organisations, and even plays a part in deciding what is considered rational and what is not.[9]

Coalitions, which may be called factions, form to protect and promote interests which are held in common. They may have a short-term focus or represent long-term alliances. They may be concerned with a narrow single issue or a range of broad issues. Probably the most visible coalitions form along departmental lines. Employees in the marketing department have a common special interest, ensuring that they obtain their share of the organisation's resources and rewards. They also have an interest in defining the organisation's problems in marketing terms. But they are not alone. Members of accounting, finance, supply chain management and every other department will have their coalitions. Coalitions, of course, are not limited to functional units. Divisional and plant managers will have their coalitions, as will different levels of middle managers and even the top management cadre and boards of directors. They may also be found at the lowest level of the organisation. And we should also not forget that coalitions may form around personalities, relationships and shared interests as well as ethnic and gender groups. Management may belong to a number of coalitions which coalesce around different issues. Coalitions are able to exert influence through collective decision making, such as by membership of committees and boards, and through problem definition and manipulation of data gathering and information flows.

dominant coalition the group within an organisation with the power to influence the outcomes of decisions

Although coalitions may form around any number of issues, the **dominant coalition** is the one that has the power to affect structure. Structure is important because of the way in which it allocates responsibility and communicates in observable form which positions and people are important in the organisation. In a small company, the dominant coalition and the owner are typically one and the same. In large organisations, top management usually dominates—but not always; politics is a constantly shifting arena based on opportunism and circumstance. Any coalition that can control the resources on which the organisation depends can become dominant, and of course uncertainty means that what is uncertain is constantly changing or is often interpreted that way.[10] A group with critical information, expertise or any other resource that is essential to the organisation's operation can acquire the power to influence the outcome of structural decisions and thus become the dominant coalition. A fuller explanation of the sources of such power appears later in this chapter.

The existence of divergent interests and coalitions leads naturally to the discussion of the role of power in organisations. Simply put, because there is rarely agreement among organisational members on preferred outcomes, coalitions are constantly vying for power and influence over decision making. The power of the various coalitions determines the final outcome of the decision process. Note that this power struggle comes about because of differing preferences over goals and outcomes and the definition of what constitutes a problem.[11] Without these differences, there would be no precondition for judgement, negotiation and the eventual politicking that occurs.

Power and authority

As power and authority are often confused the terms need clarification. In Chapter 4, we defined authority as the right to act, or to command others to act, towards the attainment of organisational goals. This right derives its legitimacy from the authority figure's position in the organisation. Authority goes with the job. All managers have a job description which defines what they are responsible for and who they answer to. These are all manifestations of authority; you leave your managerial job and you give up the authority that goes with that position. When we use the term, **power**, we mean an individual's capacity to influence decisions. As such, authority contributes to an individual's power; that is, the ability to influence, based on an individual's legitimate position, can affect decisions, but one does not require authority to have such influence.

power an individual's capacity to influence decisions

Figure 9.2 depicts the difference between authority and power. The two-dimensional hierarchical arrangement of boxes in Figure 9.2A indicates that there are levels in an organisation and that the right to contribute to decision making increases as one moves up the hierarchy. Power, on the other hand, is conceptualised best as a three-dimensional cone. The power of individuals in an organisation depends on their vertical position in the cone and their distance from the centre of the cone.

Think of the cone in Figure 9.2B as an organisation. The centre of the cone will be called the power core. The closer one is to the power core, the more influence one has to affect decisions. The existence of a power core is the only difference between A and B in Figure 9.2. The vertical hierarchy dimension in A is merely one's level on the outer edge of the cone. The top of the cone is equal to the top of the hierarchy, the middle of the cone is equal to the middle of the hierarchy, and so on. Similarly, the functional groupings in A become wedges in the cone. This is seen in Figure 9.3, which depicts the same cone in Figure 9.2B, except that it is now shown from above. Each wedge of the cone represents a functional area. Thus, if the second level of Figure 9.2A contains the marketing, production and administrative functions of the organisation, the three wedges of Figure 9.3 are the same functional departments.

The cone analogy allows us to consider the following two facts:

1 The higher one moves in an organisation (an increase in authority), the closer one automatically moves towards the power core.
2 It is not necessary to have authority to wield power, because one can move horizontally inward towards the power core without moving up the hierarchy.

Members of centrally placed unions, who have little authority in the organisation, are often very powerful because of their ability to stop production. Secretaries to

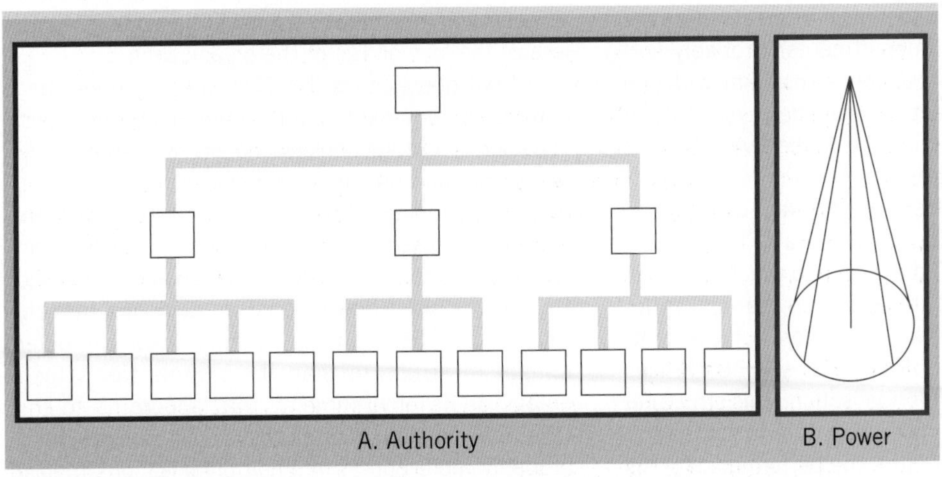
A. Authority
B. Power

FIGURE 9.2 Authority versus power

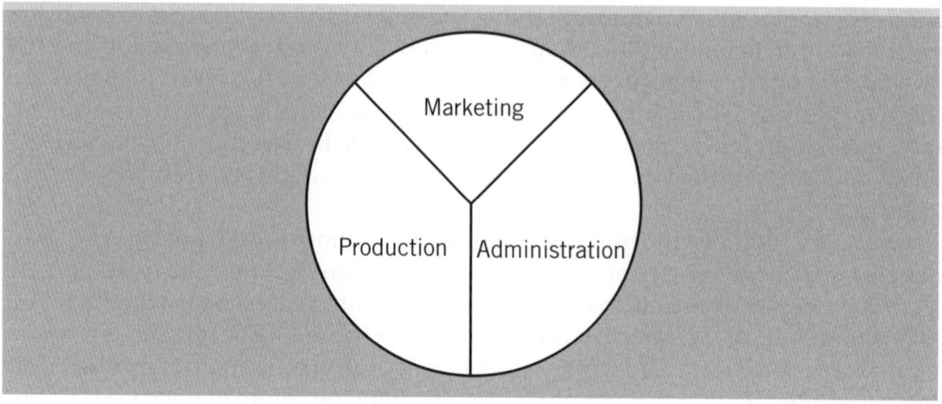
Marketing
Production
Administration

FIGURE 9.3 Bird's-eye view of the organisation conceptualised as a cone

high-place managers traditionally wield a considerable power, even though their formal position gives them little authority. Alternatively, some senior managers may have significant authority but not much power. An example of this situation may be the in-house company lawyer. Being a corporate lawyer sounds as if it would be an influential position. They may have direct access to the senior management of the

OT CLOSEUP

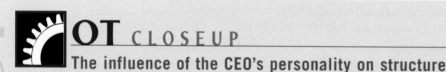

The influence of the CEO's personality on structure

Would you be surprised to find out that chief executive officers (CEOs) with a thirst for power delegate very little authority, that CEOs who are suspicious of others establish elaborate information systems so that they can closely monitor what's going on, or that CEOs with strong creative and technical interests often set up substantial research departments? Probably not! This has led to the conclusion, consistent with the strategic-choice perspective, that the personality of an organisation's CEO might be a decisive influence on determining structure.

Recent research offers confirming evidence.[12] Specifically, it has been found that a CEO's need to achieve (*nAch*)—that is, the degree to which he or she strives to continually do things better—strongly influences structure. In what way? The more achievement-oriented the CEO, the more he or she centralises power and imposes high formalisation. This structural form allows the CEO to take major credit for, and to carefully monitor and control, the performance of his or her organisation.

Does this conclusion apply to all organisations? The evidence indicates that the relationship between *nAch* and formalisation is significantly stronger in small organisations than in large ones, and in young ones than in old ones. However, the preference for centralisation by high achievers seems to be evident regardless of the size or age of the organisation.

A final question: is the CEO's personality a more powerful determinant than the traditional contingency variables of size, technology and environmental uncertainty? Yes and no! On the no side, size was found to be a significant determinant. Consistent with the research studies discussed in Chapter 6, large organisations tend to be more decentralised and formalised. On the yes side, however, is the evidence that the *nAch* of the CEO seems to be a more powerful determinant of structure than the organisation's technology or its environment. But, according to this research, this impact of the CEO's preference is probably more potent in small organisations than in large ones.

company and exist in an environment with the trappings of power and influence. But the lawyer may have few staff, if any, understand little about the company's core business, respond to a very narrow environmental segment, and be ignored once he or she moves outside their narrow area of expertise. As a result, the lawyer's capacity to influence key decisions in the organisation may be very limited. This is true of many support staff positions.

The separation of authority and power is obviously important for understanding the power-control perspective. It reminds us that those with formal authority may be able to influence decisions but, then again, others in the organisation may have created strong power bases that provide them with significant influence. Moreover, because those with the capacity to influence decisions will select criteria and preferences that promote their own self-interests, decisions are likely to diverge from those that would be made under conditions of rational decision making.

Contingencies and the nature of the organisation

There are other circumstances which challenge the contingency approach to organisational structuring. We have already discussed the cognitive difficulties in trying to comprehend the complexities of large organisations. A further problem for contingency theory is that organisations are open systems, which engage in interactions with their environment. Environmental influences may act as major limitations on decision making, as well as being a source of ideas and opportunity. Below we discuss the influence of existing organisational structures, societal influences, and fashions and fads in management thinking.

Legacy systems and large size

Legacy systems are the existing systems, rules, procedures, roles, responsibilities and ways of doing things that are accepted practice within an organisation. The word *legacy* is used to describe them because they have emerged from a stream of past decisions and become institutionalised. Organisational members become familiar with reporting relationships, ways of relating to each other, the manner in which technology is used, and how to interpret and interact with the environment. As a result, organisational structures often reflect past practices rather than current needs. They rarely reflect the future needs of the organisation. Once these practices are established and have proven successful, it takes a major management effort to change them.[13]

While legacy systems often contribute to the smooth operation of the organisation, there is a negative side. Established ways can predetermine courses of action. They can also orient managers to address problems using certain mindsets, even going so far as to define the nature of problems. The existence of legacy systems also leads to large organisations being slow to react to change. Major organisational change normally takes years, and is not undertaken lightly.[14]

The combined effect of legacy systems and large size presents a challenge to the rationality assumption of contingency theory. Organisations clearly have structures, but these structures may reflect past circumstances rather than current needs or future requirements. The fact that the organisation is probably getting by satisfactorily with its existing structure again indicates that the most appropriate structure is not a point but one of a range of possibilities.

Designing around people

The attitudes and capabilities of existing management and staff influence design outcomes. In a purely rational world, we might ignore who is at present in what position, and what their capabilities, strengths and weaknesses are. But in most cases these factors are taken into account when designing organisations. For instance, a chief finance officer with skills and interest in IT may find him- or herself with responsibility for the IT function. Another equally capable finance manager with little interest in IT would rarely be given responsibility for it. The subtle interplay of personality, skills, interests, experience, age, coalition membership, and power and politics leads to tasks being allocated that may not be optimal but which suit the skill set of management staff. Some companies, particularly in the public sector, attempt to overcome this problem by having what is called a 'spill and fill'. All positions are declared vacant. An organisation design is proposed with job descriptions for each area of responsibility. Those who feel that they have the skills and experience appropriate to a position may then apply for it.

Institutional and external pressures

In Chapter 8, we discussed institutional forces in the environment and how they may influence an organisation to adopt certain structural characteristics. These forces may be legislative in origin, such as the need to have equal opportunity officers reporting to a senior manager. But they may arise from the needs of customers or expectations of other stakeholders. For instance, the defence department often insists that its contractors adopt a matrix structure.[15] The customers of construction and civil engineering companies often require one point of contact, such as a project manager, within the organisation with sufficient executive authority to respond to issues raised. Organisations undertaking identical tasks, one a subsidiary of an overseas firm and one locally owned, may have different structural forms because of their different ownership patterns. A further example of institutional forces is the need to obtain quality endorsement (e.g. ISO 9000) with its resultant influence on organisational practices. The challenge that these external forces present to contingency theory is that the resulting structure may not reflect the imperatives we have discussed in previous chapters.

Management fashions and fads

We could have included fashions and fads when we discussed institutional theory, as it is an environmental influence, but its importance justifies separate consideration. Hardly a year goes by without a new fashion or idea being promoted as the answer to management's problems. Examples are re-engineering, strategies for the Internet, and Japanese management, lessons from Sun Tzu's *Art of War*, one-minute managing, popular books on change such as *Who moved my cheese?*. The reminiscences of prominent managers, such as those of Jack Welch, are widely read and often influence decision making.[16] Many of these books are persuasively written, often by consultants seeking to promote their own businesses. Whatever their utility—and we do not condemn these approaches as having no use—they do create social pressure to conform to their prescriptions. For instance, re-engineering was tried by a large number of companies, with mixed success.[17] Many managers no doubt tried to re-engineer their organisations because they saw others attempting it and were reluctant to be seen to be ignoring its proposed benefits. Jack Welch's approach to running General Electric, a large conglomerate based in the United States, has had a major influence on approaches to strategy. In the 1970s the matrix structure was widely adopted, generally inappropriately, in the expectation that organisations structured along matrix lines would become responsive and proactive.[18]

The above examples highlight the influence of social trends on management. If managers felt confident that their organisations were effective, perhaps they would be more resistant to fashions in management thought. But, as we have noted, organisations are difficult to understand and manage. And as organisations are composed of people and operate within a social environment, it is not surprising that social pressures exert an influence on managers.

The roads to power

How does an individual or group gain power? Certainly some power derives from personal characteristics. This section will consider the way in which power derives from the structure of the organisation.[19] It is created by division of labour and departmentalisation. Horizontal differentiation inevitably creates some tasks that are more important than others. Those individuals or departments performing the more critical tasks, or who are able to *convince* others within the organisation that their tasks are more critical, will have a natural advantage in the power-acquisition game. The authority given to those in senior management positions is also structural in origin. The evidence indicates that there are three roads to the acquisition of power: hierarchical authority, control of resources, and network centrality.[20] Let's take a look at each of them.

Hierarchical authority

In spite of our efforts earlier in the chapter to differentiate authority and power, we cannot ignore the obvious: formal authority is a source of power. It is not the *only* source of power, but individuals in managerial positions, especially those occupying senior management slots, can influence through formal decree. They can also be more open about the use of power. Subordinates accept this influence as a right inherent in the manager's position.

The manager's job comes with certain rights to reward and punish. Additionally, it comes with prerogatives to make certain decisions. Further, the higher the position a manager holds in the organisation, the more they are likely to be able to access information which is useful to them, but which is denied others, particularly subordinates. Senior management of an organisation is often exercised through committees and consultation, and the higher the position a person holds the more likely they are to sit on important committees and be consulted in relation to key decisions.

But, as we'll see, many managers find their formal influence over people or decisions extremely limited because of their dependence on others within the organisation. Also, their power is limited by restrictions placed on them by more senior managers. The power of a supervisor is obviously less than that of a general manager. Supervisors have limits on the amount of expenditure they can approve, on hiring and firing, and on the number of staff they supervise.

Those with hierarchical authority have diminished in number over the past 20 years as hierarchies have flattened. There are fewer managers in most organisations than was formerly the case and there has been a trend to devolve greater decision-making responsibility to those actually undertaking the tasks. In addition, the move to greater reliance upon market forces to assess performance has removed the need for large hierarchies which formerly assessed the value of a subordinate's work. But notwithstanding these limitations, those higher in the hierarchy have greater power than those lower down.

Control of resources and ability to reduce uncertainty

If you have something that others want, it gives you potential power over them. In an organisational setting, it also leads to you having a major influence on decisions. But the mere control of a resource is no guarantee that it will enhance your power. The resource must be both scarce and important to the organisation.[21] If a resource is scarce and important, its supply creates uncertainty for the organisation. As we have seen, organisations don't like uncertainty, so those who can reduce uncertainty by ensuring supply of a scarce resource gather power to themselves or their group.

Unless a resource is scarce within the organisation, it is unlikely to be a source of power. In most organisations, cleaners have little power. This is not because cleaners are not necessary; we would soon notice their absence. It is simply because cleaners are easy to replace; they are not scarce. Alternatively, airline pilots have typically been able to exact significant benefits from airlines because their skills are scarce and expensive to acquire. So the mere possession of a resource means nothing if that resource is not scarce. The criticality of a resource is also important. If a resource is scarce, but not critical to the organisation, then little power will accrue to those who control the resource.

If resource scarcity increases the power of the resource holder, then the proximity of relevant substitutes for the resource should also be considered. That is, a resource for which there is no close substitute has greater scarcity than one that has high substitutability. Skills provide an example. Organisations rely on individuals with a wide range of special skills to perform effectively. Those who possess a skill that the organisation needs, but that no-one else in the organisation possesses, will obviously be in a more influential position than one whose skills are duplicated by hundreds of other employees. Design engineers at aerospace firms provide a powerful coalition because it would be virtually impossible to replace their skills in the short term. Alternatively, those sewing covers for the aircraft seats would be relatively easy to replace and consequently have less power within the organisation. Skills scarcity explains why presenters such as John Laws and Jana Wendt can command such high salaries. Their abilities can raise ratings to such high levels that large advertising fees can be charged. Media owners see radio and television personalities as scarce and critical resources responsible for generating high earnings for which there is no close substitute.

Similarly, union power relative to management's is largely a function of its members' ability to restrict management's options. The most powerful unions are those which control a choke point in a supply chain, such as waterside workers and those working in warehouses. Just a few workers can halt the delivery of petrol or idle motor vehicle production lines.

What works for individuals also works for departments. Criticality emerges from the organisation's strategy and the problems it faces at any given moment.[22] Departments within an organisation take on different degrees of importance relative to the strategy the organisation is pursuing and the critical problems that arise. In an organisation that is consumer-oriented, such as Unilever, marketing personnel will be more powerful than, say, accountants or production personnel. Alternatively, we would expect accounting to be more powerful in organisations that rely heavily on financial data, such as banks and brokerage firms, or when the organisation faces critical financial or control problems.[23] The boom in the financial sector led to a large number of people being employed in recruitment, both directly by banks and in various consultancies. While there was a shortage of labour in this industry, those people who could identify and hire suitable employees could name their own terms. However, with the collapse of the boom and the contraction of the financial sector, these people very soon lost their influence.

The power of different functions can be seen in a study comparing hospitals with insurance firms.[24] The hospitals' strategies emphasised efficiency and cost control, while the insurance firms sought product and market innovation. Consistent with the role of centrality, the researcher found that the accounting, process-improvement and operations functions had the most power in the hospitals and the marketing and product-development functions had the most power in the insurance companies.

A study of a production plant in France gives us additional insight into how being in the right place in an organisation can be a source of power.[25] The researcher observed that the maintenance engineers in this plant exerted a great deal of

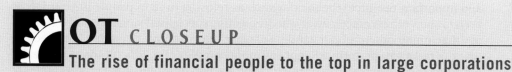

OT CLOSEUP

The rise of financial people to the top in large corporations

An understanding of power can help to explain the rise of financial personnel in recent years to positions of power in large corporations.[26]

Studies investigating the background of top managers of large companies have found that manufacturing personnel and entrepreneurs rose to the top in the early part of this century. From the late 1930s to the late 50s, sales and marketing personnel came to dominate large firms. The period 1960 to the mid-80s saw finance personnel increasingly rise to power.

This shift in the background of corporate managers largely reflects changes in the strategy and structure of organisations. These changes shifted the power of subunits within corporations, which resulted in new leaders coming out of those subunits who could best resolve the problems and uncertainties faced by the organisation.

The early years of the last century saw corporations run by entrepreneurial types and those promoted out of manufacturing. This reflected the product emphasis and single-product strategies of those firms. But over the next 30 years, large corporations began to develop multiproduct strategies and adopt multidivisional structures. This put a premium on sales and marketing expertise and increased promotion opportunities at the top for individuals with these kinds of backgrounds.

Over time, the business units of the multiproduct firms became more independent. This, together with unrelated businesses, meant that top management required less knowledge of the goods and services sold. One of the few ways to evaluate the performance of the conglomerates was to use financial information. Hence financial personnel adept at interpreting this information rose to prominence in top corporate management. Similar skills were needed during the takeover boom in the 1980s, when decisions regarding the worth of companies were largely made on financial grounds.

The trends noted above illustrate an important point—that the person occupying the top job is normally the one who has the capacity to solve the biggest problem that the firm faces. If a firm is vulnerable to takeover, a takeover defence specialist is likely to be managing director; if the biggest problem is a production problem, a production person will be in the top job. Where return on assets is low, those who can identify where the costs are lying and institute an appropriate change program generally receive the nod for the executive suite. The research referred to above reflects the fact that corporate problems tend to occur in waves and afflict all organisations in a similar manner.

influence, although they were not particularly high in the organisational hierarchy. The researcher concluded that the breakdown of machinery was the single remaining uncertainty confronting the organisation. The maintenance engineers were the only personnel who could cope with machine stoppages, and they had taken the pains to reinforce their power through control of information. They avoided written procedures for dealing with breakdowns, they purposely disregarded all blueprints and maintenance directions and so on. Not even the supervisors in the plant had adequate knowledge to check on these engineers.

As environments become more competitive, and opportunities and threats more pronounced, those in the organisation who have the knowledge to manage the resultant uncertainty gain power for themselves. Staff such as those who trade in futures and hedge markets, control complex supply chains, or understand complicated marketing arrangements and customer needs draw power to themselves. Knowledge in this case is a scarce resource because of its ability to reduce uncertainty. It consequently becomes a road to power.

The use of knowledge as a source of power provides insight into employee actions that are often seen as irrational. When placed in the context of controlling scarce and important resources, behaviour such as refusing to train people in your job or even to show others exactly what you do, creating specialised language and terminology that inhibit others' understanding of what you are doing, operating in secrecy so that the tasks you perform will appear more complex and difficult than they really are, or restricting entry to an occupation by a union or professional group suddenly appear to be very rational actions.

Network centrality

Positions within the organisation whose main function is to coordinate information flows and the work of others may be a source of power.[27] Those individuals or groups in a position of **network centrality** gain power because their position allows them to integrate other functions or to reduce organisational inefficiencies or uncertainties. It also provides them with privileged access to wide sources of information which may be used selectively to influence decisions. Those who fill these positions may be quite powerful in the organisation. For instance, consumer products companies, such as Nestlé and Procter and Gamble, have brand managers as part of their structure. Those holding this position collect and coordinate all information concerning a brand, including its position in the market, product improvements, and changes in distribution channels, promotion and advertising. Although brand managers are not particularly high in the organisation structure, they wield considerable influence, as they collect and process the only coherent body of information about a firm's products. In other industries, project managers and coordinators of various types derive their power from being in a similar position in relation to the collection and dissemination of information.

network centrality
the degree to which a position in an organisation allows an individual to integrate other functions or reduce organisation dependencies

Synthesising the power-control view

The previous discussions on non-rational decision making, dominant coalitions, divergent interests and power allow us now to synthesise the power-control view of how organisation structures are derived.

We can begin our synthesis by restating the power-control thesis: an organisation's structure, at any given time, is to a large extent the result of those in power selecting a structure that will maintain and enhance their control. As we will see, the power-control perspective does not ignore the impact of size, technology or other contingency variables. Rather, it treats them as constraints that limit what is otherwise a political process.

But a word of warning is in order. Whilst the exercise of power, and political activity, undoubtedly has an influence upon structure, there is a temptation to ascribe all residual differences in structure to the influence of power. This is misleading.[28] We have noted that effectiveness exists as a range rather than a point. Provided organisations are meeting the minimum requirements of effectiveness, there will always be a temptation for managers to make the minimal changes necessary. Often this means leaving structures as they are for as long as possible. This is not because of power considerations but because of the disruptions and inefficiencies which may emerge from constant change. Under these conditions, power may only account for a small amount of observed structural variations.

OT CLOSEUP

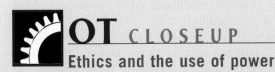

Ethics and the use of power

Are members of the dominant coalition acting unethically when they seek to use their power to enhance their control? In today's business environment—where unethical behaviour has become an increasing concern of executives, the media, academics, students of management and the general public—this question at least needs to be addressed.

Ethics refers to rules or principles that define right and wrong conduct.[29] This, then, begs the question: is the use of power, per se, wrong? Many contemporary behavioural scientists would argue that it isn't. They note that power is a natural part of human interactions—'we influence, or try to influence, other people every day under all sorts of conditions'—that carries over into organisational life.[30]

Power really has two faces—one negative and the other positive.[31] The negative side is associated with abuse—when, for example, power holders exploit others or use their power merely to accumulate status symbols. The positive side is characterised by a concern for group goals, helping the group to formulate its goals and providing group members with the support they need to achieve these goals.

If the dominant coalition chooses a structure that 'satisfices' rather than maximises goal attainment, has it acted unethically? Is 'satisficing' an abuse of the system? Does 'satisficing' exploit employees, shareholders or other relevant constituencies? Is any self-serving action by the dominant coalition that suboptimises the organisation's effectiveness an unethical act or has the dominant coalition acted ethically if the organisation's performance merely meets the 'good enough' standard? Undoubtedly, people will disagree on answers to these questions. But it is answers to questions such as these that will determine whether the power-control perspective describes unethical practice.

Structural decision making as a political process

In previous sections we have seen how structure may influence the way in which power is acquired and exercised in the organisation. However, structural decisions are often the result of political activity. Organisational politics involves activities to acquire, develop and use power and other resources to obtain a preferred outcome when there is uncertainty or disagreement about choices.[32] When we discussed the role of dominant coalitions, we saw how groups of people were more effective at achieving goals than those who act alone. This gives us some indication of the role of politics in organisations.

The challenge to the concept of organisational rationality also indicates how areas of political activity can arise. In the rational organisation goals are clear, processes and customers are well understood, and choices are made in a logical, dispassionate way. However, organisations rarely conform to the rational model. Environments and technologies change, leading to different schools of thought as to how to respond. In addition, changes in senior management may lead to different approaches to defining what the problems facing the organisation are and how to solve them. Selecting between the different alternatives gives rise to political activity in organisations. But organisations are not entirely political. The need to satisfy their various critical constituencies restricts the range of responses open to them and limits the possible options around which political activity can be carried on. Rationality therefore often constrains organisational choice.

Not everyone in the organisation is involved in political activity at any one time, although it is likely that everyone has engaged in it at some time in their career. Surveys show that the higher a person is in management, the more likely he/she is to use politics as part of their job.[33] This is not surprising, as the need to achieve consensus in uncertain situations is most common at this level. Those lower in the organisation are likely to face a more constrained set of options, which are more predictable and so can be guided by established procedures and practices.

The way we structure organisations can give rise to heightened political activity. We can identify five areas in which structure creates political arenas in organisations:

1. *Position in the hierarchy.* Status, and therefore influence, is closely attached to the position of a department head in the organisation's hierarchy. For instance, if the finance department head answers to the accounting manager, this signals that finance has a lower status in the organisation than accounting. However, if both the finance and accounting functions answer to the managing director, this signals that they are of equal status. Obviously, each department will want to report to the most senior person in the organisation.
2. *Resource allocation.* Typically, resources are allocated to departments or divisions as part of a budget. The better funded the department, the more status it has and the more likely it is to influence decisions. The allocation of resources also indicates its favour with senior managers. In addition, higher salaries can be paid, employees hired, and more influence can be exerted by the department and its head. It is therefore not surprising that resources such as budget allocations and funds for capital expenditure are subject to considerable political lobbying.
3. *Interdepartmental coordination.* Relationships between departments are part of organisational life.[34] At the lower level, these relationships are often routine and characterised by established rules and practices. Further up the management hierarchy, relationships between departments are less well defined: conflict can easily arise, as there is a high level of uncertainty and many decisions are not routine. Precedents need to be set and areas of departmental responsibility and territory defined. Political activity is often involved in seeking an acceptable outcome.
4. *Responsibility exceeding authority.* A principle of sound management is that authority should always equal responsibility. In most organisations this rarely applies. Senior managers are far more likely to delegate responsibility but withhold the authority that should go with it. This creates the situation where lower level

their maintenance of control. Organisations, therefore, will be characterised by routine technologies and environments in which uncertainties are relatively low. To enhance control further, those in power will seek to choose structures that are low in complexity and high in both formalisation and centralisation.

For review and discussion

1. 'All structures are the outcomes of power plays.' Do you agree or disagree? Discuss.
2. What are the main arguments put forward by the proponents of strategic choice?
3. What flaws can you identify in the strategic-choice argument?
4. Describe the traditional decision-making process. What assumptions does it make?
5. What is a dominant coalition and how is it formed?
6. Contrast power with authority.
7. How is it possible for someone low in the organisation to obtain power?
8. Why is being at the centre of a network of information seen as being a powerful position?
9. Why is being in control of critical resources a source of power?
10. What type of occupational background do you think would be held by individuals running large corporations at the present time? Why is this likely to be so?
11. Why is structural decision making an intensely political process?
12. Using the power-control perspective, describe how most organisations are structured.
13. Why are managers in a mechanistic structure likely to have more power than those managing in an organic structure?
14. Is it correct to ascribe those parts of structure not accounted for by the contingencies to the influence of power? Discuss.
15. At which level of the organisation does each of the contingencies have its greatest influence? Support your observations.

CASE FOR CLASS DISCUSSION

Alana's big chance

Alana was an ambitious, upwardly mobile executive aspiring to a general management position. So when she received a phone call from an executive search firm one morning sounding out her interest in managing the subsidiary of a large foreign-based company, she jumped at it. Seeing this as being a wise career move, she didn't ask too many questions about the company. But she was familiar with it and nothing that was raised in the subsequent interviews was any cause for concern. Besides, it was a move up and a chance to show what she was capable of. A spell in the executive suite running her own part of the businesses was too good an offer to refuse.

But whilst Alana was competent to handle the technicalities of the job, from the beginning things did not go entirely to plan. She found the structure of the organisation difficult to follow; the organisational chart did not bear much relationship to what actually happened in the company. The previous holder of the position, who had been in the job some time but had now retired, seemed to be able to manage the unconventional reporting relationships but she found it difficult to determine who actually had power. There was a person she reported to; that was straightforward enough. But other senior managers seemed to arrive from overseas, each with the expectation that she answer to them. Further, they expected her to take on work in areas which were not listed in her job description and which were not really in her area of expertise. When she raised this matter with them, they just laughed it off by saying that that was just the way things were done in this company.

This led to another concern for Alana: dysfunctional politics. She was responsible for local operations, but it seemed that a number of her staff reported to someone else in the organisation, ranging from the country manager to managers overseas. As a newcomer, she lacked the knowledge and the relationship base to integrate herself into this system of informal reporting. Another worry for her was that the company seemed to have settled itself into a comfortable mode of operating which did not need a lot of management input. Most initiatives and major decisions seemed to come from the overseas parent and were implemented by those lower in the organisation who had their overseas contacts and had little to do with her. As far as she could see, she essentially was there because it was conventional to have a local manager, but there was not a lot of value she could add.

Alana felt that she did not have the authority to undertake the job effectively and that the manager she answered to neither trusted her nor was prepared to stand up for her if she challenged the system. She also felt that she was held responsible for results, but did not have the autonomy or power to make any major decisions. All told, she felt powerless and after a year left the company.

QUESTIONS

1 Relate Alana's feelings of lack of power to the three sources of power described in this chapter.

2 How did structural issues influence political interplays in the organisation?

3 Why did Alana consider that the politics in the company were dysfunctional? Would all members of the organisation consider the politics to be dysfunctional?

FURTHER READING

Daniel J. Brass, 'Being in the Right Place: A Structural Analysis of Individual Influence in an Organization', *Administrative Science Quarterly*, December 1984, pp. 518–39.

John Child, 'Organization Structure, Environment and Performance: The Role of Strategic Choice', *Sociology*, January 1972, pp. 1–22.

Rosabeth Moss Kanter, 'Power Failure in Management Circuits', *Harvard Business Review*, July/August 1979, pp. 65–75.

Danny Miller & Cornelia Droge, 'Psychological and Traditional Determinants of Structure', *Administrative Science Quarterly*, December 1986, pp. 539–60.

Jeffrey Pfeffer, *Power in Organizations*, Marshfield, MA: Pitman, 1981.

Herbert Simon, *Administrative Behavior*, 3rd edn, New York: Free Press, 1976.

NOTES

1 Adapted from David Welch, 'The Car Guys Take Charge at General Motors', *Business Week*, 26 November 2001, p. 49.

2 Jeffrey D. Ford & John W. Slocum, Jr, 'Size, Technology, Environment and the Structure of Organisations', *Academy of Management Review*, October 1977, pp. 561–75.

3 John Child, 'Organization Structure, Environment and Performance: The Role of Strategic Choice', *Sociology*, January 1972, pp. 1–22; and Derek S. Pugh, 'The Management of Organization Structures: Does Context Determine Form?', *Organizational Dynamics*, Spring 1973, pp. 19–34.

4 ibid.

5 John Child, 'Strategic Choice in the Analysis of Action: Structure, Organizations and the Environment', *Organization Studies*, 18(1), 1997, pp. 43–76.
6 ibid.
7 Herbert A. Simon, *Administrative Behavior*, 3rd edn, New York: Free Press, 1976.
8 James G. March & Herbert A. Simon, *Organizations*, New York: John Wiley, 1958.
9 Jeffrey Pfeffer, *Organizational Design*, Arlington Heights, IL: AHM Publishing, 1978, p. 8.
10 Eva C. Chu, 'Dominant Coalition as a Mediating Mechanism between the Rational Model and the Political Model in Organization Theory', paper presented at Annual Academy of Management Conference, Anaheim, CA, August 1988.
11 Jeffrey Pfeffer, 'Power and Resource Allocation in Organizations', in Barry M. Staw & Gerald R. Salancik, eds, *New Directions in Organizational Behavior*, Chicago: St Clair Press, 1977, p. 240.
12 Danny Miller & Cornelia Droge, 'Psychological and Traditional Determinants of Structure', *Administrative Science Quarterly*, December 1986, pp. 539–60.
13 John Kotter & James Heskett, *Corporate Culture and Performance*, New York: Free Press, 1992.
14 ibid.
15 Stanley M. Davis & Paul R. Lawrence, *Matrix*, Reading, MA: Addison-Wesley, 1977.
16 Sun Tzu, *The Art of War*, London: Hodder and Stoughton, 1990; Spencer Johnson, *Who Moved My Cheese*, London: Vermillion, 2001; Jack Welch & John A. Byrne, *Jack: What I've Learned Leading a Great Company and Great People*, London: Headline, 2001.
17 See, for instance, Leonard L. Russell, Jr, 'Reengineering: The Missing Links', *Human Resource Planning*, 19(4), 1996, pp. 40–7.
18 Davis & Lawrence, *Matrix*; and Stanley M. Davis & Paul R. Lawrence, 'Problems of Matrix Organization', *Harvard Business Review*, 56, May/June 1978, pp. 131–42.
19 Jeffrey Pfeffer, *Power in Organizations*, Marshfield, MA: Pitman Publishing, 1981, p. 4.
20 W. Graham Astley & Paramjit S. Sachdeva, 'Structural Sources of Intraorganizational Power: A Theoretical Synthesis', *Academy of Management Review*, January 1984, pp. 104–13.
21 Pfeffer, 'Power and Resource Allocation in Organizations', pp. 248–9.
22 Donald C. Hambrick, 'Environment, Strategy and Power within Top Management Teams', *Administrative Science Quarterly*, June 1981, pp. 253–75; and M.A. Hitt, R.D. Ireland & K.A. Palia, 'Industrial Firms' Grand Strategy and Functional Importance: Moderating Effects of Technology and Uncertainty', *Academy of Management Journal*, June 1982, pp. 265–98.
23 Keith G. Provan & Germain Boer, 'Beyond Strategic Contingencies Theory: Understanding Departmental Power in Organizations', paper presented at the Annual Academy of Management Conference, Boston, MA, August 1984.
24 Hambrick, 'Environment, Strategy and Power within Top Management Teams'.
25 Michael Crozier, *The Bureaucratic Phenomenon*, Chicago: University of Chicago Press, 1964.
26 Neil Fligstein, 'The Intraorganizational Power Struggle: Rise of Finance Personnel to the Top Leadership in Large Corporations, 1919–1979', *American Sociological Review*, February 1987, pp. 44–58.
27 Daniel J. Brass, 'Being in the Right Place: A Structural Analysis of Individual Influence in an Organization', *Administrative Science Quarterly*, December 1984, pp. 518–39; and Judith D. Hackman, 'Power and Centrality in the Allocation of Resources in Colleges and Universities', *Administrative Science Quarterly*, March 1985, pp. 61–77.
28 Pfeffer, 'Power and Resource Allocation in Organizations'.
29 Keith Davis & William C. Fredrick, *Business and Society: Management, Public Policy, Ethics*, 5th edn, New York: McGraw Hill, 1984, p. 76.
30 Harold J. Leavitt & Homa Bahrami, *Managerial Psychology: Managing Behavior in Organizations*, 5th edn, Chicago: University of Chicago Press, 1988, p. 121.
31 David C. McClelland, 'The Two Faces of Power', *Journal of International Affairs*, 24(1), 1970, pp. 29–47.

32 Pfeffer, *Power in Organizations.*
33 Jeffrey Gantz & Victor Murray, 'Experience of Workplace Politics', *Academy of Management Journal*, 23, 1980, pp. 237–51; Dan L. Madison, Robert W. Allen, Lyman Porter, Patricia Renwick & Bronston T. Mayes, 'Organizational Politics: An Exploration of Manager's Perception', *Human Relations*, 33, 1980, pp. 79–100.
34 Gantz & Murray, 'Experience of Workplace Politics'; Pfeffer, *Power in Organizations.*
35 Pfeffer, ibid.
36 ibid.
37 ibid.
38 Rosabeth Moss Kanter, 'Power Failure in Management Circuits', *Harvard Business Review*, July/August 1979, pp. 65–75; and Pfeffer, *Power in Organizations.*
39 Donald J. Vredenburgh & John G. Maurer, 'A Process Framework of Organizational Politics', *Human Relations*, 37, 1984, pp. 47–66.
40 Barry M. Staw & E. Szwajkowski, 'The Scarcity-Munificence Component of Organizational Environments and the Commission of Illegal Acts', *Administrative Science Quarterly*, September 1975, pp. 345–54.
41 Richard M. Cyert & James G. March, *A Behavioral Theory of the Firm*, Englewood Cliffs, NJ: Prentice-Hall, 1963, p. 36.
42 L.J. Bourgeois III, 'On the Measurement of Organizational Slack', *Academy of Management Review*, January 1981, p. 30.
43 Pfeffer, *Organizational Design*, p. 176.
44 ibid., p. 14.
45 L.J. Bourgeois III, Daniel W. McAllister & Terence R. Mitchell, 'The Effects of Different Organizational Environments upon Decisions about Organizational Structure', *Academy of Management Journal*, September 1978, pp. 508–14.
46 Pfeffer, *Organizational Design*, pp. 73–5.
47 ibid., pp. 72–3.

PART 4

Organisations in Action

part 4

CHAPTER 10

The challenge of finding an appropriate structure

After reading this chapter you should be able to:

- explain what is required of the organisation's structure
- identify how environmental changes have led to the demand for new structures
- discuss whether bureaucracy is dead
- discuss how traditional approaches to organisational structure are evolving
- describe emerging organisational forms.

Introduction

CSR and the challenge of change

CSR, formerly the Colonial Sugar Refining Company Limited, should know a little about history: it has played a prominent part in Australia's business for over 120 years. As its name indicates, it started life as a sugar refiner and became marketer of Queensland's crop. It developed extensive sugar interests in the South Pacific and its dominant role in sugar made it one of Australia's largest companies. The sugar activities were first highly regulated by the Queensland government; later, its other businesses were protected by high tariff walls.

What were these other business interests, and why did it undertake them? By the 1950s, sugar required little additional investment and was generating a lot of cash. Overseas investment was not commonly undertaken by Australian companies, one of the main reasons being that at that time there were considerable barriers raised by countries to inward flows of capital. As well, there were plenty of investment opportunities available in a fast expanding Australia so CSR diversified at home. Over the next 30 years it became involved in industries as diverse as building materials, coal, bauxite and uranium mining, oil and gas, aluminium refining, timber and a host of lesser activities. It even owned a macadamia nut farm. In the 1980s it also entered the US market by buying quarrying and concrete interests in Florida, a move that was widely criticised because it was considered that CSR paid too much for the assets.

Most of the attempts at diversification were disastrous. By the 1980s, it had lost so much money on oil and gas that it had to sell its real estate holdings to cover the losses. By the late 1990s it had a billion dollars worth of timber assets that showed no return. Timber was not its only poor performer; many of its other investments were performing poorly. In the 25 years up to 2001, CSR had created value—that is, earned returns above the cost of capital—only in the three years from 1998. It was clear that something was radically wrong with the company. Its strategy was inappropriate: diversification had led to too many businesses that bore no relationship to each other and that were struggling to achieve economies of scale. The head office was overstretched and could not manage the subsidiaries, particularly in the area of productivity and business development. Management still had the mindset appropriate to bulk commodities and sugar and lacked the skills to improve returns by working capital harder and marketing smarter, particularly in the complex building products industry. And it found itself ill suited to compete in a globalised world characterised by fluid capital flows, demands by shareholders for reasonable returns on their capital, and almost zero tolerance for poor performance. Either CSR had to move quickly to raise its return on capital or someone else would take over the company and do it for them.

The actions taken by CSR to arrest its decline and return to growth provide a textbook example of the steps established companies have taken over the past 20 years. It cut bureaucracy, downsizing its head office from over 500 people to fewer than 50. It sold, merged or closed underperforming businesses (i.e. those showing little return). It concentrated its energies on just a few core areas such as sugar, building materials and the US businesses. It invested capital in businesses that were showing promise which, in CSR's case, was primarily its building material interests. Businesses such as energy and timber were sold. The North American construction materials company was expanded by acquisition. Management decisions were decentralised; responsibilities were focused on the divisions and each divisional manager was set performance targets to meet. Managers were then provided with the freedom to manage their businesses to reach those targets. Performance targets, mainly based on return on invested capital, reached deep into each divisional layer of management. All managers now knew how they would be assessed and that it would be on the performance of their business, not by subjective bureaucratic evaluation. Rewards, such as pay and bonuses, were now based on financial targets being met.

In 2003, CSR decided that shareholders would be best served by demerging construction materials. These were primarily associated with quarrying and cement and 70% of the assets were located in North America. The new company was called Rinker and shares were split, with shareholders receiving shares in the new company on a pro rata basis. The demerger has been a success for CSR shareholders and each company. Both companies have been able to concentrate on what they do best and investors have a clearer idea of what they are investing in.

Both firms may eventually be taken over by others who feel that they can use the capital more productively than existing management. Alternatively, they may change their investment philosophies; CSR selling its sugar interests is always a possibility. But as it has done over the last 150 years, CSR will reflect the preferences and changes in the business that it populates.

One of the themes of this book is that the structure of an organisation makes a major contribution to its effectiveness. The structure must reconcile many different demands, not the least of which is the power and political needs of top management. In this chapter we will discuss how environmental and technical changes, and changes in financial markets and societal expectations, have led to progressive changes to organisational structures. This chapter is primarily concerned with how that evolutionary process has led to contemporary practice.

Before we do that, it is worthwhile considering the purposes of an organisation's structure (see Table 10.1). This issue is not commonly addressed in the literature on organisations; it is almost as if it is taken for granted and does not need elaboration. We do occasionally gain an insight into management's thinking when structural changes are made: these are normally accompanied by statements explaining what the changes are intended to achieve. The discussion in this chapter applies to all organisations, including charities, government departments, profit-seeking businesses, and not-for-profit institutions such as schools and universities. Specifics will of course vary between organisations.

At its broadest level, structure must support the *implementation of strategy.* Strategy comprises an organisation's goals and the courses of action and the allocation of resources necessary for the organisation to achieve them. The structure must support the achievement of these plans; if it doesn't, then it indicates that the structure needs to change. For instance, if a company produces goods that are sensitive to consumer tastes but has no means of monitoring and disseminating knowledge on

TABLE 10.1 The functions of structure

Implement strategy
Define areas of responsibility
Provide control mechanisms
Facilitate the flow of production
Promote coordination and information flows
Monitor and respond to environmental change
Maintain and promote organisational knowledge

changes in consumer preferences within the organisation, we can say that there is a structural weakness in the company.

In creating a structure, we are clearly delineating *areas of responsibility*. A glance at an organisational chart easily identifies those areas which have someone responsible for them. Performance is evaluated and rewards allocated based on the areas of responsibility. This acts to powerfully direct the behaviour of managers. Resources are also allocated along responsibility lines. Through identifying areas of responsibility, we are deciding what is important and, by default, what is not. We also focus the thoughts and efforts of office holders along the lines of their areas of responsibility and direct their behaviour accordingly. As a result, areas of responsibility must reflect those which are important for the organisation.

Another function of structure, and perhaps the one we are most familiar with, is that it provides *control mechanisms*. This maintains the unity of purpose of the organisation. Command and control often has a negative connotation, but without it organisations would soon become directionless, important tasks would be neglected, decision making would slow and the quality of decisions deteriorate, and self-interest would be elevated over the organisation's interest. Command and control mechanisms also establish the chain of reporting relationships within the organisation.

Structure is responsible for *facilitating the flow of production*. All organisations produce something—cars, charitable work, government administration, air travel, hospitality services and so on. These must be produced at a cost and quality acceptable to the consumer and competitive with others doing the same thing. By creating organisational forms, promoting efficiency and using the latest technologies, we facilitate organisational competitiveness.

The structure should also *promote coordination and information flows*. Modern organisations have often been referred to as 'silos'. We are all familiar with the large concrete silos that hold grain; they comprise separate vertical components that are linked to each other structurally. But each is self-contained and they are joined only by thin membranes. In organisations, most authority structures are vertical, like silos, running from the top to the bottom of the organisation. But as production tends to flow from one department to the other—that is, across the organisation—it is important that the structure facilitate the necessary information flows which support the flow of production.

The structure must be able to *monitor and respond to environmental change*. Henry Ford, in the days of the Model-T in the 1920s, was typical of industrialists of his day. He tried to create a self-contained organisation which was insulated from its environment. He was unsuccessful, and no other organisation has managed to fully isolate itself from its environment. All organisations need to build within their structure the capacity to monitor environmental changes and to respond appropriately to them. Without this capacity—and our argument is that it is a structural feature—there will be dissonance between the organisation and its environment, and its future existence will be put in jeopardy.

Structure finally plays a part in the *maintenance of organisational knowledge and learning*. Individuals are the repository of knowledge but their knowledge is specialised. Organisational knowledge occurs when the design and production of a product or service is too complex for one person to understand. Examples are the manufacture of motor cars and aircraft and many aspects of information technology. In cases such as these, structure determines the way the specialised tasks are coordinated and brought together and information and knowledge distributed. Without structure providing this facility, the full resources of the organisation would not be used.

The origins of organisational change

It seems that it is almost impossible to write a management book for a general audience without making breathless observations about the rate of change and apocalyptic claims about the future. Is there any substance for these statements or is it merely a means of grabbing the attention of readers? There is in fact an element of truth in the observations, although many are overstated for the purpose of selling books. Businesses, and organisations, have changed very rapidly over the past 25 years (see Table 10.2), probably as much as during the previous 80 years. The period after 1980 saw the accumulation of many changes, which created new management challenges and altered the world of work. In order to identify the way in which these changes are reconstructing organisations, we need to be aware of what they are and how they have changed organisational environments. The changes have not affected all organisations equally, but there are few that have been unaffected by their influence. A number of changes have originated from government policies, while others have had their origin in technological innovation and societal expectations. In particular, government decisions in relation to privatisation, deregulation, globalisation and the promotion of competition have had a significant impact on all organisations.

Changes in government policy

During the 1980s, governments in Western countries began to introduce policies that were to have far-reaching effects. Prior to that time, government was a major owner

TABLE 10.2 Major sources of change over the past 25 years

Deregulation and privatisation
Promotion of competition
Growth of globalisation
Introduction of technological innovations
Demands for profitability
Commodification of markets
End of the public service mentality
Changes in expectations and society values

of companies, such as the Commonwealth Bank and Qantas. A number of industries, such as banking, transport, telecommunications and energy, were highly regulated: that is, the government determined who could enter the industry, what was to be charged and what the levels of competition were to be. Governments also maintained policies of industrial self-sufficiency behind high tariff walls but these were starting to be questioned as costs rose and economic growth slowed.[1]

During the 1980s these policies were progressively abandoned. Governments in most Western countries sold their trading enterprises. They deregulated industries by allowing market forces to operate and they moved to progressively lower tariff barriers. Globalisation started to accelerate, not as a product of technological change but as a result of government policy. Governments also started to question the way they managed their own operations, such as schools, universities, hospitals and government departments. They generally concluded that these were neither particularly efficient nor effective and that the bureaucratic inertia and inefficiencies present in many would need to be addressed.

Enhanced levels of competition

The result of government policies is that most organisations now experience high levels of competition. No longer do businesses have a guaranteed share of markets or the comfort of government protection. But while threats increased, so did opportunities. The dominant incumbent in many industries was a former government-owned monopoly with entrenched low productivity. The markets they operated in were attractive for entrepreneurs attempting to establish new businesses. Manufacturers faced increased competition from imported goods, leading to significant changes in practices in the sector. These included the merger or exit of many companies, and the sourcing of all or part of their product overseas. Companies found that, in competing against the world's best, they were too small to achieve economies of scale. Efficiency required the consolidation of smaller players into larger, better capitalised units.

Globalisation

The reduction of tariff barriers is only one part of globalisation. Globalisation created many opportunities for companies to expand overseas as other countries lowered barriers to goods and capital flows.[2] Those companies wanting to grow now had access to larger overseas markets. But expansion demanded management skills and knowledge that companies in many cases did not possess. They not only had to assess business prospects in unfamiliar environments, they also then had to incorporate overseas businesses into the operations of their company, which in many cases involved making major structural changes. It also exposed companies to new risks, such as differing cultural standards, currency variations and unfamiliar legal systems.

Technological innovations

Technological innovation is normally high on most people's list of environmental changes.[3] Many innovations are obvious: mobile phones, the Internet and e-commerce, reduced cost of information processing, cheap telephone interconnectivity. All of these are electronic and are based on the microprocessor. And all are readily adaptable to business use. These innovations collectively mean that we can communicate faster and cheaper and process and transmit far more information than we could previously. The uniqueness of many innovations means that their impact is difficult to determine. Some, for instance mobile phones, may be easily and quickly incorporated into day-to-day activities. For others, such as e-commerce and electronic data interchange, new strategies and organisational practices must be developed before they can make their full contribution. Competitive advantages accrue to firms which make the right choices but often late adopters benefit from the mistakes of the early adopters. Bill Gates, the founder of Microsoft, observed that we tend to overestimate technology's impact in the short term but to underestimate its long-term impact.

Demands for profitability

One of the key strategic constituencies of profit-making companies is shareholders.[4] An increasing proportion of companies are owned by professional investors such as superannuation and investment funds. These investors place heavy demands on performance; they are seeking increasing profitability and growth. They in turn require companies to perform or be sold off. As a result, management is under pressure to use resources productively and show an adequate return on assets. These demands have led to major changes in both management and the industrial relations system.

Commodification of markets

As a large number of product categories reach the mature phase of their life cycle, it is becoming increasingly difficult to differentiate products.[5] Products as diverse as motor cars, food, clothing and transport services have low rates of innovation and growth. This leads to price being the basis of most competition. In such markets, advantage goes to the producers with the lowest costs. Firms have little choice but to try to move down the cost curve by squeezing more performance out of the organisation.

End of the public service mentality

Government services, such as those of administration, health and education, although not required to show a profit, have seen the environment they operate in radically change.[6] Governments have cut budgets for education and told universities to become more entrepreneurial in raising funds. Many functions, such as IT, have been outsourced and others privatised. Governments now charge for many services that were previously provided at no cost to the consumer. New expressways are now toll roads built by private enterprise. This has led to many organisations being more aware of the need to provide value for money. Revised employment provisions have been introduced that remove jobs for life. And many services, such as metropolitan rail services, are set tight performance and financial targets to meet. Government organisations have to do more with less and both workers and managers have to focus on resource usage and efficiency issues.

Social changes and expectations

The social contract based on the male breadwinner being given a job for life in return for loyalty has ended, and new employment practices are emerging.[7] The competitive pressures we have identified in the previous sections have led to companies being far more likely to lay off surplus staff than in previous generations. Downsizing, redundancies and plant and office closures, even bankruptcies, are now common. Organisations have also had to alter established practices in order to accommodate legislative changes in relation to women and the disabled. Other legislation covers harassment, antidiscrimination, and occupational health and safety. Workers are now able to negotiate their own conditions of employment rather than work to the conditions of an award whose conditions were the same for everyone. Demographic changes, particularly the ageing of the workforce, are leading to skills shortages as older workers retire. Workforces are also becoming more diverse, forcing managers to revise management practices. Accommodating the work needs of women with young families and expectations of excessive workforce commitment are emerging issues. Society also expects high ethical standards, socially responsible attitudes and sustainable production methods, and managers must be prepared to provide these.

The changes we have identified are all the more challenging for having occurred simultaneously and within a short period of time. The rapidity and magnitude of the changes has no doubt contributed to the extensive 'paradigm shift' literature, which proposes continual and revolutionary changes in organisational structure.[8] But looking around us we can see that many traditional management practices have hardly passed from the scene. Motor vehicle production lines, banking back offices, call centres, government departments and transport companies all exhibit many of the characteristics of bureaucracy. So before we start to look at emerging organisational forms, we should ask 'Is bureaucracy dead?'

Is bureaucracy dead?

We have to answer the above question with a qualified, but firm, no! But before passing judgement, we should first explain what bureaucracy is. *Bureau* means office in French, so bureaucracy roughly translates as rule by office.

Weber's bureaucracy

The term, bureaucracy, was introduced by Max Weber, a German sociologist who wrote on a wide range of topics, extending from religion and capitalism through to Chinese social organisation. He was far from being the equivalent of a modern-day business commentator. Although he wrote around the turn of the 20th century, his writings, originally in German, were not translated into English until 1947.[9] Although the word, bureaucracy, derives from Weber's ideas, many organisations independently practised a similar system of management.

One of Weber's interests was in how to manage large industrial organisations. The modern corporation, with its large workforce and the separation of ownership and management, was one of the great organisational innovations of the second industrial revolution. Prior to its large scale emergence in the late 19th and early 20th century, most enterprises were owner-managed and business was conducted on a personal basis. The management of the modern corporation has fascinated observers, theorists, academics and practising managers for over 100 years; this book is one of many concerned with improving its effectiveness. Weber provided an early step along this road. He proposed seven principles which, when applied, would lead to rational and efficient operations. There was little that was original in these; most had already been applied in one form or another. But Weber brought them together and highlighted the key elements. A number of his proposals are structural, others are behavioural. The seven principles are:

1 *Division of labour.* Each person's job is broken down into simple, routine and well-defined tasks. This is also called job specialisation.

2 *Well-defined authority hierarchy.* A multilevel formal structure, with a hierarchy of positions, ensures that each lower position is under the supervision and control of a higher one.
3 *High formalisation.* There is dependence on formal rules and procedures to ensure uniformity and to regulate the behaviour of job holders.
4 *Impersonal nature.* Sanctions are applied uniformly and impersonally to avoid involvement with individual personalities and personal preferences of members.
5 *Employment decisions based on merit.* Selection and promotion decisions are based on technical qualifications, competence and performance of the candidates.
6 *Career tracks for employees.* Members are expected to pursue a career in the organisation. In return for career commitment, employees have tenure: that is, they will be retained even if they 'burn out' or if their skills become obsolete.
7 *Distinct separation of members' organisational and personal lives.* The demands and interests of personal affairs and kinship ties are kept completely separate from work-related activities in order to prevent them from interfering with the rational impersonal conduct of the organisation's activities.

Positive qualities in Weber's 'ideal type'

Weber's bureaucracy had a number of desirable attributes. These include the focus on merit when selecting employees; security of employment to protect employees against the exercise of arbitrary authority and changes in skill demands; rules and regulations to promote impartiality in decision making; and the establishment of clear lines of authority and responsibility.[10] Weber also sought to combat favouritism by bringing objectivity to employee selection and by reducing nepotism and other forms of favouritism by decision makers and replacing them with job-competence criteria.

The idea of tenure, or security of employment, has a positive and a negative side. The negative side is not difficult to identify: why work hard and apply yourself when your job is virtually guaranteed? Surely a guaranteed job leads to complacency? While this may be true in many cases, there is an upside to tenure. Many tasks are unique to an organisation and may take a long time to learn. Why would an employee take years to learn a highly specialised task if there was not a return obligation on the part of the organisation to provide some form of employment security? Also, security of employment allows employees to make a commitment to the organisation which is far deeper than if they are continually job-hopping. Tenure also protects the individual against capricious actions by management. Although 'jobs for life' is now an outdated management practice, most organisations still try to provide ongoing employment, although this is very much dependent on the organisation being able to afford it.

Weber's bureaucracy had its structural elements. These include division of labour, rules and regulations to cover all eventualities, and a management hierarchy with clearly defined areas of responsibility. Rules and regulations may be constraints on actions, but they also assist in identifying what you can and cannot do, introduce predicability and increase uniformity of actions. Without a policy, for instance, how does a manager know when he or she can or cannot make a decision? Absence of policy, therefore, leaves managers open to sanction for any decision made, however trivial. Similarly, if staff members do something wrong, they want to be assured that they will not be unduly penalised. Bureaucracy's high formalisation provides the mechanism with which to facilitate the standardisation of disciplinary practices.

The positive qualities of a hierarchy of management are often overlooked. Staff members know who to take problems to and how much authority a manager has, as well as their areas of responsibility. The importance of these issues is revealed in a survey of managers in industrial firms. They were found to be decidedly 'in favour of more, rather than less, clarity in lines of authority, rules, duties, specification of procedures, and so on'.[11] These managers recognised that only when the structure and relationships were clear could authority be delegated and performance assessed.

Before we leave this section we should note that much of what passes as bureaucracy has not been adopted by organisations as an act of free choice. Institutional demands in the environment promote disciplined behaviour within the organisation that has the characteristics of bureaucracy. These include the need for quality control, the requirements of safety, the necessity to follow legal requirements in employment practices, and the need to adhere to environmental legislation. All of these require extensive paperwork and the maintenance of documentation, adherence to rules, regulations and systems, and appropriate training.

Summarising Weber's contribution

The central theme in Weber's bureaucratic model is standardisation. In this we can see that many of its features are present in the machine bureaucracy we discussed in Chapter 4. The behaviour of people in bureaucracies is predetermined by standardised structures and processes. The model itself can be dissected into three groups of characteristics: those that relate to the structure and function of the organisation, those that deal with means of rewarding effort, and those that deal with protection for individual members.[12]

Weber's model stipulates a hierarchy of offices, with each office under the direction of a higher one. Each of these offices is differentiated horizontally by division of labour. This division of labour creates units of expertise, defines areas of action consistent with the competence of unit members, assigns responsibilities for carrying out those actions and allocates commensurate authority to fulfil these responsibilities. All the while, written rules govern the performance of members' duties. This imposition of structure and functions provides a high level of specialised expertise, coordination of roles and control of members through standardisation.

The second group of characteristics in Weber's model relates to rewards. Members receive salaries in relation to their rank in the organisation. Promotions are based on objective criteria such as seniority or achievement. As members are not owners, it is important that there be a clear separation of their private affairs and property from the organisation's affairs and property. It is further expected that commitment to the organisation is paramount, the position in the organisation being the employee's sole or primary occupation.

Finally, Weber's model seeks to protect the rights of individuals. In return for a career commitment, members receive protection from arbitrary actions by superiors, clear knowledge of their responsibilities and the amount of authority their superior holds, and the ability to appeal against decisions that they see as unfair or outside the parameters of their superior's authority.

The downside of bureaucracy

In the previous section we identified the positive qualities of bureaucracy. It would be misleading to leave the impression that there was not a downside and, of course, you no doubt have experienced many of these either as an employee or as a customer (see Table 10.3). As a result, bureaucracies have received more than their share of unfavourable publicity. We review these criticisms below.

TABLE 10.3 The downside of bureaucracy

Goals displacement
Inappropriate application of rules and regulations
Employee alienation
Concentration of power
Inability to adapt to change
Overstaffing
Tendency towards large size and low productivity
Non-member frustration

Goal displacement

goal displacement the displacement of organisational goals by subunit or personal goals

Bureaucracy is attacked most often for encouraging **goal displacement**—that is, the displacement of organisational goals by subunit or personal goals. One critic identified that, while rules, regulations and standard procedures introduced a high degree of reliability and predicability, the resultant conformity may be detrimental because it reduces flexibility.[13] Observation of rules and regulations becomes so entrenched that they take on a symbolic meaning of their own. The rules and procedures become more important than the ends they were designed to serve, the result being goal displacement and loss of organisational effectiveness. Another critic believed that means could displace ends as the goals of the organisation.[14] He emphasised that specialisation and differentiation create subunits with different goals. The goals of each separate subunit become the primary focus of the subunit members. This can lead to subunits trying to achieve their own goals, with consequent high levels of conflict and loss of organisational purpose. A third perspective on goal displacement proposed that rules and regulations not only define unacceptable behaviours but also define the level of acceptable performance, which is rarely exceeded.[15] That is, people will do just the bare minimum to get by.

bureaupathic behaviour adherence to rules and regulations by individuals to protect themselves from making errors

Yet another criticism of bureaucracy proposes that high formalisation bureaucracy creates insecurities in those in authority that lead to what has been called **bureaupathic behaviour**.[16] Decision makers use adherence to rules to protect themselves from making errors. But such dependence in time becomes the main focus of behaviour, leading to unadaptive and unimaginative behaviour. A further aspect of bureaupathic behaviour suggests that as people in hierarchical positions become increasingly dependent on lower-level specialists for achievement of organisational goals, they tend to introduce more and more rules to protect themselves against this dependence. That is, they use rules to maintain centralised decision making. One of the outcomes of bureaupathic behaviour is the emergence of organisations where most managers have the right to say 'no' but few have the right to say 'yes'.

Inappropriate application of rules and regulations

Related closely to the problem of goal displacement is the undesirable effect of members' applying formalised rules and procedures in inappropriate situations—that is, attempting to force the needs of a unique situation into one of a range of standard problems. This results in suboptimal performance and dysfunctional consequences.[17] We can conclude that bureaucracies' high rates of formalisation make it difficult to respond to changing conditions.

Employee alienation

employee alienation the distance an employee feels between themselves and their work

A major downside of bureaucracy is **employee alienation**. Members perceive the impersonality of the organisation as creating distance between them and their work. When one is just a 'cog in the wheel', it is often difficult to feel committed to the organisation. High specialisation further reinforces one's feeling of being irrelevant: routine activities can easily be learned by others, making employees feel interchangeable and powerless. Repetitive jobs with little challenge can also easily lead to loss of motivation and dysfunctional employee behaviour. In professional bureaucracies formalisation must be lessened, otherwise the risk of employee alienation is very high.[18]

Concentration of power

The concentration of power in senior executives of bureaucracies has been targeted by some critics. Although this criticism is subjective—it depends on whether one considers the concentration of power undesirable—it undoubtedly flies in the face of those social scientists who want to equalise power in organisations.[19] It is a fact that bureaucracy generates an enormous degree of power in the hands of a very few. If you perceive this as undesirable or counter to the values of a democratic society, as some do, you will find this attribute a negative consequence of the bureaucratic form.

Inability to adapt to change

Bureaucracies have a well-deserved reputation for being slow to change.[20] Environments can change around them, but bureaucracies tend to be always lagging in introducing new ways of doing things. This is because bureaucracies reward stability and adherence to established practices and procedures, both of which are reflected in the behaviour of workers and managers. They are rarely set up or managed to constantly monitor their environment and to respond quickly to changes. Change requires modification to the rules and regulations, which can often only be made after extensive consultations and committee meetings. As a result of their slowness to change, bureaucracies also have the tendency to maintain functions and services long after the need for them has passed.

Overstaffing

Because of the reluctance to reduce workforces, at least in former years, many bureaucracies suffer from a reputation for being overstaffed and for those employed by them being underworked.[21] This arises because technology does not stand still: new inventions and innovations are constantly reducing the numbers of people needed to undertake any given task. No organisation can go on forever without facing the need to adjust to market realities. But bureaucracies have developed a reputation for delaying the need for adjustment to their staff numbers as long as possible.

Tendency towards large size and low productivity

Until the waves of downsizing in the 1980s and 90s bureaucracies, in both business and government, had a reputation for being too big and costing too much to run. This was reflected in the size of the administrative component. The administrative component comprises those workers who are not actually producing the goods and services consumed by the customer. Large numbers of people were employed in support departments in seemingly ever-proliferating numbers. Researchers expended great effort on determining the rate at which administrative components were expanding. The growing administrative component was combined with low rates of productivity. Too many people were doing too many unnecessary things and there was enormous resistance to do anything about it.

Non-member frustration

The last negative consequence that we address relates to those outside the organisation who must deal with the bureaucracy. Bureaucracies unfortunately have a reputation for slowness and inflexibility, which can frustrate those having to deal with them. But, as we see in the next section, it is possible to breathe new life into the old form.

The greatly exaggerated death of bureaucracy

We should be fair to bureaucracy: many of the drawbacks to bureaucracy we have identified above are a result of the way in which bureaucracy has been operationalised rather than being inherent to the concept. In discussing bureaucracy we noted that it had both structural and behavioural components. We will look at each of these in turn and identify what parts of each are still relevant.

To help us answer the question 'Is bureaucracy dead?' we need only to look around us and, if we are employed, look at our place of work. We can find evidence of the structural components of bureaucracy, or at least parts of it, everywhere. The specialisation of labour is still fundamental to organised activity. Most goods and services are still mass produced in repetitive cycles. The demands of quality, efficient resource usage and safety ensure that high formalisation, in the form of rules, regulations and procedures, is fundamental to activity. There is still a hierarchy of management; there is little confusion as to who to report to and what their responsibilities are; and most employees leave voluntarily rather than through downsizing or redundancy. So, viewing bureaucracy from a structural perspective would lead to the conclusion that it is far from being a dinosaur.

Let's move on to the behavioural aspects of bureaucracy. In some ways legal changes have forced the promotion-on-merit component onto bureaucracy. The laws promoting equal opportunity oblige large organisations to select the best person for the job, but many smaller companies are exempt from the legislation. Although primarily aimed at gender equality, the provisions apply to all applicants. Obviously those 'in the know' or those who are well connected still have advantage in obtaining positions. This also highlights the impersonal nature of bureaucracy. It was an ambitious proposal on Weber's part that organisations could become impersonal. They are after all made up of people, with all their complexities of emotion, ambition and desires. It may be that few of us would want to work for an organisation that was devoid of the human touch.

There are still career tracks for employees. Most large companies have an internal labour market—that is, one where most promotions are made from within the organisation. Where there is a suitably qualified candidate from within the management ranks, he/she will generally be offered any promotion positions. Imagine if that were not the case. Would you want to work for a company in which every management position was advertised on the open market for anyone to apply? Probably not! During periods of large-scale change, some companies have what is called a 'spill and fill':

that is, every management position is declared vacant, and managers must then reapply for their old job and any other they consider they are qualified for. Even in periods as disruptive as this, most positions are filled from within the organisation. But while career tracks still exist, organisations are far from being the closed shops they used to be. Managers are regularly hired from outside the organisation, and mobility of labour is expected, especially from upwardly mobile managers.

It is in the area of separation of members' organisational and personal lives that bureaucracies perhaps fall short of current expectations. In Chapter 16, we will discuss in detail the feminist view of bureaucracy. We can summarise that discussion by observing that bureaucracies are organised with the male (or at least full-time employee) career pattern as their basic building block—that is, continuous employment combined with the application of their undivided attention to work. Some sections of the workforce, however, find it difficult to balance home and career demands. In particular, women have discontinuous work patterns, arising from child-rearing and family responsibilities. This disadvantages women in areas such as career paths and the maintenance of knowledge of the organisation, which is necessary for advancement. So, of the characteristics of bureaucracy, this particular one stands criticised more for the assumptions it makes about roles in society.

Freshening up old approaches—bureaucracy revised

The significant changes in environment and technology to which organisations have had to adapt have led to modifications to traditional bureaucracies. Before we analyse these changes, let's clarify our terminology. Weber's bureaucracy, discussed above, was proposed about 100 years ago. It did not aim to describe a structural configuration but an approach to management. In Chapter 4, we introduced the five basic structural forms. Two of these had 'bureaucracy' in their names: the machine bureaucracy and the professional bureaucracy. They were called bureaucracy because a number of elements in the forms reflected Weber's components. For the purpose of providing a starting point, we will treat the structural elements of Weber's bureaucracy and the machine bureaucracy as being very similar. These include job specialisation, high formalisation and a clear management hierarchy. So our use of the term, bureaucracy, basically refers to a machine bureaucracy.

The major structural innovations over the past 20 years have concentrated on responding to market needs, improving decision making, facilitating coordination and communication flows, focusing management's efforts on customers rather than internal processes, and using technology to lower costs (see Table 10.4). We will now examine these and relate them to the environmental changes we noted earlier in the chapter.

Focusing management effort on key responsibilities

When a structure is designed, the task of allocating responsibilities takes on importance because it identifies the areas that will receive most management effort.[22] If important areas have no one responsible for them, chances are insufficient attention will be paid to them and they will be neglected by management. The demands of competitiveness have led to greater management attention being focused on areas of importance in the environment. This often means customers, but may also include providers of inputs

TABLE 10.4 Emergent trends in organisational design

Focusing managment effort on key responsibilities
Rethinking the centralisation–decentralisation balance
Moving focus from internal processes to external adaptation
Greater use of market controls
Improving communication flows
Working back from the customer
Concentrating effort on core competencies
Improving availability of information

such as components and raw materials or other important environmental areas. In part, this does not require major structural change: we can always revise the responsibilities of existing managers. But structural changes are emerging with the creation of new divisions and units which are oriented around specialised segments. So whereas we might have had a large machine bureaucracy, we now have a divisionalised form, with each division concentrating on a product or area. For instance, a company with a machine bureaucracy form may have produced a range of building products. It would now have divisions, each with its own manager, responsible for bricks, cement and plasterboard. Each of the divisional managers would then be responsible, and accountable, for product management and satisfying the customers of their particular division. Their success in doing this would be reflected in the profitability of their division. So key management tasks have moved from being functional—that is, roles concerned with one activity such as production, accounting or sales—to being responsible for customer needs. Of course functional managers are still present, but they in turn have had their focus turned outward rather than inward.

Rethinking the centralisation–decentralisation balance

Accompanying the change identified in the previous section, has been a rethinking of the centralisation–decentralisation balance.[23] There is little point in holding managers accountable for a certain task if they have insufficient authority to operate in their role. There has thus been a move to decentralise decision making. This does not mean that all decisions are made and implemented by lower level managers but that the ideas may be generated lower in the organisation for approval by more senior managers. In turn, it may be the responsibility of lower level managers to implement them where they relate to matters close to the work flow.

The combination of greater decentralisation and responsibility for customer satisfaction puts in place one of the structural elements that is important in rapidly changing, competitive environments. It allows for faster, more appropriate decision making—faster because those responsible for decisions are clearly identified and empowered, and more appropriate because they are made by those who should be aware of customer needs.

Moving focus from internal processes to external adaptation

As we have seen, in a bureaucracy rules dominate. One of the dysfunctions of many organisations in fast-changing environments is that their focus is far too firmly set on adhering to the rules rather than responding to the needs for change. In other words, management has an inward rather than an outward focus.[24] In part, adherence to the rules is a constituent of the organisation's culture. But it is also structural, embodied in the way we define responsibilities. If we structure management responsibilities in such a way that their performance is assessed against customer- or market-focused criteria, we are likely to find that the nature of formalisation changes in order to better achieve the organisation's goals.

Greater use of market controls

One of the problems of bureaucracies is knowing which activities are making or losing money, what the return on investment is, and which activities would benefit from capital investment.[25] For a machine bureaucracy, we aggregate the cost of all activities and deduct it from revenue to arrive at profit. Of course, management accounting techniques assist in breaking down the cost of various activities, but assumptions must be made as to how fixed costs and overheads are to be allocated. In the past, the management hierarchy has undertaken this function mainly on the basis of subjective assessment. Structural changes over the past 20 years have moved towards dividing the business into mini-businesses, each with its own financial and performance goals. Managers are then made responsible for these. Where costs cannot be offset against revenue, such as for a specialised department, then budgets are set in place and managers are expected to achieve them.

We call this process moving from hierarchies to markets. Simply put, we are using monetary performance as a substitute for subjective assessment by management. This process can also be seen in subcontracting and outsourcing, where parts of the operation are put out to open tender and then undertaken on a contract basis. Transport, logistics and information technology are functions that are often outsourced. Call centres are also outsourced, sometimes to overseas countries.

Improving communication flows

The emphasis on a clearly defined management hierarchy and high formalisation presupposes that there is little need for an organisation to change, that once it is set up it can continue for a long time doing much the same as it has been doing. Few organisations have this luxury, but neither do they have the luxury of being able to dismiss the benefits of stability and bureaucracy. An emergent need therefore is to improve communication flows and promote adaptability without compromising the benefits that bureaucracy can provide. Most organisations have invested heavily in information technology to increase their ability to process information. But improved information processing is also a structural feature; managers can be specifically allocated to the task of coordination. Their role may be broadly described as crossing functional boundaries and integrating the work of specialists. For instance, a brand manager in a consumer products company is responsible for everything concerning the brand. IT coordinators liaise between the IT and user departments. Coordinators monitor progress of such disparate operations as goods in transit and material to be delivered to a city building site. These tasks could be handled in a bureaucratic manner, but it would be a very slow and inefficient process. The coordinators' main role is to speed up bureaucracy, not replace it.

Communication flows may be facilitated in the way we set out the workspace.[26] The open-plan office is almost mandatory where good communication between staff is necessary. There are few partitions between offices, and the workspace has 'chill-out' spaces with comfortable seating. There is very high usage of IT. Communication around water coolers and tea- and coffee-making facilities is encouraged. If

OT CLOSEUP

The ethics of modern management

This chapter reflects the prevailing thoughts in relation to organisational structure. The changes we have identified here, and throughout this book, point to managers having to keep a close watch on costs and to be fairly ruthless when it comes to downsizing and pruning the products and services that are making insufficient return on capital. But this can come at an enormous social cost, which is not reflected in profit reports or corporate balance sheets. We can identify three areas of concern that have been discussed in public forums: overwork, particularly by professionals and rising managers; the social dislocation caused by layoffs and downsizing; and the removal of important customer services.

It is difficult to conclude that overwork is a direct result of the way we manage organisations; workaholics have always been with us. But emerging technologies permit a person to be engaging in work-related activities 24 hours a day. Email, linkages to enable working from home, mobile phone, blueberries, and travel requirements can make work a constant activity. The potential of significant monetary rewards also contributes to a 'work must come first' attitude. The expectation of heroic efforts has become part of many management cultures rather than being an odd individual occurrence. As a result, Australian workers put in the longest hours of any industrialised country.

In Chapter 6 we discussed at some length the issue of downsizing. What was omitted in that discussion was the human costs associated with interrupted or terminated careers, unemployment and the need to look for other work, particularly for older employees. We are justified in neglecting this as the study of organisational theory precludes consideration of the micro-aspects of behaviour. But management studies generally are ill-equipped to examine such issues, because once he/she is unemployed a person is no longer a member of an organisation and hence not the subject of study. Most companies do try to handle downsizing humanely. Significant redundancy payments are generally made and help provided to find other employment. As we saw in Chapter 6, some are better off in new employment; others don't fare so well.

Critics of the large numbers of layoffs in recent years have not aimed their criticism just at companies but also at the economic and political system that has placed efficiency and resource-usage issues as the goals to which organisations must strive if they are to survive.

The removal of important customer services is most clearly seen in the actions of the big banks to close branches and to charge for what was previously not charged to the customer. Country people often find that they no longer have a bank branch in their town. Not everyone wants to use an ATM or computer to do their banking. Account fees levied by the bank fall most heavily on the poorer section of society. Alternatively, many are paying far less for banking services, particularly those who borrow large sums of money.

All of these moves make good business sense, and follow from the changes in the environment we have discussed in this chapter. But they contribute to poor public relations. As banking services are essential for all, the matter has received wide publicity that generally paints the bank in a poor light. This issue remains one to be resolved by the various stakeholders of the organisations.

privacy is required for meetings or interviews, meeting rooms are available. Previously redundant warehousing in former industrial and dockland areas is proving popular for conversion to this type of facility.

Working back from the customer

While organisations cannot actually be built around customers, responding to customer needs can become one of the design focuses of the organisation. This involves monitoring customer needs and product perceptions, then designing the organisation to respond to these. This is in contrast to placing the main emphasis on production. Of course compromises must be made: customers can never be fully satisfied, their expectations may be fickle, and there are always cost and other restraints on what can be produced. But to stay in business basic customer needs must be satisfied.

Concentrating effort on core competencies

Concentrating on core competencies sounds more like a strategy than a structure, and of course it is. But, as discussed in Chapter 5, strategy has structural implications. A core competency is something that competitors have difficulty in replicating. As the level of competition increases, most businesses are finding that they can best maximise their returns by concentrating on just a few products where they have a comparative advantage.[27] This way they can achieve economies of scale, management can focus on just a few key markets or products, and information-processing needs are reduced. As a result, we are seeing the emergence of focused organisations. The old conglomerates that had a wide range of businesses are, with few exceptions, passing from the scene. Concentration may not just be on product but may also be on a geographic area. In order to reduce complexity, management may decide to concentrate its business on just one or a few countries.

Improving availability of information

The expanding use of IT permits information to be more widely spread throughout the organisation.[28] This facilitates the flow of goods and materials and assists in serving customers. An example of this process is the bank customer service officer who can call up on their computer screen extensive information on a customer's banking history and the balances of their various accounts. The computer also highlights services which the bank feels may be of use to the customer—for instance, superannuation to the middle-aged and home loans to the young. The customer service officers can then try to sell these products to the customer. Not all information is available to everyone: most managers and workers have their access blocked to areas they are not authorised to view.

Emerging organisational innovations

Many of the environmental and technological changes we have discussed cannot be accommodated simply by modifying bureaucratic structures. We can summarise the characteristics of the 'new age' organisations as follows: the organisations tend to specialise in a small number of things, they emphasise teamwork, promote coordination, and exist as part of a network of suppliers and distributors. Table 10.5 shows what is likely to become less important in the future and what is likely to become more common.

The shifts in emphasis we have identified in Table 10.5 have led to a number of structural innovations. These are an increasing use of boundary spanners, an expanding use of adhocracies, an emphasis on teamwork and, on a broader scale, increasing divisionalisation and use of market controls. We will consider each of these in turn.

Expanded use of boundary spanners

Boundary spanners have the task of linking the environment to the organisation.[29] They identify environmental changes that are occurring and, in turn, represent the

TABLE 10.5 Trends in organisational orientation

Less of		More of
National focus	→	International focus
Internal orientation	→	External orientation
Customers and suppliers at arm's length	→	Integrating up and down the supply chain
Emphasis on hierarchy	→	Functional and cross-functional teams
Administrative control	→	Market control
Hoarding knowledge	→	Spreading knowledge
Inspecting quality in	→	Building quality in
Emphasis on physical assets	→	Emphasis on knowledge
Lifetime employment	→	Lifetime employability

Source: Adapted from Thomas Clarke & Stewart Clegg, *Changing Paradigms: The Transformation of Management Knowledge for the 21st Century*, London: HarperCollins Business, 1998.

organisation to the environment. Their increased use is linked to the rising level of competition, with its attendant uncertainties. Activities such as forming relationships with customers, managing the supply chain, monitoring the actions of competitors, seeking niches to exploit and expanding distribution channels do not occur unless there is someone responsible for them.

In the past, one of the main roles of boundary spanners was to buffer the organisation from environmental changes: that is, they protected the core operations from unwanted external shocks. Their role still includes this function, but increasingly they have the additional task of providing information to allow the organisation to adapt to external changes. To be effective, the boundary spanners must therefore be more involved in the decision making of the organisation by their inclusion in important committees and decision-making teams.

The boundary-spanning role may also be introduced by redefining role requirements. All managers have job descriptions, which identify their main areas of responsibility and the tasks associated with these. By giving these an outward orientation, we can incorporate part of the boundary-spanning role in many managers' jobs.

Variations on adhocracies

Organisations have been very inventive in grafting some of the features of adhocracy onto traditional structures. These have the effect of improving communication and facilitating innovation. We mentioned above the structural changes that have led to an increase in the ability to coordinate the various functions of the organisation. These are part of extending the use of adhocracies within organisations. The most widely spoken-of adhocracy is the matrix, but it is probably not the most common. The matrix stands as a counterpoint to the concept of unity of command and, where it is introduced in inappropriate situations or where inadequate preparations for its introduction are made, it can create major problems. A more common innovation is the use of coordinators, who integrate the work of various functional groupings. Unfortunately for such coordinators, their responsibility normally exceeds the authority given to them. This leads to a heavy reliance on communication and management skills, rather than position power, to achieve results.

Other variations on adhocracies include the use of taskforces and various committees. These are formed on an as-required basis. Taskforces are temporary in nature and have a multidisciplinary membership. They have a single-purpose function and are disbanded once this is achieved. Examples of such roles are the installation of a software package, introduction of a quality control system, or a major organisational change. Committees are generally more permanent and draw on a range of expertise relevant to their purpose. Examples include quality committees, audit committees, and occupational health and safety committees.

An emphasis on teamwork

One of the characteristics of emerging organisations is that there has been an attempt to promote more cooperative ways of working.[30] In practice, this normally means the use of teams and some form of collective responsibility. Theorists have extensively promoted the use of teams over the more common hierarchical management style. They do have practical advantages. Teams can promote effective coordination among themselves, and communication flows are often improved. Knowledge can be shared and experience more widely spread among members. They remove some of the negativity associated with hierarchical management and they can provide the support and comfort of friendships and camaraderie at work. Current practice has seen teams increasingly form the basic building block of organisational structures. However, teams do have their drawbacks. They may come under the influence of a dominant personality who may work to their own private agenda or otherwise cause dissention. If someone is not accepted into a team, then difficulties may arise. And teams may be in conflict with each other. In practice, managers are happy to delegate responsibility to teams but give them limited authority. This way they still maintain a right of veto over team decisions.

Most quality control functions require the use of teams. The shift from inspecting quality, which was the function of an inspection department, to building quality in, which requires the input and involvement of those producing the product or service, predicates that teamwork will be involved.

Even where staff are not members of a formally constituted team, organisations often try to remove communication barriers between them by team-based activities. Executive or departmental retreats, outdoor exercises such as sailing or bushwalking, Friday night drinks and sporting activities are all efforts to bring a team approach to management.

A shift towards market controls

The internationalisation of activities, high levels of competition and an increasing stress on performance have led to the need to know how each part of the organisation is performing and to focus management's attention on the organisation as a business.[31] This has seen the emergence of parts of the organisation being controlled by reference to markets. We are all familiar with hierarchical control: a manager subjectively assesses performance against a set of rules, regulations or performance criteria. In contrast, market control de-emphasises subjective assessment and continuous monitoring. In its place, performance is assessed by reference to the profit or loss of an activity or in comparison with a budget. Let's use as an example a medical centre, which may operate a pharmacy for use by the general public. The centre management could monitor the effectiveness of the pharmacy by assessing the performance of the pharmacist, the opening hours, whether staff turn up for work, the number of times medicines are not available and so on. Alternatively, it could turn the pharmacy into a business, put the pharmacist in charge, and assess perform-

Every organisation—regardless of the industry it is in or whether it is profit seeking or not—faces some degree of environmental uncertainty. This is because no organisation is completely able to generate internally all the resources it needs to sustain itself and thus completely isolate itself from environmental forces.[1] Every organisation, for example, requires financial, material and human resources as inputs and clients or customers to absorb its outputs. But just because an organisation confronts environmental uncertainty does not mean that management must just accept what the environment has to offer. As the Oxiana case illustrates, there *are* things managers can do to lessen the impact of the environment on the organisation's operations. They can attempt to *manage* their environment![2]

Management's quest to control its environment

In Chapter 1 we described organisations as open systems. Not only do they interact with their environment but successful interaction is necessary for the organisation's viability and survival. But this environment is rarely static; it is constantly changing in unpredictable and uncertain ways. However, we know that managers don't like unpredictability and uncertainty.[3] They don't like being dependent on environments they have no influence over. This arises because if external threats actually come to pass the existence of the organisation may be threatened. Steel mills without supplies of iron ore soon go out of business. Changing customer tastes provide uneven revenue streams, leading to financial risks. A charity without donations can no longer undertake its work. Motor vehicle manufacturers who have invested heavily in production plant and employ large numbers of people are looking for stability in operations to meet their obligations. If management had its way, it would prefer to operate in a completely predictable and unchanging environment. In such a perfect world, there would be no need for contingency plans because there would be no surprises, and the organisation would be impervious to influences from other organisations and environmental threats. Yet all organisations face some uncertainty, and many environments are quite dynamic and difficult to predict. It should not be surprising to find that managers want to reduce this uncertainty. But can the environment be managed?

The population–ecology perspective, presented in Chapter 8, argues that there is a limit to the extent that management can influence its environment. But as we pointed out in our critique of this theory, management does not have to accept environments as it finds them. Managers have discretion over the strategies they choose and the ways in which organisational resources are acquired and distributed. Also, in a political sense, large and powerful organisations, and even small ones, have the means to shape major elements in their environment. Further, markets have been developed that have enabled organisations to manage some of the uncertainties which may exist. These include futures markets, for everything from metals to wool and computer chips, to hedging in financial markets and insuring property.

This chapter stands as a counterpoint to the population-ecology view. Large organisations consistently demonstrate by their actions that they are not captives of their environments and that they can take active steps to lessen their environmental dependence. They enter into long-term contracts, take out insurance policies and lock in exchange rates by buying currency on futures markets. They engage in joint ventures to acquire the skills they lack. They lobby politicians to promote a favourable regulatory environment. The larger an organisation is, the more resources, skills and influence it will typically have at its disposal. However, environmental management strategies are not available only to large and powerful organisations. Many of the techniques we will discuss can be, and are, used by small and uninfluential organisations. But keep in mind that large size is positively associated with increased power to reduce environmental uncertainty.[4]

Classifying strategies

In simplistic terms, managers have two general strategies they can adopt in their attempt to lessen environmental uncertainty. They can respond by adapting and changing organisational practices to better accommodate environmental uncertainty, or they can attempt to alter the environment to fit better with the organisation's capabilities. The former we call internal strategies and the latter external strategies.

internal strategies those which adapt and change organisational practices to better fit the environment

external strategies efforts designed to alter the environment to fit better with the organisation's capabilities

Internal strategies are those which adapt and change organisational practices to better fit the environment. When management makes design changes to a product or recruits executives from its competitors, it is making internal adjustments to match its environment. The environment does not change, but the fit between the organisation and the environment is improved. The result is that the uncertainty arising from the organisation's dependence on the environment is reduced.

External strategies are efforts designed to *change* the environment. If competitive pressures are cutting a company's profitability, it can merge with another company to gain economies of scale. If changes suggested in a tax reform proposal affect superannuation companies, the large companies and their trade associations may lobby against the tax changes.

Using the internal–external dichotomy, we can categorise a number of uncertainty-reduction techniques. Table 11.1 summarises the internal and external strategies that we will now elaborate on.

Internal strategies

Management does not actually have to change the environment in order to lessen the organisation's dependence on it. The following internal strategies demonstrate that there are actions that almost any organisation—the small as well as the large—can

TABLE 11.1 Internal and external strategies

Internal strategies	External strategies
Domain choice	Bridging
Recruitment	Advertising
Environmental scanning	Contracting
Buffering	Co-opting
Smoothing	Coalescing
Rationing	Lobbying
Improving information processing	Insuring
Geographic disperson	Hedging and futures markets

take to match it better with its environment and, in so doing, lessen the impact of the environment on the organisation's operations.

Domain choice

Domain refers to that part of the environment in which the organisation operates. Organisations make deliberate choices as to which domain they operate in. Woolworths operates in the environment relevant to the mass market for groceries; Optus operates in the telecommunications environment. One action that management can take when faced with an unfavourable environment is to change to a domain with less environmental uncertainty.[5] This is a significant move, however, as it generally involves a change in strategy. Management could, for example, consider moving into an environmental niche that has the advantage of fewer or less powerful competitors; spreading its risk over a wider geographic area; introducing a new range of products or investing in research and development to gain a comparative advantage. Mining companies, for instance, can choose not to establish mines in ecologically sensitive areas, or avoid operating where there is little rule of law. As there are not many opportunities for organisations to become unregulated monopolies, most domain-choice decisions substitute one set of environmental uncertainties for another.

Multidivisional companies have a greater ability to withstand changes in their environments than single-division companies. For instance, Wesfarmers operates in fertilisers, hardware distribution and agricultural services, among others. However, OPSM has chosen to stake its future existence on the provision of eyewear. Should powerful new entrants enter the market, or surgery reduce the need for eyewear, then OPSM would face a greatly reduced market for its products. The popularity of multidivisional structures has, at least in the past, derived from their ability to operate in multiple environments, thus reducing the company-wide risk that any one environment may offer.

If management cannot change to a more favourable domain, it may choose to broaden its strategy to take a generalist format.[6] Qantas Airways, for instance, is composed of a number of airlines each catering to a specific market niche. They include mainline Qantas, Qantas Link, Jet Star, both in Australia and Asia, Australian Airlines and New Zealand based Jet Connect. Both Coles and Woolworths constantly seek to expand into different but related product lines. As a result of this strategy, they have recently begun to dominate liquor retailing. The financial resources and their management skills permit the two retailing giants to enter any field they feel may be profitable.

On the other hand, small professional firms with specific skills, such as IT companies or consultants of various types, specifically select an environmental domain that matches their knowledge and capabilities. One of the greatest threats they face is taking on a consultancy or task for which they lack the skills.

Recruitment

The recruitment of staff with appropriate skills can lessen the influence of the environment on an organisation. If an organisation faces an environmental challenge which it feels it lacks the expertise to manage, it may recruit staff with the appropriate management skills. Corporations can hire executives with skills that the company does not already possess. Investment banks entice foreign exchange dealers and those with specialist skills with offers of large salaries and fringe benefits. Senior public servants with experience in immigration are eagerly sought by immigration consultants because of their contacts within government. On their retirement from the armed forces, senior officers are often employed by defence contractors because of their knowledge of the operations of the defence establishment. High-tech firms entice scientists from other companies to gain the technical expertise possessed by their competitors. The idea behind such action is to provide the organisation with skills that can cope with environmental uncertainty.

Environmental scanning

environmental scanning scrutinising the environment to identify actions by factors that might impinge on the organisation's operations

Environmental scanning entails scrutinising the environment to identify actions by competitors, government, unions and the like that might impinge on the organisation's operations. Scanning activities also include predicting levels of economic activity and undertaking research to determine changes in fashions and demand patterns. To the extent that scanning can lead to accurate forecasts of environmental fluctuations, it can reduce uncertainty. It allows management to anticipate changes and make internal adjustments rather than react after the fact. The manufacturing firm that can correctly anticipate changes in demand for its products can plan or schedule the operations of its technical core ahead of time and thereby minimise the impact of these changes. Similarly, the consulting firm that can forecast accurately which contracts it will win during the next six months is better prepared, in having the right number and mix of consultants available to handle these projects.

boundary spanners people who operate at the periphery of the organisation, performing organisationally relevant tasks, and relating the organisation to elements outside it

Earlier chapters have introduced and discussed the role of boundary spanners. **Boundary spanners** are staff whose specific jobs require them to act as conduits between the organisation and its environment.[7] Boundary spanners function, in effect, as exchange agents between the organisation and the environment. Examples of typical boundary-spanning jobs include sales representatives, market researchers, purchasing managers, lobbyists, public relations specialists and recruitment specialists. On a broader scale, multinational firms, particularly those with operations in politically unstable areas of the world, are continuously scanning the environment to monitor risks to their operations.

What do those who occupy boundary-spanning roles do? They handle the transactions an organisation makes with its environment, filter inputs and outputs into a form that can be understood, search and collect information, represent the organisation to the environment, and protect and buffer the organisation: 'It is through the reports of boundary agents that other organization members acquire their knowledge, perceptions and evaluations of organization environments. It is through the vigilance of boundary agents that the organization is able to monitor and screen important happenings in the environment.'[8]

Senior managers also regularly scan the environment to identify threats to and opportunities for their organisation. Almost every conversation they have with outsiders, often with insiders as well, concerns things that are happening or could happen to the organisation. Attendance at lunches, trade fairs, conferences and industry gatherings, and reading business journals, are other means of scanning the boundaries of the organisation. And for those firms operating internationally regional managers act as boundary spanners, feeding information to corporate headquarters.

Buffering

buffering protecting the operating core from environmental variations in supply and demand

Buffering reduces the possibility that the organisation's operations will be disturbed by ensuring that inputs are available to the production process and that there is steady demand on the output side; it protects the operating core from environmental influences on the input or output side. This permits the organisation to operate as if it were a closed system.

On the input side, buffering is evident when organisations stockpile materials and supplies, reduce reliance on one supplier, undertake preventive maintenance or recruit and train new employees. Each of these activities is designed to protect the operations of the organisation from the unexpected. Oil refineries typically keep reserves of crude oil on hand to cover them in case of any interruptions to supply. The newspaper that buys newsprint from two or three different paper companies reduces its dependence on any one firm. Manufacturers stockpile parts in case of interruptions to supplies. Buffering can also be done with human resources. As organisations require trained personnel, the unavailability or lack of appropriate skills can mean a loss in productive efficiency. Management can meet this uncertainty through recruitment and training.

There are fewer options when buffering on the output side. The most obvious method is the use of inventories. If an organisation creates products that are not perishable, such as cars or clothing, then maintaining inventories in warehouses allows the organisation to produce its goods at a constant rate, regardless of fluctuations in sales demand. Toy manufacturers, for example, typically ship most of their products to retailers in early October for selling during the Christmas season. These manufacturers, of course, produce their toys year-round and merely stockpile them for shipping during the three months before Christmas.

The growth in the number of casuals in the workforce over the past few years is another form of buffering. It has enabled organisations to better match the supply of labour with peaks and troughs in demand. It would be highly inefficient to maintain a full-time catering workforce if the company's main business was providing food and beverages at weekend sporting events. The major supermarkets have casuals they can call on at peak times. Manufacturers often use labour hire firms to carry out their annual maintenance shutdowns or unanticipated breakdowns. By hiring casuals as needed, an organisation can be more confident of being able to meet fluctuations in demand.

Buffering provides the benefit of reduced environmental uncertainty. Management's tendency to buffer is related directly to the degree of routinisation in the organisation's technology. Where work is routine, such as manufacturing motor cars, it is possible to predict what the inputs into the system will be. As a result, we would expect buffering to be a popular strategy. However, the benefits must be appraised against the costs. The more obvious costs are those involved in warehousing and double handling the product and the risk of obsolescence inherent in stockpiling. Buffering is also of more use to those in manufacturing and those dealing in tangible products. It is difficult to buffer services; other uncertainty-reducing mechanisms may be used for this group of industries.

Smoothing

smoothing levelling out the impact of fluctuations in the environment by offering incentives to environmental units to regularise their interactions with the organisation

Smoothing seeks to level out the impact of fluctuations in the environment. This mechanism is commonly used in service industries, where the product cannot be placed into inventory or where the product is perishable. Organisations that use this technique include telecommunication providers, retail stores, car rental companies, magazine publishers and sports clubs. The heaviest demand on intercity telephone equipment is by business between the weekday hours of 8.00 am and 5.00 pm.

Telephone companies have to have sufficient capacity to meet peak demand during that period. But the equipment is still in place at other times, with most of it under used. So phone companies smooth demand by charging their highest prices during the peak period and lower rates to encourage customers to call relatives and friends during the evenings and at weekends. Airlines similarly use smoothing to charge more for travel during peak demand times. This is why you pay more to travel to Europe during July than when demand is lower during February and November, and why it is almost impossible to get a discount fare between Sydney and Melbourne at 8 o'clock on a weekday morning.

Retail clothing stores know that their slowest months are January (following the Christmas rush) and July (mid-winter). To reduce this 'trough' in the revenue curve, retail stores typically run their sales at these times of the year. Car rental companies make extensive use of smoothing. The same car that rents for $60 a day during the week is often half that price at the weekend. The reason is that business people are heavy users of rental cars during the week. Rather than have the cars sit idle at weekends, the rental companies smooth demand by cutting prices at off-peak times. Magazine publishers often give you a substantial discount—sometimes up to 50% off newsstand prices—if you take a subscription. This enables them to better predict their demand. Cut-price Tuesdays in cinemas is another example of buffering. Tuesday is a very slow day in the entertainment business, so reducing prices gives patrons an incentive to visit the picture theatre in off-peak times.

Rationing

rationing the allocation of organisational products or services according to a priority system

When uncertainty is created by way of excess demand, management may consider **rationing** products or services—that is, allocating output according to some priority system. Examples of rationing can be found in hospitals, universities, post offices and restaurants. Hospitals often ration beds for non-emergency admissions. And when a disaster strikes—a major accident, fire or flood—beds are made available only to the most serious cases. University administrators often use rationing to allocate students to popular programs. In recent years, for instance, the demand for business courses has exceeded the supply of places available at many universities. In response, entrance requirements have often been raised as a way to limit demand. The post office resorts to rationing. Priority-paid mail takes precedence and lesser classes are handled on an 'as-available' basis. It is not unusual for better restaurants to require reservations. The use of reservations acts to both ration and smooth demand for tables.

Improving information processing

One of the main causes of uncertainty is lack of information. If it is possible to improve the flow of information, uncertainty will decrease. Modern information technologies allow us to gather large amounts of data and, using appropriate software, process it into a format that can assist managers to respond to environmental changes with minimum impact on the operating core. Airlines provide a good example of this. One of their key functions is yield management. This function constantly monitors forward bookings in order to know when to offer, or not offer, discounted flights, how many seats to allocate to each class of traveller, and whether timetables should be rearranged. Through identifying trends well before time, airlines can respond with minimum disruption to their schedules while maximising returns. Other examples are the monitoring of consumer goods sales in supermarkets and stores to immedi-

OT CLOSEUP

The local pharmacy as part of a lobby group

You may wonder why your local pharmacy seems to have little competition from the large supermarket chains; the reason is because of the success of the pharmacy lobby in keeping sales of medicines firmly in local pharmacy hands. Even though Woolworths and Coles have tried on many occasions to open pharmacy facilities in their supermarkets, the Pharmacy Guild of Australia has been extraordinarily successful in preventing this. Although few would dispute that medicines should be dispensed by a pharmacist, it is less clear as to why this should be in their own shop. Further restrictions on ownership mean that what appear to be chains of pharmacies are in fact pharmacist-owned shops operating in a form of franchise agreement.

Every time the federal government has attempted to change the laws as to who can own a pharmacy, the Pharmacy Guild has argued that the public interest is best served by having the pharmacist own their own shop and that letting supermarkets establish pharmacies as part of their service would lead to a decline in standards and reduced service to the public.

It is difficult to know how long the pharmacy lobby will continue to be successful in repelling competition, particularly as many other sectors have lost their privileged status over the years. Perhaps big business could learn a lesson or two from the Pharmacy Guild; not many groups can face down the likes of Woolworths and Coles successfully year after year.

competition and enforce standards of conduct in order to keep their professions more stable. Educational institutions, hospitals, welfare associations, conservation coalitions and other single-interest groups regularly lobby parliamentarians and others to influence them to pass legislation, or to frame the budget, in their interest. Many employ specialist lobbying firms with inside information on the bureaucracy to give their lobbying efforts maximum impact.

Insuring

Organisations face many risks which are unlikely to eventuate, but which may be catastrophic if they do. Such risks may arise from a building catching fire, accidents, acts of nature such as lightning strikes, hailstorms and cyclones, riots or insurgency in overseas countries, and oil or chemical spills. Organisations also run the risk of being sued for public liability, industrial accidents, health issues and negligence of various types. Most of these events, apart from floods, can be insured against. Insurance markets grew out of individuals and organisations pooling their risk so that any one occurrence did not result in a catastrophic loss. From this beginning developed the complex insurance markets which organisations find indispensable for managing their risk. Insurance companies even insure themselves against an excessive level of claims through the reinsurance market.

Hedging and futures markets

With the deregulation of industries and commodity markets and the free floating of currencies, the level of uncertainty of many businesses has risen. New markets have consequently been developed in order to permit companies to manage their risk. Futures exchanges allow miners and commodity producers to lock in a price in advance of production and consumption. Exchange markets allow hedging against currency shifts. And investment fund managers can buy or sell shares in major companies in advance to avoid fluctuations in share prices. There are futures markets for products as diverse as electricity, wool, crude oil, aviation fuel, coffee, gold and microchips. Without such mechanisms, many companies would be unable to plan with any degree of confidence. Additionally, a significant part of an organisation's management time would be allocated to crisis management, which would be aimed at trying to ensure the organisation's survival rather than being spent on strategic matters affecting the organisation.

The use of hedging and futures markets is, however, not without risk. Predicting future states is fraught with difficulty, and many companies have lost (and gained) large amounts of money by guessing that markets would move in certain directions. There is the further problem of 'rogue traders' making large, sometimes unauthorised, bets on future product prices. A number of companies have faced bankruptcy because of failure to identify rogue traders on their staff.

OT CLOSEUP
The world's futures markets

Businesses may participate in a wide variety of futures markets around the world. These originated to enable farmers to obtain cash in order to progress their current crop and for purchasers to ensure supply at a fixed price some time in the future, hence futures markets. Although they can be, and are, used by speculators and arbitrageurs, they are essentially a legitimate business device to reduce uncertainty. Most futures markets, often called exchanges, such as the London Metal Exchange and the New York Mercantile Exchange, specialise in certain products. The Sydney Futures Exchange trades futures in commodities such as greasy wool, interest rates, the US dollar and equities futures. Other exchanges around the world deal in commodities as disparate as electricity, climate futures and aviation fuel.

Some firms, however, deliberately don't hedge their future sales. Although there is an active futures market in most minerals, many mining companies don't hedge because shareholders prefer the shares to rise and fall in accordance with the price of the commodity rather than management taking a guess at future price levels and locking in profits, or losses, at that level.

Guidelines for managing the environment

Success in managing the environment requires analysing the source of uncertainty and then selecting a strategy that the organisation can effectively implement. As we noted at the beginning of the chapter, large size facilitates environmental influence. Certainly, Telstra and Woolworths have more power in controlling their relationships with suppliers than has a small telephone supplier or a corner store. Yet most of the strategies presented in this chapter have wide applicability.

Table 11.3 presents some actions that managers can take to reduce environmental uncertainty. The examples of strategic actions are only examples; they don't purport to be *all* or the *only* options available to management. But they all share the basic premise that organisations are not just passive receivers of environmental influence. The influence works both ways; organisations in turn manage their environments to reduce uncertainty.

In this chapter we can also see the influences at work that we identified in Chapter 9 in discussing power and politics in organisations. Through reducing uncertainty by

TABLE 11.3 Matching sources of uncertainty with strategic actions

Source	Examples of strategic actions
Government	Lobby for favourable treatment
	Recruit former government officials
	Commission research to influence government
	Relocate to a different state or country
Competition	Advertise to build brand loyalty
	Select a less competitive domain
	Merge with competition to gain larger market share
	Negotiate a cooperative agreement with competition
Unions	Negotiate a long-term enterprise agreement
	Develop a single-union plant
	Build facilities in countries with a large, low-cost labour supply
	Appoint prestigious union official to board of directors
Suppliers	Use multiple suppliers
	Inventory critical supplies
	Negotiate long-term contracts
	Vertically integrate through merger
Financial institutions	Appoint financial executives to board
	Establish a line of credit to draw on when needed
	Diversify by co-opting a financial institution
	Use multiple financial sources
Customers	Advertise
	Use a differentiated price structure
	Ration demand
	Change domain to where there are more customers
Public pressure groups	Appoint critics to board
	Recruit critics as employees
	Engage in visible activities that are socially conscious
	Use trade association to counter criticism

the mechanisms we have identified, managers create a more stable internal environment. As a result, they can maintain structures that are more mechanistic and centralised, thus reinforcing their power. Managers can also justify their claim to senior positions within the organisation through an ability to understand and control external environments. There would be few CEOs who did not claim to be able to understand and respond to environmental opportunities and threats.

Summary

Every organisation faces some degree of environmental uncertainty. However, in contrast with the population-ecology view that organisations are powerless to affect their environments, this chapter has sought to demonstrate that management can reduce the impact of environmental uncertainty on the organisation.

There are essentially two approaches available to management. The first is to adapt and change its actions to fit the environment. These are internal strategies and include changing domain, recruiting executives and technical specialists with links to the environment, scanning the environment to anticipate changes, buffering the operating core, smoothing out fluctuations in demand, rationing products or services, and geographical dispersion. The second approach is to alter the environment to fit better with the organisation's capabilities. These are external strategies such as advertising, contracting with suppliers or customers, co-opting individuals or organisations through absorption, coalescing with other organisations, and lobbying to achieve favourable outcomes. Organisations also use financial instruments and hedge markets in order to reduce uncertainty. While technically only external strategies change the environment, both types of strategies together create the techniques that we say are available for *managing the environment*.

For review and discussion

1. Contrast the population-ecology view of organisations with this chapter's theme.
2. Why do organisations seek to manage their environment?
3. Which strategies—internal or external—are more likely to involve interorganisational cooperation? Why?
4. Contrast the advantages of both specialist and generalist strategies.
5. Who are boundary spanners? What role do they play in managing environmental uncertainty?
6. How does smoothing reduce environmental uncertainty?
7. Is managing the environment illegal? Explain.
8. Is product differentiation a strategy for reducing environmental uncertainty? Explain.
9. Compare co-opting and coalescing.
10. What advantages accrue to an organisation whose board members are widely interlocked with other organisations?
11. Is it easier for a profit-making business to manage its environment than it is for a non-profit-making organisation?
12. Is it easier for a manufacturing organisation to manage its environment than it is for a service organisation?
13. What do you think are the major environmental uncertainties for each of the following organisations:
    (a) a radio station?
    (b) a car dealer?
    (c) a university bookshop?
    (d) a law firm?
    (e) a large home-building firm?
14. Explain how the management of each of the previous organisations might attempt to manage its environment.
15. Why might it be more attractive to managers to manage their environment rather than adapt the organisation to the environment?

CASE FOR CLASS DISCUSSION

Westfield and its environment

Just about everyone would be familiar with Westfield shopping centres. The red Westfield signs are a common sight in Australian suburbia and increasingly throughout the world. Most people would visit a Westfield shopping mall on a regular basis. The company has come to dominate the Australian shopping centre scene by a combination of canny management and street-smart lobbying. The management of Westfield has developed a successful strategy of selecting top-class retailers for their malls and then charging premium rents. Westfield can do this because in return it can offer retailers top-quality space in well-located and maintained centres attracting high levels of passing pedestrian trade. Part of the strategy is to ensure that there is a full range of retailers in the centre so that shoppers need only visit one mall to do all their shopping. In doing this, Westfield manages to earn more income per square metre of area than comparable shopping centres.

Westfield's formula has been successfully exported. Building upon the expertise built up in Australia, it has a major operation in the United States, and it is also expanding its operations in Europe, particularly the United Kingdom. The overseas expansion allows it to spread its risks over a number of countries, as well as permitting far higher rates of growth than could be wrung from the small Australian market. Like many companies with an overseas earnings stream, Westfield has hedged part of its currency exposure in order to reduce volatility and provide a more predicable flow of income. However, investing overseas is not without its own risk. Westfield was the main retail tenant in the basement of the World Trade Center in New York and suffered considerable loss in the terrorist bombing of the building. Most of its losses were covered by its insurance policies. Westfield has financed its overseas expansion mainly by drawing upon the Australian capital market. Its long run of rising share price and record profits has meant that there is no shortage of financiers willing to subscribe new capital or provide loans.

Westfield tends to concentrate on markets it is familiar with, such as the US, the UK and New Zealand. By entering such markets it reduces the likelihood of centres not meeting targets. But the industry it is in is more than building and operating shopping centres. In effect, its success involves obtaining an appropriate parcel of land and then having development proposals approved by the local council.

Two problems arise. The first is that land is scarce and closely fought over and, second, planning permission is often hard to come by; not too many communities want large shopping centres next door to them. And competing centres close by can quickly draw customers and reduce anticipated returns. As a consequence, Westfield has finely honed its political skills in dealing with local governments and planning authorities.

This is an area which is not without risk. The zoning of land greatly influences its value and many property developers have bought land in the expectation of a quick profit when it is rezoned. In this environment Westfield is no shrinking violet when it comes to protecting its own interests. Although the shopping malls are solid enough and loom over the surrounding areas as monuments to consumerism, the changing nature of business means that the location where people do their shopping is continuously evolving. Retailers at Westfield pay high rents for the benefits of location, but some retailers now want larger areas at cheaper rents than Westfield is prepared to offer. Examples are the large hardware stores and bulky goods warehouses which sell furniture and electrical appliances. Seconds stores and factory outlets are also looking for large, low-cost retail areas. Most of these types of operations have set up in industrial areas which have been rezoned for retail activities.

Sensing the challenge that the new retail formats present to Westfield, the company has been actively lobbying politicians and public servants in an attempt to keep all retail activity close to public transport and prevent the rezoning of industrial land to retail activity.

The situation in relation to Orange Grove bulky goods centre at Liverpool, west of Sydney, provides a good illustration of the stakes involved. Originally established to sell bulky goods such as refrigerators in an industrial area, approval was granted to Orange

Grove by the Liverpool Council in 2002 to expand into a warehouse clearance outlet. This centre was popular with customers who could buy all manner of clothing and similar items at competitive prices. However, this roused the ire of Westfield who claimed that the land was not zoned for such activities and as a result the planning permission was invalid.

After considerable legal wrangling, the NSW Court of Appeal declared that the rezoning was illegal and Orange Grove should close. But Westfield was also accused of illegal contact with government ministers, with the aim of influencing the outcome of the zoning process. This was the subject of an inquiry by the Independent Commission Against Corruption, which found no illegality on Westfield's part.

This is not the first time that Westfield has been involved in such actions. Occasionally it crosses the boundary of legitimate lobbying and unethical behaviour. During 1999 it undertook an extensive campaign based on non-existent resident groups to successfully block a development in Sydney's Concord, which would have posed a direct threat to Westfield's nearby Burwood development. The managing director of Westfield, Frank Lowy, subsequently apologised for the incident.

Source: Some of the material for this case study was drawn from Robert Harley Kirela, 'Graduates from the School of Hard Knocks', *The Australian Financial Review*, 4 February 2000, p. 73; Turi Condon, 'Westfield at Large', *Business Review Weekly*, 24 January 2002, p. 32; and 'Orange Grove: A Cautionary Tale', *The Sydney Morning Herald*, Editorial, 12 August 2005.

QUESTIONS

1 Identify as many instances as you can of the ways in which Westfield controls its environment. Link them to the categories identified in this chapter.
2 Discuss the importance to Westfield of managing its environment.
3 Do you consider that when a firm engages in managing its environment it is contributing to its long-term effectiveness? Provide arguments to support your position.

FURTHER READING

Howard E. Aldrich, *Organizations and Environments*, Englewood Cliffs, NJ: Prentice-Hall, 1979.

Richard Leifer & André Delbecq, 'Organizational/Environmental Interchange: A Model of Boundary Spanning Activity', *Academy of Management Review*, January 1978, pp. 40–1.

Christine Oliver, 'Strategic Response to Institutional Processes', *Academy of Management Review*, 16, 1991, pp. 145–79.

Jeffrey Pfeffer & Gerald Salancik, *The External Control of Organizations: The Resource Dependence Perspective*, New York: Harper & Row, 1978.

NOTES

1 Howard E. Aldrich, *Organizations and Environments*, Englewood Cliffs, NJ: Prentice-Hall, 1979, p. 266.
2 Jeffrey Pfeffer, 'Beyond Management and the Worker: The Institutional Function of Management', *Academy of Management Review*, April 1976, pp. 36–46; and Jeffrey Pfeffer & Gerald R. Salancik, *The External Control of Organizations: The Resource Dependence Perspective*, New York: Harper & Row, 1978.
3 William R. Dill, 'Environment as an Influence on Managerial Autonomy', *Administrative Science Quarterly*, March 1958, pp. 409–43.
4 John Kenneth Galbraith, *The New Industrial State*, Boston: Houghton Mifflin, 1967.
5 See, for example, James D. Thompson & William J. McEwen, 'Organizational Goals and Environment: Goal-Setting as an Interaction Process', *American Sociological Review*, February 1958, pp. 23–31.

6 John H. Freeman & Michael T. Hannan, 'Niche Width and the Dynamics of Organizational Populations', *American Journal of Sociology*, May 1983, pp. 1116–45.

7 Richard Leifer & André Delbecq, 'Organizational/Environmental Interchange: A Model of Boundary Spanning Activity', *Academy of Management Review*, January 1978, pp. 40–1.

8 Dennis W. Organ, 'Linking Pins between Organizations and Environments', *Business Horizons*, December 1971, p. 74.

9 P. Neegard, 'Environment, Strategy and Management', *Accounting Proceedings of the Second European Symposium on Information Systems*, Versailles: HEC.

10 See, for example, Jeffrey Pfeffer, 'Size and Composition of Corporate Boards of Directors: The Organization and Its Environment', *Administrative Science Quarterly*, March 1972, pp. 218–28; and Mark S. Mizruchi & Linda Brewster Stearns, 'A Longitudinal Study of the Formation of Interlocking Directorates', *Administrative Science Quarterly*, June 1988, pp. 194–210.

CHAPTER 12

Managing organisational change

After reading this chapter you should be able to:

- define planned change
- distinguish between revolutionary and evolutionary change
- list factors that might precipitate structural change
- describe the four categories of intervention strategies
- explain the stages in organisational change
- explain why stability, not change, characterises most organisations
- discuss how unplanned change may be managed.

Introduction

Dairy Farmers' plans for the future

Although it seems that milk has not changed much over the years, the dairy industry has gone through rapid and unprecedented change. This has been driven by the changing economics of the industry and the impact of globalisation. The dairy industry was originally structured to provide maximum returns to the dairy farmers. In order to do this the farmers formed themselves into cooperatives which undertook the processing and distribution of milk. It was a cosy existence for many. The market was distributed between the cooperatives in order to minimise competition and there was no interstate trade in milk. Further, processing was fairly simple, involving pasteurisation and separation of cream.

As governments moved to dismantle the restrictions on trade, competition greatly increased. Also, most whole milk, which is bought in cartons, is sold through supermarkets, which force suppliers to compete intensively for the contract. This has resulted in squeezed margins and low profitability. In order to compete in such an environment, plants need to be large scale, which has led to centralisation of processing into a small number of mega-centres. But new areas of profitability are emerging. Milk that is manufactured into products such as high-quality cheeses, yoghurt and dairy desserts is highly profitable and so is attracting greater capital. But this involves new manufacturing techniques, extensive technical knowledge and an emphasis on marketing.

Globalisation has also contributed to changing the dynamics of the industry. Although many areas are protected by high tariffs and exclusion on trade, the European Union being the obvious example, the big rise in the middle class in regions such as Asia is providing significant openings for dairy products, such as cheese for cooking Mediterranean-style food. Further, the Asian countries have poorly developed domestic dairying industries, but other countries are now noting the opportunities that greater trade is offering. Argentina, for example, has the opportunity to greatly expand its dairy industry and the American farmers are fiercely competitive. So while globalisation is presenting opportunities, it is also bringing new competitive players into the market.

So where does this leave Dairy Farmers? In order to remain competitive in the new environment, Dairy Farmers introduced a major corporate restructure in early 2005. It centralised its milk processing into a smaller number of facilities over the four states it operates in. It also chose certain plants to concentrate on value-added activities. For instance, Hexam in Newcastle was chosen as the centre for sweetened condensed milk and frozen desserts and Toowoomba was chosen to concentrate on skim milk and butter. Other plants specialise in yoghurt and others in cheese. Over 700 people—more than 30% of the cooperative's staff—lost their jobs in the restructure.

Dairy Farmers has remained a cooperative owned by its suppliers for the time being. However, it is anticipated that the company will convert to a shareholding structure and be listed on the stock exchange by 2008. This would enable it to raise more capital and more freely enter into strategic alliances than would be the case under its old ownership structure.

In the management literature, change has almost become an overworked cliché. It seems impossible to write a management book without the author exhorting us to dance the dance of change, adapt to a crazy world or envision a future that bears no resemblance to the present. It would be a brave writer who offered a prescription of a future based on stability and continuation of the present ways of doing things. It is not difficult to understand why change dominates management thinking. Most of us have lived through periods of significant environmental, regulatory and technological change, which have forced organisations to radically alter their structures and established practices.

Effectiveness requires that organisations adapt appropriately to change. There is much that managers can do to facilitate change in their organisations; some of the most highly regarded managers are those who have instituted successful change programs. In this chapter we will look at how managers can actively promote change in their organisation. In keeping with the theme of this book, we will take an organisation-wide perspective rather than concentrating on its effect on individuals. An organisation-wide perspective means that we consider such factors as the environmental drivers of change, the allocation of tasks and areas of responsibility, and the processes adopted to facilitate change. The influence of change on an individual's behaviour is more appropriately considered in books dealing with organisational behaviour.

So we will first consider the different types of organisational change. Then we will look at the environmental drivers of change and the indicators of an inappropriate structure, and describe a model of change and how managers can promote innovation in organisations. We will also consider the issue of power and politics during the change process. It is not the intention to provide a comprehensive coverage of organisational change; that would take far more than one chapter to cover. Rather, we will concentrate on those issues which are relevant to the macro-approach we have adopted in this book.

The nature of change

Not all organisational change is the same. Some change alters the very nature of the organisation. Other changes may be minor and confined to one department or only part of a department. It follows that the way in which change is managed depends on the type, origin and magnitude of the drivers of change. So, in order to fully understand the nature of change, it helps to clarify the various forms that change may take. We will first consider the difference between revolutionary and evolutionary change, and then discuss planned and emergent change.

Revolutionary and evolutionary change

Sometimes, fortunately not too often, organisations are faced with a change that alters their very nature. Change of this magnitude is called *revolutionary change*. Mostly, revolutionary change emerges as a response to significant technological and environmental changes. Some examples of revolutionary change emerging from technological changes are the replacement of hot metal with electronic typesetting in newspapers, the introduction of containerisation in shipping, and the computerisation of banking. These types of technologies are called disruptive technologies. Changes in environments can also lead to revolutionary change. Deregulation and privatisation have changed the nature of a number of industries, such as electricity generation, water supply and airlines. Globalisation has had a similar effect, with heightened threats and opportunities and greater levels of competition. A further source of revolutionary change often arises as a result of mergers and acquisitions. When two companies are merged into one entity, new relationships and management systems must be established and a common way of doing things developed. Such programs are never easy to implement, and the resultant change is often traumatic.

All of these drivers have forced management to introduce comprehensive organisational change programs. Usually the *rate of change*, in contrast to the *magnitude of change*, has been such that managers have been able to plan the change program and have had the luxury of a buffer of time to introduce it. But the outcome of the change program results in the organisation being radically different after the change. Revolutionary change is often accompanied by redundancies and downsizing, shifts in power, changes in strategy and a new organisational structure. As a result of such change, employees interact with each other in different ways, adapt to new management practices and learn to use new technologies. They may also need to relate to customers in different ways. The disruption and emotional trauma caused by revolutionary change is such that it occurs only on an occasional basis. Once the organisation settles into its new pattern and people adapt to their new roles, it does not mean that change has stopped. Change then becomes evolutionary.

Evolutionary change describes ongoing minor changes that are incorporated in the existing organisational structure. Examples are adapting to a new computer program, moving to team rather than individual responsibility, introducing a new timekeeping system and upgrading the existing production process. Areas of responsibility at the top of the organisation are also often reshuffled. These changes can frequently be introduced at the level of a department or team and consequently do not have an organisation-wide impact. All employees are used to these changes—memos advising that a manager now has widened responsibilities, that a person has been appointed to take on certain tasks, that the IT department will now have a representative at each user department, or that someone has resigned and their responsibilities are being transferred to someone else. None of these changes are particularly significant by themselves but they are the normal way in which organisations consistently adapt to the changes around and within them. Without such changes, an organisation would soon stagnate and lose its fit with its environment. Most change is evolutionary change: it involves minor adjustments in response to circumstantial and unanticipated events.

Revolutionary change and evolutionary change are not self-contained categories; they are end points of a continuum. While it is quite easy to identify examples of both types of change, there will always be changes that have characteristics of both. As a result, they will fall somewhere between the two extreme cases. Examples of change between the two extremes are McDonald's extending its product range, introduction of new quality control and operations management techniques, and installation of new accounting software. In each of these cases staff have to adapt to new ways of doing things, but the nature of the work remains basically the same.

Figure 12.1 shows the contrast between evolutionary and revolutionary change. In Chapter 4 we described a set of five basic structural configurations. Each of these configurations has a common and consistent set of elements. Revolutionary change often involves moving from one basic configuration to another. It is unlikely that an organisation would adopt a sustainable form that was not one of our basic configurations, because a hybrid form would lose its internal consistency and balance. When a significant change does occur, it will probably be comprehensive.[1]

Evolutionary change	**Revolutionary change**
Evolution	Revolution
Maintain equilibrium	Seek a new equilibrium
Change individual parts or departments	Transform entire organisation
Optimise existing structure and management	Generate new structure and management
Incrementally change existing production technology	Adopt radically new production technology
Improve existing products	Introduce path breaking new products

FIGURE 12.1 Contrast between evolutionary and revolutionary organisational change

Source: Based on Alan D. Meyer, James D. Goes & Geoffrey R. Brooks, *Organizations in Disequilibrium: Environmental Jolts and Industry Revolutions*, in George Huber & William H. Glick, eds, *Organizational Change and Redesign*, New York: Oxford University Press, 1992, pp. 66–111.

This suggests that management would prefer to avoid change, if possible, because of its cost, disruptive impact and threat to management's control. If the organisation faces a dynamic environment, we would expect management first to try to reduce its dependence on that environment. However, even the largest and most powerful organisations cannot completely manage their environment, and so management has essentially two options.[2] It can change incrementally as environments change: this will achieve environmental fit but create internal inconsistencies. The other option is to delay change until it is absolutely necessary and then make it comprehensive: this maintains internal consistency but at the price of having a poor environment–structure fit for a period.

The choice between these two options could be a dilemma if it weren't for management's preference for making as few changes as possible and the reality that management does not seek to maximise organisational effectiveness. Existing structures can be adapted to new situations by making a few changes to responsibilities and reporting relationships. If the choice were between 'change' and 'no change', management would be expected to prefer the status quo; but that option is not always available. Management is going to have to accept some changes in order to maintain a 'satisficing' level of organisational effectiveness. However, when the choice is between continual change and as few changes as possible, management always aims for the steady state. As a result, most organisations are characterised by long periods of relative stability, punctuated by brief periods of dramatic and comprehensive change.

There are, of course, always exceptions to every observation. Some organisations are characterised by managers seeking the perfect structural form and as consequence they are always making structural changes. As we have noted in Chapter 4, there are a range of structures that will provide a similar outcome. Therefore, seeking the perfect structure would be a never-ending task. Other managers feel that unless change is ongoing, the organisation will succumb to bureaucratic inertia and lose its effectiveness. Everyone therefore needs to be 'on the move' in the fight against sluggishness and complacency. While many managers are no doubt motived by genuine ideals in their fight against bureaucracy, a cynic may take the view that rarely does a program of perpetual change threaten the senior managers responsible for introducing it. It may indeed assist in entrenching their position at the top of the organisation. This is particularly so if the CEO or senior manager is newly appointed and wants to make an early impression on the organisation.

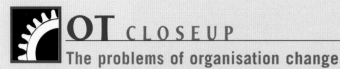

OT CLOSEUP
The problems of organisation change

Two authors have highlighted why organisational change dominates the management literature and why organisations remain such an enigma to many managers:

> For most companies, organization design is neither a science nor an art; it's an oxymoron. Organization structures rarely result from systematic, methodical planning. Rather, they evolve over time, in fits and starts, shaped more by politics than by policies. The haphazard nature of the resulting structures is a source of constant frustration to senior executives. Strategic initiatives stall or go astray because responsibilities are fragmented or unclear. Turf wars torpedo collaboration and knowledge sharing. Promising opportunities die for lack of management attention. Overly complex structures, such as matrix organizations, collapse because of lack of clarity about responsibilities.
>
> Most executives sense when their organizations are not working well, but few know how to correct the situation. A comprehensive redesign is just too intimidating. For one thing, it is immensely complicated, involving endless streams of tradeoffs and variables. For another, it's divisive, frequently disintegrating into personality conflicts and power plays. So when organization design problems arise, managers often focus on the most glaring flaws and, in the process, make the overall structure even more unwieldy and even less strategic.

Quoted from: Michael Goold & Andrew Campbell, 'Do you have a well-designed organization?', *Harvard Business Review*, March 2002, p. 117.

Planned and unplanned change

Another way in which change may be classified is whether it is planned or unplanned. Planned change refers to situations in which organisations have adequate time to anticipate and formulate a response to the drivers of change. An example of planned change is the introduction of new equipment or processes. In this case, management can draw up schedules for installation of the equipment, undertake job redesign and reallocate management tasks. Management may not, of course, do this entirely successfully, but at least the opportunity for planning for the introduction of new equipment is present. The objective of planned change is to maintain the viability of the organisation and respond with minimum disruption and cost.

In contrast, unplanned change emerges as a response to an unanticipated threat or event. The impact on airlines, broking houses, insurance companies and others of the World Trade Center attack is an example of unplanned change. Most companies survived in one form or another, but their ability to adapt was sorely tested. Perhaps less spectacular examples of unplanned change are machinery and computer breakdowns, the collapse of a major supplier or customer, the impact of weather such as drought or cyclone, and even the resignation or death of a critical person in the organisation such as the chief executive. The unanticipated actions of competitors and the introduction of technical innovations that threaten core activities are also examples of unplanned change. These include the impact of TV news services on newspapers, e-commerce on existing distribution channels and the effect of competition from road transport on railways.

An unwelcome takeover or merger proposal generally also leads to unplanned change. The organisation undertaking the takeover normally wants to impose its way of doing things, and often has a different strategy from that of the company being taken over. It is also likely to be keen to extract synergies from the merger. This normally results in changes being introduced, which often include changes in top management.

The collapse of Ansett illustrates the ultimate in unplanned change—that of insolvency. Insolvency, or the threat of it, means that change in one form or another is unavoidable and will take a form that is often unanticipated. Responses may range from the dissolution of the company through to parts being sold off as stand-alone companies or merger with other organisations.

Categorising change

Through combining the two dimensions of change we can develop a matrix which categorises the various forms of change. This is important because management of change varies with each category. The matrix is shown in Figure 12.2, along with examples of the change we can expect in each quadrant. *Adaptive change* is the least difficult change to manage. It generally does not affect everyone in the organisation, and presents management with choice as to how and when it will be implemented. Management also has discretion as to the timing and nature of change and has time to undertake extensive negotiation with affected parties. Plans may be drawn up which allow for the orderly introduction of change. *Systemic change* is the type of change we are most used to reading about. It forms the basis of most management writing on change. It is organisation-wide and touches on most areas of the organisation's operations. As it is planned change, however; it does not emerge from a shock to the system, but as management's response to changes in the environment or perceived organisational effectiveness. It is often undertaken only after extensive consultation among senior management and the board of directors. Outside consultants are also often involved in discussions. Because of the enormous amount of effort and disruption caused by systemic change, it is undertaken only as a matter of necessity. While *transitory change* is unplanned, it is not necessarily unanticipated. Most commodity producers, such as those of metals and agricultural products, know that the price of their product is subject to wide swings in price. Retailers often have bad seasons and are often hard hit in times of economic downturn. Key managers can leave or new competitors emerge. All of these require a response that normally involves some type of organisational change. But most change is not far-reaching unless the organisation's existence is threatened: selective layoffs, reallocating responsibility, concentrating on reducing costs or increasing flexibility are typical responses. These may be unplanned but manageable in the sense that they are easily grasped and implemented. The final type of change, *chaotic change*, is every manager's nightmare. It is unanticipated, threatens the organisation's existence, and arrives so fast that adequate planning is not possible. Examples are the activities of terrorists, violent weather, unanticipated hostile

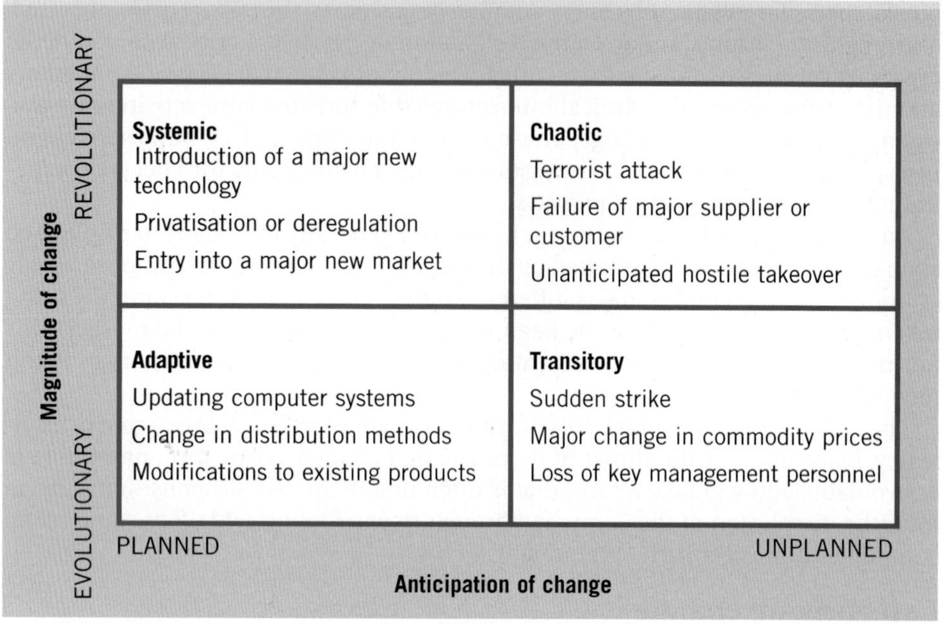
REVOLUTIONARY
EVOLUTIONARY
Magnitude of change
Systemic
Introduction of a major new technology
Privatisation or deregulation
Entry into a major new market
Chaotic
Terrorist attack
Failure of major supplier or customer
Unanticipated hostile takeover
Adaptive
Updating computer systems
Change in distribution methods
Modifications to existing products
Transitory
Sudden strike
Major change in commodity prices
Loss of key management personnel
PLANNED
UNPLANNED
Anticipation of change

FIGURE 12.2 Change classification scheme

takeovers, financial collapse, sudden interruptions to the supply chain or loss of important customers, and accident or misadventure involving critical assets. Handling the situation entails management going into crisis mode.

This chapter will concentrate on planned change. Because organisations are open systems—dependent on their environments—and because the environment does not stand still, organisations must develop internal mechanisms to facilitate planned change. Change efforts that are planned—that is proactive and purposeful—are normally what we mean by *managing* change. It is also the type of change in which managers generally have sufficient time to anticipate the nature of the change and what its effects are likely to be. It is aimed at keeping the organisation current and viable. In keeping with the focus of this book, we will further concentrate on structural change. Structural change is a specific part of the change process, which will be discussed in the next section. Unplanned change will be briefly considered later in the chapter.

What makes you think that you may need a new structure?

Many of the problems and challenges that confront organisations do not necessarily require a structural change. For problems such as poor morale, high absenteeism or inadequate skill levels, changing the structure may even make existing problems worse. So what are the indications that a new structure may be called for? We can summarise these in the following three areas:[3]

1 *Decision making is slow or inappropriate.* There may be a number of structural causes for this problem. One of the most common is that adequate information is not reaching the right person or group at the right time. The input of important or knowledgeable people may be excluded, or there may be too many people who

OT CLOSEUP

The Uniting Church and change

The organisations which are facing some of the most significant environmental challenges in Australia and New Zealand are the long-established churches. Although we live in a secular age, religion still provides fundamental support, comfort and meaning for many in society. The organised religions are also the oldest established organisations in Australia and, if the historical roots in Europe are taken into account, have a history going back many centuries. But herein lies the problem for many churches; their liturgy, ritual and order of service have changed little over the past centuries and to many in society look a little dated and bear little relevance to the way they live their lives.

New churches with innovative methods of worship, such as the evangelical churches, are greatly expanding their congregations whilst existing churches are faced with emptying pews. This presents a problem for church leadership; the existing congregations are fairly conservative and are happy with exiting rituals and forms of worship but future congregations are looking for something more relevant to their lives.

The Uniting Church has proposed that, in future, congregations may need to move away from traditional church buildings and worship in hotels, living rooms and shopping malls to remain relevant and reconnect with the wider population. The churches' moderator in NSW has warned that the traditional steepled sandstone church with stained glass windows and traditional religious imagery and language will have to change. There is also an economic reason for the churches' concern. Traditional churches, particularly historic ones, are expensive to maintain and building new ones in new housing estates often stretches the budget.

Introducing change in organisations as traditional as churches is very difficult, made all the more so by many members of the congregation being volunteers who can walk away if things don't suit them. Also, intense passions are involved and any change often strikes at the heart of a worshipper's sense of being. Moreover, there is no guarantee that moving into shopping malls and public halls would necessarily result in increased congregations or would reach those who are at present alienated from the church. Although change in churches is of a different nature to that of businesses, it is probably the most emotional change program to undertake and one of the longest.

must agree on the decision. The extent of delegation may not suit the situation. Decision makers may be overloaded and not allowed sufficient time to consider issues or gather the required information. Decision makers may not have latitude to make the decision they feel is appropriate: they must abide by inflexible rules. A further decision-making problem experienced in many organisations is that too many managers are given the authority to say 'no' but not enough are permitted to say 'yes' when a decision is necessary. Decisions may therefore be easily blocked and inertia in decision making sets in. As a result, important opportunities, and time, may be lost. At its extreme, organisational processes may be so inflexible that management systems do not recognise that a problem exists.

Overcoming this problem may involve improving information flows and clarifying areas of responsibility. It may involve hiring people with specific skills or removing superfluous people or departments. Job responsibilities may need reviewing. However, if the problem is that of the inadequacies of an individual, then the structure should not be changed to adapt to that individual. People problems need people solutions.

2 *The organisation is not responding innovatively to environmental change.* Indications of this may be that the organisation's products may be out of date or

technologically inferior to competing products. Other companies may be able to bring products to market faster or more cheaply. Important demographic changes may be overlooked. The company may not be keeping current with changing fashions or consumption patterns. Important changes, such as a low inflationary environment or the globalisation of business, may not be understood and consequently the organisation is unprepared for their impact. This indicates that the organisation's structure is not adequately monitoring these changes or that mechanisms do not exist to incorporate environmental changes in the decision-making process. Structural changes may therefore be necessary to align responsibilities with important organisational needs, or to improve communication channels.

3 *All important tasks should have someone responsible for them.* Environments change over time, and each important segment of the environment should have someone responsible for dealing with it. The rise of environmental specialists and Aboriginal liaison officers in mining companies is relatively recent. Without constant monitoring of these sectors, mining companies would very soon find themselves dealing with major public relations disasters. Since privatisation, the nature of Qantas's relations with the federal government has changed. Instead of dealing with the government as owner, it now must continually place profitability first. This has necessitated structural change within Qantas as areas of responsibility have changed.

But there are also areas within an organisation which must have someone responsible for them. For example, someone must be responsible for IT, sales, and supply chain management. In a good organisational design, all important areas will have a person with appropriate levels of authority responsible for them.

The tendency towards stability

Organisations, by their very nature, are conservative.[4] Once procedures and systems have been established, they act as a disincentive to change. You do not have to look far to see evidence of this phenomenon. Government agencies want to continue doing what they have been doing for years, whether the need for their service changes or remains the same. Organised religions are deeply entrenched in their history; attempts to change church doctrine and liturgy require great persistence and patience. Many charities and environmental groups find it difficult to alter their philosophies in the face of evolving circumstances. The majority of business firms, too, appear highly resistant to change.

Why do organisations resist change? There are at least four explanations. First, members fear losing what they already have. Those in power—who are in the best position to initiate change—typically have the most to lose. Second, most organisations are bureaucracies. Such structures have built-in systems and procedures that work against change. Third, many organisations can manage their environment and hence can reduce the pressures for change. For managers it is often easier to manage the environment than to introduce a change program. Finally, organisation cultures resist pressures for change. Let us elaborate on each of these points.

Any change can become a threat to employees' economic wellbeing, security, social affiliations or status. Change can result in the loss of money, friends, work group associates or even their jobs. As employees have a high investment in specific skills, change also threatens employee self-interest. Few people are prepared to throw away years of job preparation and experience. However, probably the greatest fear is loss of position and privilege by those in the managerial ranks. Top management can legitimately

OT CLOSEUP

The environmental drivers of change over the past 50 years

Organisations are constantly evolving and changing for all manner of reasons. But every age has an environmental driver of change which most firms must respond to. It is possible to identify what these environmental pressures are and how firms have responded. Not all organisations respond in the same way and some operate in environmental segments which are different from those of the majority of organisations. Neither is all change driven by these pressures. But they do indicate the themes which recur at any particular time.

1950s–1970s. Protectionism was high and most firms were domestically focused. Expansion took the form of entering new domestic markets with unrelated products. This was a period of great economic growth and expansion and organisations struggled to meet demand. Industrial disputation was high, often as a result of the tedious nature of work associated with mass production. As a consequence, most organisational change efforts were aimed at improving the quality of working life for those lower in the organisation.

1970s–1980s. The main influence upon organisational change at this time was the increasing sophistication of information technology. The early applications of computers were aimed at undertaking routine tasks and simple record keeping. By now, however, they were undertaking more sophisticated tasks and, in the early 1980s, desktop computers started to find an application. Organisations had deferred large-scale layoffs arising from the application of computers, but rising competitiveness and cost pressures forced organisations to take drastic action to reduce their number of employees. This ushered in the era of downsizing in which head counts were sometimes reduced by up to 50%. One of the challenges of this time was keeping morale and commitment high in what were uncertain and difficult times.

One structural change which was often played with, rather than fully embraced, was the matrix structure. It became very fashionable in the 1960s and 1970s as a possible way to break the bureaucratic inertia typical of most large organisations. The matrix permits an organisation or unit to respond to two environmental segments at once. But in many cases it was not applied with this in mind; it was hoped that organisations would become more responsive generally. Given this, it is not surprising that the matrix raised the levels of confusion and the outcomes were often disappointing.

The late 1970s and early 1980s saw a rise in imports from lower wage countries, particularly Japan. Many Western firms directly facing this competition, such as those in the motor vehicle and electronics industries, were shaken by the efficiency of their Japanese competitors and sought to emulate many of their management practices, particularly operations management techniques. The concept of corporate culture as a major factor in competitiveness also emerged from the study of Japanese companies. And quality techniques were widely applied during this period.

1980s–1990s. This period was one of continuous and disruptive change, which led to major structural changes; there was probably more change in the 1980s and 1990s than in the preceding 80 years. Many of these have been covered in Chapter 10. Most of the changes emerged from an environment of heightened competition. This competition was largely the result of government policy. First, governments had moved to deregulate and privatise industry with the aim of increasing competition. Second, again as a result of government policy, globalisation was gaining momentum. This presented both the challenge of increased import competition and the opportunity of expanding into new markets.

The general structural response of firms was to reduce the number of businesses they were in and concentrate upon their core competencies. There was also a shift from hierarchical control to market control. Many companies entered foreign markets for the first time, in the process climbing a steep learning curve. The overseas operations often changed the companies significantly as management grappled with new challenges, including the search for economies of scale.

Middle-management levels had been greatly reduced in previous downsizings and this, combined with new communication and information technologies, permitted far more operational decisions to be made by operatives and those lower in the organisation.

claim to have a great deal to lose from change. One author has noted why senior managers especially are prone both to resist change and to misinterpret signals that change is needed:[5]

> . . . they have strong-vested interests; they will be blamed if current practices, strategies, and goals prove to be wrong; re-orientations threaten their dominance; their promotions and high statuses have persuaded them that they have more expertise than other people; their expertise tends to be out-of-date because their personal experiences with clients, customers, technologies, and low-level personnel lie in the past; they get much information through channels which conceal events that might displease them; and they associate with other top managers who face similar pressures.

Add to this the fact that major restructuring almost always includes large-scale replacement of the top managers and it is not surprising to find senior managers being critical impediments to change.

Bureaucracies endure as the most common structural design in our society, with their popularity deriving from their ability to handle routine activities efficiently and their strong command and control emphasis. Even though writers and commentators promote the emergence of new organisational forms, most organisations, particularly large ones, exhibit many of the elements of bureaucracy. A significant shift away from bureaucracy is unlikely to have a widespread following. Specifically, bureaucracy's standardised technologies, high formalisation and stability-based reward systems, which strongly penalise risk-taking and mistakes, discourage doing things differently.

Chapter 11 described how organisations manage their environment. Clearly, many large and powerful organisations use their strength to reduce dependence on their environment and so protect their core activities. In doing this, they reduce their need to adapt to changes in that environment.

The organisation's culture also acts to impede change. Every organisation has a culture that defines what behaviours are appropriate and inappropriate. Once employees absorb their organisation's culture—and this need not take a long period of time—they know the way things are supposed to be done. Although culture helps employees understand what is important and what is not, it also creates a consistency of behaviour that becomes entrenched and highly resistant to change.

In summary, it appears that large-scale change receives far more attention in textbooks than it does in practice. The forces against change, and the inertia surrounding existing practices, result in far more stability than the rational-change literature describes. Of course, inertia is not all bad. Organisations need some resistance qualities, otherwise they might respond to every perceived change in the environment. Organisations need stability to function effectively. If an organisation was in a state of perpetual change, it would lose the consistent, goal-directed behaviour that makes a group of people into an organisation, and effectiveness would soon be lost.

A model for managing planned organisational change

Figure 12.3 represents a model for organisational change and shows how change may be broken down into a set of steps. Change is initiated by forces that generally originate in the environment. Occasionally, however, the forces for change may be internally generated, such as when an organisation seeks to commercialise an invention or discovery it has made itself. Introducing new technology also changes the organisation. The forces for change must be identified and interpreted by management, which then decides how the organisation should respond. In some cases the responsibility for the change is delegated to a change agent, while in others a management team will take responsibility for the change. Either way, there is someone, or some group, that is identified with introducing the change. The party responsible for the change determines the nature and type of change. This generally takes the form of a plan of action. The intervention requires that the change group must decide whether the change is a one-off occurrence or whether processes should be put in place to

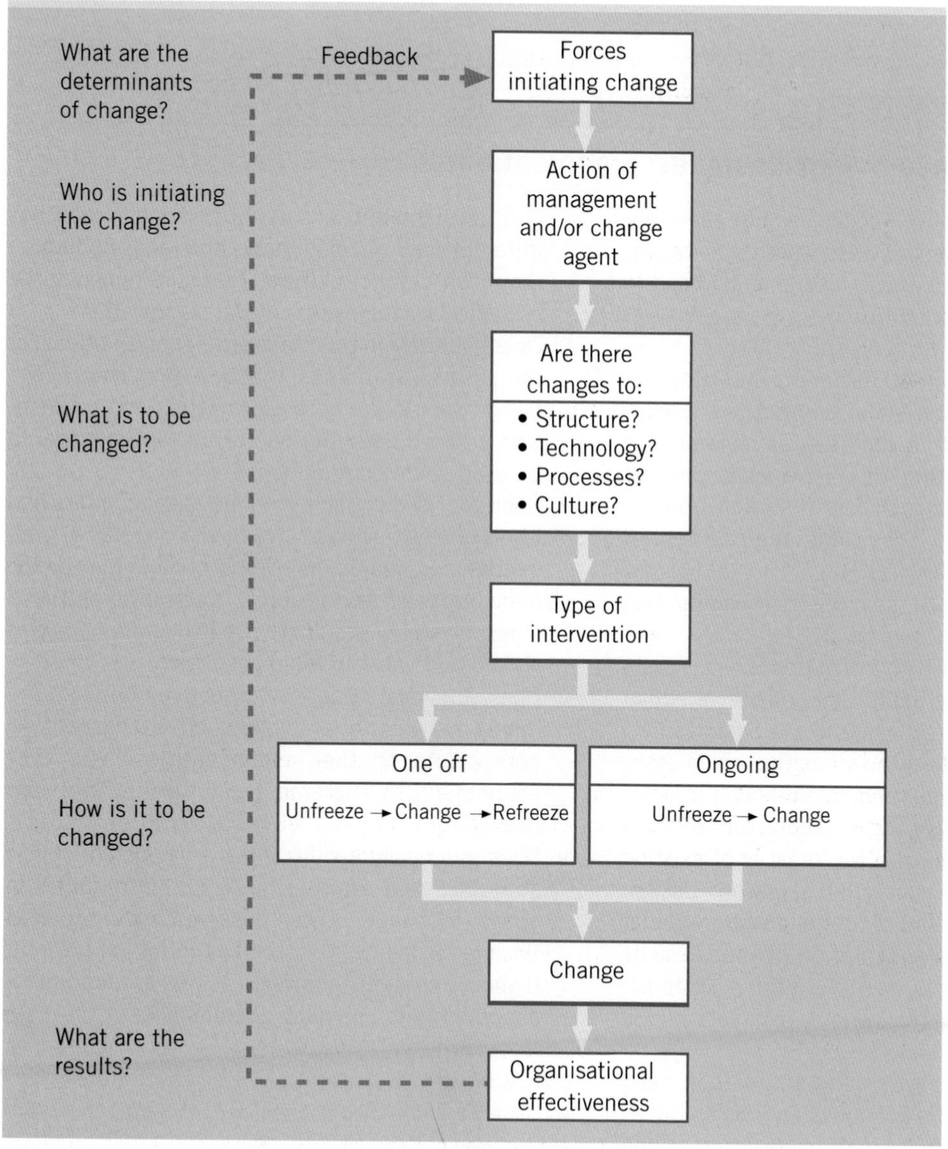
What are the determinants of change?
Who is initiating the change?
What is to be changed?
How is it to be changed?
What are the results?
Feedback
Forces initiating change
Action of management and/or change agent
Are there changes to:
• Structure?
• Technology?
• Processes?
• Culture?
Type of intervention
One off
Unfreeze → Change → Refreeze
Ongoing
Unfreeze → Change
Change
Organisational effectiveness

FIGURE 12.3 A model for managing organisational change

promote self-regeneration and continuous adaptation. Where it is only a one-off change, the process involves unfreezing the status quo, movement to a new state and refreezing the new state to make it permanent. Where continuous adaptation is involved, the change process omits the refreezing and attempts to make change an ongoing process. Implementation also includes the way in which the change agent or group chooses to put the change process into effect. The change itself, if successful, improves organisational effectiveness. Of course, changes do not take place in a vacuum; a change in one area of the organisation is likely to initiate new forces for other changes. The feedback identified in Figure 12.3 acknowledges that this model is dynamic. The need for change is presumed to be both inevitable and continual.

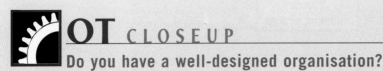

OT CLOSEUP

Do you have a well-designed organisation?

Goold and Campbell have suggested that there are nine tests to guide observers as to whether an organisation is well designed. These tests may be used to evaluate an existing structure or design a new one. The tests are:

1 Does your design direct sufficient management attention to your sources of competitive advantage in each market? A good test as to whether a structure is achieving this is if each market segment is receiving sufficient attention from an organisational unit. If it is not, then structural changes are indicated.
2 Does your design assist the corporate headquarters to add value to the organisation? Too often corporate headquarters become a drag upon the divisions rather than assisting them. Corporate-level activities should provide real value to the organisation.
3 Does your design reflect the strengths, weaknesses and motivations of your people? Although it is not a wise policy to design organisations around individuals, the strengths and weaknesses of existing employees should be considered in any new design.
4 Have you taken account of all the constraints that may impede the implementation of your design? Such constraints may be information systems, existing cultures or the various interests of the organisation's stakeholders.
5 Does your design protect the units that need distinct cultures? Different activities develop different cultures. Examples of these are sales, research and development, and product design; each has different ways of doing things and tends to develop their own distinct culture. This culture should be protected by the design of the organisation.
6 Does your design provide coordination solutions for the unit-to-unit links that are important? The design should promote coordination and cooperation and a clearly defined arbitration process to be used when conflicts arise.
7 Does your design have too many headquarters and levels of responsibility? If each division has a headquarters, as well as the company, there may be too many areas of responsibility. Each level and area of responsibility should have a distinct function and should add value to the organisation.
8 Does your design support effective controls? Are there clear areas of accountability? Are the controls appropriate to the responsibilities? Are they economical to implement and do they motivate managers?
9 Does your design facilitate the development of new strategies and provide the flexibility required to adapt to change? A well-designed organisation is flexible for the future as well as fit for the present. It should promote innovation as well as allowing for adaptability to changing circumstances.

Source: Drawn from Michael Goold & Andrew Campbell, 'Do you have a well-designed organization?', *Harvard Business Review*, March 2002, pp. 117–24.

Forces leading to change

All organisations change at some time during their life. This is particularly so for business organisations which face a constantly changing environment. Opportunities present themselves, technologies evolve, competition becomes more pronounced, and expectations of management and other critical constituencies change over time. These opportunities and problems may arise either from within the organisation or from outside it, or both.

The factors capable of initiating structural change are countless. While it is tempting to create several categories into which most of the factors fall neatly, such efforts quickly show that the impetus for change can come from anywhere. Table 12.1 summarises a number of the more visible reasons for an organisation considering a change in structure. This list, of course, is far from comprehensive. The origins of structural change may emerge from an unlimited set of sources. But changes in strategy, size, technology, environment or power can be the source of structural change. It is part of the skills set of upper-level management to interpret the drivers of changes and how to respond to them.

It is at times when major changes are necessary that organisations are vulnerable to introducing inappropriate change. One of the problems with the issue of change is that markets and environments generally change faster than organisational members' ability to grasp what is actually happening. For instance, few managers understood the impact of the low inflation of the 1990s on their organisations: they had to experience it for a number of years before its influence could be grasped. Similarly, technological change is typically either oversold as a panacea for all problems, or its introduction leads to unexpected consequences for the organisation. The opportunities and threats of globalisation took some time to actually become apparent. Organisations whose managers interpreted the environment correctly had an advantage over their competitors.

Organisations are continuously absorbing changes in environments and technologies with little in the way of structural change. Most modern structures, with the exception of those of the most rigid bureaucratic type, are designed to absorb ongoing changes of a minor nature. This capacity for self-design permits a wide variety of behaviours and capabilities to exist within the same structure and indicates that not all environmental change leads to major structural change. It is only when the organisation has lost the capacity for self-design that major structural change occurs.

Interpretation of the forces

Interpreting changes in the environment and the impact of new technology is not an exact science. There is always disagreement over the environmental changes taking place and what they mean for the organisation. Decision makers bring with them mindsets which predispose them to certain ways of interpreting events and happenings. These can range from ignoring them through to considering that they presage catastrophe for the organisation.

Either way, interpreting the problem accurately goes part way to determining an appropriate response. This process is not only fraught with the difficulties associated with interpreting facts and events, it is also highly political. Groups and individuals bias their interpretations in ways that favour them and their coalition. This need not be something that consciously occurs; it may be the outcome of the way that different professions view and interpret problems. Other influences upon perception may arise from the impact of management fashions and fads and attachment to strategies or trends in the industry.

TABLE 12.1 Some determinants of structural change, with examples

Change in objectives. Consistent with the strategy imperative, if an organisation chooses to move from being an innovator to being a mass producer, it is likely that its structure will need to become more mechanistic.

Purchase of new equipment. New equipment and technological processes often lead to changes in power and reporting relationships within the organisation. It can also make an organisation more mechanistic, as there is a greater capital intensity within the organisation.

Implementation of a sophisticated information-processing system. When organisations introduce sophisticated information processing, the centralisation dimension of structure is typically altered. It also permits new organisational forms which may previously have been too expensive to introduce.

Government regulations. The passage of new laws creates the need to establish new departments and changes the power of current departments. Governments also deregulate industries. In this case, government control of an industry is removed.

Globalisation. The lowering of tariffs and freeing of capital flows have led to organisations seeking higher efficiencies by focusing more on their core competencies, and disposing of peripheral businesses. It has also greatly increased the number of companies with overseas operations.

Changes in industrial relations. The move to enterprise bargaining has led to individual business units taking responsibility for industrial relations matters. The former system of centralised industrial relations meant limited freedom for individual businesses.

Increased pressure from consumer-advocate and environmental groups. In response to pressure from consumer and environmental groups, some organisations have created or expanded their public relations department, whereas others have upgraded the authority of personnel in the quality-control function. Changes in product ranges have also occurred.

Mergers or acquisitions. Duplicate functions will be eliminated, and new coordinating positions are typically created. Intense political activity can emerge.

Actions of competitors. Aggressive action by competitors can lead to the expansion of boundary-spanning roles and an increased focus on costs.

Sudden internal or external hostility. Temporary crises are typically met by management's centralising decision making.

Decline in profits. When a corporation's profits fall, management often resorts to a structural shake-up. Personnel will be shuffled, departments added and/or deleted, new authority relationships defined and decision-making patterns significantly altered.

Reduction in layers of management. As organisations can offer few promotions to employees, they must consider changes in tasks and responsibilities in order to broaden employees' skills and keep them interested in their jobs.

aesthetics, and wind testing. The adhocracy designing the car was made possible only by the technology used.

Conversely, any introduction of new technology will lead to organisational change. Some technological changes may be foreseen and planned for. Call centres provide a good example. Emerging communication technologies made it possible to concentrate all telephone enquiries into large centres which could be located anywhere. The actual physical presence of the firms, in the form of bank branches or insurance company shopfronts, could be wound back. The influence of other technological changes is more subtle and difficult to interpret. Emails, for instance, have changed communication patterns in ways that were unanticipated. Traditional travel agents have also been slow to embrace Internet bookings and to respond to what this technology means for their industry.

Organisational processes

The final strategy considers changing organisational processes, such as decision-making and communication patterns. If, for instance, a change program introduces taskforces into a machine bureaucracy with the intention of improving the transmission of information between functional units and allowing representatives from each unit to participate in decisions that will affect all of them, it will have altered the organisation's decision-making processes.

Changing culture and behaviour

Changing culture and behaviour is more the concern of organisational behaviour than organisational theory, although culture will be considered in the next chapter. It is included here because changing culture and behaviour forms an essential part of any change program. Often behaviour can be changed by changing structure, technologies and processes; one of the aims of changing structure is, in fact, to induce a behavioural change on the part of office holders. But behaviour and attitudes may be the main focus of the change program and attempts may be made to change these in the absence of other changes. Often this fails to lead to satisfactory outcomes. Texts on organisational behaviour cover this aspect of change in greater detail.

In addition to actions, the plan should incorporate elements of the expected outcomes of the change program and how these are to be measured or assessed. Some change programs may have an element of speculation; organisations know that they cannot keep on doing things in the same way but have only a fuzzy idea of what the outcome of the program will be. But other outcomes are capable of being measured or, at minimum, subjective outcomes made as to success.

Implementation of the change plan

Referring again to Figure 12.3, once forces for initiating change have been identified and those responsible have drawn up a change plan, the next phase in the change program is implementation. The method of implementation depends upon whether it is intended that the change program be a one-off event or part of an ongoing change program. Most change programs are one-off events, although some do aim to be part of an ongoing process of change, as we have seen in the Boral example above. One-off change programs follow a three-step process of preparing the organisation for change, changing the organisation and then incorporating the changes within the processes of the organisation. This process has in the past been referred to as unfreezing–changing–then refreezing. We begin by looking at the steps in the change process. Then we turn our attention to implementation tactics.

The change process

The three-step process recognises that change will not be successfully accomplished without unlearning the old ways, learning the new, and then incorporating the new ways as part of established practice. Unlearning is the mental process involved in the realisation that the old ways of doing things are no longer applicable. They are not forgotten, but in changed circumstances they no longer apply.

It is useful to view implementation as being a juxtaposition of two forces: those resisting change and those promoting change. Forces resisting change may emerge from comfort and familiarity with established practices; lack of understanding of what is involved in the change; the influence of important centres of power, which resist change or modifications to existing power structures; aversion to new roles or relationships which may be associated with the change; suspicion that new practices are unworkable; dismay at the loss of skills and doubts about the ability to learn new ones; and the influence upon attitudes of key opinion leaders. Managers will also resist change if they feel that their autonomy or areas of responsibility will be affected or, as may occur, their job will be lost. Sources of resistance will differ depending upon the situation.

But those managing change do have some powerful forces they can use to promote the change. Forces promoting change may include the power to change structure, that is, to redefine areas of authority and responsibility, create rewards, exercise legitimate authority, fund training and information sessions, co-opt respected leaders to promote the changes, introduce technological changes and make physical changes to workplaces and locations. Seven tactics that managers may use for dealing with resistance to change are described in Table 12.3.

Assuming that change has been implemented, it is necessary to ensure that the organisation does not revert to its former ways. Unless this last step is attended to, there is a very high likelihood that the change will be short-lived and employees will attempt to revert to the previous equilibrium state. There are a number of key factors that determine the degree to which a change will become permanent. One review of change studies identified a number of relevant factors.[9] The *reward allocation system* is critical. For instance, if rewards fall short of expectations over time, the change is likely to be short-lived. If a change is to be sustained, it needs the *support of a sponsor*. This individual, typically high in the management hierarchy, provides the change with legitimacy and charismatic leadership. Evidence indicates that once sponsorship is withdrawn from a change project, there is strong pressure to return to the old equilibrium state. It is also important that managers close to the employees be seen to support the change. People need to know what is expected of them as a result of the change. Therefore, *transmitting information* about expectations should reduce the degree of springback to the former ways; on the other hand, failure to do so would have the opposite effect. *Cultural change* and *group forces* are other important factors. As employees become aware that others in their group accept and sanction the change, they become more comfortable with it. *Commitment* to the change should lead to greater acceptance and permanence. As noted earlier, if employees participate in the change decision, they can be expected to be more committed to seeing that it is successful. Change is less likely to become permanent if it is implemented in a single unit of the organisation. Therefore, the more *diffusion* in the change effort, the more units that will be affected and the greater legitimacy the effort will carry.

TABLE 12.3 Tactics for dealing with resistance to change

Education and communication. Resistance can be reduced through communicating with employees to help them see the logic of a change. This tactic assumes basically that the source of resistance lies in misinformation or poor communication. If employees receive the full facts and get any misunderstandings cleared up, the resistance will subside. This can be achieved through one-on-one discussions, memos, group presentations or reports.

Participation. It's difficult for individuals to resist a change decision in which they have participated. Assuming that the participants have the expertise to make a useful contribution, their involvement can reduce resistance, obtain commitment and increase the quality of the change decision.

Facilitation and support. Change agents can offer a range of supportive efforts to reduce resistance. When employee fear and anxiety are high, counselling and therapy, new skills training or short, paid leaves of absence may facilitate adjustment.

Negotiation. This tactic requires the exchange of something of value for a lessening of the resistance. For instance, if the resistance is centred in a few powerful individuals, a specific reward package can be negotiated that will meet their individual needs.

Manipulation and co-optation. Manipulation refers to covert influence attempts. Twisting and distorting facts to make them appear more attractive, withholding undesirable information or creating false rumours to get employees to accept a change are all examples of manipulation. Co-optation is a form of both manipulation and participation. It seeks to 'buy off' the leaders of a resistance group by giving them a key role in the change decision. The advice of those who have been co-opted is sought only in order to get their endorsement, not to ensure a better decision.

Coercion. This tactic is the application of direct threats or force to the resisters. Examples include threats of transfer, loss of promotion, negative performance evaluation or a poor letter of recommendation.

Realigning staff profiles. This may involve both the dismissal of those who actively oppose the change and the hiring of new managers who support and reflect the values of the change.

Adapted from: John P. Kottler & Leonard A. Schlesinger, 'Choosing Strategies for Change', *Harvard Business Review*, March/April 1979, pp. 106–14.

These factors highlight that the organisation is a system, and that planned change will be most successful when all the parts in the system support the change effort. Successful and enduring change programs generally change more than just one aspect of the organisation. What is more, successful change requires careful balancing of the system. The consolidation of three divisional units into a single region obviously carries with it a wide range of reverberating effects. But the impact of even small changes (as when a multi-billion-dollar consumer products firm creates a new department of public affairs staffed with only a handful of personnel) can be expected to be widespread. Other departments and employees may feel threatened. Still others will feel that a portion of their responsibility has been taken from them. All changes, regardless of how small, will have an impact outside the area in which they were implemented. No change can take place in a vacuum. A structural modification in unit A will affect other structural variables within unit A, as well as structural variables in units B, C and so forth.

The systems perspective highlights that those responsible for change consider any and all interventions as having a potential impact that is far wider than the specific point where the change was intended. Large-scale change projects often don't try to change the whole organisation simultaneously: change is introduced in one part, or subsystem, of the organisation which may be supportive of the change. The benefits are then disseminated throughout the organisation, with different parts picking up on the change as the benefits and problems are better understood. As a result, in large organisations change often proceeds at different rates, with some subsystems adopting change faster than others.

We mentioned earlier that refreezing may not always be a good idea. In many cases the aim of the change may be to create a more flexible and adaptable organisation. This may involve a greater reliance on teamwork, introducing improved coordination devices and pushing responsibility lower down the management hierarchy. Here, the refreezing process will be aimed at reinforcing relationships and reducing barriers to communication flows rather than stressing formalisation and hierarchical relationships.

Implementation tactics

Appropriate tactics for implementing change are critical to success. Those responsible for the change must make decisions about how the planned change is to be brought about. Research has identified that four basic tactics summarise those that are most commonly used. One author has called these tactics intervention, participation, persuasion, and edict.[10]

The intervention tactic is characterised by change agents *selling* their change rationale to those who will be affected. They argue that current performance is inadequate and that new standards and procedures must be established. They cite comparable organisations or units with better performance to justify the need for change, and then often explicitly describe how current practices can be improved. To assess more fully inefficient or poorly designed procedures, change agents using the intervention tactic often form taskforces made up of those subject to change. The taskforces can work backwards from a desired state, identifying the best means of achieving what is desired. This co-opting technique utilises the expertise of those who know the job best while reducing resistance to change. But change agents retain power to veto any of the taskforce's recommendations.

In participation, change agents *delegate* the implementation decision to those who will be affected. They stipulate the need for change or the opportunities change can provide, create a taskforce to do the job, assign members to the taskforce, and then delegate authority for the change process to the taskforce with a statement of expectations and constraints. Change agents who use this tactic give full responsibility to the taskforce for implementation and exercise no veto power over its decisions. This tactic is often used in large organisations, where the senior managers decide on the need for change while leaving the actual process to others.

Some change agents handle change by essentially *abdicating* the decision to experts. Change agents identify the need or opportunity for change. But because they are disinterested, lack knowledge or feel that others can handle the job better, they

For review and discussion

1 What is the traditional view of change in organisations?
2 What does 'managed change' mean?
3 Why do organisations resist change?
4 Describe five determinants of change.
5 Describe the three types of intervention strategies.
6 Contrast driving and restraining forces in unfreezing.
7 What would make managers think that their organisation needed a new structure?
8 Review the various tactics for dealing with resistance to change in power-control terms.
9 Explain why organisations have an inherent bias towards stability.
10 'Bureaucracies have survived because they have proved able to respond to change.' Do you agree or disagree? Discuss.
11 'Pressure for change originates in the environment, whereas pressure for stability originates within the organisation.' Do you agree or disagree? Discuss.
12 'Resistance to change is good for an organisation.' Do you agree or disagree? Discuss.
13 Why would the results of a major change program take years to become clear?
14 How might an organisation respond to unplanned change?
15 How would you modify Figure 12.3 to reflect the descriptive and power-control views of organisational change?

CASE FOR CLASS DISCUSSION

Coles Myer's 'Operation Right Now'

Coles Myer is one of Australia's perennially underperforming companies. It was formed by the 1985 merger of Coles supermarkets and discount stores and the department store chains of Myer and Grace Brothers. The major stores owned by Coles Myer include Coles supermarkets, Liquorland, Target, Kmart, Myer department stores and Officeworks. The idea was to create a large retailing group which would benefit from significant economies of scale. For instance, costs could be greatly reduced if all bed linen for the group was purchased by one central purchasing department and processed through a common supply chain management system.

However, these savings have been difficult to achieve. A string of chief executives have always 'had a plan' to capture the economies but none has worked as anticipated. Powerful heads of the separate store chains were reluctant to cede power and control to centralised buying, and warehousing groups and excessive bureaucracy and overstaffing at head office slowed structural change. In short, the interaction of the problems of large size and disparate product range were difficult to overcome. Just when it seemed that progress could be made, at least one of the major businesses had problems, which dragged down the performance of the group. Myer department stores have had endless troubles finding the right mix of merchandise and service, Kmart allowed its costs to rise so that it was no longer a cheap shopping destination, while Target tried to reinvent itself as a homewares store. These problems were compounded by overstocking, and the subsequent disposal of excess merchandise impacted profits. About the only solid business in the group consisted of Coles supermarkets.

In order to overcome the performance shortfall, a new chief executive, John Fletcher, was appointed in 2001. A former respected chief executive of Brambles, he had no retailing experience; indeed, one of his first statements on taking over the position was that he had not been in a shop for 20 years. However, he felt that most of the problems facing Coles Myer were structural and ones of process and that specialist retailing knowledge was not needed to address them. Fletcher's plan was called 'Operation Right Now'. It aimed to create a sharper focus for each business group. A whole new layer of top management was recruited, mostly from overseas, and they brought in new ideas and were free of commitment to the existing Coles Myer culture. These new managers headed each of the major store chains.

Another major part of Fletcher's plan was to create shared service units in areas such as warehousing, logistics, buying and supply chain management. Economies of scale could then be obtained by reducing the number of warehouses and movements of merchandise. He is also trying to improve decision making by reducing the size of the head office bureaucracy and moving personnel into the operating divisions.

But although some progress has been made since the program was introduced, a number of the overseas appointments did not work out and resignations occurred, setting back strategic decision making in some key business units. Consolidating warehousing proved more difficult to implement than anticipated. Deriving economies from reduced inventories and storing and moving the millions of different items of stock required the introduction of sophisticated information technology. This also proved more difficult to implement and there were extensive cost overruns and delays in the program.

QUESTIONS

1 Identify the ways in which the case illustrates the multidimensional nature of change.

2. Why is achieving economies of scale for such a retailing enterprise proving difficult?

3 Why would a program such as Operation Right Now take at least five years to implement?

4 Why would strong fiefdoms delay the implementation of a change program? How did Fletcher overcome this source of change?

FURTHER READING

John Child, *Organization*, New York: Harper & Row, 1977.

Leonard Goodstein & Warner Burke, 'Creating Successful Organizational Change', *Organizational Dynamics*, Spring 1991, pp. 5–17.

Rosabeth Moss Kanter, *When Giants Learn to Dance*, London: Routledge, 1989.

Rosabeth Moss Kanter, Barry Stein & Todd Jick, *The Challenge of Organizational Change: How Companies Experience It and Leaders Guide It*, New York: Free Press, 1992.

Andrew Pettigrew, *Innovative Forms of Organizing*, London: Sage, 2003.

NOTES

1 Henry Mintzberg, *The Structuring of Organizations*, Englewood Cliffs, N.J.: Prentice-Hall, 1979.

2 William H. Starbuck & Paul C. Nystrom, 'Designing and Understanding Organizations', in P.C. Nystrom & W.H. Starbuck, eds, *Handbook of Organizational Design*, vol. 1, New York: Oxford University Press, 1981.

3 John Child, *Organization*, New York: Harper & Row, 1977.

4 Richard H. Hall, *Organizations: Structure and Process*, 3rd edn, Englewood Cliffs, NJ: Prentice Hall, 1987, p. 29.

5 William H. Starbuck, 'Organizations as Action Generators', *American Sociological Review*, February 1983, p. 100.

6 Jeffrey Pfeffer, *Power in Organizations*, Marshfield, MA: Pitman Publishing, 1981, pp. 142–6.

7 Albert Dunlap, *Mean Business*, Singapore: Butterworth Heinemann Asia, 1996.
8 Daniel Katz & Robert L. Kahn, *The Social Psychology of Organizations*, 2nd edn, New York: John Wiley, 1978, p. 679.
9 Paul S. Goodman, Max Bazerman & Edward Conlon, 'Institutionalization of Planned Organizational Change', in Barry M. Staw & Larry L. Cummings, eds, *Research in Organizational Behavior*, vol. 2, Greenwich, CN: JAI Press, 1980, pp. 231–42.
10 Paul C. Nutt, 'Tactics of Implementation', *Academy of Management Journal*, June 1986, pp. 230–61.
11 Nutt, ibid.
12 Nutt, ibid.
13 This section is based on Jeffrey Pfeffer, *Organizational Design*, Arlington Heights, IL: AHM Publishing, 1978, pp. 190–2.

CHAPTER 13

Managing organisational culture

After reading this chapter you should be able to:

- define organisational culture
- list organisational culture's key characteristics
- differentiate between the dominant culture and subcultures
- identify the characteristics of a strong culture
- explain how a culture is sustained over time
- describe how employees learn an organisation's culture
- explain how culture affects the success of mergers and acquisitions
- list conditions that favour the successful changing of a culture.

Introduction

NAB tries to build a new culture

The National Australia Bank is one of the pillars of corporate Australia. As one of the strongest banks to emerge from the late 1980s financial crisis, it became comfortable with its position of dominance.[1] During the 1990s, a strong managing director, Don Argus, exerted tight control on the company and a culture of deference to a strong CEO developed.

But this was not the only trait which characterised the NAB's culture. The culture was characterised by arrogance and delusions of grandeur and a belief that no one could teach the bank anything, and as a result there was nothing to learn. Believing its own legend and the image it had of itself, it went on a buying spree around the world: banks in the United Kingdom and, particularly, Homeside in the United States. None of these purchases was worth the price paid and the NAB legend started to look extremely shaky when Homeside was sold at a loss of $4 billion.

The reaction to this loss revealed the weaknesses in NAB's culture. Shareholders were not told the reasons for the losses, no one in the bank took responsibility and, in fact, one of the outside advisers who recommended that NAB go ahead with the purchase of Homeside was hired as head of risk management at the bank.

In short, NAB had developed a culture which viewed itself as infallible: mistakes were always someone else's fault, no one took responsibility when something bad happened but were always around for any rewards that were given out, and shareholders were considered an annoying necessity. Not surprisingly, this set the bank up for its next debacle: the foreign exchange losses. In 2003, rogue foreign exchange traders lost $360 million on unauthorised trades. Subsequent enquiries revealed further aspects of an arrogant culture. It disclosed a culture of fear and intimidation, where profit was king, and deference to a domineering management was common. The board was revealed as being ineffectual and failing to exercise their duties.

Major shareholders were not prepared to let the situation continue so it was clear that the culture of NAB had to change. An almost entirely new board of directors was appointed, as was a new managing director. Almost all of the senior layer of management was sacked and new outside appointments made. A start was made on creating an organisation with a candid culture in which people took responsibility for their actions, with less focus on bureaucratic processes and procedures. Rather than the previous 'good news culture', staff were encouraged to talk about problems and issues and to be innovative in seeking answers. Teamwork was encouraged.

This process was expected to take some time; after two years into the program the managing director stated that maybe it would be another five years before permanent improvements would be seen.

This chapter introduces the idea that organisations have personalities. We call these personalities organisational cultures. Researchers and commentators have linked the culture of modern business organisations with their success, thus ensuring continuing interest in culture as an organisational variable. But ever since antiquity, leaders have intuitively understood that organised activity involved commonality of belief and behaviour and it was this that contributed to creating a disciplined organisation as distinct from an unfocused random group.

Culture is a common feature of organisational life, even if it is stronger and more obvious in some organisations than others. In this chapter we concentrate upon culture in modern business organisations. We build an argument that culture has an important influence on an organisation's effectiveness. We also examine how cultures originate, and discuss the difficulties of managing culture and cultural change.

What is organisational culture?

There is no shortage of definitions of organisational culture. It has been described, for example, as 'the dominant values espoused by an organisation',[2] 'the philosophy that guides an organisation's policy toward employees and customers',[3] 'the way things are done around here',[4] and 'the basic assumptions and beliefs that are shared by members of an organization'.[5] A closer look at the wide array of definitions does uncover a central theme—**organisational culture** refers to a system of *shared meaning*. In every organisation there are patterns of beliefs, symbols, rituals, myths and practices that have evolved over time.[6] These, in turn, promote common understanding among members as to the purpose of the organisation and the way its members are expected to behave. Without such understanding, which channels behaviour into certain patterns and promotes a common understanding amongst members, organisational life as we know it would not be possible.

organisational culture a system of shared meaning within an organisation

But there is more than this. Culture does not just refer to present actions: it is also one of the main mechanisms through which the behaviour and actions of new members of the organisation are shaped. A long-time researcher of organisation culture, Edgar Schein, has proposed the following definition:[7]

> Organisational culture is the pattern of basic assumptions that a given group has invented, discovered or developed in learning to cope with its problems of external adaptation and internal integration, and that have worked well enough to be considered valid, and, therefore, to be taught to new members as the new way to perceive, think and feel in relation to those problems.

A close study of Schein's definition identifies some key concepts of organisational culture. First, it is composed of beliefs and assumptions. Beliefs and assumptions form the mental concepts of what we consider reality. This in turn affects how events are perceived around us and the interpretations placed upon them. We take our beliefs and assumptions for granted, rarely questioning or evaluating them. Indeed, so embedded are they that many of us may be unable to identify what our basic assumptions and beliefs are. In many cases, we become aware of them only when we move to a different social system, such as a country or company, where our beliefs and assumptions are no longer the dominant ones. Where the beliefs and assumptions are shared amongst a population, communication is facilitated and the exercise of control becomes easier.

Schein's definition also highlights that the beliefs and assumptions we apply at work are part of the social processes that have emerged from the way in which organisations adapt to their environment. In other words, cultures do not emerge as a random set of beliefs and thoughts. They have a purpose, and that purpose is to enable the organisation to survive in the environment in which it operates. It does this by providing a common set of values, which facilitates understanding among members. This provides members with a collective identity and enables them to work well together. Just as importantly, the culture of the organisation should be congruent with—in other words, it should fit—the external environment in which the organisation operates. Further, the emergent culture of the organisation is transmitted through a process of socialisation of new members.

Organisational cultures exist because the conditions that foster their creation are commonly found. These conditions may be identified from Schein's definition. They are stability of membership and a repetitive cycle of events, which leads to a stable pattern of interaction among members. Further, there is a need for at least some measure of organisational success, typically organisational longevity, as this indicates that the actions being taken are appropriate and should be transmitted to new members.

terminal values the desired end-state or outcome that people try to attain

instrumental values desired modes of behaviour

The culture of an organisation is expressed in the values and behavioural norms of organisational members. There are two types of values: terminal and instrumental.[8] **Terminal values** refer to the desired end-state or outcome that people try to attain. Examples of terminal values may be achieving certain quality or performance levels, alleviating the effects of poverty, providing clean drinking water or providing aids for the disabled. **Instrumental values** refer to desired modes of behaviour. Examples are the standards of conduct of organisational members, professional standards, attitude towards work, the nature of cooperation within an organisation, and values that influence certain patterns of communication. 'Norms' are derived from the word 'normal', and that should provide a good idea as to what they are. *Norms* are behavioural and attitudinal standards that are taken as accepted for a given group.

This discussion indicates that culture exists at two levels. These are shown in Figure 13.1. The first is outward manifestations of the culture, which are observable and capable of some form of interpretation. For instance, we can identify the symbols of the organisation, the pattern of communications, the physical arrangement of work spaces and the ways in which power is expressed. We can also listen to the stories that are told and observe the bonding ceremonies that members participate in. The second level of culture is composed of the deeply held values, beliefs, assumptions, attitudes and feelings that underlie behaviour. Beliefs and assumptions at this level are difficult to identify and hence interpret and understand. As a consequence, they present complexities for managers and researchers alike. Even organisation members may be unable to articulate what the values and beliefs of the organisation are. It is the visible level of culture that is more amenable to measurement and change, and consequently it is this that has attracted the greater part of management attention.

Researchers have identified that culture is not just an instrumental feature of an organisation whose sole purpose is to achieve environmental adaptation. It also satisfies a deeper human need by providing a sense of meaning and belonging to organisational members. This has been called the symbolic-interpretive approach to culture.[9] Membership of an organisation provides more than just economic rewards. It also affords a source of identification upon which people may build significance within their lives. Organisations that impart this for their members have been called social movements. The term 'clan' has been used to describe organisations which, in an industrial setting, exhibit many of the control and identification functions of self-sufficient preindustrial groups.[10] While many prominent businesses provide this identification for their members, it can also clearly be seen in the not-for-profit sector. Religious organisations, those engaged in environmental lobbying such as Greenpeace, charities, overseas aid organisations and sporting bodies have a deep

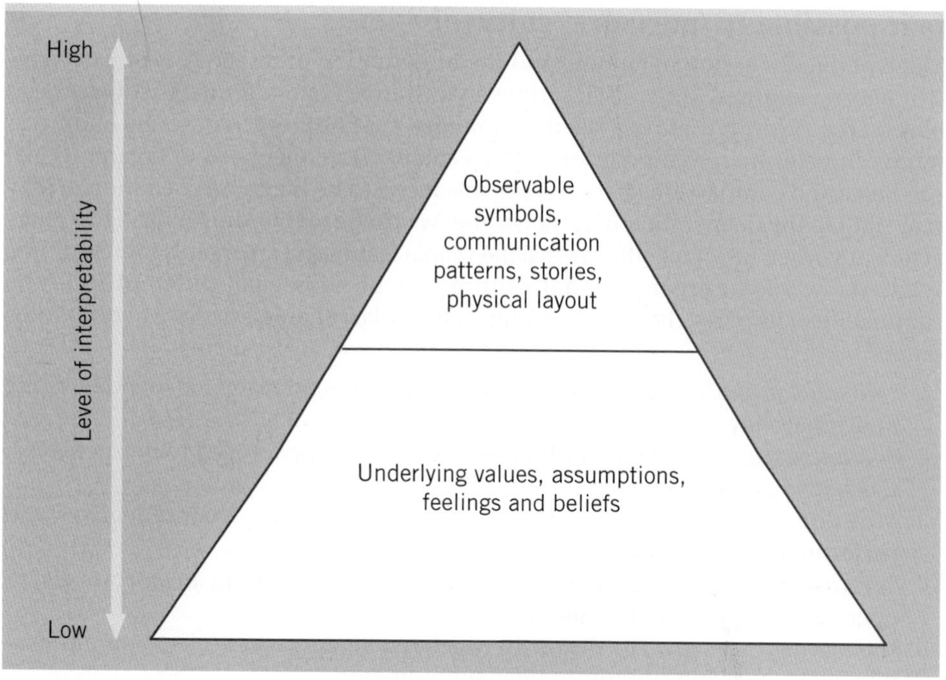
High
Low
Level of interpretability
Observable symbols, communication patterns, stories, physical layout
Underlying values, assumptions, feelings and beliefs

FIGURE 13.1 The different levels of culture, showing how interpretability varies with each level

symbolic meaning for their members. In many cases, members of these organisations are happy to give their services free of charge because of their close identification with the basic purposes of the organisation. Needless to say, this presents challenges to the management of these organisations that are not encountered in profit-oriented businesses.

The discussion of culture so far should not leave us with the idea that all organisations have strong and distinctive cultures which may be readily distinguished from each other. Culture exists to facilitate the organisation's movement towards its goals. Many organisations have similar goals and operate in similar environments; the large banks provide a good example. So it is not surprising that the cultures of many businesses are very similar. A distinctive culture takes a long time to evolve and learn and the fact that employees move seamlessly between organisations and can quickly become productive in another organisation indicates similarity between organisational cultures.

A further influence promoting cultural similarity is commonality of environment. As open systems, organisations are influenced by their environment, and groups of organisations facing a similar environment absorb characteristics of that environment. It is unlikely that an organisation would develop a culture which was radically different from the environment of which the organisation was a part. Further influences promoting similarity of cultures include common education and training systems, legislation requiring certain forms of behaviour, for instance, anti-discrimination laws, and high levels of labour turnover. In addition, national cultures are reflected in organisational cultures. As a result, we are likely to find that organisations located in the one country and undertaking similar tasks are likely to exhibit similar cultures.

Is it possible to 'measure' culture?

Much of the discussion of culture, and the presentation of research, is of a descriptive nature: in other words, it describes in narrative form features that have been observed. However, there is a need for managers and others to describe culture in more concrete and measurable terms. This enables both diagnosis of organisational problems and comparisons between organisations to be made. So even though they may not tap the deeper meanings of culture, we propose that the following 10 characteristics, when taken together, reveal the visible features of an organisation's culture. While the whole of organisational culture may be somewhat different from the summation of its parts, the following represent the key characteristics where cultures differ:[11]

1. *Individual initiative.* The degree of responsibility, freedom and independence that individuals have.
2. *Risk tolerance.* The degree to which employees are encouraged to be aggressive, innovative and risk-seeking.
3. *Direction.* The degree to which the organisation creates clear objectives and performance expectations.
4. *Integration.* The degree to which units within the organisation are encouraged to operate in a coordinated manner.
5. *Management support.* The degree to which managers provide clear communication, assistance and support to their subordinates.
6. *Control.* The number of rules and regulations and the amount of direct supervision that are used to oversee and control employee behaviour.
7. *Identity.* The degree to which members identify with the organisation as a whole rather than with their particular work group or field of professional expertise.
8. *Reward system.* The degree to which reward allocations (i.e. salary increases and promotions) are based on employee performance criteria in contrast to seniority, favouritism and so on.
9. *Conflict tolerance.* The degree to which employees are encouraged to air conflicts and criticisms openly.
10. *Communication patterns.* The degree to which organisational communications are restricted to the formal hierarchy of authority.

These 10 characteristics include both structural and behavioural dimensions. For example, management support is a measure of leadership behaviour. Most of these dimensions, however, are closely associated with an organisation's design. To illustrate, the more routine an organisation's technology and the more centralised its decision-making process, the less individual initiative employees in that organisation will have. Similarly, machine bureaucracies create cultures with more formal communication patterns than do simple or matrix structures. Close analysis would also reveal that integration is essentially an indicator of horizontal interdependence. What this means is that organisational cultures are not just reflections of their members' attitudes and personalities. A large part of an organisation's culture can be traced directly to structurally related variables.

Do organisations have uniform cultures?

Organisational culture represents a common set of beliefs held by the organisation's members. This was made clear when we noted that culture was a system of *shared*

OT CLOSEUP

How cultures are seen by business people

We have listed above the variables that academics have used to define culture. But business people and journalists have their own language to describe culture. The following descriptors, and their meanings, are among those commonly used in business journals:

Entrepreneurial culture. Constantly seeking new markets and products.
Conformist culture. Low tolerance of dissent.
Clubby and paternalistic culture. Exclusive, with the company looking after employees.
Cosy culture. Comfortable and stress-free.
Insular and consensus-driven. Isolated, inward-looking and agreement-seeking.
Slow-moving and arrogant. Slow to change and contemptuous of others.
Bureaucratic. Dominated by adherence to rules and procedures.
Complacent, sluggish and inward-looking. Uncaring of the organisation's environment and not prepared to change.
Blokey. Dominated by male interests such as sport and male banter.
Performance-based. Goal- and target-driven behaviour.
Culture of hubris. Proud and dismissive of other organisations.
Shareholder culture. Seeking to maximise shareholder gains.
Hidebound, politics-ridden culture. Narrow-minded and conspiratorial.
Plodding, perfectionist culture. Stodgy but seeking constantly to improve products.
Aggressive culture. Pushy and assertive.

meaning. We should expect, therefore, individuals with different backgrounds or at different levels in the organisation will tend to describe the organisation's culture in similar terms. However, this does not prevent different parts of the organisation developing their own distinctive subcultures. It is unlikely that sales and research and development would exhibit the same culture because they are subject to different pressures and time frames. As a result, most large organisations have a dominant culture and numerous sets of subcultures which differ in varying degrees from the dominant culture.[12]

A **dominant culture** expresses the **core values** that are shared by a majority of the organisation's members. When we talk about an *organisation's culture*, we are referring to its dominant culture. It is this macro-view of culture that gives an organisation its distinct personality. Top management is often closely associated with either promoting or carrying the dominant culture.

dominant culture the overiding core values shared by the majority of an organisation's members

Subcultures tend to develop in large organisations to reflect common problems, situations, technologies or experiences that members face. These subcultures can form vertically or horizontally.[13] When one product division of a divisionalised form has a culture uniquely different from that of other divisions of the organisation, a vertical subculture exists. Multinational companies also have vertical cultures, where different cultures exist in different countries. When a specific set of functional specialists—such as accountants or research and development personnel—have a set of common understandings, a horizontal subculture is formed. Of course, any group in an organisation can develop a subculture. For the most part, however, subcultures tend to be defined by department, occupation or geographic location. The purchasing

core values the primary values expressed by an organisation's dominant culture

subcultures separate cultures encompassed within organisational subunits

department, for example, can have a subculture that is uniquely shared by members of that department. It will include the core values of the dominant culture plus additional values unique to members of the purchasing department. Similarly, a department or unit of the organisation that is physically separated from the organisation's main operations may take on a different personality. Again, the core values are essentially retained but modified to reflect the separated unit's distinct situation.

If organisations had no dominant culture and were composed only of numerous subcultures, the influence of culture on organisational effectiveness would be far more difficult to determine and manage. This is because there would be no common culture to identify. It is the 'shared meaning' aspect of organisational culture that has attracted the attention of researchers and commentators and makes it such a powerful management tool. However, we cannot ignore the reality that many organisations, and almost all large ones, also have distinct subcultures. This raises questions when studying an organisation's culture as to what should be the main focus of research. Should it be assumed that the organisation's culture is strong enough to overcome those of departments or occupational groups, or should the focus be on various subcultures of the organisation in the expectation that these are stronger drivers of behaviour?

Culture and organisational effectiveness

What impact does culture have on organisational effectiveness? To answer this question, we need first differentiate between strong cultures and weak ones.

strong culture a culture characterised by intensely held, clearly ordered and widely shared core values

A **strong culture** is characterised by the organisation's core values being intensely held, clearly ordered and widely shared. The more members that accept the core values, agree on their order of importance, are highly committed to them and whose actions are guided by the culture, the stronger the culture will be. Organisations that have constant turnover among their members, almost by definition, will have a weak culture because members will not have shared enough experiences to create distinctive common meanings.[14] This should not be interpreted as implying that all mature organisations with a stable membership will have strong cultures, as the core values must also be intensely held.

Religious organisations, cults and Japanese companies are examples of organisations that have very strong cultures.[15] In extreme forms, these are very instructive about the role that culture can play in an organisation. Many religious organisations, such as monasteries, require little in the way of control because the values of the order are so intensely held that members can always be relied upon to act in the best interests of the organisation. Other examples of extreme culture control are military organisations, which take recruits from a wide variety of backgrounds and then isolate them for months while moulding them into an efficient fighting force. Of course, the strong cultural influences that can lead to organisations with little control or the formation of elite military units can be harnessed to create successful organisations such as Blue Scope Steel and Virgin Blue—although, of course, the extreme mechanisms used by organisations such as military services must be modified in commercial organisations. Additionally, commercial organisations may not seek to develop such a deep culture within their organisations.

If the culture is strong, how will it influence the organisation's effectiveness? In Schein's definition of culture given at the beginning of the chapter, we identified culture as playing an important role in internal integration and in the external adaptation of the organisation to its environment. We can see that effectiveness requires that an organisation's culture, strategy, environment and technology be aligned with the organisation's goals.[16] The stronger an organisation's culture, the more important it is that culture be congruent with the other variables.

The successful organisation will achieve a good *external fit*—its culture will conform to its strategy and environment. Market-driven strategies, for instance, are more appropriate in dynamic environments and will require a culture that emphasises individual initiative, risk-taking, high integration, tolerance of conflicts and high horizontal communication. In contrast, product-driven strategies focus on efficiency, work best in stable environments, and are more likely to be successful when the organisation's culture is high in control, minimises risk and conflict, and emphasises conformance to standards. Successful organisations will also seek a good *internal fit*, with their culture properly matched to their technology. Routine technologies provide stability and work well when linked to a culture that emphasises conformance to process, centralised decision making and limited individual initiative. None of us would be keen to fly with an airline that promoted and rewarded risk-taking! Non-routine technologies require adaptability and are best matched with cultures that encourage individual initiative and free-flowing communication and where control is de-emphasised. Advertising agencies are good examples of this type of cultural fit.

Environments are rarely stable. Technology and the actions of competitors are constantly changing. Expectations of stakeholders, such as customers, shareholders, employees, communities and government, change over time. And with the expansion of globalisation a whole new range of complexities has entered the organisation's external environment. From our definition we can see that the organisation's culture influences its ability to adapt to these changes. This indicates that the appropriateness is likely to change over time. As environments and technologies change, so too must the organisation's culture in order for the organisation to maintain its effectiveness. As we shall discuss later, the stronger the culture, the more difficult it is to change.

Many Australian and New Zealand companies that were in regulated industries or were government monopolies are faced with having to change strong cultures. In many cases, although the butt of many jokes about efficiency, these organisations (e.g. Telstra, the various water supply authorities, port authorities, and electricity generation and supply organisations, to name a few) were strongly imbued with the ethic of service to the public. The stability that regulation had given them, combined in many cases with fairly static technology and a highly centralised and structured industrial relations system, led to very fixed and rigid ways of doing things. Any proposed change in the organisation's operations had to contend with the inertia of many layers of management and massive industrial relations issues. However, now that most of these organisations have been either deregulated or privatised, they must alter their way of operating in order to accommodate change more readily. Layers of management have been cut and labour awards negotiated on an enterprise basis. Whole organisations have had to come to terms with the fact that it is no longer sufficient just to get the job done, and that efficiency measures have to be met as well. In addition, technological change in telecommunications is relentless. The competitive marketplace is unforgiving of those organisations that do not use their resources effectively or fail to adapt to change. In the new environment, the old culture was a liability, and a new culture of cooperation and wider job skills and responsibilities had to be learnt by those wishing to avoid redundancy.

OT CLOSEUP

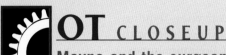

Mayne and the surgeons: or the tricky business of hospital culture

One of the perennial underperformers on the Australian stock market is the former Mayne Nickless, now known as Mayne Group. As one of the conglomerates which dominated Australian business, Mayne has constantly struggled to determine what its core competencies are and, in turn, extract reasonable returns from them. Its main businesses have been reduced to transport, logistics and health care, its major division, which is based on 58 private hospitals and supporting diagnostic and pathology services.

After years of strategy changes and attempts at cost cutting, in 2001 the board of Mayne appointed Peter Smedley as managing director. Smedley established his reputation as a turnaround expert at Colonial Mutual, which he built from a sleepy insurance company to a major funds manager, which was subsequently sold to the Commonwealth Bank for $10 billion. Much of the growth at Colonial took place through acquisitions from which he extracted considerable synergies. Smedley, and the management team he brought with him, was expected to work a similar magic at Mayne.

However, running a large health care group proved to be a far more difficult task than Smedley had possibly imagined. The main reason for this was that the culture of the health industry proved to be radically different from that of banking and funds management. Hospitals are a service business and the group which refers the patients to the hospital are the surgeons. Most patients are not really concerned with the hospital they attend; they follow the surgeon's advice. The patients pay the surgeons and the health funds reimburse the patient for their costs, or at least some of the costs. Keeping the surgeons happy, therefore, becomes the key to profitability. The surgeons are not employees who can be managed using command and control techniques; they must be kept satisfied in other ways.

If anyone went out of their way to antagonise the surgeons, it is unlikely that they could have done a better job than Mayne. Notwithstanding the fact that the hospitals were spread throughout the country, Smedley's first structural move was to centralise all decision making in the Melbourne head office. The aim was to cut costs through reducing management input at the local hospital level and through centralising purchasing. But it had the consequence of leaving little decision making at the local level. Surgeons were advised that if they wanted to speak to management they would have to write a memo and wait for a reply from Melbourne, a complete contrast to just walking up to the hospital manager's office to discuss patient care. Many surgeons complained that their telephone calls to hospitals were rarely answered and important meetings never held. Needless to say, relations with medical staff deteriorated rapidly.

Another important downside of the centralisation strategy was that critical local issues were not identified and acted upon in time. Further, the remote management strategy gutted hospital management of its knowledge base and its links with local communities.

Other health professionals were put offside by constant cost cutting, which many staff claim treated patients like cans off a conveyer belt, and the concentration on the bottom line also shifted the focus from patient care. Partly this was attributed to Smedley and his team having little experience in managing a service industry like health. Ultimately, a culture built on quality service to a patient did not take too kindly to bureaucratic-type cost cutting. So widespread was the dissatisfaction in the industry with Mayne that other health care companies were reluctant to merge with the company, virtually ending its strategy of growth by acquisition.

Mayne eventually made attempts to devolve decision making to the hospitals but too much damage was done for it to be a success. Talented managers had left in dismay and were reluctant to rejoin the company; others were discouraged by the reputation which Mayne had acquired. Eventually, the hospitals were sold, only for the new owners to restore the hospitals' fortunes and on-sell them for double what they paid for them.

Mayne itself didn't survive, announcing in 2005 that the company would be split and cease to exist as a single entity.

Source: Adapted from Beth Quinleven, 'Medicine Man', *Business Review Weekly*, 4 April 2002, pp. 46–53; and David Roe & Tom Noble, 'How Dissatisfied Doctors Cost Mayne $1 Billion', *The Age*, 27 April 2002, p. 1.

Culture: a substitute for formalisation?

A further effect of a strong culture is that it promotes behavioural consistency.[17] We know that high formalisation, such as the application of rules and regulations, acts to standardise employee behaviour. High formalisation in an organisation creates predicability, uniformity and consistency. A strong culture does the same but without any need for written documentation or obvious exercise of management power.

Moreover, a strong culture may be more potent than formal controls, because culture influences thought processes as well as organisational members' actions. Once a culture has been established, behaviours which breach the standards of the culture attract social sanction. A person may be excluded from key activities or they may be spoken to about their actions or snubbed in some other way. If the breach continues, and it is sufficiently serious, then a person may be excluded from the social system. If a person acts in a way which is not in accordance with the culture of the organisation, they may feel guilt and shame, which may lead to their not repeating the behaviour. It is through these mechanisms that culture contributes to uniformity of behaviour.

Many organisations that undertake work for which high levels of reliability are required have found that one of the most effective ways in which reliability is promoted is by the development of a strong culture.[18] Such organisations operate nuclear power plants, oil rigs and air traffic control systems. As in most organisations, it is almost impossible to predict every eventuality and write a rule to cover it. This problem can be overcome by instilling a culture of reliability, which promotes making meaning of small changes or errors that may occur, and accommodates latitude for interpretation, improvisation and actions for which a precedent has not been set.

Some features of organisational culture can provide an intrinsic sense of belonging for the individual. Much of what is discussed as culture refers to the features of a modern form of tribe or clan, acting as a source of identification and mutual support for the individual employee.[19] Being a member of the organisation provides psychological support through a sense of shared goals, values and behaviour standards with other organisation members. This guides action through providing a set of sanctions and rewards to ensure that the organisation's behavioural norms are being adhered to. Where such sharing of values is deeply embedded in the minds of organisational members, the need for management virtually ceases to exist.

Many voluntary and not-for-profit organisations also have strong cultures which substitute for formalisation. Charities, environmental groups and local community associations have remarkably few rules and regulations and have low levels of coordination, hierarchy and formal management input. In such cases those involved are guided by their identification with the goals of the organisation, and are prepared in many cases to self-manage their efforts.

It seems entirely appropriate to view formalisation and culture as two different roads to a common destination. The stronger an organisation's culture, the less management need be concerned with developing formal rules and regulations to guide employee behaviour. Those guidelines will have been internalised by employees when they learned the organisation's culture. But as we have seen, the downside of a strong culture is that, if it becomes inappropriate over time, it can be extremely difficult to change, and in some circumstances will be so resistant to change as to threaten the organisation's existence.

OT CLOSEUP

The Macquarie Bank culture

One of the most admired companies in Australia is Macquarie Bank. Known colloquially as the 'millionaires factory', it has grown exponentially over the last 20 years. Its particular strength as an investment bank has been bundling together various infrastructure assets into trusts and then listing them on the stock market.

It is probably a truism that no company becomes as successful as Macquarie by chance; an appropriate strategy is accompanied by a supporting culture. So what is Macquarie's culture? It has been described as a savage meritocracy in which anyone with the talent to make money will rise to the top. The naked pursuit of wealth is a given. But the collaborative culture of small business exists within this larger organisation. Those in leadership positions remember what it was like to be a part of a smaller business, and they have organised the company so that small business style entrepreneurship still exists within this now much larger organisation.

This is fostered through a philosophy called freedom within boundaries. This means that the organisation seeks to centrally control a small number of key risks but to give as much freedom as possible to the people who are involved in the relevant business, and this even extends to them recommending their own strategies.

In such an organisation, it is important that egos don't run away with themselves. In this Alan Moss, the managing director, sets the tone. Moss is Australia's highest paid executive, receiving $18 million in 2004. Outwardly, he is far from arrogant or ostentatious. He is the dreamy genius who is notoriously clumsy, bumping into things and tripping over wires; he is known to colleagues at Macquarie as 'the bumbling professor'. He is renowned for his egalitarianism in the workplace. He eschews the local celebrity circuit and shuns executive toys and accessories. He drives a modest Mercedes and lives in one of the less imposing water frontages on Sydney's North Shore. His socialising is mostly done outside banking circles.

The example is clear and strong; accolades derive from being smart and making money, not from the flashy show of wealth and status symbols.

Source: Adapted from Paul Ham, 'Macquarie's Masterminds', *The Sunday Times*, 21 August 2005, p. 9; and Lachlan Colquhoun, 'The Architect Who Shaped the Macquarie Model', *South China Morning Post*, 19 September 2005.

Creating, sustaining and transmitting culture

An organisation's culture doesn't emerge without human influence and, once established, it rarely fades away. What forces influence the creation of a culture? What reinforces and sustains these once they are in place? How do new employees learn their organisation's culture? The following summarises what we have learned about how cultures are created, sustained and transmitted.

How a culture begins

An organisation's current customs, traditions and general way of doing things are largely due to what it has done before and the degree of success it had with those endeavours. This leads us to the ultimate source of an organisation's culture—its founders.

The founding fathers or mothers of an organisation traditionally have a major impact on establishing the early culture. They have a vision or mission as to what the organisation should be. They are unconstrained by previous ways of doing things or by ideologies. In many cases they are energetic people with firm views as to how any organisation they establish should operate. The small size that typically characterises any new organisation further facilitates imposing the founders' vision on all organisational members. Because the founders have the original idea, they also typically have biases about how to implement the idea. The organisation's culture results from the interaction between the founders' biases and assumptions and what the original members who the founders initially employ learn subsequently from their own experiences.[20]

Sir Hudson Fysh of Qantas, Harry Seidler with his architectural firm and Franco Belgiorno-Nettis of Transfield are just some of the individuals who have had an immeasurable impact on the shaping of their organisation's culture. For instance, Sir Hudson Fysh's ideals in relation to taking the then risky venture of flying and applying modern technology and management methods to establish an airline is celebrated within Qantas' folklore. The late Harry Seidler specialised in the design of large buildings and managed to bring individuality to difficult architectural challenges. Franco Belgiorno-Nettis has recognised that the strength of his company is in construction, and it has never strayed from developing its skills in using people to manufacture and construct, even through the speculative boom of the 1980s.

Of course, not all firms that are founded by visionary individuals survive in the long run. And many that do need to undergo a cultural change along the way. As Bill Gates of Microsoft has found, the urge to be super-competitive and to dominate may have given his company an edge in the early stages of its formation and growth. But the culture developed to achieve this end proved to be a burden to Microsoft once this goal had been reached. Indeed, it contributed to constant investigation of the firm by regulators suspicious of anti-competitive activity.

Keeping a culture alive

Once a culture is in place, there are forces within the organisation that act to maintain it by giving employees a set of similar experiences. The four forces that play the most important part in sustaining a culture are the organisation's selection practices, the actions of top management, the organisation's socialisation methods, and the use of appropriate rewards and punishments.[21] These are shown in Table 13.1.

Selection practices

The stated goal of the selection process is to identify and hire individuals who have the knowledge, skills and abilities to successfully perform the jobs within the organisation. But typically, more than one candidate will be identified who meets any given job's requirements. When that happens, it would be unwise to ignore the fact that the final decision as to who is hired will be significantly influenced by the decision maker's judgement as to how well the candidates will fit into the organisation. This attempt, purposely or inadvertently, to ensure a proper match results in the hiring of people

TABLE 13.1 Ways in which a culture is sustained

Selection practices
Actions of top management
Socialisation
Use of appropriate rewards and punishments

who have common values (ones essentially consistent with the organisation's) or at least a good portion of them, and who are likely to acquire those that they do not have.[22] Moreover, the selection process provides applicants with information on the organisation. Candidates learn about the organisation and, if they perceive a conflict between their values and the organisation's, they can self-select themselves out of the applicant pool. Selection, therefore, becomes a two-way street, allowing either employer or applicant to withdraw from the process if there appears to be a mismatch. In this way, the selection process sustains an organisation's culture by selecting out those individuals who might attack or undermine its core values.

For example, Macquarie Bank will hire only graduates with distinction averages. To get a distinction average, most students must be prepared to work hard, have ambition, be attuned to competition and have a fair measure of intelligence. These characteristics are those required by the bank of people who will work in the more complex areas of banking and finance, developing new products, interpreting financial trends and providing financial advice. In contrast, the police forces for many years avoided hiring graduates. They preferred to educate the recruited rather than recruit the educated. Their idea was that those with just a basic education would be more easily socialised into the organisation and inculcated with police ways of thinking.

Actions of top management

Top management has a symbolic influence on an organisation's culture.[23] The actions and attitudes of the chief executive, or the divisional general managers, are closely observed for guides as to what behaviour is acceptable and how the problems of the organisation should be approached. Indeed, the chief executive is even viewed as being the person to define the problems of the organisation and what business it should be in. Although in a large organisation the chief executive is rarely seen, the pronouncements from the executive suite are often made available through annual reports, company profiles, emails, and even videos for staff consumption. So important is this group in influencing the culture of the organisation that they have been termed 'culture carriers'. In extremely large organisations, senior managers such as divisional heads and country managers may be the important culture carriers.

The chief executive also has a major impact on culture through deciding who is hired and fired and who is disciplined and for what.[24] Virtually all of the senior management of the organisation is chosen or approved by the chief executive. Those chosen almost always reflect the culture that the chief executive wants to promote.

Socialisation

No matter how good a job the organisation does in recruitment and selection, new employees are not hired fully indoctrinated into the organisation's culture. Perhaps most importantly, because they are least familiar with the organisation's culture, new employees are potentially most likely to disturb the beliefs and customs that are in place. The organisation will therefore want to help new employees adapt to its culture. As noted in Chapter 4, this adaptation process is called socialisation.

The army provides an extreme example of the socialisation process. All new recruits must go through recruit training. Recruit training camps are in country locations, such as Singleton or Puckapunyal, far from the family and society supports that have determined recruits' behaviour up to the time they enlisted. Once these supports are no longer there to fall back on, it is far easier for the army to mould the behaviour of the new recruit, so that the new, desired behaviours are more likely to dominate a soldier's actions.

Most firms do similar things, in a very mild form, through such means as induction courses. These are designed to provide new employees with an understanding of what is expected of them, to tell them about the standards of dress and presentation required, how to treat customers, and to give them other information relevant to their job. They then acquire further socialisation by working with others on the job.

Socialisation continues throughout an employee's career in an organisation. However, socialisation is most explicit when a new employee enters an organisation. This is when the organisation seeks to shape the outsider into an employee 'in good standing'. Once on the job, a manager or senior colleague often becomes a coach to further guide and mould the new member. In some cases a formal training program will even be offered to ensure that the employee learns the organisation's culture.

Use of appropriate rewards and punishments

Rewards and punishments send a powerful message to organisational members. Employees are constantly observing events that are going on around them as well as experiencing praise and rebukes themselves. Such praise and rebukes may not be obvious: they can be as subtle as a glance or tone of voice. Events such as who is hired and fired, who is promoted and why, and actions that result in approval or admonition both channel and direct behaviour. If employees find that they cannot or will not change their behaviour to suit what they see around them, chances are they will have to leave the organisation.

Learning the deeper aspects of a culture

In addition to explicit orientation and training programs, culture is transmitted to employees in a number of other forms, the most potent being stories, rituals, material symbols and language.

Stories

If you worked at the Ford Motor Company during the 1970s, you would undoubtedly have heard the story about Henry Ford II reminding his executives, when they got too argumentative, that 'It's *my* name that's on the building'. The message was clear. Henry Ford II ran the company!

Stories such as this circulate through many organisations. They contain a narrative of events about the organisation's founders, key decisions that affect the organisation's future course and actions of top management. They anchor the present in the past and provide explanations and legitimacy for current practices.[25]

Stories serve a more important function than just being a narrative of occurrences or promoting coordination. Many events occur in organisations that defy logical analysis or simple behavioural explanation. Stories permit the explanation and interpretation of events and situations that are too complex for traditional linear analysis to explain.[26] Narratives and stories have been the main way in which humankind has passed on its experiences—and hence its culture and sense of meaning—since time immemorial. They allow the reconstruction of scenarios in a manner which enables them to be understood, interpreted and incorporated in the individual's belief- and sense-making system. They often interweave individual variables and organisational pressures to explain and understand behaviour. Whenever members of an organisation get together to relax, telling such stories is commonplace. They therefore provide a strong understanding of the organisation–individual interface, which assists members in making sense of the milieu in which they operate.

Rituals

We reviewed rituals in Chapter 4 in our discussion of formalisation. Just as rituals are used as a formalisation technique, so are they a means of transmitting culture. Activities such as recognition and award ceremonies, weekly Friday afternoon drinks and annual company picnics are rituals that express and reinforce the key values of the organisation, what goals are important, which people are important and any changes in power bases.[27]

Material symbols

In many cases, material symbols are used to transmit and reinforce the culture of an organisation. Anyone walking into a Kmart or Target store can see that it is obviously different from a David Jones or Country Road store. The workers in these chains know that working in each one is different as well. A David Jones employee acts differently towards customers and is expected to do different things from a Kmart employee.

An industry has arisen in recent times around generating image through office decoration and layout. Interior decorators design and fit out offices to reflect the values and business philosophies of the client. Legal firms seek to create an image of high probity and low risk through muted tones and the isolation of staff. The decoration of an advertising agency tends to reflect originality, creative skills and the frenetic pace of the industry. It was traditional in older companies that the senior executive offices be wood panelled, which led to lower level staff referring to the accommodation as 'mahogany row'. Turn-of-the-century banking chambers were lofty, solid affairs, with substantial fittings, to reflect an atmosphere of stability and permanence. Even the outsides of the buildings were made of heavy stone, with solid Doric columns. In contrast, businesses such as Nike and Microsoft have built their offices in the style and form of universities, and have even gone as far as calling them campuses rather than offices.

Even such factors as the type of car driven by the senior management of the organisation reflect its standards and values. The advertising industry is famous for the number of executives who drive BMWs and Porsches. University vice-chancellors, however, drive far more sedate top-of-the-line Fords and Holdens.

Through the above means messages are conveyed to employees regarding such factors as who is important, the degree of egalitarianism desired by top management, and the kinds of behaviours (i.e. risk-taking, conservative, authoritarian, participative, individualistic, social) that are appropriate.

Observation and experience

Human beings are innately suited to functioning as members of social systems. Much of what they learn in organisations is a result of observation and experience. This is often a far more powerful teacher than written mission statements and policy and procedures manuals, which are often studied only at a superficial level and generally induce acute boredom. Where there is a conflict between what is observed and experienced and what is written, observation and experience will have the greater impact.

Language

Many organisations and units within organisations use jargon and terminology as a way to identify members of a culture or subculture. By learning language in this way, members attest to their acceptance of the culture and, in so doing, help to preserve it. In many cases the distinctive language of a culture or subculture derives from the tasks undertaken and the technology used by the group.

The kitchen personnel in large hotels use terminology foreign to people who work in other areas of the hotels. Members of the army sprinkle their language liberally with jargon that readily identifies its members. Many organisations, over time, develop unique terms to describe equipment, offices, key personnel, suppliers, customers or products that relate to their business. New employees are often overwhelmed with acronyms and jargon that after six months on the job become a natural part of their language. But once assimilated, this terminology acts as a common denominator that unites members of a given culture or subculture.

When cultures collide: mergers and acquisitions

The contrast between two cultures is highlighted when organisations merge and an attempt is made to generate a common culture.[28] Cultural differences need not be confined to organisational culture but may include national culture as well. Not all mergers and takeovers result in culture clashes; in many cases, a business is taken over and run as an autonomous division. In this case there is generally not a great pressure to change the existing culture. This may be seen in the US operations of the building materials companies, Boral and Rinker, which have little interaction with the Australian operations. This is possible because the technical core of the organisation can be split into self-contained parts. However, many mergers are aimed at attaining economies of scale, which may only result from merging two organisations into one entity. In this case the merging of cultures cannot be avoided and the success of the merger depends upon how effectively this is achieved.

Generally, senior managers don't underestimate the difficulties of merging cultures but their reservations are subsumed by the need to achieve economies in other areas. These economies may be derived from sharing design costs, obtaining access to distribution channels, more intensive use of capital equipment or better supply chain management. The motivation of senior management varies greatly. Often there is a dominant manager who pushes the merger against opposition. The potential benefits of the merger are often oversold in order to bring doubters on side. Top managers are frequently overcome by the rush of emotion surrounding the deal and are anxious to leave a larger company as their legacy. In this atmosphere, it is unlikely that the full difficulty of merging the two cultures is given sufficient consideration.

Few mergers meet the expectations held of them. One of the difficulties arises from integrating the two organisations in a way that achieves the anticipated economies and benefits. There have been a number of high-profile and widely publicised mergers that highlight the difficulties that are often encountered. One which has dominated the business press is that between Hewlett Packard and Compaq.[29] Hewlett Packard was a long-established research-based company, with a deeply rooted egalitarian research culture, which had a competitive line of computer peripherals such as printers, amongst other products. Compaq was a more recent start-up, which manufactured personal and low end computers. It had a tougher, sharper culture, which was honed during years of intense competition and layoffs. It was felt that a merger of the two would bring economies of scale and create a stronger combined business. The benefits of the merger were promoted by a high-profile, telegenic CEO, Carlton (Carly) Fiorina. The sales-oriented Fiorina was never fully at home in the engineering culture of Hewlett Packard, and now she had the difficult task of merging two radically different companies. When attempts to integrate the businesses were made, significant areas of resistance emerged, encouraged by the resistance to the merger from significant powerbrokers and stakeholders. Eventually, as the economies expected from the merger proved hard to achieve, Carly Fiorina was forced from office. It became clear that any economies would quickly be subsumed by losses generated by lack of cultural synergies and

OT CLOSEUP

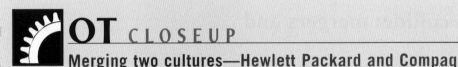

Merging two cultures—Hewlett Packard and Compaq

The IT industry is renowned for the high price paid for acquisitions and the failure of most to achieve anticipated economies from the merger. With this as background, the merger of Hewlett Packard and Compaq was the most intensely planned and anticipated in modern times.

The merger was never going to be easy. Both Compaq and Hewlett Packard were struggling computer companies with slightly different strengths. Hewlett Packard was strong on peripherals and imaging and Compaq had the edge in personal computers. The two companies found themselves squeezed between the high end consulting companies such as IBM and Accenture, which offer comprehensive service contracts to large clients, and the ferociously competitive PC makers such as Dell. By merging it was felt that economies could be gained in PC manufacture and the resulting company would also be sufficiently large and diverse to compete with the likes of IBM.

The planning for the merger was extensive and meticulous. Half a million hours of planning were expended on integration issues even before the merger was approved by shareholders. Key managers of business units were identified and they were involved in the planning process from the start. Up to 600 staff members from the two companies formed integration teams for each of the four main business units. Other teams dealt with general issues such as IT, finance and human resource issues.

The working groups were given clear principles on how to proceed. One of these was 'adapt and go', a process where each of the two companies' systems was evaluated in relation to any particular process and the most appropriate adopted. This avoided the problem of trying to invent something new and then sell it to the business divisions. If the working groups could not agree, a consultant was called in to adjudicate. More difficult decisions were passed to a 'steering committee' composed of the two company's most senior managers, who met for a half a day a week. The Internet assisted integration by keeping everyone informed, and the collaboration groups made extensive use of collaboration tools such as online spreadsheets and calendars.

Notwithstanding the cultural differences—Hewlett Packard had an engineering culture where managers thought long and hard before making a decision, while Compaq, being a PC company, was more used to being quick on its feet—the merger proceeded well. But it must be considered to be a failure because the expected benefits in the way of sales and profitability did not emerge. It was a case of two weak companies not making a strong one.

Source: Drawn from 'Planning to Prove Them Wrong; Hewlett Packard and Compaq', *The Economist*, 9 March 2002, p. 81.

strategic miscalculations, and that building a new company would take many years of patient, disruptive effort.

An Australian example is that of the merger in 2000 of two wine companies, Rosemount and Southcorp.[30] Rosemount was a young, privately owned and, unusually in the wine industry, profitable company. It was a sales-driven organisation, with estimates of the likely demand for wine in the coming season being matched by production of predominantly young, fresh wine. In contrast, Southcorp had a stable of long-established and respected brands, including Penfolds, the manufacturer of Grange, Australia's finest wine. Southcorp was a product-driven firm where the winemakers made good quality wines and worked hard to maintain the integrity of their brands and the traditions associated with them. In fact, it probably had too many brands to manage effectively. Profitablity was poor and sales growth was sluggish. As Rosemount was seen to have superior management, Southcorp suggested a merger which would place Rosemount managers in charge of the merged companies.

The merger subsequently took place but Rosemount management proved not to be as effective as anticipated. Almost all senior Southcorp managers were dismissed, including those with extensive knowledge of the company and its markets. Senior winemakers with 30 or more years experience were made redundant, to be replaced by young winemakers virtually just out of college. The many prestigious brands were heavily discounted and sold through inappropriate channels, and their reputation suffered. The merged company lost hundreds of millions of dollars in the first two years of operation. Morale slumped, and it became clear that the existing management were not in a position to turn the company around. They in turn were dismissed and outside mangers appointed. But too much damage had been done to be repaired easily and the company was taken over by Fosters in 2005, leading to further downsizing.

These experiences are not typical of all mergers. Many of the problems that arise are manageable, given good will on both sides. Many other mergers do not present major problems from a culture perspective: the merged companies may not have to work closely together, or the cultures may not be substantially different from each other and may be easily blended. The merger of BHP and Billiton, covered in the case for class discussion, is an example of a successful merger.

When culture clashes occur during a merger, they are generally well anticipated and discussed beforehand. Senior management is usually optimistic that any problems are manageable and that an appropriate and supportive culture will emerge. This is often wishful thinking. In the Hewlett Packard case, culture differences were widely discussed as potential threats to the success of the merger and, in both cases, informed opinion counselled that the mergers not proceed. However, a strong and charismatic CEO pushed the merger proposal against stiff opposition and carried the majority of opinion with her. Her job depended upon the outcome of economies from the merger being stronger than the losses from forcing two different cultures into a close working relationship. Unfortunately for the CEO, in the short term the losses proved stronger, so she lost her job. But the widespread airing of potential cultural problems probably encouraged those within each company to resist the change more than they otherwise might have.

The forces driving mergers often reflect the confidence that everything may be managed. Business always contains an element of risk. Sometimes this can be easily assessed and incorporated into the business model; insurance companies are doing it all the time. But the merging of cultures is a far more difficult task and the problems are often downplayed in the optimism associated with doing a deal. A sales mentality often brushes aside concerns as something that the future will take care of. But merging cultures cannot proceed by formula and considerable judgement is called for in implementing the change program. In many cases optimism runs ahead of more sober consideration of the difficulties involved.

One attempt to overcome resistance to change is to dismiss most of the top managers in the weaker partner in the merger and replace them with mangers from the dominant party. The expectation is that this will triumph over centres of resistance and quickly stamp the new culture on the weaker company. It also gives a great sense of power and control, as well as providing a symbolic gesture as to who holds the power. This often proves counterproductive. Valuable experience and corporate memory are often dispensed with and new managers may not be as competent as the old. Dismay at seeing valued and respected managers being dismissed for no apparent reason, apart from symbolic ones, can quickly feed into lack of cooperation and distrust, which can fester for some time. Air New Zealand dismissed many of Ansett's senior managers when it took over the company and replaced them with Air New Zealand staff. But the Air New Zealand managers were unfamiliar with Ansett's environment and the problems it faced. Ansett soon folded and Air New Zealand walked away considerably humbled by the experience and poorer for it; its losses were so great that it had to be taken over by the New Zealand government.

If the cultures of both companies are weak, then chances are that culture will not be an impediment to a successful merger. Neither side will feel the need to dominate or resist integration. In most of the cases we have mentioned in this section as presenting problems—Southcorp, Hewlett Packard, Compaq and Ansett—strong cultures existed, which generated a tribal style of bonding resistant to the merger. Weaker cultures generate no such loyalty and are more receptive to integration techniques.

As with many issues relating to culture, it is difficult to be specific about the best way to merge two different cultures. Most successful mergers involve most of the following attributes:

- support from the top management of both companies
- selection of the best manager for the jobs available
- creation of integration teams not dominated by managers from one of the companies, which concentrate on issues relevant to each area of the combined business
- imposition of time limits aimed at limiting debate and promoting problem solving.

Globalisation has added complexity, with many mergers now occurring across borders as companies seek to expand market share or achieve economies of scale. What looks on the surface to be a sound strategic move often proves difficult to implement. French-based Renault's acquisition of the Japanese-based Nissan, Daimler's acquisition of Chrysler and BP's merger with Amoco are just a few of the high-profile international mergers that have occurred recently. There are many smaller cross-border mergers that escape notice. Each of these mergers presents the additional problem of coping with the integration of those with different national cultures. In some cases firms don't try too hard to seek close integration; they run their overseas operations as separate divisions. CSR's and Boral's large-scale building materials operations in the United States are run autonomously, with little day-to-day contact with the Australian operations. Most Australian overseas investment is aimed at operating as an insider in overseas markets, with very little integration with the Australian operations. This avoids many of the problems arising from differences in national culture.

In a merger or acquisition, if one or both of the organisations have weak cultures, the marriage is more likely to work, as discussed above. This is because weak cultures are more malleable and can therefore adapt better to new situations. Two strong cultures, on the other hand, can create real problems. The banking industry provides a good example of this. Realising that reliance on low-margin traditional banking services would not deliver the growth desired, the large multi-product banks have, over the past 20 years, attempted to move into the higher margin investment banking area. Investment banks provide such products as advising on mergers and acquisitions, managing funds, and providing general corporate advice. However, attempts by the large banks to merge with the investment banks have almost invariably resulted in failure. The reason for the failure was not a flawed strategy but the inability of the two cultures to merge. Mainstream banking promoted a culture of high control, application of rules and regulations, and risk avoidance. In contrast, investment banking relied on the skills of very talented, high-paid, fast-moving individuals who would act on a perceived opening, which in many cases they themselves identified in the market. When the large banks tried to impose their culture of close control on the investment bankers, the latter felt restricted and unable to operate at their optimum level. High levels of defection and resignation among the investment bankers contributed to the failure of most of the mergers.

The merging of two strong cultures need not present problems if the cultures are very similar. BHP merged with the Utah minerals division of General Electric with a minimal amount of trauma. Both firms had strong cultures, but their compatibility was high and Utah enjoyed considerable autonomy in day-to-day operations. Thus, strong cultures are likely to hinder effectiveness in the newly merged organisation only when the cultures are at odds.

The incompatibility of two cultures need not be a problem when mergers are not within the same industry. For instance, when one company is taken over and added to another company as a division, the interaction with the rest of that company may be minimal. In such cases, the new acquisition becomes a subculture of the larger organisation. Many of the conglomerates of the 1980s, such as the Adelaide Steamship Company, were made up of differing subcultures, which made additions and disposals easier to accomplish. There is little interaction between Foster's beer and wine operations, allowing each to develop its own strong culture.

Although, in many cases, mergers are promoted as being the amalgamation of equals, this is rarely the case. One company generally emerges the stronger and manages to impose its will on the other. This is sometimes obvious from the financial strength of the companies concerned. But it can also be linked to the power plays surrounding who will become chief executive. Obviously, there can be only one chief executive, and the one that emerges triumphant normally gets to stamp his or her personality on the merged company. Naturally, this means that the company from which the chief executive emerges is the stronger.[31]

How can cultures be managed?

We now turn to the essential issue in this chapter: can cultures be managed? Earlier we discussed that organisations operate as open systems which are characterised by environmental interaction. A major contributor to organisational effectiveness is a high degree of congruence between the culture of an organisation and the demands placed by the environment upon the organisation. As environments are constantly changing, cultures must change to suit them. But is it possible to change an organisation's culture? And, if so, how difficult is it?

An organisation's culture has a marked influence on its employees. As we have seen, this influence is not only on the visible and measurable aspects of employee performance and behaviour. Culture can also operate at a deeper level, which provides both meaning and a guide to action to employees. Because it is so deeply embedded in either personality or beliefs, or both, this contributes to making culture the organisational characteristic that is probably most difficult to change. It is far easier to change reporting relationships, introduce new technology, draw up a budget or adopt a new strategy than to manage the supporting cultural changes. A further reason for this is that many features of culture are not easily understood or interpretable and hence not amenable to conventional management techniques.

Further difficulties arise for managers in that culture is 'owned' by all members of the organisation and is not purely within management's capacity to change. In many cases management only plays a part in creating the culture, with the organisational members themselves making a major contribution to many of its features. As a result, there is a temptation to consider that culture should be treated as a given, in which case managers would be advised to try to understand their organisation's culture but to remember that there is very little they can do, at least in the short term, to change it.[32]

As knowledge and experience of management has expanded, however, we realise that there are actions that managers can take to facilitate cultural change. Indeed, current thinking is that proactive steps should be taken by management to align the organisation's culture better with the organisation's strategy and environment. Many of those who are most admired in the business community are those who have introduced and sustained a program of cultural change in their organisations—although it must also be said that there are many cases of failure in this area.

managing culture changing the organisation's culture

When we discuss **managing culture**, we mean *changing* the culture. This has grown to become the prevailing definition, yet, as one writer has noted, managing culture need not be the same as changing culture.[33] In a time of transition, for instance, managing an organisation's culture may entail sustaining or reinforcing the present culture rather than making any change. So, in a very strict sense, managing a culture could entail stabilising the status quo as well as inducing a shift to another state. For our purposes, however, we will treat *managing* culture and *changing* culture as synonymous.

What factors are likely to influence a cultural change program?

The foregoing discussion suggests that there may be circumstances which make culture easier for managers to change.[34] This leads us to a situational analysis of conditions that are necessary for, or will facilitate, cultural change. The ideas we offer are based on observation as well as substantive research. However, there seems to be increasing agreement among theorists about the importance of the following situational factors. These are often events which 'unfreeze' the organisation, contributing to the understanding that established ways are unsustainable if the organisation is to adapt to environmental changes. Table 13.2 summarises the factors influencing cultural change.

have failed to adapt to these changes. Their senior management, through its review processes, has come to the realisation that major changes need to be made to the way its organisation operates, and this involves cultural change. It is part of management's cultural change program to create a sense of crisis in the organisation when none is necessarily felt by the majority of employees.

Leadership turnover

As top management has a major influence in transmitting culture, a change in the organisation's key leadership positions facilitates the imposition of new values.[37] But new leadership, per se, is no assurance that employees will accept new values. The new leaders must have a clear alternative vision of what the organisation can be; there must be respect for their leadership capabilities; and they must have the ability to translate their alternative vision into reality. New leadership without an alternative set of values is unlikely to result in any substantive change in the organisation.[38]

Leadership turnover must encompass the organisation's chief executive. But it is not limited to this position. The likelihood of successful cultural change typically increases with a purge of all major management positions. Rather than having previous executives accept the new leader's values, it is usually more effective to replace them with individuals who have no vested interest in the old culture. Of course, it is undesirable for all top managers to be replaced: some continuity is necessary for the ongoing health of the organisation. But selective replacement of key managers sends a powerful signal to the rest of the organisation, particularly if they are associated with centres of resistance.

Life-cycle stage

Cultural change is easier when the organisation is in transition from the formation stage to the growth stage and from maturity into decline. As the organisation moves into growth, major changes will be necessary. These changes are more likely to be accepted because the culture is less entrenched and embodied in rules, regulations and practices. Additionally, a growing organisation is more likely to be hiring new employees, which gives management the opportunity to place those whose values are desired in key positions. However, other factors will facilitate acceptance of the change. One writer, for instance, has proposed that employees will be more receptive to cultural change if the organisation's previous success record is modest, employees are generally dissatisfied, and the founder's image and reputation are in question.[39] By contrast, organisations such as Microsoft and Nike can grow fast because their culture is attractive and easily transferable to those who seek employment with those companies.

The other opportunity for cultural change occurs when the organisation enters the decline stage. Decline typically requires cutbacks and other retrenchment strategies. Such actions are likely to highlight to employees that the organisation is experiencing a true crisis.

Age of the organisation

Regardless of its life-cycle stage, the younger an organisation, the less entrenched its values will be. We should therefore expect cultural change to be more acceptable in an organisation that is only 5 years old than in one that is 50 years old. The reason for this includes the fact that young organisations have no long-serving employees and lower levels of formalisation.

Size of the organisation

We propose that cultural change is easier to implement in a small organisation because, in such organisations, it is easier for management to reach employees. Communication is clearer, and role models are more visible in a small organisation, thus enhancing the opportunity to disseminate new values.

Strength of the current culture

The more widely held a culture, and the higher the agreement of its values among members, the more difficult it will be to change. Conversely, weak cultures should be more amenable to change than strong ones. For instance, changing the culture of a call centre, where many of the employees are short-term hires on part-time contracts, should be easier than changing the culture of an organisation where the average employee has 20 years service.

Absence of subcultures

Heterogeneity increases members' concern with protecting their self-interest and resisting change. This observation is drawn from the power-control viewpoint. Therefore, we would expect that the more subcultures there are, the more resistance there will be to changes in the dominant culture. Trying to change three cultures is always going to be more difficult than changing one. This thesis can also be related to size. Larger organisations will be more resistant to cultural change because they typically have more subcultures.

What management techniques are available to change culture?

In describing culture, we noted that many of its aspects are either difficult to observe or understand or are otherwise not interpretable. This presents a problem for managers, as it is difficult to change something that is intangible. But managers have little alternative but to work with the mechanisms available to them. As a consequence, those managers who successfully change cultures tend to concentrate on changing behaviour rather than values.[40] Changes in values will, it is hoped, emerge with changes in behaviour.

One study of cultural change in large organisations found that only a small number of the attempts at cultural change could be counted as a success.[41] Cultures were found to have a strong 'springback' quality: that is, they very quickly reverted to what they were originally. Those attempts at cultural change that were successful were multidimensional: that is, attempts to change the culture focused on a number of key variables which mutually supported the change process. These included changes in structure, rewards and leadership, as well as in key personnel.

So how can cultural change be successfully undertaken? The following are those factors that have been found to be important when attempting a cultural change program and are summarised in Table 13.3.

Applying firm leadership

No successful attempts at cultural change have been made without strong leadership driving the change at the top of the organisation. As leadership is generally covered in organisational behaviour texts, we have paid little attention to it in this book. But it is of such fundamental importance to cultural change that it must be raised in this section. It is the role of a leader to raise fundamental questions in relation to the organisation. To do this a leader should have a good understanding of the present

TABLE 13.3 Techniques of managing organisation culture

Applying firm leadership
Seeking political support
Changing key personnel
Implementing structural changes
Avoiding micro-managing the details
The need to be patient
Applying appropriate management skills

state of the organisation and a vision of the characteristics of the emerging culture. An extensive study of the leader's role in cultural change found that the leader often introduced cultural change by asking basic questions that challenged the status quo—for example, 'Are we meeting customers' needs better than the competition?', 'Can we produce product more efficiently?', 'Do our products incorporate the latest changes in technology?'. In many cases, the leaders themselves had to create a sense of crisis in what may have been a complacent organisation. The leader should be capable of communicating his or her vision to a wide variety of people and take every opportunity to do so.

Effective leadership cannot be imposed from the top of the organisation. Leadership lies in creating conditions in which people are inspired to follow. Consequently, leaders must work hard—communicating to a wide audience and constantly talking about and sharing their vision. The role of leadership is so important that rarely, if ever, does cultural change emerge as a bottom-up initiative from those lower in the organisation. To be effective it must always be initiated and nurtured from the very top of the organisation.[42]

It is not surprising that leadership is so important in effecting cultural change, as it mirrors the intangible nature of culture itself. It draws on fundamental and poorly understood human values and perceptions and acts on us in ways that are difficult to define. The function of interpersonal influence is as old as humanity, and cannot be replaced by a computer program or a rule manual.

Seeking political support

Leaders cannot function without some political support in their organisation. We have seen that political activity is heightened during periods of organisational change. Not all of this activity need be aimed at resisting the proposed changes. Leaders introducing cultural change constantly seek out political support, either from individual managers or departments, as a base from which influence may spread. They often seek out early successes in which the benefits of the new culture may be observed by others and be adopted by the wavering.

Changing key personnel

It is inevitable in periods of cultural change that changes in management and other personnel take place. Those associated closely with the old culture are generally moved aside and newer, more sympathetic managers appointed. This even applies to the CEO, as very few cultural change programs are initiated without changes at the very top of the organisation.

Implementing structural changes

We have noted the tendency for cultures to resist change by reverting to their original characteristics. One of the ways in which managers can counteract this is by making supporting structural changes. Structure influences the ways in which people behave in organisations. The structure of an organisation allocates responsibilities, determines reporting relationships, defines tasks and determines the size of the management hierarchy. It also becomes the framework within which performance is assessed and rewards are allocated in the organisation.

Cultural difficulties that can be addressed by structural change include problems arising from a large head office, which is primarily involved in checking, emphasis on the application of rules and regulations rather than an outward focus on the customer, senior managers receiving out-of-date and filtered information, and managers being remote from markets and customers. It can also include lack of ownership of results on the part of managers.

So how can structural changes assist in addressing these problems? Reducing layers of managers can reduce the checking mentality prevalent in many organisations. It can also reduce the numbers involved in making decisions, leading to faster decision making. Reallocation of responsibilities can decrease the number of managers who can say 'no' but not 'yes'. By creating divisions and other profit centres managers become more responsible for results. By emphasising the close link between customer satisfaction and performance, managers should become more responsive to customer demands. If they do not, it becomes apparent from the poor results of their division.

Avoiding micro-managing the details

It is not possible for senior managers to micro-manage the details of cultural change. Micro-management is concerned with managing the small details of day-to-day processes and events. Senior management have little alternative but to create the conditions that establish and nurture the new cultural values and to constantly sell the advantages of a new way of doing things. As a result, it is unreasonable to expect managers to manage myths, values or meanings. Organisational members, be they management or operatives, will create their own values, myths and meanings according to their own needs and experiences. Senior managers are limited to trusting that the deeper meanings of the new culture, as expressed in the values, myths and meanings, are aligned with what they are trying to promote in the organisation.

The need to be patient

All cultural changes take time; the bigger the change and the larger the organisation, the longer it takes. Large companies like General Electric have been working on cultural change for upwards of 15 years and still regard it as an ongoing process. In a large organisation little in the way of sustainable cultural change can be accomplished in less than five years. This means that the change must often be steered by a number of successive senior managers. It also follows that one of the characteristics of successful leaders of cultural change is to have a good appreciation for what can be accomplished in any given period of time. Work too slowly, and momentum and interest in the change is lost. Work too fast, and the old culture is destroyed without replacing it with the new, more appropriate culture. Disillusionment and confusion is the result, followed by a loss of organisational effectiveness.

Applying appropriate management skills

The skills to introduce a major cultural change are not commonly possessed by managers. As a consequence, many companies faced with the need to quickly address the problem of a cultural change specifically appoint a chief executive whose task it is to quickly shake up the old culture and implant the new, and then leave the task of consolidating the new culture to managers whose skills are more appropriate to this task. Al Dunlap, who has earned the nickname 'Chainsaw' for his rapid and ruthless cost cutting, is such a manager. George Trumbull, the managing director of AMP from 1994 to 1999, is another example. Both operated with considerable speed in deconstructing much of the old culture, while leaving it to others to undertake the longer term implementation and consolidation of the new culture.

Culture and the way ahead

This chapter has introduced and discussed the concept of organisations having cultures. Culture is, however, a tricky concept to define, as well as being difficult to measure and manage. Further, research is making only small advances in reducing what is a very complex issue into something that is more readily understandable. But research has highlighted that an organisation's culture makes a major contribution to effectiveness and that culture needs to change over time, just as the organisation must change over time to adapt to changes in its environment.

It is difficult to successfully change an organisation's culture without changing other organisational features, such as its strategy, structure and management. Whichever way we approach it, changing a culture is a major task, involving significant upheaval over long periods of time. It requires leaders with outstanding communication and persuasion skills who have a good grasp of the problems facing the organisation and the way in which they may be solved.

Beneath the obvious surface of symbols, artefacts and structure lies a dense web of interactions drawing on, and satisfying, basic human needs. Managers have little alternative but to concentrate on those features of culture which can be manipulated, while realising that the success of any cultural change lies very much in changing the deeper levels of culture.

Summary

Organisations have personalities, just like individuals. We call these personalities organisational cultures. An organisational culture is a system of shared meaning. Its key characteristics are individual initiative, risk tolerance, direction, integration, management contact, control, identity, rewards, conflict tolerance, and communication patterns.

Organisations have dominant cultures and subcultures. The former express the core values shared by a majority of the organisation's members, though most large organisations have additional values, expressed in subcultures. Strong cultures are those where values are intensely held, clearly ordered and widely shared. Strong cultures increase behavioural consistency and can therefore act as substitutes for formalisation.

The ultimate source of an organisation's culture is its founders. It is sustained by the organisation's selection and socialisation processes and by the actions of top management. It is transmitted through stories, rituals, material symbols and language.

The key debate surrounding organisational culture concerns whether or not it can be managed. Cultures can be changed, but there appear to be a number of conditions necessary for bringing about such change. Even where conditions for change are favourable, managers should not expect any rapid acceptance of new cultural values. Cultural change should be measured in years rather than months.

For review and discussion

1 Define *organisational culture*. Which of its key characteristics are structurally based? Which are behaviourally based?
2 Can an employee survive in an organisation if he or she rejects its core values? Explain.
3 What forces might contribute towards making a culture strong or weak?
4 Identify those parts of culture which are visible and interpretable and those which are hidden.
5 How is an organisation's culture maintained?
6 What benefits can socialisation provide for the organisation? For the new employee?
7 Can you identify a set of characteristics that describe your educational institution's culture? Compare them with those of your peers. How closely do they match?
8 What is the relationship between culture and formalisation?
9 Why do management theorists and consultants have a vested interest in demonstrating that organisational cultures can be managed?
10 'Culture may change, but the change may not be planned or precipitated by management.' Discuss.
11 What factors work against changing an organisation's culture?
12 At what stage in an organisation's life cycle is cultural change most likely to be accepted? Why?
13 What condition is most necessary for cultural change to be accepted? Why?
14 Describe the conditions that would be most conducive to initiating cultural change.
15 A senior executive from a major corporation has hired you to give advice on how to change the organisation's culture. How would you approach this assignment?

CASE FOR CLASS DISCUSSION

The problems of building a common culture at BHP Billiton

The merger in 2000 of BHP of Australia and Billiton of South Africa, although headquartered in London, was not undertaken because the organisations were similar. It took place in order to build scale and financial size, linking BHP's profitable long life and established assets with Billiton's more growth-oriented projects. Although they were both mining companies, the cultures of the two companies were very dissimilar. BHP reflected the Australian cultural traits of openness, mateship and questioning authority. Billiton, although previously owned by Shell, reflected its South African heritage. It had a reputation for being strictly hierarchical, with a culture that demanded respect for authority. There was little openness, a lack of exposure to outside criticism, and almost no experience of confrontational unions. Senior management at Billiton consisted of a small coterie of hard-driving men who worked autonomously. BHP's senior management was more consultative, calculative and methodical in style and used to working under a strong board of directors.

This indicates a further reason for the merger and that was to access the talents of Billiton's management team. It was felt that the style and aggression of Billiton's managers would shake up BHP's more staid management style and lead the combined company on a path to fast growth.

Merging the cultures was never going to be easy. It was complicated by the nature of the chief executive's role. Initially, Paul Anderson, the American boss of BHP, was chief executive, but he was replaced in 2002 by Brian Gilbertson, the chief executive of Billiton. Seen as a talented opportunist, Gilbertson had risen to success mainly through takeovers. The rest of the senior management team were mainly Gilbertson's colleagues from Billiton days.

To assist in merging the cultures at the operating levels of the company, BHP Billiton adopted a process known as 'feathering'. This involved alternating the placement of former BHP and Billiton staff throughout its organisational structure in an attempt to break down old company allegiances. Early emphasis was given to quickly combining key HRM processes, such as remuneration and performance management. Integration teams consisting of managers from each company were formed very soon after the merger. They were encouraged to abandon preconceived ways and to consider only what was good for BHP Billiton.

Integration was assisted to a certain extent by structural changes accompanying the merger. Both companies had designed their structures around their mining operations. But after the merger the focus was changed to the customer, and businesses were built around customer groupings.

However, the culture clashes in the executive suite far outweighed those at the operating level. Brian Gilbertson was an aggressive and ambitious executive who wanted to double BHP Billiton's size in a short time. This could not be achieved by organic growth; it had to come through acquisition. Brian Gilbertson was always on a plane trying to do deals, but he failed to keep the BHP board informed of his actions and confided more in his close Billiton colleagues. It was a case of staid methodical decision making meeting aggression and risk taking.

In a showdown with the board at the end of 2002, Gilbertson was asked by the board to leave. After a few months, his three most senior Billion colleagues had also left the company. The significant premium BHP paid to access Billion's management proved to be wasted.

Source: Adapted from Stewart Oldfield, 'BHP Billiton Is No Feather Bed', *The Australian Financial Review*, 18 July 2001, p. 15; Tim Treadgold, 'Falling out of Bed', *Business Review Weekly*, 6 July 2001, pp. 54–7; and Malcolm Maiden, 'Blend of Cultures Fails at the Top', *The Sydney Morning Herald*, 7 January 2003, p. 25.

QUESTIONS

1 What does the case tell you about how cultures originate and are sustained?

2 Evaluate the extent to which the cultural change program conforms to suggestions on managing culture discussed in this chapter.

3 Drawing upon the case, discuss why there is likely to be a high turnover of managers when different cultures are merged.

4 Drawing upon the material in the case, show how different cultures can co-exist in the same organisation.

5 Why are culture clashes in the executive suite likely to be resolved by one group leaving the organisation?

FURTHER READING

Paul Bate, *Strategies for Cultural Change*, Oxford: Butterworth Heinemann, 1995.

Terrence E. Deal & Allan A. Kennedy, *Corporate Cultures: The Rites and Rituals of Corporate Life*, Reading, MA: Addison-Wesley, 1982.

John P. Kotter & James Heskett, *Corporate Culture and Performance*, New York: Free Press, 1992.

Edgar H. Schein, 'The Role of the Founder in Creating Organizational Culture', *Organizational Dynamics*, Summer 1983, pp. 13–28.

Edgar H. Schein, *Organizational Culture and Leadership*, San Francisco: Jossey-Bass, 1985.

NOTES

1 This section is draw primarily from Tim Hughes, 'Lessons from the NAB Debacle', *The Courier Mail*, 26 January 2004, p. 17; and Duncan Hughes, 'Join Our Cultural Revolution, NAB Chief Asks Staff', *The Age*, 22 May 2004, p. 2.

2 Terrence E. Deal & Allan A. Kennedy, *Corporate Cultures: The Rites and Rituals of Corporate Life*, Reading, MA: Addison-Wesley, 1982.

3 R.T. Pascale & A.G. Athos, *The Art of Japanese Management*, New York: Simon & Schuster, 1981.

4 Marvin Bower, *The Will to Manage*, New York: McGraw-Hill, 1966.

5 Edgar H. Schein, *Organizational Culture and Leadership*, San Francisco: Jossey-Bass, 1985.

6 Linda Smircich, 'Concepts of Culture and Organizational Analysis', *Administrative Science Quarterly*, September 1983, p. 339.

7 Edgar H. Schein, 'Coming to a New Awareness of Organizational Culture', *Sloan Management Review*, Winter 1984, p. 7.

8 M. Rokeach, *The Nature of Human Values*, New York: Free Press, 1992.

9 Clifford Geertz, *Interpretation of Cultures*, New York: Basic Books, 1973.

10 William Ouchi, 'Markets, Bureaucracies and Clans', *Administrative Science Quarterly*, 25(1), 1980, pp. 129–41.

11 Based on George C. Gordon & W.M. Cummins, *Managing Management Climate*, Lexington, MA: Lexington Books, 1979; and Chris A. Betts & Susan M. Halfhill, 'Organization Culture: Theory, Definitions, and Dimensions', paper presented at the National American Institute of Decision Sciences Conference, Las Vegas, NE, November 1985.

12 See, for example, K.L. Gregory, 'Native-View Paradigms: Multiple Cultures and Culture Conflicts in Organizations', *Administrative Science Quarterly*, September 1983, pp. 359–76.

13 Meryl Reis Louis, 'Sourcing Workplace Culture: Why, When, and How', in R.H. Kilmann, M.J. Saxton & R. Serpa, eds, *Gaining Control of the Corporate Culture*, San Francisco: Jossey-Bass, 1985, p. 129.

14 Schein, 'Coming to a New Awareness of Organizational Culture'.

15 Charles A. O'Reilly III, 'Corporations, Cults and Organizational Culture: Lessons from Silicon Valley Firms', paper presented at the 42nd Annual Meeting of the Academy of Management, Dallas, 1983.

16 Bernard Arogyaswamy & Charles M. Byles, 'Organizational Culture: Internal and External Fits', *Journal of Management*, Winter 1987, pp. 647–59.
17 Karl E. Weick, 'Organizational Culture as a Source of High Reliability', *California Management Review*, Winter 1987, pp. 112–27.
18 ibid.
19 Ouchi, 'Markets, Bureaucracies and Clans'.
20 Edgar H. Schein, 'The Role of the Founder in Creating Organizational Culture', *Organizational Dynamics*, Summer 1983, pp. 13–28.
21 See, for example, Yoash Wiener, 'Forms of Value Systems: A Focus on Organizational Effectiveness and Cultural Change and Maintenance', *Academy of Management Review*, October 1988, pp. 541–3.
22 Benjamin Schneider, 'The People Make the Place', *Personal Psychology*, Autumn 1987, pp. 437–52.
23 Renato Tagiuri & G.H. Litwin, *Organizational Climate*, Boston: Harvard University Graduate School of Business Administration, 1968; Jerome L. Franklin, 'Down the Organization: Influence Processes across Levels of Hierarchy', *Administrative Science Quarterly*, June 1975, pp. 153–64; and 'Handing Down the Old Hands' Wisdom', *Fortune*, 13 June 1983, pp. 97–104.
24 Ralph H. Kilmann, 'Five Steps for Closing Culture Gaps', in Kilmann et al., *Gaining Control of the Corporate Culture*, p. 357.
25 Andrew M. Pettigrew, 'On Studying Organizational Culture', *Administrative Science Quarterly*, December 1979, p. 576.
26 Karl Weick & L.B. Browning, 'Arguments and Narration in Organizational Communication', *Journal of Management*, 12, 1986, pp. 243–59.
27 Pettigrew, 'On Studying Organizational Culture'.
28 See, for instance, 'The Daimler Chrysler Emulsion', *The Economist*, 29 July 2000, pp. 65–6.
29 This information was drawn from Peter Burrows, 'What Price Victory at Hewlett Packard', *Business Week*, 1 April 2002, p. 36; and Ben Elgin, John Cady & Andrew Park, 'Carly's Challenge', *Business Week*, 13 December 2004, p. 98.
30 This article is drawn from Colleen Ryan, 'Blood on the Vine', *The Australian Financial Review*, 31 December 2003.
31 See, in relation to the BHP Billiton merger, Tim Treadgold, 'Falling out of Bed', *Business Review Weekly*, 6 July 2001, pp. 54–7.
32 Schein, *Organizational Culture and Leadership*, p. 45.
33 Caren Siehl, 'After the Founder: An Opportunity to Manage Culture', in Peter Frost et al., eds, *Organizational Culture*, Beverly Hills, CA: Sage Publications, 1985, p. 139.
34 Joanne Martin, 'Can Organizational Culture Be Managed?', in Frost et al., *Organizational Culture*, pp. 95–6.
35 Pettigrew, 'On Studying Organizational Culture', pp. 570–81.
36 John P. Kotter & James Heskett, *Corporate Culture and Performance*, New York: Free Press, 1992.
37 See, for example, W. Gibb Dyer, Jr, 'Organizational Culture', in W.G. Dyer, ed., *Strategies for Managing Change*, Reading, MA: Addison-Wesley, 1984.
38 Pettigrew, 'On Studying Organizational Culture', pp. 570–81.
39 Siehl, 'After the Founder: An Opportunity to Manage Culture', pp. 128–9.
40 This section is drawn from Kotter & Heskett, *Corporate Culture and Performance*.
41 ibid.
42 ibid.

CHAPTER 14

Managing organisational growth and decline

After reading this chapter you should be able to:

- identify four reasons why organisations seek growth
- describe the five-phase model of organisational growth
- discuss the applicability of the phases of growth
- define organisational decline
- describe environmental forces that might precipitate organisational decline
- explain how decline affects the administrative component
- outline the steps management is likely to follow in response to decline
- identify the potential problems managers face when organisations decline.

Introduction

Foster's—the brewer that has seen it all

It may have been true at some stage that Australians were great beer drinkers and that you could not go broke owning a brewery, but Foster's experience challenged the myth. Over the past 20 years, Australia's per capita beer consumption has been slowly declining and Foster's has faced the challenge of how to maintain growth in a flat and falling market. It has also been close to being insolvent on at least one occasion.

The first Foster's Lager was brewed in 1888 and in 1907 Foster's merged with Carlton Brewery to form Carlton and United Breweries, shortened to CUB. CUB subsequently became a Melbourne icon. The managers of the main brewers in Australia, called the beer barons, carved the Australian market up between them, creating comfortable monopoly positions in their home market. This cosy existence was interrupted in the early 1970s by governments ruling such practices illegal.

But the breweries had a high cash flow, which attracted the attention of the corporate raiders of the 1980s. With low levels of debt and conservative and risk-averse management, the breweries were attractive to the brash entrepreneurs who could borrow against the security of assets and high cash flows and use the borrowed funds to expand the company. CUB was taken over by John Elliot's IXL, which had great plans to 'Fosterise' the world. In the process, during the 1980s and early 1990s, Foster's bought breweries in the US and the UK and chains of hotels in Australia and the UK and promoted Foster's as a world brand.

Foster's was caught up in the financial engineering of the late 1980s and early 1990s and was at one time part owned by BHP, a relationship which did not finally end until 1997. Unfortunately, Elliot also used the cash flow from Foster's to fund his other interests and by the early 1990s, when Foster's emerged from Elliot's control, it was struggling under a heavy debt burden. And the problem of falling beer consumption had not gone away. Strategies had to be developed to both reduce debt and move into other alcoholic drink areas. Because of its high debt levels, Foster's Brewing Group, as it was then called, missed some promising acquisition opportunities in the 1990s as the international brewing industry consolidated. But it did make a number of important acquisitions in the wine industry, including Berringer in the US and Mildara Blass in Australia. It also established breweries in China, India and Vietnam.

However, returns on overseas operations, including the Chinese breweries, were poor and could not provide the growth needed to replace faltering beer sales in Australia. It became clear that its ownership of hotels was drawing capital that could be used more profitably in other areas. Also, its wine operations needed scale to compete on a worldwide basis. Foster's share price was static and making the company vulnerable. Without action being taken to address these issues, Foster's would have fallen to a predator, probably one from overseas, and been broken up.

By the early 2000s debt had been reduced to a manageable level and the hotels and other distracting interests disposed of. The opportunity to buy Southcorp, a large Australian wine company, presented itself in 2005 and Foster's Group, as it was now named, grabbed at the opportunity. Influencing its strategy was the belief that the world wine industry was ripe for consolidation and that in the future it would be dominated by just a few companies enjoying worldwide scale. It wanted to be one of those companies and leader in the consolidation, not a reactor to it.

Organisational decline: accepting the new reality

Despite all the reasons that managers have for favouring growth conditions, organisational decline is becoming a fact of life for an increasing number of organisations, especially those in mature industries.[14] For example, most large organisations have engaged in some form of downsizing in recent years. In industries such as clothing and footwear, there have been large-scale plant closures, and almost every type of industry, including the service industries, has felt the need to rationalise by closing branches or factories, with consequent reduction in employment. This does not necessarily mean that the output of the organisation is falling, rather that productivity in many cases has risen and there is need for fewer workers.

Twenty years ago, few managers or organisational theorists were concerned about decline. Growth was the *natural* state of things, and decline, when it occurred, was viewed as an aberration—the result of errors by poor management or merely a brief setback in a long-term growth trend. What, then, has changed? Have we merely ignored reality in the past, or have more organisations actually entered the decline stage of their life cycle?

Clarifying definitions

Before we look at the causes that may lead to organisational decline, let us clarify our terminology. When we refer to **organisational decline**, we refer to a long-lasting and ongoing decrease in the overall activity of the organisation. This can involve loss of customers or market share, a decline in competitiveness, or obsolescence in a firm's key technology, product or service. It is *not* meant to describe temporary slowdowns arising from changes in economic conditions or minor adjustments due to market forces.

organisational decline a long-lasting and ongoing decrease in the overall activity of the organisation

Another term closely aligned with organisational decline, and sometimes used interchangeably with it, is *downsizing*. But, as we have seen in Chapter 6, this term has a more specific meaning. By **downsizing**, we mean a reduction in the size of the organisation through the reduction of the number of employees and organisational positions. Downsizing reduces the staff count, widens the organisation's average span of control and pushes authority downwards. When you hear about management reorganising to become 'lean and focused', the organisation is typically engaged in downsizing.

downsizing planned reduction in an organisation's staffing levels

The causes of decline

The empirical research into organisational theory which was conducted between the mid-1940s and the mid-1970s was largely growth oriented.[15] Coincidentally, this same three-decade period was one of relatively uninterrupted growth in Western economies. It should not be surprising, therefore, to find that the organisation theory literature is heavily growth oriented, focusing almost exclusively on problems or benefits associated with expansion. However, since about the mid-1970s, we have seen a distinct increase in the number of organisations shrinking their operations. The obvious question is, why? The reasons are often complex and multicausal, that is, they have a number of causes which often act together to exert a powerful force. The causes will be divided below into those external to the firm and then those that are internal.

Environmental causes

Environmental causes are those events which occur in the firm's environment and over which the firm has little control; it must react to them as it sees fit. These causes are typically those considered in studies of organisational strategy. The first is *mature markets*. For instance, the appliance manufacturer, Email, now owned by Electrolux, has found the Australian market for its products static. Everyone who wants a washing machine or refrigerator has one, and the market is limited to replacement sales. For many manufacturers, significantly lower production costs overseas have been an obvious factor precipitating a decline in demand for their goods. Since 1980, approximately 300 000 manufacturing jobs have been lost in Australia to offshore competition. In some cases whole industries, such as consumer electronics, no longer exist in Australia. At one stage in the late 1960s Australia had more than 10 manufacturers of television sets. It now has none. Personal computer manufacturers are facing similar market maturity, leading to a round of mergers among some, while others prefer to exit the market. Under such conditions, it is those organisations with better access to resources and better management that survive.

Some organisations, especially those with a single product or those where a single product dominates sales, have been hit by *technological obsolescence*, arising from the introduction of a disruptive technology. Manufacturers of vinyl records, steam locomotives, aircraft propellers and asbestos products are just four examples of companies which have had to face a loss of growth expectations. The end of the product life cycle does not apply only to product categories. The computer industry has seen the rise and decline of many innovative companies which dominated their field until new products were introduced by competitors. Examples of firms that have experienced decline caused by new product offerings by competitors are Wang, Digital and even IBM during the late 1980s.

Some organisations are forced to cut back as a result of *loss of market share*. The total market for their product or services may not be shrinking, but their failure to sustain their share of that market creates the need to retrench. Ford's loss of market share in the car market is such a case. Discount airlines have led to the near elimination of interstate bus and rail services as mass movers of passengers. Deregulation has also had a major effect on Telstra as new players such as Optus have entered the industry.

Globalisation has introduced a whole new dynamic to business. It has had the effect of raising the levels of competition from both domestic and foreign businesses and of creating new opportunities overseas for Australian-based companies. The increase in competition has led to many firms realising that they have neither the scale nor the scope to survive. They can seek merger partners or go out of business. But another effect has been for organisations to divest themselves of non-core businesses, allowing them to concentrate on those areas in which they have a comparative advantage. The resulting organisation structure is more centralised and focused on a fewer number of products.

The recent spate of *mergers and acquisitions* has created redundancies in many companies. When banks merge or Mobil acquires Esso, efficiencies often dictate consolidating operations and staff personnel in functions such as legal, accounting, purchasing and human resources.

Local, state and federal government departments have additional problems to worry about. Changes in government priorities have led to a reduction in expenditure on public broadcasters such as the ABC and SBS. Forcing government business enterprises to compete has led to a major shift in the way they conduct their operations, in many cases involving large job losses. Privatisation (e.g. of the Commonwealth Bank or Qantas) has forced managers to become more market focused. Even universities have been forced to seek more of their income from students and services to industry. In addition, previously protected industries such as electricity generation and gas distribution have been opened to competition.

Institutional rigidities may also contribute to organisational decline. This refers to the existence in the environment of forces such as laws, agreements or powerful groups such as unions, which are not under the control of management but which may be contributing to firms' decline by making change difficult to enact. The commitment of General Motors to providing pensions and health care to retirees is an example of institutional rigidity. (See case for class discussion at the end of the chapter.) Another example is the barriers which many European governments place upon firms laying off workers.

In Chapter 8, we discussed the application of *population ecology*. This approach seeks to identify characteristics in the environment which contribute to organisational failure. It uses statistical techniques to identify association between variables rather than seeking sources of causation. The following contributors to failure have been identified by their research.[16]

The first is *population density*. Although the relationship is not entirely clear, the more organisations there are in a population, the more likely it is that failure will occur. This is associated with carrying capacity of an environment. Returning to the white goods example in Chapter 8, where we looked at the number of refrigerators sold in Australia and then compared this with the size of a factory necessary to achieve economies of scale, we can see that there is room for only one or at most two refrigerator manufacturers in Australia. The limitation on the number of firms highlighted by density issues applies to industries as diverse as airlines, building materials suppliers and suburban hairdressers. It helps explain, for instance, why duopolies, that is, two dominant firms, are so common in Australian industry.

However, a denser population may provide higher levels of environmental support. Important providers of resources, such as financiers and suppliers, may be more familiar with the industry and used to dealing with firms in it. Alternatively, a new start-up in an unfamiliar industry may have difficulty in attracting resources because of unfamiliarity with what it is trying to achieve.

Population ecologists have also identified the *organisational life cycle*, which we described in Chapter 1, as a cause of decline. This is because it is environmental factors that are the main contributors to the life cycle. The life cycle is seen to be inevitable and not easily amenable to managerial intervention.

Research has also shown that the probability of failure is higher when an organisation is *new and young*. This has been termed the liability of newness. It is argued that as new organisations find it difficult to create new routines and management structures, they are more vulnerable than older companies which have already developed coping and adaptation mechanisms. New organisations also have fewer slack resources and less environmental support. Researchers have identified that the liability of newness also extends to those firms undergoing significant organisational change. When a new strategy and structure are adopted, an organisation is vulnerable as it learns new ways of doing things and managers adapt to new roles.

Associated with newness is size; small firms are more likely to fail than large ones. Mortality of firms decreases as they grow larger. The problems facing small firms have

OT CLOSEUP

Why do companies fail?

The reasons for company failure are often difficult to determine. Researching the topic is fraught with methodological difficulties. Few managers of failing companies write memoirs explaining their role in their company's failure. They are often reluctant to give interviews, and those who do have a natural tendency to paint their statements in a positive light. Additionally, when a company fails, the staff of the company disperse and can be difficult to find. Contrast this with researching the histories of successful companies. The managers are more than willing to talk about the success of their organisation and their contribution to it. The organisation is still in existence, so managers and others are easy to trace. As well, archives and historical documents are readily to hand.

This does not mean that we do not have a good idea of why companies fail. One journal has identified the following six causes as contributors to organisational failure.[17]

1. *Identity crisis.* Senior management often does not have a clear idea of the business it is in and what makes it tick. Managers are often ill-informed as to the fundamentals of their business and what has made the business successful. They are therefore unaware of what actions need to be taken to ensure that the business grows.
2. *Failure of vision.* Few managers prepare their company for likely environmental or technological changes. Most do not anticipate threats to their core technology, such as diesels replacing steam locomotives and networked PCs replacing mainframes.
3. *High levels of debt.* Management and boards of directors often feel that unless they load their company with debt for expansion, the performance of the company will suffer and opportunities for expansion will be missed. Servicing the debt often becomes unsustainable during times of economic downturn and high interest rates, leading to corporate failure.
4. *Adhering to past practices.* Many companies continue to adhere to established customs and practices long after the circumstances that gave rise to them have passed. As a result, organisations find themselves out of alignment with actions of competitors and changes in market demand. This tendency increases with the size of the company.
5. *Failure to stay close to the customer.* This is an obvious failing and one which is the subject of dozens of management books and articles. But even companies that need to monitor customer demand, such as those in entertainment and fashion, still manage to get this fundamental wrong.
6. *Beware of the enemies within.* While the aphorism that employees are a company's greatest asset is true, many companies have been brought down by the actions of their own employees. Poor industrial relations, lack of incentives, misaligned rewards, uncontrolled risk taking, alienation and poor people management can lead to hostility and lack of cooperation from the workforce. Few organisations can thrive under these conditions.

been linked to shortage of capital, difficulties in attracting skilled workers and managers, higher administrative costs and lack of legitimacy amongst important stakeholders.

To summarise, population ecologists consider that the industry and the environment are more important than a firm's strategy. Environments change faster than organisations and, as a result, it is the environment that determines whether the firm declines or not, rather than the firm's strategic choice.

Although providing valuable insights into why organisations decline and fail, population ecology provides no insight into how the management of firms may have contributed to the decline or suggestions as to what behaviours or actions should be taken to proactively address the problem. These are discussed in the next section.

The behavioural dimensions of decline

The previous section concentrated on factors in the environment of the organisation which can contribute to organisational decline. But decline has perceptual and behavioural dimensions which greatly influence outcomes. Although not strictly part of organisational theory, decline cannot be understood without mentioning the influence of behavioural factors.

Researchers have identified an unusual contributor to organisational decline: it can be the result of a *self-fulfilling prophecy*.[18] In simple terms, this means that if important groups expect that decline will happen, they will act in a way that promotes it. For instance, the greater the tendency for managers to consider decline inevitable, the less likely they are to invest in equipment, processes and personnel to combat decline. This in turn leads to a reduction in the capacity for organisational renewal. Further, if important external stakeholders consider that the organisation is declining, they will be disinclined to provide the resources and support to assist in turning the organisation around. Thus loss of confidence and an institutional expectation of failure can contribute to a lack of effort to take necessary corrective action. Decline and failure thus become inevitable.

The much discussed phenomenon of *groupthink* can blind management to potential problems and creative responses.[19] Groupthink occurs when a highly cohesive team generates conditions in which high levels of unanimity are required. Any 'naysayers' and holders of alternative opinions are marginalised and information which does not fit the mindset and world view of the dominant group is excluded. It is easy to see under these conditions that important information would not be considered by key decision makers. Strong autocratic leaders can also generate conditions in which alternative views and opinions are excluded.

Decline and *management perceptions* are also closely related.[20] Some managers find it difficult to actually understand and interpret the sources and progress of decline. Often they rely upon filtered data. Summary reports from subordinates, accounting summaries and overviews from various sources are useful in that they cut down the amount of data to be processed. But they are only summaries and they lack richness and depth of meaning. Similarly, accounting and production reports follow well-established traditional formats. However, such summaries only identify trends and associations between variables and they generally fail to identify what may be causing changes in the organisation.

Managers are also prone to *selective perception*; that is, they only concentrate on certain parts of the environment to the exclusion of others. This may be sources of information which have been useful in the past, but have outlived their usefulness. Limited understanding of environmental and technological changes can also be a problem; in fact, understanding technological changes presents particular problems. All technologies when they are first introduced are clumsy, embryonic and provide limited utility. As a result, they can be easily dismissed. But often, as they develop, they present major challenges to existing technologies. This can be seen in technologies as different as aircraft, the personal computer and mobile phones. Reading the impact of these changes presents considerable difficulties to management.

Top management's actions may also conform to the *rigidity effect*. This proposes that individuals, groups and organisations tend to behave rigidly in threatening situations and seek to maintain the status quo. As a result, managers do not change their focus in response to an external threat and act as if it does not exist. Obviously, the causes of this condition lie in complex psychological phenomena and, as such, are not the main focus of this book. But the existence of this and other similar conditions explain why management's response, or lack of response, to crises fails to improve matters for the organisation.

A final behavioural problem is that of *framing* the decline accurately, that is, putting it into its appropriate context and formulating an appropriate response. Once decline is perceived by important stakeholders, be they inside or outside the organisation, pressure for action builds. Managers come under pressure to 'do something'. This is a time for strong nerves and clear thinking. Many managers fail this test.

The points raised in this section indicate that there is a strong behavioural element to decline. This implies that the actions of different managers will lead to different outcomes. It also explains the existence of turnaround managers who specialise in returning organisations to a growth path, and why, when decline is identified, existing management is often replaced. A different mindset is important to perceiving the situation in different ways and a prerequisite to formulating corrective action.

Is managing decline the reverse of managing growth?

Until recently, there was little research into the decline process. This was undoubtedly due to the emphasis on growth and the reality that organisations undergoing contraction can rarely afford the luxury of sponsoring reflective research. Moreover, management does not see much gain in permitting outsiders to chronicle its organisation's decline.[21] Further, in the fast-moving and constantly turbulent business world, defunct companies soon disappear and are rarely thought of again. But the struggle of many companies to combat stagnation, decline and changing market conditions is widely reported in the business press and has relevance for investors and employees, even if organisation theory researchers are reluctant to expend much time on the issue. Business disciplines such as strategy are rich in research on organisational turnarounds, much of which is not relevant to the area covered by this book. The organisation theory literature on organisational decline is essentially based on some preliminary research evidence and a good deal of insightful speculation.

We begin with the observation that the management of decline is not merely a matter of reversing the process of managing growth. An organisation cannot be reduced piece by piece simply by reversing the sequence of activity and resource-building by which it grew.[22] There is evidence to conclude that activities within same-sized organisations during periods of growth and decline will not correspond directly. As a generalisation, there is a lag that typifies the rate of change in structure during prolonged decline that is not evident in growth.[23] As discussed in Chapter 6, changes in size have a significant impact on structure. But those conclusions were drawn from organisations that were all changing in the growth direction. During decline, size has an impact on structure, but it is not the reverse of the growth pattern. This lag results in the level of structure being greater in the same organisation for a given level of size during decline than for the same level of size during growth.[24] Referring to Figure 14.2, the lag thesis would state that at a given size, *X*, points *a* and *b* are not equal. More specifically, at point *b* in time, the organisation should have a greater degree of structure. For instance, we could expect a lag in the degree of formalisation. Typically, when an organisation goes from 100 employees to 1000, there is an increase in formal rules and regulations. But this is not easily reversible. We predict, there-

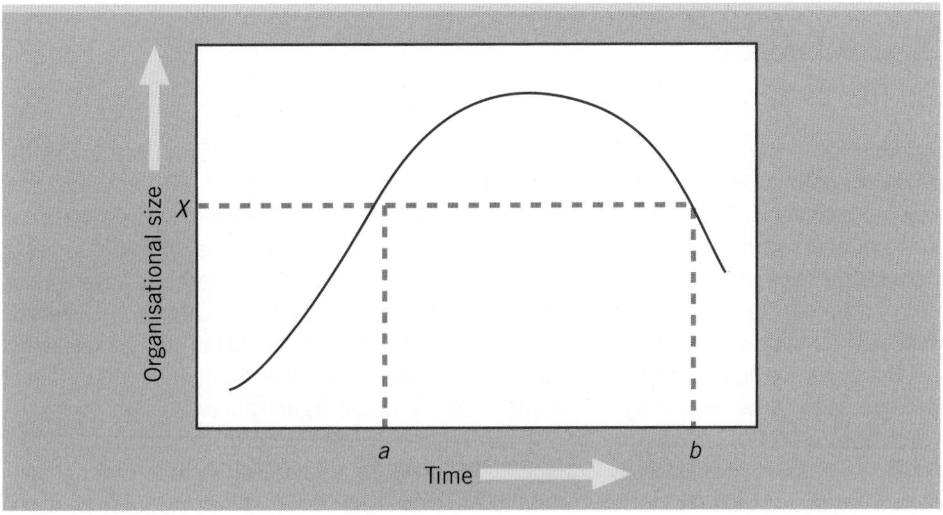
Organisational size
X
a
b
Time

FIGURE 14.2 The organisation's life cycle

fore, that when an organisation is contracting, it will tend to have a higher degree of formalisation at each size level than it had at the same level in its growth stage. This lag factor is most evident in recent studies of the administrative component in declining organisations.

The administrative component

The administrative component refers to the number of people in an organisation who engage in support activities. If there is a lag in decline, one would expect the administrative component to shrink at a slower rate than the whole organisation. Studies confirm this expectation.[25] In some cases, evidence has been found that the administrative component actually grew while organisations declined.[26] Although the exact nature of the relationship is not well established, it is clear that the relationship between size and the administrative component is different during decline from that during growth. Interestingly, either a lag or an increase would be consistent with the conclusion that organisational politics distorts the effect of the decline process on the administrative component.[27] The administrative support group, because of its power, is more effective in resisting cutback pressures. As a result, the ratio of supportive staff to operatives will be higher at the same level of total organisational size in the decline stage.

Organisational size is a major factor in determining an organisation's structure during growth, but not during decline. Thus, our conclusions in Chapter 6 on the size–structure relationship appear to be relevant only on the upside of an organisation's life cycle.

An enhanced case for power-control

While the evidence is incomplete, we offer the following hypothesis: size is a key determinant of structure during growth, but it is replaced by power-control in decline. The actions of vested interest groups to maintain or enhance their power are not nearly

OT CLOSEUP

Decline and the public sector

Many public sector organisations, such as local councils, have an infinite life; they never cease to exist no matter how badly they are managed. Poorly run public sector organisations are also not in a state of perpetual decline; they obviously have some regenerative capacity. Research in the United Kingdom provides a good illustration of the process of adaptation by such organisations. Public sector organisations undertake functions which are seen to be necessary and socially desirable and failure to deliver them efficiently or effectively does not absolve government from undertaking the relevant tasks; rubbish removal is a good case in point. Ideas as to what constitutes good performance vary. Organisations exist within an environment of powerful stakeholders who have within their own minds what constitutes good performance. And concepts of good performance vary over time in line with current thinking and political ideals. As public-service performance is typically difficult to define, subjective assessment becomes an important source of assessing effectiveness. For instance, when planning was being promoted for local government, those councils without a plan were considered to be poorly managed compared to those that had developed a plan, no matter how irrelevant the plan was.

In examining local councils, the researchers found that public organisations typically exhibit variations in performance over time. No organisation is consistently good or consistently poor, but like football clubs in a long-running competition, move up and down according to situational factors. Further, institutional values and norms in the environment influence perceptions as to how an organisation is performing at any particular time.

A further finding was that organisations such as local councils are loosely coupled, leading to considerable variation between levels of performance of the component parts. (Loose coupling refers to the situation where one part of an organisation has little interaction with, or dependence upon, other parts). For instance, one local council may run the library extremely well but maintain roads poorly. Another may provide superior services to the elderly and children but have a poor record in approving building applications. As a result, public sector organisations rarely fail comprehensively; parts of them may not make the grade, which draws attention to the whole organisation.

A turnaround in poorly performing public sector organisations will be undertaken by existing management to the extent that it recognises that poor performance exists and it has sufficient leadership capacity to manage effective change. This implies that the need for change must be recognised and that the current management and leadership have the resources—political, conceptual and physical—to introduce change.

Finally, for those organisations which seem to be perpetually failing, turnaround will be effective to the extent that external pressure from important stakeholders is able to promote the necessary leadership capacity to ensure improvement. This may be by such means as providing additional funds, replacing existing management or providing expert assistance.

One of the great insights of this research is that decline is not a continual downward trajectory; it proceeds in cycles and it is possible for public sector organisations to return to effectiveness. It also stresses that assessment of effectiveness is greatly influenced by fashions and fads in thinking exhibited by important stakeholders. These reveal themselves in institutional pressures placed upon organisations.

Source: Drawn from Pauline Jas & Chris Skelcher, 'Performance Decline and Turnaround in Public Organisations: A Theoretical and Empirical Analysis', *British Journal of Management*, 16, 2005, pp. 195–210.

as visible during growth as they are in decline. A growing organisation allows most people to achieve at least part of their goals. In addition, there are more resources in the organisation, resulting in minimisation of conflicts. Confrontations may be resolved by all parties' getting what they want. However, when the organisation is contracting, resources become scarce, leading to intense political activity over control of what few there are. Administrative rationality, which can explain the size–structure relationship in growth, is replaced by a power struggle explanation in decline. In decline, therefore, structure is more likely to reflect the interests of those in power, for they are best able to succeed in a political struggle.

Decline follows stages

Decline is not a continuous process originating from some starting point through to the eventual dissolution of the organisation.[28] As environments and technologies are constantly challenging an organisation's legitimacy, all organisations will eventually face circumstances that can lead to decline. But there is nothing inevitable about decline. Management can and does have choices which, when exercised wisely and appropriately, can end or slow the decline process. The reason that organisational change is such a common part of management practice is that it is often associated with attempts to combat decline.

A useful model of organisational decline, proposed by Weitzel and Jonsson, views decline as consisting of five stages. At each stage, except the last, it is possible for management to take corrective action to end the decline process. The model, shown in Figure 14.3, identifies five stages of decline, with each stage having a corresponding action that the organisation can take to arrest the decline.

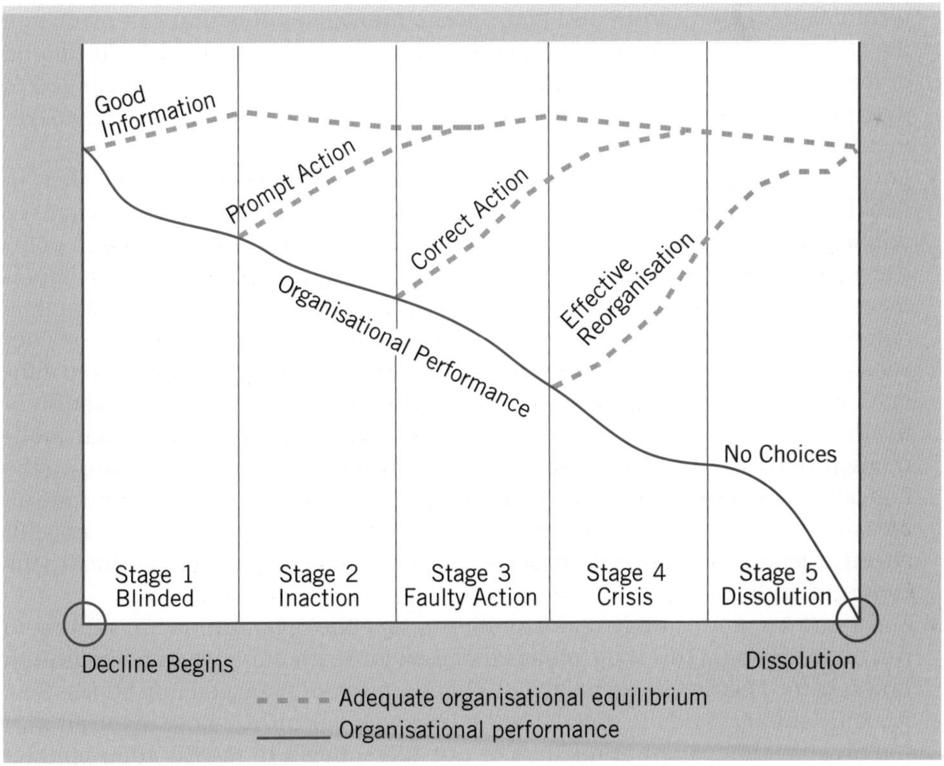
Good Information
Prompt Action
Correct Action
Effective Reorganisation
Organisational Performance
No Choices
Stage 1 Blinded
Stage 2 Inaction
Stage 3 Faulty Action
Stage 4 Crisis
Stage 5 Dissolution
Decline Begins
Dissolution
Adequate organisational equilibrium
Organisational performance

FIGURE 14.3 Stages of decline and the widening performance gap

Source: William Weitzel & Ellen Jonsson, 'Decline in Organisations: A Literature Integration and Extension', *Administrative Science Quarterly*, 34(1), March 1989, p. 102.

- *Stage 1: Blinded decline.* In this stage the organisation fails to anticipate or detect internal or external influences which can threaten the organisation's survival. Some of the signs that are often overlooked are the build-up of excessive numbers of personnel, tolerance of incompetence, cumbersome administrative procedures, disproportionate staff power, poor productivity, unclear goals and decision benchmarks, fear of embarrassment and conflict, loss of effective communication, and an outdated organisational structure. One of the reasons for these signs being overlooked is that managers are trained to be attentive to quantitative changes in commonly gathered data, such as accounting measures of performance. But these data are historical, in that they reflect past performance. Decline may have set in long before it is reflected in performance statistics. Another feature of this stage of decline is that organisations often tend to focus their attention on meeting internal benchmarks and adhering to procedures rather than concentrating on adapting to the environment. However, management can overcome the problems of blinded decline by seeking good information; once this is obtained, overcoming the problems leading to decline is straightforward.
- *Stage 2: Inaction.* During this stage the signs of decline are apparent but the organisation chooses to do little or nothing about them. In profit-making organisations the signs can include declining sales, stagnant profits and surplus inventories. If the organisation is older and longer established, the inaction stage is likely to be more pronounced and longer lasting. Decline during this stage is by no means terminal, because prompt and appropriate management action can overcome the causes of the decline. One of the risks of this stage, however, is the likelihood of management increasing commitment to courses of action that contributed to the problem in the first place. This is why there is often turnover in senior management during this stage.
- *Stage 3: Faulty action.* This stage sees the multiplication of the external signs of decline, even though action is being taken to arrest the decline. Differences of opinion regarding courses of action proliferate. This leads to an increase in political activity and power plays in the organisation as each faction lobbies to implement its preferred course of action. Employees experience uncertainty and morale deteriorates. Staff turnover increases. Organisation leaders are forced to consider substantive changes to ensure organisational survival. However, there is often difficulty in determining the most appropriate course to return the organisation to health. There is also pressure for quick action and decisions rather than well-thought-out ideas. Decisions may also be faulty because they concentrate on the indicators rather than the causes of the decline. Solutions may also concentrate on areas where slack resources are greatest or the power of resistance weakest. But effective action is still possible at this stage, provided that it correctly addresses the causes of decline.
- *Stage 4: Crisis.* At this stage opportunities to save the organisation are starting to run out. Survival at this stage means that a major reorientation and revitalisation is necessary. This inevitably involves a change in senior management. Staff suffers from divisiveness and the social fabric begins to break up. All those involved with the organisation, whether insiders or outsiders, begin to restrict their contact with it. As talented employees leave, turnaround becomes that much harder. Risk-taking increases as options run out. Customers and suppliers begin to desert the organisation. At this stage it may be subject to takeover if it has assets of value to other organisations, but this is not necessarily the case. Products may be old or out

of date, technology or capital equipment obsolete, and brand names or market positioning of little worth.

- *Stage 5: Dissolution.* Decline at this stage is irreversible. The loss of capital, markets, reputation and talented personnel takes its toll and eventually the organisation collapses. Closing ceremonies, get-togethers and barbecues are often a feature of organisations that are closing up shop, and part of the skills of managing this stage of decline is in instituting constructive leave-taking processes.

Not all organisations follow precisely the stages identified in the model. In the case of a sudden shock, for instance, an organisation may find itself in stage 4 without going through the previous stages. An airline that experienced the crash of one of its aircraft for which it was found negligent would be a case in point. But the model does distinguish between actual decline, the perception of that decline, and the actions necessary to restore the organisation to health. Differentiating between these is very much influenced by perception and appropriate response relies on important stakeholders of the organisation reading the situation correctly and taking appropriate remedial action. Reversing decline also requires that institutional support from the environment be available. Once an organisation loses the support of its bankers, for instance, decline can be extremely fast. A bank itself can be put out of business in a week if depositors lose confidence in the bank's solvency. Organisations also rely on support from suppliers. Once this is lost and suppliers either won't supply their goods or require cash in advance, the end of the organisation will not be far off.

Movements betweeen growth and decline are common

Any long-established organisation can identify periods in its history where management has had to take proactive measures to return the organisation to a growth path. These tend to recur over time and are part of the normal process of adapting to the environment. They also reflect changes in expectations of important stakeholders, which can view organisations as being in crisis or decline when the only thing that has changed has been their own attitudes and values. The changes in the perception of nuclear power generation and uranium mining over the past 20 years are instructive of the importance of stakeholder perceptions.

A further contributor to poor performance is the 'success breeds failure' syndrome.[29] When organisations, either through good management, luck or some other factor, grow fast, or are considered to be successful, management often tends to repeat actions which led to past success even though they may not be appropriate in the changed circumstances. The organisation tends to fall into comfortable ways of doing things, in the process letting opportunities slip and competitors take advantage of environmental changes. Eventually, poor performance cannot be ignored and corrective action needs to be taken. Generally this means appointing new management.

Organisations may therefore be seen to be constantly moving between growth and decline phases which are capable of being appropriately managed. In this sense, the use of the word 'decline' is perhaps misleading; 'cycle' may be a more appropriate term.

Potential managerial problems when organisations decline

Some like the challenge of managing in adversity. Others merely find themselves in a leadership position when facts dictate that the organisation has entered its decline phase. While it is undoubtedly easier to manage an organisation during growth than

TABLE 14.1 Dysfunctional consequences of organisational decline

Centralisation	Decision making is passed upwards, participation decreases and control is emphasised.
No long-term planning	Crises and short-term needs drive out strategic planning.
Innovation curtailed	No experimentation, risk-aversion and scepticism about non-core activities.
Scapegoating	Leaders are blamed for the pain and uncertainty.
Resistance to change	Conservatism and turf protection lead to rejection of new alternatives.
Turnover	The most competent leaders tend to leave first, causing leadership anaemia.
Low morale	Few needs are met, and infighting is predominant.
Loss of slack	Uncommitted resources are used to cover operating expenses.
Fragmented pluralism	Special-interest groups organise and become more vocal.
Loss of credibility	Leaders lose the confidence of their subordinates.
Non-prioritised cuts	Attempts to ameliorate conflict lead to attempts to equalise cutbacks.
Conflict	Competition and infighting for control predominate when resources are scarce.

Source: Adapted from Kim Cameron, David A. Whetten & Myung U. Kim, 'Organizational Dysfunctions of Decline', *Academy of Management Journal*, March 1987, p. 128; with permission.

during decline, the fact remains that decline is a reality, and that when it occurs managers must be prepared to cope with its consequences. Table 14.1 lists some of these consequences. The remainder of this chapter looks in greater detail at some of these problems and considers what managers can do about them.

Increased conflict

A manager has the opportunity to really test his or her conflict-management skills during organisational decline. As we have noted before, growth creates slack, and that acts as an emollient to smooth over conflict-creating forces. Management uses this slack as a currency for buying off potentially conflicting interest groups within the organisation. Conflicts can be resolved readily by expanding everyone's resources. However, in the decline phase, conflict over resources grows because there are fewer resources to divide up. For instance, conflict has been found to be higher in declining school districts than in growing districts.[30]

The increased conflict evident in decline is not necessarily dysfunctional. If managed properly, it can be directed towards slowing the decline. Out of the conflict can come changes that may revitalise the organisation: selection of a new domain, creation of new products or services, and cost-cutting measures that may make the downsized organisation more efficient and viable.

Increased politicking

Less slack also translates into more politicking. There will emerge many organised and vocal groups actively pursuing their self-interest. As we noted earlier in this chapter, structural changes during decline are more likely to be determined by which coalitions win the power struggle for organisational control than by rational determinants such as size, technology or environment. Politically naive managers will find their jobs difficult, if not impossible, as they are unable to adjust to the changing decision-making criteria. Remember, in declining conditions the resources pie is shrinking. If one department can successfully resist a cut, the result will typically be that other departments have to cut deeper. Weak units will not only take a disproportionate part of the cut, but may be most vulnerable to elimination.

Further politicking occurs over how to interpret the symptoms of decline and what strategy to adopt to respond to it. There will no doubt be different schools of thought on whether the decline is permanent or temporary, what is causing it and how the diminishing amount of resources should be spent in responding to it. In these circumstances only one opinion can prevail, thus providing a sharp edge to the politics involved.

Increased resistance to change

An organisation responds more slowly to environmental change in decline than in growth.[31] In its effort to protect itself, the dominant coalition fights hard to maintain the status quo and its control. Vested interests thwart change efforts.[32] Preparing the organisation for change becomes extremely difficult, as there is a genuine fear of the consequences of change. Generally, change in declining companies means redundancies and loss of status and position. Resistance to change seems to be related to the previously discussed 'stages of decline'.[33] Early in the decline, individuals follow a pattern of 'weathering the storm'. This is characterised by intensified efforts to follow the old, established procedures and may result in slowing the decline. But if it is truly of the prolonged variety, at best it can only delay the inevitable. Thus the early part of decline is a period of high resistance to change. Resistance should be reduced as it becomes clear that the decline is not temporary. It is part of management's task during decline to communicate the implications of decline widely.

One writer has noted that a major force for resisting change during the initial phase of decline will be those vested interests which have benefited most from growth.[34] As their power base is challenged, they are motivated to continue to push for growth-related policies, even though it no longer makes sense.

Loss of top management credibility

During decline, members of the organisation will look to some individual or group on which to place the blame for retrenchment. Whether or not top management is directly responsible for the decline, it tends to become the scapegoat. This leads to a loss of confidence in top management and doubts that they have the ability to remedy the situation. Employee morale can also suffer and there are an unlimited number of ways that disaffected employees can withdraw their voluntary cooperation from management. In large organisations, once this occurs, management faces an almost impossible task to reclaim its credibility. Important stakeholders, such as shareholders, often step in at this stage and insist on a change of management as a prerequisite for further support. Also, as shareholders own the company, they can effect management change at any time by changing the composition of the board of directors.

Change in workforce composition

Retrenchment requires workforce cuts. One common criterion for determining who gets laid off is seniority: that is, the most recent employees are the first to go. Laying off personnel on the basis of seniority, however, tends to reshape the composition of the workforce. As newer employees tend to be younger, seniority-based layoffs create an older workforce. If the industry is mature, large-scale layoffs of this nature can lead to a rise in the average age of the workforce of up to 10 years. The problems arising from this is compounded by the naturally ageing workforce as baby boomers reach retirement.

More recently, companies have been using voluntary redundancy, or variations of it, to reduce numbers. Although conventional wisdom has it that younger employees and those with more marketable skills are more likely to accept the packages offered, the results of research in the area are mixed. Many longer serving employees, who often receive larger financial packages through the schemes, are attracted to them. Versions of early retirement schemes are also used to downsize the workforce, leaving a younger profile overall. One of the downsides of this is that the company loses valuable experience and corporate memory. One method used to avoid the problem of changes in workforce composition is to make positions, and therefore their holders, redundant rather than specific individuals.

Increased voluntary turnover

Voluntary resignations are the other side of employee departures. This becomes a major potential problem in organisational decline, because the organisation will want to retain its most valuable employees. Yet some of the first people to voluntarily leave an organisation when it enters the stage of decline are the most mobile individuals, such as skilled technicians, professionals and talented managerial personnel. These, of course, are typically the individuals that the organisation can least afford to lose. Managers with an eye on their career are particularly prone to seek higher profile employment when it is clear that the growth days of the company are over. The opportunities for advancement and increased responsibilities are obviously reduced greatly during decline. The upwardly mobile executive will look for an organisation where his or her talents are more likely to be used. This suggests that senior management will be challenged to provide incentives to ambitious junior managers if it is to prevent a long, slow decline from snowballing into a rapid descent.

Decaying employee motivation

Employee motivation is different when an organisation is contracting from when it is enjoying growth. During growth, motivation can be provided by promotional opportunities and the excitement of being associated with a dynamic organisation. During decline, there are retrenchments and reassignments of duties that often require absorbing the tasks that were previously undertaken by others, and similar stress-inducing changes. It is usually hard for employees to stay focused when they are uncertain whether they will still have a job next month or next year. When their organisation is experiencing prolonged decline, managers are challenged to function effectively in an organisational climate typified by stagnation, fear and stress.

What's the solution to organisational decline?

There are no magic techniques available to management that can overcome the many negative outcomes associated with organisational decline. However, some things seem to work better than others.[35] These include aligning the organisation's strategy with environmental realities, increasing communication, centralising decision making, redesigning jobs and work practices, and developing innovative approaches to cutbacks. Management also needs to improve the organisation's chances of survival by meeting the needs of critical constituencies in the environment.

Management needs to concentrate upon the ambiguity that organisational decline creates among employees. This is best done by clarifying the organisation's strategy and goals. Where is the organisation going? What is the organisation's future and potential? By addressing these questions appropriately, management demonstrates that it understands the problem and has a vision for what the new, smaller organisation will look like. Employees generally have a broad idea of what the organisation's problems are, or at least can understand when told about them. They want to believe that management is not content to sit back and run a 'going-out-of-business' sale. If management loses credibility among the employees, it will be so much harder to turn the organisation around.

Organisational decline demands that management do a lot of communicating with employees. The primary focus of this communication should be downward—specifically, explaining the rationale for changes that will have to be made. But there should also be upward communication to give employees an opportunity to express their fears and frustrations and have important questions answered. Remember, management's credibility is not likely to be high. Moreover, rumours will be rampant. This puts a premium on management making every effort to explain clearly the reasons for, and implications of, all significant changes. That is not going to eliminate employee fears, but it will increase the likelihood that management is perceived as honest and trustworthy, which may be the best one can hope for.

During decline, organisations also need to sharpen their focus and clarify strategy. This may mean that unwanted or secondary businesses or undertakings are sold in order for management and workers to concentrate on what is worthwhile salvaging. This implies that it is common for managers to centralise decision making when a serious attack on decline begins. At such times, there is a significant need for the direction generated by strong leadership. This is reinforced by centralised decision making. Motivating and keeping staff focused requires extensive communication, but this does not imply an involvement in decision making.

You may also be thinking, wouldn't decentralisation and an increase in participation be a better solution? After all, participation is often proposed as a powerful vehicle for facilitating change. We argue against participation during decline, especially in tough resource allocation and cutback decisions, because of the evidence that people cannot be rational contributors to their own demise.[36] The self-interest of participants is just too great to provide benefits that exceed the costs. Participation and decentralisation should be reintroduced only when it is clear to everyone that the decline has stabilised.

When cuts are made in personnel, there is an opportunity for management to consolidate and redesign jobs. If the decline appears to have been arrested and fears of further layoffs have subsided, the redesign of jobs to make them more challenging and motivating can turn a problem—eliminating functions and reassigning workloads—into an opportunity. For example, if the variety of work activities is expanded and people are allowed to do complete jobs, employees can find their new assignments offering a greater diversity of activities and develop a greater identification with their work.

Our final suggestion for managing organisational decline is for management to look for innovative ways to deal with the problems inherent in cutbacks. Some organisations, for example, have offered attractive incentives to encourage employees to take early retirement; have provided outplacement services to laid-off employees; and have set others up as contractors or suppliers to the organisation.

All of the above actions indicate that strong leadership is necessary if an organisation is to stop and reverse the decline process. The leader provides a focus for action and generates new ideas and courses of action. Leadership at this time may be even easier than in an organisation experiencing expansion. During decline, organisational members actively look to those in a leadership position for guidance and even hope. In times other than decline, the leaders may have difficulty getting those in the organisation to listen to them.

Summary

Growth and decline—the two most significant stages in the organisation's life cycle—create distinctly different problems and opportunities for managers.

The organisational theory literature has had a growth bias. 'Bigger is better' is consistent with that bias. So too are the beliefs that growth increases the likelihood of survival, is synonymous with effectiveness and represents power. This bias can be seen in Greiner's model of organisational growth. In this model, an organisation's evolution is characterised by phases of prolonged and calm growth, followed by periods of internal turmoil. Hanks' model of growth for high-technology firms does recognise that growth is not an inevitable outcome. It is only when firms start to expand beyond the start-up and early growth stage that organisational matters begin to be of importance for survival.

Managing organisational decline is not merely reversing what was done during growth. There is a lag that typifies the rate of change in structure during prolonged decline that is not evident in growth. This lag causes the level of structure to be greater in the same organisation for a given size during decline than during growth. In turn, this projects into a larger administrative component during decline; the increased importance of the power-control perspective in explaining structure; and the tendency for management to first ignore decline, then to treat it as an aberration and to respond appropriately only after some delay.

In decline, managers are likely to confront higher levels of conflict, increased politicking, stronger resistance to change, loss of credibility, changes in workforce composition, higher levels of voluntary turnover and decaying employee motivation. Suggestions for managing decline include clarifying the organisation's strategy, increasing communication, centralising decision making, redesigning jobs and developing innovative approaches to cutbacks.

For review and discussion

1. Why do Australian values favour growth?
2. How does growth increase survival?
3. How can growth be conceived as power?
4. In Greiner's model, what crisis does creativity create? Delegation? Coordination?
5. Discuss the applicability of Hanks' growth model to those organisations in other than high-tech industries.

6 Compare organisational decline and downsizing.
7 Describe how organisational decline can be interpreted as a reduction in organisational effectiveness.
8 Is decline more likely to occur in public-sector organisations than in business firms? Explain.
9 'Decline doesn't reduce slack; it increases it! In decline, organisations have more personnel and physical resources than they need.' Do you agree or disagree? Discuss.
10 How does the administrative component in decline differ from that in growth?
11 Describe how management typically responds to decline.
12 Why might a manager prefer to work in a growing organisation than in one that is in decline?
13 What positive outcomes, if any, might retrenchment provide for an organisation?
14 What solutions, other than those mentioned in this chapter, might management implement to manage decline better?
15 Contrast the role of the imperatives in determining an organisation's structure (discussed in Chapters 4–8) during growth and during decline.

CASE FOR CLASS DISCUSSION

General Motors—the struggles of an American icon

Companies don't come much bigger than General Motors of the US, the owner of Holden amongst many other brands. Emerging as one of America's industrial icons in the 1930s, General Motors (GM) employs over 500 000 people and is the world's largest car maker. It is also close to filing for bankruptcy. How did GM get into this position?

Like all old established companies, GM has to battle its history. The 1960s and 1970s were good times for GM, with brands such as Chevrolet, Buick, Oldsmobile and Cadillac dominating the US market and producing fat profits. But the seeds of GM's problems were sown at that time. It was slow to respond to rising petrol prices and the inroads of the smaller Japanese cars. With so much productive capacity in place for large cars, and with the mindset of managers fixated on existing ways of doing things, GM let companies such as Toyota establish a strong foothold in the US market.

The unions, mainly the United Auto Workers Union (UAW), managed at this time to extract from GM highly beneficial wage and condition agreements, including a generous company-funded pension plan, full health cover, and guarantees against redundancy. They also managed to obtain a veto on plant closures and a large measure of control over how work was to be carried out. One of the reasons facilitating union strength was the heavy concentration of GM plants in Michigan and other northern industrial US states.

As the 1980s progressed it was clear that GM had significant problems. Its costs of production were high, rates of innovation were low, and its key brands were tired and mainly associated with an ageing customer base. It first tried to tackle the inertia generated by GM's notorious bureaucracy, typified by its large head office in Detroit. The aim was to speed decision making and to reduce the inward focus of the company. This generally was successful, but whilst focusing on this problem, new product development slowed so that its cars started to develop a dated feel. And problems started to emerge from other quarters.

Toyota and other manufacturers had built new green-fields factories in southern states, such as Kentucky, with far more productive labour contracts than those at GM. GM began to suffer from overcapacity as it could not close its northern state factories. The UAW was proving uncooperative in any of its dealings with GM. By the end of the 1990s the only money GM was making was on its SUVs and pick-up trucks, and from its finance arm. As the new decade progressed and petrol prices rose, the reputation of GM cars as being gas guzzlers further depressed sales and GM products accounted for barely 25% of the US market, down from 45% 30 years before. Cars were discounted heavily just to keep factories operating.

By 2005, GM faced the possibility of filing for bankruptcy. The big advantage for GM was that, once this was done, it automatically terminated existing industrial agreements and could shed much of its high-cost labour. But it still would be left with the problem of tired brands, unappealing cars, Japanese competition and the emerging threat of cheap cars from China.

QUESTIONS

1 How has GM's history influenced the problems that it faces?
2 To what extent can management free a company from its historical agreements and traditions? Discuss this in relation to GM's case and another company with which you are familiar.
3 How closely does the GM case conform to Weitzel and Jonsson's model of decline?
4 In contrast to decline, could GM's situation be described as one of failure to handle growth? Discuss.
5 Drawing upon the case, discuss the proposition that decline is inevitable for companies.

FURTHER READING

Larry E. Greiner, 'Evolution and Revolution as Organizations Grow', *Harvard Business Review*, July/August 1972, pp. 37–46.

Steven Hanks, Colin Warson, Eric Jansen & Gaylen Chandler, 'Tightening the Life-Cycle Construct: A Taxonomic Study of Growth Stage Configurations in High-Technology Organizations', *Entrepreneurship Theory and Practice*, 18(2), 1993, pp. 5–29.

Michael T. Hannan & John H. Freeman, 'Internal Politics of Growth and Decline', in Marshall W. Meyer & Associates, eds, *Environments and Organizations*, San Francisco: Jossey-Bass, 1978, pp. 177–99.

Pauline Jas & Chris Skelcher, 'Performance Decline and Turnaround in Public Organisations: A Theoretical and Empirical Analysis', *British Journal of Management*, 16, 2005, pp. 195–210.

Kamel Mellahi & Adrian Wilkinson, 'Organization Failure: A Critique of Recent Research and a Proposed Integrative Framework', *International Journal of Management Review*, 5–6(1), 2002.

William Weitzel & Ellen Jonsson, 'Decline in Organizations: A Literature Integration and Extension', *Administrative Science Quarterly*, March 1989, pp. 91–109.

NOTES

1 James D. Thompson, *Organizations in Action*, New York: McGraw-Hill, 1967, p. 89.
2 'How Mergers Go Wrong', *The Economist*, 22 July 2002, p. 19.
3 Jeffrey Pfeffer, *Organizational Design*, Arlington Heights, IL: AHM Publishing, 1978, p. 114.
4 David A. Whetten, 'Organizational Decline: A Neglected Topic in Organizational Science', *Academy of Management Review*, October 1980, p. 578.
5 William G. Scott, 'The Management of Decline', *Conference Board Record*, June 1976, p. 57.
6 Jeffrey Pfeffer & Gerald R. Salancik, *The External Control of Organizations*, New York: Harper & Row, 1978.
7 'How Mergers Go Wrong', op. cit.
9 Pfeffer, *Organizational Design*, p. 115.

9 Steven Hanks, Colin Warson, Eric Jansen & Gaylen Chandler, 'Tightening the Life-Cycle Construct: A Taxonomic Study of Growth Stage Configurations in High-Technology Organizations', *Entrepreneurship Theory and Practice*, 18(2), 1993, pp. 5–29.

10 David A. Whetten, 'Organizational Growth and Decline Process', in Kim S. Cameron, Robert I. Sutton & David A. Whetton, eds, *Readings in Organizational Decline*, Cambridge, MA: Ballinger Publishing, 1988, p. 36.

11 Larry E. Greiner, 'Evolution and Revolution as Organizations Grow', *Harvard Business Review*, July/August 1972, pp. 37–46.

12 Hanks et al. 'Tightening the Life-Cycle Construct: A Taxonomic Study of Growth Stage Configurations in High-Technology Organizations'.

13 David Terpstra & Philip Olsen, 'Entrepreneurial Start-Up and Growth: A Classification of Problems', *Entrepreneurship Theory and Practice*, 17(3), 1993, pp. 5–20.

14 See, for instance, William Weitzel & Ellen Jonsson, 'Decline in Organizations: A Literature Integration and Extension', *Administrative Science Quarterly*, March 1989, pp. 91–109.

15 A good classification of the contributors to decline is given in Kamel Mellahi & Adrian Wilkinson, 'Organization Failure: A Critique of Recent Research and a Proposed Integrative Framework', *International Journal of Management Review*, 5–6(1), 2002.

16 Ibid.

17 Kenneth Labich, 'Why Companies Fail', *Fortune*, 14 November 1994, pp. 152–68.

18 John Edwards, William McKinley & Gyewan Moon, 'The Enactment of Organizational Decline: The Self-Fulfilling Prophecy', *International Journal of Organizational Analysis*, 10(1), 2002, pp. 55–75.

19 Mellahi & Wilkinson, 'Organization Failure: A Critique of Recent Research and a Proposed Integrative Framework'.

20 This section is drawn from Vincent L. Baker, '111 Traps in Diagnosing Organization Failure', *Journal of Business Strategy*, 26(2), 2005, pp. 44–50.

21 Whetten, 'Organizational Decline: A Neglected Topic in Organizational Science', p. 579.

22 Charles H. Levine, 'More on Cutback Management: Hard Questions for Hard Times', *Public Administration Review*, March/April 1979, pp. 179–83.

23 Jeffrey D. Ford, 'The Occurrence of Structural Hysteresis in Declining Organizations', *Academy of Management Review*, October 1980, pp. 589–98.

24 ibid., p. 592.

25 John H. Freeman & Michael T. Hannan, 'Growth and Decline Processes in Organizations', *American Sociological Review*, April 1975, pp. 215–83; William McKinley, 'Complexity and Administrative Intensity: The Case of Declining Organizations', *Administrative Science Quarterly*, March 1987, pp. 87–105; and John R. Montanari & Philip J. Adelman, 'The Administrative Component of Organizations and the Ratchet Effect: A Critique of Cross-Sectional Studies', *Journal of Management Studies*, March 1987, pp. 113–23.

26 Jeffrey D. Ford, 'The Administrative Component in Growing and Declining Organizations: A Longitudinal Analysis', *Academy of Management Journal*, December 1980, pp. 615–30.

27 Michael T. Hannan & John H. Freeman, 'Internal Politics of Growth and Decline', in Marshall W. Meyer & Associates, eds, *Environments and Organizations*, San Francisco: Jossey-Bass, 1978, pp. 177–99.

28 William Weitzel & Ellen Jonsson, 'Decline in Organisations: A Literature Integration and Extension', *Administrative Science Quarterly*, 34(1), March 1989, pp. 91–186.

29 William Starbuck & Bo Hedberg, 'Saving an Organization from Stagnating Environments', in H. Thorelli, ed., *Strategy+Structure=Performance*, Bloomington, IN: Indiana University Press, 1977.

30 Hannan & Freeman, 'Internal Politics of Growth and Decline'.

31 ibid.

32 John Gardner, 'Organizational Survival: Overcoming Mind-Forged Manacles', in John F. Veiga & John N. Yanouzas, eds, *The Dynamics of Organization Theory: Gaining a Macro Perspective*, St Paul, MN: West Publishing, 1979, pp. 28–31.

33 B.L.T. Hedberg, Paul C. Nystrom & William H. Starbuck, 'Camping on Seesaws: Prescriptions for a Self-designing Organization', *Administrative Science Quarterly*, March 1976, pp. 41–65.
34 Whetten, 'Organizational Decline: A Neglected Topic in Organizational Science', p. 582.
35 These suggestions are derived from Ronald Lippitt & Gordon Lippitt, 'Humane Downsizing: Organizational Renewal versus Organizational Depression', *S.A.M. Advanced Management Journal*, Summer 1984, pp. 15–21; Lee Tom Perry, 'Least-Cost Alternatives to Layoffs in Declining Industries', *Organizational Dynamics*, Spring 1986, pp. 48–61; Cynthia Hardy, 'Strategies for Retrenchment: Reconciling Individual and Organizational Needs', *Canadian Journal of Administrative Sciences*, December 1986, pp. 275–89; and George E.L. Barbee, 'Downsizing with Dignity: Easing the Pain of Employee Layoffs', *Business and Society Review*, Spring 1987, pp. 31–4.
36 Charles H. Levine, 'More on Cutback Management: Hard Questions for Hard Times'.

CHAPTER 15

Innovation, knowledge management and organisational learning

At the end of this chapter you should be able to:

- discuss the importance of innovation and knowledge management to organisations
- identify the ways in which innovation may be promoted within organisations
- understand the common forms of knowledge-management techniques
- understand the importance of organisational learning
- describe the organisational learning cycle
- understand how the organisational learning cycle may be broken.

Introduction

How General Electric retains its competitiveness

Few companies are admired as much as General Electric, often known by its initials, GE. For almost 30 years its sales and profits have grown consistently faster than the market and it is showing little sign of slowing. GE has achieved this whilst having a wide spread of businesses, unfashionable in today's world of focus and adherence to core competencies. GE's products range from aircraft engines, railway locomotives and medical diagnostic equipment through to financial services and electrical generation equipment. All told, there are over 350 different business segments.

It would be very easy for GE to lose its leading edge across its product range if it did not make the most productive use of its resources. Traditionally this would have meant concentrating on tangible management issues such as machine utilisation rates, inventory levels, tight financial management and close control of the supply chain. But there is another resource which GE has harnessed and that is knowledge. GE employs some of the brightest engineers, scientists and commercial people around, but if only part of what they know stays in their head, then a valuable resource is not being used. In the competitive world in which GE operates loss of innovative edge would have serious consequences for its business.

So how does GE promote the use of knowledge? The challenge of harnessing and using knowledge has been placed into greater focus by the Internet, which enables greater storage, retrieval and dissemination of information than was ever possible to previous generations of workers. So the use of intranets (internets within the company) based upon communities of practice is part of the solution that GE has adopted. They come with the usual Internet features of chat rooms, links and postings by members. Training modules are also placed on the Web. In addition, video-conferences are held frequently during which best practices are shared and top executives communicate with employees.

But the Internet itself is a limited tool if staff lack the interest, motivation and incentive to use it appropriately. The organisational structure must also support the free flow of ideas and the implementation of innovations which emerge from them. In other words, there must be a culture and structure which supports knowledge management.

GE promotes this culture through intensive socialisation and the movement of personnel throughout the company. Every employee is indoctrinated with the core GE values within three months of hiring. Key people within the organisation are connected with each other. GE runs a company university at Crotonville, which promotes networking throughout the organisation. In addition, there is a high degree of movement of managers between the business units, which encourages the spread of knowledge around the company. All of these actions have contributed to GE being a leader in all of the many areas in which it operates.

The 1980s began a period of sustained change for all organisations. Levels of competition increased as changes in government policy and the rise of globalisation began to take effect. Moreover, major innovations in information processing began to fundamentally change the way that organisations were managed. One response by business was to reduce costs; it was difficult to raise prices above those of competitors or lower priced imports. Another was to differentiate products in some way in order to make them more attractive to consumers, and thus enable higher prices to be charged. High rates of innovation were linked with the emerging information technology sector—loosely known as high tech. Information technology was also progressing beyond its application to routine tasks and IT industry leaders were contemplating the next big industry leap towards computers being linked to each other and also assisting with the conceptual work of the organisation.

Another factor affecting competitiveness was increasing globalisation. Foreign competitors became an ever-present feature of the market. But globalisation also presented companies with an opportunity to enter new overseas markets either through exporting or by setting up subsidiaries. Either way, they were coping with a new set of risks and developing new management techniques. Even the not-for-profit sector, such as government departments and charities, found that they needed to be more proactive in dealing with their environment and more innovative in responding to problems.

Service industries were also expanding and many of these differed fundamentally from the traditional businesses which dominated most of the 20th century. Many, such as consultancies and professional practices of various kinds, required employees with high levels of education and an ability to solve complex and unique problems. Such people could not be managed in the same way as an industrial workforce staffing a production line. Further, their knowledge base needed to be kept up to date and continuously expanded.

Other organisational problems were becoming apparent. Many large corporations, such as IBM and DuPont, ran significant research facilities as part of their business. But their record of turning inventions into new products was poor. For instance, IBM operated a world-leading research laboratory but it was constantly beaten to market by new start-up companies which seemed to outmanoeuvre it at every turn—Microsoft being the most obvious example. Time was another area in which many companies found they were losing out to competitors. In General Motors, for instance, it took five years to bring a new car from concept to production; at Toyota it was two years and falling.

Highlighting these problems was the example of a subset of Japanese companies which were super-competitive. These companies—Toyota, Sony, Panasonic—appeared to be managed in a fundamentally different way from their Western competitors. In particular, they managed to capture the ideas and knowledge of their workforce and then apply them in ways which increased their competitiveness.

These developments drew the attention of managers, consultants and scholars to the need to improve the capabilities of organisations, not just the ability to produce more of the same, but to raise 'mental capacities' so that organisations could compete more effectively in a range of areas simultaneously. It was recognised that more could be done to draw upon the ideas and capabilities of the various parts of the organisation and combine them in ways which would produce innovative solutions to problems.

This quest, and the research which emerged from it, has led to the emergence of the three topics which are the feature of this chapter—*organisational innovation*, *organisational knowledge* and *organisational learning*. These are discussed in the same chapter as they are interrelated concepts. But first, a definition of each!

Definitions

organisational innovation a process by which a new and significantly improved good, service, product or practice, which is intended to be useful, is introduced

Organisational innovation is a process by which a new and significantly improved good, service, product or practice, which is intended to be useful, is introduced. The definition highlights that innovation is more than just invention; innovation is the process by which an invention is moved through the various stages of development until it is applied in practice. Its obvious application is in reference to the introduction of new products and changes to existing ones. But organisational innovation has a wider application. It may refer to new ways in which an organisation perceives and responds to problems or the introduction of a major new IT application, a program of organisational change or a revised corporate strategy. There is a distinction between invention and innovation. Invention is thinking of an idea and taking the first steps towards building a prototype or applying the idea in some way. Innovation is the far more complex process of invention combined with development and commercialisation; that is, turning the idea into a marketable product or organisational practice. That innovation requires a high level of cooperation and coordination amongst various parts of an organisation makes it the more complex process.

organisational knowledge the collective knowledge of members of an organisation, which is available for others to access and apply

Organisational knowledge is not easy to define and few have attempted to do so. But the fact that it is an abstract concept does not infer that it does not exist. For our purposes, we will define **organisational knowledge** as the collective knowledge of members of an organisation, which is available for others to access and apply. Scholars have often been fascinated by the challenges and opportunities posed by the interface of the individual and the organisation. And managers have often been frustrated by their inability to access the full capabilities of their workforce to improve competitiveness and profitability. An individual has certain capabilities, but so too does an organisation. One of the reasons that organisations exist is to undertake work which is far more complex and mentally challenging than can be undertaken by an individual acting alone. Building cars and ships are examples. Such tasks require co-ordinated effort and the contribution of the knowledge of many individuals. But individuals who comprise an organisation are also capable of extending their capacities, abilities and knowledge base. This may include undertaking more complex tasks or reducing lead time for new products. So organisational knowledge has two main components—improving the opportunity for individuals to contribute to the organisation and improving the capabilities of the organisation. Organisational knowledge also includes improvement in the ability to interpret and respond to environmental changes and in decision making.

organisational learning the process of improving organisational action through better knowledge and understanding

Organisational learning defies easy definition, which is surprising given that it has been one of the main areas drawing organisation theorists' attention over the past 20 years. It is an abstract concept which is fairly easily understood in general terms, but is difficult to narrow down and be specific about. Organisational learning is a slightly misleading term; it is individuals who learn, not organisations. But the phrase taps into the metaphor of the organisation having human characteristics; as humans learn, so do organisations. Organisational learning comprises elements of learning to adapt to the environment and individual responses, which are collectivised into organisational action. So we will define **organisational learning** as the process of improving organisational action through better knowledge and understanding. Whilst individuals learn from their experience, the structure and management processes of the organisation may prevent this learning being translated into organisational action. So organisational learning implies that the actions of the organisation have been changed in response to past experiences. No change, no learning! The capacity of the organisation to learn has major implications for its ability to adapt to changing environments and technologies. It not only implies that new knowledge must be incorporated into organisational practice, but also that old ways must be recognised as being no longer useful, a process called *unlearning*. The recognition of the redundancy of past practices facilitates new learning.

Each of these important areas will be covered in turn.

Organisational innovation

The bureaucratic form dominates organisation structure. However, it performs best in stable conditions and this can be a problem in an era of changing environments and technologies when innovation is necessary. So in order to better understand the difficulties in promoting organisational innovation, we will start by examining why bureaucracy is linked to low rates of innovation. We will then examine how innovation may be enhanced.

OT CLOSEUP

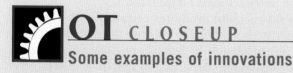

Some examples of innovations

When the word, 'innovation', is applied in common usage, it connotes that we should see the results of the innovation on a shop shelf or in the services we consume. Whilst this is often the case, it may also apply to the internal processes of the firm. The following examples indicate the range of innovations which have been made by companies in recent years.

Australia Post. Faced with a decline in its letter business, Australia Post has moved to make greater use of its extensive branch network. Customers may now pay bills, buy air tickets, transfer money and purchase a wide range of stationery and even mobile phones at their local, generally franchised, post office.

Air New Zealand. As Australians and New Zealanders are amongst the tallest people in the world, Air New Zealand has introduced what it calls Pacific Premium Economy, which has slightly longer leg room than the standard economy seat but costs far less than business class.

Woolworths. Project Refresh has cut up to $1.7 billion from operating costs, mainly by concentrating on supply chain and inventory management.

BankWest. This Perth-based bank, owned by the Bank of Scotland, used the Internet to introduce a high interest rate savings account.

Australian Taxation Office. In order to identify those who avoid paying their share of taxes, the ATO has introduced IT-based anti-avoidance measures. These include computer profiling of taxpayers against others in order to identify those with low tax payments, matching financial transactions with declared income and declared capital gains with property sales.

Ford Australia. In order to gain a share of the SUV market, the company developed the Ford Territory, which was based upon the Ford Falcon, and as a result costs of design and manufacture were kept low.

Brisbane Airport Corporation. As the owners of airports are exempt from local land zoning, the owners of Brisbane airport are developing an extensive commercial, retail and industrial precinct on airport land.

Bureaucracy and innovation

If you asked most people their reaction to the word, 'bureaucracy', chances are their comments would be negative. Inefficient, rule bound, resistant to change and inward looking would probably feature in most responses. But as we saw in Chapter 10, bureaucracy does have its upside. Its actions are predictable, rules contribute to transparency, and it can protect customers and organisational members from capricious behaviour. Of relevance to us in this section is what it is about bureaucracy that makes it difficult to change and resistant to innovation. Once the factors which inhibit innovation have been identified, it is possible to propose structures and management practices which facilitate more adaptive behaviour.

The downsides of bureaucracy have long been studied by researchers.[1] Much of the research and many of the observations are a number of decades old. This research was appropriate for the 1950s and 1960s as most organisations could be considered to be more 'bureaucratic' than they are now. In one sense, large bureaucratic enterprises are a thing of the past. The extensive environmental changes which have occurred over the past 20 years have meant that organisations have either had to adapt or go out of business. Even government agencies such as water supply authorities and providers of administrative services have had to radically change the way they provide services. But many of the factors identified resonate with many organisations at the present time: after all bureaucracy is far from dead.

We have seen that bureaucracy favours and promotes certainty. It has a strict hierarchy of authority in which expertise is assumed to increase the higher placed a manager is. There is a clear-cut division of labour which makes possible a high degree of specialisation. Employees are organised into departments and divisions, largely based upon occupation, and often their primary loyalty is to their department rather than to the organisation.

So how may features such as these lead to attributes which may inhibit innovation? Thompson suggested that as organisations become more complex there is a growing gap between the right to decide, emerging from a manager's position in the hierarchy, and their ability to decide, which depends upon their technical skills.[2] The growing imbalance between the right to decide and the ability to decide creates tensions and exposes insecurities in the system and has serious effects upon management behaviour. Management may develop an exaggerated need for control, a heightened emphasis upon rules and regulations, and resist any change to the status quo.

In bureaucracies, a manager's responsibility almost always exceeds their authority. This limits the ability of decision makers to support projects, provide approval to expend money and push ideas throughout the company. It also leads to the situation where many people can block innovation at various stages but few have the authority to push it through against resistance. Expressed in terms that managers often use, 'Ninety-nine managers can say no but only one can say yes'.

A further problem is that bureaucracies have poor mechanisms for dealing with conflict. Innovation has political consequences and these may be disruptive. Moreover, innovation is often multidisciplinary and occurs at the intersections of departments and disciplines. Many managers view relationships between divisions and departments as win–lose situations: one department's gain must lead to another department's loss. Conflicts can easily arise where this belief prevails.

Information is a source of power and many managers and individuals tend to hoard it. This is anathema to the innovating organisation, which depends upon free flow of information and cooperative effort.

Managers often speak of their organisations as being silos where one part does not communicate well with the other. Silos may refer to either departments or divisions. This problem arises from organisations being structured (that is, forming departments) along disciplinary, product or area lines, with consequent difficulties in getting them to act together. When the tendency to hoard information is combined with rewards that favour stability, it is easy to see how silos emerge. It needs more from management than just talk for silos to be broken down.

Promoting organisational innovation

Although no two organisations will act in the same way, the following are the main means by which innovation can be promoted. These are summarised in Table 15.1.

Endorsement of a supportive culture

Facilitating innovation requires multiple strategies, but all initiatives will fail unless the culture of the organisation reflects appropriate attitudes and values.[3] Such a culture is tolerant of new ideas and risk taking, promotes cross-disciplinary cooperation and open communication, and discourages politicking and defensive behaviour. It stresses the importance of the organisation's goals and values over individual and departmental interests.

Such a culture does not happen naturally, particularly in large organisations; it must be fostered by top management. It takes time to implement; if it is absent, years of patient effort may be required just to move part of the way towards a desired culture. And if it is not continuously supported, the organisation can easily revert to its former bureaucratic ways. Chapter 13 discussed the ways in which culture change may be effected. But for promoting innovation, the emphasis should be on the organisation rather than individual departments. Conferences, social gatherings and functions which bring together disparate elements of the organisation are useful but have limited value if they remain one-off events.

Implementation of appropriate reward systems

Reward systems must also align behaviour with desired outcomes. This is often achieved through company-wide rewards, rather than rewards based upon unit or department performance. Where departmental or divisional rewards are given, it removes the incentive to cooperate with others in the organisation as behaviours are seen to be a win–lose transaction. Companies often operate share-incentive or

TABLE 15.1 Ways of promoting organisational innovation

Promoting a supportive culture. Such a culture is tolerant of ideas and risk taking, promotes cross-disciplinary cooperation and discourages politicking and defensive behaviour.

Providing appropriate rewards. Rewards should be aligned with the desired behaviour and should reward cooperation.

Supporting ideas regardless of their worth. It is important that the organisation is supportive of ideas even though they may not be implemented.

Creating boundary-spanning positions. These positions assist coordination and information flows.

profit-sharing schemes which tend to reduce the tendency for parts of the organisation to look after their own narrow interests.

Appropriate rewards need not be expensive. Managers and workers often value recognition and respect from their peers, and just seeing their ideas being recognised by being implemented is sufficient reward for many.

Tolerance of ideas which are not implemented

Not all innovations are successful and many ideas which look good at the time, or may be an individual's favoured project, for various reasons do not reach the implementation stage.[4] This is an important time for managers as the way in which they handle 'failure' sends a powerful message to the organisation. Organisations that are successful at innovation are generally tolerant of ideas which don't make the implementation stage. It is still possible to recognise effort and to thank those who tried. If the message to workforces is that suggestions that are not implemented will be ignored or not recognised, or worse, those who propose them receive a negative reaction, then others will be discouraged from putting forward ideas and will withdraw to their comfort zone.

Creation of boundary-spanning positions

Innovation often occurs at the intersection of disciplinary areas.[5] It is a convention in organisations that communication flows up and down the organisational structure, but communication which flows across the organisation is important for innovation. In order to overcome blocks to the flow of information across the organisation, boundary-spanning roles are often created. Boundary-spanning positions have the responsibility of gathering and consolidating cross-disciplinary information, promoting communication, sharing ideas and coordinating effort. There are a number of ways of achieving this. The position of project or program manager may be created to facilitate new processes or product development. Or an organisation may appoint a multidisciplinary team, committee or taskforce to work towards a goal. Although they are the bane of many managers, formal meetings often provide a useful forum for reviewing progress, sharing ideas and reviewing bottlenecks.

One of the advantages of formal mechanisms, such as creating a new position, is that top management signals through the appointment that the area of responsibility is important. To be effective, the holder of the position should have clearly defined authority rather than just relying upon persuasive powers and goodwill.

The combination of structural positions and an appropriate culture highlight the dependence of innovation upon information flows. Culture creates the environment upon which flows of information may be based, while the formal positions provide its direction and focus. If neither is present new ideas rarely get beyond the idea stage.

Innovation has become well established in organisational discourse. It is viewed as a central ingredient in an organisation's capacity to introduce new products and services, remain competitive and adapt to the environment. The techniques involved in managing innovation are fairly well understood and have emerged as a fundamental part of good management practice.

Once innovation was mastered, theorists and managers turned to a deeper stage of thinking, namely that of organisational knowledge. And it is to this area of concern that we now turn.

OT CLOSEUP

Knowledge management at McKinsey and Company

McKinsey and Company, a leading management consultancy, was an early adopter of knowledge-management techniques. Famous for its high-level consulting—rumour has it that it will only deal with chief executives—McKinsey's business rides on the way that it accumulates and applies knowledge. Although it only hires the best and brightest from leading business schools, its consultants must maintain professional and technical skills and learn from the experience of others.

In order to promote this, in the early 1980s McKinsey's introduced a knowledge-management program. Given that McKinsey's was a large worldwide consultancy and the Internet did not exist, this was no easy task. It established working groups to develop knowledge in two key areas that were important to its practice: strategy and organisation. It developed company-wide, industry-based client sectors, such as banking and consumer products, which brought together experience from all the different countries and regions which McKinsey's served. It also began hiring some consultants with specialist industry knowledge rather than the usual broad problem-solving skills. In addition it introduced 15 centres of competence in areas such as change management and systems.

But there was a cultural problem which prevented full benefit being derived from the databanks. Most of the knowledge gleaned from various consultancies remained undocumented because of a suspicion held by many consultants that McKinsey's was trying to package ideas into one-size-fits-all applications. As McKinsey's prided itself on the originality of the advice it provided, a standard formula response was seen to be anathema to the reason for its existence.

In 1987, McKinsey launched a more comprehensive knowledge-management project, in which the experience and knowledge accumulated from client work was entered into a common database. In order to overcome cultural resistance, the system was intended to rely heavily upon staff using it, in other words it became a demand–pull model. The system succeeded because the data in it was constantly changing, it was driven by staff and the culture empowered everyone to ask for information.

Since its introduction, the system has been modified in order to take advantage of advances in communication technologies. Each team must appoint an 'historian' to document the work. This is then transferred to a knowledge database that contains a record of the experience of every assignment, including names of team members and client reactions. This database is searchable and accessible by anyone in the company, no matter where they are located. It is being constantly expanded and provides McKinsey and Company with a powerful repository of knowledge, which remains with it, regardless of who leaves the company.

Introducing an appropriate structure

Structuring to facilitate knowledge mainly involves removing barriers to communication and facilitating information sharing.[8] As we saw earlier in the chapter, many traditional structural options inhibit this process. Contemporary management techniques stress the importance of teamwork, and introduce management structures which promote sharing of information rather than hoarding it. These management techniques have a long history in military services but tend to be newer in businesses. Air forces in wartime, for instance, faced with a need to spread knowledge and experience quickly, made the mess room the focal point for airmen who spent much of their time, including their off-duty hours, discussing various aspects of their task. There was an important added incentive: their survival often depended upon drawing upon the knowledge of others.

Sometimes teams form naturally but they are most effective if constantly nurtured. Shared social occasions, dinners, team sports, outdoor exercises and regular meetings are some of the team-maintenance activities often used. Senior and middle management support is also critical for communication lower in the organisation. Sometimes cross-departmental and interdisciplinary communication requires a more formalised response. In this case, as we have seen, an organisation may introduce a position, such as project or program manager, specifically to facilitate communication. Such roles often have as their aim soliciting inputs from a wide variety of organisational members and the feedback and sharing of information.

Many organisations, particularly those providing professional services, have introduced the position of *knowledge manager*. This follows the design dictum that all important tasks should have someone responsible for them. It also signifies that knowledge is important to the organisation and provides a focal point for queries or issues related to knowledge management.

A further advantage of having a person 'responsible' for knowledge arises from its intangibility. Knowledge is not something which may be observed or counted in an organisation. Further, deficiencies in knowledge management take a long time to become apparent. They will not manifest as something that is immediately obvious or that presents a straightforward solution. If cleaners stop work, the workplace will soon become messy, and the cause will be obvious and a solution easy to arrive at. There is no obvious and simple way to determine if firms are not using knowledge to best advantage. We may infer its absence from low rates of product innovation, or slipping market share or profitability. But these problems may not point to appropriate remedial action. The advantage of having a knowledge manager is that the long-term decline associated with the poor use of knowledge may be constantly combated.

What are the attributes of successful knowledge managers? Many are organisational insiders and they are aware of the location of the repositories of knowledge and how harnessing knowledge may make a difference to the organisation. They must be good communicators and have the respect of the staff they are likely to deal with. To be effective they should report to a manager senior in the organisation. The reason for this is partly political: reporting to someone in a senior position signifies the importance of the position to the organisation. Direct access to a senior manager also helps unblock any problems or areas of resistance which may be encountered. You may identify that there is a contradiction between the democratic emphasis of knowledge management and the political nature of the appointment. But on closer inspection, you will see that there is little contradiction. Every manager in an organisation needs a source of power to be effective. This applies both to the exercise of their responsibilities and to their contribution to wider decision making. As the position of knowledge manager is relatively new, senior managers indicate its importance by taking a direct interest in the area. As knowledge management becomes more firmly established, reporting relationships may be reviewed. Most companies that have created the position of knowledge manager are professional consultancies or rely heavily upon spreading knowledge throughout the consultancy for their competitiveness. Most of the literature concentrates upon knowledge management in this type of organisation.

So what are the typical tasks of a knowledge manager? Bear in mind that few organisations actually have such a position and there is no consistency as to what the position is actually called. The role of knowledge manager has no predetermined functions because each organisation, and the challenges it faces, is unique and the knowledge manager must work within this unique environment.

The broadly defined tasks of knowledge management are:[9]

- identification of corporate knowledge and the barriers that prevent its collection and utilisation, including cultural and organisational factors
- creation of infrastructure that facilitates and encourages individual development, group learning and corporate sharing
- introduction of processes to trap and interpret, package and present, and integrate into the work processes and culture the knowledge of the organisation.

Where the role is new three steps are required: preparing the organisation, managing the knowledge assets, and leveraging knowledge.

Given the wide variety of organisations which may appoint knowledge managers, we can only generalise as to how this responsibility may be translated into specific actions. Team building, particularly at the top of the organisation, is at the core of the activity. As the knowledge manager does not work alone, the early stages of the implementation of a knowledge-management program should include a team drawn from important areas of the organisation. This team will know where knowledge resides and the dynamics of how the organisation works and will play a coordinating role in the program's introduction. The knowledge manager keeps the change focused and resists it being hijacked by sectional interests or otherwise neglected. One writer summarises the role of the knowledge manager in the following way:

> They manage the environment which optimises knowledge, encourages information sharing between people, stores codes and makes information available in a way which adds value to an individual's work, benefits the organisation and creates a community of trust and common purpose.[10]

The introduction of the knowledge manager may be viewed as a form of organisational change, and change does not occur without people. Evidence suggests that successful knowledge managers are those who have greater people skills than information technology skills.[11] But part of the knowledge manager's task is to make the maximum use of emerging information technologies which facilitate knowledge sharing.

Making appropriate use of technology

Knowledge may exist in a number of forms in an organisation.[12] The most obvious repository is in employees' heads. But other sources are in electronic form in databanks, in physical form in storage facilities such as filing cabinets, and even in bits of paper on desks. Information technology can provide useful tools to categorise and make this knowledge available. Information technology also links employees so that knowledge may be easily shared. This feature is of particular importance for those who don't work within coffee-drinking or meeting distance.

We are all familiar with the use of computers as a database; information is added to the computer in various fields and folders and we selectively draw upon whichever field, or combination of fields, to suit our purpose. But the computer does not think for itself; it must be told what is wanted from it. As a result, much of the information contained within databanks remains unused. This is part of the problem of turning information into knowledge.

One of the responsibilities of the role of the knowledge manager is to select and introduce appropriate programs to tap into the existing database of the firm. In doing this, the information must be presented in a format which is of use to the person or group to whom it is directed. This process is called *data mining*. You are probably familiar with the way insurance companies use their databanks to determine their pricing. The cost of insuring a motor vehicle, for instance, varies with the age of the driver, where the car is garaged, the type of car and the claim record of the policy-holder. The price of these risks has been determined by mining the data of past claims to appropriately reflect the risk which the insurance company is taking on. Mining the data also enables them to identify accident black spots and times of day when accidents are most likely to happen.

Most organisations have databanks which they can put to similar use. Maintenance records can identify vulnerable equipment; banks can identify their most profitable customers; the on-time running of rail systems may be assessed; and eduction systems may identify the sources of the more successful students and any group which appears to be underperforming.

A further use of information technology is linking people within the organisation. Many IT companies promote software which encourages communication amongst workers as a comprehensive answer to knowledge management. Whilst many claims are marketing spin, the software designers do have a point in that people communicating is important to knowledge management and the application of appropriate communication tools certainly promotes this. Typical proprietary software used in knowledge management is Lotus Notes and Novell's GroupWise. Such software includes email, discussion board and conferencing features. But many large companies, particularly those which are geographically dispersed, promote the use of an *intranet*. An intranet has many of the features of the Internet but is directed at those inside the organisation. Each department, region, occupational speciality or even individual can have their own home page with news, chat rooms, discussion boards, requests for information and so on. Intranets have search engines which enable staff to seek out information or ideas relevant to their problem. Needless to say, access to an intranet is not available to those outside the organisation.

Essentially, knowledge-management technology overcomes time and distance limitations and brings together people, and their ideas, no matter where they may be located. The ideal may be to have staff located close together in order to achieve this, but in many companies this is not possible. An alternative is to bring various groups together for a conference using another form of technology, aircraft. As mentioned earlier, with the decline in the cost of air travel, it has become more common for dispersed staff to meet on a regular basis to share information, swap ideas, and through intensive socialisation remove barriers to communication. Staff who otherwise may have only been in contact by email have a chance to meet face to face. Such conferences have the advantage of removing barriers to communication and facilitating flows of information.

Once an organisation has developed its capacity to manage knowledge, it then faces the difficulty of incorporating the new knowledge within the collective memory of the organisation ready to be drawn upon as required. We call this process organisational learning.

Organisational learning

One of the challenges facing organisations is developing ways to adapt to the external environment. Another is to improve their effectiveness by continuously improving processes by avoiding mistakes and errors of the past. Both of these important responses involve organisations learning from their experiences and incorporating that learning into their corporate memory. So increasing a firm's capacity to learn from past actions will improve an organisation's ability to adapt to the changing environment and thus increase its survival prospects.

Organisational learning has been defined as the process of improving organisational action through better knowledge and understanding.[13] This definition identifies that organisational learning is concerned with the way that an organisation senses changes and signals in its external and internal environment, adapts accordingly, and then incorporates what has been learned from the adaptation within the organisation's learning.

Schools of thought on organisational learning

As organisational learning is a difficult concept, it is not surprising that there is considerable theorising around the topic, but given the abstract nature of much of the theorising, there is a paucity of empirical work in the area. Further, those who study organisational learning do so with different applications in mind. These range from adapting to environmental shocks through to new product development, human resource management, organisational change and marketing, to name just a few. Even though there is a general lack of consensus, it is possible to identify four different schools of thought through which to approach organisational learning. These are the economic school, the developmental school, the managerial school, and the process school (see Table 15.3).[14] We will discuss each of these approaches in turn.

The *economic school* views organisational learning as a tool to promote the efficiency of the organisation. Take, for example, a motor vehicle production line. Through application of continuous improvement techniques, quality circles and technological innovation it is possible to reduce production costs. This is achieved through incremental gains in know-how, which adds to the stock of knowledge of the organisation. Managers often use the phrase, 'moving along the experience curve', to describe this process.

This type of learning has been termed *single loop learning* by Argyris and Schon.[15] Single loop learning is learning that does not alter established practices and procedures of the organisation and leaves the basic strategies of the organisation unchanged. It is the simplest form of organisational learning. The product of this form of learning may be contained in formal rules, regulations, and established practices and procedures, but sometimes problem solving rules may also be enhanced. The challenge for management is to facilitate conditions which contribute to individuals expanding their capacity to learn job-related matters.

TABLE 15.3 Schools of thought on organisational learning

Economic school. Aims at improving existing processes through better use of knowledge and experience.

Developmental school. Studies how organisations learn as they pass from one stage of development to another.

Managerial school. Examines how managerial actions may increase an organisation's capacity to learn.

Process school. Closely links learning to supportive technologies such as information technology.

The *developmental school* links learning to the organisational life cycle. As we discussed in Chapter 1, many organisations pass through a number of predictable stages, ranging from establishment, through growth and maturity, to decline and eventual dissolution. The development school focuses on the significance of each of these stages for organisational learning. As the firm grows and matures, it acquires experience, management depth and more resources for generating new ideas and problem solving. These are termed the firm's dynamic capabilities and logically such capabilities are greater in a large firm with more resources than in a smaller one. Learning occurs as a series of sequential and related steps which makes it difficult to 'leap ahead' of competitors.

A further interpretation of the developmental school is the idea that the organisation moves towards a goal or end state. In contrast to the life-cycle model, there is no fixed path to follow to achieve the end state (in other words, it is not path dependent), but in the process of moving towards the goal, experience and learning accumulate. As there are different goals and end states, no two organisations will follow the same learning path. Past behaviour and learning is also seen to influence, and restrict, strategic options available to the organisation. The developmental school tends to reject the idea that learning is closely linked to managerial intervention. Rather it sees it as emerging from the autonomous activities of organisation members as they solve problems associated with life-cycle issues.

This type of higher level learning has been called *double loop learning* by Argyris and Schon.[16] Higher level learning in organisations originates in a less structured environment in which the possibilities are both greater and more creative than for single loop learning. Such learning leads to changes in assumptions, norms, beliefs and theories that members apply in the organisational setting.

As with evolution in biology, learning is considered to proceed through a repetitive and cumulative sequence of variation, selection and retention episodes in a resource scarce environment. Each cycle builds upon, and is constrained by, previous cycles of learning and change. Such learning cycles may take place as an organisation evolves from one stage to another in its development, but they may also take place as a result of generational changes between stages or within a stage during a period of equilibrium.

An unexpected crisis or external shock is often a stimulus to organisational learning as well. Examples of shocks are shortages or steep price increases of key inputs, a major accident which reveals poor safety management techniques, a sudden loss of market share, or an unexpected innovation by a competitor. Such crises may also include the onset of a pandemic, such as bird flu, or a terrorist attack. Circumstances such as these provide the impetus for organisations and their management to question established practices and norms and re-evaluate whether new ways need to be discovered and adopted.

The *managerial school* has emerged from the extensive literature aimed at improving learning by management intervention. It is a process where single loop and double loop learning combine to form what Argyris and Schon call *deutero-learning*.[17] This is a form of learning which acknowledges the role of management in creating the conditions for organisational learning to take place.

The development of the managerial school has greatly accelerated since the 1980s and it reached the height of its popularity with the publication of Peter Senge's *The Fifth Discipline*.[18] From the early 1980s, both public and private sector organisations have come under increasing competitive pressures from deregulation and globalisation. As a result, mechanisms to facilitate change and adaptation, such as organisational learning, have found a wide readership.

The managerial school considers that learning is dependent upon certain conditions or circumstances; left to their own devices, organisations will revert to lower level incremental learning of the economic type or perhaps fail to learn at all. Managers can overcome this tendency towards entropy (winding down) by creating the conditions necessary for higher level learning.

Most writers in this area propose a set of prescriptions for managers to follow. Senge's popular work, for instance, identified five disciplines which must be applied for organisational learning to take place (see OT Closeup). Although the details of the various prescriptions vary, the learning organisation is seen to possess a supportive culture, a shared vision, low power distances between members of the organisation, a team focus and an acceptance that there is mutual benefit in sharing information. Many of these attributes form the basis of successful organisational change programs.

One problem with the managerial school is its tendency to promote a 'one size fits all' solution. This is particularly so of the work of popular management writers. Managers are attracted to the prescriptive nature of the managerial school, with its

OT CLOSEUP

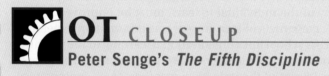

Peter Senge's *The Fifth Discipline*

Most academic research into business follows concepts and ideas which have been introduced by managers to solve problems or address other issues which are of importance to them. Often ideas are subject to disciplined research by academics once they have been popularised. Unusually, the idea of organisational learning originated in academic circles and later became better known to a wider audience of managers as they realised the importance of it to organisational practice.

One of the popularisers of the concept was Peter Senge who wrote *The Fifth Discipline*, a book on organisational learning, which was widely read in the 1990s. He proposed that organisational learning was the key to organisations creating their own future. The five disciplines are:

1 *Systems thinking.* Senge proposes that we should look at the patterns that connect the larger system. Careful attention should be paid as to how different tasks and functions interact. Systems thinking allows patterns of interplay to be revealed, thus identifying important issues.
2 *Personal mastery.* Senge stresses the importance of personal discipline and capacity as a contribution to organisational success. This is linked to clarifying our personal vision, concentrating our energies and focusing on reality.
3 *Shared vision.* This discipline stresses the importance of all organisational members having a clear idea of what the organisation is trying to achieve and where it should be in the future.
4 *Team learning.* Senge claims that the capacity of teams is always greater than that of individuals who make up the team. Tapping into the capacity of teams is achieved through open communication and team-building promotions.
5 *Mental models.* All of us carry mental models of how the world, and our organisation, works. They embody unquestioned assumptions, generalisations, and mental maps that influence how we understand the world. Since how we act is based on our impressions of our surrounding environment, it is important that we understand and reassess our mental models and preconceived assumptions.

Source: Drawn from Peter Senge, *The Fifth Discipline*, New York: Doubleday, 1992.

provision of checklists and targets. Such an approach is called *normative*; that is, it promotes the idea that application of the techniques will provide a certain outcome. However, normative approaches tend to ignore the complexity and subtle nuances common to organisations, which often confound such an approach. They also tend to ignore contingencies such as environment, technology and the size of the organisation. For instance, the learning needs of an organisation producing a single, simple product, such as generating electricity or manufacturing cement, will be different from those of a large multinational, with an extensive product range, operating in diverse environments. One way in which large, complex organisations break their learning needs into manageable components is by focusing on parts of the organisation which have something in common, for example, occupation or product groupings. These parts are called *communities of practice.* This observation leads us to the final approach to organisational learning, which focuses upon the cognitive abilities of organisation members.

The *process school* of organisational learning concentrates upon the centrality of information processing to learning. In this instance, information processing refers to the capacity and capability of the individual to learn, rather than its more common IT association. Individual learning proceeds through the cycle of information acquisition, dissemination, interpretation and memory. If organisational learning is to be enhanced, then the capacity of the individual to learn must be improved. This is achieved by attending to the constructs of learning such as information generation and dissemination. The process school links organisational learning to the cognitive and behavioural capabilities of individual members. The organisation's learning capabilities emerge from the capabilities of the individual members. As a consequence, the capabilities of the individual assume greater importance than in the other schools. Individual capabilities are limited by such behavioural factors as bounded rationality and the tendency to 'satisfice' (see Chapter 9). The process school considers that organisational learning is a replication of the individual learning cycle and that this produces organisational cognition.

Learning is viewed by the process school as a socially constructed phenomenon which is influenced by the quality and nature of social relations within the firm. Management initiatives aimed at promoting learning should concentrate on improving communication between individuals and departments, exposure of individuals to new stimuli and experiences, and the quality of interpersonal interaction. As the way to promote this will vary from organisation to organisation, the process school is not as prescriptive as the management school. As a result, it is more sensitive to individual company and industry differences. Because of its less precise nature, this school is less well known amongst practising managers. But the approach does suggest that a sustained competitive advantage may be obtained by developing unique networks of social relationships and knowledge repositories, which may be difficult to replicate by competitors.

A difficulty which the process school faces is that, in concentrating on the role of the individual in organisational learning, it neglects the importance of higher order learning. It does not automatically follow that, if the capability of the individual to learn is improved, the capacity of the organisation to learn will be increased.

Coexistence of the organisational learning schools

The four schools of organisational learning have been introduced and described as if they were separate entities. But this is a convenience to bring clarity to a diverse

James G. March & Johan P. Olsen, 'The Uncertainty of the Past: Organizational Learning under Ambiguity', *European Journal of Political Research*, 3, 1975, pp. 147–71.

Ken Starkey, Sue Tempest & Alan McKinlay, eds, *How Organizations Learn: Managing the Search for Knowledge*, 2nd edn, London: Thompson, 2004.

NOTES

1 The literature on the influence of bureaucracy is quite voluminous, but see Victor Thompson, *Modern Organizations*, New York: Knopf, 1961.

2 ibid.

3 Michael L. Tushman & Charles A. O'Reilly III, *Winning through Innovation: A Practical Guide to Leading Organizational Change and Renewal*, Boston, Mass.: Harvard Business School Press, 1997; and E.C. Martens & F. Terblanche, 'Building Organizational Culture that Stimulates Creativity and Innovation, *European Journal of Innovation Management*, 6(1), 2003, pp. 64–75.

4 Ken Dovey & Richard White, 'Learning about Learning in Knowledge Intense Organizations', *The Learning Organization*, 12(3), 2005, pp. 246–61.

5 Abdelkader Daghfous, 'Absorptive Capacity and the Implementation of Knowledge-Intensive Best Practices', *S.A.M. Advanced Management Journal*, 69(2), 2004, pp. 21–8.

6 Ikujiro Nonaka & Hirotaka Takeuchi, 'The Knowledge-Creating Company: How Japanese Create the Dynamics of Innovation', New York: Oxford University Press, 1995.

7 There is quite an extensive literature on knowledge management and culture, but see for instance Arun Hariharan, 'Implementing Seven KM Enablers at Bharti', *Knowledge Management Review*, 8(3), 2005, p. 2.

8 Christine Soo, Timothy Divinney, David Midgley & Anne Deering, 'Knowledge Management: Philosophy, Processes and Pitfalls', *California Management Review*, 44(4), 2002, p. 129.

9 Jay Liebowitz, *Knowledge Management Handbook*, Boca Raton, Fl: CNC Press, 1999; and Angela Abel & Nigel Oxbrow, *Competing with Knowledge: The Information Professional in the Knowledge Management Age*, London: Library Association, 2001.

10 ibid.

11 Abel & Oxbrow, *Competing with Knowledge: The Information Professional in the Knowledge Management Age.*

12 There are numerous publications in which IT is linked to organisational knowledge. See, for instance, Elias Awad & Hassan Ghazari, *Knowledge Management*, Upper Saddle River, NJ: Pearson Education, 2001.

13 C.M. Fiol & M.A. Lyles, 'Organizational Learning', *Academy of Management Review*, 10(4), 1985, pp. 803–13.

14 Simon Bell, Gregory Whitwell & Bryan Lukas, 'Schools of Thought in Organizational Learning', *Academy of Marketing Science Journal*, 30(1), 2002, pp. 70–86.

15 Chris Argyris & Donald Schon, *Organizational Learning: A Theory of Action Perspective*, Reading, Mass.: Addison Wesley, 1978.

16 ibid.

17 ibid.

18 Peter Senge, *The Fifth Discipline: The Art and Practice of the Learning Organization*, New York: Doubleday, 1992.

19 James G. March & Johan P. Olsen, 'The Uncertainty of the Past: Organizational Learning under Ambiguity', *European Journal of Political Research*, 3, 1975, pp. 147–71.

CHAPTER 16

Gender and organisations

After reading this chapter you should be able to:

- explain why gender in organisations is a widely debated and important topic
- describe how workforces become gender segmented
- identify the main barriers to women's promotion
- examine the main schools of feminist thought in relation to organisations
- describe feminist research methodologies
- identify the characteristics of masculine and feminine management
- identify the characteristics of equal opportunity programs
- evaluate whether organisations can become gender free.

Introduction

Women and the law

The professions are an area where the experiences of men and women are often in stark contrast.[1] In particular, the legal profession, with its hierarchical structure leading to judicial appointment, is one which draws considerable commentary. This is for two reasons. The first is the glaring lack of women at the top of the profession: partners in top law firms, senior barristers and judges. The second is the fact that the law is not just about numbers or inert objects; its practice, and the decisions made by leading practitioners, have a significant influence on the nature of the society we live in.

So why does women and legal practice present such a conundrum? The most obvious reason is the disparity between the numbers of women studying law and those who reach the peak of the profession. Over 50% of law students are female, but female representation in the judiciary rarely reaches 15%. Similarly, only about 15% of top barristers are women. Only a small proportion of female solicitors reach partnership in the top law firms. Women also tend to be involved in shorter cases and those involving family and criminal law.

Various reasons have been proffered for this situation. The demands of the law can be grindingly hard, making it difficult for women involved with raising families. Offices rarely close at 5.00 pm and law firms' lights burn late into the night. But that is not the only reason that has been suggested for the disparity. The masculine social networks, with drinking rituals and football-tipping competitions, have also come in for criticism for alienating women. However, research has not identified clear reasons for the lesser representation of women in top positions in the law, and indeed in any other profession or organisation, with the exception of women's role in child rearing.

The experiences of women in the legal profession form part of the wider study of gender in organisations. However, the bulk of research has concentrated upon women in management, and often when we speak of gender, this is the common conception which comes to mind. It is this topic on which this chapter is based.

Take a look at most organisations, and chances are that the board of directors, the managing director and most of the senior management will be male. The more senior the management, the fewer the number of women you are likely to see. Look at the studies quoted in this book, and most of them, with the notable exception of Woodward's studies quoted in Chapter 7, have been undertaken by men. Not surprisingly, you may be left with the impression that men have both defined and operationalised management and the way organisations are structured, and that they have done so in a way that has promoted male interests. In the process, this has excluded the participation of women.

The impact of gender on the way organisations are structured and managed forms the subject of this chapter. We have called it 'Gender and organisations', although it draws primarily on studies concerning women. In part, this is because most of the literature on gender in organisations exists in the feminist literature, and women have largely defined the nature and content of gender studies. The implications are that existing organisational knowledge, as it has been largely male dominated and practised, reflects the male position. There have been many studies and theoretical writings about women in organisations. Few have men as their main source of inquiry.[2]

Most studies regarding women's participation in the workforce have concentrated on their absence from managerial and other positions of influence. In this area the statistics are quite clear: the higher the managerial position, the fewer women are to be found. In a recent Australian study it was found that 71% of supervisors were women, but women comprised only 13.7% of junior managers, 14% of middle managers and 1.3% of senior managers.[3] Notwithstanding legislative provisions and equal employment programs, this situation, according to some studies, is not changing. It is not as if women do not have the educational background for higher levels of responsibilities: in 1996, of those enrolled at universities, 53% were women.

But first we need a few definitions and explanations. **Sex** is a biological concept, which refers to whether we are male or female. **Gender** is a broader concept which, although including sex, addresses the various actions and roles of men and women in organisations and in society generally. It includes the different life experiences of men and women in terms of social conditioning, family roles and community expectations, and the thought processes and orientations that can arise from these.

A branch of gender studies is feminism. There is no shortage of opinions as to what feminism is and what its impact has been over the past 25 years. It is more difficult, however, to come up with a definition that is acceptable to all parties. However, we shall define **feminism** as an active advocacy of the claims and aspirations of women. As with all social movements, feminism has adherents ranging from strong and politically vocal advocates through to those who espouse sympathy, but little else. Feminism also has a negative image among some sections of the population, women included. But what is common to all interpretations of feminism is a promotion of the rights and interests of women. These rights and interests extend to all aspects of modern life, from political decision making to equal employment opportunity. A close reading of our definition identifies that you do not have to be a woman to be a feminist, although of course feminism is widely regarded as an exclusively female orientation. There are many men who adopt attitudes that are feminist in nature, just as there are many women who reject them.

sex a biological concept, which refers to whether we are male or female

gender a concept which addresses the various actions and roles of men and women in organisations and in society generally

feminism an active advocacy of the claims and aspirations of women

In keeping with the theme of this book, we will look at feminism as it applies to organisations. The literature on feminism has grown extensively over the past 25 years, with only part of it being relevant to organisation theory. In this chapter, we address two streams of feminist literature. The first is the feminist attack on rational scientific inquiry and methodology. And the second is the position that considers organisations having been developed and run as a patriarchy which marginalises female participation.

It is difficult to isolate the organisational theory aspect of organisations from that of organisational behaviour. After all, all organisational life is behavioural life. As with the chapter on culture, we will cross the boundaries between organisational behaviour and organisation theory in order to better understand the subject.

Why should we be concerned with gender and organisations?

The types of organisations discussed in this book have a central part to play both in the economy and in shaping society. Not only do they perform the essential functions

OT CLOSEUP

Masculinities in organisations

It might not be apparent from reading the literature on gender but there are actually two genders, one female and one male. Feminists have been highly successful politically in publicising their claims and having supporting legislation passed. But statistics still show continuing inequality of outcomes within organisations. Although they join organisations in equal numbers to men, their progression up the management ladder is slower. In particular, they remain stubbornly under-represented in the executive suite. But on a more mundane level, the gender segmentation of the workforce is obvious from everyday experience. Men are giving up becoming educators in droves, with teaching becoming an increasingly feminised profession. Similar outcomes can be seen in the health industry, with men rarely seen in nursing and allied health occupations. Welfare positions such as social work are almost exclusively female.

Why do we see such segmentation? This has been the subject of considerable theorising and research, but a valuable insight may be provided by studying masculinities—in other words, what defines and motivates men as a gender. This is not a new area of research, and increasing attention is being paid to it. One of Australia's leading researchers on masculinities is Professor Amanda Sinclair of the University of Melbourne. She notes that men are often not comfortable talking about themselves and other men but yet their experiences are crucial to understanding organisational life. She considers that this may be because the male management experience is considered the norm, and hence not worthy of separate consideration. Men regard most management theory as being deducted from the research of men and deserving of no special male focus. This is compounded by the fact that men in dominant positions have generally not thought of themselves as a category or identity group; gender is something women have and race and culture something non-whites and immigrants have. Men in prominent positions can also be defensive, bearing the brunt of criticism ranging from being a 'suit', being white, being male, being senior and running exploitative corporations.

Not discussing masculinities leaves much of organisational life opaque, inaccessible and beyond negotiation and change. It also means that we can revert to familiar stereotypes such as 'the glass ceiling' and 'the pipeline' to understand what is going on. To contribute to greater understanding, Sinclair has identified three key areas that are revealing of masculinities in organisations. These are the role of heroic leadership, men's role in the new economy, and teamwork and the exclusion of diversity.

Male managers relate the management task to that of *heroic leadership*. They view management, and leadership, as demonstrating endurance, emotional toughness, self-reliance and a rejection of the feminine. The more endurance and stamina demonstrated as a leader, the more status is accrued to the person as a man. Sinclair sees this as deriving from the frontier mentality of history. She sees success in this culture as providing the attribute of invincibility and almost mythical status. Where professional heroic cultures have been defined by the absence of women, problems of invincibility can arise. Where leadership is defined by the myth of invincibility, alternate viewpoints are not considered and the organisation becomes inflexible. For women to succeed in this culture, they must exhibit traits similar to those of the dominant male culture. Of course, there are other masculine subcultures within organisations, but that of the heroic leader dominates the executive levels.

The *new economy* presents a more complex picture for masculinities. On the one hand, new communication technologies are reducing status, racial and gender barriers to communicating. Alternatively, it is possible to work 24 hours a day, with work overflowing into personal and family life. Travel for work is common and answering emails is expected to be done in the evening and at weekends. Research indicates that under these conditions the emerging masculinities are as excluding of women as traditional work, but they may be more accommodating of racial and cultural diversity. Successful employees are those without a family and for those for whom work and play merge in a desire to be at the technological frontier.

Teamwork is also revealing of masculinities. Although Australian workplaces are diverse, the composition of teams within them is very homogeneous, particularly at the middle and senior levels.

This homogeneity often extends to the way in which teams operate. Team behaviour is limited by the traditional and narrow template of expected behaviours and interactions, including strong leadership, which rewards verbal assertiveness and certainty as evidence of knowledge. This has emerged as part of the heroic and stoic culture of management in Australia. Many teams also function in hierarchical ways, where everyone knows their place and who is boss. As well, teams often recruit members who are like themselves. Sinclair considers that, in this culture, the contributions of women are often marginalised and women's ways of doing things are rarely experienced.

Source: Adapted from Amanda Sinclair, 'Caution: Men at Work', *The Australian Financial Review*, Weekend Review, 5 January 2001, p. 1.

of deciding what and how much to produce, but they are also the main mechanism for distributing income to the various sectors of the population. Most people's income and status are largely derived from the positions they hold in business and government organisations. If a section of society is excluded from holding positions of influence and power, then that section of society is disenfranchised from many of the benefits that society can provide. Also, significant decisions concerning the direction of society are not made by people representative of that society. It is, of course, no secret that women have been underrepresented in positions of formal power in the past. And through being the main carers and nurturers of children as well as the elderly, they have typically had a lower status in the community.

Further, to exclude, either by design or accident, one section of the population from the full range of opportunities available to members of society is an affront to the rights of the individual. Very few members of the workforce rise to senior management or decision-making positions, but it should be open to all members of society to aspire to such positions, or any other occupation, on the basis of their merits. Additionally, by widening the pool of available applicants we make the best use of the talent available, thus improving the chances of putting the best person in the job.

Another reason for taking gender in organisations seriously is that the issue has been highly politicised. Few readers are unaware of the extent to which women's issues have been publicly raised and discussed. None of the issues discussed in this book carries the same political, or emotional, connotations as that of gender. It is hard to imagine parliaments giving their attention to organisational size, technology or culture. But highly skilled lobbying on the part of feminist activists has led to a raft of legislation that obliges organisations to take issues relating to women seriously. Managers are not able to ignore the legislative requirements, or community attitudes and expectations.

What has led to the gender segmentation of the workforce?

Australia has traditionally had one of the most gender-segmented workforces of the industrialised countries.[4] This has applied not only to occupations but also to the dominance of men in management. And, particularly as far as participation in management is concerned, women's inroads seem to be stalling.[5] It is useful to consider how this segmentation came about and why it appears to be perpetuated. In this book we have considered many different points of view about the influence of variables on organisation structure; equally there are debates about why organisations have come to be male dominated. (From the factors we discuss, you can probably make your own evaluation as to their relative influence.)

We also draw a distinction between political and legal equality and the participation of women in business and employment. This distinction highlights the different stages in the progress of the women's movement. Feminists have been active for over 150 years in promoting legislation that treats men and women equally. Many protests in years gone past have been violent and disruptive. Suffragettes, those seeking the vote for women, often used to chain themselves to iron fences in London and throw away the key. One suffragette threw herself under the king's horse in a race at Ascot and was killed. In the early part of the 20th century, the women's suffrage movement dominated political discourse. So the legislation we have seen emerge over the past 25 years promoting equality in the workplace is the result of a long period of feminist activism. In Western countries up to the early part of the 20th century, the women's movement concentrated on the rights of women to own property and to vote. From 1883 in the various Australian colonies, legislation was passed to allow married women the same legal position in relation to property as unmarried women. Prior to this, the property of all married women could be claimed by their husbands. However, divorce and inheritance laws recognised women's dependence and provided income support for them. They were also provided with widows' pensions on the premature death of their husband.

Australia, along with New Zealand, was one of the first countries to give women equal voting rights with men. South Australia was the first colony to allow women the right to vote (called suffrage) in 1894. The other colonies, known as states after federation in 1901, progressively followed, with Victoria being the last to grant female suffrage in 1908. Women were allowed the right to vote in the first federal elections in 1903. By contrast, universal female suffrage was not introduced in the United States until 1920, and not until 1928 in the United Kingdom.

Despite legal and political progress, women saw little move to equality in the employment area. This arose from a combination of factors, both social and institutional. By institutional we mean that the barriers existed in legislation and in accepted organisational custom and practice. Societal expectations were such that women were primarily mothers and keepers of the household. Until 40 years ago, this demanded a fair amount of time. Family sizes were larger than today, leading to the care of children extending over a longer period.[6] Health standards were also poorer.[7] Few of the labour-saving devices we now take for granted existed. Washing machines, vacuum cleaners, refrigerators and motor cars did not reach full-scale commercialisation in Australia until the 1950s. Microwave ovens, take-away food and all-night shopping were well in the future. The better-off households could afford domestic help, but this was mostly provided by other women.

The notion of the 'housewife' and women and domesticity was entrenched in the social structures and expectations of the day. It was reinforced by advertising and the popular press, with many women's magazines promoting the role of the woman as housewife and mother. The etiquette and social standards of the day saw men and women treated differently. Men always raised their hats to women, stood for women in public transport and opened doors for women. As attitudes changed in the 1970s, these actions were interpreted by feminists as being condescending, and they eventually died out.

To complement the caring role of women, men had their specialised tasks in relation to providing income and family support. In many cases, men were seen to be the

chances of promotion. In many cases, money spent on the education of women was considered to be wasted, as their participation in the workforce was expected to be short. These attitudes also led to the expectation of women being submissive and for it to be inappropriate for them to aspire to higher levels of responsibility. Nursing, teaching and secretarial work were the main career paths for women wanting more than domestic service and factory jobs.

Barriers through organisational practices

The reasons for the paucity of women in top management have been a subject of considerable theorising. The statistics are clear, but the reasons behind them are often clouded. Most organisations, particularly large ones, have transparent management selection and promotion processes, and most senior managers genuinely believe that their organisations are free of discrimination. Although the visible impediments that women face in recruitment and promotion have been removed, they are still greatly underrepresented in the highest levels of management. The final hurdle has been called the *glass ceiling*, referring to the fact that the barriers are invisible and difficult to identify, but real nonetheless. A complicating factor in determining the reasons for the paucity of women in senior management is that traditional research techniques seem inadequate to the task. Subtleties in organisational practices and attitudes are difficult to identify and interpret. Actions may be motivated by unconsciously held beliefs, which are complex and puzzling. These subtleties of course are as much applicable to women as to men. It may be that, as one researcher has noted, many managers realise that environments may not be conducive to women, but suppress any moves to do anything about it because the whole issue is too messy.[12] Regardless of these difficulties, there has been sufficient research undertaken to provide a good guide to the particular problems faced by women in male-dominated organisations. Theorists have also been active in generating explanations. So while the research has been seen as confusing, episodic and contradictory, we can at least be confident that many barriers we identify do exist in many organisations.[13] To put this section into perspective, it should be stated that promotion positions in organisations are scarce. Many aspire to such positions, but in large organisations only a tiny proportion of the workforce of either gender reach top management.

Barriers deriving from male management and behaviour standards

As men dominate management, it is not surprising that their preferred management style has come to dominate organisations. Rosabeth Moss Kanter reported a classic study of organisational gender segmentation in 1977, which identified many of the arguments as to why male management is self-perpetuating.[14] The organisation she studied had a bureaucratic approach to management, with a tall hierarchy of many management layers. Female jobs were concentrated in secretarial and lower grade clerical work. She found that the senior management of the company, which was almost exclusively male, tended to reproduce itself because people tended to understand, and trust, people who were most like themselves. As the management team required such trust, the cloning of management from one generation to the next became common, leading to men promoting other men. In other words, managers were reluctant to take a risk in promoting someone who was different from themselves.

Linguistics can also assist us in identifying why male management may become entrenched.[15] Shared language is an important guide to who is included, or excluded,

OT CLOSEUP

Sexual harassment in the workplace

An issue that often surfaces when integrating women into a predominantly male workforce is that of sexual harassment. Although it is not only women who are subject to it, it is the women's movement that has largely defined what constitutes sexual harassment. It is this interpretation that has been incorporated in the *Sex Discrimination Act*. This considers such harassment as unwelcome sexual advances or requests for sexual favours, or engagement in unwelcome conduct of a sexual nature in which a reasonable person having regard to the circumstances would have anticipated that the person harassed would be offended, humiliated or intimidated.

The purposes of the provisions of the Act were laudable, namely the protection of vulnerable women from intimidation in the workplace. Sexual harassment can include personally offensive verbal comments, sexual or smutty jokes, unsolicited letters, obscene phone calls, being followed from work to home, offensive hand or body gestures, provocative posters with sexual connotations, repeated comments or teasing about a person's private life, or stares and leers. It can also include general discussion of sexual matters in the presence of those who may find it offensive.

Whereas there is broad community acceptance that certain behaviours are clearly unacceptable, there is a large grey area that makes it difficult for even a reasonable person to decide whether sexual harassment has taken place. This problem was broadly discussed by a Senate Standing Committee into alleged sexual harassment aboard HMAS *Swan* during its Asian deployment in 1992. The navy started to integrate female sailors into its crews in the early 1990s and there were a number of female sailors on HMAS *Swan* during this deployment. At the conclusion of the voyage a number of serious allegations of sexual assault and harassment were made, which were investigated by various boards of inquiry and finally the Senate Standing Committee. A number of charges were laid and censures made against naval officers, most of which were subsequently withdrawn. There were enormous emotional costs to all involved, including the complainants, a number of whom suffered ill health from the ordeal of repeatedly having to give evidence. Matters were not made easier for them by the wide publicity given to the case in the mass media.

One of the problems for the Senate Standing Committee was determining what actually constituted sexual harassment. It noted that there were a number of problems with the definition and its implementation. First, under the Act, whether sexual harassment had taken place was the subjective judgement of the person being harassed. This put sexual harassment into a different category from all other areas of the law, in that innocent intention was no defence. Given the wide variation among people in society, it is inevitable that different people would interpret the same act by a person in different ways. The committee also found that either sex could experience difficulties in the behaviour of the opposite sex. For instance, if copies of *Penthouse* are offensive in the workplace, are copies of *Cleo* or *Cosmopolitan* also offensive? Persons from different cultures, too, have different interpretations of behaviour, including touching and comforting.

In reviewing the committee's deliberations, Beatrice Faust, a feminist from the University of New South Wales, considers that one of the main problems with EEO and sexual harassment cases is that they accept a very low threshold for an offence to have occurred.[16] By contrast, the prevailing community threshold appears to be much higher. For instance, popular shows and films such as *Sex/Life*, *Basic Instinct*, *Fatal Attraction*, *Sleepless in Seattle* and *Sex and the City* assume that women are more sexually autonomous than EEO legislation acknowledges. She considers that legislation is a top–down remedy which, if it is to succeed, must be met by a bottom–up change in values, attitudes and expectations. Often skilful lobbying by special-interest groups will lead to reform in an area which may result in a disjunction between the law, attitudes and practices.

Stung by the HMAS *Swan* case, the navy realised that it had had handled the integration of women into ship's crews poorly. It realised after the event that it required major organisational change rather than an approach to problems on a piecemeal, ad-hoc basis. The whole culture of the navy needed to be changed, from proper preparation for both men and women for seagoing appointments to changes in navy regulations. The expectations of men and women needed to be more clearly defined and genuine problems, such as the different physiology of men and women, openly addressed rather than assumed away. In a perverse way, the experience of the women on HMAS *Swan* led to improved working conditions for all concerned. Previously the navy was very much a macho environment, which expected too much of people and consistently breached reasonable occupational health, safety and ergonomic limits. Now emphasis is placed on better standards of supervision, ergonomic factors at work and improved avenues for addressing complaints.

from a group. (By language, we are referring to the subtle nuances and word usage that are part and parcel of shared experience and close working relationships.) One of the ways we can identify the sharing of a corporate culture is by the use of language. Kanter found that those in the management group in the organisation she studied spent most of their time in face-to-face communication. Time pressure was such that they had to derive as much as possible from the time spent communicating. This led not only to importance being placed on communication ability, but also to the sharing of a common symbolism, inflection and meaning, which disadvantaged those outside the group. This of course included women.

Such symbolic language in organisations often draws on male interests.[17] For instance, football analogies and references to war are frequently used to make meanings of situations. 'Doing battle', 'no man's land', 'bringing the big guns to bear', 'going head-to-head', 'doing the hard yards' and 'taking your eye off the ball' are often used to describe management problems and responses. The use of words such as 'chairman' and 'foreman' also gives management a masculine flavour.

Needless to say, the linguistics associated with management has been mainly originated and defined by men, so it is not surprising that women might feel intimidated by the communication used in the executive suite. The failure to share the meaning of symbolic language and phraseology is a familiar way to make women feel excluded and marginalised. Feminists would argue that, even though procedures and policies may make an organisation 'facially neutral', in practice factors such as language perpetuate gender segregation in the workplace.[18]

Choice of decoration may also act to make women feel intimidated in the executive suite. Dark tones and colourings, pictures reflecting male interests, furnishings to suit male tastes and a general bonhomie among the men can act to make even the most determined woman feel out of place. Many simply give up trying to achieve high levels of management and settle for a position with a greater comfort zone.

The male approach to management has also been identified as contributing to the paucity of women in management. Later in this chapter we consider in some detail the differences in management styles that have been attributed to men and women. We could summarise this research, however, by identifying that women have been linked to a management style that stresses teamwork, empathy and relationship building. Men, on the other hand, have been identified as emphasising results, placing great importance on control, and stressing the primacy of the task at hand. While these management styles are only generalisations (we do not have to look too hard to find exceptions) they do represent styles that are difficult to practise simultaneously. The male management style that tends to dominate in most organisations presents a challenge to women to adapt. Some women resolve the problem by leaving the organisation rather than fighting, many starting their own businesses where they can practise their preferred management style.

Women have found that the barriers to promotion are lower in those organisations which operate in fast-changing industries and those which are new start-ups.[19] In each of these types of organisations there are fewer entrenched practices and institutional barriers to change, hence promotion decisions are more likely to be made according to ability. But there is a contrary position, and that is that new start-up companies, particularly those in information technology, place heavy and irregular demands upon those associated with them, as does the role of entrepreneur, and this places many women at a disadvantage in such companies.

Politics as a necessary skill for breaking down barriers

A further reason offered for the paucity of women in the executive suite is the subtlety of political skill which is played out at that level.[20] In this context, by political skill we mean the use of influence, connections to the right networks and the manner in which power is exercised. Political skills include social astuteness, interpersonal influence, networking ability and sincerity, and they are becoming increasingly important the higher the position in the organisation. The inability to successfully negotiate this type of politics may inhibit women's careers. Without access to political networks and skills to operate in them, it is difficult to gain the inside information necessary for career positioning and the leveraging of their social capital for success. Glass ceilings, maternal walls, tokenism, exclusion from informal networks and lack of developmental opportunities are some of the barriers which require highly developed political skills to negotiate.

Management selection processes as barriers

It is fair to say that in most large organisations considerable effort has been expended on creating discrimination-free selection and promotion criteria. But women are still underrepresented in promotion positions, particularly in senior management. What causes this situation is difficult to establish, as the subtleties stretch existing research methodologies. Theorists have of course been active in generating explanations, and there has been some research that has provided useful information. From these sources, the following indicate some of the barriers faced by women. Of course, men face many of the barriers as well, but they appear to be more pronounced in the case of female employees.

Uneven allocation of assignments

While selection and promotion criteria may be impartial, the allocation of challenging tasks that may lead to promotion is inequitable.[21] Track record and task accomplishments are important to promotion; candidates can point to these as evidence of capacity. It is also true that assignments that build a strong track record are hard to come by. It is at this level that women appear to be disadvantaged, as they are given fewer stretch assignments. As a result, when the time comes to apply for promotion, they are less able to demonstrate competence. Such tasks might be membership of key committees and taskforces, responsibility for introduction of new technology or management techniques, coordination or liaison roles, and management responsibilities. The importance of these additional tasks is highlighted by the vague and ill-defined nature of management selection criteria. Such phrases as 'demonstrated competence', 'ability to communicate' and 'analytical skills' are tricky to nail down and assess. Selectors usually rely on a candidate being able to demonstrate that he/she is able to do these things through previous assignments.

or how the participation of women in the industry could be increased. We have already noted that many women in senior management positions do not have children. We need further qualitative research to determine what the reasons for this may be.

Are gender-free organisations possible?

Notwithstanding affirmative action and equal opportunity programs, there is still a wide gulf between the roles of men and women in organisational life. Drawing on the research that has been undertaken, and examining the literature, we can build a case both for and against the possibility of organisations becoming gender-free.

We should be clear in our mind about what we mean by the term, 'gender-free'. There are two components that can be identified when considering this issue. The first refers to an organisation as being 'gender-blind': that is, in matters of gender, men and women are considered equally under its policies, procedures and culture, and no weight is placed on the gender of an employee. It would also include special provisions for women by taking into account their child-care role. The second component is statistical equality between men and women at all levels in the organisation. This would see an end to the typical rise in the proportion of men holding senior positions in organisations.[44]

We could raise the following points to support the argument that organisations will become gender-free:

- The active promotion of equal opportunity and affirmative action will inevitably see more women move into the full range of organisational life, including senior management. Their positions as decision makers will ensure that the interests of women are considered and that female approaches to management and organisational structuring are accommodated and given a far more sympathetic hearing in the organisation.
- Modern human resource practices try to avoid the situation where women with children are absent from the workforce for long periods of time after having children. Even where women prefer to stay at home with children, attempts are being made by businesses, such as banks, to keep employees up to date, through providing part-time work for instance. This ensures continuity in their career. The long career breaks that previously put women at a disadvantage in promotion will no longer be a feature of corporate life. And, of course, families are becoming smaller and fewer women are choosing to have children.
- New technologies allow women to compete equally with men in the labour force. For instance, using computers does not require strength or stamina, unlike shovelling coal. And automation and labour-saving devices have removed physical barriers to the employment of women in lower level positions from which they can gain promotion. Also, with less gender segregation in the workforce men and women use the new technology equally, unlike the days when women were often restricted to using typewriters.
- The new management paradigms are closer to those associated with female management styles than with the male management style. Such management behaviours as the promotion of teamwork, empathy, cooperation and a lower emphasis on control will favour women as managers. We will therefore see more women promoted on their skill as managers.
- Organisations reflect societal attitudes, and as societal attitudes change, then organisational practices will change. Women are participating more in education,

and now form over half of university enrolments, as well as performing better at school. As more women move into the higher levels of organisational activity, so gender practices will become less of an issue.
- Many feminists have overstated the case regarding discrimination against women in organisations. They have let their dislike of the business system generally, and in many cases dissatisfaction with male management styles, portray organisations as male-dominated patriarchies intent on perpetuating women's disadvantage. Such perceptions are not supported by the progress of women in organisations, and society, over the past 25 years.
- Organisations are realising that there is much to be gained by having a staff profile similar to their customer base. For instance, women and men both buy cars and use banks, but the senior management of both car manufacturers and banks is heavily male dominated. More women in senior positions would create products better suited to the substantial female clientele.

The case for organisations remaining gendered may be summarised as follows:

- New technological developments are not favouring women. Since the Industrial Revolution in Europe, the nature of technological and scientific progress has been determined by men, and new technology is no different. The Internet is dominated by men;[45] men are shaping the nature of the new technologies, ranging from computers to biotechnology, and thus defining what is classified as progress. In addition, men dominate the older, established technologies based on the car, aircraft, railways and telecommunications. In turn, women are still concentrated in the 'caring' professions such as health, welfare and education. As the dominant determiner of new technology, men define the organisations they create to serve them in their own image.
- Societal attitudes still devalue women's work. The greater the proportion of women in a profession, the lower its status.[46] Infant and primary school teaching indicates this trend. Also, the greater the number of women in a profession or occupation, the lower its pay. Social workers, occupational therapists and psychologists are examples. This devaluation of the attitudes and values of women has organisational implications. As society devalues women's work, so do organisations.
- Organisational size is not really under the control of management. In order to achieve economies of scale, it is not possible to have a small bank, car plant or oil refinery. Where the size of the organisation is determined by the needs of the technological core, rather than being a reasoned decision of management, there is a need for the traditional management skills of control through hierarchies and unemotional, rational, analytical decision-making styles to optimise the performance of the organisation. These are characteristics attributed to male management.
- Because of their nurturing and physical make-up, women and men are equal but different. It is natural that these differences in biology and nurturing would have an impact on the performance and interests of men and women in an organisation. Even where women are reaching the top rung of management, this is typically in human resources and other 'caring' areas of the organisation.
- New organisational forms are acting as a deterrent to women's participation. Writing creative software, for instance, requires a discontinuous work pattern, with intense periods of work over weeks, often with workers not returning home for days on end. There may then be long breaks in the work. This pattern is common in many creative enterprises. Depending on the cooperation from her partner, this

clearly doesn't suit a woman with family responsibilities. Women in similar situations are limited in their freedom to travel and take up overseas postings. Because women are the primary carers in the family, men are far less limited by time constraints. Promotion is therefore more difficult for women to come by.

- There is little evidence that the female management style will find much applicability in the emerging organisational environment. The opening up of the world economy, and the emphasis of governments on competition and microeconomic reform, has created highly competitive organisations and workplaces. In this environment, choosing appropriate strategies and using all the resources in the organisation as productively as possible becomes important. There is little in the feminist literature that claims women are superior in all-round management to men: the feminist position relies on more sympathetic management of people than the management of resources. But the way the physical resources of the organisation are used is of major importance to the profitability of the organisation.
- Despite over two decades of equal employment opportunity, labour markets remain stubbornly segmented.[47] Some, such as school teaching, are developing greater gender inequality rather than less. Women still show disdain for many of the lower level jobs typically undertaken by men. Men are still not moving into areas such as nursing, welfare services and part-time work which are dominated by women and form the major area of workforce growth. As technological change has eliminated many typically 'male' jobs but created new positions in those typically filled by women, men as a gender have been the biggest losers.

Summary

Over the past 25 years, the role of gender in organisational structuring and operation has been the subject of considerable discussion and research. Part of the reason for this is that organisations form the core of power and reward in society, and women felt they were being disadvantaged by being denied equality of access to management and other senior positions. The removal of barriers to women's participation within organisations falls within the liberal feminist point of view. However, other feminist perspectives would view both the structure of business and the way organisations are run as being incapable of serving women's interests. Feminists have also criticised scientific methodology as failing to reveal the full extent of discrimination that occurs in organisations.

The gender segmentation of the workforce has a number of historical origins, but the evidence is that it is persisting beyond what could be expected given affirmative action legislation. Management is still dominated by men. And women still find themselves disadvantaged through their child-caring responsibilities.

Research has failed to reveal a uniquely or dominant female style of management, although a feminine, as opposed to a masculine, approach to management is often referred to in the gender literature. Feminine styles are based on cooperation, empathy and intuition, while masculine styles emphasise control through hierarchical structures and a stress on winning.

Whether an androgynous, or gender-free, way of organising and managing is likely to emerge is not clear. Whereas there is progress in some areas, such as in minimising the absence of women from the workforce because of family responsibilities, there seems to be little progress in others. Management is still dominated by men, and the concept of 'male' and 'female' jobs still influences many members of the workforce.

For review and discussion

1. Define sex, gender and feminism.
2. Why should we be concerned with gender in organisations?
3. Identify and describe three factors that have led to gender segmentation of the workforce.
4. Debate with other members of your group the following proposition: 'The male patriarchy will never let women rise to top management'.
5. How has technological change assisted women's progress in the workforce?
6. Discuss the extent to which you feel that child-rearing and family responsibilities may disadvantage women who seek top management positions.
7. Identify barriers that may exist to the promotion of women in an organisation you are familiar with.
8. Is male and female language likely to be different, and if so how? Give illustrations. How is this likely to affect the roles of each in the workforce?
9. Contrast the approaches of the liberal feminist, radical feminist, psychoanalytic feminist and anti-capitalist feminist theories to women's expectations of access to management positions.
10. Identify the strengths and weaknesses of the feminist approach to research.
11. Build an argument either supporting or rejecting the proposition that men and women manage differently.
12. What are the differences between equal opportunity and affirmative action programs?
13. Argue a case either supporting or rejecting the proposition that affirmative action programs disadvantage men.
14. Why are men reluctant to enter traditionally female occupations?
15. Do you consider that gender-free organisations are possible? Be prepared to discuss your position.

CASE FOR CLASS DISCUSSION

Gender inequality goes underground

A conference on 'Women, Management and Employment Relations' came to the conclusion that gender *inequality* in the workplace hasn't vanished—it's just gone underground. And without a concerted effort to change the fundamentals of organisations, including addressing the culture and behaviour of those in management, little will change that will benefit women. Further, one of the greatest problems was that many believed that the case for gender equality and diversity had already been addressed.

Ann Sherry, a senior Westpac manager, claimed that most male managers '. . . do not see a problem. The frame of reference that our managers bring is the same as for many corporates. They're middle aged, they're male, many went to private schools and they spend their weekends hanging out with each other. If you attack this group with a hectoring, punishing approach it does not work. It actually sends the problem underground. They don't disagree openly, they close their minds and stop participating'. She went on to say that women's achievements are in danger of being mere talk if they are not underpinned by a framework that achieves sustainability, and this means making major cultural changes in organisations.

She claimed that achieving equality is easier when problems are more visible. The discrimination is now subtle, where what appears to be the status quo provides many barriers to women's progression. Work practices and cultural forms that may appear unbiased can create a subtle pattern of systemic disadvantage that blocks all but a few women from career advancement. Too often, sustaining diversity relies on the efforts of individuals, and once they leave there is no legacy in the company to sustain the transformation that is taking place.

Source: Ann Sherry's comments were reported in Catherine Fox, 'Gender Inequality Goes Underground', *The Australian Financial Review*, 24 July 2001, p. 50.

QUESTIONS

1. Why would changing an organisation's culture be necessary for improved equality for women? Identify what you think the barriers to such sustained cultural change would be.
2. What does Ann Sherry mean by the problems of gender inequality going underground?
3. What would be the likely characteristics of an organisation's culture with which women felt comfortable? Would men feel comfortable in this culture? If not, how can the two be reconciled?
4. Discuss whether it is possible to have a caring, supportive organisation in a demanding and unforgiving environment.

FURTHER READING

Marta Calas & Linda Smircich, 'The Women's Point of View: Feminist Approaches to Organisational Studies', in Stewart Clegg, Cynthia Hardy & Walter R. Nord, eds, *Handbook of Organisation Studies*, London: Sage, 1996.

Colleen Chesterman, *Senior Women Executives and the Cultures of Management*, Sydney: Women's Executive Development Program, University of Technology, 2004.

D. Collinson & J. Hearn, *Men as Managers, Managers as Men: Critical Perspectives on Men, Masculinities and Management*, London: Sage, 1996.

Susan Halford & Pauline Leonard, *Gender, Power and Organisations*, Houndmills, Basingstoke: Palgrave, 2001.

Sally Helgeson, *The Female Advantage: Women's Ways of Leadership*, New York: Doubleday, 1990.

Rosabeth Moss Kanter, *Men and Women of the Corporation*, New York: Basic Books, 1977.

Albert Mills & Peta Tancred, eds, *Gendering Organizational Analysis*, Thousand Oaks, CA: Sage, 1992.

Judy Wajcman, 'Desperately Seeking Difference: Is Management Style Gendered?', *British Journal of Industrial Relations*, September 1996, pp. 333–49.

NOTES

1. This section is drawn from an address by Justice Michael Kirby to the Victorian Women's Lawyers Association, 20 August 2001, viewed 24 October 2005, <www.hcourt.gov.au/speeches/kirbyj/kirbyj-vicwomen.htm>.
2. However, see David Collinson & J. Hearn, eds, *Men as Managers, Managers as Men: Critical Perspectives on Men, Masculinities and Managements*, London: Sage, 1996; and Cliff Cheng, ed., *Masculinities in Organizations*, Thousand Oaks, CA: Sage, 1996.
3. Leonie Still, Cecily Guerin & William Chia, 'Women in Management Revisited: Progress, Regression or Status Quo?', in Alexander Kouzmin, Leonie Still & Paul Clarke, eds, *New Directions in Management*, Sydney: McGraw Hill, 1994.

4 See, for instance, Australian Bureau of Statistics, *Labour Force*, cat. no. 6291.0.40.001, Canberra: ABS.
5 Leonie Still, Cecily Guerin & William Chia, 'Women in Management Revisited: Progress, Regression or Status Quo?'.
6 In 1900 the average family consisted of four children.
7 In 1900 the average life expectancy was 55 years of age for women and 52 years of age for men. In 1992 the figures were 80 and 75 respectively.
8 Asbestosis, dust diseases of the lungs and industrial deafness were the three most common. To these were added muscular and skeletal problems arising from labouring and lifting. The average life expectancy of a working-class man up to 1945 was 65 years of age. Women who worked in factories also suffered from many industrial diseases, particularly in the 19th century. Smoking-related illnesses were common. Working-class people of both genders suffered from poor diet.
9 John Gunn, *Challenging Horizons: Qantas 1939–1954*, Brisbane: University of Queensland Press, 1987.
10 Sharon Moore, 'Closing the Gender Gap', *Australian Accountant*, 68(1), 1998, pp. 20–1.
11 Nigel Piercy, David Cravens & Nikala Lane, 'Sales Manager Behaviour Control Strategy and Its Consequences: The Impact of Gender Differences', *Journal of Personal Selling and Sales Management*, 21(1), 2001, pp. 39–49.
12 Stephen Linstead, 'Comment: Gender Blindness or Gender Suppression? A Comment on Fiona Watson's Research Note', *Organization Studies*, 21(1), 2000, pp. 297–303.
13 Peter York, 'The Gender Agenda', *Management Today*, October 1999, pp. 56–63.
14 Rosabeth Moss Kanter, *Men and Women of the Corporation*, New York: Basic Books, 1977.
15 D. Tannen, 'The Power of Talk', *Harvard Business Review*, September/October 1995.
16 Beatrice Faust, 'Sexual Harassment and HMAS Swan: A Case History', *Policy*, Autumn 1995, pp. 44–8.
17 R. Evered, 'The Language of Organizations', in Louis R. Pondy, Peter J. Frost, Gareth Morgan & Thomas C. Dandridge, eds, *Organizational Symbolism*, Greenwich, CT: JAI Press, 1983, pp. 125–43.
18 For women in non-traditional occupations, see Silvia Gherardi & Barbara Poggio, 'Creating and Recreating Gender Order in Organizations', *Journal of World Business*, 36(3), 2001, pp. 245–59.
19 Anna Smith, 'Gender Defender', *Management—Auckland*, 46(4), 1999, pp. 20–2.
20 Pamela Perrewe & Debra Nelson, 'Gender and Career Success: The Facilitative Role of Political Skill', *Organizational Dynamics*, 33(4), 2004, pp. 366–78.
21 Judith Oakley, 'Gender-Based Barriers to Senior Management Positions: Understanding the Scarcity of Female CEOs', *Journal of Business Ethics*, 27(4), 2000, pp. 321–34.
22 Catherine Fox, 'Gender Inequality Goes Underground', *Australian Financial Review*, 24 July 2001, p. 50.
23 ibid.
24 ibid.
25 ibid.
26 See Australian Bureau of Statistics, *Workforce Statistics* (such as cat. nos 4113, 6104 and 6259*)*. In 1995 over three-quarters of jobs created were part-time or casual, and women filled most of these.
27 This section has been drawn from Marta Calas & Linda Smircich, 'The Women's Point of View: Feminist Approaches to Organisational Studies', in Stewart Clegg, Cynthia Hardy & Walter R. Nord, eds, *Handbook of Organisation Studies*, London: Sage, 1996.
28 See Claire Burton, *The Promise and the Price*, Sydney: Allen & Unwin, 1991.
29 Fred Kerlinger, *Foundations of Behavioral Research*, 3rd edn, New York: CBS College Publishing, 1986.
30 This term is commonly used in the feminist literature. But see Jeanne de Bruijn & Eva Cyba, *Gender and Organizations: Changing Perspectives*, Amsterdam: VU University Press, 1994.

31 The points in regard to methodology are drawn from the following sources: Gloris Bowles & Renate Klein, eds, *Theories of Women's Studies*, London: Routledge & Kegan Paul, 1983; Sandra Harding, *Feminism and Methodology*, Indiana: Indiana University Press, 1987; Sandra Harding, *The Science Question in Feminism*, Ithaca, NY: Cornell UP, 1986; Mary Fonow & Judith Cook, eds, *Beyond Methodology*, Indiana: Indiana University Press, 1991; Ruth Bleier, *Feminist Approaches to Science*, New York: Pergamon Press, 1986; Judy Wajcman, *Feminist Confronts Technology*, Cambridge: Polity Press, 1991; and S. Reinharz, *Feminist Methods in Social Research*, Oxford: Oxford University Press, 1992.

32 An early study using participant observation was L. Williams, *What's On the Worker's Mind*?, New York: Charles Scribner & Sons, 1920.

33 See, for example, Huw Beynon, *Working for Ford*, 2nd edn, Harmondsworth: Pelican, 1984; and Brian McVeigh, *Life in a Japanese Women's College*, London: Routledge, 1997.

34 Sally Helgeson, *The Female Advantage: Women's Ways of Leadership*, New York: Doubleday, 1990.

35 Helen Brown, *Women Organising*, London: Routledge, 1992; and Judith Pringle, 'Feminism and Management: Critique and Contribution', in Alexander Kouzmin, Leonie Still & Paul Clarke, eds, *New Directions in Management*, Sydney: McGraw Hill, 1994.

36 See, for instance, Judy Wajcman, 'Desperately Seeking Difference: Is Management Style Gendered?', *British Journal of Industrial Relations*, September 1996, pp. 333–49.

37 de Bruijn & Cyba, *Gender and Organizations: Changing Perspectives*.

38 Eric Trist & K.W. Bamforth, 'Some Social and Psychological Consequences of the Longwall Method of Coal Getting', *Human Relations*, 4, 1951, pp. 3–38.

89 For the Volvo experiments in teams, see J. Matthews, *Tools of Change*, Sydney: Pluto Press, 1989; and J. Pontusson, 'The Politics of New Technology and Job Redesign: A Comparison of Volvo and British Leyland', *Economic and Social Democracy*, 11, 1990, p. 311.

40 A. Sinclair, 'The Tyranny of Teams', *Working Paper No. 4*, Melbourne: Graduate School of Management, University of Melbourne, 1989.

41 Kathy Ferguson, *The Feminist Case Against Bureaucracy*, Philadelphia: Temple University Press, 1984.

42 See the various publications of the Affirmative Action Agency, as well as the relevant legislation.

43 See, for instance, Ferguson, *The Feminist Case Against Bureaucracy*; de Bruijn & Cyba, *Gender and Organizations: Changing Perspectives*; and Rosabeth Moss Kanter, *Men and Women of the Corporation*.

44 For suggestions as to what constitutes gender-free management, see Alice Sargent, *The Androgenous Manager*, New York: Amacom, 1981.

45 Dale Spender, *Nattering on the Net: Women, Power and Cyberspace*, Sydney: Spinifex Press, 1995.

46 de Bruijn & Cyba, *Gender and Organizations: Changing Perspectives*.

47 'Tomorrow's Second Sex', *The Economist*, 28 September 1996, pp. 25–30.

Case studies

1 Coles Myer Limited

2 Mayne—and the perils of getting structure right

3 Organisational change in the navy

4 Shell—from committee to streamlined responsibility

5 Sony—the remaking of an icon, or along, slow decline?

6 Tell your friends about One.Tel

7 The car manufacturer that rules the world—or why 26 million Corollas can't be wrong!

8 'Which Bank' reinvents itself—perhaps!

CASE STUDY 1

Coles Myer Limited

Coles Myer is one of those unhappy companies that make the headlines for all the wrong reasons; for over twenty years it has had to react to the competition, primarily Woolworths, and it has never achieved the financial returns expected of it. It was formed in 1985 by the merger of G.J. Coles, a Melbourne-based downmarket general goods and supermarket retailer, with Myer Limited, an upmarket department store chain which was part of the Melbourne establishment. It created a monster retailer, including Coles supermarkets, Liquorland, Myer and Grace Bros department stores as well as Kmart and Target discount chains. The merger was predicated upon the significant cost savings from sharing services and overheads. This included purchasing, warehousing, information technology, property and so forth. But from the start these benefits failed to materialise. Burdened with poor management, bad strategic decisions and internal conflict, the group had reached an all-time low by 2000. The share price was faltering, lagging behind a resurgent Woolworths and profit had been stagnant for the previous three years. The board realised that it had one more chance to try to get the whole group performing at a satisfactory level or it would have to be broken up and sold, with each part going its separate way.

In September 2001 the board appointed John Fletcher as chief executive. Fletcher was well known to the Australian business community as the man who had done so much to turn Brambles into a successful international company. His first comment on being appointed chief executive was that he had not been inside a supermarket for 25 years, but that did not matter in his job: he was a change agent, and his task was to manage the company in order that it reach its potential.

So what were Fletcher's priorities? Doing something about Coles Myer's share price was the first one. But that would rise only when investors, particularly institutional investors, saw some improvement in the business and felt that the company had got on top of its strategic and structural problems.

His first move was the sale of non-core businesses, such as Red Rooster fast foods and World 4 Kids. These were small businesses by Coles Myer standards, and distracted management from the main task of improving the larger businesses.

Fletcher also made it clear that he wanted to break down the bureaucratic culture at Coles Myer. The inappropriate culture was personified by the headquarters of Myer in the Melbourne suburb of Tooronga. Nicknamed 'Battlestar Galactica', it was built in the early days of the combined group as a statement of purpose, place and status. It had a foyer reminiscent of a garish five-star hotel, vast executive office space, and a floor plan that emphasised status differences rather than the promotion of communication. Fletcher could not move out of the building because of contractual commitments but he made symbolic changes. For instance, he turned the executive office floor into accommodation for 79 staff rather than the four it previously held, and he converted the foyer into something more appropriate for a company that dealt in fast moving/low margin goods.

On the merger of Coles and Myer, several 'silos' were allowed to develop, each with its own ethos, loyalties and culture. None of the silos cooperated with each other and this was exacerbated by the heads of the main business units being new overseas appointments.

Fletcher moved to dismantle the silos to make it a one culture/one company business, something which previous managers had failed to achieve. This was understandable as successfully dismantling silos and moving towards a single culture is one of the most difficult tasks for management. This was made more difficult, and indeed almost impossible, by the diversity of the businesses, each with their own separate customs and practices and customer base.

Trying to define where each business fitted was also a challenge for Fletcher. They each struggled to establish a coherent strategy. Each new manager changed the strategy with the result that the consumer was not clear as to where each store fitted within the retail offering. The changes were so rapid that often the employees and lower level managers were confused. After constant interference from various previous managements, they settled on the brand positioning they had a number of years previously. The role of the supermarkets was fairly obvious. Kmart was confirmed as a deep discounter, Target was to concentrate on apparel and homewares with much of its stock being its own branded goods, and Myer Grace Bros was to operate in the middle and upper market. The roles of Officeworks and Liquorland remained unchanged.

Costs were also to be tackled. In fast moving/low margin goods, such as in supermarkets, costs were critical and Woolworths had a head start in managing its supply chain more effectively. In September 2001 Coles Myer introduced 'Operation Right Now' with the aim of saving up to $150 million in the non-food businesses. This involved optimising the supply chain by removing duplication in purchasing, processes and operational structures. Coordination among the various functions was also to be improved. IT was to be standardised in order to simplify business processes and to enable all computers in the group to be linked with common software. This was to promote coordination of worldwide sourcing and allow common supply-chain and logistics planning.

Clear structures, roles and responsibilities were defined so as the performance of each business unit, and manager, could be assessed. One of the obvious areas for savings appeared to be in purchasing. Myer, Kmart and Target all sell common items, such as shoes and manchester. It seemed logical to create a common buying team for all the stores which can obtain greater discounts from suppliers. But early experimentation showed little promise: Kmart's needs were different from those of Myer. So it was decided that a better outcome could be achieved by improving coordination and communication between buyers for the chains rather than by having a common purchasing function.

Tackling the bureaucracy also meant downsizing. Up to 1000 back-office staff were made redundant in the first wave, and others followed. Fletcher extended his number of direct reports from three to eight. A number of these were hired from outside the company. Coles Myer's senior management is a disparate group of expatriate managers, who run the major businesses, and local managers further down the hierarchy.

Developing a consistent strategy for each of the businesses was important. Coles supermarkets mainly required good tactics; an emphasis on costs, fresh food and an efficient supply chain. But the strategies for the other businesses lacked consistency, often changing from year to year as managers repositioned stores and changed stock levels and product ranges in an attempt to hit upon a successful formula. Consumers became confused and staff disillusioned.

Developing a common culture for such a diverse range of businesses is also fraught with difficulty. Morale can decline. Productivity can fall as people's thoughts turn inward, and new roles must be learned while old ones are unlearned. Good people can resign or inadvertently be sacked, and the clash between the old and new staff—and those who benefit and those who lose—can be extremely disruptive. Fletcher undertook this task while every analyst and reporter watched and assessed his moves.

One of the Coles Myer businesses which has consistently under-performed is the Myer department store chain. Department stores have struggled to find a profitable niche in the modern retailing environment. But notwithstanding this, David Jones managed to establish a competitive edge over Myer. It had a consistent product offering which customers could understand and, subject to the normal ups and downs of consumer spending, was consistently profitable. This was more than could be said for Myer. It struggled to find a market niche and acceptable profitability. On the one hand it consumed a lot of corporate time and effort to try to fix the problem whilst suffering from unfocussed management. On the other it had to compete for capital and management attention with other parts of the group.

By 2006, the twenty-year attempt by Coles Myer to turn the Myer stores into a profitable part of the group was finally abandoned. Myer was put up for sale and was bought by a private equity group for $1.4 billion. The expected economies arising from merging functions were never achieved, senior management was always distracted by the constant need to quickly turn around the chain and internal politics meant that they were always second guessing what senior management was thinking. Further, the culture of running an up-market department store never really fitted into the culture of Coles Myer which was dominated by a mass merchandising mentality.

With Myer disposed of, Fletcher moved towards a more hands-on role in the company. His previous role at Brambles was characterised by careful management of capital. In practice, this meant seeking a return on funds greater than the cost of capital, being clear as to where you are making and losing money, and either fixing businesses or selling them. But it also means identifying areas for growth. Supermarkets have heavy traffic and can be used to sell other products, from financial services to bill paying. Tapping into these new sources of growth is fundamental to the future health of the company. And Coles still has to get its costs as low as Woolworths, which will be a difficult task given Woolworths' advantages in this area. With the Myer distraction now disposed of, and with the extra capital which it brought being able to be deployed, Fletcher can now roll his sleeves up and get involved in hands-on management.

QUESTIONS

1 What is an appropriate method of assessing the effectiveness of Coles Myer? Using the method you have nominated, how effective has Coles Myer been since it was formed?

2 Compare and contrast the changes proposed at Coles Myer with the model of change discussed in Chapter 12.

3 What would be easier to change, culture or business processes? Why?

4 Undertake sufficient research to determine to what extent Coles has achieved its goals since the case was written.

CASE STUDY 2

Mayne—and the perils of getting structure right

Most organisations as they age face problems in adapting to evolving environments. Many face considerable turmoil as they seek to adjust to changes in fashions and technologies and the emergence of energised competitors less burdened by legacy costs and practices. Many don't survive the process. The former Mayne Industries provides a telling example of this process.

Two entrepreneurs, John Mayne and Enoch Nickless, established a parcel delivery company in Melbourne in 1885. In subsequent years, it grew into a nationwide general transport and logistics company which became part of the Melbourne establishment. By the 1970s growth had slowed and, in accordance with the trend in management thinking at the time, the directors decided that growth should be sought by expanding overseas and also by entering industries that seemed to offer greater growth prospects than their existing businesses. The security business, principally armoured cars to move cash, provided one diversification, computer applications and telecommunications another (it was a founding shareholder in Optus when it was established in 1991) and it also had businesses in waste management. In the early 1980s it expanded into health care by purchasing a number of hospitals, health being seen to be a growth area. It is the fortunes of the health operations which forms the major part of this case.

The strategy of diversification brought few benefits to Mayne. It was a company which was divisionalised along product lines—each product grouping formed a division, and as new products were added, new divisions were created. There were structural problems: a centralised bureaucracy attempted to maintain tight control, leading to slow and inappropriate decision making, and duplication of functions led to high costs. Each division had its overseas operations, which had little to do with each other. Top managers struggled to understand the disparate array of businesses. Rather than fully understand them, the temptation was to reduce them to a set of numbers and compare performance year to year. But just as importantly was a strategic problem: each business was too small to achieve economies of scale. In the fast consolidating and globalising world of the 1990s, in order to be profitable, companies had to either have economies of scale or dominate market niches. Conglomerates such as Mayne had to restructure and concentrate on just a few things, but do them well and achieve economies in order to compete with better capitalised and more specialised competitors. Mayne's financial performance during the 1990s reflected these problems; although it had its ups and downs depending upon the economic conditions, the long-term trend in profitability was downwards. Performance generally disappointed, and shareholders were becoming impatient for the always promised up-turn to occur. Mayne's board of directors did what most boards in these circumstances do; it appointed new management. In 2000, the manager they chose was Peter Smedley, one of Australia's turnaround experts, who brought with him, as is usual, a team of like-minded assistants.

Smedley takes the helm

Smedley came with a solid reputation as a turnaround expert. A former Shell executive, he had turned the sleepy Colonial Mutual insurance company into a leader in the finance industry. This was achieved by eliminating waste, rationalising processes and making strategic acquisitions which built scale and broadened the product range. Colonial was finally sold to the Commonwealth Bank in 2000 for over $9 billion. Smedley was also expected to continue with the disposal of non-core businesses, a process which had already started. Most of the overseas operations had gone prior to Smedley's arrival, as had the waste business and Mayne's share of Optus, which was floated in 1998. In future, Mayne was to concentrate on the fragmented health industry. The strategy was to boost returns through acquisition, consolidation and synergies gained through providing a complete set of medical services which fed into each other.

Mayne started to build upon its ownership of hospitals by acquiring general practice clinics, pathology and radiology laboratories, and pharmaceutical distribution firms. The aim was to control the total medical supply chain. GPs in the clinics would use Mayne diagnostic tests, specialists would use Mayne hospitals to operate and patients would consume Mayne-supplied pharmaceuticals. Costs were also tightly controlled. Mayne owned hospitals in all mainland states, and previously they had enjoyed a fair amount of autonomy in how they operated. This now ended as almost all decisions were centralised in the Melbourne head office. Local management were dismissed and new staff hired to implement the new system. Purchase and supply of medical items, such as surgical gloves and consumables, were centrally controlled. What was left of local management had virtually no input into running the hospitals or decision making.

The business plan relied upon integrating a fragmented medical process, centralising management to push costs down and directing one part of the 'supply chain' into the other. As an industrial model, it could certainly be justified, but as part of providing medical services, it proved to be flawed—so flawed that Smedley lost his job and left the company in early 2002 with his reputation tarnished.

Reasons for Smedley's fall from grace

The immediate reason for Smedley's departure was the disastrous fall in profitability arising from doctors refusing to use Mayne's hospitals. It is here that the defect in the Mayne model was to be found. Mayne's customers were not the patients but their doctors, and the doctors went to where they felt they could provide the best service to their patients. Medical specialists, such as surgeons, could not be ordered around like employees in a bureaucracy; they were used to being listened to by the managers at the hospitals where they operated and their needs, such as for specialist materials, being met. Now they were being asked to write a memo to be forwarded to an anonymous head office for consideration. Mayne was also accused of 'cherry picking' patients, by discouraging those who were frail and elderly in favour of younger, healthier patients who could be turned around more quickly. Whilst this accusation was never proved, it was widely reported at the time and further riled the medical profession, always wary about the intersection of profit and medicine.

Mayne also fell out with other health professionals. The culture of the health industry is that the quality of medical care is more important than money. Although everything has its price, doctors prefer to have choices so that they can respond to the individual needs of patients; the Mayne model limited their options to company provided alternatives. Managers with little experience in specialised areas such as pathology were put in charge of pathology laboratories in order to cut costs and organise services along industrial lines, again provoking a backlash from users. And accusations were made that Mayne was moving to replace large numbers of nurses with semi-skilled operatives in order to save money.

Stumbling into the future

The flaws in the business plan indicated that little could be done to save it; making minor modifications and fine tuning the system was not an option. After Smedley's departure, his deputy, Stuart James, took over as CEO. He decentralised hospital administration so that it resembled more its former structure. But the results were only partially satisfactory as the damage to Mayne's reputation had been done. As a result, the hospitals were sold to a combination of management buyout and private equity groups for $900 million. After restoring the relationship with doctors, and making other management improvements, they were in turn sold 18 months later for $1.3 billion.

So what was Mayne to do now? In the early stages of Smedley's tenure, Mayne had purchased a long-established Adelaide-based pharmaceutical company called Faulding. Along with a pharmaceutical business it also ran an injectable drugs division, which offered considerable promise. So it was decided to turn Mayne into a company which specialised in injectable pharmaceuticals of various types, with a concentration on anti-cancer drugs. In building this business a number of successful acquisitions were made and the company showed a promising future provided it was appropriately managed. It had also moved well along the way to having a global reach. It had a high level of risk but the returns had the potential to be impressive.

However, Mayne still had the remnants of its failed domestic health plan: diagnostics and radiology, pharmaceutical distribution and a generic drugs manufacturing operation. This was a low-risk, low-return operation where management of operations were important. It was considered that the management skills and capital profile of each were too dissimilar to operate as one company so, in 2005, Mayne was split in two. The domestic-oriented businesses became Symbion Health and the injectable businesses became Mayne Pharma. The shares in Mayne were split, with shareholders receiving shares in each business. They could then choose which company provided them with returns to suit their needs.

This case was drawn from a number of sources but the main ones were Malcolm Maiden, 'Mayne Strategy to Drive Business Has Backfired, *The Age*, 25 April 2002; and David Wroe & Tom Noble, 'How Diversified Doctors Cost Mayne $1 billion', *The Age*, 27 April 2002.

QUESTIONS

1 Identify and explain the various structural issues raised in the case study.
2 Drawing upon the information in the case, discuss how structure may contribute to the success or failure of an organisation.
3 Discuss whether the case supports or rejects Chandler's argument that strategy follows structure.
4 Compare and contrast Mayne's experience with a model of growth or decline.

CASE STUDY 3

Organisational change in the navy

From the early 1990s, women were able to serve on all vessels of the Royal Australian Navy except submarines. Integrating women is a major change for any organisation, but this particularly posed the navy enormous problems. Virtually all naval vessels were built to be manned by men, or at least one gender. To embark women, ships up to 40 years old had to be modified to provide toilet, ablution and sleeping facilities for both sexes. This led to the women having either better or worse facilities than the rest of the ship's company. It even involved such details as whether to allow women more water for washing their hair.

If the integration of women into a ship's company was to be a long-term success it was imperative that women be seen to be doing a job that was equal to that of male crew members. This was not just a matter of training: there were obvious physiological differences between men and women. Men were stronger in areas such as the shoulders and arms and women were more likely to suffer leg injuries in carrying heavy loads or shifting material.

The navy was the archetypal masculine environment. For hundreds of years, warships had been the preserve of men. Cramped into confined spaces for months on end, jocularity often centred on sexual references and exploits. Bad and lewd language accompanied virtually every conversation. Even tattoos often had a sexual connotation. It was also the natural home of the macho management style. Top-down, directive, tough, uncompromising and often abusive with little show of emotion or compromise, it was justified on the basis that war situations demanded such management behaviour.

Any aggravation festered in the environment of a warship at sea. The same people in a cramped, sometimes non-air-conditioned space, operating 24 hours a day often at the limits of physical endurance, tested the levels of tolerance. Crew members were isolated from home comforts and there was emotional trauma in separation from loved ones. Seasickness was often a problem. Any difference was grasped at as a source for releasing frustration. Introducing women into such an environment was always going to be hard.

Perhaps the greatest potential area of difficulty was that of sexual harassment. The language commonly used on a warship would not be acceptable in a mixed workplace in civilian life. Given the nature of seagoing life, the possibility of unwelcome sexual advances would be high. But within the confined spaces of a warship people often have to brush past one another or otherwise inadvertently come into physical contact. Handling complaints arising from this would be difficult. Another problem was fraternisation (a services codeword for sexual relationships). Harassment was harassment only if it was unwelcome. Fraternisation involved consenting adults. The possibility of fraternisation splitting the crew and creating havoc with morale could not be discounted.

Given all of the above considerations, it was considered that no woman should be allowed at sea without other female members of the ship's company as support. The navy relied on the divisional system to identify and correct any problems. The divisional system basically relies on the hierarchy of command identifying and acting on problems.

It was not as if women were new in the navy. The WRANS (Women's Royal Australian Naval Service) had long been a feature of service life. Women joined the WRANS as a branch of the service but had female officers and were close to their own support network. What was being attempted by the navy was their seamless integration into all branches of the service.

In the early days of women at sea, the navy basically relied on people knowing what was right and doing it. In many cases common sense prevailed and this worked well. In other cases it failed. A woman being transferred between ships at sea almost fell in the water because crew members were reluctant to grab hold of her to steady her. They had been told that any touching of women was tantamount to sexual harassment. Female sailors watched as men did the heavy work, leading to resentment among the men. Sometimes men did not know which way to look as a female sailor let forth with a string of bad language.

During the time it was trying to integrate women into the service the navy had other major problems on its hands. It was introducing a complex quality control system and was grappling with program budgeting. It was faced with a high attrition of skilled staff and had had its funding allocation cut. At the same time, more was expected of it.

In 1992 the events on HMAS *Swan* (briefly described in the OT Closeup in Chapter 16) revealed that the navy's approach to integrating women was flawed. In subsequent inquiries it became clear that events on HMAS *Swan* were the product of a whole range of factors coming together on the one ship. Allegations of sexual harassment intermixed with discontent over the working conditions of female crew members. Standards of supervision and handling of complaints were found wanting. Some women were poorly trained for their job and others inadequately prepared for seagoing life. Men were often confused and unsure of what was acceptable conduct and what was not. In some areas of the ship standards of management were poor, and these happened to be those where women were present. Some of the male officers' language and conversation in the wardroom drew complaints even from male colleagues.

The captain of the ship was censured by the Chief of Naval Staff for the events that occurred on HMAS *Swan*. However, this was later seen to be an exercise of looking for someone to blame in order to send a powerful message to the rest of the service that sexual harassment was not to be tolerated. The Senate Standing Committee inquiring into the affair found that making a scapegoat of someone who had tried to do his best and did not deserve censure was hardly an appropriate message to send to the fleet. Most officers felt that any reasonable person would have acted the same way as the captain, and were relieved that they were not in his shoes. The real problem was the culture of the navy and the management system it supported.

Source: Adapted from 'Sexual Harassment in the Australian Defence Force', *Report of the Senate Standing Committee on Foreign Affairs, Defence and Trade*, AGPS, August 1994.

QUESTION

1 Assume that it is 1990 and you have been appointed by the navy to advise them on how to successfully integrate women into their ships. The first women are to be posted to ships in 1992. It is to be a navy-wide project. Draw up a plan of action identifying the main points you feel need addressing and how you will tackle them. The navy has approximately 12 000 members, of whom 12% are women.

CASE STUDY 4

Shell—from committee to streamlined responsibility

As befitting one of the companies which dominates the oil industry, the familiar red and yellow Shell logo is one of the world's most recognisable commercial symbols. Amongst those who study business, Shell is also well known because of its unusual ownership and management structure, which sets it apart from other companies. Shell was formed in 1907 by the joining of Royal Dutch Petroleum, established in 1883 to exploit the oil potential of The Netherlands East Indies (now Indonesia), and Shell Transport and Trading, a long-established London company which originally started selling sea shells in the 1840s, but had branched out into oil trading amongst other ventures. The joining of the companies was not an actual merger; shares could be bought in Royal Dutch Petroleum in The Hague or Shell Transport and Trading in London. They were two separate companies.

The unusual ownership structure was presided over from its founding until the 1930s by a doyen of the European oil industry, Sir Henri Deterding. He virtually ran the company single-handedly out of an office in London and was knighted for supplying the Allies with petroleum during the First World War. However, Deterding's behaviour became increasingly erratic during the latter part of his career and he engendered considerable controversy in the early 1930s by agreeing to supply the Nazis in Germany with a year's supply of oil on credit. As a result, he was forced to resign from the board in 1936.

Deterding's actions had far-reaching implications for Shell. Chastened by the experience, the directors decided that no longer would they allow one executive to acquire as much power as Deterding had done. Henceforth, the company would be managed by a series of committees, each overlapping, with some based in London and others in The Hague, in the Netherlands. Positions would be duplicated, with two chief executives, one for each company, and agreement had to be reached by both managements before any major decisions could be made. It was the ultimate in decentralised decision making.

Decentralisation of management seeped into the DNA of Shell. Shell managed a global business before the words became popular and it did so in an era of poor communications. It often operated in remote areas, drawn to where the oil deposits were to be found, and in regions where local knowledge was important. As a result, local managers were given considerable autonomy. But this was only possible by building a strong culture, which provided the behavioural controls necessary for entrusting local managers with important decisions.

Shell's management development heavily relied upon all potential managers spending time supervising its far-flung operations. Shell's management had always been admired for their shrewdness, professionalism and expertise, and to be hired by Shell was the goal of many graduates. Promising managers were identified early in their career and posted to field locations far from head office. Once they had experienced the rigours of managing in different countries, they were then posted to head office with a grandiose title. But they did have a good sense of the business and understood the difficulties of managing a global company.

Shell's strategy differed from most of the oil majors. In the 1960s and 1970s, the US oil companies received a setback, as Middle Eastern countries, and others which gained independence, confiscated their oil interests. Shell had few interests in the Middle East and so was not greatly affected by these actions. But as many exploration areas were closed to it, it concentrated on discovering and developing natural gas and on its marketing and downstream oil interests, such as refining and distribution. Both of these strategic moves proved to be of long-term benefit to Shell.

Shell's structure at this time was a classic worldwide matrix. It consisted of a mixture of both country managers and product managers. Strangely, this structure was appropriate to Shell's committee system and its ponderous decision making. A matrix almost inevitably leads to extensive consultation and negotiation and this could be blended with the committee system.

By the 1990s, problems were surfacing, which were damaging Shell, both as a business and as a brand name. It was experiencing problems in Nigeria where local opposition to its operations was gaining

The new CEO—an outsider from the valleys of Wales

In March 2005, the Sony board felt that, after 10 years of promises but little in the way of results, it was time for Nobuyuki Idei to step aside. In his place they appointed none other than Sir Howard Stringer to head the company. The new boss, a long-time media executive, had run Sony's business in America from 1997. Whilst it was not unknown for a non-Japanese to head a significant Japanese company—foreigners had headed both Nissan and Mazda—it was rare that one should head an icon such as Sony. It was also an acknowledgement by the board that significant changes were needed.

Stringer assured everyone that he took both the legacy and the future of Sony's electronics business seriously. He identified two main goals: simplification of Sony's management so that it could start making electronic devices more profitably; and solving the long-running challenge of how to make Sony's hardware and content work together well enough so that consumers would pay a premium price for them. In this he was pushing convergence as the strategy that Sony should adopt.

Is Howard Stringer the right man for the job? Certainly compared with the inward-looking change-resistant managers running Sony, he was a distinct improvement. It was not as if he was an outsider brought in to turn the company around. As the head of the American unit, he had already overseen the turnaround of Sony's media business and helped to deliver an impressive degree of consistency in an industry known for its ups and downs and variable cash flows.

He was already familiar with many of the problems in the electronics business. His managers in America, in their efforts to improve Sony's performance, had lobbied Sony's engineers in Japan to design their products to be simple and more customer-friendly. As well, Sony USA had some success in getting the engineers in Japan to think outside of their vertical silos. Sir Howard conceded that turning the electronics operation around would be difficult. The attempt to recapture Sony's one-time status as the world's leading electronics brand would involve cutting a large number of jobs from Sony's bloated corporate structure and reducing the level of bureaucracy, which stifled decision making,

Stringer's proposals

Howard Stringer's strategy to reinvigorate Sony falls into two main categories: product and structure.

Product

Deep in Sony's culture is the idea that it is the leading electronics company with the best technology and the world's leading researchers and product developers; competing on price in a crowded marketplace is anathema. It follows from this cultural self-perception that Sony should have its own standards, which are the industry's best, and that as a result premium prices could be charged. Whether achieving this is possible becomes the critical question surrounding strategy. Certainly Sony is using this strategy to regain a premium place in relation to product. Sony is now directly competing with Apple with a range of new music players and the PSP, a new portable PlayStation device, launched in Japan in December 2004, which went on sale in America in 2005. Although it is primarily a portable games console (its name is short for PlayStation Portable), the PSP is being promoted as a portable entertainment system, since it also doubles as a music player, photo viewer and video player. The product also reflects Sony's obsession with convergence.

Although it is a versatile product, the PSP reflects Sony's aims of producing proprietary products. Music tracks must be stored on a plug-in memory card and the PSP's memory slot supports only Sony's proprietary Memory Stick Duo format. This is widely seen as a not very subtle attempt to get consumers to buy expensive Memory Stick cards from Sony. Similarly, the PSP uses a proprietary disc format, called UMD, to store movies. While Sony will release its own movies, including *Spider-Man*, in UMD format, which is difficult to pirate, there is reluctance in the movie industry to support a proprietary format. Once again, Sony's determination to protect its interest in content, that is, movies and music, is restricting its new technology offerings.

Sony has also developed what it calls Cell architecture, which includes new chips and software. This has the potential to transform Sony's electronics business. Sony's upgraded PlayStation 3 is the first product in which Sony intends to use the Cell chip. The chip is also well suited to other sorts of media processing. The idea is that Cell chips will also find their way into high-definition televisions (which need lots of processing power), personal video recorders and other devices—even, perhaps, desktop computers. As usual, Sony hopes to establish a new standard: its goal is to become the Intel of the living room. The involvement of IBM and Toshiba, which also plan to use the chips, means that this goal is not perhaps as unrealistic as it may seem.

Another attempt by Sony at making its proprietary technology the dominant standard is the video-disc player based on Sony's new Blu-ray high-definition standard, which had already been backed by big PC makers like Dell, Hewlett-Packard and other electronic industry heavyweights. But Toshiba's rival HD-DVD format, which is also in the running to succeed DVD as the dominant video-disc standard, is cheaper, and has received fresh backing from Microsoft and Intel. Attempts to unify the two standards early in 2005 came to nothing, so a bitter standards war, akin to the battle 30 years ago between the VHS and Betamax video-cassette standards, now seems inevitable.

This means that Sir Howard is taking the reins just as the electronics division is placing two huge bets. Sony is attempting to establish two proprietary technologies—the Cell chip and Blu-ray discs—as dominant standards. He is hoping that Sony's position as a producer of entertainment content will somehow help it to sell gadgets more profitably. Sony has not only failed so far to demonstrate this, but its attempts have often involved proprietary standards that make its gadgets overly complicated and reduce their appeal to consumers. Consumers are reluctant to buy a product, such as an MP3 player, which forces them to buy content from one supplier.

Structure

The hope that Sony has for its proprietary technology cannot disguise the fact that major structural changes are needed. The first problem is that costs are high. Stringer already has a reputation as a cost cutter and is expected to accelerate the process along the lines he introduced in the US where he cut 9000 jobs in an attempt to save A$900 million a year. He also struck two huge entertainment deals, buying MGM Studios, and merging Sony Music with Bertelsmann AG to create Sony BMG, the world's second largest music company.

He will attempt to pursue the same disciplined approach to electronics that he has used with music and films. He does not seem to be worried about getting Sony's engineers to accept similar discipline. The key, he says, is to let them be creative while treating them the same as everyone else in the company. If this approach can work with film and music moguls, then using it on Japanese engineers at least seems possible.

In 2005, Sony cut the number of corporate executive officers—the company's top executive layer—from 13 to 7. Sony is also reducing the kinds of top posts available, as well as the number of ranks those executives can hold—big steps in title-sensitive corporate Japan.

But his plan involves more than just cutting costs; there are other expectations. The hope is that by reducing the number of managers and merging responsibilities for different business lines it will be easier for Sony's independently minded business groups to work together. In the past, lack of cooperation within the company has been a liability for Sony. It is a big company, with over 1000 products, and its bureaucracy has grown to prodigious size and slowed decision making. Thinking is compartmentalised into silos, which don't communicate with each other very well. As a result, control over product strategy, product development, product design and software integration has become increasingly complicated. The idea is to reduce bureaucracy and create an environment with open communication which is more dynamic and focused, but open to innovation. Some see the diverse nature and sheer size of Sony's operations as part of the problem—it is hard to come up with a unifying strategy to get so many disparate elements to work together.

Sony also aims to start the process of bringing the two sides of the company, entertainment and technology, together in order to promote convergence. In the past they have not worked as closely as they should have and this has led to missed opportunities. As well, Sony has not responded to changes in consumer lifestyles as quickly as it should have done.

Sony will also shut down 11 of its 65 plants around the world and shed 10 000 jobs, or about 7% of its workforce. It will stop making a few unprofitable products, although it has yet to determine which. Overall, the firm says, this will cut costs by A$2 billion by March 2008. That should help to raise Sony's poor operating profit margins in electronics to

4%. Even this modest boost, however, depends on Sony meeting an ambitious target of increasing electronics revenues by 5% a year.

Conclusion

Critics have generally been unimpressed by the reforms proposed, describing them as timid and not cutting deep enough. Stringer has responded that American-style business rationalisation is simply not possible in the more consensual and less brutal environment of Japan. He also claims resistance from inside Sony has prevented him from doing anything too bold. The financial markets seem to be siding with the critics, with Sony's share price continuing to decline.

Sir Howard has already ruled out one step that would fundamentally reshape the company: he insisted in 2005 that he would never break up Sony by dividing its media division (responsible for hits such as the *Spider-Man* films) from its electronics business. For now, therefore, he is pursuing the same vague, steady-as-she-goes strategy as his predecessor, Nobuyuki Idei, in which a phalanx of cost-cutting initiatives is flanked by some wishful thinking and risky gambles on opaque strategies.

Sir Howard's timid reforms mean that he is, in effect, betting that Blu-ray, the Cell chip or the PlayStation 3 will put the company back on its previous growth trajectory. If this does not happen, the cuts he will have to make will make the present ones look very small indeed.

Source: Drawn primarily from 'Behind the Smiles at Sony', *The Economist*, 12 March 2005, p. 83; Brian Bremner, Cliff Edwards & Ronald Grover, 'Sony's Sudden Samurai', *Business Week*, 21 March 2005, p.28. Other sources have been consulted as appropriate.

QUESTIONS

1 Briefly identify the main challenges facing Sony's senior management. Identify and describe the origins of the challenges.
2 Why would a change program at Sony take at least three years to show results?
3 This case study was written in mid 2005. Undertake research in order to bring the events at Sony up to date. From your research, evaluate the success of the change plan so far adopted by Sony.
4 Discuss the reasons why changing the entertainment part of Sony based in the US (mainly films and music) would be different from changing the electronics part based in Japan.

CASE STUDY 6

Tell your friends about One.Tel

Organisations contain within them many contradictions which management must try to resolve or at least live with. One of the most enduring is that of the theoretical ideal working conditions for employees and the reality of having to run a business with responsibility to various stakeholders. Commentators, academics and a plethora of social analysts praise conditions which favour personal responsibility and autonomy, the removal of drudgery and the promotion of innovation. But the reality of business life for most employees is dictated by the discipline of systems, detailed planning, budgeting and account keeping, and attention to quality issues.

The former telecommunications company, One.Tel, provides a good illustration of how a dissonance between culture and systems can have disastrous consequences. One.Tel was established in 1995 to take advantage of the deregulated telecommunications environment. It was not surprising that budding entrepreneurs were attracted to the industry, which was dominated by the then government-owned Telstra which was widely viewed as being unpopular, bureaucratic, slow moving and easy to beat in the marketplace. But Telstra and its new competitor, Optus, owned most of the infrastructure to connect the calls, so One.Tel was initially a reseller of the other networks' capacity.

However, One.Tel had grander plans than just being a seller of other networks' capacity. Eventually it hoped to build its own network and to undertake extensive overseas expansion by taking its business model, which relied heavily upon its marketing expertise, offshore. From its founding, One.Tel was not a company that was to be conservatively managed and built slowly and patiently piece by piece. Jodee Rich, the main founder of the company, had already one failed business venture behind him, a computer software company called Imagineering. His close associate, Brad Keeling, who undertook much of the day-to-day management of One.Tel, had similar thoughts in relation to the company.

In start-ups, such as One.Tel, the biggest problem is not ideas but money; the bills must be paid until the business expands to become cash flow positive. In many cases this is a race against time; costs such as wages, rent, lease payments and so on are often large even before sales can be made. Normally this would indicate close monitoring of costs against expenditure and the careful management of resources.

One.Tel was essentially a marketing company and its symbol was the 'dude', a cartoon character who was young, hip but not too bright. He urged customers to 'tell your friends about One.Tel'. It was a pointer that the culture at One.Tel was not in the bureaucratic Telstra or Optus style, dominated as they were by engineers in grey cardigans. It was to be different because One.Tel was intended to be a different company. But it was its culture as much as anything else that led to One.Tel's demise.

One.Tel's culture

One.Tel was primarily a young person's company. Most people hired were in their 20s, and few had reached their 40s. In the early days of One.Tel, sales greatly exceeded expectations and new staff were appearing every day. Jodee Rich created a culture based upon building camaraderie between employees, which was useful given the significant number of new hires who were appearing. The aim of the company was to be fun and friendly for the people who worked there. In the early days of the company, everyone sat together. They were all on one floor without partitions or offices. Everyone took turns at wearing a 'fireman's hat' for the day. This meant that they had to run around for everyone else, loading paper in the copiers, running errands and fixing problems. There were teams and champions and the champs had their pictures painted onto the wall.

Paul Barry, who chronicled the One.Tel story, described other aspects of the culture:

> There was also the One.Tel story which everybody had to know in case Jodee made them recite it. New recruits were asked to define a team player, to which the correct answer was someone who enjoyed other's success and shared. A cartoon on the wall labelled 'Vitamin C' encouraged everyone to give tablets to one another—an allegory for sharing what you knew.

CASE STUDY 8

'Which Bank' reinvents itself—perhaps!

During the 1990s, the Commonwealth Bank introduced an advertising campaign promoting the virtues of the bank that ended with the phrase 'Which Bank?' Regardless of the campaign's success, 'Which Bank' has been associated with the Commonwealth ever since. The 1990s were a mixed decade for banks such as the Commonwealth; their profitability increased out of sight as they cut staff, closed branches, and generally substituted IT transactions and call centres for the more expensive face-to-face contact. But this came at an enormous cost to the banks' reputations. Country towns were deprived of banks and customers had to travel suburbs away in the cities to find a branch, only to wait in queues that snaked out the door. Low-income customers had to get used to the idea of bank fees and long-serving staff shook their heads in frustration.

All the while the banks fretted that their traditional source of income—the interest spread between deposit and lending rates—was being eroded because of competition and they needed new sources of income. Margins (the profitability) of traditional products such as mortgages were falling and increasingly savers were using superannuation products to accrue wealth rather than put their money into low-interest bank accounts. The banks thought the way out of their predicament was to expand into wider wealth management, that is funds management and various superannuation products, and become 'all finance' organisations. The banks would use their extensive branch network, or what was left of it, along with their brand name and goodwill, again what was left of it, to cross-sell products. So someone walking into a branch, for instance, could be quickly assessed as to their potential as a customer and offered anything from a student loan to a superannuation product depending upon their standing, or potential, as a customer and their life stage.

In 2000, in support of this strategy, the managing director of the Commonwealth, David Murray, paid $9 billion for the funds management and superannuation operations of Colonial Group. The acquisition proved to be of dubious worth. As soon as the Commonwealth moved in, the star funds managers left Colonial, leaving a void which was not easy to fill. Cross-selling of Colonial products proved to be more difficult in practice than it was as a management concept, and customers generally treated the whole process with indifference.

By 2003, the bank was faced with having to introduce a major change program or watch its growth potential disappear. Staff morale was falling and customer-service levels were reported as the lowest of any of the big four banks. Costs were high and increasing. So the Commonwealth introduced the 'Which New Bank' program which was intended to promote major changes in the way that the bank operated. It was a comprehensive program which combined changes in attitude and employee orientation with changes in systems and processes. Specifically the bank aimed to:

- redesign branches so that they had a more contemporary appearance and to facilitate shorter queue lengths
- replace existing ATMs with more modern, functional machines
- speed up decision making—decision times for changes to loan conditions were to be reduced from 10 days to 3 and provisional approval for home loans could be given by the branches in 4 hours
- stress a unified culture in the disparate business units of the bank in order to facilitate cross-selling.

There was to be further investment in systems and processes with the aim of cutting costs and simplifying processes. New IT systems were to give staff an accurate profile of the customer in order to promote cross-selling opportunities. But over half of the $1.5 billion project was allocated to staff development and funding redundancies. Over 3700 staff, mainly from the back office, processing and head office functions, were to be made redundant. But new staff were to be hired in customer-service areas and existing staff were to be put through rigorous training in order to upgrade their customer-service skills and product knowledge. Bank managers were to be retrained so that they spent less time in supervision and up to 80% of their time with customers. The program was intended to take three years and yield significant cost benefits which would show up directly as increased profit.

Uncertain delivery

No change program goes entirely according to plan, and there are always legions of critics expressing opinions from the sidelines. Specifically, those made redundant could hardly be expected to be supporters. But 'Which New Bank' appeared to be more poorly perceived and executed than many change programs.

Some difficulties were obvious; a number of very high-profile senior managers and champions of the change program left the bank early in the program and proved difficult to replace. On the other hand, progress in branch redesign and refit and replacement of ATMs could be measured against the plan. This aspect of the change program did not cause major problems. Most criticism was directed towards the staff aspect of the program.

Quite a number of senior branch managers left the company, citing a litany of complaints. They claimed that, whilst the rhetoric supported increased customer service, resources to the branches were actually cut, making improving customer service more difficult to achieve. Experienced staff who left, or were made redundant, were being replaced by inexperienced new hires who did not have sufficient skills or product knowledge to provide good service. On a more general level, strikes increased and there was general agitation by the union. The program itself was not seen to be the problem—it would be almost impossible to argue with its aims—but staff considered it to be under-resourced. If anything queues at branches got longer rather than shorter! And rather than staff with improved skills, inadequately trained tellers were being rushed into customer-service roles.

Perhaps one of most strident criticisms by lower level staff was that no one was listening to complaints. It was as if complaints, suggestions and comments hit a brick wall before they got anywhere near the executive suite and no one at the top of the company wanted to hear any bad news. The only reports lower level employees got to hear from the executive suite were those indicating that the program was going well and targets were being met, and how great the bank would be when it was all over. Those in the branches felt an immediate dissonance between what was being said and what was being experienced.

Source: Drawn from various Commonwealth Bank media releases from 2003 onwards, <www.commbank.com.au>; and James Kirby, 'The "Which Bank" Trials', *Business Review Weekly*, 22 July 2004, pp. 37–43.

QUESTIONS

1 Drawing upon the case study, demonstrate how major change programs involve not just structure, but all aspects of the business. Discuss the importance of this for the Commonwealth Bank change program.

2 The case highlights the dissatisfaction of many experienced frontline staff with the change program. What implication has this for the success of the change program? Should senior managers take note of their concerns? Discuss whether senior managers may have been happy for frontline staff to leave the bank.

3 The originators of the change program left the bank before the program was fully completed. Almost the whole top management of the bank, including the managing director, also resigned or left for various reasons. Discuss the implications of this for the change program.

4 How could senior managers evaluate the success or failure of the change program? How long would it take for such indications to emerge?

Glossary

Adaptive activities Change activities that allow the system to adapt over time.

Adhocracy An organisational form characterised by high horizontal differentiation, low vertical differentiation, low formalisation, intensive coordination and great flexibility and responsiveness.

Administrative innovation The implementation of changes in an organisation's structure or its administrative processes.

Analysers Organisations whose strategy is to move into new products or new markets only after their viability has been proven.

Appeals system The right of redress on grievances through formal channels.

Authority The formal rights inherent in a managerial position to give orders and expect the orders to be obeyed.

Autonomy The degree to which a job provides substantial freedom, independence and discretion to the individual in scheduling the work and in determining the procedures to be used in carrying it out.

Balance of maintenance and adaptive activities To be effective the system must ensure that its subparts are in balance and that it maintains its ability to adapt to the environment.

Balance scorecard The balanced scorecard seeks to balance the various demands on the organisation with its capabilities.

Biological school A work-design approach that emphasises the comfort and physical wellbeing of the worker.

Boundary spanners People who operate at the periphery of the organisation, performing organisationally relevant tasks, and relating the organisation to elements outside it.

Bridging The process by which managers endeavour to regulate their environments through negotiation, cooperation, exchange of information and other forms of mutual benefit.

Buffering Protecting the operating core from environmental variations in supply and demand.

Bureaucracy An organisational form characterised by division of labour, a well-defined authority hierarchy, high formalisation, impersonality, employment decisions based on merit, career tracks for employees and distinct separation of members' organisational and personal lives.

Bureaupathic behaviour Adherence to rules and regulations by individuals to protect themselves from making errors.

Business-level strategy Refers to those strategies adapted by business units of the organisation.

Capacity The degree to which an environment can support growth.

Centralisation The degree to which decision making is concentrated in a single point in the organisation, usually top management.

Change agents Those in power, and those who wish either to replace or constrain those in power.

Closed system A self-contained system that has no interaction with its environment.

Coalescing The combining of an organisation with one or more other organisations for the purpose of joint action.

Complexity The degree of horizontal, vertical and spatial differentiation in an organisation.

Computer-integrated manufacturing A manufacturing process controlled by computers, which brings together all aspects of the production process.

Configuration A complex clustering of elements that are internally cohesive and where the presence of some elements suggests the reliable occurrence of others.

Conglomerate A divisional structure where the autonomous units engage in diverse businesses and are completely independent.

Contracting Protects the organisation from changes in quantity or price on either input or output side.

Co-opting The absorption of those individuals or organisations in the environment that threaten a given organisation's stability.

Coordination The process of integrating the objectives and activities of the separate units of an organisation in order to achieve organisational goals efficiently.

Core values The primary values expressed by an organisation's dominant culture.

Corporate-level strategy Attempts to define the nature of the businesses in which the firm seeks to operate.

Cost-leadership strategy Aims to achieve the lowest cost within an industry.

Craft technology Containing relatively difficult problems but with a limited set of exceptions.

Critical theory An approach to studying organisations which concentrates on their perceived shortcomings and deficiencies.

Cyclical character The system consists of repetitive cycles of events.

Defenders Organisations whose strategy is to produce a limited set of products directed at a narrow segment of the total potential market.

Differentiation Task segmentation and attitudinal differences held by individuals in various departments.

Differentiation strategy Aims to achieve a unique position in an industry in ways that are widely valued by buyers.

Disturbed-reactive environment An environment characterised by many competitors, one or more of which may be large enough to influence that environment.

Division of labour Functional specialisation; jobs broken down into simple and repetitive tasks.

Divisional structure A structure characterised by a set of self-contained, autonomous units, coordinated by a central headquarters.

Domain An organisation's niche that it has staked out for itself with respect to products or services offered and markets served.

Dominant coalition The group within an organisation with the power to influence the outcomes of decisions.

Dominant culture The overriding core values shared by the majority of an organisation's members.

Downsizing Planned reduction in an organisation's staffing levels.

Employee alienation The distance an employee feels between themselves and their work.

Enactment A process where structures and process take form through the actions of individuals.

Engineering technology Containing a large number of exceptions, but can be handled in a rational and systematic manner.

Entropy The propensity of a system to run down or disintegrate.

Environment Those institutions or forces that affect the performance of the organisation but over which the organisation has little or no direct control.

Environment awareness The organisation consistently interacts with its environment

Environmental change Ranges from static (little change) to dynamic.

Environmental complexity The degree to which the environment is concentrated on just a few elements.

Environmental scanning Scrutinising the environment to identify actions by factors that might impinge on the organisation's operations.

Environmental uncertainty The degree to which an environment is characterised by a large number of heterogeneous and rapidly changing factors.

Equifinality A system can reach the same final state from differing initial conditions and by a variety of paths.

Evolution Prolonged and calm growth.

Evolutionary mode A strategy that evolves over time as a pattern in a stream of significant decisions.

Explicit knowledge Codified knowledge, which may be transmitted in formal systematic language.

External strategies Efforts designed to alter the environment to fit better with the organisation's capabilities.

Feedback Receipt of information pertaining to individual or system effectiveness.

Feminism An active advocacy of the claims and aspirations of women.